5555 9438

World Terrorism

Volume 2

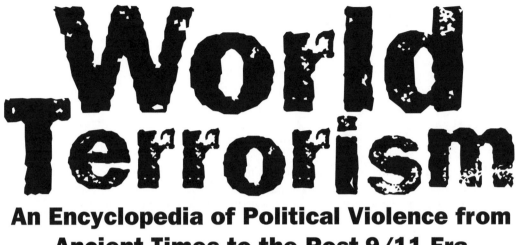

World Terrorism

An Encyclopedia of Political Violence from Ancient Times to the Post-9/11 Era

Second Edition

Volume 2

James Ciment, Editor

SHARPE REFERENCE

an imprint of M.E. Sharpe, Inc.

SHARPE REFERENCE

Sharpe Reference is an imprint of M.E. Sharpe, Inc.

M.E. Sharpe, Inc.
80 Business Park Drive
Armonk, NY 10504

Library of Congress Cataloging-in-Publication Data

World terrorism: an encyclopedia of political violence from ancient times to the post-9/11 era / James Ciment, editor—2nd ed.
   p. cm.
 Includes bibliographical references and index.
 ISBN 978-0-7656-8284-0 (hardcover : alk. paper)
 1. Terrorism—History—Encyclopedias. I. Ciment, James.

HV6431.W67 2011
363.32503—dc22

2011006073

Publisher: Myron E. Sharpe
Vice President and Director of New Product Development: Donna Sanzone
Vice President and Production Director: Carmen Chetti
Executive Development Editor: Jeff Hacker
Project Manager: Angela Piliouras
Program Coordinator: Cathleen Prisco
Editorial Assistant: Lauren LoPinto
Cover Design: Jesse Sanchez
Typesetter: Nancy Connick

Contents

World Terrorism

Volume 2

Japan: Radical Attacks, 1960s–1980s

From the late 1960s to the mid-1970s, three closely linked Japanese terrorist groups—the Red Army Faction (RAF), the United Red Army, and the Japanese Red Army—conducted a campaign of hijacking, bombing, and hostage taking as part of a struggle for a communist revolution. This took place against a background of unrest among Japanese left-wing students during the 1950s and 1960s. Determined to crush the unrest, the government passed a law in August 1969 to control the demonstrations. By this time, though, the left-wing movement had begun to lose momentum and had started to question its future.

Red Army Faction

The Sekigun-ha (Red Army Faction) was formed in September 1969 in response to this left-wing uncertainty. Established by dissident communists, it was far more militant than other radical groups. The RAF's ideology of worldwide communist revolution, of which a Japanese uprising would be just a part, called for the creation of a revolutionary army to wage war on the government.

The group's initial activities were mere skirmishes, with little impact. It soon realized that significant training would be required if they were ever to function as a real army. The RAF's leader, Takaya Shiomi, proposed establishing bases in communist countries, including North Korea and Albania, and in Western countries, including the United States and West Germany. RAF activists would receive military training there and would then return to Japan with the aim of taking over the country. At the same time, the group sought alliances with sympathetic organizations throughout the world. It viewed the terrorist acts of other rebel forces, such as the Palestinians in the Middle East, as victories for the RAF. The group considered itself in the front line of a struggle for a global revolution. Defeats by the police at home mattered less if the struggle for the world was being won.

In November 1969, however, the RAF was dealt a severe blow when fifty-three of its members were arrested in the mountains west of Tokyo. They had been training for an attack on the prime minister's residence, but after this setback, the RAF opted for small-scale guerrilla terrorism. Meanwhile, police activity against the group continued, and in March 1970, Shiomi was arrested.

Later that month, the RAF made the headlines when it carried out Japan's first-ever airplane hijacking. Nine of its members, armed with swords and knives, captured a Japan Airlines jet on a domestic flight. They flew to North Korea, where they expected support from the communist leader, Kim Il Sung. Instead, the North Korean government immediately declared the hijackers "uninvited guests." Nevertheless, several of the hijackers remained in exile in the country for many years.

The absence from Japan of the group's leading members left a vacuum at the top of the RAF. Eventually, the group came under the control of Tsuneo Mori, a radical who concentrated the group's activities along more domestic lines. Between February and July 1971, the group robbed eight banks in Japan, raising around $200,000. The group also announced "the age of bombs," and it began to use high-power explosives against the police.

Once again, the RAF sought cooperation with guerrillas in other countries. Its aim, as before, was to organize an army and prepare for a coup d'état, so the group's Central Committee established bases in the Middle East and the United States. In February 1971, Central Committee member Fusako Shigenobu was sent to Palestine to make contact with the Popular Front for the Liberation of Palestine (PFLP). The two groups quickly formed an alliance, and in October 1971, a member of the Central Committee of the PFLP came to Japan to announce the joint Red Army Faction–PFLP "Declaration of World War."

United Red Army

In January 1972, the RAF merged with the Keihin Anpo Kyoto (KAK). The KAK, also founded in 1969, was more nationalistic than the internationalist RAF, advocating a pro-Chinese, anti-American, one-country revolution. Despite the ideological differences between the RAF and the KAK, both groups believed in challenging political power with arms. Together, they established the United Red Army (URA) and formed a Central Committee of seven members.

Driven by police pressure, URA members fled to the mountains of central Japan to train to be what they termed "true revolutionaries." During the winter of 1972, fourteen URA members were murdered in violent internal fighting and buried in shallow graves.

In February 1972, Mori and Yoko Nagata, another Central Committee member, were arrested as they returned to the group's hideout. In retaliation, five URA men took a woman hostage in a mountain cottage. Hundreds of police surrounded the cottage and, after the longest hostage incident in Japanese history, all five terrorists were arrested. The siege lasted nine days. It had cost the lives of two police officers and one civilian. It also virtually destroyed the URA. The organization had made no efforts to rally support for its campaign, and after the siege, it found itself alienated from the general public. It split into three major factions, amounting to about 100 members in all, but was no longer a serious terrorist threat.

New Foreign Red Army

By this time, the RAF had established a group in the Middle East, which started to act independently. After initially calling themselves the Arab Red Army, they took the name Japanese Red Army (JRA). In May 1972, three JRA members massacred twenty-six people and injured seventy-six in a gun and grenade attack at Lod Airport in Tel Aviv, Israel. It was a suicide mission, and two JRA activists, including Shigenobu's husband, were killed. The sole survivor of the operation, Kozo Okamoto, was arrested by Israeli police, tried, and sentenced to life imprisonment.

Following the ill-fated Tel Aviv operation, the JRA acquired international notoriety with a string of terrorist activities. In July 1973, one member of the JRA and four from the PFLP hijacked a Japanese jumbo jet en route from Amsterdam to Tokyo. The PFLP leader accidentally dropped a grenade and killed herself. Since only she knew what the group's demands were, the terrorists, unsure of what to do next, forced the aircraft to fly to Dubai in the United Arab Emirates, and then on to Benghazi, Libya. The terrorists released all the passengers, blew up the plane, and surrendered to the Libyan government.

In January 1974, two PFLP and two JRA terrorists attacked Shell Oil facilities in Singapore and subsequently seized a ferry and five hostages. The next month, five members of the PFLP took over the Japanese embassy in Kuwait. They captured the ambassador and fifteen other hostages and demanded a plane for the terrorists involved in the Singapore incident. The Japanese government sent a plane to pick up the terrorists and hostages in Singapore so they could join the others in Kuwait. They then flew to Aden, South Yemen, where the terrorists surrendered to the authorities.

In September 1974, three members of the JRA seized the French embassy at The Hague in the Netherlands and held nine hostages, including the French ambassador. They demanded the release of Yoshiaki Yamada, who had been arrested in France in July. After he had been exchanged for the hostages, the terrorists flew to Damascus, Syria, and surrendered.

In August 1975, to coincide with the Japanese prime minister's visit to the United States, five members of the JRA seized the U.S. consulate and the Swedish embassy (in the same building) in Kuala Lumpur, Malaysia. They held more than fifty people hostage, including the U.S. consul general and a Swedish diplomat. They demanded the release of seven JRA members held in Japanese prisons. The Japanese government released five (two refused to leave) and flew them to Kuala Lumpur. After joining with the others, they flew to Tripoli, Libya, where they surrendered. In September 1977, five members of the JRA hijacked a Japanese airplane flying from Paris to Tokyo and forced it to land in Dacca, Bangladesh. They

KEY DATES

September 1969 Dissident former communist activists establish Sekigun-ha (Red Army Faction; RAF).
November 1969 Japanese security forces arrest fifty-three RAF members.
February–July 1971 RAF terrorists rob eight banks in Japan.
May 1972 Terrorists of the Japanese Red Army (JRA), a Middle Eastern offshoot of the RAF, massacre twenty-six persons at Lod Airport in Tel Aviv, Israel.
September 1977 JRA hijackers seize a Paris-bound Japanese jumbo jet, taking more than 150 hostages; the Japanese government agrees to pay their $6 million ransom demand.
1986–1988 Several high-profile arrests of remaining JRA members shut down the declining organization.

took 151 hostages and demanded $6 million and the release of nine JRA members jailed in Japan. The Japanese government again caved in and released six (three refused to leave), and flew them to Dacca with the money. After the released prisoners joined the hijackers, they all flew to Algeria and surrendered to the authorities.

Change of Direction

After a spectacular success at Dacca, the JRA paused to reexamine its tactics. Between December 1977 and June 1983, the JRA published a small English-language newspaper in Beirut, Lebanon, called *Danketsu,* meaning "solidarity." In this paper, the JRA appealed to so-called New Left groups in Japan for solidarity and called for the establishment of a "Japanese Revolutionary Congress."

In 1982, internal troubles in the Palestinian movement disrupted the JRA's activity, and the group temporarily moved to Syria and southern Lebanon. In January 1984, JRA members returned to northern Lebanon to rebuild their headquarters. Between 1986 and 1988, several leading JRA members were arrested in Japan, effectively ending Red Army's campaign of violence.

Tadashi Kuramatsu

See also: *Definitions, Types, Categories*—Left-Wing and Revolutionary Terrorism. *Modern Terrorism*—Japan: Aum Shinrikyo Terrorism.

Further Reading

Farrell, William R. *Blood and Rage: The Story of the Japanese Red Army.* Lexington, MA: Lexington Books, 1990.

Katzenstein, Peter J., and Yutaka Isujinaka. *Defending the Japanese State: Structure, Norms and Political Responses to Terrorism and Violent Social Protest in the 1970s and 1980s.* Ithaca, NY: Cornell University Press, 1991.

Steinhoff, Patricia G. "Portrait of a Terrorist: An Interview with Kozo Okamoto." *Asian Survey* 169 (September 1976): 830–45.

Jordan: Palestinian Nationalism and Islamic Fundamentalism, 1960s–2000s

With its close proximity to Israel and its large population of Palestinians—most of them refugees and descendants of refugees from the 1948–1949 Arab-Israeli War (known by Israelis as the War of Independence)—Jordan has both been a base for and a target of Palestinian nationalist and Islamist terrorism since at least the 1960s.

Expulsion of the Palestine Liberation Organization

In September 1970, Jordan's King Hussein—fearful of Israeli reprisals and worried over the loyalties of his Palestinian subjects—expelled the Palestine Liberation Organization (PLO) from his kingdom, a move that led directly to the creation of one of the Middle East's most effective terrorist groups, the Black September Organization. The developments of September 1970 grew from two events. First, in late 1967, Israel clamped down on

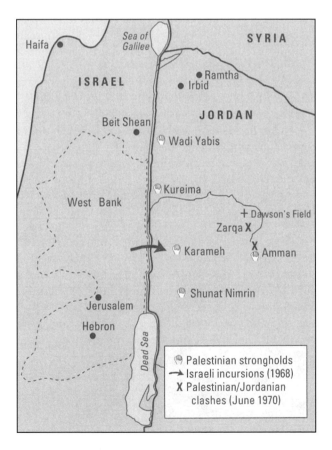

Palestinian strongholds and Israeli incursions leading up to the expulsion of the PLO from Jordan (September 1970–July 1971).

the Palestinian guerrillas who had been operating inside the West Bank since the end of the 1967 war. The guerrillas involved fled to Jordan, from where they raided the West Bank, attracting Israeli reprisals against their hosts. Second, certain elements in the PLO believed that the use of Jordan as a launchpad for liberating western Palestine could occur only with the overthrow of the king. The Popular Front for the Liberation of Palestine (PFLP) declared on its founding that "the road to Jerusalem goes through Amman [the capital of Jordan]."

Israeli Reprisals

The Israelis responded to attacks by Jordanian-based Palestinians by bombarding the border area. In March 1968, the Palestinians attracted much greater retribution when they mined the road linking Tel Aviv with the Negev Desert. The mine detonated beneath a school bus, killing two children and injuring twenty-seven more. With the Israeli public clamoring for revenge, an Israeli army formation crossed into Jordan and attacked the village of Karameh, which housed much of Fatah's organization; founded by Yasir Arafat and others in 1959, Fatah has become the leading party within the PLO. Although they suffered heavy casualties, the Palestinians, supported by the Jordanian army, repelled the attackers, and Fatah claimed a victory. However, Israel was also hitting Jordanian civilian targets in retaliation for Palestinian attacks, including the East Ghor Canal irrigation project. Although not seeking to undermine Jordan, Israel was sending King Hussein a clear message to take action against the Palestinian terrorists.

Hussein in Danger

Hussein's rule was already in great danger. In parts of the country, Palestinian terrorist groups were in control, and many Palestinians—in particular radical groups such as the PFLP—believed that the king should be deposed. In November 1968, a round of clashes and demonstrations led Hussein to get tough with the Palestinians. The army surrounded two refugee camps near Amman and shelled them for three days.

Hussein's control over his kingdom continued to diminish, however. Then, in February 1970, he clamped down on the Palestinians once again, issuing a list of restrictions that included a ban on firearms and demonstrations. Clashes between the Palestinians and the king's forces left 300 dead. The king turned to conciliation, withdrawing his restrictions. This further encouraged the leftist Palestinian leaders, who believed Hussein's throne was ripe for the taking.

Riots in Amman in April 1970 were instigated by the PFLP to abort the proposed visit of Joseph Sisco, the U.S. undersecretary of state for the Middle East. Some 10,000 people were brought out onto the streets, shops and homes were ransacked, and foreigners were taken hostage. On June 9, after clashes between Palestinians and the army in Amman and nearby Zarqa, Hussein narrowly escaped death when Palestinians opened fire on his motorcade near Amman. The king again tried conciliation, declaring, "We are all fedayeen [Arabic for "martyr," but loosly meaning guerrilla fighter]," replacing his cousin Sharif Zaid bin Shakr as commander of the Third Armored Division, and assembling a "pro-Palestinian" government. On July 10, Hussein made a peace pact with the Palestinians.

The tide was about to turn against the Palestinians, however. Israel and the United States were both becoming increasingly concerned about the deteriorating situation in Jordan and the threat to Hussein's throne. Then, on July 23, 1970, President Gamal Abdel Nasser of Egypt accepted an American proposal for a cease-fire between his country and Israel. The Palestinians were furious: an agreement between an Arab country and the archenemy Israel was intolerable to them. The Palestinians accused Nasser of treachery and demonstrated against Hussein, believing that Jordan was also moving toward peace with Israel.

Dawson's Field

In Amman, under pressure from his army to act, Hussein warned the Palestinians to stop challenging his authority. Clashes followed, as did another assassination attempt on September 1. Palestinian nationalist leader George Habash's PFLP then threw oil on the fire by seizing three aircraft on September 6. The terrorists hijacked one to Cairo, Egypt, and destroyed it; two were flown to Dawson's Field, an abandoned airfield outside of Amman. Three days later, the PFLP hijacked a fourth aircraft, which was also taken to Dawson's Field. The terrorists held more than 300 people hostage at the airfield and demanded the release of fedayeen from European and Israeli jails. On September 12, the terrorists blew up the three planes at Dawson's Field and released all the passengers apart from fifty-four Israelis and American Jews. They in turn were released in exchange for the imprisoned Palestinian terrorists.

Black September

The hijackings and subsequent destruction of the airliners made the Palestinian cause headline news all over the world. However, the PFLP operations also gave Hussein the opportunity to turn his tanks on the fedayeen. On September 17, he sent in the army to crush the PLO bases in Palestinian refugee camps and killed several thousand fighters. The king then expelled the PLO from Jordan—a process completed by July 1971. These events led Palestinians to call September 1970 "Black September."

After its expulsion from Jordan, the PLO moved its operational base to Lebanon. The whole episode had been a defeat for the policy of PLO chairman Yasir Arafat, who had been negotiating behind the scenes and trying to cooperate with the Arab states. Now negotiation did not seem to make sense, even to many of Arafat's own Fatah party. The Arab neighbors of Israel, vulnerable to counterattack, were unwilling to countenance raids from their territory. Elements within Fatah decided to move against softer, international targets.

Black September Organization

The result of this new direction was the formation of the Black September Organization. It was an offshoot of Fatah, or more precisely, a terror cell within Fatah, formed by those who saw military action rather than diplomacy as the appropriate tactic after the devastation in Jordan that gave the group its name. The Black September Organization's key figures were Abu Iyad, a deputy of Arafat's, and Ali Hassan Salameh.

Black September's first terrorist act was the murder of the Jordanian prime minister, Wasfi al-Tal, in Cairo in November 1971. The killing had the immediate result of boosting the number of volunteers ready to take a militant line against Arab regimes. Black September's next act was a failed assassination attempt on the Jordanian ambassador in London, in December 1971.

Black September was not simply a terror group committed to the belief that armed struggle was the only way to liberate Palestine. The notion that it was just a convenient front for Arafat's military option is also questionable. Taking the struggle into Europe, for which Black September became notorious, was a desperate tactic more in keeping with those whose recklessness had triggered the debacle in Jordan. In truth, Black September was a loose terror group led by Fatah men who wanted to give vent to their frustrations. The group was not a formal part of Fatah nor was it subject to its leadership; however, its ability to use Fatah structures, and the fact that its leaders were part of the Fatah organization, made it difficult for Fatah to disown Black September.

Massacre in Munich

In May 1972, Ali Hassan Salameh, Black September's head of European operations, organized the hijacking of a Belgian Sabena aircraft and forced it to land at Tel Aviv. However, the four terrorists were taken completely by surprise when Israeli commandos of the Sayeret Matkal unit, disguised as white-coated airport technicians, stormed the plane. The commandos killed two terrorists and captured the other two but also killed one passenger and wounded five more in the process. This was the first instance of a hijacked plane being stormed by an elite counterterrorist unit.

It is the massacre at the 1972 Olympics in Munich, West Germany, for which Black September is most notorious. Abu Iyad, at the time chief of security and intelligence services for both Fatah and the PLO, is the man most commonly linked to this incident. His closeness to Arafat ensured that the PLO chairman is still widely seen as at fault. Abu Iyad was obliged by his position to assume executive responsibility for this and other Black September operations, and he defended the organization's actions privately as well as publicly. Abu Iyad was involved in the planning of the kidnappings. It seems likely that Arafat gave the go-ahead but kept a careful distance in order to ensure that the buck would stop with the PLO's security chief.

At 4 A.M. on September 5, 1972, two security guards patrolling the Olympic Village spotted eight track-suited men climbing over a security fence. The guards took the intruders to be athletes returning after a night out. They were in fact Black September terrorists, armed with grenades and Kalashnikov assault rifles, on a mission to take the Israeli Olympic team hostage.

The terrorists moved into Building 31, where the Israeli team was staying. After a violent struggle, in which weightlifter Joseph Romano and wrestling coach Moshe Weinberg were killed, nine athletes and officials were taken hostage. The remainder of the Israeli team managed to escape through windows or out the rear door. Shortly afterward, Building 31 was surrounded by armed police and negotiations began.

The Israeli government refused to comply with the terrorists' demands for the release of prisoners and did not wish the West Germans to continue negotiations. However, West Germany saw its hosting of the Olympics as proof that it was accepted back into the community of nations after the Nazi atrocities of World War II. The kidnapping of Jewish hostages on German soil was thus a disaster for the West Germans.

German security forces devised a plan to free the hostages. They ruled out an assault on Building 31, as it would almost certainly end in the death of the hostages. Consequently, the German forces appeared to accept the terrorists' demand for a plane to fly them and their hostages to Tunisia. The Germans' plan was to mount an attack on the terrorists before they boarded the plane.

At 10 P.M., the terrorists and their bound and blindfolded hostages were taken by bus to a helicopter pad. Three helicopters took off for Fürstenfeldbruck airport, two carrying terrorists and hostages, the other carrying German negotiators. The helicopters landed 165 yards (150 meters) from the escape plane. Two terrorists walked over to inspect the aircraft while another two dismounted

with the pilots. As the first two returned from the plane, a Bavarian state police marksman began shooting and three terrorists were killed. The other terrorists immediately opened fire on the hostages and on the control tower where the police had hidden, killing one marksman.

There was then stalemate for a short time, but just after midnight, one of the terrorists leapt from a helicopter and flung a grenade back into it, setting it ablaze. He and another terrorist were then shot dead. The remaining three were captured by security forces in armored cars. All nine hostages were dead.

However, the operation was a failure for Fatah: another "Black September." The terrorists' demand that 200 PLO prisoners be released in exchange for the hostages had failed, and the world was horrified. Furthermore, the Bavarian police had been shown to be inadequately trained to deal with terrorists, which led many countries to create special counterterrorist units. In addition, Israel set up hit squads under Operation Wrath of God to track down Black September members.

Final Acts of Terror

The next Black September operation was to send mail bombs, one of which killed an Israeli consul. After this, there was the hijacking, on October 29, 1972, of a Lufthansa aircraft, which secured the release of the three surviving terrorists from Munich. Although the result of this operation was a propaganda coup, Israeli retaliation into Lebanon and Syria meant that the governments of these countries put great pressure on PLO groups to stop Black September actions.

In February 1973, the Israelis shot down an off-course Libyan airliner, killing 106 people. President Muammar Gadhafi of Libya then helped Black September set up another strike. Eight Black September terrorists took over the Saudi Arabian embassy in Khartoum, Sudan, on March 1. They demanded the release of of all Palestinian prisoners, as well as Sirhan Sirhan, the Palestinian who killed Robert Kennedy, and Kozo Okamoto, the surviving member of the 1972 Lod massacre terrorists, a group of Palestinian and Japanese terrorists who killed 26 persons at Israel's main international airport.

The terrorists also demanded the release of prisoners belonging to the West German Baader-Meinhof terrorist gang. U.S. president Richard Nixon refused point-blank to negotiate, and the terrorists mercilessly machine-gunned to death the U.S. ambassador, the U.S. chargé d'affaires, and a Belgian diplomat in the embassy compound.

By now, the Fatah leadership, including Abu Iyad, agreed that Black September's conduct had gotten out of hand. Israeli reprisals were also in full swing. In April, Israeli troops killed seventeen Palestinians in Beirut, including three leading Black September members. Fatah was also distancing itself rapidly from Black September.

In September 1973, Black September seized the Saudi embassy in Paris in an unsuccessful attempt to secure the release of Abu Daoud, the former Palestinian militia commander now imprisoned in Jordan. Arafat unequivocally condemned the attack.

In the last recorded Black September mission, in September 1973, Italian police arrested five terrorists armed with Soviet SAM-7 ground-to-air rockets. They had taken a house on the flight path to Rome and were planning to shoot down an Israeli El Al airliner.

The 1973 Arab-Israeli War opened up a new chapter in Middle East negotiations. The Arabs now had the "oil weapon," which put them in a strong bargaining position. Arafat wanted Fatah to be accepted as a part of Middle East negotiations, so he formally renounced terrorism. He achieved a major aim when he was allowed to address the General Assembly of the United Nations in November 1974. However, he had also alienated some former supporters, such as Abu Nidal. The Black September Organization, though, was no longer in operation.

Abu Nidal and Radical Islam

In 1987, two bombs went off in Amman. Responsibility for them was claimed by Black September, at this time no more than a cover name for the Abu Nidal Organization.

Terrorism erupted again in Jordan in 1991 at the time of the Gulf War. An Islamic extremist group calling itself the Prophet Muhammad's Army emerged, made up of militants who had defected from the Muslim Brotherhood. The group admitted responsibility for the murder of a Jordanian intelligence officer, for two car bombings, and for planning attacks on Western embassies. Eight members of the group were convicted and sentenced to death, though the sentences were later commuted to prison terms. Other groups were probably behind a number of attacks on business and diplomatic targets belonging to countries involved in the coalition against Iraq.

In 1992, two Jordanians were convicted of membership in a group calling itself Vanguard of the Islamic Youth. The group had reportedly been funded by Iran via the Popular Front for the Liberation of Palestine—General Command. It had planned to attack Western embassies in Amman and launch cross-border raids into the West Bank. In November, the two defendants were sentenced to twenty years' hard labor, although King Hussein of Jordan gave them amnesty a few days later. In 1993, Jordanian security forces discovered a plot to assassinate King Hussein by members of the banned opposition Islamic Liberation Party. In November, three gunmen allied with the Egyptian group al-Gamaa al-Islamiyya (the Islamic Group) were killed when they tried to attack a Jordanian army post near the West Bank.

KEY DATES

1967 Israel defeats Jordan and other Arab states in the Six-Day War, seizing control of the West Bank and East Jerusalem from Amman.
1970 After Palestinian nationalists seize three commercial aircraft and force them to land at Dawson's Field, in Jordan, King Hussein decides to oust the Palestine Liberation Organization from his territory, sparking a bloody civil war known as Black September.
1972 Members of the Black September terror group seize Israeli athletes and coaches at the Munich Olympics, killing eleven of them.
1973 Terrorists of Black September seize the Saudi embassy in Paris and the Saudi embassy in Khartoum.
1987 Black September, now little more than a cover name for the terrorist organization run by Palestinian Abu Nidal, sets off two bombs in Amman.
1994 Jordan becomes the second Arab nation, after Egypt, to sign a peace treaty with Israel.
2005 Al-Qaeda suicide bombers attack three hotels in Amman, killing sixty persons, most of them Jordanian.

In January 1994, suspected members of the Prophet Muhammad's Army carried out more attacks in Jordan, bombing cinemas in Amman and Zarqa. The police made twenty-five arrests and claimed that some of those detained were former mujahideen who had fought in Afghanistan. Those arrested were charged with a plot to overthrow the government. Eleven received death sentences and seven were sentenced to hard labor. Also in 1994, the authorities arrested thirty others suspected of terrorism, including fifteen members of the Abu Nidal Organization.

In that same year, Jordan signed a peace treaty with Israel, the second Arab country to do so, after Egypt. While this largely brought a cessation of Israeli attacks on the country, it also fomented outrage among more extremist Islamist elements in the Middle East. In addition, the country became more active in rooting out terrorist cells on its soil. In 2000, for example, it sentenced six Islamist terrorists to death for plotting attacks on U.S. and Israeli targets. Four years later, it handed down death sentences against eight Islamist militants convicted of killing a U.S. government official in 2002. Such moves made Jordan a target. In 2005, some sixty persons were killed when suicide bombers of al-Qaeda attacked three international hotels in the capital, though no incident on this scale has occurred since.

Neil Partrick and Andrew Rathmell

See also: *Definitions, Types, Categories*—Islamist Fundamentalist Terrorism. *Modern Terrorism*—Palestine: PLO and the Arab States.

Further Reading

Cobban, Helena. *The Palestine Liberation Organization: People, Power, and Politics.* New York: Cambridge University Press, 1983.

Groussard, Serge. *The Blood of Israel: The Massacre of the Israeli Athletes, the Olympics, 1972.* New York: William Morrow, 1975.

Klein, Aaron J. *Striking Back: The 1972 Munich Olympics Massacre and Israel's Deadly Response.* New York: Random House, 2005.

Livingstone, Neil, and David Halevy. *Inside the PLO: Covert Units, Secret Funds, and the War Against Israel and the United States.* New York: William Morrow, 1989.

Melman, Yossi. *The Master Terrorist: The True Story Behind Abu Nidal.* New York: Adama Books, 1986.

Mishal, Shaul. *The PLO Under Arafat Between Gun and Olive Branch.* New Haven, CT: Yale University Press, 1986.

Robins, Philip. *A History of Jordan.* New York: Cambridge University Press, 2004.

Kenya: Mau Mau Uprising, 1952–1956

The Mau Mau was a secret society that led a terrorist campaign against colonial rule in the British African colony of Kenya. Like many secret societies in Africa, the Mau Mau was based on a single tribe and evoked supernatural powers.

It is unclear how ancient the Mau Mau was or what its name meant. However, by the late 1940s, the society had a political message. It taught that the white farmers who had grown prosperous through raising cash crops had built their success on the backs of the Kikuyu tribesmen. Many unemployed men, seeing the wealth of the whites, joined the movement.

Magical Oaths

The main increase in Mau Mau numbers came in 1949, as the society carried out an aggressive recruitment campaign. Kikuyu were persuaded, or forced, to take an oath, or *thenge*, in a ceremony that often included ritual self-scarring with knives. The recruits swore to carry out Mau Mau instructions on pain of death at the hands of supernatural beasts. The violent deaths of a few recruits served to convince any uncertain tribesmen.

The rising number of initiation ceremonies led the Kenyan colonial government to ban the Mau Mau in 1950. However, by 1952, the society had organized a guerrilla army and begun a campaign of violence. The aim was to overthrow the colonial regime and replace it with Kikuyu supremacy over neighboring tribes.

The forests and mountains north of Nairobi were home to around 12,000 Mau Mau guerrillas, armed mostly with traditional spears and clubs. About 30,000 tribesmen in villages formed the "passive wing," which sent supplies to the guerrillas. Most of the other Kikuyu were bound by magical oath to support the movement. In Nairobi, a central committee gathered information, coordinated activity, and issued orders to the guerrillas. The command structure was loose and relied on obedience to the oath for its efficiency.

During 1951 and 1952, the Mau Mau carried out attacks on isolated white-owned farms and murdered several Kikuyu who opposed the movement. These attacks became so frequent that the government declared a state of emergency in October 1952. At first the authorities could do little because of the lack of troops and poor intelligence work. In January 1953, the Ruck family (husband,

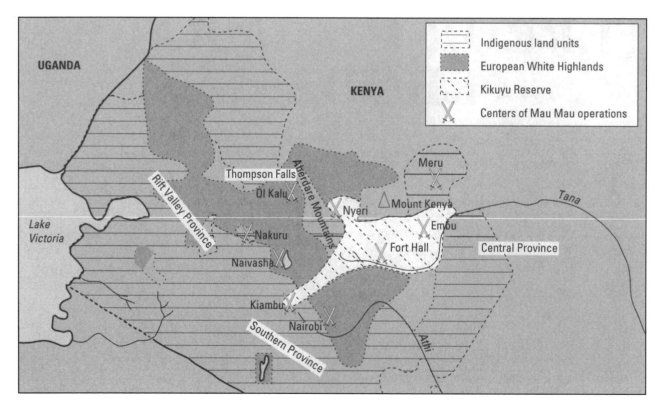

Kikuyu reservations and areas of Mau Mau activity.

wife, and six-year-old son) were hacked to death, an act that outraged the settlers.

In response, the colonial regime imprisoned the leaders of the Kenya African Union, the legal political party representing the Kikuyu. It also increased the British military strength in Kenya, called up native home defense forces, and strengthened the police. In 1953, a conventional military campaign against the Mau Mau began but achieved little. The Mau Mau, which now numbered up to 15,000 fighters, proved an elusive enemy and suffered few losses. Mau Mau guerrilla attacks on villages continued, and the bodies of victims were often mutilated in ritual fashion.

In early 1954, the new British commander, Sir George Erskine, introduced counterinsurgency tactics used in Malaya. He set up propaganda and psychological warfare staffs, improved intelligence gathering, and ensured cooperation between the military and the police.

The first major mission under this new initiative was Operation Anvil in April 1954. The Kikuyu population of Nairobi, some 30,000 people, were rounded up and interrogated. Hooded informants were used to identify Mau Mau activists, who were placed in detention camps. Operation Anvil effectively broke the central committee and ended coordinated activity among the different groups of Mau Mau guerrillas.

Meanwhile, the British declared the denser forests of Kenya to be war zones in which the security forces could shoot on sight, and they often did. The Kikuyu villages were searched for Mau Mau supporters and surrounded by stockades. These measures seriously reduced the Mau Mau's ability to continue its terrorist campaign. Another effective tool was the introduction of cleansing oaths to counter the Mau Mau oath of obedience. Once the British hired witch doctors to cleanse large numbers of Kikuyu in this way, the Mau Mau lost its base of unwilling support.

Clearing the Forests

In 1955, British military raids forced the guerrillas to split into small groups and flee the forest, making them easier to eliminate. Attempts were made to negotiate surrenders. Captured Mau Mau leader General China persuaded guerrillas to surrender, and 1,200 members of the passive wing were arrested. Allegations of torture were brought against the security forces. A total of 430 detainees were shot "trying to escape," and more than 1,000 executions had been carried out by 1956.

The Mau Mau also found itself faced with "countergangs." These gangs, made up of native soldiers and cleansed Mau Mau fighters, posed as Mau Mau to locate groups of guerrillas. They successfully made contact with the guerrillas that the large-scale sweeps missed. These tactics effectively destroyed the Mau Mau by November 1956.

Kenya gained its independence in 1963 under Jomo Kenyatta, who had been arrested as a leading member of the Kenya African Union during the crisis. Kenyatta, a Kikuyu, rapidly established his tribe in power, though without the radical land policies of the Mau Mau.

John Finlayson

See also: *Definitions, Types, Categories*—Ethnonationalist Terrorism; State vs. Nonstate Terrorism.

Further Reading

Barnett, D. *Karari Njama: Mau Mau from Within.* New York: MacGibbon and Kee, 1966.

Egerton, Robert B. *Mau Mau: An African Crucible.* New York: Ballantine Books, 1991.

Elkins, Caroline. *Imperial Reckoning: The Untold Story of Britain's Gulag in Kenya.* New York: Henry Holt, 2005.

Majdalani, F. *State of Emergency: The Full Story of Mau Mau.* Boston, MA: Houghton Mifflin, 1963.

Kenya and Tanzania: Embassy Bombings, 1998

On August 7, 1998, highly trained al-Qaeda strike units simultaneously exploded two powerful truck bombs at the U.S. embassies in Nairobi, Kenya, and Dar es Salaam, Tanzania, resulting in the deaths of 224 people, 12 of them U.S. citizens, and the wounding of more than 4,000 others. These high-impact bombings were consistent with Osama bin Laden's fatwa of February 23, 1998—under the International Islamic Front for Jihad Against Crusaders and Jews—to kill Americans wherever in the world they were found, and his later declaration of holy jihad in May 1998 in the London-based newspaper *Al-Quds al-Arabia* against the United States, Israel, and the Western allies.

Historical Background

The historical origins of al-Qaeda's political and military involvement in the East African region date back to the early Islamic and Muslim objective of penetrating East Africa and sub-Saharan Africa and converting all Africans to the Islamic faith in the early modern era. The realization of these strategic objectives by militant radical Islamists and their allies was particularly important in the East African region composed of Kenya, the Sudan, Tanzania, Uganda, and Zanzibar, where Islam already had a very powerful foothold. In the summer of 1991, Osama bin Laden and the al-Qaeda leadership secretly met with the Sudan's supreme spiritual leader and head of the National Islamic Front in the Sudan, Hassan al-Turabi, and debated the best means to remove U.S. and Western influence from East Africa and sub-Saharan Africa, and to push the East African region closer to the Islamic world.

At the operational level, Hassan al-Turabi, bin Laden, and Ayman al-Zawahiri agreed that defeating the insurgency of the Sudanese People's Army (SPA) against the Islamic government in Khartoum had first priority and that it could be done by discouraging East African states from materially supporting the SPA's political and military activities in the Sudan through a campaign of subversion, bombings, and terrorism. In early 1993, a high-level al-Qaeda military trainer, Ali Mohammad, began the advanced training of al-Qaeda operatives in the Sudan for regionwide terrorist attacks in East Africa, targeting Kenya, Tanzania, and Uganda. In spring 1993, Ali Mohammad's al-Qaeda training camps in Somalia began preparing the warlord Mohammad Farah Aidid's gunmen to resist the coming United Nations (UN) and U.S. peacekeeping operations in Somalia. However, the loss of U.S. Special Forces personnel to Aidid's gunmen and the al-Qaeda strike force in a large ambush in Mogadishu was a major tactical victory for al-Turabi, bin Laden, and other foreign militant radical Islamists in the region (including Iran, whose strategic objective was to improve Islam's profile in East Africa and embarrass the United States in the region at all costs). Nonetheless, the withdrawal of U.S. Special Forces in October 1993 from Somalia—and the reluctance of its warlords to embrace al-Qaeda and militant radical Islamist doctrine—convinced al-Turabi and bin Laden to begin advanced strategic planning for high-profile terrorist operations against U.S. targets in East Africa to further embarrass the United States, to encourage East African states not to materially assist the SPA in the Sudan, and to convince East African states to move into the Islamic orbit.

Establishment of Al-Qaeda Cells

To satisfy these strategic objectives, Ali al-Rashidi, the senior military commander in Kenya and one of the leaders of an elite al-Qaeda strike team against American Special Forces in Somalia, began building up the clandestine al-Qaeda network throughout the East African region. He focused on building both support networks (smuggling, money laundering, and logistical assistance) and operational networks (assassination, bomb making, and weapons acquisition) to allow al-Qaeda operatives in the region to deal with all eventualities, including an increasing coordination of efforts by American, Egyptian, and Kenyan authorities against them.

In May 1996, al-Rashidi died in a boating accident in Kenya, delaying for a period the building of the East African network. In this context, the rebuilding of the support and operational networks in East Africa was initially located in Somalia but was later facilitated by al-Qaeda operative Mohamed Sadeek's move to Mombasa, Kenya, and by al-Qaeda member Walih el Hage's move to Dar es Salaam, Tanzania (although Hage's front would be severely compromised by the intervention of the Federal Bureau of Investigation [FBI] and Kenyan security services, forcing Hage's exit from Kenya altogether in 1997). Both of these hardened al-Qaeda chiefs would use legitimate businesses as fronts to both rebuild the networks and plan the terrorist bombing strikes against U.S. embassies in Nairobi and Dar es Salaam. The strengthening of the African and Arab Islamic cell systems in East Africa and other regions of sub-Saharan Africa with significant Islamic populations resulted in

The U.S. embassy in Nairobi, Kenya, smolders after a massive truck bomb explosion on August 7, 1998. The U.S. embassy in Dar es Salaam, Tanzania, was struck simultaneously. The attacks were attributed to Osama bin Laden's al-Qaeda network. *(Associated Press)*

an increased al-Qaeda strike capability, much to the satisfaction of bin Laden of al-Qaeda, al-Turabi of the Sudan, and Iran's leaders. The terrorist cells were highly organized, well financed, motivated by highly trained leaders and field operatives, and capable of doing great material damage in the African states in which they were operating. In 1997, Subhi Abdul Aziz Abu-Sitta, a close confidant of al-Zawahiri and of the now deceased Ali al-Rashidi, was appointed as the new East African military commander by al-Qaeda. Staying in the shadows, he functioned as the operational link between al-Qaeda's leadership cadres in Afghanistan and Pakistan and the al-Qaeda strike groups in the East Africa region. It was these existing terrorist cell systems located throughout Kenya and Tanzania that the al-Qaeda leadership turned to for the development of planning for the U.S. embassy bombings in East Africa.

Al-Qaeda's Forward Terrorist Planning

From the available evidence, it is clear that the forward terrorist planning by al-Qaeda's leaders in the East Africa region was highly professional in content, organizationally compartmentalized, extremely meticulous logistically, and very well financed. They also practiced sophisticated operational security procedures, utilizing code names and false names for terrorist strike personnel. In retrospect, it is clear that they were dedicated to maximizing the collateral bomb damage against U.S. embassies in Kenya and Tanzania simultaneously. In July 1998, Ali Saleh—chief military planner of the

terrorist bombings of the U.S. embassies in Nairobi, Kenya, and Dar es Salaam, Tanzania—finalized the operational planning.

A hardened Egyptian veteran of the Afghanistan war, Ali Saleh passed on his operational battle plan to senior al-Qaeda supervisors for critical review in mid-July 1998. His plan approved, Ali Saleh informed key multinational al-Qaeda personnel in Kenya and Tanzania to begin final tactical bombing preparations, secretly contacting affected personnel at disparate cells around the world: Wadih El Hage (the United States), Mohamed Rashid Daoud al-Owhali (Yemen), Mohammed Sadiq Odeh (Jordan-Palestine), Abdallah Nacha (Lebanon), and Abdallah Mohammed Fazil (Egypt). While U.S., Kenyan, and Egyptian counterterrorist activities against al-Qaeda in the East African region were increasing in both intensity and frequency by mid-1998, the al-Qaeda strike teams went forward with the final secret preparations for the U.S. embassy strikes, including stepped-up reconnaissance and observations of the U.S. and Israeli embassies in Nairobi, Kenya, bomb design and bomb-making preparations, and exit and escape planning in the postbombing event.

The Attacks

In July 1998, Ali Saleh and Abdallah Mohammed Fazil moved quickly to prepare for the U.S. embassy strikes in Kenya and Tanzania, with a routine emphasis on qualitative information assessment by senior al-Qaeda leaders on all phases of the coming bombing operations in Kenya and Tanzania, including multiple reconnaissance and observations of the U.S. embassy sites, the design and assembly of the bomb (TNT with traces of the high explosive Semtex-H), transportation and placement of the bomb, and the exit and escape of the al-Qaeda bombing teams. On August 7, 1998, the Nairobi operation commenced after some diversion, and 1,800 pounds of military-high-explosives bomb were detonated, destroying the U.S. embassy and causing the deaths of American and Kenyan embassy personnel and civilians, as well as the wounding and mutilation of many more. At exactly the same time in Dar es Salaam, a military high explosive weighing several hundred pounds (TNT reinforced with tanks of oxygen, gas, and acetylene) detonated at the U.S. embassy with deadly impact, causing death and mayhem. In hindsight, the tightly organized and extremely secretive al-Qaeda cell in Dar es Salaam remains an enigma. It was activated by the al-Qaeda leadership in June 1998 and commanded by Mustafa Mohammad Fadhil (Egypt). From available evidence, the al-Qaeda unit in Dar es Salaam worked efficiently, quietly, and with great purpose. The al-Qaeda operatives in the Dar es Salaam bombing included Rashid Saleh Hemed (Tanzania/Zanzibar), Mustafa Mohammed Fadhil, Ahmad Khalfan Ghailani (Tanzania/Zanzibar/Oman), Khalfan Khamis Mohammed (Tanzania/Zanzibar), Fahad Mohammed Ali Msalam (Kenya), Sheikh Ahmed Salim Swedan (Kenya/Yemen), and Ahmed the German (Egypt).

KEY DATES

February 1998 Osama bin Laden issues a fatwa—or religious command—to kill Americans wherever they might be found around the world.

May 1998 Bin Laden issues a call for a jihad, or holy war, against the United States in a London-based Arabic-language newspaper.

July 1998 Ali Saleh, chief military planner for al-Qaeda, finalizes plans for the bombing of the U.S. embassies in Kenya and Tanzania.

August 1998 Two suicide attackers set off truck bombs at the U.S. embassies in Nairobi, Kenya, and Dar es Salaam, Tanzania, killing 213 people in the former city and 11 in the latter; the vast majority of the victims are Africans.

Trials

Since the August 1998 U.S. embassy bombings in Kenya and Tanzania, the federal judicial proceedings in Courtroom 318 of the U.S. District Court in Manhattan against the al-Qaeda operatives Mohammed Saddiq Odeh, Wadih El Hage, Rashid Daoud al-Owhali, and Khalfan Khamis Mohammed, all of whom faced a 302-count indictment, revealed much about Osama bin Laden and al-Qaeda. The federal trial would reveal U.S. intelligence failure to penetrate al-Qaeda in the East African region, as well as the porous security at the U.S. embassy sites in Kenya and Tanzania.

Presided over by U.S. District Judge Leonard B. Sand, the federal trial was extremely tense and noted for its extraordinary security measures inside and outside the courtroom, as well as revealing to federal authorities al-Qaeda's planning sophistication, its ability to secretly transfer large sums of money to operational terrorist units in the field, the excellent military training and dedication of its leadership and operational personnel, and its marked ability to coordinate terrorist activities across locations. After a contentious trial, all four al-Qaeda defendants were convicted and sentenced. Although the conclusion of the trial gave the public some closure on the U.S. embassy bombing events, it did nothing to lessen the grief of Americans and Africans who suffered by al-Qaeda's actions.

Michael J. Siler

See also: *Definitions, Types, Categories*—Domestic vs. International Terrorism. *September 11 Attacks*—Al-Qaeda.

Further Reading

Alexander, Yonah, and Michael S. Swetman. *Usama bin Laden's al-Qaeda: Profile of a Terrorist Network.* Ardsley, NY: Transnational, 2001.

Bodansky, Yossef. *Bin Laden: The Man Who Declared War on America.* Roseville, CA: Prima, 2001.

Clarke, Richard. *Against All Enemies: Inside America's War on Terror.* New York: Free Press, 2004.

Pirio, Gregory Alonso. *The African Jihad: Bin Laden's Quest for the Horn of Africa.* Trenton, NJ: Red Sea Press, 2007.

Post, Jerrold M. *Military Studies in the Jihad Against Tyrants: The al-Qaeda Training Manual.* London: Frank Cass, 2002.

Korea: Korean War, 1950–1953

From 1910 to the end of World War II in 1945, Korea was a colony of Japan under a harsh military regime. The largest protests against Japanese rule took place on March 1, 1919, when more than a million Koreans demonstrated peacefully all over the country. In response, the Japanese executed more than 7,000 Koreans in order to terrorize the population into submission. An increasingly pervasive police force continued to practice state terror. By 1941, there was one security officer for every 400 people.

After the Japanese surrender in 1945, Koreans hoped that their country would achieve immediate independence. People's committees arose spontaneously, taking on the role of government throughout the peninsula. These committees included all political groups, except those that had collaborated with the Japanese. The groups tended to be dominated by the Left, though not by the communists. The Left had popular support because it had opposed the Japanese and sympathized with the desire of many rural Koreans for land reform.

All hopes of independence were thwarted, however, by the immediate arrival of Soviet forces in North Korea and American forces in South Korea, with the occupation zones being divided at the 38th parallel.

The Soviet forces had made some preparations for the occupation. For example, they brought with them credible anti-Japanese Korean figures, including the communist former guerrilla leader Kim Il Sung. The Soviets initially worked through the people's committees, only gradually placing their own nominees in positions of power. In 1946, Kim became chairman of the North Korean Interim People's Committee and implemented the popular measure of land redistribution. The regime used intimidation against right-wing politicians, former collaborators, landowners, and Christians to force them off the land.

By contrast, the U.S. forces were not prepared for occupying Korea. They believed that the radical people's committees were communist fronts and refused to recognize them. They guaranteed a return to order in Korea by working through the existing Japanese government structure, which most Koreans hated. In so doing, the U.S. occupation was forced to support politicians of the extreme Right. These politicians offered the most reliable opposition to communism but represented only a narrow section of Korean society. Many who had collaborated with the Japanese occupiers were allowed to remain in their positions. For example, more than 75 percent of the senior police officers serving in November 1946 had previously worked with the Japanese colonial police.

UN Involvement

Toward the end of 1947, the United States decided to remove its occupation force. It tried to involve the United Nations (UN) in order to strengthen the legitimacy of the government it left behind. In May 1948, a UN commission supervised and then endorsed elections. Seventy-five percent of voters participated, and southern leader Syngman Rhee and his supporters emerged as the largest group in the new National Assembly. As a result, the commission recognized Rhee's pro-Western Republic of Korea, commonly referred to as South Korea, as the legitimate government of Korea in the southern zone.

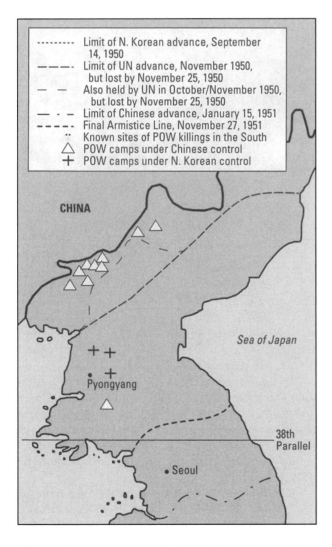

Military advances by the armies of North and South during the Korean War, and the many prisoner-of-war camps on the peninsula.

The reality of the elections, however, was a long way from what might have been expected, given the endorsement of the UN commission and all that it implied. There was left-wing disruption and right-wing intimidation, and the polls were controlled by right-wing police auxiliaries, many of whom were still in their Japanese uniforms. During the forty days of campaigning for the elections, nearly 600 people were killed in the widespread disturbances.

The northern zone responded with its own elections. Little is known about how these elections were run. Much can be assumed, though, from the claimed 99.97 percent participation rate and the universal victory of the communist candidates of the North Korean Labor Party. The Democratic People's Republic of Korea was declared in the north in October 1948, and Soviet forces, their task complete, then withdrew.

From 1948 to 1950, the populations of these competing regimes were subject to widespread terrorism. In North Korea, resistance to the government seems to have been comparatively small, partly because of the popularity of measures such as land reform, and partly because many of the government's opponents had fled to the south.

In South Korea, by contrast, the communists continued to oppose the regime, gaining popular support because of the lack of social reforms instituted by Rhee's government. The government was also implicated in the assassination of politicians who refused to support it. In 1949, for example, an army lieutenant murdered Kim Ku, South Korea's leading moderate. The killer was sentenced to life imprisonment but released within months. Later, he was promoted to lieutenant colonel.

The largest uprising against Rhee's government came on the island of Cheju during 1948–1949. The government responded with a program of state terror. The authorities destroyed all the villages in the interior of the island and massacred their inhabitants or moved them to refugee camps on the coast. About 30,000 people, or 10 percent of Cheju's population, were killed in the suppression of the revolt.

Terror in the South and North

In early 1949, North Korea launched a campaign of propaganda and cross-border raids aimed at weakening South Korean confidence in Syngman Rhee's government. However, by 1950, it was plain to the North Koreans that this campaign was not going to be enough to bring about the South Korean government's collapse. So, on June 25, 1950, North Korea launched an invasion across the thirty-eighth parallel. It is now clear that this attack was begun at North Korea's own instigation. The Soviet Union, however, gave the enterprise its blessing and provided the necessary equipment.

The North Koreans hoped that South Korea would fall before the intervention of the United States. However, the U.S. led a swift UN intervention. North Korea occupied 90 percent of the Republic of Korea during the summer of 1950 but was then forced back. The UN forces rapidly occupied 90 percent of North Korea between October and December 1950. At this point, the Chinese entered the war and forced the UN back. By the summer of 1951, the battle line was close to the thirty-eighth parallel, where it remained until the armistice of July 1953.

North Korea sought to legitimize its invasion by extending reforms in South Korea during the brief period of occupation. However, to demonstrate the price of opposition, it also conducted a purge of those who had collaborated with Rhee's government. Many target groups fled, but thousands of policemen, officials, landlords, and their families were executed without trial. Killings increased as the North Koreans retreated and tried to eliminate people who might collaborate with the UN forces. An estimated 20,000 to 23,000 people were executed during this period, including 300 U.S. prisoners of war.

In addition to this "red terror," there was a "white terror" enacted by South Korean security forces before the North Korean invasion. At the time of the invasion, up to 58,000 suspected communist sympathizers were languishing in southern jails. When war broke out, many of these prisoners were executed—estimates are as high as 50,000—because they were considered security risks. The chief of the South Korean police admitted to only 1,200 executions in the first three weeks of fighting. However, a French missionary witnessed the execution of 1,700 prisoners at Taejon early in the war. Before their execution, a British journalist saw 700 prisoners chained at Pusan and gathered that this process had been "going on for months." A figure of 50,000 deaths is probably too high, but it is possible that as many died in this terror as in the communist occupation.

When Republic of Korea security forces reoccupied their country in October 1950, they unleashed terror on an even greater scale in their search for anyone suspected of having cooperated with the communists. Those defined as cooperating included people who had simply continued in their jobs during the occupation.

In his memoirs, U.S. diplomat Gregory Henderson claimed that "tens of thousands—probably over 100,000—were killed without any trial whatsoever when [South Korean] soldiers . . . re-captured . . . areas of leftist repute." UN officials discounted the massacres publicly, but in private they were prepared to admit the scale of the killings.

The problem continued when UN forces entered North Korea in October 1950. UN officials hoped that by taking responsibility for the occupation they might avoid the excesses that had taken place in the South. However, South Korean troops made up half the UN army, and all the American and British forces were required at the front. This meant that the occupation of North Korea was left in the very biased hands of the South Koreans. Needless to say, the fiercely anticommunist South Koreans were brutal in their methods. Their militia units were often under minimal central control. Additionally, all but one of the South Korean army's senior officers had previously served with the Japanese military, and many of the junior officers were from the dispossessed families of refugees from North Korea.

The South Koreans also had to cope with an extensive guerrilla campaign in areas occupied by the UN forces. This was waged by scattered bands of North Korean troops, who were ruthless in their exploitation of the civilian population, using children to carry ammunition and refugees to cover their assaults.

Toll on Civilians

The result of all this terror was that an enormous number of civilians died at the hands of South Korean forces. North Korea has claimed that the civilian death toll amounted to 170,000, with the majority killed when UN forces were forced to retreat after China's intervention in the war. The accuracy of this claim is impossible to verify. However, given the scale of killing undertaken by South Korean forces, it seems likely that tens of thousands were killed. Again, significant eyewitness evidence exists to indicate the extent of the brutality.

Other UN forces, which were overwhelmingly American, were not immune to the oppressive atmosphere created by this savage civil war, the stress of guerrilla warfare, and racial isolation. Understandably, morale was lowest in retreat. Unable to tell friend from foe, many became suspicious of all Koreans and were ready to shoot at the slightest provocation. Suspicion, coupled with weak discipline in some U.S. units early in the war, led to many Korean civilian casualties. The situation improved dramatically from December 23, 1950, when American general Matthew Ridgway took command of the UN forces. He imposed the highest standards of discipline.

From spring 1951, the war became steadily less mobile, with the two Korean states maintaining control of their own territories. Both sides continued to use violence and arbitrary executions to suppress any elements of the population suspected of disloyalty. This was particularly the case after periods of enemy occupation, when allegiances became especially open to doubt. However, there were two other elements of terror associated with the latter part of the war: the treatment of prisoners of war and the air attacks.

Torture and Execution

Prisoners on both sides suffered terribly. In the communist camps, South Korean prisoners were very badly treated, but 2,701 of the 7,140 U.S. personnel taken also died in captivity. Many died early in the war because of the primitive conditions in the camps, while others were executed. Those prisoners who would not cooperate in communist propaganda were tortured. The methods of torture included being forced to stand for long periods on tiptoe with a taut noose around the neck.

Prisoners in UN hands were guarded largely by South Korean troops. The troops were frequently left alone to physically abuse prisoners. British observers claimed that U.S. troops involved were often inclined to "regard the [prisoners] as cattle." As the war progressed, the prisoners polarized into pro- and anticommunist groups. UN and Chinese agents were placed among the prisoners in order to encourage the different factions. The leaders of both sides used terror to coerce prisoners to join their groups. This included beatings, mutilations, and executions. At one point, UN troops tried to screen the prisoners to see which of them wished to return to China and North Korea. Rejecting repatriation, the procommunists rioted. In the ensuing battles, several UN troops and hundreds of prisoners were killed, some by their own comrades when they tried to surrender.

Further allegations of the use of terror emerged from UN air operations. Raids were restricted to defined military targets until the Chinese intervention.

After this, the definition of a military target was broadened, in the words of U.S. secretary of state Dean Acheson, to include "every means of communication, installation, factory, city, and village in North Korea." North Korea accused the UN of terror bombing. The UN responded that only military targets were attacked, but this claim avoided the issue of the all-inclusiveness of such targets. Frustrated that the industries that supported the communist war effort were outside the country, the UN launched some raids simply to increase the strain of the war. British prime minister Winston Churchill wrote, with regard to the use of napalm against Korean cities, that he would take no responsibility "for the indiscriminate use of napalm not in warfare but to torture the civilian population." The final civilian casualty toll is uncertain, although estimates by U.S. High Command of 2 million killed or injured may be exaggerated.

Terror was a major aspect of policy during the Korean War. Ultimately, North Korea's population probably was terrorized to a greater degree than the South Korean population. However, in the postconflict period, communist North Korea conducted a terrorist campaign against a much stronger U.S.-aided South Korea that included bombings and the assassination of prominent figures, such as President Park Chung Hee in 1979.

Stephen Prince

See also: *Modern Terrorism*—Korea, North: WMD Threat.

Further Reading

Cumings, B. *The Origins of the Korean War.* Vol. 2, *The Roaring of the Cataract, 1947–1950.* Princeton, NJ: Princeton University Press, 1990.

Foot, Rosemary. *A Substitute for Victory: The Politics of Peacemaking at the Korean Armistice Talks.* Ithaca, NY: Cornell University Press, 1990.

Halberstam, David. *Coldest Winter: America and the Korean War.* New York: Hyperion, 2007.

Knox, D. *The Korean War: An Oral History—Pusan to Chosin.* New York: Harcourt, Brace, Jovanovich, 1985.

MacDonald, C. "So Terrible a Liberation: The UN Occupation of North Korea." *Bulletin of Concerned Asian Scholars* 23:2 (1991): 3–19.

Korea, North: WMD Threat, 1980s–Present

North Korea, known as the world's only unreconstructed Stalinist country, was accused of state-sponsored terrorism long before Afghanistan decided to give shelter to Osama bin Laden. It was placed on the U.S. Department of State's list of states supporting international terrorism in 1988, following the 1987 bombing of a South Korean airliner by North Korean agents, which killed 119 people. A female North Korean agent, arrested soon after the attack, told South Korean security officials that she was directly ordered by North Korean leader Kim Il-sung to participate in the bombing of Korean Airlines flight 858.

North Korea has not been conclusively linked to a terrorist attack since the 1987 Korean Airlines bombing incident. However, the state continues to be a challenge to regional and global security because of the following factors: (1) North Korea's pursuit of weapons of mass destruction (WMD) and long-range missiles; (2) its readiness and eagerness to sell missiles and other armaments to states that have dubious international credentials; (3) its intransigence in refusing to hand over Japanese Red Army hijackers of Japanese airliners they have sheltered since 1970; (4) its abysmal human rights record and state repression of its own people; and (5) its continued provocation of neighbors, including the testing of missiles over Japanese airspace in 1998 and 2009 and the alleged sinking of a South Korean navy ship in May 2010, with the loss of forty-six sailors.

WMD Threat

North Korea has pursued a nuclear weapons program since the 1980s. In 1985, the U.S. intelligence agencies reported that North Korea was constructing a 200 megawatts electric nuclear reactor at Yongbyon, which is located approximately ninety kilometers north of the country's capital city, Pyongyang. Following this revelation, the international community, led by the United States, pressured North Korea to sign the Nuclear Nonproliferation Treaty (NPT). However, even after signing the NPT, until January 1992, North Korea declined to provide access for international nuclear safeguards arrangements, under which it was required to allow unrestricted inspections of its nuclear facilities by the International Atomic Energy Agency (IAEA).

In 1991, the states of North and South Korea signed an agreement on the denuclearization of the Korean Peninsula and followed it up with the signing of the nuclear safeguards agreement with the IAEA in 1992. In 1993, however, North Korea halted the IAEA nuclear inspections program by refusing access to unreported nuclear facilities that were suspected of holding nuclear waste. When subjected to pressure by the international community, North Korea, on March 12, 1993, announced its withdrawal from the NPT. This event led to a serious security crisis on the Korean Peninsula. The United States responded by holding high-level talks with North Korea, which led to the U.S.–North Korea Agreed Framework in 1994. This agreement called for North Korea to freeze its existing nuclear development program in return for an attractive international economic package.

North Korea has subsequently complied with the Agreed Framework. However, it has declined to account for approximately 24 kilograms of plutonium it is suspected to have extracted from its nuclear facilities during 1987–1991—before these facilities were closed under the 1994 U.S.–North Korea Agreed Framework. Some experts estimate that with this unaccounted plutonium, North Korea would be capable of producing at least two to three nuclear bombs, thereby endangering regional security.

In October 2002, the worst fears of experts were corroborated when Pyongyang admitted that it had been secretly enriching uranium for possible use in nuclear weapons in violation of its 1994 agreement with Washington. While some North Korea observers believed that the country made its admission in anticipation of a U.S. exposure of Pyongyang's secret nuclear efforts, others believed that the revelation may have been President Kim Jong-il's way of showing that his country was now trying to cooperate with Washington. In November 2002, North Korea threatened to resume missile tests if bilateral talks on normalizing relations between Japan and Korea failed. While the Japanese did not take the threats seriously, in November 2002 the United States and its East Asian and European allies voted to suspend oil shipments to North Korea. After the announcement of suspended fuel shipments, Pyongyang subsequently issued a statement that its claim to have nuclear weapons was a translation mistake, further confusing the issue. But things became clearer in 2003, when North Korea first announced its withdrawal from the NPT and then said it had enough plutonium on hand to start assembling at least six nuclear bombs.

Meanwhile, desultory talks began that same year, with North Korea, the United States, Japan, Russia, South Korea, and China, Pyongyang's only significant supporter, convening to discuss North Korea's nuclear program and ambitions. The talks would start and stop over the next several years, usually as the result of Pyongyang's erratic commitment to them. More provocative behavior followed in July 2006, when North Korea test-fired long- and medium-range missiles capable of carrying nuclear weapons, though U.S. officials said the tests were largely failures. The ultimate fear for the region, however, came when North Korea announced that it had tested its first nuclear weapon in October 2006, though there were some doubts as to whether or not it involved a true nuclear chain reaction.

Despite this setback, the six-party talks resumed in February 2007, leading to some significant break-throughs, including an October 2007 commitment by Pyongyang to disable three of its nuclear reactors and mothball all its nuclear programs by the end of the year. In the end, North Korea failed to live up to its commitments, though it did make its long-awaited declaration of nuclear assets in June 2008. In response, the United States announced that it would remove North Korea from its list of countries that sponsor terrorism if Pyongyang allowed for full access to its nuclear facilities by international inspectors.

Progress on the nuclear front with North Korea was always a matter of two steps forward and one step back. As international talks failed to make progress and the United States suspended energy aid, part of a deal to get North Korea to stop its nuclear program, Pyongyang in 2009 moved forward on efforts to develop its nuclear arsenal further, announcing in May that it had carried out its second underground nuclear test. Then, with the sinking of the South Korean naval vessel in March 2010, the United States announced new sanctions against the North Korean regime and launched naval exercises with South Korea. Pyongyang in July denounced these moves as provocations, even threatening a nuclear response if the exercises got too close to North Korean shores.

North Korean nuclear weapons are the most significant concern for both the United States and the country's neighbors, but not the only one. Even as it has pursued such weapons, Pyongyang has also had a functioning chemical weapons program, which is believed by the U.S. intelligence community to include the capability, since 1989, to produce bulk quantities of nerve, blister, choking, and blood chemical agents, as well as a variety of filled munitions systems. North Korea has eight industrial facilities that can produce chemical agents and about six storage facilities located in mountain tunnels dispersed all over the country. North Korea's chemical stockpiles are reportedly estimated to be 5,000 tons (4,536 metric tons).

In addition, since 1960, North Korea has been pursuing research and development related to biological warfare. Available biological warfare resources presently include a rudimentary (by Western standards) biotechnology infrastructure that is sufficient to support the production of limited quantities of toxins and biological warfare agents such as anthrax, plague virus, yellow fever, and smallpox. North Korea's National Defense Research Institute and Medical Academy is currently involved in biological warfare research. North Korea is also a signatory to the 1987 Biological Weapons Conventions.

Missile Development and Sales

North Korea has a well-developed missile program, including the Scud (175–200 miles), Hwasong (175–435 miles), Nodong (840–930 miles), Taepodong-1 (1,240–1,370 miles), and three-stage Taepodong-2 (2,500–3,750 miles). Almost all North Korean missiles are capable of delivering WMD munitions. North Korea is also actively involved in global missile proliferation. It has sold missiles, missile components, and technology to countries including Iran, Syria, Egypt, Libya, and Pakistan. Most vexing to the international community has been a series of ballistic weapons tests and underground nuclear tests; the UN Security Council issued resolutions in 2006 and 2009 that condemned such testing and imposed punitive sanctions. Beyond that, Pyongyang is also believed to have sold weapons to terrorist groups including the Moro National Army of the Philippines, the Liberation Tigers of Tamil Eelam of Sri Lanka, and the United Wa State Army, a drug trafficking group active in Burma.

Harboring Terrorists

The North Korean government continues to refuse to hand over to Japan four Red Army terrorists who have been sheltered in Pyongyang since 1970. These Red Army terrorists are accused of hijacking a Japan Airlines jet and diverting it to North Korea. The U.S. Department of State has demanded expulsion of the terrorists as a key condition for removing North Korea from its list of countries sponsoring terrorism. North Korea calls these terrorists political refugees and has refused their extradition.

Human Rights and Domestic Repression

North Korea is a totalitarian regime led by Kim Jong-il. The regime's military-first policy (North Korea spends 18 to 24 percent of its gross national product on the military) has led to a nearly bankrupt national economy, with people living under conditions of abject poverty and deprivation. Reports indicate that some North Koreans have fled for economic reasons to neighboring China and the far east of Russia. The North Korean government uses harsh measures against people accused of unauthorized emigration, including torture and even summary executions. According to its 1999 annual report, Amnesty International stated that the North Korean Security Service pursues North Korean refugees in the Russian Federation and sometimes apprehends them and forcibly returns them to North Korea.

North Korea has extended its support to the ongoing

The worst horrors the regime has unleashed have been against its own citizens. Outside human rights experts say Pyongyang has jailed hundreds of thousands of persons on largely political and social offenses and executed thousands more. In addition, many in the international community hold it responsible for the death of millions of its citizens through incompetent economic practices, which resulted in widespread starvation after devastating floods in the late 1990s and again in 2007. Some believe the regime may have blundered when it devalued its currency in 2009, wiping out the savings of millions of its citizens overnight, forcing it to ease restrictions on private markets, a rare about-face for a regime that has always seemed to maintain a rigid control over its citizens. Outsiders in the country at the time of the devaluation reported ordinary North Koreans expressing dissent for the first time.

Surinder Rana and James Ciment

See also: *Modern Terrorism*—Korea: Korean War. *Tactics, Methods, Aims*—Weapons, Nuclear and Radiological.

Further Reading

Amnesty International. "Democratic People's Republic of Korea (North Korea): Conditions of Detention," March 24, 1999. www.amnesty.org.

Bandow, Doug. "Nuclear Issues Between the U.S. and North Korea." In *North Korea After Kim Il Sung,* ed. Dae Sook Suh and Chae Jun Lee. Boulder, CO: Lynne Rienner, 1998.

Bermudez, Joseph. *Terrorism: The North Korean Connection.* New York: Taylor and Francis, 1990.

Chang, Gordon. *Nuclear Showdown: North Korea Takes On the World.* New York: Random House, 2006.

Chung, Wook Chong. "Mass Organization and Campaigns." In *North Korea Today: Strategic and Domestic Issues,* ed. Robert A. Scalpino and Jun Yopkim. Berkeley: University of California, Berkeley, Institute of East Asia Studies, Center for Korean Studies, 1983.

Holden, Simon. *North Korea's Nuclear and Ballistic Weapons.* Hauppauge, NY: Nova Science, 2009.

Oberdorfer, Don. *The Two Koreas: A Contemporary History.* Lexington, MA: Addison Wesley, 1997.

Vick, Charles P. "North Korean Missiles." Federation of American Scientists (FAS), March 27, 2002. www.fas.org.

U.S.-led global war on terrorism. However, the current North Korean regime continues to perpetrate repression of its own people, and also harbors international terrorists. Moreover, North Korea's position as longtime rogue state was bolstered by revelations, issued by Pyongyang during a visit there by Japanese prime minister Junichiro Koizumi in September 2002, that North Korea had kidnapped thirteen Japanese citizens during the Cold War to serve as language teachers and cultural instructors for North Korean spies, eight of whom had died under suspicious circumstances. In October 2002, North Korea allowed the remaining five to return to Japan for a two-week visit, further outraging Tokyo when it retained children and spouses of the five kidnapped Japanese as hostages to ensure their return. Pyongyang relented later in October, allowing the five kidnapped Japanese and their families to permanently move to Japan. Its soldiers were also responsible for the shooting death of a South Korean woman at the Mount Kumgang special tourism area in July 2008 and the seizure of two American journalists in June 2009, though it eventually released them after the intercession of former president Bill Clinton two months later.

Lebanon: Civil War, 1975–1990

Lebanon is a state containing many religious groups. Until the mid-1970s, there was a practical consensus about how the government of the country should be managed so that no one group became too powerful. In 1975, however, this system of power sharing broke down under the impact of Israeli raids and the presence of Palestinian guerrilla groups. The result was a horrific civil war. The old Lebanese state was destroyed, and this set the scene for a further round of terrorism in the 1980s.

The Maronite Christians were the dominant religious-political group, representing about 25 percent of the Lebanese population. A major element of the Maronite community was the extreme right-wing Phalangist Party. The conservative Sunni Muslims were the dominant Muslim group, even though they made up only about 20 percent of the population, compared with the Shiite Muslims' 30 percent. The Shiite Muslims traditionally had little political influence. In the mountains was an Islamic sect, the Druze, who had great political influence, although they made up just 7 percent of the population. Smaller groups included the Greek Orthodox and Armenian Christians.

Palestinian refugees entered this mix in the 1940s, and after the Palestine Liberation Organization (PLO) was expelled from Jordan in 1970–1971, it set up its headquarters in Lebanon, from where the movement struck at Israel. While PLO terror continued, Israel felt free to launch preemptive strikes in Lebanon. Israel targeted Palestinians both in southern Lebanon and in the Lebanese capital, Beirut. Besides attracting Israeli attacks, the Palestinian presence also politicized the previously dormant Shiite Muslims. They began to protest about their exploitation by the wealthy Maronite Christians and in 1973 established the Movement of the Dispossessed.

War for Fishing

The Lebanese Maronite Christian leaders were prepared to protect their interests with force, however. The beginning of the civil war in 1975 is usually seen as a dispute over fishing rights in the coastal town of Sidon. Before long the local Muslim mayor had been fatally wounded defending Muslim fishermen, and the situation escalated. The main conflict was between the Christian Maronites, in particular the Phalangists, and the left-wing Lebanese National Movement, which united the Druze-led Progressive Socialist Party, smaller communist groups, and the Shiite Movement of the Dispossessed. Both sides had private militias.

In April 1975, a key event took place when Pales-tinian gunmen shot the bodyguard of Phalangist leader Pierre Gemayel. The Christians retaliated by massacring twenty-seven Palestinians and injuring nineteen men on a bus in the Beirut suburb of Ain El Remmaneh. Druze leader Walid Jumblatt declared that he would no longer accept the presence of Phalangists in the cabinet, effectively tearing up the old constitutional arrangements. Some Palestinians teamed up with the Lebanese Sunni Muslim Mourabitoun militia in Beirut and took the lead in fighting the Phalangists.

In January 1976, Christian Maronite militias besieged Palestinian refugee camps in Karantina and Tel al-Zaatar. PLO leader Yasir Arafat had no choice but to affirm his commitment to war on the side of the Lebanese

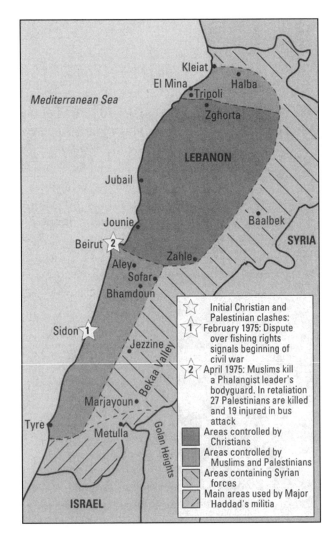

Areas controlled by protagonists in the Lebanese civil war, 1975–1977.

National Movement. It was probably inevitable that the PLO would ally itself politically with fellow Muslims in Lebanon. The Maronites, for whom the maintenance of the status quo meant everything, regarded the Palestinians as a destabilizing force.

Arafat's PLO was drawn into what became a mire of bloodletting and terror. PLO forces pushed north toward Beirut from their bases in the south of the country. On January 20, the PLO and Lebanese National Movement forces conducted a bloody raid on the tiny Christian coastal town of Damour, massacring much of the population. Control of the country was slipping from the Maronites' grasp.

In order to prevent a complete Palestinian victory, which might provoke Israeli intervention in Lebanon, President Hafiz al-Assad of Syria moved against the Palestinians. His troops encountered stiff resistance but managed to rescue the Maronite forces from destruction. While the Palestinians were occupied with the Syrians, the Maronites took the opportunity to destroy two Palestinian refugee camps in Christian territory: Jisr al-Pasha and Tel al-Zaatar. The latter held out for fifty-three days against the Phalangists, who massacred most of the inhabitants when the camp finally fell on August 12.

In October 1976, the Arab states agreed that a predominantly Syrian peacekeeping force should remain in Lebanon. By then, order had all but collapsed in Beirut and a large number of small, armed groups were causing mayhem throughout the country. In March 1977, for example, Druze leader Kamal Jumblatt, father of Walid, was assassinated. Druze slaughtered the Christian inhabitants of a nearby village in revenge. The villagers were almost certainly innocent. All existing evidence points to Syrian involvement in Kamal Jumblatt's killing.

While Lebanon submerged into terror, PLO groups continued raids into Israel. On March 11, 1978, terrorists from Fatah, the main Arafat-controlled party in the PLO, took a busload of Israelis hostage. Thirty-five hostages were killed and eighty-two were wounded before the terrorists themselves were killed in a shoot-out in Tel Aviv giving Israel a perfect reason for entering Lebanon.

On March 14–15, some 20,000 Israeli troops crossed into Lebanon. They pounded Palestinian bases and communities as far north as Tyre. Operation Litani, as the punitive raid was code-named, lasted seven days. During this period, the Israelis created "Free Lebanon," a strip of south Lebanon that served as an Israeli "security zone," controlled by a Christian Lebanese militia under Major Saad Haddad.

Terror in Lebanon, 1980–1987

The fighting that took place in Lebanon during the period 1980–1987 included a series of terrorist acts. Indeed, terror was an integral part of the tactics used by all sides as the country collapsed into a number of armed camps, in a moral twilight during which sworn enemies met to plan assassinations, and avowed opponents—such as the United States and fundamentalist Iran—colluded in arms trafficking.

The situation in Lebanon had been relatively quiet since the 1975–1978 civil war, although there were a number of terrorist incidents. In January 1979, for example, the Israelis detonated a bomb that killed Ali Hassan Salameh, the head of Yasir Arafat's bodyguard Force 17 and the man thought responsible for planning the terrorist attack on Israeli athletes at the 1972 Munich Olympics. The bomb also killed six innocent passersby.

In 1981, there were heavy exchanges of fire between Palestinians and Israelis. Arafat's forces rained down rockets on northern Israeli towns, while Israeli warplanes and artillery pounded Palestinian camps. After letting off steam, and with little hope of matching the Israeli carnage being wrought in Lebanon, the PLO chairman soon put a stop to the rocket attacks. Arafat agreed to a ceasefire despite formidable Palestinian resistance. The PLO leader was fearful that Israel's Prime Minister Menachem Begin just wanted another pretext to send troops into Lebanon to drive out the PLO. Meanwhile, Syrian-controlled terrorists were trying to break the cease-fire. And once Begin was reelected in August 1981, the likelihood of intervention in Lebanon increased, especially once Ariel Sharon, considered a hardened "hawk," became defense minister.

Operation Peace for Galilee

On June 6, 1982, Israeli forces did indeed drive into Lebanon in what it dubbed "Operation Peace for Galilee." Although the government announced that it wished only to establish a demilitarized zone to prevent rocket attacks on northern Israel, it seems unlikely that Begin did not know of Sharon's intention to go all the way to Beirut. If Operation Litani, the limited incursion of 1978, had been insufficient, then taking control of Lebanon four years later would seem logical. Destruction of the PLO and knocking out Syria before establishing a proxy Christian regime in Beirut were the undoubted objectives.

The attempted assassination of Shlomo Argov, Israeli ambassador to London, on June 3, probably was not the final straw, as some have argued. Israel knew that agent provocateur and archenemy of the PLO Abu Nidal had orchestrated the attack—to which Israeli chief of staff Rafael Eitan responded, "Abu Nidal, Abu Shmidal. We have to destroy the PLO."

Fighting alongside Bashir Gemayel's Phalangist militias, Israel overran the country in six days. Having pushed most of Syria's troops north after destroying its air force in the Bekaa Valley, Israel now closed in, holding Muslim West Beirut in a siege, starved of food, fuel,

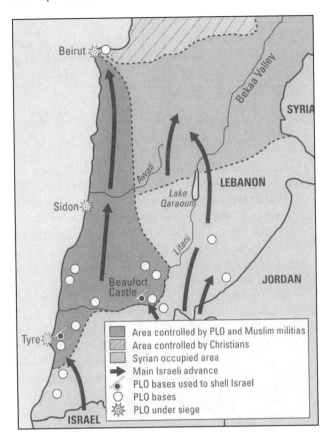

Operation Peace for Galilee, the Israeli invasion of Lebanon in June 1982. Israel's objective was to set up a demilitarized zone to protect its northern border.

and water. Indiscriminate Israeli aerial bombardment—civilians accounted for an estimated 90 percent of all casualties—continued until August 12. At this point, the Ronald Reagan Administration called for a cease-fire. The United States played a much publicized part in brokering the cease-fire and securing the evacuation of PLO and Syrian soldiers from Beirut by September 1, 1982.

Refugee Camp Massacres

Bashir Gemayel, closely connected to Israel, was elected Lebanese president by the Chamber of Deputies, and Syria signaled its military weakness by signing the cease-fire with Israel on September 11, 1982. However, whatever plans the Israelis may have had now began to unravel. The first problem was that its ally Bashir Gemayel was killed on September 14 by a bomb most likely planted by Syrian agents. The second problem was the international outcry when Israeli troops allowed Phalangist militia to enter the Palestinian refugee camps of Sabra and Shatila in West Beirut, where they massacred hundreds of Palestinian refugees while Sharon's men looked on. The Phalangists had been the Israelis' military allies and supposed political puppets. However, their action

so besmirched the Israelis and their Lebanon policy that in many ways the beginning of the Israeli withdrawal can be traced to this incident. It also signaled the point at which U.S. troops—uniformed as international forces in the U.S.-dominated Multinational Force (MNF)—moved into Lebanon.

The Israelis remained in Beirut, withdrawing to the south of the city and then toward the frontier only in 1983. Not until 1985 did they finally withdraw from Lebanon, and even then they left a zone of southern Lebanon dominated by the South Lebanon Army, a Christian force that they controlled. The U.S. component of the MNF remained until February 1984, and the last European contingent of French troops left in 1986.

The main loser in this fight was the PLO. Under attack from an alliance of the Syrians, dissident PLO elements, and Christian militias, Yasir Arafat was forced into the northern Lebanese town of Tripoli and finally had to evacuate his headquarters from that city in 1983. The PLO headquarters moved to Tunis, in Tunisia—far from the frontiers of Israel.

For the rest of the 1980s, there was constant fighting in Lebanon. The main protagonists were the Christian militias (who were themselves split, principally in a feud between Phalangist Lebanese Forces and the Zghorta Liberation Army); the Syrians and the Israelis, who both had ambitions to mold Lebanon into a client state; the Shiite Amal militia, originally the armed wing of the Movement of the Dispossessed; the Palestinians, who had begun infiltrating back into Lebanon after the evacuation of 1982–1983 and who were allied with the Sunni Muslim militia, the Mourabitoun; and the Islamic fundamentalist group Hezbollah.

Party of God

Hezbollah (literally "Party of God") had emerged in Lebanon in 1982. Its origins lay in Iran, and there were confirmed reports that Iranian Revolutionary Guards were operating in Lebanon in the early 1980s. Although the inspiration for Hezbollah came from Tehran, it was assisted by Syria and led by Lebanese Shiite clerics.

There were two tactics that made Hezbollah so effective and so notorious. The first was the use of suicide bombers, young men who were prepared to drive a car or truck loaded with explosives into an enemy headquarters and blow themselves up in pursuit of their cause. The Israeli headquarters in Tyre was struck twice by suicide bombers: in November 1983 and November 1984. The members of the MNF were also targets. A suicide bomb attack against the U.S. embassy in Beirut in April 1983 killed 16 Americans. The most effective of such attacks took place on October 23, 1983. A suicide bomber broke through the security at the U.S. Marine barracks near the

Beirut airport; the resultant blast killed 241 Marines. The same day, another bomber drove into the barracks of the French contingent and killed 58 soldiers. These terror attacks helped intensify the pace of the U.S. and Israeli withdrawal from Lebanon.

However, the emergence of Hezbollah was of grave concern to other states too. In March 1985, a massive car bomb exploded outside the Beirut headquarters of Hezbollah. It killed 80 people but failed to injure its target: Hezbollah's spiritual leader, Sheikh Muhammad Hussein Fadlallah. There was much debate over who planted this bomb. The most common explanation was that the CIA and Saudi Arabia had funded a Maronite Christian group to assassinate Fadlallah.

Hijacking and Hostages

Lebanese Shiite militants staged an international airplane hijacking in revenge against the CIA car bomb. On June 14, 1985, TWA flight 847 was taken over, and an American serviceman among the passengers was killed. However, Hezbollah did not undertake further hijackings, and settled down as a guerrilla resistance group fighting the Israeli presence in the "security zone," having assisted in their removal from the rest of the country.

The second tactic used by Hezbollah was the taking of hostages—particularly high-profile Western hostages. Hostage taking had been part of the civil war of the mid-1970s; the first U.S. hostage to be taken was Colonel Ernest Morgan in June 1975. In the early 1980s, however, hostage taking increased greatly. In 1985, it is estimated that Hezbollah took nineteen hostages, including four Americans; in 1986, the figure was fifteen, followed by ten in 1987. Among those taken hostage were two Americans, CIA station chief William Buckley and Marine lieutenant-colonel William Higgins, who were subsequently killed by their Hezbollah captors.

Negotiations between U.S. officials and the Iranians over the sale of arms to Iran generated a great deal of publicity. Hezbollah took advantage of this widespread interest to further its cause in 1987, by taking hostage British envoy Terry Waite, who was negotiating for the release of other hostages. Hostage taking proved to be a short-lived tactic, though. By the end of 1991, the last Western hostages had been released. However, Hezbollah had made its mark.

Later Stages of the War

The war in Lebanon during the late 1980s was marked by infighting between radical Muslim groups, as well as by terror against all religious groups. For example, when Israel moved out of the Chouf mountains in 1983, Muslim forces moved in. As a result, tens of thousands of Christian villagers had to leave their homes and be-

come refugees. Amal, the militia with its roots in the Shiite Movement for the Dispossessed, had become the major indigenous Lebanese armed force by 1984. Over a two-year period from mid-1985, the Amal militia attempted to capture the Palestinian refugee camps in Beirut in what is known as the "War of the Camps." The clandestine reentry of some Fatah fighters into Lebanon made the Palestinian refugee community a target for attacks by Shiite Muslims. Brutal fratricide ensued as Amal militiamen besieged Palestinian camps using rocket launchers and artillery to try to batter the defenders into submission. The Palestinians held out, and the siege ended in January 1988.

Having engaged in a confrontation with the Palestinians, Amal next became engaged in a war with Hezbollah. There had been disputes between the two groups over the hijacking of TWA flight 847 in June 1984, and large-scale fighting broke out in April 1988, initially in southern Lebanon. The conflict soon spread to Beirut, however, where indiscriminate shelling of opposition-controlled areas led to hundreds of deaths. As a result, Amal suffered a heavy defeat and had to be rescued by Syrian intervention. This was the end of major fighting, although many small-scale terrorist acts continued in a country that had been effectively pulled apart by war.

In 1989, all major parties in the civil war signed the Taif Agreement ending the conflict, though limited fighting continued into 1990.

Neil Partrick

See also: *Definitions, Types, Categories*—Ethnonationalist Terrorism. *Modern Terrorism*—Lebanon: Hezbollah; Lebanon: Post–Civil War Era; Palestine: PLO and the Arab States.

Further Reading

Brynen, Rex. *Sanctuary and Survival: The PLO in Lebanon.* Boulder, CO: Westview, 1990.

Deeb, Marius. *The Lebanese Civil War.* New York: Praeger, 1980.

Fisk, Robert. *Pity the Nation: Lebanon at War.* 3rd ed. New York: Oxford University Press, 2001.

Harris, William W. *The New Face of Lebanon: History's Revenge.* Princeton, NJ: Markus Wiener, 2005.

Hirst, David. *Beware of Small States: Lebanon, Battleground of the Middle East.* New York: Nation Books, 2010.

Kramer, Martin. *Hezbollah's Vision of the West.* Washington, DC: Washington Institute for Near East Policy, 1989.

Sahliyeh, Emilie, ed. *Religious Resurgence and Politics in the Contemporary World.* Albany: State University of New York Press, 1990.

Shehadi, Nadim, and Dana Haffar Mills, eds. *Lebanon: A History of Conflict and Consensus.* New York: St. Martin's, 1992.

Lebanon: Hezbollah, 1982–Present

Hezbollah (or Party of God) is an extremist political-religious movement based in Lebanon. The movement was created and sponsored by Iran in July 1982, initially as a form of resistance to the Israeli presence in southern Lebanon.

Hezbollah's followers are Shiite Muslims who took their lead from the Ayatollah Ruholla Khomeini, then Iran's leader. They are strongly anti-Western and anti-Israeli and are unswervingly dedicated to the creation of an Iranian-style Islamic republic in Lebanon and the removal of all non-Islamic influences in the area. To this end, Hezbollah's militia has carried out a number of successful terrorist acts, including more than ninety hostage takings in Lebanon, in other parts of the Middle East, and in Europe and South America.

The scope and nature of Hezbollah's terrorist campaign reflect its close dependence on Iranian support, at both an ideological and a financial level. Examples of its terrorist acts include the abduction of Western hostages in 1982 and suicide attacks on the U.S. Marine and French military barracks in Beirut the following year.

Hezbollah was established under the spiritual leadership of Sheikh Muhammad Hussein Fadlallah, a Shiite cleric. The movement joined forces with smaller Shiite political parties and Dawah, the Lebanese branch of Iraq-based Hizb al Dawa al-Islamiyya, and with dissatisfied members of the older Islamic Amal. Iranian officials actively supervised and assisted the movement. The formation of Hezbollah was crucially assisted by the arrival of Iranian Revolutionary Guards (Pasdaran) in Baalbek in the northern Bekaa Valley of Lebanon. This 1,200-strong Pasdaran contingent not only fought against the Israelis and the South Lebanon Army based in southern Lebanon, but also provided Hezbollah's fighters with a combination of ideological indoctrination, vast financial support and military training, and equipment. The Iranian presence was a key factor in Hezbollah's transformation from a loose network into a well-organized and highly disciplined movement with a sophisticated guerrilla force.

Structure

Hezbollah is run by a consultative council (Majlis al-Shura), twelve clerics led by a secretary-general, with specialized committees dealing with ideological, military, political, judicial, informational, and social affairs. In turn, the consultative *shura* and these committees are replicated in each of Hezbollah's three main regional and operational areas in Lebanon: the Bekaa Valley, Beirut, and southern Lebanon. All Hezbollah activity is regulated by decisions taken by the main consultative council, which issues general directives to the regions. The regions, in turn, are left to implement decisions on the operational level. Major decisions are made collectively by the consultative council and approved by Iran.

Within the military committee of Hezbollah's main consultative council there also exists a separate body, the so-called Special Security Apparatus (SSA), which is responsible for intelligence and security matters. The SSA is itself divided into three subgroups: the central security apparatus, the preventative security apparatus, and an overseas security apparatus. The preventative security apparatus is responsible for the personal protection of its most senior clerics. The central security apparatus is the clandestine unit responsible for most of the hostage taking of Westerners as well as the car-bomb and suicide attacks of the early 1980s. The overseas security apparatus was activated when the organization pursued terrorist operations abroad, often in close operational coordination with Iran.

The overall decision to take a hostage is made by the consultative council in liaison with Iranian officials.

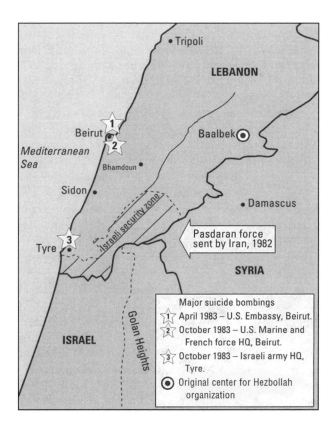

Sites of major Hezbollah suicide car-bomb attacks in Lebanon, 1983.

The instructions are then passed down to the commanders of the SSA. In the execution of the abductions, the SSA maintains a close liaison with Iran's embassies in Beirut and Damascus, which provide intelligence on targets, and with the Pasdaran contingent, which supplies weaponry and training. To maintain security, the core SSA group responsible for Western hostage taking is composed of a dozen men from various Hezbollah clans. In major terrorist operations, the SSA receives support from Hezbollah's military wing, the Islamic Resistance, which is composed of more than 5,000 well-trained and well-armed fighters.

Goals

Hezbollah's worldview, published in a 1985 manifesto, states that all Western influence is detrimental to following the true path of Islam. In its eyes, the West, and particularly the United States, is the foremost corrupting influence on the Islamic world today; thus, the United States is known as "the Great Satan." In the same way, the state of Israel is regarded as the product of Western imperialism and Western arrogance. Hezbollah believes that the West installed Israel in the region in order to continue dominating it and exploiting its resources.

Thus, Israel represents the source of all evil and violence in the region and is seen as an outpost of the United States in the heart of the Islamic Middle East. In Hezbollah's eyes, Israel must therefore be eradicated. Hezbollah sees itself as the vanguard of oppressed and dispossessed Muslims. The movement's ideological hostility toward its enemies has been translated into a series of central goals that explain the nature and scope of its use of terrorism.

The first goal is the establishment of an exclusively Shiite Islamic state in Lebanon, with Iran as its model. This was the driving force behind Hezbollah's hostage taking and suicide bombings during the 1980s.

The second goal of Hezbollah is the complete destruction of the state of Israel and the establishment of Islamic rule over Jerusalem and Palestine—this is deemed a religious obligation. As such, the movement carries out attacks on the Israeli army occupying part of southern Lebanon, launches rocket attacks at the civilian population in northern Israel, and carries out attacks on Israeli targets abroad, such as the bombings in Buenos Aires of the Israeli embassy that killed 29 people in 1992 and of a Jewish cultural center that killed nearly 100 in 1994.

The third goal, linked to the destruction of Israel, is Hezbollah's implacable opposition to the Middle East peace process, which it tries to sabotage through terrorism. The movement aligns itself with Palestinian Islamic movements, such as Hamas and Islamic Jihad, in their struggle against Israel "from within." The uncompromising spirit of Hezbollah's ideology is clearly reflected in the organization's emblem: a raised arm bearing a rifle against the background of the globe, with the slogan "The Party of God Is Sure to Triumph" (the Koranic verse from which Hezbollah adopted its name) on top, and the motto "The Islamic Revolution in Lebanon" at the bottom.

Timetable of Terror

In June 1982, Israel began its occupation of southern Lebanon. One month later, Hezbollah began its terrorist attacks against both the Western and Israeli presence in its country. Hezbollah's initial acts of hostage taking were carried out partly to prevent U.S. involvement in the Iran-Iraq War of 1980–1988 on the Iraqi side. The movement also took hostages to use as bargaining tools to obtain supplies of U.S.-made weapons for its "sponsor," Iran. Only one U.S. hostage, David Dodge, was taken between July 1982 and February 1984. Instead, the movement focused its activities on suicide car-bomb attacks against Western targets, aimed at eliminating them in Lebanon. In April 1983, a suicide car-bomb attack on the U.S. embassy in Beirut killed 49 and injured 120. In October that same year, Hezbollah carried out suicide car-bomb attacks on the U.S. Marine and French forces headquarters in Beirut, killing more than 300 servicemen, and on the Israeli army headquarters in Tyre, killing more than 50 soldiers.

In February 1984, Hezbollah increased its hostage-taking activities. Five Americans and one Frenchman were taken hostage by Hezbollah. This terrorist act was a direct response to the arrest and trial of Hezbollah members in Kuwait, who had been responsible for perpetrating a string of bombing attacks against the American and French embassies in late 1983. Subsequently, throughout the 1980s, the movement used these hostages as a bargaining tool in its efforts to gain the release of its members held in Kuwait.

Hezbollah continued to take Westerners hostage between March and June 1985, although its motives varied. For example, the kidnapping of American journalist Terry Anderson was a response to the failed assassination attempt on Sheikh Fadlallah in Beirut. In another instance, five Frenchmen were abducted, both in response to France's arms shipments to Iraq (with whom Iran had been at war since 1980) and in an attempt to gain the release of a convicted Iranian terrorist imprisoned in France. Finally, Hezbollah hijacked an American airliner, TWA flight 847, in an effort to gain the release of 766 Shiites held by Israel. As a result of this terrorist act, the prisoners were released.

The hostage taking continued during early 1986. Seven French citizens were abducted in response to several disputes between Iran and France, ranging from the French policy of supplying arms to Iraq to the repayment of an outstanding loan to Iran. Hezbollah also initiated a bombing campaign in Paris in March 1986, timed to

U.S. Marines stand guard amid the rubble of their command building in Beirut, which was destroyed in a truck bombing on October 23, 1983. A total of 241 American soldiers were killed in what was one of the first major terrorist attacks by Hezbollah. *(Associated Press)*

coincide with the French national elections. Hezbollah also kidnapped two British citizens in response to their country's tacit participation in the American bombing raid on Libya in April 1986.

In November 1986, a Beirut-based magazine revealed that U.S. president Ronald Reagan had secretly supplied arms to Iran in exchange for American hostages. The Irangate affair, as it came to be known, shocked the world. For Hezbollah, the tactic of taking American hostages had proved successful in damaging U.S.-Iranian relationships.

Hezbollah's activities continued through 1987, bolstered by continuing military aid from Iran. When U.S. authorities asked for the extradition of a leading Hezbollah SSA operative arrested in Germany, Hezbollah responded by taking hostage four American teachers and two Germans in Beirut. Additionally, in January 1987, Terry Waite, the British envoy to the archbishop of Canterbury, was taken hostage by Hezbollah. Ironically, Waite was on a humanitarian mission to gain the release of other hostages. At this point, however, Syria intervened. Previously, Syria had found Hezbollah to be a useful instrument of pressure against both Israel and the pro-Israeli South Lebanon Army. However, Syria was now anxious to prevent Hezbollah from gaining political monopoly among other Shiite groups. For example, Syria encouraged the Islamic Amal group to attack Hezbollah fighters in southern Beirut.

However, Hezbollah continued to carry out acts of terrorism. In February 1988, Lieutenant-Colonel William Higgins, an American United Nations (UN) officer, was abducted by Hezbollah to put pressure on Israel to release 400 Shiite prisoners. He was later killed. At the same time, the movement hijacked Kuwaiti airliner KU-422 and again demanded the release of its imprisoned members held in Kuwait.

1990s and 2000s

The death of Iran's Ayatollah Khomeini in 1989 and the conclusion of the Taif Accord, which brought peace to Lebanon after fifteen years of civil war, were the crucial factors that ended the spate of hostage taking. Hezbollah's involvement in hostage taking finally drew to a close in late 1991, with a three-way swap brokered under UN auspices, which involved the return of 450 Lebanese and Palestinians detained by the Israelis. They were exchanged for seven dead or captured Israeli servicemen and the remaining Western hostages. Hezbollah then switched from terrorist acts against Western targets and began escalating its guerrilla confrontation against Israeli forces in southern Lebanon.

Hezbollah's activities in the 1980s were funded by vast financial aid from Iran: the organization could depend on receiving between $60 million and $80 million annually from Iranian sources. Hezbollah used these funds to expand its influence over the Shiite community. When the movement participated in the 1992 Lebanese national election, it won eight of the twenty-seven seats reserved for Shiites. Although in the mid-1990s Hezbollah focused mainly on increasing its guerrilla struggle against Israel's occupation of southern Lebanon, the organization continued to rely on terrorism as a means to exact retribution against its enemies abroad. When Israel assassinated the secretary-general of Hezbollah, Sheikh Abbas al-Musawi, in a helicopter attack in 1992, the movement responded a month later with the car-bomb attack on Israel's embassy in Buenos Aires, killing 29 and wounding more than 100.

Hezbollah continued with its uncompromising stand against Israel's right to exist. In 1991, al-Musawi had declared that while Israel remained in Lebanon, the movement would not lay down its arms. In 1993, the killing of two Israeli soldiers led to massive retaliation by Israel, which left 130 people dead and 300,000 homeless.

By the late 1990s, Hezbollah was giving more ideological and moral support to the radical Palestinian Islamic movements Hamas and Islamic Jihad in their terrorist campaign against Israel. That and continued Hezbollah rocket attacks on northern Israel prompted the latter to launch a massive aerial assault in 1996—known as Operation Grapes of Wrath—at the organization's bases in southern Lebanon, the Bekaa Valley, and the southern parts of Beirut. The two-week-long assault resulted in a

```
┌─────────────────────────────────────────────┐
│               KEY DATES                       │
│                                               │
│ 1982  Hezbollah is founded, partly with the   │
│ aid of the Islamic government in Iran, to     │
│ resist Israel's presence in southern Lebanon. │
│                                               │
│ 1983  Hezbollah suicide bombers launch        │
│ attacks on U.S. and French military targets   │
│ in Lebanon, killing hundreds.                 │
│                                               │
│ 1985  The party issues a manifesto declaring  │
│ its opposition to Western influences within   │
│ the Islamic world and its opposition to       │
│ Israel as a proxy for Western imperialists.   │
│                                               │
│ 1986  A Lebanese newspaper reveals that the   │
│ Ronald Reagan Administration traded arms to   │
│ Iran for the release of American hostages     │
│ held by the Iranian-backed Hezbollah.         │
│                                               │
│ 1996  To stop continued rocket fire on its    │
│ northern territory, Israel launches a major   │
│ aerial assault on Hezbollah targets in        │
│ southern Lebanon, the Bekaa Valley, and       │
│ Beirut's suburbs.                             │
│                                               │
│ 2005  Anti-Syrian prime minister Rafik        │
│ Hariri is assassinated, allegedly by agents   │
│ of Damascus.                                  │
│                                               │
│ 2006  Following an assault by Hezbollah       │
│ militants on one of its border military       │
│ outposts, Israel launches a massive air and   │
│ ground assault against the party's forces     │
│ across Lebanon.                               │
│                                               │
│ 2008  Hezbollah and progovernment militants   │
│ engage in armed clashes that leave dozens     │
│ dead, provoking fears of a new civil war in   │
│ Lebanon.                                      │
└─────────────────────────────────────────────┘
```

U.S.-brokered "understanding between Hezbollah and Israel, wherein the former agree not to attack civilians within Israel but would retain the right to defend itself against Israeli occupation forces in southern Lebanon." While the Lebanese and Syrian governments did not sign on to the agreement, a Israel-Lebanon Monitoring Group, consisting of members from the United States, Lebanon, Israel, and Syria, was set up to see that the terms of the understanding were respected.

In the years following the operation, Hezbollah began an offensive against the South Lebanon Army, leading to the latter's collapse by May 2000. The South Lebanon Army's demise forced Israel to move forward its planned date of troop withdrawal from southern Lebanon. While Jerusalem called the withdrawal strategic, Hezbollah and its supporters declared it a victory for their side, increasing the party's stature within both Lebanon and the larger Arab world.

These events also left Hezbollah as a main power in southern Lebanon. In 2006, Hezbollah militants used their position to once again go on the offensive against Israel, which they claimed was conducting raids on Lebanese territory, at a place called Shebaa Farms. Israel claimed the territory as its own. In July, Hezbollah launched rocket attacks on northern Israel as a diversion for an attack on Israeli soldiers, which left three of the latter dead and two captured. The Jewish state responded with an even more powerful assault than that of a decade earlier. The so-called Israeli-Hezbollah War of July and August 2006 left about 1,000 Lebanese and 160 Israelis dead. Although Hezbollah suffered large casualties, it was once again able to declare itself the victor, having survived the might of the Israeli Defense Forces, increasing its sway within Lebanese politics. Meanwhile, to ensure the peace, the UN dispatched a 15,000-strong force along the country's southern border with Israel.

While peace has generally been maintained between Hezbollah and Israel since the 2006 war, the party has made its presence felt inside Lebanon. Sometimes its opposition to the government in Beirut, which it has charged with sidelining the needs of the country's Shiite citizens, Hezbollah's main constituency, has been conducted peacefully, as was the case with mass demonstrations and sit-ins in 2007. At other times, however, party members have clashed violently with progovernment factions, as happened in 2008. Hezbollah also suffered a setback with the withdrawal of Syrian troops from Lebanon—the Damascus government is one of Hezbollah's leading allies, along with Iran—in 2005, following the assassination of anti-Syrian prime minister Rafik Hariri, which many blamed on Syria.

Magnus Ranstorp and James Ciment

See also: *Definitions, Types, Categories*—Islamist Fundamentalist Terrorism. *Modern Terrorism*—Lebanon: Civil War; Lebanon: Post–Civil War Era.

Further Reading

Azani, Eitan. *Hezbollah: The Story of the Party of God.* New York: Palgrave Macmillan, 2009.

Carusso, Ileana M. *Hezbollah and Lebanon.* Hauppauge, NY: Nova Science, 2011.

Harris, William, W. *Faces of Lebanon: Sects, Wars, and Global Extensions.* Princeton, NJ: Markus Wiener, 1995.

Ranstorp, Magnus. *Hizb'allah in Lebanon.* New York: St. Martin's, 1996.

Salem, Elie Adib. *Violence and Diplomacy in Lebanon.* New York: St. Martin's, 1995.

Winslow, Charles. *Lebanon: War and Politics in a Fragmented Society.* New York: Routledge, 1996.

Lebanon: Post–Civil War Era, 1987–Present

After a long-running civil war (1975–1990), Lebanon has struggled to reestablish its economy by attracting investments, restore its lost sovereignty by regional diplomacy, and establish law and order by building a representative government. Lebanon's civil war not only devastated the socioeconomic and political infrastructure of the country but also contributed immensely to the insecurity of the Middle East. In addition, since the end of the civil war, intervention by Syria and Israel as well as the continued presence of Palestinian refugee camps has hindered Lebanon's ability to stabilize and to exercise full sovereignty within its borders.

Lebanon was the international epicenter for terrorist training, weapons procurement, and planning operations throughout the civil war. The Syrian-controlled Bekaa Valley in Lebanon trained two dozen Middle Eastern, European, and Asian guerrilla and terrorist groups. After receiving state-of-the-art training, these recruits fought against the Israeli and other security forces in southern Lebanon.

Civil War

With the outbreak of violence in 1975, the most devastating terrorist attack in the Middle East occurred in Lebanon when the U.S.-led multinational force suffered heavily on October 23, 1983. The Lebanese Hezbollah (Party of God), a radical Shiite militia, conducted coordinated simultaneous suicide attacks against the U.S. Marine barracks and the French paratrooper headquarters in Lebanon, killing 241 Americans and 58 Frenchmen. Although Hezbollah also planned to conduct a suicide attack against the Italian headquarters, they were prevented from doing so because the Italian troops were not living in a single structure but in isolated tents. As a result of the devastating attacks in Beirut, the multinational force withdrew and the United States disengaged itself from the Middle East for nearly a decade. Militias, guerrillas, and terrorists sponsored by Libya, Iran, and Syria conducted a series of assassinations, car bombings, and kidnappings, with a particular focus on Americans and Europeans as targets.

Although Hezbollah was established in 1982 by the Iraq-educated Shiite cleric Sheikh Muhammad Hussein Fadlallah, from southern Lebanon, it followed the Iranian line. Ayatollah Ruholla Khomeini wanted Lebanon to become another Islamic state like Iran, and therefore he strengthened Hezbollah and exhorted and guided its leaders to achieve that aim. But Lebanon's influential Christian population made such efforts impractical and unattainable. Nevertheless, its young, radical, and poor recruits, who were ever willing to sacrifice their lives, remain committed to Islamist goals—both in Lebanon and overseas.

Post–Civil War

The ending of Lebanon's civil war, the Oslo Accords, and the dramatic decline of Arab state sponsorship of terrorism in the region forced the gravity of terrorism to shift to Afghanistan. After the Soviets' withdrawal from Afghanistan in 1989 and the West's disengagement in the early 1990s, a period of lawlessness developed in central and southwest Asia, which created the conditions for cooperation between Middle Eastern and Asian groups.

The most virulent and tenacious outcome of the civil war was the creation of Hezbollah. Supported by Iran and Syria, Hezbollah emerged as the most powerful and deadliest terrorist group in the 1980s and a group with a global reach in the 1990s. Hezbollah's head of security, Imad Mughniyah, developed ties with Osama bin Laden when al-Qaeda was headquartered in Sudan. Al-Qaeda transformed itself from a guerrilla group to a terrorist group with the support of the specialized training provided by Hezbollah and its Iranian Revolutionary Guards in southern Lebanon, Iran, and Sudan in the early 1990s. Today, Hezbollah, a Shiite group, and al-Qaeda, a Sunni group, are cooperating in Asia, Latin America, the Middle East, and Europe to work against a common enemy: the United States.

As partial implementation of the Taif Accord, a plan for national reconciliation, commenced there were attacks and counterattacks by pro-Syrian and anti-Syrian elements. For instance, the pro-Syrian Palestinian leader Jihad Jibril—the son of Ahmed Jibril, the leader of the Popular Front for the Liberation of Palestine (PFLP)—was killed in May 2002. That same month, the body of an anti-Syrian Christian leader, Ramzi Irani, was recovered with gunshot wounds to his head. These sporadic attacks reflected the tensions between the multiple domestic and foreign-armed factions still operating in Lebanon.

Syria maintained a presence of 25,000 troops in Beirut, North Lebanon, and the Bekaa Valley until 2005, when a twenty-nine-year Syrian presence was brought to an end. Lebanese Christians and the Druze had become increasingly vocal against the Syrian presence in their country. Meanwhile, Syrian hawks perceived Lebanon as

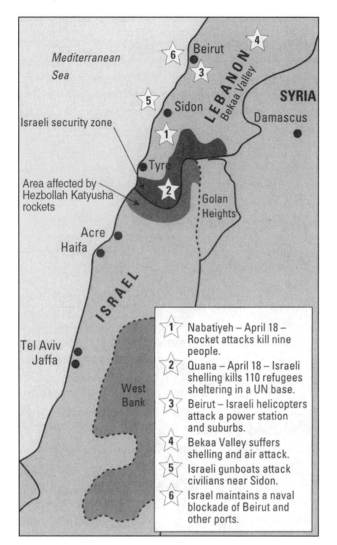

Nabatiyeh – April 18 –
Rocket attacks kill nine
people.

Quana – April 18 – Israeli
shelling kills 110 refugees
sheltering in a UN base.

Beirut – Israeli helicopters
attack a power station
and suburbs.

Bekaa Valley suffers
shelling and air attack.

Israeli gunboats attack
civilians near Sidon.

Israel maintains a naval
blockade of Beirut and
other ports.

Israel's Operation Grapes of Wrath in 1996 targeted Hezbollah terrorists and their bases in Lebanon.

a buffer between Israel and itself. Those who viewed the Lebanese armed forces as weak and the political institutions as still in the making perceived the Syrian presence to be legitimized by the Arab League and the Taif Accord. In response to public criticism, Syria initially redeployed its forces from Beirut to the eastern region of Lebanon, the area closer to Syria, before an eventual full withdrawal of military forces, but not intelligence assets, in 2005.

Despite continued attempts at reconciliation, Lebanese politics were challenged with the familiar foe of sectarian violence from 2004 to 2009, until finally achieving some respite from the troubles with the unity government that emerged under Saad Hariri in November 2009. For example, former prime minister Rafik Hariri—Saad's father—was among a number of Lebanese politicians and media figures who were adamantly opposed to Syria's involvement in Lebanon and were then assassinated. Harari was murdered in 2005, as were members of parliament—Walid Eido and Antoine Ghanem in 2007—along with General François al-Hajj in 2007 and Christian politician Pierre Gemayel in 2006. Many in Lebanon and the international community accused Syria of involvement in the killings. In fact, a Special Tribunal for Lebanon opened on March 1, 2010, to investigate the assassination of Hariri.

Hezbollah, which is credited with having forced Israel to withdraw from southern Lebanon in May 2000, is today waging a similar campaign to recover the Shebaa Farms. Abbassieh and Shebaa Farms are part of the mountainous territory at the Lebanese-Syrian border occupied by Israel since 1967. The Shebaa Farms area, where Hezbollah long concentrated its activities, is about 0.4 square miles (1 square kilometer), and the demarcations were—and are—nonexistent. Both Israeli posts and border patrols have come under Hezbollah mortar and antitank fire. Furthermore, Hezbollah maintains a visible presence to project its image as the defender of Lebanon. The Lebanese government has refrained from deploying its forces along the Israel-Lebanon border, as it does not wish to enter into a confrontation with Hezbollah guerrillas. In July of 2006, Hezbollah militia forces kidnapped two Israeli soldiers in a daring border raid. Israel responded with an invasion of Lebanon and subsequent thirty-four–day military operation designed to destroy Hezbollah strongholds along the Lebanese-Israeli border.

Cooperation between Hezbollah and Syria and Iran has also been a source of regional tension. In April 2010, the United States warned Syria of serious consequences of providing Scud missiles to Hezbollah. Iranian president Mahmoud Ahmadinejad's visit to Lebanon in October 2010 coincided with increased sectarian tensions and a large Hezbollah rally near the Israeli border.

Terrorist and Guerrilla Organizations

In addition to Hezbollah, several other foreign and domestic terrorist and guerrilla groups operate in Lebanon. Fatah, the military wing of the PLO, has a significant presence, especially among the 350,000 Palestinian refugees in Lebanon. Lebanon's largest refugee camp, Ein al-Hilweh, is fully controlled by Fatah and by elements of the al-Aqsa Martyrs Brigade. Of the Islamist groups, Hamas and Palestinian Islamic Jihad maintain a presence and a working relationship with Hezbollah and Iran. In Lebanon, the links between Hamas and Hezbollah have continued to deepen. In May 2000, the Hamas monthly *Falastin al-Muslima* and its Web site reported a quote from the semi-official Palestinian newspaper *al-Hayat al-Jadida*: "O Lebanese joy, spread your delicious disease among us!"

Three other Islamist groups that maintain a presence in Lebanon are Asbat al-Ansar, al-Gamaa al-Islamiyya, and Ziad al-Jarrah. Asbat al-Ansar operates in Ein al-Hilweh, a refugee camp in southern Lebanon. Reportedly, the group worked closely with al-Qaeda's Jordanian cell planning millennium bombings. In January 2000, during the riots in northern Lebanon between the Sunni Islamists and the Lebanese government, Asbat al-Ansar clashed with the Lebanese military. In addition to generating support for its own activities, Asbat al-Ansar maintains al-Qaeda interests in Lebanon. Asbat al-Ansar has also conducted several terrorist operations in Lebanon, including the assassination of four judges in Sidon in 1999 and the attack on the Russian embassy in 2000.

Ziad al-Jarrah, inspired by al-Qaeda, is most notable for its presence in southern Lebanon and strategy of firing Katyusha rockets into Israel. Although not a terrorist group, Hizb ut-Tahrir (the Islamic Liberation Party), a nonviolent Islamist group, is actively politicizing and recruiting among Palestinians also in northern Lebanon. Although secular leftist groups like the PFLP have a presence, increasingly their influence in Lebanon has diminished. Nonetheless, Damascus continues to maintain links and to aid PFLP, PFLP—General Command, the Democratic Front for the Liberation of Palestine, and the Abu Nidal Organization, all of which maintain an organizational presence in the Bekaa Valley. Although none of these groups engages in terrorism inside Lebanon, they have all infiltrated the Palestinian communities for the purpose of recruitment and building political support.

The political instability that resulted from the sectarian violence that began in 2005 created a political vacuum that allowed terrorist groups to infiltrate Lebanese society. Al-Qaeda–influenced groups, such as Asbat al-Ansar and others associated with Fatah, targeted the Palestinian refugee camps as an opportunity to expand their activities. Positive signs, however, emerged from the unity government of late 2009 under Saad Hariri. First on Hariri's agenda was a strengthening of the Lebanese armed forces in order to deal with threats of terrorism and sectarian violence. Lebanon also increased cooperation with the United States on security issues. Hariri supported the disarmament of Hezbollah but insisted it must be accomplished through a national dialogue. One controversial element of the national dialogue strategy was the inclusion of Hezbollah representatives in the unity government. Hariri's ouster in early 2011 by forces allied with Hezbollah has placed many of his accomplishments in jeopardy, with few experts willing to predict the country's future course. Long the subject of international intervention, the future of Lebanon nevertheless remains intimately linked to its capacity to maintain sole sovereignty within its borders and the ability of Lebanese politicians to avoid the sectarian violence that attracts foreign meddling and political violence.

In brief, Lebanon has much to do to establish the conditions that would discourage the development of terrorism. Until the quality of life improves in this region, especially in the areas of employment, education, travel, and health care for refugees, and until a level of public security is established for the eventual renewal of general civil order (i.e., one conducive to business operations and even foreign investment), terrorist groups will no doubt flourish, and they will have a steady flow of recruits. Notwithstanding that reality, if peace is to ever effectively return to the area, the mandate of the United Nations Interim Force in Lebanon should at least include the authority to act decisively against these groups.

Rohan Gunaratna and Matthew H. Wahlert

See also: *Modern Terrorism*—Lebanon: Civil War; Lebanon: Hezbollah.

Further Reading

Dagher, Carol. *Bring Down the Walls—Lebanon's Post-War Challenge.* New York: St. Martin's, 2002.

El-Khazen, Farid. *The Breakdown of the State in Lebanon, 1967–1976.* Cambridge, MA: Harvard University Press, 2000.

Fisk, Robert. *Pity the Nation: Lebanon at War.* New York: Oxford University Press, 2001.

Harris, William W., and Rudolf Steiner. *Faces of Lebanon, Sects, Wars, and Global Extensions.* Princeton, NJ: Markus Wiener, 1996.

MacFarquhar, Neil. *The Media Relations Department of Hizbollah Wishes You a Happy Birthday: Unexpected Encounters in the Changing Middle East.* New York: Public Affairs, 2009.

KEY DATES

1975 Civil war breaks out in Lebanon among various factions of Christian and Muslim Lebanese.

1982 Israel invades Lebanon in a successful effort to oust the Palestine Liberation Organization.

1983 Hundreds of U.S. and French military and diplomatic personnel are killed in suicide bombings by Hezbollah militants.

1990 Civil war ends.

2000 Israel ends its occupation of southern Lebanon.

2005 Lebanese prime minister Rafik Hariri is assassinated, allegedly with Syrian involvement.

2006 In an effort to destroy the Hezbollah infrastructure, Israel invades Lebanon.

2009 Saad Hariri, Rafik's son, is elected prime minister and pursues an inclusion policy toward Hezbollah.

2011 Billionaire businessman Nijab Mikati succeeds Hariri as prime minister; he is largely seen as a caretaker, until new parliamentary elections can be held.

Libya: State Sponsorship of Terrorism, 1970s–2000s

Libyan leader Colonel Muammar Gadhafi has supported terrorists fighting for anti-imperialist and Arab nationalist causes since he seized power in 1973. However, the U.S. air strike against Libya and Gadhafi personally in 1986, in response to alleged Libyan support for the bombing of a Berlin disco frequented by U.S. servicemen, forced him to act more cautiously. Gadhafi was careful after 1986 to operate secretly through others who could be blamed instead.

Gadhafi was also more careful to support groups that could give him value for money—that is, those that could genuinely hurt his enemies, rather than just repeat anti-imperialist slogans. At the same time, he was eager to take revenge on the United States, and on Britain, which had provided bases for the American bombers.

Libyan support for terrorism was multifaceted. The country gave funds, for instance, to Saiqa, a Syrian-backed Palestinian splinter group, and to Palestinian Islamic Jihad. Some $1 million was paid to the Popular Front for the Liberation of Palestine—General Command (PFLP-GC) in 1990 alone. The Communist Party of the Philippines' New People's Army received more than $7 million between 1987 and 1991. Libya's Anti-Imperialism Center provided a coordinating point for aid to revolutionaries. Established in 1982, it held conferences of radical groups and acted as a recruiting agency for potential terrorists and guerrilla groups from as far afield as Colombia, Chile, Costa Rica, Peru, Haiti, and the Philippines, as well as those from the Middle East and Europe, who received training, funds, and arms. Training camps included al-Qalah, occupied by the Abu Nidal Organization (ANO); the Seven April and Bin Ghashir camps, for Africans and Latin Americans; and the Ras al-Hilal camp, for Palestinian fighters.

Palestinian groups often receive payments directly into third-country bank accounts; Libyan diplomats

The bombing of a West Berlin discotheque frequented by U.S. servicemen killed three people and injured hundreds of others in April 1986. After the Libyan government was linked to the attack, President Ronald Reagan ordered retaliatory air strikes on that country. *(Associated Press)*

and Anti-Imperialism Centers often dispense funds; and sometimes couriers are used to hand out money. Libya has a number of front organizations through which it aids radical groups. Since 1986, it has been careful to make less use of Libyan People's Bureaus (embassies), since these have been closely monitored by host governments.

Libyan support for terrorism in the late 1980s was of three kinds: sponsorship of operations against hostile states—notably the United States, Great Britain, and France; support for radical Palestinian groups that operated both on Libya's behalf and according to their own agenda; and attacks on Libyan exiles and political dissidents abroad.

Attacks Against the West

The state airline, Libyan Arab Airlines, has frequently been used to assist terrorists. In 1986, for example, a Libyan Arab Airlines flight from Cyprus smuggled aboard six terrorists who had just raided a British base. Other front companies have smuggled arms and explosives across borders or provided intelligence services. Such companies, according to the U.S. government, have included Exo-Commerce, Sarra, and Neutron International. The Islamic Call Society, a Libyan religious philanthropic foundation, has also been used to recruit and fund radicals, notably in Benin, Africa.

In 1987, Libya sponsored a series of attacks on French targets in retaliation for France's military support for the Chad government. With French help, Chad defeated a rebel insurgency backed by Libya, which wanted control of resource-rich northern Chad. A Libyan-backed Palestinian group, the Popular Struggle Front, bombed a café in the former French territory of Djibouti on the Red Sea, killing eleven people, five of them French citizens. In October, the Armenian Secret Army for the Liberation of Armenia, a group with ties to Libya, killed two French gendarmes in Beirut, Lebanon. In November 1987, the ANO, operating on Libya's behalf, hijacked the yacht *Silco* in the Mediterranean. Five French and Belgian passengers were taken hostage. They were not all finally released until 1991.

Direct attacks on American targets were less frequent. The U.S. government, however, linked the organization Egypt's Revolution to Libya. This group tried to kill three U.S. diplomats in Egypt. Also, in October 1987, a bomb went off at the offices of an American charity, World Vision, in Chad.

Libya's retaliation against Britain was more extensive. In April 1987, two Libyan-supported terrorists shot at a British soldier near Limassol in Cyprus, wounding him and a companion. In October, the French authorities seized a freighter, the *Eksund II,* carrying 150 tons of arms and explosives from Libya to the Provisional Irish Republican Army (IRA). The shipment turned out to be the fifth such consignment.

Attacks on Dissidents

Libyan agents also carried out at least three attacks on dissidents in 1987. In January, a dissident was murdered in Athens. In May, an agent failed in an attempt to kill a dissident in Vienna. In June, two agents of Libya's Revolutionary Committees killed a senior official of the opposition National Salvation Front for Libya.

In 1988, Libya engaged in a public policy of moderation. It did not attack any dissidents and even invited exiles to return. The U.S. government, however, linked a number of attacks on American targets to Libya, arguing that a wide variety of terrorist groups had received Libyan aid to mark the second anniversary of the U.S. reprisal attack on Tripoli, Libya. On April 14, the Japanese Red Army (a left-wing anarchist terrorist group) bombed a club in Naples, killing five people including a U.S. servicewoman. On the same day, the Colombian terrorist group M-19 bombed a U.S. Information Service (USIS) building. The following day, a U.S. Air Force post in Spain was bombed. On April 16, the Peruvian Tupac Amaru Revolutionary Movement (MRTA) bombed two USIS centers. On April 19, terrorists in Costa Rica bombed an American cultural center. In addition, Senegal arrested two Libyan agents smuggling arms aboard a flight to Benin. They were believed to have been planning to hit Western targets. Subsequently, Benin expelled the head of the Libyan People's Bureau.

Libya and Abu Nidal

An important aspect of Libya's support for terrorism during 1988 was its evolving relationship with the Abu Nidal Organization. Libya had given aid to the ANO since the 1970s, and since the ANO transferred its main base to Libya in 1987, the relationship had flourished. Most ANO members were based in Libya; they trained in the al-Qalah camp south of Tripoli; and they were provided with weapons and Libyan passports. Abu Nidal (the code name of Sabri al-Banna) himself lived in Tripoli.

However, the Libyan government did not call all the shots. The ANO was experienced enough as an organization to retain its independence. Therefore, several of its operations could not be directly linked to Libya. A case in point was the July 11, 1988, hijacking of a Greek cruise ship, *City of Poros.* Terrorists fired and threw grenades at passengers as the ship approached port in Athens. Nine Europeans were killed and 100 wounded. Earlier, a bomb had exploded prematurely in a parked car at the pier, killing the two occupants. The ANO did not claim responsibility; only subsequent investigations implicated the group and identified Libyan weapons used in the raid.

In 1989, Gadhafi responded to international criticism

by reining in Libyan-sponsored groups. As part of his diplomatic activity to end his country's isolation, he called on Palestinian groups to attack only Israeli targets. Nonetheless, the ANO remained in Libya, while the MRTA again attempted to bomb the USIS center in Peru to mark the third anniversary of the U.S. air attack on Libya.

In 1990, Libyan-backed groups carried out further attacks. The Palestine Liberation Front team that carried out a seaborne raid on Tel Aviv, Israel, had been trained at Libya's Sidi Bilal port and received extensive support for the raid. The mother ship for the raiders, the *Tiny Star,* was owned by a Libyan front company. Costa Rica accused Libya of training all fifteen members of the Santamaria Patriotic Organization, which planned grenade attacks on U.S. facilities in the country. Ethiopia expelled two Libyan diplomats for alleged involvement in the March 30 bombing of the Addis Ababa Hilton.

Lockerbie and Niger Bombings

The most notorious cases of alleged Libyan sponsorship of terrorism were the destruction of Pan Am flight 103 over Lockerbie, Scotland, on December 21, 1988, and of UTA flight 772 over Niger on September 19, 1989. Two hundred and seventy people were killed in the Pan Am attack and 171 in the UTA bombing. On October 30, 1991, a French magistrate issued arrest warrants for four Libyan officials accused of masterminding the UTA attack. On November 14, Scottish and American courts issued indictments against two Libyans for their role in the Pan Am attack.

The UTA flight had been flying from Brazzaville, Congo, to Paris via N'djamena, Chad. The French arrest warrant charged that three Congolese had been recruited by Libya to place a suitcase bomb on the aircraft. One of the Congolese is in jail in Congo and another in Zaire. The French magistrate accused four Libyans of organzing the plot: Abdallah Sanussi (a brother-in-law of Gadhafi and deputy commander of Libyan intelligence), Ibrahim Nayli (Libyan intelligence representative in Athens), Abd al-Azragh (first secretary in the Libyan People's Bureau, or embassy, in Brazzaville), and Abbas Musbah (a Libyan intelligence officer in Brazzaville). In addition, the magistrate issued international lookout notices for Musa Kusa, the deputy foreign minister, and another suspect.

The Scottish indictment accused Abdelbaset al-Megrahi, a senior intelligence officer, and Lamen Fahimah, a former manager of the Libyan Arab Airlines office in Malta, of planning the Pan Am bombing. The United States has claimed that the operation was planned at the highest levels of the Libyan government. Washington has accused Said Rashid, a leading organizer of Libya's subversive operations and a confidante of Gadhafi, of orchestrating the attack. The Scottish American case against Libya consists of evidence linking the accused to the attack and argues that the Libyan government

was responsible since the accused had senior positions in Libya's intelligence services.

Evidence of Libyan Involvement

The indictment charged that Megrahi and Fhimah deposited the suitcase bomb on Air Malta flight 180 from Valetta, Malta, to Frankfurt, Germany, where it was routed to New York via London on Pan Am flight 103. The bomb timer, marked MST-13 and manufactured by Swiss electronics firm Meister et Bollier, was one of a batch delivered to the Libyan External Security Organization (ESO) in 1985. The Senegalese authorities found similar timers when they arrested two Libyan terrorists in 1988. The U.S. government claims that the accused acted with the direct backing of senior Libyan officials. Megrahi is a long-serving associate of the ESO. In 1987, he became director of the Center for Strategic Studies, an ESO research unit that worked on covert arms procurement and on building ties with Latin American radicals.

The alleged, but unindicted, mastermind was Said Rashid, Megrahi's cousin. Rashid was a senior ESO officer and member of Libya's Revolutionary Committees Bureau. In 1980, he was briefly jailed in France for his role in the murder of a Libyan dissident in Italy. In the same year, he led a team to Togo to assassinate the Chadian president, Hissen Habré. In the early 1980s, Rashid planned attacks on U.S. targets, including planning an attempt to smuggle a cigarette-carton bomb onto a Pan Am flight from Istanbul. In the mid-1980s, according to the U.S. State Department, Rashid planned a series of attacks on U.S. targets. He was responsible for buying the MST-13 timers.

Libyan Denials of Responsibility

Libya denied its responsibility for the bombings and refused to hand over the suspects. Gadhafi launched a diplomatic counteroffensive, accusing Britain and the United States of engaging in a political campaign against him. At the same time, he promised to end support for terrorist groups such as the Provisional IRA. According to Libya, a Libyan judge investigated the case and placed the two suspects in detention. A Libyan offer to discuss the matter with Scottish or American judges was turned down.

In response to the Libyan attitude, the UN Security Council adopted Resolution 731 on January 21, 1992, which demanded that Libya hand over the Lockerbie suspects, acknowledge responsibility for the attack, and cooperate fully with the French investigation. Libya asked the International Court of Justice to declare the resolution illegal but was turned down. On March 31, the UN Security Council passed Resolution 748, imposing mandatory economic sanctions on Libya. All civilian air links were cut and arms supplies banned. In response, angry mobs attacked Western embassies in Tripoli.

KEY DATES

1973 Radical colonel Muammar Gadhafi seizes power in a coup.

1987 Libya sponsors a series of attacks on French targets.

September 19, 1989 Terrorists linked to the Libyan government down a French UTA jet over Niger, killing all 171 people aboard.

December 21, 1989 Terrorists linked to the Libyan government, including Abdelbaset al-Megrahi, plant a bomb aboard a Pan Am flight between the United Kingdom and the United States, downing the jet over Lockerbie, Scotland, and killing all 270 people aboard.

1993 The United Nations issues sanctions against Libya in response to the two jetliner bombings.

1999 Gadhafi agrees to turn over the two suspects in the Lockerbie bombing to a Scottish special court in the Netherlands.

2001 Megrahi is found guilty of the Lockerbie bombing and sentenced to life in prison; the other suspect is found not guilty.

2003 Libya agrees to pay compensation to the Lockerbie victims' families; the UN votes to lift sanctions against the country; Gadhafi announces he is suspending his country's nuclear program.

2009 A Scottish court releases the dying Megrahi, allowing him to return to Libya, angering Lockerbie victims' families and the general public in the United Kingdom and the United States.

2011 Rebels rise up against Gadhafi in eastern Libya in February, triggering a military crackdown by the regime and threats of mass killings; the United States, France, the United Kingdom, and ultimately NATO launch air attacks on Gadhafi's forces.

Libya offered to hand over the suspects to an Arab state, but the UN renewed sanctions in 1993, despite protests in the Arab world. Britain and the United States demanded that Libya hand over the suspects by October 1. Gadhafi refused, attempting various ploys to derail the deadline. When no progress was made, the American, French, and British UN delegations submitted a draft Security Council resolution imposing harsher sanctions on Libya. On November 11, Resolution 883 was adopted. It froze Libyan assets abroad, banned sales of certain oil and gas equipment, and closed down Libyan Arab Airlines' offices abroad.

In 1994, Gadhafi declared his willingness to hand over the suspects to the International Court or to a Muslim court in Britain or the United States. However, Britain and the United States demanded that the suspects be tried in Scotland. The UN continued to renew the sanctions, but European nations resisted U.S. pressure to intensify the embargo.

Doubt over Responsibility

Although the British and American governments remained firm in their campaign to force Libya to hand over the Lockerbie suspects, a variety of critics countered the Scottish and American charges. One theory was that the Pan Am flight 103 attack was the work of the PFLP-GC, sponsored by Iran in retaliation for the destruction of an Iran Air flight, shot down in error by the U.S. Navy cruiser *Vincennes* over the Gulf in 1987.

The most prominent of those convicted was an experienced PFLP-GC bomb maker jailed in 1991 for bombing American troop trains. Critics also argued that the investigation initially pointed the finger at Syria and Iran but that during the Gulf War of 1990–1991, it became politically more convenient to blame Libya, since the West needed Syria and Iran to cooperate in the war against Iraq. Critics of the official line include relatives of the Lockerbie victims and a former senior U.S. intelligence official. The Scottish and U.S. courts stuck by their accusations, however, and few disagreed that Gadhafi had been a major sponsor of terrorism.

Improved Relations with the West

In 1999, Gadhafi made a dramatic about-face and turned over the suspects for trial in the Netherlands, but under Scottish law. As result, UN sanctions against the country were suspended and the United Kingdom restored diplomatic relations with Tripoli. In January 2001, the special Scottish court in the Netherlands found one of the suspects, Megrahi, guilty and sentenced him to life imprisonment, while his codefendant, Lamen Fahimah, was found not guilty. A year later, the United States and Libya opened talks to mend relations, after years in which Washington had charged the government in Tripoli with sponsoring terrorism.

After Libya agreed to provide $2.7 billion in compensation to the Lockerbie victims' families in August 2003, the UN Security Council voted to lift sanctions against the country. Libya also agreed in January 2004 to pay compensation to the families of victims killed in the French passenger aircraft downing in Niger that was linked to the Tripoli government. Meanwhile, in December 2003, Gadhafi agreed to suspend its nuclear program, removing the last obstacle for the country's full integration back into the international community of nations.

But the improved ties with the West did not last long. Problems emerged in August 2009, when a Scottish court allowed a dying Megrahi to return to Libya. The cheers that greeted him upon his return to Libya, and the fact that he remained alive as of early 2011, angered both Lockerbie victims' families and the international community. Then in early 2011, anti-Gadhafi rebels rose up in the eastern part of the country, inspired by successful revolts against authoritarian regimes in neighboring Tunisia and Egypt. Unlike his counterparts there, however, Gadhafi refused to concede power, turning his armed forces against the rebels and threatening wholesale slaughter should he emerge victorious in the struggle. In response, several Western countries—including the United States, France, and the United Kingdom—launched an air assault against Gadhafi forces, quickly turning over authority for the campaign to NATO.

Andrew Rathmell

See also: *Tactics, Methods, Aims*—State-Sponsored Terrorism.

Further Reading

Chasey, William C. *Pan Am 103: The Lockerbie Cover-Up.* Carson City, NV: Bridger House, 1995.

Davis, Brian L. Qaddafi, *Terrorism, and the Origins of the U.S. Attack on Libya.* New York: Praeger, 1990.

Grant, John P. *The Lockerbie Trial: A Documentary History.* Dobbs Ferry, NY: Oceana, 2004.

Martinez, Luis. *The Libyan Paradox.* Trans. John King. New York: Columbia University Press, 2007.

Simons, Geoff. *Libya: The Struggle for Survival.* New York: St. Martin's, 1993.

Malaysia (Malaya): Anti-British Conflict, 1948–1960

In response to a rising wave of terrorism by guerrillas of the Malayan Communist Party (MCP), the British colonial government in Malaya declared a state of emergency in June 1948. It lasted until 1960. Emergency regulations allowed for detention, deportation, and even death for insurgency-related offenses.

The communist guerrillas, organized after the Japanese invasion of 1941, were drawn largely from Malaya's Chinese community. The British encouraged the MCP during the war, sending in arms, supplies, and advisers until it fielded some 7,000 guerrillas. Led by the tactician Chin Peng, the MCP scored some successes over the invaders.

Setting Up a Terrorist Wing

After the war, however, the MCP aimed to overthrow the colonial government and set up a communist regime in Malaya. The organization infiltrated labor unions and attempted a Soviet-style revolution through strikes and protests, some violent. In 1948, it accepted that the tactic had failed and launched an armed revolt.

The MCP's military wing was originally called the Malayan People's Anti-British Army. It was renamed the Malayan Races' Liberation Army (MRLA) in 1949 in order to appeal to the non-Chinese majority populace.

In May 1948, Chin Peng mobilized eight regiments using weapons saved from the war. Guerrillas ambushed civilian and military buses, trains, and trucks. They murdered government supporters and informers, abducted businessmen, and extorted bribes. On June 29, terrorists shot up Jerantut township, 20 miles (32 kilometers) from Kuala Krau, burned down the police station, and took Chinese and Malay prisoners.

In the meantime, communist cells on British-owned rubber plantations and in tin mines orchestrated strikes and takeovers. On July 12, communist terrorists attacked the police post at Batu Arang, Malaya's only coal mine, overwhelming the occupants and cutting the telephone wires. The terrorists managed to sabotage machinery before colonial police reinforcements could get to the mine. In response to the agitation and violence, the government banned the MCP.

Although there was substantial support for the insurgency among the Chinese community in Malaya, the general popular uprising that the communist leadership predicted did not occur. This disappointment, coupled with the strong response of the colonial police and army, forced the MRLA into the jungle, where they established bases near weapons stashes. The bases were often located near Chinese settlements so that the MRLA could obtain supplies and information from a network of supporters known as Min Yuen.

New Terrorist Attacks

Malaya was comparatively calm during the guerrilla reorganization, but by the end of 1949, the terrorists were back in business. The terrorists mostly attacked village police posts, but towns and farming estates were also raided. Attacks were often large-scale. On September 11, a force of 300 communist terrorists raided the town of Kuala Krau, killing four police officers, two British railway engineers, and two Malayan women. The following month, 200 terrorists struck at an isolated rubber plantation in Pahang, setting fire to several buildings.

By early 1950, the MRLA communists had built an organization capable of protracted warfare. They had a hierarchy of military-type units that ranged from terror and sabotage sections in populated areas to village guerrilla units, up to regular units. Food supplies and intelligence were provided by the political organization and the Min Yuen, so military camps in the jungle had to be within a few hours' walking distance of populated areas. Communication between the settlements and the jungle camps was a weak link.

The guerrillas increased their activity until incidents were occurring at the rate of 400 a month—twice their 1948 rate. The terrorists singled out the British planters and their families for particular attention. One family withstood no less than twenty-five terrorist attacks on their plantation in a two-week period in 1951, including three in one night.

The terrorists also took to machine-gunning the "new villages," set up by Lieutenant General Sir Harold Briggs, the British director of operations in Malaya. Briggs's plan was to separate the MRLA from its supporters in the community, so he resettled the Chinese into newly constructed villages away from the old settlements. Here, housing and sanitary conditions were far superior than in the old shanties, and many Chinese welcomed the change. Briggs also imposed strict allocations of rice. There was little left over to pass to the MRLA, so the terrorists were forced into the open to find food. At the same time, the British army, including the Special Air Service, was getting used to finding and dealing with the terrorists.

By late 1951, the terrorists had been forced to come up with a new strategy. They split their large military units into smaller groups and withdrew deeper into the jungle to rest and retrain.

Ambush and Assassination

Nonetheless, terrorist incidents continued to take place. In fact, on October 6, 1951, the terrorists pulled off their most notorious operation of the campaign—the assassination of the British high commissioner, Sir Henry Gurney. The terrorists ambushed Sir Henry on the road to Fraser's Hill, a rest station where British officers and officials could get away from the heat and humidity of the Malayan plains. The road was steep and winding for the last 20 miles (32 kilometers) to the station and was bordered by thick jungle and, in some places, high cliffs. The heavily armed terrorist force chose a 200-yard section of this part of the road as their killing zone and settled down to wait.

At about lunchtime, some twenty-seven hours after the ambush was set, Sir Henry's motorcade came in sight. When it left the capital, Kuala Lumpur, the convoy had consisted of an armored car, a radio vehicle, an unarmored Land Rover, and the high commissioner's Rolls-Royce. Unfortunately, the radio truck had broken down en route and the armored car had stopped to help, leaving the limousine only lightly guarded.

As the convoy reached the ambush site, the terrorists opened fire, making short work of the escort before turning their attention to the official car. Trapped in the vehicle in a hail of gunfire, Sir Henry opened the door,

possibly to try to make cover. He was killed instantly. Only the arrival of the armored car, machine guns blazing, saved his wife and his private secretary from the same fate. The high commissioner's assassination stunned Malaya.

Soon, the terrorists again struck in spectacular fashion. On October 8, the mail train from Johore to Kuala Lumpur struck a terrorist mine near Johore Bharu. The explosion derailed the train, killing the driver and wounding two railwaymen and three passengers. That same autumn, the terrorists gained their first British female fatality, ambushing a British tin miner's wife on the Taiping to Selama road.

Some attacks were particularly brutal. On November 25, with her parents away in Kuala Lumpur, a plantation owner's daughter was out for a ride in the family Land Rover with the estate cook. Terrorists sprang an ambush, shooting the girl through the head. She was only two years old.

Although the insurgency continued for a further nine years, the end of 1951 marked a turning point. Until then the terrorists had been effective. Now, with the guerrillas starved of food and support from the population and suffering high numbers of casualties, the government went on the attack. Using a combination of conventional military force and psychological warfare, including leaflet drops and broadcasting propaganda from aircraft, the British closed in. Many guerrillas turned their backs on communism and accepted British bribes to turn in their fellow terrorists. Malaya was granted independence from Britain on August 31, 1957, and it was only the tenacity of the few remaining hard-line guerrillas that kept the emergency in place until 1960.

Chris Marshall

See also: *Historical Roots*—European Colonial Expansion Conquests. *Modern Terrorism*—United Kingdom: Decolonization and Post-Decolonization Struggles.

Further Reading
Clutterbuck, Richard. *The Long, Long War: Counterinsurgency in Malaya and Vietnam.* New York: Praeger, 1966.
Dewar, Michael. *Brush Fire Wars: Minor Campaigns of the British Army Since 1945.* New York: St. Martin's, 1984.
Stubbs, Richard. *Hearts and Minds in Guerrilla Warfare: The Malayan Emergency 1948–1960.* New York: Oxford University Press, 1989.

Mexico: Narco-Terrorism, 2000s–Present

One of the major successes in the U.S. war on drugs during the 1990s was the near total destruction of the Medellín and Cali cartels in Colombia. Unfortunately, this led to more violence even closer to the United States, as Mexican criminal cartels became increasingly involved in the drug trade, in the process undergoing an explosive growth in size and in their capacity for violence in the last decade.

In the first decade of the twenty-first century, a cluster of narcotics-trafficking cartels in Mexico began engaging in ruthless competition with one another, while also terrorizing authorities of the Mexican state. In the last three years of the decade, the conflict increasingly destabilized the border area of the United States and Mexico. From December 2006 to August 2010, at least 24,000 people died as a result of narco-terrorism by Mexican cartels, virtually all of them in Mexico.

"Narco-terrorism" is a protean term, defined by different persons in different ways for different contexts. Although it is sometimes used to describe the widespread phenomenon of terrorist group involvement in the narcotics trade, the term originated in 1983 with Peruvian president Fernando Terry to describe terrorist-style attacks by participants in the narcotics industry against the authorities of a state. The classic example was the *plomo o plata* ("lead or silver") approach taken by the Medellín cartel under Pablo Escobar against the Colombian government in the 1980s. Community leaders, senior police officers, judges, and other figures were offered the choice of bullets (lead) or bribery (silver) as an inducement for noninterference in the cartel's activities. While both offerings are inimical to the functioning of civil society, narco-terrorism pertains to the use of lead.

Classic narco-terrorism lies outside the usual definition of terrorism in that the primary goal for those who wage it is not to seek and exercise political power, other than to dissuade authorities to pursue anti–drug trade actions and policies. While many terrorist groups, from the Basque Euskadi Ta Askatasuna (ETA) and the Palestine Liberation Organization (PLO) through to the Taliban and the Liberation Tigers of Tamil Eelam (LTTE) have used narcotics to fund their activities, their ultimate stated goal is the achievement of political power. The cartels of Mexico, like the Medellín and Cali cartels before them, instead seek to profit from narcotics while preventing any effective political order from interfering with them.

To achieve this end, narco-terrorists use the techniques of terror to intimidate politicians, police and military officers, journalists, and community leaders. They do

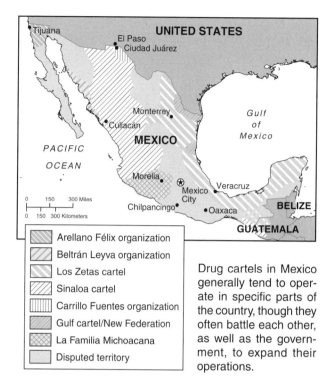

Drug cartels in Mexico generally tend to operate in specific parts of the country, though they often battle each other, as well as the government, to expand their operations.

not seek the destruction of the state or its infrastructure, appreciating the benefits of good roads, reliable water and electricity, good hospitals, and so on. Nor do they seek the complete erosion of the state's authority, because they need respect for their government's sovereignty as a shield against action by the authorities of foreign powers. Insofar as there is a definition for narco-terrorism, it should be the use of terroristic techniques against lawful authority to inhibit actions taken against the perpetrators' narcotics-related enterprises.

Rise of Mexican Cartels

There is a long history of transnational crime along the U.S.-Mexican border. In recent decades, particularly since the 1960s, the shipment of marijuana and hashish and the smuggling of illegal immigrants from Mexico into the United States have been common. As U.S. interception of South American cocaine shipments in the Caribbean increased during the 1980s, Colombian drug smugglers increasingly turned to Mexican criminal gangs to smuggle their product into the United States. By forging links with the expanding gang culture inside American cities and utilizing a small portion of the growing number of Mexican immigrants in the country, the criminal gangs also gained access to a ready distribution network.

As U.S. and Colombian authorities made inroads on the Medellín and Cali cartels in the 1990s, Mexican gangs became increasingly active in the drug trade. Already receiving enormous profits for moving tons of cocaine into the United States every year, highly experienced crime bosses, such as Pedro Aviles Perez of Sinaloa State, expanded their drug-smuggling activities. Thus, continuing success in Colombia only accelerated the growth of Mexican cartels, and as this occurred, four trends concerning their growth were revealed.

First came fragmentation, as an increasing number of new players appeared on the scene, often arising out of old smuggling networks. By 2010, there were nine major cartels in a shifting array of alliances. Some were old players, such as the Sinaloa or Tijuana cartels; others were new on the scene, such as the brutal gunmen of Los Zetas, a group of former Mexican Special Forces military personnel once hired as enforcers by other cartels.

Second, the infrastructure of the smuggling and transborder trafficking networks kept pace with the growth of the Mexican cartels. Thus, while the price of cocaine in the United States dropped only slightly, supply continued to seem plentiful. For example, as of 2009, one distribution hub in Chicago apparently accounted for two tons of cocaine distributed in the United States every month. Overall, Mexico is the source for 70 percent of all foreign narcotics and 90 percent of all cocaine consumed in the United States, generating approximately $31 billion a year in revenues.

Third, with the near destruction of the Colombian cartels, their Mexican counterparts were quickly able to act as the transshipment and distribution agents for the leftist guerrilla movement, the Revolutionary Armed Forces of Colombia (FARC), and—given the increasing role of Hezbollah in the cocaine trade out of Venezuela—likewise for the Islamist fundamentalists.

Finally, and most spectacularly, beginning in 2006, the cartels increased the violence of their own rivalries while becoming much more aggressive in their attacks on Mexican authorities.

Terrorism as an Instrument of Destabilization

Although Mexican cartel violence had grown steadily from 2000 to early 2006, President Felipe Calderón's attempt to curb escalating violence in Michoacán State in December 2006, with the deployment of 6,500 troops, is widely regarded as the start of the Mexican narcotics war. In the years that followed, the number of troops deployed against the cartels grew to at least 61,000.

Until that time, the cartels typically preferred bribery over bullets as the method of controlling the police. Indeed, there were numerous episodes in which police and prison guards were identified as working on behalf of various cartels. According to several reports, they participated in kidnapping squads, worked as bodyguards for senior drug lords, and, according to one 2010 allegation, hired out cartel hit men who had been incarcerated in their facilities. Meanwhile, other law-enforcement officers were intimidated into becoming inside intelligence sources for the cartels or simply were cowed into inaction.

Balanced against these examples are hundreds of Mexican police officers who followed the line of duty and died for it. In 2005, one new chief of police in the border town of Nuevo Laredo was gunned down barely hours after taking office. In 2007, rogue police officers unsuccessfully ambushed their new chief of police in Rosarito, killing his bodyguard. In 2008, Edgar Millán Gómez, the acting chief of the Mexican federal police, was assassinated in Mexico City. Cartelistas have gone so far as to murder police cadets in training. As hundreds of police officers have been suspended for apparent receipt of cartel payments, police cadets represent the potential of the Mexican government to create new, "clean" police departments. The families of police and military personnel have also been occasionally murdered.

But the violence does not end with law enforcement, the military, and their families. In 1993, gunmen from the Tijuana cartel gunned down Cardinal Juan Posadas Ocampo and seven other people. The Cartelistas claimed they had mistaken the outspoken cardinal for a rival dealer, but he was hit by fourteen bullets in the attack. The Catholic Church has continued to be outspoken in its condemnation of cartel violence and drug dealers and, as a result, has seen dozens of priests murdered. While some cartel members adhere to the forms and practices of Catholicism, others are self-declared Satanists and have taken to attacking the church with particular enthusiasm. Mormon and Protestant activists have also been attacked and killed.

From the beginning of 2000 to August 2010, at least sixty-four Mexican journalists also were murdered by various cartels. The total number of journalist homicides related to cartels was climbing every year, according to the international journalist advocacy group Reporters Without Borders; the organization described Mexico as "the most dangerous state in the Americas" for journalists to work in. In addition to the shooting deaths, there were grenade attacks on a number of newspaper offices and television stations. Indeed, many Mexican news outlets stopped allowing journalists to cover cartel-related issues.

Attacks on politicians also escalated, particularly with the June 2010 assassination of Institutional Revolutionary Party (PRI) candidate for governor Rodolfo Torre Cantú by Los Zetas gunmen in Tamaulipas State. Six other people were killed alongside him, including a state legislator. The Juarez cartel is widely believed to have been behind the 1994 assassination of PRI presidential candidate Luis Donaldo Colosio in Tijuana.

Municipal police in Juárez, Mexico, carry the casket of a fellow officer murdered by members of a drug cartel in 2008. Shootings, kidnappings, and a general fear of violence have run rampant in Juárez, the epicenter of Mexican narco-terrorism. *(Shaul Schwarz/Getty Images)*

There have also been purely terroristic attacks, as when grenades were tossed into the middle of an Independence Day rally in 2008 in Morelia, Michoacán State, killing eight people and injuring 100. The attack, blamed on Los Zetas, was meant to showcase the inability of the Mexican president to safeguard ordinary citizens. There have been attacks on drug rehabilitation clinics in several Mexican towns, and cartel gunmen have murdered dozens of would-be illegal migrants on the U.S. border who had refused to work for them. Musicians have been a prominent target, especially composers of popular ballads (called *narcorridos*) lauding particular drug lords; among them have been such popular performers as Valentín Elizalde and Sergio Gómez.

The vast majority of the victims of cartel violence are members of rival cartels. In contrast to the narcotics terror perpetrated by Colombian gangs, the Mexican organizations are much less monolithic and much more competitive. Some observers question the level of destabilization in Mexico, suggesting that the murderous internal habits of the cartels inhibit their ability to seriously undermine the state. Yet all of the cartels have focused some of their energies on the authorities and their own critics.

Cartel violence favors spectacular attacks, often with indiscriminate automatic fire from several gunmen.

A cultural bias toward developing distinctive styles is sometimes reflected in the manner in which they deal with murdered enemies, often mutilating the dead or posting footage online of macabre ways of disposing of dead bodies. In 2010, cartel gunmen began to use grenade launchers, antitank rockets, and their first car bombs.

External Aspects

The immense profitability of the Mexican cartel trade routes and market distribution has attracted some external involvement from other organized criminal societies around the world. In 2008, police in the United States, Italy, Mexico, and Guatemala arrested some 200 people associated with Los Zetas and the 'Ndrangheta Calabrese Mafia for smuggling and distributing cocaine and methamphetamines into Europe.

Various groups, purportedly including the Russian Mafiya and Asian gangs, were reported to be supplying arms to Mexican cartels, though most evidence pointed to U.S. gun shops, shows, and underground suppliers as the source of much of the weaponry used by the cartels. In addition, authorities also believe that the cartels may be supplying other services to outside criminal organizations, such as money laundering and the trafficking of their narcotics, including methamphetamines and heroin.

KEY DATES

1980s U.S. authorities crack down on the Caribbean smuggling routes of Colombian drug cartels.

1990s Under increasing pressure from Colombian and U.S. law enforcement, Colombian drug cartels shift their smuggling routes to Mexico, establishing relations with Mexican criminal gangs.

2006 With Mexican drug cartels growing in size and power, President Felipe Calderón dispatches thousands of troops, a decision many experts say marks the beginning of the country's "drug war."

2006–2011 Authorities say more than 24,000 Mexicans have been killed in drug violence and the security crackdown on drug cartels.

Not since the Mexican Revolution of the first years of the twentieth century has Mexico faced worse internal violence than that presented by the cartels. While the cartels are mainly preoccupied with taking territory from—and fighting with—each other, their ability to corrupt and intimidate police, politicians, clergy, reporters, and ordinary citizens is already significant and could worsen considerably, causing further destabilization of the Mexican state. At the same time, according experts, they are inhibiting Mexican industry and economic growth and could achieve the same effect in the U.S. Southwest should their influence be felt there in coming years.

John Thompson

Fears that the Hezbollah was being drawn into involvement in the Mexican cartel wars appear to have been confirmed by a series of arrests in Tijuana in the 2000s. Hezbollah has a growing involvement in cocaine production and refinement in Venezuela and is facilitating the trafficking of cocaine into Europe and Africa.

Finally, cartel activity has begun to spill over Mexico's northern border, with a growing presence in the U.S. border regions. In 2010 Mexican cartels were responsible for the murder of American citizens on U.S. soil and directly threatened U.S. law enforcement officers on several occasions. U.S. authorities fear that the influence of the cartels may spread to other American criminal organizations and, along with it, their violent methods.

See also: *Modern Terrorism*—Colombia: Guerrilla Warfare and Narco-Terrorism. *Tactics, Methods, Aims*—Drug Trafficking and Organized Crime Connections.

Further Reading

Bonner, Robert. "The New Cocaine Cowboys." *Foreign Affairs* (July–August 2010).

Cook, Colleen W., ed. *Mexico's Drug Cartels.* Washington, DC: Congressional Research Service Report for Congress, 2007.

Freeman, Laurie. *State of Siege: Drug Related Violence and Corruption in Mexico.* Washington, DC: Washington Office on Latin America, 2006.

Grayson, George W. *Mexico: Narco-Violence and a Failed State?* New Brunswick, NJ: Transaction Publishers, 2010.

Mexico: Zapatista Uprising, 1994–2000s

Prior to January 1, 1994, few Mexicans and even fewer people around the world had heard of the Zapatista National Liberation Army (EZLN). On that day, the rebels attempted to seize the towns of San Cristóbal de las Casas, Altamirano, Las Margaritas, and Ocosingo in the southern Mexican state of Chiapas. The EZLN, comprised mainly of Mayan Indian peasants dissatisfied with the poor living conditions and extreme poverty in Chiapas, also threatened to capture a regional Mexican Army headquarters and garrison on the outskirts of San Cristóbal de las Casas. The Zapatistas, on behalf of some of the most impoverished people in Mexico, both indigenous and nonindigenous, demanded land, work, decent wages, housing, access to health care, free schools, an end to racism, liberty, democracy, peace, and justice in Chiapas. They also called for the president's resignation and for sweeping political, social, and economic changes throughout Mexico.

The attack surprised the Mexican government, but after a twelve-day delay, its army and air force counterattacked, taking back control of the towns and chasing the Zapatistas back into their jungle and mountain retreats. This battle, in which more than 100 persons were killed, brought allegations against members of the military of human rights abuses. In response, Mexican president Carlos Salinas de Gortari (1988–1994) declared a unilateral cease-fire, sent a negotiator to initiate peace talks with the Zapatistas, and offered amnesty to the rebels on January 12, 1994. National and regional party officials in Chiapas were dismissed.

Economics and Revolution

For 500 years, indigenous peoples were pushed off their lands by the expansion of plantations owned by descendants of Spanish settlers. At the beginning of the twentieth century, the indigenous people in Chiapas were farming the sloping, rocky soils of the highlands. After the Mexican Revolution (1910–1917), the dominant political party, the Institutional Revolutionary Party (PRI), implemented a vast program of land reform, which distributed Mexico's land to peasant farmers, preventing the emergence of large private farms.

In the 1980s, a severe economic crisis forced the Mexican government to initiate several reforms to help stabilize the economy. Agriculture reform, necessary for Mexico to farm on an efficient scale, included laws to allow foreign ownership of Mexican land and firms and reconcentration of land so as to achieve a competitive level of productivity.

In 1992, the Mexican government rewrote Article 27 of the Mexican constitution, bringing an end to the land-reform policies that had helped shape the relationship between the government and the peasants. In a 1994 interview, Subcomandante Marcos, the leader of the EZLN, stated that this change in Article 27 had persuaded the rebels to take up arms against the government. In contrast to his impoverished and poorly educated followers, Marcos was a university teacher and son of a well-to-do furniture dealer. Although the Zapatista movement demanded traditional human rights for the native Indian population, Marcos made use of portable computers and the Internet to bypass the government blocks on communications.

The peasant farmers, such as those in Chiapas, saw the economic reforms of the 1980s and the changes in Article 27 as threats to their agrarian way of life. These economic reforms effected major political changes in agricultural

The Zapatista National Liberation Army seized control of much of the Mexican state of Chiapas in early 1994.

states such as Chiapas. The peasants in the Mexican rural and agricultural states historically supported the PRI, and in return the state provided subsidies and the goods and services necessary for their survival. As the dominant political party in Mexico since 1917, the PRI took the rural peasant support for granted, not seeing a need for much political reform in these areas. Antistate and anti-PRI sentiments were fueled largely by peasant landlessness, land scarcity, and the widening gap in living standards between Chiapas and the rest of Mexico.

In the 1980s, the northern financial and industrial sector emerged as a major political force. Coincident with this development, Mexican public policy refocused from the traditional socialist economic orientation of the Mexican Revolution, which benefited peasants, to the moderate and conservative policies of the modern presidential administrations. This change gave political weight to the business and financial sectors of society at the expense of the peasants, who felt abandoned by the PRI. During this period of economic reform, the Zapatistas began recruiting peasants to their cause and timing their uprising to coincide with the inauguration of the North American Free Trade Agreement (NAFTA), with the possible consequence of stemming the flow of capital investment into Mexico.

Zapatista Goals

Although a rebellion in name, the Zapatista philosophy of rebellion differs from many, because its followers struggle not for power and government overthrow but for democracy, liberty, and justice—regardless of who is in power. The movement is named after Emiliano Zapata, a hero of the Mexican Revolution, who also led a landless peasant army against those who took their lands. The Indian peoples of Chiapas enjoyed self-government until the 1970s, when a series of governors, landowners, and cattle barons began taking their lands, driving them further into the jungle and up the mountains into desperate poverty.

Although the rebels were mainly Chiapas peasants, the level of the EZLN's tactical skill during their surprise attack suggested a non-Indian, external leadership, who were probably urban, professional, and university educated. Their main rebel spokesman, Subcomandante Marcos, was thought to be well educated and not an ethnic Indian. The EZLN's demonstrated competence in the performance of military-oriented activities indicated the probability that former military officers and guerrillas with combat experience were members, possibly originally from Guatemala's left-wing revolutionaries. Although the Zapatistas fought for an ancient way of life, they used modern instruments for the dissemination of their ideology. The EZLN was credited with the first use of the Internet as an instrument of political dissent, and since 1994, Subcomandante Marcos has regularly issued communiqués through this medium.

Escalation of Violence

In September 1994, 20,000 Tojolabal Indians, organized by the independent Union of Agricultural Workers (CIOAC), declared themselves autonomous. Shortly afterward, on October 10, Marcos temporarily broke off contact with the government negotiator. Violence escalated as peasants armed themselves against the attacks of paramilitary forces organized by ranchers. One group of angry peasants kidnapped the interim governor, Javier López Moreno, holding him hostage for several hours. On the eve of his inauguration on December 8, governor-elect Eduardo Robledo offered to resign if the guerrillas laid down their arms. They did not do so. On October 19, the guerrillas, who by this time controlled about one-fifth of the state, demonstrated their ability to slip through the army cordon. They erected roadblocks, proclaimed "liberated areas" where government forces were not allowed to enter, and occupied the town of Simojovel and thirty-seven other municipalities. The government had advance warning of this move and, on October 21, attempted to take advantage of the situation to devalue the peso, the unit of currency, while placing the blame on the guerrillas.

Within twenty-four hours, while fresh troops and tanks moved into place around the guerrilla bases, the devaluation had revealed the flaw in the Mexican economy: its dependence on short-term loans. As capital flooded out of the country, the government lost control of the financial situation. The peso fell to unprecedented depths, precipitating a crisis of confidence.

By contrast, the rebels appeared to gain legitimacy. In the circumstances, the new president, Ernesto Zedillo, prudently decided to start fresh negotiations with the rebels. Dialogue was resumed by the new government and continued during the early weeks of 1995, but sporadic attacks on the insurgents continued at the same time. It was not always clear whether the army was following government orders or acting on its own initiative. A government peace offer on March 1 was quickly rejected by the insurgents. However, six further rounds of negotiations finally led to an agreement on September 11, 1995, after the Zapatistas had agreed to participate in dialogue.

After the Cease-Fire

On January 18, 1996, the San Andrés accords, an agreement between the Mexican government and the EZLN, were negotiated. The accords recognized indigenous peoples' right to self-determination, as well as the judicial, political, social, economic, and cultural rights that would stem from this self-determination. However, the troubles continued because the Mexican government refused to implement the elements of the accords.

After the cease-fire in 1994, President Ernesto Zedillo sent 40,000 troops, about one-third of the Mexican Army, to Chiapas to protect oil and uranium reserves and to prevent the spread of the Zapatista movement to neighboring states. On December 22, 1997, paramilitary attackers massacred forty-five men, women, and children in the Chiapas village of Acteal. This massacre was precipitated by months of political tension because the local PRI had lost much of its support to the rebel sympathizers and other opposition groups. It is widely believed that the paramilitary groups responsible for the Acteal massacre were funded by PRI party loyalists. Masked Zapatista guerrilla commanders met in November 1998 with a congressional peace commission in Chiapas, with hopes of renewing peace talks between the rebels and the Mexican government. In general, the government wanted to negotiate because it sought to find a way to avoid: (1) a costly conflict that might erode the morale of the army and diminish the national treasury; (2) an ongoing international embarrassment for a Mexico that was desperately trying to escape an image of political instability and economic chaos and to appear more modern and democratic; and (3) the real possibility that the nascent rebellion in Mexico's southern states could take hold elsewhere and thereby contaminate the young and disaffected in Mexico City and the poor peasantry throughout the country. For their part, the Zapatistas wanted social justice and political power, and they knew that the government was not prepared to fight them indefinitely.

In the context of the subsequent talks, the Zapatistas insisted on being accorded respect. They complained about the lack of decent food, accommodations, and security provided by the commission, and they referred to these actions or slights as racism against the indigenous population of Mexico. Because neither side appeared ready to compromise, the peace process reached an impasse. Thereafter, the Zapatista commanders informed the commission that unless the government implemented the peace accords (which had been signed by Zedillo but never submitted to Congress), there would be no return to the negotiating table.

The PRI's loss of political power to the conservative Partido Acción Nacional broke the seventy-six-year, one-party rule, providing some hope that reform was possible. After President Vicente Fox took office in December 2000, the law drafted in 1996 was finally sent to Congress. Subsequently, the indigenous rights

KEY DATES

January 1996   The Mexican government and Zapatista leaders sign the San Andrés accords, promising the country's indigenous peoples more self-determination.

November 1998   Zapatista leaders meet with a Mexican congressional peace commission in Chiapas.

December 2000   As President Vicente Fox takes office, an indigenous rights law is sent to the Mexican Congress; the bill passes in 2001.

law, passed in 2001, granted Mexico's 10 million Indians the political autonomy and control over natural resources that were initially provided for under the 1996 accords. The law became caught up in a succession of legal challenges but eventually won approval by the Supreme Court. In 2001, President Vicente Fox closed seven military bases in Chiapas that were built to monitor guerrilla strongholds. This gesture was intended to encourage the Zapatistas to negotiate an end to their eight-year rebellion.

In the years since, the EZLN has become an activist political organization, conducting peaceful protests and actions in defense of Mexican workers and peasants. In addition, it has reached out to groups around the world in defense of indigenous peoples' rights. By 2011, its days as an insurgency force were long over.

Manuel S. Romo and Peter Calvert

See also: *Definitions, Types, Categories*—Ethnonationalist Terrorism; Left-Wing and Revolutionary Terrorism.

Further Reading

Collier, George A. "Zapatismo Resurgent." *NACLA Report on the Americas* 33:5 (March–April 2000): 20–27.

Di Piramo, Daniela. *Political Leadership in Zapatista Mexico: Marcos, Celebrity, and Charismatic Authority.* Boulder, CO: FirstForum, 2010.

Harvey, Neil. *The Chiapas Rebellion: The Struggle for Land and Democracy.* Durham, NC: Duke University Press, 1998.

Hayden, Tom, ed. *The Zapatista Reader.* New York: Thunder's Mouth Press/Nation Books, 2001.

Ierardi, Anthony R., and Casey Wardynski. "The Zapatista Rebellion in Chiapas." *Military Review* 74:10 (October 1994): 64–76.

Namibia: Anti–South African Struggle, 1960–1990

During World War I, South Africa conquered the neighboring German colony of South West Africa on behalf of the Allies. At the war's end, the League of Nations granted South Africa a mandate to govern the territory. In 1946, the League's successor, the United Nations, recommended that South Africa prepare the region for independence.

The South African government in Pretoria, however, continued to govern it as a part of its own country and introduced apartheid—the system of legal racial discrimination. This attitude antagonized many and, in October 1966, the United Nations General Assembly recommended that the mandate be revoked. In June 1968, the assembly renamed the territory Namibia, instructing South Africa to grant independence. Finally, in July 1971, the International Court of Justice declared South Africa's presence there illegal.

Pretoria's control was also challenged by Namibian nationalist movements, most notably the South West Africa People's Organization (SWAPO), founded in April 1960 and drawing most of its members from the Ovambo tribe. The South African authorities soon took repressive measures against SWAPO. Many members fled to Tanzania to organize the People's Liberation Army of Namibia, which led an insurgency combining guerrilla warfare, terrorism, and political activity.

South African army bases in Namibia and the Ovamboland region where SWAPO was active.

In late 1965, the first trained insurgents set up camps in Ovamboland. These activists attacked security forces and progovernment blacks and sabotaged installations. In 1966, SWAPO also carried out a number of terrorist attacks on white civilians. In response, Pretoria arrested and convicted thirty-seven Namibians for supporting terrorism. From the first clash with South African forces on August 26, 1966, until 1975, the insurgents made little progress militarily. But their political activities gradually made gains, as SWAPO exploited disquiet over apartheid.

SWAPO's prospects improved after 1975, when the Portuguese withdrew from Angola. Independent Angola allowed SWAPO to use that country as a base. By now SWAPO was gaining greater international recognition, including a declaration of support from the United Nations in December 1976. SWAPO gained more recruits, got better weapons from the Soviet Union, and received better training by Cuban and Eastern bloc personnel in Angola. From 1975, SWAPO tried to extend its campaign beyond Ovamboland.

While SWAPO used traditional guerrilla techniques, it also sometimes resorted to terrorist attacks. According to South African reports, on December 20, 1976, terrorists shot dead a white farmer's wife and her twelve-year-old son near Grootfontein, northern Namibia. Moreover, on New Year's Eve 1976, in Oshandi, Ovamboland, in northern Namibia, ten terrorists fired at shoppers, killing two civilians.

South African troops responded with counterinsurgency operations, attacking SWAPO bases in southern Angola. These missions were effective, with SWAPO allegedly suffering ten times as many dead as the security forces. Pretoria also sought to undermine the guerrillas by promising Namibia eventual independence. The insurgents also failed to extend their influence beyond

Ovamboland, since ethnic groups other than the Ovambo did not see SWAPO as liberators.

In early 1988, SWAPO again resorted to terrorism as part of its insurgency campaign. On February 19, 1988, the insurgents exploded a bomb in a bank at Oshakati, in Ovamboland, killing twenty-one civilians.

In 1988, the Soviet Union and the United States sponsored a settlement linking a South African withdrawal from Namibia to a Cuban and Eastern bloc withdrawal from Angola. In the November 1989 elections, SWAPO's political wing won the most votes, albeit not an absolute majority, and in March 1990 SWAPO formed the first government of the new independent state of Namibia.

Henry Longstreet

See also: *Definitions, Types, Categories*—Ethnonationalist Terrorism. *Modern Terrorism*—Angola: Civil and Separatist Wars; South Africa: Antiapartheid Struggle.

Further Reading

Beckett, Ian F.W., and John Pimlott, eds. *Armed Forces and Modern Counterinsurgency.* New York: St. Martin's, 1985.

Herbstein, Denis, and John A. Everson. *The Devils Are Among Us: The War for Namibia.* Atlantic Highlands, NJ: Zed Books, 1989.

Leys, Colin. *Namibia's Liberation Struggle: The Two-Edged Sword.* Columbus: Ohio University Press, 1995.

Nepal: Maoist Uprising, 1996–2006

Nepal became a united kingdom in the late eighteenth century, under the rule of the Gorkha prince Prithvi Narayan Shah. The Shah family ruled through a period of turmoil and military defeat at the hands of the British until 1846, when the Rana family made the post of prime minister, which they held, hereditary. In the process, the monarch was reduced to a figurehead, while the Rana ministers established a strong centralized autocracy that kept Nepal independent but economically and politically isolated.

In 1950, King Tribhuvan, a direct descendant of Prithvi Narayan Shah, fled to India, where he instigated an armed revolt that overthrew the Rana regime and brought the Shah dynasty back to absolute power. Over the next several years, he worked with political parties to frame a constitution and institute democratic reforms. In 1959, under King Mahendra, this effort culminated in a written constitution and Nepal's first democratic elections for a national assembly. The Nepali Congress Party, modeled loosely on the Congress Party of India, won a majority of seats in the assembly. B.P. Koirala was democratic Nepal's first prime minister.

The arrangement lasted only eighteen months. Citing the need to adhere more closely to Nepali tradition, King Mahendra dissolved the assembly and issued a new constitution that abolished political parties, replacing them with a pyramidal *panchayat* (council) structure. Rising from a base of village assemblies to the National Parliament, the new structure preserved ruling-class privilege and put the king firmly back at the pinnacle of absolute power.

Democracy and the People's Revolution

Mahendra's son, King Birendra, faced popular unrest and demands for democratic reform almost from the time he succeeded his father in 1972. In 1991, a popular and largely peaceful "People's Revolution" forced King Birendra, after an initial violent crackdown, to accept a constitution. The pact transferred a large part of the monarch's power to an elected parliament, lifted the ban on political parties, and freed political prisoners.

Constitutional rule has not brought the benefits that its supporters envisioned to much of largely rural, agrarian Nepal. In the twenty years during which parliamentary democracy has been in place, life has not noticeably improved in the countryside or for the poorest segments of the population. Remnant feudalism and the rigid Hindu caste system imposed by the early Shah kings account for at least some of this inertia, while endemic official corruption at all levels of government prevents any real reform or progressive agenda from taking hold. The Nepali Parliament has been plagued by feuds within and among political parties, instability, and a swift succession of ineffectual ministerial governments.

Nepal ranks as one of the world's poorest countries. Subsistence farmers, a third of them landless sharecroppers, produce 37 percent of the country's gross domestic product (GDP) on the 20 percent of Nepal's total land that is arable. Villages are linked by narrow, eroded paths that wind and climb among precipitous hills; food and supplies are carried in—and agricultural products are carried out—on the backs of animals or people. Deforestation for fuel and water pollution due to lack of infrastructure have become life-threatening ecological disasters throughout much of the country. Literacy stands at 52 percent for men and 18 percent for women; schools in rural areas can be hard to get to or nonexistent. Average life expectancy for both men and women is below sixty years, and even less in the lower castes.

Like all societies composed of many ethnic and cultural groups, Nepal struggles with the dichotomy of national unity versus representative diversity. On the one hand, the imposition of majority norms from above can lead to the repression of minorities, while on the other hand perfect equality can lead to political fragmentation around narrow agendas. Despite Nepal's official characterization as the world's only Hindu kingdom, a significant portion of its indigenous and immigrant populations is not Hindu. Since the 1991 People's Revolution, a number of groups have arisen to promote indigenous rights and social reforms aimed at increasing the profile of poor and marginalized groups. Only very recently, mostly thanks to pressure from international human rights groups, has the Nepali government finally acknowledged the devastating traffic in young girls from poor villages, who end up in brothels or as virtual slave laborers in India.

Massacre in the Palace

Ten years into constitutional rule, Nepal became headline news around the world on June 1, 2001, when the British Broadcasting Company announced that eight members of the royal family, including King Birendra and Queen Aishwarya, had been massacred during a family dinner at the royal palace. The Nepalese people listened in disbelief to the news that Crown Prince Dipendra, in a fit of drunken rage over his mother's refusal to allow him to marry the woman of his choice, had attacked his family with an array of automatic weapons that had been loaned to him for testing by the army. After a half-hour rampage during which some family members were gunned down as they fled through the palace gardens, Dipendra allegedly turned a gun on himself. In a bizarre denouement, the accused assassin was declared king according to the laws of succession as he lay in a coma at a nearby army hospital; he died there two days later.

In a matter of minutes the Shah dynasty's line of direct succession, which had passed from father to son unbroken for eleven generations, was shattered forever. Gyanendra, brother of the murdered king, succeeded to the throne upon Dipendra's death. Meanwhile, police sought to control tense crowds that massed outside the palace and throughout the capital Kathmandu demanding more information about the killings.

The palace embarked on a series of confusing, contradictory, and ultimately unsatisfying explanations of what had happened that night. After first blaming the crown prince, officials retracted the "drunken rage" explanation and put out an improbable story that the whole thing had been an accident. When this news was met with predictable disbelief, the new king appointed a Probe Commission to investigate. After ten days, the commission publicly reiterated the first story—that Dipendra had acted alone to kill his family and then committed suicide. Many Nepalis found this conclusion hard to accept and wondered why, in the heavily guarded palace, the rampage had gone unchecked for a full half hour. Where were the bodyguards? Why, among the dozens of people in the area where the shootings occurred, were no one but royals killed and wounded? What happened to the forensics reports of the crime scene, and why were postmortems not carried out according to law?

Although rumors flew and important questions remained unanswered, no competing explanation of the events of June 1 has been widely accepted. In the face of silence from the palace and a spreading communist insurgency that hit a new level of violence after the tragedy, it is likely that the full truth of the palace massacre will remain hidden.

Maoist United People's Front

The Communist Party of Nepal (CPN) has been a strong and credible force in Nepali politics since the early 1950s. It is represented by a number of factions that came together as the United Left Front to help organize the People's Revolution of 1991. Since then, the CPN has consistently made a strong showing in parliamentary elections. The CPN (Maoist) is one of the most radical branches of the CPN. This group demanded nothing less than the abolition of the monarchy and the establishment of a secular republican government, as well as an end to all foreign "imperialist" influence in Nepal. Once the CPN (Maoist) leaders concluded that the political system was not going to satisfy their demands for a communist republic, they began to plan

for a popular peasant uprising along the lines of classic Marxist-Leninist dialectical thinking. This uprising was launched in the countryside on February 13, 1996.

Borrowing from Mao Zedong's People's Liberation Army and Peru's Shining Path, the Nepali Maoists began a campaign of "liberation" in Nepal's mountainous western provinces aimed at overthrowing "the bureaucratic-capitalist class and state system." To Westerners, the insurgents' agenda, with its promotion of Marxism-Leninism-Maoism and calls for revolution at any cost, seems chillingly anachronistic. By spring 2002, that cost had risen to an estimated 3,000 to 4,000 lives.

By May 2002 the insurgents had managed to capture roughly a third of Nepal's seventy-five districts through a combination of force, coercion, and, most important, populist law enforcement that often proved more effective and efficient than that which the local governments provided. Wealthy landowners saw their deeds burned; banks—and the farmers' loan records in them—were blown up; women found justice against abusive husbands. Women, in fact, make up a large part of the insurgent army. The poorest and most marginalized sector of Nepali society, young rural women, found a means to escape the oppressive life of the farm and to gain a measure of power in their own right, with the help of an AK-47.

The rebels often are characterized as "Robin Hoods" and praised for bringing a semblance of justice and order to parts of Nepal ignored and forgotten by the central government. The dark side of the movement lies in its resemblance to the Khmer Rouge of Cambodia. Teachers and other "intellectuals" are among those routinely targeted for assassination in the villages. Operatives infiltrate Kathmandu, extorting "protection" money from anyone perceived to have ties to the West. Those who refuse are threatened with death, and many successful businesspeople flee the country to seek asylum elsewhere. Groups of foreigners are surrounded and shaken down for money and valuables while hiking, and in at least one instance visitors at a popular tourist hotel in the foothills were robbed en masse. Several general strikes sporadically have paralyzed the major cities. There was little evidence that Comrade Prachanda, the rebel leader, or his lieutenants, had thought beyond winning the armed conflict to the actual governance of the country.

A large portion of Nepal's foreign exchange used to come from tourism. Adventurous travelers from all over the world flocked to Kathmandu both to trek into the Himalayas, which form the northern border of the country, and to enjoy the exotic (to a Westerner) ancient Nepalese culture and superb handcrafts. Permits bought by Everest climbers are another important source of government revenue. Although the insurgents so far have been careful not to hurt foreign travelers, the increasing violence has virtually shut down Nepal's tourist industry and helped send the country's weak economy into free fall. This development was applauded by the Maoists as another means to bring down the government, although its repercussions naturally hit the poorest the hardest.

The insurgents stepped up their attacks on villages and police outposts after the royal massacre, surrounding and slaughtering the poorly trained and equipped district police by the tens and hundreds. Factions within the government began to call for negotiations, which began in August and September 2001. Government representatives met with their revolutionary counterparts three times before the talks broke down over intractable demands on both sides. Cease-fires were declared and broken. In November, Prime Minister Sher Bahadur Deuba, through the king, declared a national state of emergency in an effort to control general strikes instigated by the rebels, and to crack down on media his government considered threatening. The army, which had been kept out of the conflict on the principle of *posse comitatus*, was mobilized against the rebels at the end of the year, but without noticeable result other than a dramatic increase in casualties.

In May 2002, Prime Minister Deuba, bolstered by promises of arms and money from the United States and Britain as part of the larger war on terrorism in South Asia, declared that the time for negotiation was over. Critics charged that outside military aid would do nothing to alleviate the poverty and corruption that laid fertile ground for the insurgency in the first place, but would simply widen the war. In that same month, Great Britain also committed itself to sending ground forces into Nepal, a potentially destabilizing move with the potential to raise tensions in the region considerably.

During the insurgency, which largely came to an end in 2006, credible evidence surfaced that the rebels received substantial financial and material help from Pakistan's secret intelligence branch, the Inter-Services Intelligence (ISI), in a bid to draw some of India's security forces away from the border war in Kashmir. India had a powerful interest in keeping Nepal stable and under its wing and had been in close consultation with the Nepali government over the course of the uprising. The roots of Nepal's insurgency, however, were indigenous and arose directly from the country's extreme poverty and lack of responsive government. Although the insurgents called themselves Maoists, area experts agreed that China itself had no motive to help destabilize Nepal, which has long acted as a useful buffer between the two nuclear-armed rivals, India and China.

At the beginning of 2003, there appeared to be a breakthrough in the conflict as the two sides declared a cease-fire in January. But hopes were dashed when the rebels pulled out of the agreement in August and launched renewed attacks on government forces. At the same time, clashes intensified between student groups and police in the capital. Facing a rural insurgency and

KEY DATES

February 2, 1996   An uprising by the Maoist Communist Party of Nepal is launched in the Nepalese countryside.

June 2001   Crown Prince Dipendra, in a fit of drunken rage, murders eight members of the Nepalese royal family, then turns the gun on himself, dying from the wounds two days later.

May 2002   Maoist insurgents reportedly control one-third of Nepalese territory; bolstered by U.S. and British support, Prime Minister Deuba announces that negotiations with guerrillas are over.

November 2006   Maoist insurgents and the government sign the Comprehensive Peace Agreement, ending ten years of conflict.

May 2008   A month after Maoists win the largest bloc of votes in parliament, the legislative body votes to end the monarchy, turning Nepal into a republic.

May 2009   The coalition government falls apart as the Maoists pull out over a dispute about how to integrate former rebel fighters into the national army.

civil unrest in urban areas, King Gyendra dismissed the government and imposed a state of emergency in February 2005, only to lift it under international pressure three months later. In late 2005 and early 2006, all sides agreed to a cease-fire as a means to restore democracy to the country. The cease-fire led directly to the Comprehensive Peace Agreement of November 2006, which brought the decade-old insurgency to an end and allowed members of the Maoist party to enter parliament.

The Maoists, however, insisted that the monarchy was not acting in good faith and pulled out of the government in September 2007. Simultaneously, three bombs went off in Kathmandu, the first attack on the capital since the end of the insurgency nearly a year before. The Maoists agreed to participate in elections in April 2008 and won the largest bloc of seats in parliament, but not enough to establish a ruling majority. The following month, parliament voted to end the monarchy and establish a republic. In May 2009, the coalition government, headed by Maoist leader Prachanda (nom de guerre for Chhabilal Dahal), fell apart as the Maoists pulled out over disputes regarding the integration of rebel fighters into the national armed forces. Out of government, the Maoists continued to press their demands by seizing land in the west of the country, provoking clashes that left four persons dead in December 2009. Such incidents aside, the country remained largely at peace as the new decade began, though the governing coalition remained at odds with the Maoist opposition over the form a new national constitution would take.

From the mid-1990s to the mid-2000s, the peaceful kingdom of Nepal was forced onto the world scene at gunpoint. The forces that tore it apart were rooted deep in the country's own history and fueled by the regional rivalries swirling around—and across—its borders. By the mid-2000s, it had become clear that neither side was likely to win the upper hand through conflict, and the two ultimately came to an agreement to share power. That outcome was aided by the fact that much of the Nepali population had turned against the repressive and unresponsive monarchy, which had been the strongest advocate for conflict. Once the Maoists became the dominant party through elections, the monarchy ceased to exist—though the country remained politically divided and tense.

Elizabeth Skinner and James Ciment

See also: *Definitions, Types, Categories*—Left-Wing and Revolutionary Terrorism.

Further Reading

Hutt, Michael, ed. *Himalayan People's War: Nepal's Maoist Rebellion.* Bloomington: Indiana University Press, 2004.

Lawoti, Mahendra, and Anup K. Pahari, eds. *The Maoist Insurgency in Nepal: Revolution in the Twenty-first Century.* New York: Routledge, 2010.

Lecomte-Tilouine, Marie. *Hindu Kingship, Ethnic Revival, and Maoist Rebellion in Nepal.* New York: Oxford University Press, 2009.

Nicaragua: Revolution and Counterrevolution, 1974–1990

In Nicaragua, terror tactics were used by both sides during the fighting that led to the overthrow of the Somoza regime and the installation of a Sandinista government in 1979. Carlos Fonseca Amador organized the Sandinistas as a guerrilla movement in 1961. He took inspiration from the left-wing Cuban revolutionary model of Fidel Castro and Che Guevara. The group's title, the Sandinista National Liberation Front (FSLN), indicated its anti-U.S. stance by paying homage to General Augusto Sandino, the hero of guerrilla resistance against the United States in the 1920s and 1930s. However, after the withdrawal of U.S. forces in 1933, National Guard commander Anastasio Somoza García ordered the murder of Sandino and took power in 1936.

Somoza ruled Nicaragua until 1956 and was succeeded by the elder of his two sons, Luis Somoza. Fonseca planned to follow Sandino's example and set up a rural guerrilla movement in the northern hills. However, with poor organization and inadequate secrecy, the campaign was quashed, and many guerrillas, including Fonseca, were arrested.

In 1967, Somoza's younger son, Anastasio Somoza Debayle, took over as president. His power was based on the National Guard, which he kept as his private army. In 1973, he amended the Nicaraguan constitution so he could rule indefinitely.

Meanwhile, the Sandinistas had reorganized in the cities, but their success appeared short-lived. In 1969, the Sandinista leadership was identified. Five of the seven members of the group, including its leader, Julio César Buitrago, were killed in a shoot-out in downtown Managua, the capital of Nicaragua. Shortly afterward, Fonseca was arrested and imprisoned in Costa Rica. He was freed the following year, when Sandinista guerrillas hijacked a Costa Rican aircraft and demanded his release.

Shattered by Earthquake

On December 23, 1972, an earthquake devastated Managua. Although aid poured in from around the world, it became clear that no one would receive any money except the Somozas and their followers. The National Guard openly looted ruined buildings. The Sandinistas gained support, especially after staging a few outrageous acts of moneymaking. In one such raid on December 27, 1974, a thirteen-strong Sandinista commando unit, armed with M1 carbines, hunting rifles, and grenades, burst in on a party held by the U.S. ambassador in Managua. They seized the embassy, taking as hostages government ministers, the city mayor, two ambassadors, and leading businessmen. The siege lasted sixty hours, until the government gave in. It released political prisoners, including senior Sandinista Daniel Ortega Saavedra, increased wages for industrial and rural workers, and paid a massive $2 million ransom.

The government's reaction was swift and brutal. More than 400 people were murdered in the reprisals that followed. Horror at these state killings served to unite the conventional political parties, most of which, like the Sandinistas, were illegal. But the Sandinistas were divided as to how to respond, and after Fonseca's death in December 1975, they split into three factions. The smallest, Prolonged Popular War (GPP), favored a Maoist strategy of rural-based guerrilla activity. The second group took a Leninist line and opted for mass insurrection led by a small band of urban-based militants. Daniel Ortega led the third faction, which became known as the "Terceristas." He argued for immediate insurrection, but in alliance with other disenchanted elements. With the support of the majority of the combatants, Ortega launched a national offensive against the government on October 13, 1977.

Opposition Joins Forces

Legal opposition to the government, including elements of the Catholic Church, had long supported the Sandinistas, but the core of this opposition was the Conservative Party. The remains of Nicaragua's traditional two-party system had been retained by the Somozas for appearances, but the Chamorros, the leading Conservative Party family, had never accepted their Somoza rivals.

The signal for insurrection came in January 1978, when a gunman killed Pedro Joaquín Chamorro, editor of *La Prensa* newspaper. Chamorro had been increasingly critical of the regime. His murder, believed to be the work of the National Guard, cemented unity among opposition groups. A general strike was called. Attacks were launched simultaneously from the north by the Sandinistas and from the south by a democratic opposition front sponsored by Costa Rica and Panama.

In another spectacular event, senior Sandinista Edén Pastora, known as Commander Zero, led twenty-five insurgents in Operation Pigsty. They attacked Managua's National Palace and held top politicians among their 100 hostages. The regime was forced to hand over $500,000 ransom and release scores of political prisoners. Once again, the Sandinistas escaped.

By mid-September, Nicaragua was facing full-scale civil war. The National Guard fought viciously to retain its power and privileges (rewards for service included appointments as governor of a department, which was a license to collect local taxes). Outside the National Guard, the Somozas lacked support. They had appropriated much of Nicaragua's wealth and had left little for anyone outside their circle. The National Guard's terrorist tactics alienated what little support they had.

U.S. Alarm

President Jimmy Carter viewed this chain of events with concern. His administration had tried to distance itself from the Somozas, but his instructions had not been followed. By the time U.S. diplomats tried to engineer a transfer of power to a compromise candidate, it was too late. The Sandinistas were expecting such a move. They had already joined the other opposition forces in proclaiming a new provisional government from Costa Rican soil. When Somoza fled Nicaragua on July 17, 1979, members of the Sandinista-dominated Junta of National Reconstruction and its provisional governing council flew in to take charge on July 20.

Over the next year, the Sandinistas shared power with non-Marxist groups, but as Marxist hard-liners consolidated control, toleration of other groups ended. In 1980, state-controlled mobs attacked a rally organized by Nicaraguan Democratic Movement leader Alfonso Robelo. In a speech, Ortega threatened to unleash these *turbas divinas* (divine mobs) on any opponent. Mobs attacked the homes and businesses of Sandinista opponents, often beating the victims as well. During March 1981, mobs painted insults on the house of Violeta Chamorro, widow of editor Pedro Chamorro. Mobs also destroyed Robelo's home.

During these same two years following the revolution, the provisional government embarked on a series of reforms, including a literacy campaign, the provision of free medical care, and the abolition of the death penalty. However, President Ronald Reagan feared that the insurrection in neighboring El Salvador was part of a worldwide communist conspiracy. The Reagan Administration thought the conspiracy was supported by the Soviet Union through Cuba's capital, Havana, and Managua.

Formation of the Contras

In November 1981, President Reagan authorized the formation of a clandestine force to launch a counterrevolutionary guerrilla campaign in Nicaragua from bases in Honduras. Although the title chosen by the CIA was the Nicaraguan Democratic Force (FDN), the force became known as the Contras (an abbreviation of the Spanish word for counterrevolutionaries).

By 1981, American financial backing and military training for the Contras were under way. Attacks on Nicaraguan economic targets began in March 1982. Most military activity involved small-scale raids into northern Nicaragua, causing considerable loss of life and economic damage. These raids, however, resulted in the local population uniting behind the Nicaraguan army and establishing their own militias in support.

By 1983, covert U.S. aid had reached $20 million a year and some 150 CIA operatives were believed to be in the area. On January 3, 1984, forces coordinated by a U.S. warship attacked oil facilities at Nicaragua's Puerto Sandino. On February 25, the Contras made similar attacks on the Atlantic port of El Bluff and the Pacific harbor of Corinto. They laid mines, damaging four freighters, one of Soviet registration. On April 5, the United States vetoed a United Nations resolution condemning the mining. Meanwhile, at a press conference, President Reagan claimed that the Nicaraguan provisional government was "exporting revolution" and stated, "We are going to try and inconvenience the government of Nicaragua until they quit that kind of action."

The failure of the Contras stemmed partly from personnel. They were mostly former members of Somoza's National Guard, chosen more for their anticommunism than for their competence. Despite extensive training, they were unable to gain the trust of the local populace. Contra incursions into Nicaragua left a trail of murder, rape, torture, and robbery. In addition, after an Argentine hit squad killed Somoza in Paraguay in 1980, the Contras lacked leadership. Consequently, the CIA sponsored a second opposition force in the south.

Another Contra Force

At the same time, another movement, called the Democratic Revolutionary Alliance (ARDE), was established in Costa Rica, Nicaragua's southern neighbor, by Contras who rejected association with the Somoza dictatorship. One such member was the disaffected ex-Sandinista Edén Pastora, who became its leader. Pastora, who enjoyed the popular appeal that the FDN Contras lacked, began operations in September 1982. By April 1983, ARDE was making incursions into southern Nicaragua. In September 1983, ARDE sent out light aircraft to launch a rocket attack on Managua's airport.

Because of U.S. aid, the usual balance of insurgency and counterinsurgency was reversed in that the insurgents had the superior weaponry. Air attacks and naval commando raids devastated economic targets, particularly oil facilities, and gasoline rationing was introduced in October 1983. Despite their aerial and naval superiority, however, the Contras needed a decisive victory on land. Between August 1983 and January 1984, ARDE and FDN Contra forces launched a series of offensives involving 10,000 troops, but the Nicaraguan army, bolstered by local militias, had increased in number to

> ## KEY DATES
>
> **1972**   An earthquake devastates the capital of Managua; the dictator Anastasio Somoza and his cronies steal much of the international aid that pours into the country.
>
> **1974**   Commandos from the Sandinista National Liberation Front (FSLN) seize the U.S. embassy, marking the beginning of the revolution to oust Somoza.
>
> **1979**   Besieged Somoza and his followers flee Managua, marking the triumph of the FSLN-led revolution; President Jimmy Carter begins small-scale support to anti-FSLN forces.
>
> **1981**   The inauguration of President Ronald Reagan sees a large-scale increase of support to counterrevolutionary forces, known popularly as the Contras and based in neighboring Honduras and later Costa Rica.
>
> **1984**   Contra forces, aided by the U.S. military, attack oil installations in Nicaragua.
>
> **1986**   Costa Rican president Oscar Arias begins the peace process to end the civil war in Nicaragua.
>
> **1990**   The victory of opposition leader Violeta Chamorro over FSLN president Daniel Ortega signals the end of the war.

50,000. Neither the FDN in the north nor ARDE in the south was able to hold territory for long, although with U.S. support, they could continue to operate with losses indefinitely. The United States concluded that since the Contras appeared unable to defeat the Sandinistas, they would pursue a war of attrition.

Election of Ortega

In May 1984, Pastora was seriously injured by a bomb. The blast destroyed his headquarters and killed four people, including a visiting U.S. journalist. In June, the U.S. Congress voted to cut off aid. In November, a free election was held, and Daniel Ortega, representing the united Sandinista party, was elected president.

Ortega's election did not end the terror. An unidentified terrorist threw a grenade onto a crowded dance floor in September 1985, killing seven and wounding thirty-five. Hostility continued between the United States and the Sandinista regime. Ortega rejected calls for negotiations with the Contras at the UN General Assembly. Since the coffee harvest had been completed with no casualties, he felt the Contras now posed little threat. But the Contras' very existence encouraged hard-line elements within the Sandinista regime. Personal liberties in Nicaragua were curtailed, and Nicaraguan troops took the war across the border. An incursion into Honduras in March 1986 gave Ortega's opponents an opportunity.

The United States had continued to give covert aid to the Contras, using funds that had been obtained through the illegal sale of arms to Iran. After the Honduras incursion, though, Congress was again prepared to give open support to the Contras. The Sandinista response within Nicaragua was the curtailment of liberties. This included the closure of the opposition newspaper *La Prensa*, and the expulsion of the pro-Contra bishop Pablo Antonio Vega.

When the news of the Iran-Contra scandal broke in Washington, D.C., in November 1986, the Contra threat to Nicaragua, starved of funds, was already subsiding. Thereafter, the next phase of insurgency, from 1986 to 1990, consisted of negotiations involving Nicaragua, the United States, and other interested parties.

A plan drawn up in 1986 by Costa Rican president Oscar Arias called for an immediate cease-fire in all civil wars in Central America, cessation of aid to guerrilla groups, a general amnesty, and negotiations among all parties. It also imposed a series of deadlines. By the first of these, November 7, 1987, much of the plan had already been achieved.

Nevertheless, the Contras launched a spring offensive in 1988. Attacks on civilian targets alienated opinion at home and abroad. Sandinista troops repelled the attacks, and Contra leaders accepted the offer of negotiation as stipulated in the Arias plan.

Ortega's concessions included the reopening of the opposition newspaper *La Prensa* and the Catholic radio station, along with promises of free elections in 1990. However, the war against the Contras had been a great strain on an already troubled economy, and on February 25, 1990, voters rejected Ortega in favor of Violeta Barrios de Chamorro. She responded to the Contras' presence by engaging the archbishop of Managua as a peace mediator. The final demobilization of the Contra forces took place on June 27, when 19,197 troops surrendered under the auspices of the United Nations.

The conflict seemed to be resolved in 1990, with the election of Violeta Chamorro as president and the formal demobilization of the Contras under UN auspices. However, with no jobs or land available for demobilized soldiers, land disputes resumed between former Contras and Sandinistas. Terrorism also continued. In August 1991, sixteen civilians were killed when their truck drove over a Contra land mine. Contra commanders recruited veteran soldiers, and the Sandinistas rearmed. In the first year of Chamorro's rule, more than 100 died in fighting. As one commentator noted, "Wars don't just end—especially in Third World countries."

In 2006, the FSLN won national elections, obtaining the largest bloc of seats in the national assembly and returning Ortega to the presidency. But it was no longer a revolutionary organization; instead, it has pursued moderate, left-of-center social and economic policies ever since. Critics, however, complain that both Ortega and the FSLN are stifling political dissent.

Peter Calvert

See also: Definitions, Types, Categories—Left-Wing and Revolutionary Terrorism; Right-Wing and Reactionary Terrorism. *Modern Terrorism*—El Salvador: Civil War.

Further Reading

Kinzer, Stephen. *Blood of Brothers: Life and War in Nicaragua.* Cambridge, MA: David Rockefeller Center for Latin American Studies, Harvard University, 2007.

Kornbluh, Peter. *Nicaragua, The Price of Intervention: Reagan's Wars Against the Sandinistas.* Washington, DC: Institute for Policy Studies, 1987.

Morley, Morris H. *Washington, Somoza, and the Sandinistas.* New York: Cambridge University Press, 1994.

Pastor, Robert A. *Condemned to Repetition: The United States and Nicaragua.* Princeton, NJ: Princeton University Press, 1987.

Rogers, Miranda. *The Civil War in Nicaragua: Inside the Sandinistas.* New Brunswick, NJ: Transaction Publishers, 1993.

Thomas, W. Walter. *Reagan Versus the Sandinistas: The Undeclared War.* Boulder, CO: Lynne Rienner, 1993.

Nigeria: Antigovernment Violence and Christmas Day Bomber, 1960s–2000s

Nigeria's experience with terrorism is atypical for Africa but significant. Nigeria does not have a debilitating insurgency, nor does it possess a weak state structure—both of which are common characteristics of African countries and factors that are thought to facilitate the incidence of international and transnational terrorism. However, Nigeria's ethnic divisions and its rich natural resources (i.e., a comparatively large population of approximately 125 million, comprising over 250 ethnic and linguistic groups and split nearly evenly between Sunni Muslims and Christians, combined with dispersed pockets rich in oil and minerals) constitute conditions that precipitate internecine conflict and political violence.

Political Background Since 1960

Nigeria gained independence from the United Kingdom on October 1, 1960, but the elected civilian government was soon overthrown by a military coup. A succession of coups interspersed with brief respites of civilian rule totaling only twelve years came to characterize Nigerian politics. The advent of elections and conformance to a new constitution from December 1998 to February 1999 appeared to provide a basis for political stability and some promise for the extended civilian rule of former military ruler General Olusegun Obasanjo.

To a great extent, the earlier military regimes forged and enforced a variety of compromises among various ethnic and linguistic groups and between Christians and Muslims—all of which are beginning to unravel early in the twenty-first century. For example, conflicts have erupted between the Egon and Tiv groups and between the Hausa and Yoruba groups. In addition, by 2002 the twelve northern Muslim majority states of Nigeria had implemented the sharia (Islamic law), alienating and angering local Christians. Clashes between these religious groups have resulted in up to 7,000 deaths and an increasingly political polarization of society. This has resulted in much violence during election seasons since the early 2000s.

Further Incidents

Nigeria's experience with terrorism from 1993 to 2002 was episodic and relatively unorganized. No formal group appeared to coordinate a campaign of terrorism, to communicate a particular political message, or to achieve a particular end. For example, the Nigerian Movement for the Advancement of Democracy, the United Front for Nigeria's Liberation, and a group un-

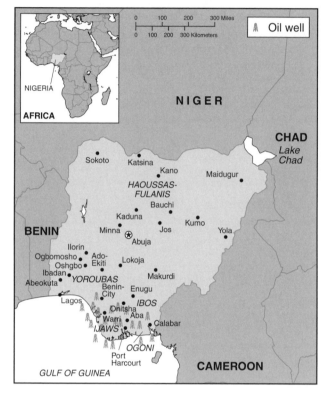

Since winning its independence from Great Britain in 1960, Nigeria has been torn by ethnic and religious infighting, particularly in the Muslim north and oil-rich southeast. The latter was the site of the unsuccessful Biafran uprising of the late 1960s.

der the banner "Enough Is Enough in the Niger Delta" each claimed responsibility for a relatively spectacular attack, only to quickly fade from public attention when claims were unverified or ignored.

Among certain ethnic groups and youth movements in the oil-rich regions of Nigeria, however, the terrorist tactic of kidnapping foreigners, including the abduction of U.S. oil-company workers for ransom demands or political statements, gained popularity after 1997. Often protesting exploitation by foreign oil firms or the use of the Nigerian military, these seemingly uncoordinated renegades frequently resorted to seizing oil platforms and drilling rigs. As many as sixty such attacks occurred from 1997 to 2002. Nonetheless, hostages were nearly always released unharmed, and demands were generally left unmet.

The September 11, 2001, terrorist attacks against the United States have contributed somewhat to the polarization of religious groups in Nigeria. To a lesser extent, America's massive military response in Afghanistan has fostered anti-Western sentiment and sparked occasional acts of violence in a few Nigerian communities. Yet the Nigerian government has taken steps to increase its international cooperation against terrorism with a number of bilateral and multilateral antiterrorism agreements.

Although Nigeria's numerous potential conflicts have remained well contained, strong tensions continue to simmer. Alarmingly, the United Nations reports that a Nigerian physicist who supported the Biafran secessionist efforts of the late 1960s obtained, but then lost, a significant amount of radioactive material in Europe for use in a planned bombing attack of the capital city, Lagos. Thus, Nigeria's large, well-educated diaspora, spread throughout the world, offers a potential network of support for increasingly disillusioned groups within this important country in sub-Saharan Africa.

Perpetrators

The Movement for the Advancement of Democracy (MAD) was created under the leadership of Maalam Jerry Yusuf in mid-1993 following the annulment of the June elections. Yusuf studied at an Islamic university in Nigeria, joined the Nigerian Army, and lived in Germany from 1973 to 1977 prior to going into business. Yusef's MAD sought support from the Campaign for Democracy, a coalition of some forty Nigerian humanitarian groups, but was rejected.

This small group amounted to little more than an anticorruption cult known only for a 1993 aircraft hijacking. On October 25, 1993, four terrorists claiming to belong to the Nigerian MAD hijacked a Nigerian Airways Airbus 310. Conflicting reports indicate that the hijackers sought to divert the plane to Frankfurt, Germany, or Ndjamena, Chad, but ultimately landed in neighboring Niamey, Niger. The hijackers' demands had included a corruption trial for former president Ibrahim Babangida, the resignation of Nigeria's interim government, and the lifting of press restrictions. After three days and the release of two groups of passengers, police stormed the aircraft and captured the four hijackers but killed one crew member. Subsequently, three other MAD members, including the group's legal adviser, were arrested for planning the hijacking. The group has not perpetrated any terrorist acts since then.

A shadowy group called the United Front for Nigeria's Liberation (UFNL) claimed responsibility for the plane crash of January 17, 1996, which killed President Sani Abacha's son Ibrahim. Though Abacha had assumed the presidency in a military coup in 1993 and led a repressive regime, investigators found no evidence of sabotage, and so the UFNL's claim was subsequently ignored.

Another shadow movement emerged in 1996. In June 1996, five heavily armed youths from a group calling itself Enough Is Enough in the Niger Delta attacked a Shell Oil drilling facility. They destroyed property, hijacked a helicopter, took hostages, and secured a ransom for their release. Although the group was never subsequently identified, "Enough Is Enough" is a slogan often used in propaganda by a variety of ethnic autonomy movements in the oil-rich regions of Nigeria. Interestingly, this attack fits the modus operandi of a more general and seemingly uncoordinated youth movement from the Ijaw region of Nigeria.

Perpetrators of many of the oil-company kidnappings and attacks have been identified as radical ethnic Ijaw youths, but details are seldom provided. For example, young Ijaw militants targeted foreign oil company workers as early as 1997. As a protest to redrawn regional boundaries, in two attacks the youths captured and eventually released at least 127 oil company workers. In 2000 alone, groups seeking a greater share of the country's oil revenues took more than 300 hostages, but they were all released unharmed. Finally, in April 2002, twenty Ijaw youths seized control of an offshore oil rig, taking eighty-eight workers hostage for up to five days before releasing them unharmed.

In December 1998, a meeting under the leadership of Felix Tuodolo and Timi Kaiser-Wilhelm Ogoriba led to the formation of a group called the Ijaw Youth Council (IYC). This group issued the Kaiama Declaration, which called for, among other things, autonomy, the withdrawal of the Nigerian military forces from the Ijawland, and control of land and natural resources—especially oil reserves and subsequent revenues. The IYC was formed by twenty-five Ijaw organizations representing more than 500 communities from more than forty clans. It sought to "coordinate the struggle of Ijaw peoples for self-determination and justice." The group's warning included the following statement: "Any oil company that employs the services of the armed forces of the Nigerian State to 'protect' its operations will be viewed as an enemy of the Ijaw people."

Between 2006 and 2008, militants in the Niger Delta once again launched assaults on oil pipelines and drilling facilities, as well as kidnapping foreign oil workers, as a means of forcing the government to return a greater share of the hydrocarbon wealth of the region. The attacks were perpetrated by a number of militant groups, some affiliated with the IYC and some in opposition to it. Among the most significant of these was the Movement for the Emancipation of the Niger Delta, though it suffered a setback when two of its leaders were extradited from Angola to face terrorism charges for attacks on oil facilities and kidnappings of oil workers.

Counterterrorism Efforts

Although nearly all terrorist attacks in Nigeria are domestically based, many of those attacks have targeted foreign interests. In addition, Nigeria has felt the effect of foreign-based or "global" international terrorism. Nigeria suffered at least one dead and four missing citizens in the World Trade Center attack in 2001, but the U.S. counterattack against al-Qaeda and Taliban forces in Afghanistan has polarized Nigerian Muslim-Christian relations and sparked some sectarian violence. The Iranian-sponsored terrorist group Hezbollah is known to have sought to develop a presence among the country's 60 million Muslims, and some of the al-Qaeda suspects implicated in the 1998 African embassy bombings had been based for a time in Nigeria. This fact has led some officials to conclude that al-Qaeda terrorist cells are likely to be active in the country.

In response to these and other terrorist threats, the Nigerian government has strengthened bilateral, regional, and international counterterrorism efforts. As early as 1993, Nigeria extradited Omar Mohammed Ali Rezaq to the United States for the 1985 hijacking of Egypt Air flight 648. Rezaq, a member of the terrorist Abu Nidal Organization, had been indicted on air-piracy charges stemming from the hijacked plane in Malta in which sixty people died, including one American. Three years later, on July 19, 1996, the U.S. district court in Washington, D.C., convicted Rezaq of air piracy.

In other important efforts, President Olesegun Obasanjo fostered bilateral antiterrorism, antinarcotics, and anticorruption efforts on his trip to India in 2000. Regionally, Nigeria plays a prominent role in the Organization of the Islamic Conference's counterterrorism measures. In addition, the Nigerian government has signed a few international agreements to combat terrorism, including the 1963 Tokyo Convention, the 1970 Hague Convention, and the 1971 Montreal Convention, all relating to airline safety, as well as the International Convention for the Suppression of the Financing of Terrorism, adopted by the General Assembly of the United Nations on December 9, 1999.

Specifically in response to the September 11 attacks, Nigeria finally ratified a bilateral anticrime treaty with the United States originally signed in 1989 that fosters cooperation on antiterrorism and drug efforts. Other antiterrorism measures introduced by President Obasanjo (a southern Christian) have angered Muslims. As recently as October 2001, U.S. troops engaged in training exercises with Nigerian military forces, sparking large public protests. The federal government initiated a profiling program that targets Muslims with ties to radical Islamic groups or states and even restricts the banking practices of those suspects. Finally, Nigerian civil libertarians warned against the government's steps to revive its antiterrorism police squad, which was first created under the military regime but was deactivated upon civilian rule in 1999. In the 2000s, the government has also launched a series of offensives against militant groups in the Niger Delta in an effort to stop the armed attacks on oil facilities and the kidnapping of foreign oil workers for monetary ransom and to exact concessions from the central government, which has made only limited moves to return more of the revenues to the region, as the militants have been demanding for more than two decades.

Christmas Day Bomber

Nigeria found itself uncharacteristically in the international limelight in the war on terrorism in late 2009, when one of its nationals, Umar Farouk Abdulmutallab, attempted to blow up a Northwest Airlines jet en route from Amsterdam to Detroit on Christmas Day. Aged twenty-three at the time, Abdulmutallab was a member of the country's elite, son of the former chairman of the First Bank of Nigeria and high-ranking economics official in the government. More significantly, Abdulmutallab grew up in Kaduna, a central Nigeria city on the border between the Muslim north and the Christian south, and site of numerous outbreaks of religious violence in recent years that left hundreds dead. By the time he reached his late teens, the already pious Abdulmutallab had become radicalized, attending an Arabic-language school in Yemen. After studying business and economics in London, he returned to Yemen in the summer of 2009, where he soon broke off all contact with his family. Concerned, his father contacted Nigerian authorities in November and was told to contact the U.S. embassy, where he spoke with Central Intelligence Agency officers. Despite such warnings, the U.S. government failed to prevent Abdulmutallab from getting on the U.S.-bound jet with plastic explosives hidden in his underwear. Fortunately, the bomb failed to go off. After the attack, Abdulmutallab told investigators that he had been trained for the attack by al-Qaeda members and had obtained the explosives in Yemen. Two weeks after the attack, the young Nigerian was indicted on six charges, including attempted use of a weapon of mass destruction.

KEY DATES

1997 Young militants of the Ijaw tribe begin taking oil company workers hostage in the Niger River delta.

1998 Following the bombings of the American embassies in Kenya and Tanzania, it is reported that some of the alleged al-Qaeda organizers of the attack were based in Nigeria.

October 2001 The presence of U.S. troops, engaged in training Nigerian forces, sparks large public protests.

April 2002 Twenty Ijaw youths seize control of an offshore oil rig, taking eighty-eight workers hostage for five days before releasing them safely.

December 2009 A Nigerian national named Umar Farouk Abdulmutallab attempts to blow up a U.S. airliner bound from Amsterdam to Detroit on Christmas Day.

For much of the 1990s and 2000s, Nigeria's great terrorism threat lay within, as evidenced by the numerous indigenous attacks against foreign-owned assets and foreign-born workers and the sectarian violence in its central region. The country nevertheless continued to strengthen bilateral and multilateral counterterrorism measures even as the civilian government in place since 1999 sought to forge a balance between civil liberties and domestic security. Despite his failure to blow up the airliner, the Christmas Day bomber, as Abdulmutallab came to be called, did create one major casualty: Nigeria's reputation as a country not particularly prone to jihadist-style terrorism. In the wake of that attempt, the U.S. government placed Nigeria on its list of fourteen countries of interest in the war on terrorism. This prompted the Nigerian government to introduce tougher antiterrorism legislation, particularly aimed at terrorist financing, though the bill remained stuck in parliamentary debate as of the summer of 2010.

James T. Kirkhope and James Ciment

See also: *Definitions, Types, Categories*—Ethnonationalist Terrorism; Islamist Fundamentalist Terrorism.

Further Reading

"American Airline Attack: Terror in the Sky." *The Economist*, December 26, 2009.

Crenshaw, Martha, ed. *Terrorism in Africa*. New York: G.K. Hall, 1994.

Falola, Toyin. *Violence in Nigeria: The Crisis of Religious Politics and Secular Ideologies*. Rochester, NY: University of Rochester Press, 1998.

Okonto, Ike, and Oronto Douglas. *Where Vultures Feast: Shell, Human Rights, and Oil in the Niger Delta*. New York: Verso, 2003.

U.S. Department of State. *Patterns of Global Terrorism, 2000*. Washington, DC: U.S. Government Printing Office, 2001.

Pakistan: Islamist Struggle, 1947–Present

A persistent domestic conflict between fundamentalists and moderate Islamists in Pakistan eventually resulted in Pakistan's decision to allow the fundamentalists to use its territory as a base for a global jihad movement.

Problems

In 1947, the British left the Indian subcontinent and partitioned India into two countries: India and Pakistan. The concept of Pakistan was rooted in the demand of the Muslims of India for a separate homeland. However, the country's beginning was inauspicious.

First, the new country consisted of two distinct areas, East and West Pakistan, separated by 995 miles (1,600 kilometers) of Indian territory. East Pakistan would eventually declare independence in 1971 and form a new state—Bangladesh.

Second, Pakistan inherited a territorial patchwork of ethnic populations, each concentrated in a region. Punjabis, who live in Punjab and speak Punjabi, are the largest group. They dominate the upper echelons of the military and civil service and in large part run the central government, thereby creating resentment among other ethnic groups. Pashtuns, as Pashto speakers are called, reside in the North-West Frontier Province. Sindhis, who speak Sindhi, live in the province of Sindh. (Zulfiqar Ali Bhutto and his daughter Benazir Bhutto are famous Sindhi leaders.) The Baloch live in Balochistan and speak Baloch or Brohi. The Muhajirs, Muslim migrants from India, live in the urban areas of Karachi and Hyderabad and speak Urdu. Pakistan has persistently been plagued by Muhajir militancy, Sindhi and Baluchi nationalism, and Pashtun separatism.

Third, Pakistan was born in bloodshed. In 1947, following the British partition of India, some 12 million refugees crossed the new border, with the Muslims leaving India for Pakistan and the Hindus and Sikhs crossing over from Pakistan to India. It is estimated that 2 million refugees were killed in the communal frenzy that accompanied the mass exodus. Mohammed Ali Jinnah, popularly known as the Quaid-i-Azam (great leader), the founder of Pakistan, was appalled by these communal riots. Although he had led the movement to create a separate homeland for Muslims, his vision for newly independent Pakistan was secular. He envisioned equal rights and protection for all minorities. Jinnah's death in September 1948—just thirteen months after independence—was to have long-term consequences for Pakistan's identity and nationhood. During the past six decades, the country has struggled in vain to define the basis of interaction between Islam and politics in Pakistani society. Consequently, the military has often taken over the governance of the country. Since its independence, Pakistan has had five constitutions and four military governments under Ayub Khan, Yahya Khan, Mohammad Zia-ul-Haq, and Pervez Musharraf, intermittently interrupted by civilian governments.

Fourth, since its inception, Pakistan has had to survive in a harsh security environment. Not only is it surrounded by heavily populated and powerful neighbors (India, China, and Russia), but its own ethnic populations extend into neighboring countries. India and Pakistan have gone to war three times since 1947: immediately after independence, again in 1965, and during the Bangladeshi war of independence in 1971. Kashmir remains a contentious issue between them. The territory of Jammu and Kashmir, which has a majority Muslim population, is presently divided, with one-third under Pakistan and two-thirds under Indian jurisdiction. Pakistan claims that Kashmir is a disputed territory and that its status—whether it should be a part of India or Pakistan—should be decided through a plebiscite. India, on the other hand, claims that Kashmir is an integral part of India by virtue of a treaty of accession signed by the Hindu ruler of the state after partition. The nuclear weapons tests of May 1998, first by India and then by Pakistan, have heightened the tensions between the two countries.

Islam

Each of Pakistan's constitutions has defined Pakistan as an Islamic state. Although there is a general consensus that Pakistan is an Islamic society, views as to the implications of Islamic law for the Pakistani society and polity diverge greatly. There has been a constant struggle between the fundamentalists, who want to implement all provisions of Islamic law, and the modernists, who advocate restricting the scope of the religion. Under General Zia-ul-Haq's military rule (1977–1988), the fundamentalists gained the upper hand. In 1979, the general announced a set of reforms—Nizam-i-Mustafa (rule of the Prophet)—which were to bring all existing laws into conformity with Islamic principles. Islamic punishments were introduced, such as amputation of the left hand for theft, stoning to death for adultery, and eighty lashes for the consumption of alcohol. In addition, the compulsory collection of *zakat* (a charity tax) and *ushr* (an agricultural tax) was imposed. The money collected through these taxes was to be redistributed to the poor. In 1981, a new educational policy was introduced making Koranic and Islamic courses compulsory in educational institutions. Arabic was introduced as a compulsory foreign language, and it was proposed that women's educational institutions be separate from those of men.

The fundamentalists in Pakistan have been largely successful in implementing their orthodox agenda through a network of traditional Islamic schools called madrassas. According to unofficial reports, there are about 70,000 madrassas in the country. Most madrassas are in the private sector; they are supported both by the community through trusts and endowments and also, heavily, by the *zakat*. Each madrassa is under the control of an individual *ulema*, who acts as both owner and manager. Since the 1980s, these schools have become a breeding ground for sectarian violence, particularly against the Shia Muslim minority, and a recruitment center for a global Islamic jihad movement. Pakistan's leading religious party, Jamaat-i-Islami, took the lead by using foreign funds for the Afghan jihad movement to establish a network of madrassas in the North-West Frontier Province and Balochistan. It was in these madrassas that Afghani opposition, including the Taliban, was educated and trained. It is now well-known that several madrassas in Sindh, Punjab, and the North-West Frontier Province have also provided armed training in terrorist activities to the activists of groups such as Sipah-i-Sahaba Pakistan, Jamiat-ul-Ulema, Ahl-i-Hadith, Harkat-ul-Ansar, and Lashkar-e-Taiba.

Relations with Afghanistan

Pakistan became a frontline state during the Soviet occupation of Afghanistan, which began in 1978. It reluctantly became home to 3 million Afghan refugees. Such a massive inflow of refugees created problems of public health, deforestation, overgrazing by more than 3 million livestock brought by the refugees, and an illegal arms and drug trade. In addition, Pakistan allowed its frontier provinces bordering Afghanistan to be used for the training of Afghan mujahideen (freedom fighters). The Afghan resistance made its base in the Pakistani cities of Peshawar and Quetta. The United States shared the burden of refugees by providing substantial humanitarian aid. In addition, the United States passed on weapons and economic and financial assistance to the mujahideen through the Pakistan government and Pakistan's intelligence agency, the Inter-Services Intelligence.

After the Soviet withdrawal from Afghanistan, Pakistan remained involved in Afghanistan. The Inter-Services Intelligence actively courted the Taliban, who received Pakistani assistance in recruiting and training Pakistani Taliban and in supplying weapons and ammunition. According to one source, at the height of the Taliban regime in Afghanistan, the movement included more than 10,000 Pakistani soldiers. Several radical Pakistani Islamic organizations such as Jamiat-ul-Ulema, Hizb-ul-Mujahideen, Harkat-ul-Ansar (later known as Harakat-ul-Mujahideen), and Tehrik-i-Jihad actively recruited Pakistanis for the Taliban movement.

Some of these recruits also moved on into Indian Kashmir, where a secessionist movement has been in existence since 1989. Since 1996, the initially homegrown and widely mass-supported secessionist movement in the Kashmir Valley has come to be controlled by Pakistani and Afghani jihad militants. Fedayeen suicide attacks have become their latest and perhaps most dramatic strategy against the Indian state. In October and December 2001, the suicide squads of Jaish-e-Mohammed and Lashkar-e-Taiba conducted attacks on the Jammu and Kashmir legislative assembly in Srinagar, the capital city of the state, and the Indian Parliament in New Delhi, respectively. Even more deadly was the latter's attack on Mumbai in 2008, which left 164 dead. Despite strong pressure from the United States and President Musharraf's measures to ban and sanction these terrorist groups, the attacks have intensified in Indian Kashmir, increasing the likelihood of armed conflict between India and Pakistan.

Pakistan was one of only three countries to recognize the Taliban regime. When it became known to the U.S. government that Osama bin Laden was responsible for the bombing attacks of the U.S. embassies in Nairobi, Kenya, and Dar es Salaam, Tanzania, in 1998, it asked Pakistan's assistance to force the Taliban to hand over bin Laden. Fearing major domestic repercussions, Pakistan was unable to assist the U.S. government. Nor did Pakistan weigh heavily in U.S. foreign policy concerns. When the United States launched its cruise missile attack against bin Laden's training camps in Afghanistan in August 1998, the U.S. government did not inform Pakistan beforehand. However, since the September 11 attack on America, Pakistan has emerged as an important ally of the United States in fighting the war on terrorism. President Musharraf provided his country as a springboard for the offensive against the Taliban. He purged senior members of the Inter-Services Intelligence, the mentor and benefactor of the Taliban, so that he could ensure the support of the intelligence agency in assisting the United States to curb Taliban activity within Afghanistan and Pakistan. Despite the organized opposition of Islamic extremist groups, President Musharraf was able to contain the dissidents to the war on terrorism.

During January 2002, there was a crackdown on the extremist religious groups in Pakistan, in the form of ordinances whereby the government was authorized to regulate the activities of all religious institutions, trusts, and endowments. President Musharraf required the registration of the madrassas with the government and asked for the modernization of their syllabi. Despite these efforts, terrorist activities have continued in Pakistan, including the killing of the *Wall Street Journal* reporter Daniel Pearl and an attack on a church in Islamabad. In exchange for its support for the war on terrorism, Pakistan has received specific economic rewards. The Western countries have lifted their sanctions against Pakistan, imposed after the 1998 nuclear tests; they have rescheduled repayments on Pakistan's $38 billion debt; and the U.S. government released $300 million by way of reimbursement for Pakistan's role in Operation Enduring Freedom in Afghanistan. Reports from the U.S. State Department confirm that hundreds of terror suspects have been killed or captured in Pakistan since 2001. Yet Pakistan's flirtation with Islamic militants, dating to the support of the mujahideen against the Soviet Union and support for the Taliban regime, along with its historic inability to control its border with Afghanistan, continues to draw questions regarding the veracity and likelihood of success of Pakistani antiterror efforts.

The threat of terrorism toward the Pakistani government became quite obvious in 2003. That year, al-Qaeda called for the overthrow of the Pakistani government and labeled it a main enemy. Al-Qaeda rhetoric was not without action, as December 2003 saw two assassination attempts on President Musharraf. As a result of the more direct and overt threat posed by the militants on the Afghan-Pakistani border, Musharraf launched a number of military and political initiatives aimed at reducing the number of terrorists and those sympathetic to their cause. The significant geographic front for fighting militants has always been the largely lawless Federally Administered Tribal Areas (FATA), the border region of Afghanistan and Pakistan. The Pakistani Army Frontier Corps in 2004 successfully destroyed a number of al-Qaeda camps in the South Waziristan Agency of FATA. Musharraf followed with political negotiations and economic development plans concerned with gaining the support of the antigovernment-minded tribes of the region.

International Antiterrorism Cooperation

In 2004, Pakistani cooperation in efforts to deal with militant Islamic terrorism was not limited to FATA. In fact, Pakistan cooperated in the key arrests of the Heathrow bomb plot suspect, Naeem Noor Khan, as well as the arrest of both a suspect in the 1998 bombing of the U.S. embassy, Ahmed Khalfan Ghailani, and the alleged murderer of Daniel Pearl, Amjad Farooqi. In addition, Pakistan began earnestly attempting to crack down on Harakat-ul-Mujahideen and Harakat-ul Jihad Islami. Many analysts trace this more aggressive Pakistani approach to the threat from al-Qaeda and the assassination attempts on Musharraf.

Pakistan continued to provide increased cooperation against Islamic militants in 2005. Approximately 80,000 Pakistani troops were sent to the border regions on the eve of Pakistani parliamentary elections. Meanwhile, government attacks on al-Qaeda strongholds continued in both North and South Waziristan. Operations in the region even claimed the life of the chief of external operations for al-Qaeda, Hamza Rabia. Continued intransigence in Balochistan led to Pakistani military intervention to enforce Pakistani sovereignty in the province. Following the July 7 subway bombings in London that left fifty-two dead, Musharraf called for a "jihad against extremism" in a national speech. Musharraf pledged to crack down on banned groups and their sources of funds, limit and more closely examine foreign madrassa students, and increase registration and financial reporting requirements for the Islamic schools.

As Pakistani attempts to drain the proverbial swamp of terrorists continued, the U.S. State Department, in its 2006 country report, indicated that Pakistan was both a safe haven and a source for leaders and militants of extremist Islamic groups. At the same time, the State Department also labeled Pakistan a "frontline partner" in the war against terrorism. Terror attacks within Pakistan numbered approximately 650 in 2006 alone. Geographically, the trouble regions continued to be Balochistan, FATA, and the North-West Frontier Province. Once again, Musharraf attempted to reduce sympathy among the tribes for Islamic militants by calling for Pakistani government agencies to examine the possible ways to address both economic and social development in the region. By the end of the year, the FATA Sustainable Development Plan had been completed was undergoing a thorough review. Continued cooperation between Pakistan and the Americans and British led to the arrest of Rashid Rauf, who had planned to bomb London-Heathrow Airport. Bombings in Varanasi and Mumbai, India, led to Musharraf's denouncing terrorism in India and making efforts to end Pakistani support for militants in Kashmir. In fact, Musharraf and Indian prime minister Manmohan Singh managed to meet privately at the Non-Aligned Movement Summit in Havana, where they agreed on an institutional mechanism to inform each other on terrorist threats. Fighting between the Balochistan Liberation Army and Baloch nationalists against Pakistani government forces began to escalate. By April, Pakistan had designated the Balochistan Liberation Army as a terrorist organization.

Increasing Lethality of Terrorist Attacks

The number and complexity of terror attacks within Pakistan increased again in 2007. Many of the attacks could be traced to either al-Qaeda or groups inspired by al-Qaeda. The lethality of attacks also increased. For example, the U.S. State Department counted twenty-two suicide attacks in Pakistan from 2002 to 2006 and forty-five in 2007. October 18 was the date of the deadliest suicide attack in Pakistan history, when 130 were killed during a homecoming celebration for former prime minister Benazir Bhutto. Bhutto would be assassinated on December 27 of that same year. At the same time, al-Qaeda–inspired terrorists attempted to reassert their control in South Waziristan. Some 200 Pakistani troops were seized and held as hostages. Areas near FATA—including Swat, Tank, and Dera Ismail Khan—also became regional targets for extremist groups. Government operations in Swat concentrated on militant Maulana Fazlullah after he had seized authority from Pakistani law enforcement officials and began to implement sharia law. The Pakistani government continued to struggle in exerting its authority in FATA even though it had almost 100,000 troops in the region. That said, Pakistani efforts to reduce attacks in the Kashmir region appeared to be having some effect, as the number of attacks, according to the U.S. State Department, fell about 50 percent since 2006. At the same time, some of the Kashmiri militants, most notably Lashkar-e-Taiba, began to focus on support of attacks in Afghanistan. Successes of that year included the death of Nawabzada Balach Marri—leader of the Balochistan Liberation Army—and the creation of the FATA Development Authority. The equivalent of US$120 million was set aside for FATA economic development. Pakistan's overall efforts in addressing terrorism and militant Islam resulted in it being the third-largest recipient of U.S. aid.

A particular issue with regard to the continuing war on terror was Pakistani adherence to United Nations Security Council Resolution 1267, which called on governments to freeze assets of terrorist groups linked to al-Qaeda or the Taliban. A presidential decree in 2007 enacted an anti–money-laundering law, which led to the creation of a Financial Management Unit. Critics of the law noted that it failed to comply with key components of Resolution 1267. *Hawalas*, informal money changers, were required by law to register with the Pakistani government. Long a secretive banking system used for terrorist money laundering, hawalas have heretofore managed to escape the Pakistani authorities.

Parliamentary elections in February 2008 resulted in Musharraf supporters losing to members of the Pakistan People's Party and the Muslim League. Musharraf resigned in August 2008 after both the Pakistan People's Party and Muslim League launched impeachment proceedings. Asif Ali Zardari accepted the office of president on September 6, 2008 in the name of his martyred wife, Benazir Bhutto. Zardari immediately pledged to deal with the issue of Islamic militancy.

The lion's share of Pakistani-related terror targets in 2008 continued to be centered in FATA, North-West Frontier Province, and Balochistan regions. Some militants, however, began to increasingly target the more

The famous Taj Mahal hotel was one of ten sites in Mumbai, India, targeted for a series of coordinated attacks by members of the Pakistan-based militant Islamic organization Lashkar-e-Taiba beginning on November 26, 2008—events referred to as "26/11." *(Associated Press)*

urban areas of Lahore, Islamabad, Peshawar, and Rawal-pindi. A number of bombings occurred that drew inter-national news coverage. On September 20, sixty people died when the Marriott Hotel in Islamabad was attacked by a suicide bomber; the Danish embassy was bombed on March 15; and an Italian restaurant in Islamabad was also attacked on March 15. The bombing of an ammunitions plant on August 21 resulted in seventy deaths. Militants increasingly attacked hard, or defended military and se-curity, targets as the March 11 bombings at the Federal Investigation Agency in Lahore attest.

In late 2007 and early 2008, one militant, Baitullah Mehsud—an al-Qaeda–inspired extremist who formed the Tehrik-i-Taliban (TTP)—began to increase his group's presence throughout FATA. Much of the popu-larity of TTP, according to the U.S. State Department, comes from its promise of filling the role of lackluster and ineffective government agencies. TTP soon spread to Kurram, Swat, and North and South Waziristan. By August, Pakistani officials banned the TTP and seized its funds. The TTP became best known for its strategy of targeting foreign officials, media, and aid workers for either kidnapping or assassination. Nevertheless, Pakistan continued to force the issue with military op-erations targeting South Waziristan, Darra Adam Khel, Bajaur, and Swat. In addition, local militias committed to eradicating the Islamic threat have emerged to pro-vide some assistance to Pakistani forces. On the Kashmir front, relations between India and Pakistan appeared to be heading in a positive direction. Trade, closed for the previous sixty years, opened.

The small positive steps taken were quickly erased with the November 2008 terrorist attacks in Mumbai, India. Pakistani nationals launched a well-coordinated attack on ten targets in Mumbai, which included the Taj Mahal Hotel. The lone terrorist survivor later admitted the group was associated with the Pakistani-based Laskhar-e-Taiba and its fund-raising arm, known as the Jamaat ud-Dawa. Pakistan responded by arresting approximately fifty members of Lashkar-e-Taiba and Jamaat ud-Dawa. Pakistan pledged to bring to justice anyone who assisted in the planning or implementation of the attacks. Progress made in Indian-Pakistani cooperation quickly was over-taken by the traditional rivalry of the two countries. For its part, Pakistan was slow to admit that the terrorists were of Pakistani origin, while India complained that Pakistan did not fully cooperate with its investigation.

Pakistan's efforts to more firmly control Balochistan, FATA, and the North-West Frontier Province led to retaliatory strikes by Islamic extremists in 2009. Oc-tober attacks on a military headquarters in Rawalpindi and a security force location in Lahore and a December mosque attack in Lahore were all seen as retaliation for the Pakistani military forays into Swat and FATA. In a reaction against modern education, terrorists also began a

KEY DATES

1947 Pakistan wins independence from Britain; violent par-tition of the country from India leads to over a million deaths; much of Muslim-dominated Kashmir is awarded to India.
1971 With the military support of India, East Pakistan breaks away from West Pakistan to form the country of Bangladesh.
1979–1989 During the Soviet occupation of Afghanistan, the mujahideen resistance sets up bases in—and receives support from—Pakistan.
2001 In the wake of the September 11 terrorist attacks, the United States recruits Pakistani aid in fighting the Taliban in Afghanistan.
2007 Former prime minister Benazir Bhutto is murdered.
2008 Pakistani-based Kashmiri Islamist terrorists launch attacks on Mumbai, India, killing more than 175 persons.

strategy of attacking schools—especially female schools. Systematic terror attacks were also aimed at Inter-Services Intelligence offices in Peshawar and Lahore and the Inter-national Islamic University in Islamabad. Awami National Party (ANP) politicians and activists were also targeted by Islamic militants of the TTP. Ethnically Pashtun, the ANP's support and cooperation with the U.S. invasion of Afghanistan made it a particularly inviting target for the TTP. ANP officials also allege that the Pakistani govern-ment has been complicit in the growth of the TTP.

Pakistani forces moved a long way to answering some of the ANP charges when TTP leader Baitullah Mehsud died and Pakistan attacked TTP enclaves in South Wa-ziristan in an all-out offensive called Raah-i-Nijatt (in English, "the way of riddance"). By the end of 2009, much of the TTP had been cleared from South Waziristan, while engagements continued in Orakzai Agency against TTP and in Khyber Agency against Lashkar-i-Islam. As of 2010, Pakistan faced a number of terrorist threats from Taliban-related organizations. Al-Qaeda, of Osama bin Laden and Ayman al-Zawahiri infamy, is based in North Waziristan, while the Taliban of Mullah Omar utilizes a base in Quetta, Pakistan. Another faction of the Taliban, the Haqqani network, targets NATO, Afghan, and Indian locations from its base in North Waziristan. Gulbuddin Hekmatyar's Hizb-e-Islami also targets NATO, the United States, and Afghan facilities from bases in Afghan-istan, as well as from Afghan refugee camps in Peshawar, Pakistan. The TTP continues to be based in North and South Waziristan and Orakzai and, in addition to NATO, United States, and Afghan targets, has launched attacks against the Pakistan Army. The Swat and Bajaur Taliban face a similar set of foes from Pakistan's Swat Valley and Bajaur. In addition, terror organizations based in Kashmir and Punjab, including Lashkar-e-Taiba, Sipah-i-Sahaba Pakistan, Lashkar-e-Jhangvi, and Jaish-e-Mohammed, also remain active.

The capability and good faith of Pakistan's antiterrorist operations came into question in May 2001, when U.S. special forces succeeded in killing al-Qaeda founder Osama bin Laden at a residential compound deep inside Pakistan where he had been living for years. The compound was located in the garrison town of Abbottabad, the home of the nation's military academy and less than 40 miles (65 kilometers) from the capital of Islamabad. The U.S. government did not inform Pakistan of the raid on its territory and, in the aftermath, demanded to know who in the Pakistani government, armed forces, or intelligence service might have known of bin Laden's presence in the country.

Reeta Chowdhari Tremblay and Matthew H. Wahlert

See also: *Definitions, Types, Categories*—Islamist Fundamentalist Terrorism. *Modern Terrorism*—Afghanistan: Rise of the Taliban; Afghanistan: Soviet War; Afghanistan: Terrorist Haven Under the Taliban; Afghanistan: U.S. Invasion and War; India: Kashmir Struggle. *September 11 Attacks*—Pursuit and Death of Osama bin Laden.

Further Reading

Baxter, Craig, Yogendra K. Malik, Charles H. Kennedy, and Robert C. Oberst. *Government and Politics in South Asia.* 5th ed. Boulder, CO: Westview, 2002.

Bennet Jones, Owen. *Pakistan: Eye of the Storm.* New Haven, CT: Yale University Press, 2009.

Bose, Sugata, and Ayesha Jalal. *Modern South Asia: History, Culture, and Political Economy.* London: Routledge, 1998.

Haider, Ziad. *The Ideological Struggle for Pakistan.* Stanford, CA: Hoover Institution Press, 2010.

Rashid, Ahmed. *Descent into Chaos.* New York: Viking, 2008.

Shaikh, Farzana. *Making Sense of Pakistan.* New York: Columbia University Press, 2009.

Ziring, Lawrence. *Pakistan in the Twentieth Century: A Political History.* New York: Oxford University Press, 2000.

Palestine: Beginning of International Terrorism, 1968–1970

The 1967 Arab-Israeli War revealed to Palestinian nationalists the failure of their strategy of reliance on the Arab states to achieve their ends. In the wake of the war, Palestinian activists began to organize themselves more efficiently, but the debate continued over the most effective methods the Palestinian activists could use. Small-scale cross-border raiding, which had been the main tactic in the 1950s and early 1960s, had had little effect. However, it was not Fatah, the leading party within the Palestine Liberation Organization (PLO), that initiated the move to international terrorism; instead it came from Arab nationalist groups, such as the Arab Nationalist Movement (ANM).

First Terrorist Cells

In 1963–1964, the ANM formed secret terrorist cells, at first with the Land, an underground and illegal group of nationalist Arabs in Israel. The ANM carried out reconnaissance and sabotage, but it mostly planted "sleeper" agents, who had organizational and intelligence roles in Israel alone. As early as September 1964, the ANM resolved that Palestine could be freed only through armed struggle, and only with the help of worldwide revolutionary groups. The ANM divided into national leaderships in the various Arab states and an international leadership based in Beirut, the capital of Lebanon. Before the 1967 war, the international leadership included George Habash, Wadi Haddad, Hanni al-Hindi, and Muhsin Ibrahim, who later led the Syrian-backed Saiqa organization. However, as Habash was a Christian, he could not attract the Muslim following of PLO leader Yasir Arafat.

Aftermath of the 1967 War

The Arab defeat by Israel in the 1967 war created a ferment in Palestinian thought. There were meetings between the various Palestinian groups. Habash said that the war "brought a full revolution in our thought. We decided to adopt the Vietnamese model: a strong political party, complete mobilization of the people, the principle of not depending on any regime or government. We were preparing for 20 or more years of war against Israel and its backers." This was the inspiration for the 1967 formation of the Popular Front for the Liberation of Palestine (PFLP).

Habash became the leader of the PFLP. The group's members believed in international revolution and a change in the world order leading to the establishment of a Palestinian state. This led to PFLP involvement in the internal politics of various Arab states. It also meant that its directors looked at international methods for striking at Israel. At a PFLP meeting in December 1967, Wadi Haddad, the operational commander, urged the group to abandon smuggling men and weapons across the Jordan River. The Israeli army, he said, had to be hit in a "qualitative, not a quantitative way. . . . We have to hit the Israelis at the weak points. I mean spectacular, one-off operations." This would focus world attention on the Palestinian problem and hurt the Israelis.

Haddad proposed the hijacking of an Israeli airliner. This annoyed Habash, who preferred to emphasize leftist politics over terrorism, to convince somewhat hesitant supporters such as the Soviet Union, who were long on verbal support but short on material aid for the resistance movement. But because Habash had been imprisoned by Syria before the 1967 war and Haddad had had him freed, Habash was indebted to Haddad and had to defer to him on the terrorism issue.

First PFLP Hijackings

As a result, on July 22, 1968, Haddad's three-man team hijacked a plane belonging to El Al, the Israeli national airline, and forced it to land in Algiers. The terrorists believed that General Ariel Sharon, who had commanded Israeli armored forces in Sinai in 1967, was aboard the flight and that the pilot carried a diplomatic pouch. Neither was true.

In Algiers, the Algerian government handled the negotiations with the PFLP. The terrorists rapidly released all the hostages with the exception of twelve Israeli passengers and crew. On July 25, the PFLP announced that it had acted to "remind the world" that many Palestinians, imprisoned and tortured in Israel, deserved to be freed. It was not until August 31 that the Algerian government finally freed the plane, securing the release of the hostages in exchange for the release of some Palestinian prisoners, as well as the freedom of the hostage takers themselves.

Besides striking at Israel and making headlines around the world, the PFLP was trying to make a point to Arafat and Fatah: cross-border guerrilla attacks, costly in casualties and ineffective, did not pay, whereas hijacking did. After this first hijacking, the PFLP and other Palestinian groups continued to carry out "external operations," as they termed these acts of international terrorism. On December 26, 1968, two PFLP men at the Athens airport shot up another El Al aircraft, killing a retired Israeli naval officer aboard, wounding two people, and badly damaging the plane. An Athens court imprisoned the attackers for fifteen years.

Israel declared Lebanon responsible because the two attackers had spent time in refugee camps in Lebanon and had taken off for Athens from the Beirut airport. In retaliation, Israeli special forces, flown in by helicopter, attacked the Beirut airport on December 28. Without causing casualties, they burned thirteen airliners belonging to or on loan to Lebanon's Middle East Airlines and Trans-Mediterranean Airways.

On February 18, 1969, a PFLP team and an El Al security guard exchanged fire outside an El Al plane at Zurich airport, killing the pilot and one terrorist and wounding the copilot. Two days later, the PFLP bombed a Jerusalem supermarket, killing two Israelis and injuring more than twenty. A woman later was jailed for life, both for this attack and for causing a bomb blast in the cafeteria of Jerusalem's Hebrew University.

On March 4, 1970, Habash announced that attacks on Israeli civilian targets would go on "if the Israelis continue to practice atrocities against us." He called the airport assaults "answers to acts of savagery by the Israelis against Arabs in the occupied territories." On August 29, 1969, Leila Khaled, a female refugee from Haifa who had joined the ANM at sixteen and had had guerrilla training with the PFLP, led the hijacking of a TWA airliner. She forced it to land in Damascus, Syria. The Syrian-based terrorists held two Israeli passengers for forty-five days. One was a professor at the Hebrew University, and the PFLP believed that the other had tortured fedayeen (Palestinian fighters) prisoners during interrogations. Pressure from governments and the International Federaton of Airline Pilots' Associations secured their release. The hijackers were detained by the Syrians for forty-four days, partly because of an old quarrel between the ANM and the Ba'ath, party in which forces of the former tried to launch a coup against the latter.

The tactics of international terrorism certainly gained worldwide publicity and were copied by other groups. In October 1969, in a copycat operation, five Palestinians of the Libyan- and Syrian-backed Popular Struggle Front (PSF), a small group under the PLO umbrella and headed by Bahgat Abu Gharbiya, a Palestinian linked to Egyptian intelligence, exploded a grenade in the El Al office in Athens. One Greek child was killed and another wounded. The PSF apologized and sent money to the victims' families, but this action won over no Greek hearts and minds to the Palestinian cause.

Two months later, Arab terrorists chose Athens as

KEY DATES

1963–1964 Arab nationalists in Israel form secret cells collectively known as the Arab Nationalist Movement.

1967 Israel defeats its Arab neighbors in the Six-Day War, giving it East Jerusalem, Gaza, and the West Bank; the war reorients Palestinian nationalists away from dependence on Arab states; radical Palestinian nationalist George Habash forms the Popular Front for the Liberation of Palestine (PFLP).

1968 In its first high-profile international act of terrorism, the PFLP hijacks an El Al plane; in another attack, PFLP terrorists shoot at an El Al plane in Athens; Israel blames Lebanon and retaliates by burning thirteen Lebanese airliners in an attack on the Beirut airport.

1969 The PFLP launches several attacks on Israel and Israeli nationals abroad.

1970 PFLP leader George Habash announces further attacks on Israeli civilians, as long as Israel continues "atrocities" against Palestinians.

---

the starting point for another terrorist operation. This time, Greek police arrested three Arabs as they tried to board a TWA airliner in Athens on December 21, 1969. The three were carrying guns, grenades, and a declaration that the aircraft was being seized on behalf of the PFLP.

Two years after the shattering defeat of 1967, Palestinians had found, in international terrorism, a way of striking out that gave them world headlines. It also, however, led to a great crisis. King Hussein of Jordan, fearful of the consequences, was struggling to stop his country from becoming an uncontrolled terrorist base, a situation that led directly to a showdown with the Palestinians in September 1970.

John Cooley

See also: *Modern Terrorism*—Israel: Raids on the PLO; Israel: Response to Terrorism; Israeli-Palestinian Conflict; Jordan: Palestinian Nationalism and Islamic Fundamentalism; Palestine: Birth of Fatah and the Palestine Liberation Organization. *Tactics, Methods, Aims*—Hijacking.

Further Reading

Cobban, Helena. *The Palestine Liberation Organization: People, Power, and Politics.* New York: Cambridge University Press, 1983.

Khaled, Leila. *My People Shall Live: The Autobiography of a Revolutionary.* New York: Bantam Books, 1974.

Mishal, Shaul. *The PLO Under Arafat: Between Gun and Olive Branch.* New Haven, CT: Yale University Press, 1986.

Palestine: Birth of Fatah and the Palestine Liberation Organization, 1948–1969

Arab historians refer to the defeat in the 1948–1949 Arab-Israeli War (also called the Israeli War of Independence) as the *nakhba* (the disaster). Terrorism and violence erupted in the Arab states and societies that had taken part in the war. There was no Palestinian state, and Palestinian territory still in Arab hands was divided. The West Bank and East Jerusalem was under Transjordanian rule, while the Gaza Strip was under Egyptian control.

A major reason for the Arabs' defeat was the confusion in Arab aims. The Palestinians had no effective political organization in 1948; even if one had existed, it would have been opposed by King Abdullah of Transjordan, who claimed that Palestine was part of his kingdom. Palestine's other major neighbors, Syria and Egypt, also had their own agendas, which did not necessarily coincide with those of the Palestinians.

The Arab world in the 1950s was in ferment, with nationalists, modernizers, and fundamentalists working with (and often against) one another. From this, a Palestinian resistance movement arose among small groups of Palestinian refugees, mainly students and university-educated people. By 1970, the resistance movement was a central force in the Middle East and was undertaking its own terrorist campaigns. How this came about is in large measure the story of the movement for Palestinian nationalism, of its leading figure, Yasir Arafat, and of the Fatah organization.

Murder of King Abdullah

The first major act by Palestinians after the 1948–1949 war was a terrorist attack. By 1951, the kingdom of Transjordan was involved in secret peace talks with Israel. King Abdullah met with Golda Meir, a senior member of the Israeli leadership, seeking a permanent peace. On July 19, 1951, the king inaugurated the Royal Jordanian Air Force at a ceremonial parade in Amman. The next day, at the entrance to the Great Mosque in Transjordanian-held East Jerusalem, a Palestinian terrorist shot and killed Abdullah, setting back by generations the chances of a permanent peace between Transjordan and Israel—just as the killer had intended.

The most important development in the Arab world from the Palestinian point of view was the overthrow of the Egyptian monarchy in 1952 by General Mohammed Naguib, Lieutenant-Colonel Gamal Abdel Nasser, and a group of like-minded nationalist and reformist army officers. Naguib in turn was replaced by Nasser in 1954. From this time until the 1967 war, the Palestinian resistance was closely linked with Egypt, which still occupied the Gaza Strip, where half a million Palestinian refugees lived in crowded camps.

Although the coup was carried out by reformists, the most important organization within Egypt for the Palestinians at this stage was the Muslim Brotherhood, set up in 1928. The Brotherhood believed in government by religion (theocracy) and formed open and clandestine chapters in Arab nations and former Palestinian territory in the early 1950s. Its aim was to create an Islamic state, first in Egypt, then elsewhere, including Palestine. Brotherhood members tried unsuccessfully to assassinate President Nasser in 1954 (they disagreed with his more secular philosophy), and many members fled to Saudi Arabia.

In the 1950s, young Egyptians and other Arabs were recruited by the Muslim Brotherhood to carry out terrorism against British troops in the Suez Canal Zone in Egypt. The Muslim Brotherhood and the conservative Islamic elements in Egypt and Saudi Arabia nurtured Palestinian aspirations: in 1953, the Muslim Brotherhood formed an Islamic Council for the Palestine Question, and Muslim Brotherhood spokesmen urged that the anti-British armed struggle in the canal zone be extended to Israel.

Some Palestinians were already taking action, and, from his viewpoint, President Nasser was also beginning operations. Nasser later told *New York Times* correspondent Kennett Love that he had withheld fedayeen (Palestinian fighters) raids on Israel until August 25, 1955. That was the day he also decided to buy arms from Czechoslovakia, in the Soviet bloc, the United States and Britain having refused to sell Egypt weapons. In fact, from late 1954, Nasser had sponsored what one Arab military historian called "organized, attritive, and relentless fedayeen raids into Israel from the Gaza Strip and from Jordan."

Terror and Counterterror

In reprisal against these terrorist attacks, the Israelis made a major attack on an Egyptian Army base in Gaza in February 1955 and hit other bases at Khan Yunis on September 1 and at Sabha on November 2. Between February 1955 and the Suez Crisis of October 1956, the Israelis carried out fifteen major reprisal raids, not only against Arab army camps and police posts, but also against border villages. The largest such attack was against the West Bank village of Qalqiliya on October 10, 1956.

Israeli counterterrorist activity (as distinct from full-scale military operations) also began in Gaza before the 1956 Suez Crisis. Two Egyptian intelligence officers supervising fedayeen activities, Salah Mustafa and Mustafa Hafez, were assassinated by Israeli counterterrorist action, the first in a bombing raid and the second by means of a package bomb.

In April 1955, an important fedayeen commando unit was set up under the supervision of the Egyptian Army in Gaza. It included about 700 men, some of them Palestinians. Many had fought against the British in the canal zone. Palestinians in this unit (which included Khalil al-Wazir, one of the founders of Fatah) later formed the initial complement of Fatah's military wing.

Yasir Arafat

Yasir Arafat was born in Jerusalem in 1929 to upper-middle-class Palestinian parents. His father died when Arafat was young. By the age of fifteen, Arafat was running guns for the Arab irregulars formed to fight the Israeli army and Zionist terrorist bands. In late 1947, he apparently served in the Arab Army of Salvation. When they realized that the 1948–1949 war was lost, Arafat and his family fled to Gaza, where they experienced the grim life of refugees. Cairo was the easiest Arab capital to reach from Gaza, so Arafat enrolled at the university there in 1951. He joined the Muslim Brotherhood, and in 1954, when President Nasser deported the Muslim Brotherhood's leadership, Arafat left for Beirut, Lebanon, and later Kuwait, where he worked for an engineering and contracting firm. He was allowed to return to Cairo in 1955, where he enrolled in an Egyptian Army commando training course.

Just before the 1956 Suez Crisis, Arafat visited friends in Gaza, who helped him to create a new Palestinian nationalist organization, Fatah. He and his friends laid the logistical and financial groundwork by enlisting bankers, contractors, and other wealthy Palestinians. Gaza became the breeding ground for the new group, and by 1959, the first fully operational cells had taken root there and in Kuwait. The name "Fatah" is a reverse Arabic acronym for Harakat al-Tahrir al-Watani al-Falistini, or Palestine National Liberation Movement. The word "fatah" itself means "conquest."

Fatah adopted the conservative Islamic values coupled with respect for Western technology that characterized the Muslim Brotherhood, Fatah's major source of inspiration in the 1950s. In the 1960s, practical support for Fatah in logistics and organization, as well as the influence of different views, came from the more radical left-wing Arab nationalist groups. These groups included Algeria's National Liberation Front (FLN), victorious in the war for independence from France in 1962, and Syria's Ba'ath Party, which seized power in Damascus in 1963.

Yasir Arafat, the leader of the Palestinian nationalist movement and co-founder of the anti-Israeli guerrilla group Fatah, became chairman of the broader Palestine Liberation Organization (PLO) in 1969. He held that position until his death in 2004. *(Stringer/AFP/Getty Images)*

Arafat became friendly with Muhammad Khidder, one of the Algerian revolution's toughest organizers and the FLN treasurer. The two set up fund-raising, recruiting, and training for Fatah in Algeria after 1962. Selected Palestinians trained at the Algerian military academy. One of Arafat's associates who developed strong links with the Algerians was Khalil al-Wazir.

Arafat needed a secure base near Israel. After the Suez Crisis of 1956, however, Nasser was no longer in any position to help and in fact repeatedly warned other Arab leaders that the Arab world was not ready to fight Israel. He stated also that he would not be dragged into war by Palestinian guerrilla or terrorist action "before we are ready to choose the time and place of the battle." Neither Jordan nor Lebanon would help. Both were imprisoning Palestinians known for affinities with Arafat and Fatah.

Syria and Ba'athism

Fatah now turned to Syria and the new government there. On March 8, 1963, a group of Syrian officers who belonged to the secretive Ba'ath (Arab Socialist Resurrection) Party had seized power in Damascus. The Ba'ath Party had an ideology that mixed Arab nationalism, Marxism, and nineteenth-century Germanic Romanticism, conceived largely by Michael Aflaq, a Damascus schoolteacher. One of its main principles was the "liberation of Palestine."

Arafat and his brain trust, especially Khalil al-Wazir (who later took the nom de guerre Abu Jihad) and Salah Khalaf (Abu Iyad), reckoned correctly that their concept of a revolutionary war to regain Palestine suited Ba'athist ideology and propaganda. Arafat accordingly found support from two Syrian officers, Colonel Abd al-Karim al-Jundi, head of military intelligence, and Colonel Ahmed Sweidani, the chief of staff. By the summer of 1963, Arafat had shifted Fatah's base of operations to Syria.

Arafat's men began to mount covert missions into Israel, and in 1964, the Fatah leaders met to discuss a starting date for guerrilla operations. A minority of Fatah's ruling revolutionary council, then numbering about twenty, insisted that conditions were still too unfavorable. Further meetings reached no decision.

Apart from Fatah, there was an important radical branch of Palestinian nationalism. After refugee George Habash reached Beirut in the early 1950s to study medicine, he and other Arab intellectuals, including Hanni al-Hindi, a Syrian, and Ahmed al-Khatib, a Kuwaiti, formed a discussion group. This merged with the Arab Nationalist Movement (ANM), founded in Jordan in 1953 by another medical graduate, Wadi Haddad. The prestige Habash and others had among radical young Palestinians led to the formation of one the first secret terrorist organizations, the Phalange of the Redeemers.

By the late 1950s, Habash had finished medical school in Beirut and opened a clinic, treating the poor for free. Gradually, he abandoned medicine for politics. The roots of what Habash and his sympathizers called "the internationalization of the Palestinian resistance," and what the rest of the world came to know as international terrorism, began to grow out of ANM cells. Graduates formed the cells in Aden (then capital of British-ruled South Arabia; after 1967 it became the capital of South Yemen), in Kuwait, and in what was then the pre-Gadhafi kingdom of Libya.

In Jordan, the ANM developed more medical clinics for the poor, and started schools to supplement those established by the government and the United Nations to fight widespread illiteracy. Everywhere, ANM cells preached against Israel and Western "imperialism." ANM members also took part in Nasser-controlled fedayeen operations in Gaza in the mid-1950s.

The ANM believed that Arab unity was necessary if the Palestinians were to regain their homeland and

supported countries it thought might bring the Arabs together. During the 1956 Suez Crisis, the ANM cooperated with Egypt. Its founders viewed Syria's Ba'athists, who were supporting Fatah, as partners in Arab nationalism. "From 1956 to 1964," Habash asserted, "we worked for Arab unity, in order to bring about a state encircling Israel."

Birth of the PLO and the 1967 War

During the early 1960s, Palestinian raids against Israel continued and were met with Israeli retaliation. Three events had huge significance for the future of terrorism, however. These were the foundation of the Palestine Liberation Organization (PLO); its subsequent takeover by Yasir Arafat's Fatah, the organization's dominant group; and the defeat of the Arab states in the 1967 war with Israel.

The PLO was founded almost as an afterthought during a conference hosted by Egypt's President Gamal Abdel Nasser in January 1964 to discuss Israel's plan to divert water from the Jordan River. Israel's new national water system was based on a pipe carrying water from the Jordan River in Galilee to the Negev Desert, to permit

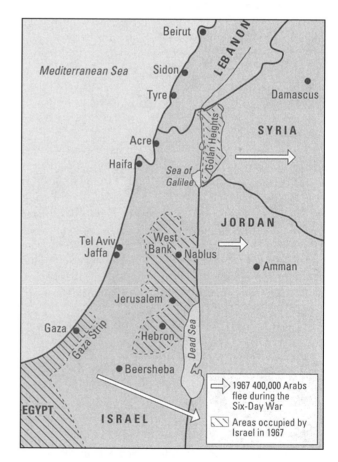

Exodus of Palestinian Arabs during the Six-Day War of 1967.

new agricultural settlement there. In the end, the conference took no direct action at all on the water question. Instead, it decided on the creation of the PLO as the Arab League's official Palestinian entity. Its declared purpose was to give the Palestinians direct responsibility for their own liberation and future.

The intention in founding the PLO was to draw together the terrorist and political groups that had emerged in the dispossessed Palestinian refugee communities. The PLO's first leader was a verbose Palestinian lawyer, Ahmed Shuqairy. He proved to be an asset to Israeli publicists and Western journalists, who would repeatedly quote his words (which he denied ever saying) about "throwing Israel into the sea." Israeli spokesmen used such statements to argue that the PLO, which developed a vast network of banks, trade unions, student associations, and other organizations for social and charity work, was in reality only a "terrorist" organization.

The PLO's founding conference convened in East Jerusalem, then still governed by Jordan, in May 1964. The 422 participants endorsed two documents: a constitution and the Palestinian National Covenant, or Charter, issued on May 28. Several of the clauses committed the PLO to the destruction of Israel. This commitment would remain in force until April 1996.

PLO Disputes with Jordan

Internal controversy within the PLO and friction with its Arab creators arose almost at once. On July 2, 1964, Shuqairy released a statement in the Jordanian capital, Amman, claiming that the whole territory of the Hashemite Kingdom of Jordan (formerly Transjordan), including the part east of the Jordan River, was part of Palestine. This seriously offended the PLO's Jordanian hosts. It was one cause of King Hussein's determination to keep PLO chapters formed in the West Bank disarmed, despite their constant demand for weapons.

In addition, many Arabs, especially in Egypt, were skeptical that the PLO had a useful role to play. In their view, the PLO had been created not to further the Palestinian cause, but mainly to lift the burden of confronting Israel from the shoulders of the Arab regimes, in particular that of President Nasser in Egypt. Nor did groups such as Arafat's Fatah take the new organization at all seriously.

The PLO leadership also established a fighting force, the Palestine Liberation Army (PLA), for operations against Israel in time of war. It was intended to give the PLO a regular military force. This Palestinian army evolved as an independent force, with its own budget, cadres, training, and sources of supply. Almost from its start, the army's leadership contested the PLO's control. In the Lebanese civil war after 1975, for example, the army's Hittin Brigade, based in Syria, fought the PLO in Lebanon.

Recruitment to the Palestinian Army

Because of concern that the Palestinian army might threaten its host governments, only Egypt and Iraq permitted recruitment of small Palestinian units under the host's military command. A unified Arab command was supposed to supervise the army, although its main headquarters was set up in Damascus, Syria, and would remain there until Arafat ordered it moved to Beirut in 1976. King Hussein allowed no formal army presence in Jordan and only symbolic PLO offices. In addition to severe restrictions on its weapons, the PLO was not allowed to tax or to recruit Palestinian refugees in Jordan. Lebanon did not permit the Palestinian army on its territory, though it did allow Palestinians living in Lebanon to join. However, once a Lebanese Palestinian had joined the PLA, he was no longer allowed to return to Lebanon, even to visit his family.

The Palestinian army had four separate brigades, attached to the host armies, and recruited first from Palestinians, including professional officers already serving with the Egyptian, Syrian, and Iraqi armies. One brigade was recruited directly from the Gaza Palestinians. This was the only Palestinian unit to play a military role in the 1967 war, fighting a desperate and sometimes suicidal holding action against the Israeli army on June 5 and 6, 1967. Some survivors formed guerrilla and terrorist cells to resist Israeli occupation.

Since the Soviet Union was unwilling to supply arms to the PLO or its army directly, Shuqairy and the Fatah leaders together (although Fatah and the army were in some respects rivals) turned to China. Arafat, Shuqairy, and others traveled to Beijing in 1965. The Chinese offered arms and financing, complementing what was already trickling in from a few Arab governments, especially Algeria. By 1966, Chinese equipment was arriving, including rifles, grenade launchers, mortars, some aging field guns and rocket launchers, and some old M-48 tanks and armored cars. Training before the 1967 war went on in Gaza, Syria, China, and North Vietnam. By June 1966, there were 4,000–6,000 recruits training in Syria and 8,000–9,000 in Gaza.

Terror from "the Storm"

Meanwhile, a majority of Fatah's ruling revolutionary council, with their Syrian mentors' approval, voted to start independent armed action on January 1, 1965, despite a dire lack of funds, training, arms, and leadership. The Algerians, Arafat argued, had begun their revolution on the eve of All Saints' Day 1954 under the same conditions and, by 1962, had succeeded in wresting independence from France. Fatah dissenters insisted that military operations begin under a cover name, so that in case of failure, Fatah could then continue secret operations without being compromised.

Thus using the name al-Asifa (the Storm, or Tempest), Fatah's military wing launched the first operation on New Year's Eve 1964 against Israel's national water system near al-Himma, on the Jordanian border where the Jordan River water flowed into the Israeli pipeline. This first "official" attack was a military failure but served as a warning to Arab governments that Fatah had begun operations that the Arab governments had not dared to undertake.

Predictably, both Jordan and Lebanon (but not, at this stage, Fatah's host, Syria) increased their efforts to prevent Palestinians from using their countries as bases for operations against Israel. Jordan especially had suffered too many destructive Israeli reprisal raids for previous cross-border movements to want any more. One of the two fedayeen carrying out the New Year's Eve raid—the first was killed by the Israelis—was captured by a Jordanian army patrol as he returned across the river. On King Hussein's orders, Jordanian prime minister Wasfi Tal's government began a merciless manhunt for fedayeen. Ten days after the first operation, a Jordanian soldier killed another al-Asifa guerrilla, Ahmed Musa.

From January 1965 until the war of June 1967, Fatah issued seventy-three military communiqués on sabotage raids conducted by al-Asifa. Some were directed personally by Arafat, who began making clandestine trips, sometimes disguised as a woman or a peasant, into Israel, including some to Jerusalem. Most of these operations started from Syria; a few, without King Hussein's authorization, were from Jordan.

Israeli Retaliation

In retaliation, on November 13, 1966, Israel struck hard, not at Syria, but at the remote West Bank Jordanian hamlet of Samua, 10 miles (16 kilometers) south of Hebron and 4 miles (6 kilometers) north of the Israeli border in the Negev Desert. Jordanian army reinforcements who were rushed in against the Israeli incursion ran into an Israeli ambush; twenty-one Jordanian soldiers were killed and thirty-seven wounded.

Hussein remained adamant in his opinion that the Samua raid, the most destructive of a series of Israeli reprisals that had begun at the West Bank town of Qibya in 1953, was inevitable. He regarded the raid as the direct result of the refusal of the PLO command to function under the operational control of the Unified Arab Command. This body was largely dominated by Egypt, but other Arab countries, including Jordan, were represented.

The Samua raid might have halted clandestine PLO operations from Jordan, but Fatah continued its incursions from Syria. Israeli chief of staff General Yitzhak

Rabin and other senior officials threatened that Israeli forces might enter Syria to "teach a lesson" to the Ba'athist regime in Damascus, which was protecting the terrorists. Arab unity, tenuous at best, was further damaged by a vicious argument between Jordan and the rest of the Arab states. There were increasing Arab threats against Israel, especially by the PLO's Shuqairy and to a lesser extent by Nasser's Egypt.

Incidents multiplied on the Syrian-Israeli border, especially on and around Lake Tiberias (the Sea of Galilee). In a serious aerial clash in April 1967, six Syrian MiG fighters were shot down by the Israeli air force. In mid-May, Israeli prime minister Levi Eshkol issued a "serious warning" to Syria either to curb Fatah or to face the consequences.

Buildup to the 1967 War

On May 15, Egyptian president Nasser, influenced by Arab and Soviet intelligence reports of Israeli buildups and partial mobilization, began his precipitate moves into war, which went counter to his earlier judgments. He ordered a maximum alert of the Egyptian armed forces and instructed the UN forces stationed in Sinai and Gaza to withdraw, which they did on May 19. Nasser next closed the Straits of Tiran, running between Sinai and Saudi Arabia and controlling Israel's Red Sea lifeline to Eilat.

Although reluctant to become embroiled in another Arab-Israel war, King Hussein of Jordan was under great pressure from the Palestinians that made up 50–60 percent of East Jordan's population. Jordan also had endured the worst of the Israeli reprisals since the 1950s. On May 30, Hussein visited Nasser in Cairo to sign a mutual defense pact with Egypt and Iraq, committing Jordan to defending the Arab cause if another signatory was attacked. This step convinced Israeli defense minister Moshe Dayan that Israel should go to war.

On the night of June 3–4, the Israeli cabinet issued orders to attack Egypt and Jordan early on June 5, 1967. The Israeli government believed Israel's national existence was endangered and that war was the only way to end fedayeen attacks. The Israelis struck on June 5, wiping out much of the Egyptian, Syrian, and Jordanian air forces on the ground and moving deep into Gaza and Sinai. The Arab world was unprepared militarily, economically, morally, and philosophically for the punishing lightning war that followed.

The Palestinian army played only a small role in the war, tightly controlled by the Syrian high command. Al-Asifa combat units operated separately and claimed a few successes against Israeli positions near the Syrian frontier. Some Palestinians fought the Israelis in al-Quanytirah (Kuneitra), a Syrian city of more than 70,000 people at the western edge of the Golan Heights, but the Syrians failed to give the Palestinians the arms they needed to fight effectively. In Jordan, a small Egyptian Army fedayeen unit slipped between the Israeli forces and penetrated Israel almost to Tel Aviv's Lod Airport. Israeli units detected and destroyed them. In Gaza, some 15,000 army "regulars" and a mixed group of PLO guerrillas fought stubbornly, but Israeli armor and infantry quickly overwhelmed them.

By June 11, when the final cease-fire took effect, Israeli armies had taken the Gaza Strip and Egypt's Sinai, Syria's Golan Heights, and, most crucially for King Hussein and the Palestinians, the Jordanian West Bank and East Jerusalem. The walled city was formally annexed by Israel and subsequently proclaimed Israel's eternal capital. Although terrorist violence had earlier done much to bring about the war, neither guerrilla nor terrorist action played any significant role in the war's conduct.

At the war's end, Arafat had still not emerged as Fatah's clear leader. The organization had a collective leadership, and journalists found very few Palestinian insiders willing to be interviewed about the postwar disarray or any future plans.

President Nasser's June 9 admission of defeat, and his declined offer to resign, cast gloom among the Palestinian leaders. They were forced to acknowledge that their dependence on Nasser and the Arab governments had gained them nothing. At the end of June 1967, Arafat, Khalil al-Wazir, and about twenty other Palestinians held a meeting. Arafat argued for resuming armed action as soon as possible. Most of the others present disagreed.

PLO Organizes Within Israel

While Arafat's group resolved to resume operations, Arafat himself, accompanied by a deputy, Abu Mi Shaheen, slipped in disguise into the occupied West Bank and established a clandestine headquarters at Qabatiya, near Jenin. Here they recruited followers, stored arms, and tried to create a network of safe houses and sympathizers. But most of the comfortable middle-class Palestinians living in cities such as Nablus, Ramallah, and Jerusalem, let alone the small but wealthy patrician class of nonrefugees in Gaza, had no stomach for clandestine revolutionary work.

What was more, during the war the Israeli army had captured Jordan's army intelligence files on the PLO and fedayeen sympathizers in the West Bank, together with detailed biographical sketches and many photographs. By October 1967, Israeli security had knocked out the Fatah networks. Reprisals and interrogations were harsh. Amnesty International and other human rights groups documented many cases of torture and beatings by Israeli forces.

Battle of Karama

In March 1968, Arafat scored a significant propaganda victory. The Palestinians were regularly firing Katyusha rockets into Israel from Jordan, and the Israelis decided to retaliate with an attack on Karama, a settlement housing about 35,000 of the refugees from Arab-Israeli conflicts since 1948.

Early on March 21, 1968, Israeli paratroopers landed behind fedayeen lines in the Ghor hills behind Karama, and three brigades of tanks and infantry crossed the Jordan. They encountered a small unit of the Popular Front for the Liberation of Palestine and, to their surprise, the Jordanian army. Both the Jordanian army and the fedayeen were prepared. Jordanian army artillery halted the Israeli armor, while in the banana groves near the river, a section of eighteen fedayeen destroyed several Israeli tanks, at the cost of all but one member of the Palestinian unit. Arafat's personal guard was later named Force 17 to commemorate the event.

General Amar Khammash, the Jordanian commander in chief, could do nothing to rescue guerrillas trapped in bunkers and shelters in Karama. Many were killed by the Israelis in hand-to-hand fighting. However, the Jordanians stood their ground and repulsed the Israeli armored thrust. After destroying most of Karama, the Israelis withdrew in the late afternoon, taking about 100 prisoners.

Karama (which means "dignity" in Arabic) gave Palestinian forces credibility. On March 23, for example, King Hussein reversed his earlier coolness toward the fedayeen: "The time may come . . . when we will all be fedayeen," he said. The battle became a symbol of Arab steadfastness for the Palestinian resistance. Thousands of recruits streamed to Jordan to join guerrilla organizations. The prestige of Karama enhanced Arafat's position within Fatah, and Fatah's role within the PLO.

KEY DATES

1948–1949 Israel defends itself against neighboring Arab states in its War of Independence; Jewish victories lead to the exile of hundreds of thousands of Palestinians.

1951 A Palestinian terrorist assassinates Jordan's King Abdullah, setting back a possible peace agreement between Israel and Jordan for decades.

1956 Israel battles Egypt in the Suez War.

1959 Yasir Arafat and other Palestinian nationalists form Fatah in Kuwait.

1964 The Palestine Liberation Organization (PLO) is founded in Egypt, under the tutelage of President Gamal Abdel Nasser.

1967 Israel defeats its Arab neighbors in the Six-Day War, seizing East Jerusalem, Gaza, and the West Bank in the process.

1968 Fatah forces the defeat of Israeli commandos at the Battle of Karama, Jordan, enhancing Arafat and his Fatah party's position within the PLO.

1969 Arafat becomes chairman of the PLO.

Fatah's leadership announced on April 16, 1968, that Arafat would henceforth be "its official spokesman and its representative for all official questions of organization, finance, and information." At a full meeting of the Palestinian National Council, in Cairo in July 1968, Arafat and his companions secured the cooperation of some of the smaller fedayeen groups and organized the Palestine Armed Struggle Command. At Palestinian National Council meetings in February and June 1969, Arafat secured control of the main PLO bureaucracy and established a PLO-Fatah military command.

In February 1969, Arafat became the PLO chairman. His executive committee would provide the core of the PLO for a generation to come. It included Muhammad al-Najjar of Fatah; Farouk al-Khaddoumi of Fatah; Khaled al-Hassan of Fatah; and Ibrahim al-Bourji of Saiqa (the Thunderbolt), an official Syrian fedayeen organization. Another key member was treasurer Abdul Hamid Sho-man. The PLO was now an effective organization, ready to control its own strategy.

John Cooley

See also: *Modern Terrorism*—Israel: Raids on the PLO; Israel: Response to Terrorism; Israeli-Palestinian Conflict.

Further Reading

Abu Iyad. *My Home, My Land: A Narrative of the Palestinian Struggle.* New York: Times Books, 1978.

Ciment, James. *Palestine/Israel: The Long Conflict.* New York: Facts on File, 1997.

Cobban, Helena. *The Palestine Liberation Organization: People, Power, and Politics.* New York: Cambridge University Press, 1983.

Mishal, Shaul. *The PLO Under Arafat: Between Gun and Olive Branch.* New Haven, CT: Yale University Press, 1986.

Ovendale, Ritchie. *The Origins of the Arab-Israeli Wars.* 2nd ed. New York: Longman, 1992.

Palestine: First Intifada, 1987–1992

The mass civil unrest in the occupied territories of the West Bank and the Gaza Strip, known as the "intifada" (an Arab word literally meaning "shaking off"), broke out in December 1987. An Israeli truck driver in the Gaza Strip crashed into a car carrying Palestinian workers. Harsh Israeli repression of the rioting that followed sparked off widespread mass protests, which spread rapidly to the West Bank. The uprising undermined Israeli control. Protesters' tactics ranged from noncooperation, such as nonpayment of taxes and strikes, to demonstrations, riots, and attacks on Israeli soldiers and settlers. On the whole the protesters were armed with stones and similar implements, but as the struggle went on, they increasingly used weapons such as Molotov cocktails, explosives, and firearms.

Fight for Liberation

The intifada was characteristically fought and led by Palestinian youths who, having grown up since 1967 under Israeli occupation, were frustrated at the failure of the established Palestinian groups to liberate their lands. The uprising was in many ways directed as much against the traditional Palestinian leaders as it was against the Israelis who were confiscating land and permanently settling in the occupied territories. The movement was only informally organized, though a Unified National Leadership of the Uprising did emerge. This body coordinated strike calls and issued statements after discussion among the various nationalist factions.

In 1988, 11 Israelis and more than 360 Palestinians were killed in clashes. In 1989, 432 Palestinians were killed, 304 by the Israeli Defense Forces (IDF) and Israeli settlers in the occupied territories, and the remainder by other Palestinians. Thirteen Israeli soldiers and civilians died. In 1990, 140 Palestinians were killed by the IDF and settlers, compared to 10 Israelis. Casualties fell as a result of a lower profile adopted by the IDF early in the year, but tensions mounted after Saddam Hussein's invasion of Kuwait in August 1990. On October 8, Israeli border guards killed 17 Palestinians in a running battle on the Haram al-Sharif (Temple Mount) in the Old City of Jerusalem. In 1991, mass violence fell as a result of tight Israeli security measures imposed during the Gulf War and the opening of Palestinian-Israeli peace talks.

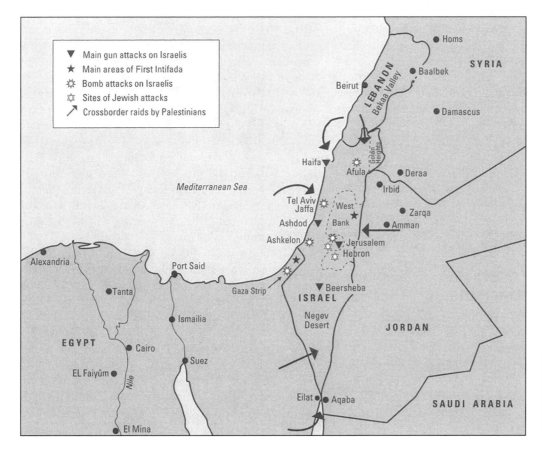

Main areas of the intifada and other terrorist activity in Israel and Palestinian territory, 1987–1996.

Nevertheless, 101 Palestinians were killed by Israeli troops or settlers, and Palestinians killed 12 Israelis.

Terrorism in the Intifada

The majority of the casualties sustained during the intifada did not arise from terrorism as such. Most of the incidents came under the heading of civil violence. Even in cases where specific armed attacks were carried out against people or property, the diffuse nature of authority in the uprising's leadership made it hard to attribute responsibility for some attacks. Many of them were carried out by individuals only loosely, if at all, linked to organizations.

However, there is no doubt that terror was an integral part of the intifada. Stabbing, for example, became common. In three separate incidents in March, May, and September 1989, Palestinians stabbed to death five Israelis and injured five others. In July, a young Palestinian forced an Israeli bus off the road along the Jerusalem–Tel Aviv highway, killing sixteen passengers. In the following years, many stabbing attacks took place, some carried out by individuals and others for which groups claimed responsibility.

In 1990, protesters stabbed to death three Israelis in Jerusalem in October and injured another three in Tel Aviv in December. On May 18, 1991, the Palestinian Islamic Jihad claimed responsibility for a knife attack wounding three Israelis. In 1990 and 1991, organized and armed groups carried out a growing number of attacks, and bombings occurred with increasing regularity. Between May and July 1990, three pipe bombs exploded in different Israeli cities, killing two people and injuring thirty-three, including foreign tourists.

In 1991, numerous small bombs and arson attacks signaled Palestinian support for Iraq and Saddam Hussein in his war against the American-led coalition. In September, a bomb at a market in Beersheba injured several people. Firearms were also used: in October, gunmen opened fire on an Israeli bus in the West Bank, killing two Israeli settlers and wounding six. Both the Popular Front for the Liberation of Palestine and the Palestinian Islamic Jihad claimed responsibility. In 1992, the use of guns and explosives by radical groups increased as popular unrest waned. At least 24 Israelis were killed in 1992, while 158 Palestinians were killed by Israeli forces.

Effects of the Uprising

The intifada irrevocably changed the nature of the Palestinian-Israeli conflict. For the Palestinians, the uprising took the initiative out of the hands of the Palestine Liberation Organization (PLO) leadership in exile abroad and brought to the fore the interests of the Palestinians living in the occupied territories. Many of the "insiders" were amenable to compromise—willing to settle for a two-state solution, in which a Palestinian

---

KEY DATES

December 1987 An Israeli truck driver crashes into a car carrying Palestinian laborers in Gaza, sparking the beginning of the First Intifada.

1988 In the first year of fighting, 11 Israelis and more than 360 Palestinians are killed in clashes.

October 8, 1990 Israeli border guards kill 17 Palestinians in a running battle on the Temple Mount (Haram al-Sharif).

1992 As support for the intifada wanes in its final year, Palestinian militants turn increasingly to guns and explosives, resulting in the deaths of 24 Israelis; 158 Palestinians are killed by Israeli security forces.

---

state was set up alongside Israel, rather than fight for the dream of an Arab state in the whole of Palestine. The PLO leadership was forced to pay less attention to the interests of the Palestinian refugees in Lebanon, who insisted on no compromise with Israel. (Israeli intelligence, however, believed that a key PLO leader, Abu Jihad, had organized the initial outbreak of intifada violence.)

On the Israeli front, years of policing the intifada eroded public morale and international support. The IDF and Israeli public came to realize that they could not maintain their hold over the occupied territories, except by engaging in the sort of repressive internal security policing that they found distasteful and dangerous. As the economic, military, social, and moral cost of repressing the Palestinians escalated, so the sentiment grew in Israel that, at the least, Gaza and some of the West Bank towns should be handed over to the Palestinians. At the same time, international opinion turned against the Israelis. Repeated television pictures of IDF troops beating Palestinian youngsters eroded international, and especially American, respect for Israel and contributed to a climate in which U.S. policy makers could propose reducing American support for Israel, if only tentatively. The combination of these factors meant that some in the Israeli political establishment and public were more willing to agree to a compromise solution.

Although these factors were important in the emergence of a negotiated solution to the conflict, their importance should not be exaggerated. By 1991, the intifada was weakening through sheer exhaustion. Three years of hardship caused by a combination of Israeli repression, strikes, and economic problems had hit morale in the occupied territories. The Israeli forces also began to adopt a less aggressive stance, helping to reduce civil unrest. However, increasingly radical Palestinian youths had started to organize themselves on paramilitary lines and carry out attacks on Israelis. Meanwhile, Israeli intelligence had created a class of Palestinian collaborators who served to break up Palestinian unity. In 1990, the number of alleged Palestinian collaborators killed by Palestinian activists (165) outnumbered those killed in clashes with the IDF and settlers (140). By 1992, the number of Palestinians killed by their fellows had risen to almost 200, greater than the number killed by Israel (158). The intifada not only had changed the nature of Palestinian-Israeli politics, but, partly through its use of terror, had also brought the possibility of compromise closer.

Andrew Rathmell

See also: *Modern Terrorism*—Israeli-Palestinian Conflict; Palestine: Islamist Fundamentalism.

Further Reading

Freedman, Robert O. *The Intifada: Its Impact on Israel, the Arab World, and the Superpowers.* Miami: Florida International University Press, 1991.

Hunter, Robert F. *The Palestinian Uprising: A War by Other Means.* Berkeley: University of California Press, 1991.

Khaled, al Hassan. "The PLO and the Intifada." *American-Arab Affairs* 31 (Winter 1989–1990): 42–48.

Palestine: Islamist Fundamentalism, 1980s–Present

Between 1980 and 1987, following the Islamic Revolution of 1978–1979 in Iran, the Muslim faith became a far more significant element in the Palestinians' struggle for a nation-state. Iranian arms and money contributed to the growth of Islamic politics throughout the Middle East. The assassination of President Anwar Sadat of Egypt, in October 1981, was the most striking single example of the new Muslim fundamentalism. Sadat was killed for having recognized the state of Israel and for having signed a peace agreement with it. Members of the Egyptian Islamic Jihad carried out the assassination. They would soon have imitators all over the Arab world, and they played a crucial role among Palestinians.

Muslim Brotherhood and Jihad

Islamic Jihad had its roots in the Muslim Brotherhood, a fundamentalist movement founded in Egypt in 1928. At one stage, the movement numbered 500,000 active members, and it influenced Palestinians such as Yasir Arafat during the 1950s. President Gamal Abdel Nasser banned it after its members tried to assassinate him in 1954. The ban remained in place until after Nasser's death in 1970. Nasser's successor, Sadat, restored legality to radical Muslim groups in an attempt to counter the influence of left-wing political parties.

The Muslim Brotherhood traditionally maintained a strong base around Gaza, where it had retained a presence since spreading there in the 1930s from its Egyptian base. From 1979 onward, the Muslim Brotherhood began to present a strong challenge to the secular nationalists in student elections held in universities across the occupied territories (the West Bank and the Gaza Strip). It formed electoral alliances where convenient—on occasion with Fatah against the powerful communists—and made a formidable showing in professional bodies such as the Engineers Association, which elected a majority of Muslim Brotherhood supporters in 1981. However, electoral pacts soon gave way to campus clashes between supporters of the Muslim Brotherhood and Fatah, primarily, between late 1981 and 1985. The focus was the Islamic University in Gaza, founded by the Muslim Brotherhood in 1978; An-Najah National University in Nablus; and, to a lesser extent, Hebron and Birzeit universities.

Growth of Islamic Radicalism

The existence of radical Egyptian Muslims—the Egyptian Islamic Jihad—encouraged a Palestinian equivalent. In the early 1980s, small, more radical groups of fundamentalists began to emerge in Palestine from within those influenced by the Muslim Brotherhood. Although they professed dissatisfaction with the Muslim Brotherhood's refusal to embrace violence, there was often more in common between them and the Muslim Brotherhood than they were prepared to admit, and there was a considerable common membership.

In 1980, these radical Palestinian Muslim Brotherhood members founded the Palestinian Islamic Jihad, which argued that the Muslim Brotherhood's policy of tying the liberation of Palestine to the transformation of the whole Arab world was pointless because Palestine should play the primary role in any Arab liberation struggle. Young fundamentalist leaders such as Fathi Shiqaqi and Palestinian Islamic Jihad's spiritual leader, Abdel Aziz Auda, believed they could challenge the secular (nonreligious) nationalism of the Muslim Brotherhood, especially since the Palestine Liberation Organization's (PLO's) armed struggle was showing no concrete results. The fundamentalists took advantage of the fact that the PLO leaders seemed concerned more with gaining international diplomatic recognition than with achieving their official objective of liberating Palestine.

Hamas

Hamas emerged in 1987 out of the ranks of the Muslim Brotherhood. When the intifada (civil unrest in the occupied territories) broke out, Sheikh Ahmed Yassin, founder of the Gaza Islamic Center, and a number of other Muslim Brotherhood leaders in Gaza, called for resistance to Israel. Their first leaflet was issued on December 14, 1987, but they did not identify themselves as Hamas until January 1988.

The Hamas charter, issued on August 18, 1988, insists that Palestine is in the trust of the Muslim world and that "it is not right to give it up nor any part of it." Hamas calls for the uprooting of Israel and the establishment of an Islamic state in its place. It characterizes peace initiatives as a waste of time and an absurdity and calls for all Muslims to engage in jihad, or holy war.

Hamas's popularity grew during the late 1980s and early 1990s because it was able to provide schools, medical centers, and social welfare activities that were otherwise lacking in the occupied territories.

Hamas also both benefited from, and promoted a return to, traditional Islamic values that appealed to many of the disoriented Palestinian youth. At the same time, its uncompromising stance toward Israel attracted many

Palestinians who did not agree with the compromise approach of PLO chairman Yasir Arafat and who wanted to continue the fight against Israel. With its daring military operations and use of suicide bombers, Hamas appeared to many to be the main defender of Palestinian rights during a period when many Palestinians perceived the peace process as being weighted against them.

Recruiting in Gaza

The overpopulated and poverty-stricken Gaza Strip became Hamas's main base and recruiting ground. However, the movement also gained a following in the West Bank and among Palestinians in Jordan and Lebanon.

Hamas enjoyed support from Syria and Iran, although it remained unclear exactly how much help was given. The movement certainly had offices in both countries, and the governments in both Damascus and Tehran gave it verbal backing. Much of Hamas's funding came from supporters in the West and in other Muslim countries, notably Saudi Arabia. As a movement advocating a return to Islamic social values, Hamas could call on sympathy among Muslims worldwide opposed to the secular attitude of the PLO.

Divide and Rule

At first, Israel was prepared to encourage the Islamic fundamentalists, allowing them to build their institutional base—and even surreptitiously funding Muslim Brotherhood mosques—in order to divide and rule. Supporting Muslim fundamentalist groups seemed a way of reducing PLO support, especially in Gaza, and at this stage there was no apparent armed fundamentalist threat. While the PLO factions tried to gain control of whatever civil structures the Israelis allowed in the occupied territories, Islamic Jihad consolidated its own power base. The fundamentalists gathered increasing support in student unions, professional associations, and mosques. Hamas was also supported by the Israeli authorities. At first, the group emphasized its social activities over its military aims, and the Israelis viewed it as a useful counter to the PLO. But this strategy of divide and rule backfired. By the early 1990s, Hamas, with perhaps 40 percent of the popular support in Gaza, had become Israel's deadliest enemy.

Meanwhile, the members of Islamic Jihad had split from the Muslim Brotherhood over the national question, believing that a Palestinian Islamic state could be created without an Islamic revolution in the rest of the Arab world. Support for Islamic Jihad's armed actions would eventually weaken support for the Muslim Brotherhood's nonmilitant line in some of the professional unions. However, the Muslim Brotherhood encouraged students to organize under the electoral umbrella of the Islamic bloc. The Muslim Brotherhood also conducted pioneering social, cultural, and educational work under the authority of the Islamic Center in Gaza—headed by its founder, the Gaza Muslim Brotherhood leader, Sheikh Ahmed Yassin.

Islam was becoming a potent political challenge to the PLO's dominance of the Palestinian national cause, although as yet it lacked any prominent leadership. From 1984 onward, however, radical fundamentalists, calling themselves Islamic Jihad, began a series of small attacks on Israeli settlers in the Gaza Strip. They constituted a self-styled armed "Islamic vanguard."

On October 16, 1986, sixty-eight army recruits were injured and one soldier's father was killed when two Palestinians threw hand grenades at an army inauguration ceremony at the Western Wall in Jerusalem's Old City. The Islamic Jihad claimed responsibility, as did several Fatah groups, for the "Gate of the Moors" attack. However, despite these claims, the incident was most certainly the work of Islamic Jihad.

Islamic Jihad terrorists were also responsible for a number of knife attacks during the intifada and later mounted a variety of assaults and suicide attacks on Israeli targets. In February 1990, Islamic Jihad terrorists ambushed an Israeli tour bus in Egypt. They killed nine Israelis and wounded seventeen other people. The group also carried out raids into Israel and threatened U.S. targets.

As the PLO-Israeli peace process advanced, Hamas and Islamic Jihad became more violent. Hamas concentrated at first on operations against Israeli military forces. In early December 1992, it ambushed soldiers in Hebron and Gaza, killing four. In mid-December, an off-duty border guard was kidnapped just outside Tel Aviv and killed. In retaliation, Israel deported some 400 fundamentalist leaders to Lebanon, but they were not allowed into the country and were forced to set up camp on border hillsides. Half the deportees were allowed to return in September 1993, and most of those remaining were returned in December 1993.

At the same time as the last deportees returned, Hamas and Islamic Jihad intensified their operations in an attempt to derail the peace process. The two groups were responsible for the majority of Israeli casualties in the year—some 65 dead and 390 injured. Between September and December, Hamas claimed thirteen attacks, several of them suicide bombings. On October 4, 1993, a Hamas bomber rammed his explosive-laden car into an Israeli bus, injuring 30 people.

During 1994, Hamas killed more than 50 Israelis and wounded more than 150. Thirteen soldiers and settlers were killed in individual knife, ax, and shooting attacks. On April 6, 1994, Hamas took revenge for the Hebron massacre with a car bomb in Afula that killed 7 Israelis. Another bomb in Hadera also killed 7 people. Israel responded by sealing off the occupied territories of the West Bank and Gaza Strip in order to hurt the Palestinian population economically and to prevent bombers from entering Israel proper.

In October, Hamas kidnapped an Israeli Defense Forces (IDF) soldier and demanded the release of Hamas founder Sheikh Ahmed Yassin, who had been jailed in 1989, as well as 200 activists. In a botched rescue mission by IDF commandos on October 15, 3 kidnappers were killed, along with the hostage and an IDF officer. On October 9, Hamas opened fire indiscriminately on the streets of Jerusalem, killing 2 people and wounding 14. On October 19, a Hamas suicide bomber blew himself up with 22 passengers in a Tel Aviv bus, wounding at least 48 other people. On December 25, Hamas bombed an IDF bus in Jerusalem, wounding 13 people.

Hitting Islamic Jihad

On November 2, 1994, Israeli agents killed an Islamic Jihad leader, Hani Abed, in Gaza with a car bomb. Islamic Jihad retaliated with a suicide bicycle bomber, who killed three IDF officers near the settlement of Netzarim in the Gaza Strip. Earlier in the year, in April, Islamic Jihad had shot dead two Israelis at a bus stop in Ashdod. In response to the Hamas and Islamic Jihad attacks, Israel demanded that Arafat's Palestinian Authority (PA) crack down on Hamas and Islamic Jihad activists in the area controlled by Arafat.

Arafat was happy to take on Islamic Jihad since he regarded them as Iranian-backed extremists with no popular base. He recognized, however, that Hamas had wide support. During 1994, he tried to reach an accommodation with Hamas's political wing while reining in the group's terrorist activities. Arafat's main concern was to avoid a Palestinian civil war, but his crackdowns nearly caused a surge of violence. In November 1994, the PA's forces killed sixteen demonstrators while dispersing a fundamentalist rally in Gaza.

On January 22, 1995, two Islamic Jihad suicide bombers killed 20 Israeli soldiers and a civilian at Beit Lid, injuring 68 others. In April, six Palestinians were killed in an explosion in a Gaza City apartment complex. The dead included top Hamas military man Kamal Kahil, who was wanted in Israel for a series of bombings and by the Palestinian authorities for the murder of 16 collaborators. A week later, fundamentalist suicide bombers killed 8 Israelis in two attacks in the Gaza Strip. In response, Arafat arrested around 200 suspects. Hamas, however, went on with its campaign. On July 24, 1995, a suicide bomber killed 6 Israelis on a Tel Aviv bus. In a similar attack on August 21, 6 more Israelis died.

Meanwhile, Arafat demanded that Israel speed up the redeployment of its troops as agreed earlier. On September 24, 1995, Israel and the PLO signed an interim agreement at the Egyptian resort of Taba. The agreement extended the PA's rule in the occupied West Bank, effectively giving it control of more than 1.3 million people.

The agreement led to the Israeli army withdrawing from 6 West Bank towns and more than 440 villages, although it remained in Hebron to protect 415 Jewish settlers living in the middle of the town. The Taba agreement paved the way for the Palestinian elections held on January 20, 1996. In these elections, Arafat was elected president of the PA and Fatah supporters won a majority of seats in the eighty-eight-member legislative council.

This electoral victory gave Arafat more authority in his dealings with Hamas. The fact that 75 percent of the Palestinian population had voted despite Hamas's call to boycott the poll enabled Arafat to negotiate from a position of strength. However, splits within Hamas had begun to emerge between the Hamas leadership, who were prepared to open a dialogue with Arafat, and the hard-core members of the movement, who were strongly opposed to any such peace negotiations. These splits within Hamas and the continued activities of Islamic Jihad undermined Arafat's authority and soon provoked a crisis in the peace process.

On October 26, 1995, Fathi Shiqaqi, Islamic Jihad's founder, was shot dead in Malta by suspected Mossad agents. He had been in transit between Libya and Damascus. Two IDF medics were killed in an ambush in the West Bank by the hitherto unknown group Mujahideen al-Islami. However, the combined Israeli-PA offensive against Hamas and Islamic Jihad appeared to bear fruit during late 1995. The Palestinian authorities rounded up hundreds of fundamentalist activists and pressed the Gulf States to end their financial support for militant Palestinian Islamic groups. With Palestinian intelligence help, Israel rounded up Hamas military cells in the West Bank. Meanwhile, Arafat began to engage in a dialogue with Hamas's political leadership. A cease-fire was enforced from mid-1995 until early 1996 and the PA arranged an amnesty for some Hamas activists in Palestinian jails.

On January 5, 1996, Yahya Ayyash, Hamas's top bomb maker, who was involved in many of the suicide bombings, was killed by a booby-trapped cellular phone. Israel did little to hide the fact that Shin Bet, the Israeli security service, was behind the operation. Revenge attacks predictably followed. On February 25, Hamas claimed two suicide-bomb attacks. One in Jerusalem ripped apart a bus, killing twenty-five and injuring fifty-five people. An hour later, a second suicide bomb in Ashkelon injured some thirty-five Israelis. Hamas claimed that the bombs were in retaliation for the 1994 Hebron massacre as well as for the assassination of Ayyash.

In the wake of the bombings, Israel imposed a clampdown on the Palestinian areas, and the United States and Israel called on Arafat to dismantle Hamas. Arafat condemned the attacks as terrorism and launched his police forces against Hamas's military wing, the Izz al-Din al-Qassam Brigades. The PA arrested more than 470 suspected militants.

Hamas Halts the Peace Process

On March 3 and 4, 1996, a second wave of suicide bombings struck at the heart of Israeli society, again carried out by militants in Hamas and Islamic Jihad. The bombings killed 32 people in Jerusalem and Tel Aviv. The Tel Aviv bomb exploded in the heart of the town's Dizengoff shopping area during the Jewish festival of Purim. Thirteen people died, and about 125 were wounded. A caller to Israeli radio stated that "today's attack is a reply after the government of the so-called prime minister and defense minister Shimon Peres declared war on Hamas. Let him know that if he does not negotiate with Hamas and if he tries to destroy it there will be even bloodier attacks."

These devastating attacks halted the peace process and led to a major crisis. Israeli troops entered PA-controlled areas and imposed an internal closure on the Palestinian areas, which meant that the IDF controlled all movement between villages and towns in Gaza and the West Bank. All adult males were rounded up and questioned in several towns. Israeli president Ezer Weizman justified these collective punishment measures, saying, "if we cannot find the needle" of Hamas, then "we must burn the haystack" of the Palestinian people. Israeli troops also detained more than 250 suspects and destroyed the homes of the families of suicide bombers.

The Israeli government began to implement a plan to separate Israel once and for all from Palestinian areas. Israeli troops and police began to set up a mile-wide buffer zone separating the West Bank from Israel. Part of this zone was to be fenced off, and the rest controlled by patrols and surveillance devices.

Arafat Ends Dialogue with Hamas

Since the Hamas militants had successfully quashed any opportunity for a peace dialogue between Arafat and the Hamas moderates, Arafat had no choice but to join in Israel's declared "war" on Hamas. On March 3, the PA banned six Palestinian militias, including Hamas's Izz al-Din al-Qassam Brigades and Palestinian Islamic Jihad's Qassam militia. He declared that he would "cooperate fully with Israel to wipe out terrorism." On March 6, PLO official Mahmoud Abbas also declared "there is now no dialogue with either Hamas's political or military wings." Several days later, after being briefed by the CIA, Arafat told a Palestinian rally that he believed the recent suicide operations had been ordered by Iran. This statement reflected his new determination to treat Hamas as a foreign-inspired enemy.

In well-publicized operations, Palestinian police raided mosques, Islamic centers, and universities and detained hundreds of suspects. The Izz al-Din al-Qassam militia responded by promising more violence. On March 9, it issued a statement saying, "Qassam has decided to resume its martyrdom attacks against the Zionists." It warned that the PA's actions "will completely destroy any understanding or future agreement" between Hamas and the PLO. These statements showed that the political leaders had lost control of their military counterparts. Hamas political leader Mahmoud al-Zahar told a Gaza press conference that "we are demanding a stop to the military actions against Israeli targets," but added, "we have no organizational relation to the military wing." His calls accordingly had no effect.

Second Intifada and Conflict with Fatah

In 2000, a second intifada against Israeli rule broke out in both Gaza and the West Bank, triggered by the visit of former defense minister Ariel Sharon—accompanied by hundreds of security personnel—to the grounds of the al-Aqsa Mosque in Jerusalem, considered one of the holiest sites in Islam. Over the course of the next two years, terrorists from Hamas and Islamic Jihad conducted a wave of suicide bombings against targets in Israel, killing hundreds of civilians in the process. To stop such attacks, Israel launched a massive military incursion in both Gaza and the West Bank to destroy the terrorist infrastructure. At the same time, it began to build a security barrier within and around the West Bank to prevent further terrorist attacks. Even after it withdrew most of its troops from the two territories, it continued to launch air attacks on suspected Islamist militant strongholds there. The strategy worked, as terrorist assaults on the Jewish state plunged.

In 2005, Sharon, now prime minister, unilaterally pulled Israeli settlements and troops out of Gaza, leaving the territory to the PA. In January of the following year, the political wing of Hamas won a landslide victory in Palestinian legislative elections, leading many Western countries to cut off aid to the PA. Opposition to the group was partly a function of its barrage of rockets launched against Israel, which resulted in few deaths but produced a state of terror in southern parts of the country. In response, Israel launched missile attacks and occasional armed incursions into areas of Gaza from which the majority of the rockets were launched.

Hamas's belligerence toward Israel and its challenge to Fatah's hegemony in the PA—Fatah was the secular nationalist party founded by Arafat in the 1960s and was the main party within the PLO—led to growing tensions between the two parties. By the summer of 2006, the two sides were engaged in gun battles, which ultimately resulted in a split between Gaza and the West Bank, with the former falling under the control of Hamas and the latter under Fatah. While Fatah continued to pursue a negotiated two-state settlement with Israel, Hamas refused to participate, insisting that Israel had no right to exist and refusing to denounce the use of violence—including

KEY DATES

Late 1970s Islamic Jihad of Palestine emerges among radical Islamists in Gaza.

1987 Members of the Muslim Brotherhood form Hamas; Palestinians launch the First Intifada rebellion against Israeli rule.

1993 The Palestine Liberation Organization (PLO) signs a peace deal with Israel, establishing the Palestinian Authority (PA).

2000 The Second Intifada is launched; Hamas and Islamic Jihad accelerate their terrorist bombing campaign against Israel.

2002 Israel launches an invasion of Gaza and the West Bank to destroy the Islamist terrorist network.

2006 Hamas wins the PA elections, eventually triggering a conflict with the PLO that leaves Hamas in control of Gaza and the PLO in control of the West Bank.

2008 To stop rocket attacks by Hamas and other Islamist militants, Israel launches an invasion of Gaza.

2010 Hamas opposes U.S.-sponsored peace talks between Israel and the PA.

2011 Hamas signs a merger agreement with its longtime rival, Fatah, the largest political faction of the PLO.

terrorist attacks—against the Jewish state. Among its tactics was the increased use of improved rockets, which could reach farther into Israel. Finally, in December 2008, Israel launched a massive invasion of Gaza in an effort to shut down the rocket launches. Widely condemned in the international community, Operation Cast Lead resulted in the deaths of more than 1,000 Palestinians in Gaza, many of them civilians. The incursion, however, dramatically slowed the rate of rocket attacks.

At the same time, Israel continued its embargo on Gaza, refusing to allow all but essential items to be imported into the territory. Hamas and other groups responded by digging tunnels under Gaza's border with Egypt, which Israel tried to shut down—largely ineffectively—with air attacks. Through 2010, Hamas remained defiant toward Israel and icy toward Fatah, denouncing the latter's peace talks with Israel, sponsored by the United States. The peace talks broke down over new Israeli settlements on the West Bank, and, in May 2011, Hamas and Fatah ended their longstanding conflict and signed a reconciliation agreement. Brokered by Egypt, the accord called for the creation of a joint transitional government for Palestine and elections to the Palestinian Authority in one year. For Israel, which still recognized Hamas as a terrorist organization, the merger made the prospect of a negotiated two-state solution even more remote.

Neil Partrick, Andrew Rathmell, and James Ciment

See also: *Definitions, Types, Categories*—Islamist Fundamentalist Terrorism. *Modern Terrorism*—Israeli-Palestinian Conflict. *Tactics, Methods, Aims*—Suicide Attacks.

Further Reading

Abu Amr, Ziad. *Islamic Fundamentalism in the West Bank and Gaza: Muslim Brotherhood and Islamic Jihad.* Bloomington: Indiana University Press, 1994.

Benvenisti, Meron. *Intimate Enemies: Jews and Arabs in a Shared Land.* Berkeley: University of California Press, 1995.

Chehab, Naki. *Inside Hamas: The Untold Story of the Militant Islamic Movement.* New York: Nation Books, 2007.

Dekmejian, R. Hrair. *Islam in Revolution: Fundamentalism in the Arab World.* Syracuse, NY: Syracuse University Press, 1995.

Gunnin, Jeroen. *Hamas in Politics: Democracy, Religion, Violence.* New York: Columbia University Press, 2008.

Halabi, Rafik. *The West Bank Story: An Israeli Arab's View of Both Sides of a Tangled Conflict.* New York: Harcourt Brace Jovanovich, 1982.

Kardelj, Nejc, ed. *Israel vs. Hamas.* New York: Nova Science, 2010.

Sivan, Emmanuel, and Menachem Friedman. *Religious Radicalism and Politics in the Middle East.* New York: State University of New York Press, 1990.

Palestine: PLO and the Arab States, 1970s–Present

The relationship between the Palestine Liberation Organization (PLO) and the Arab states had a tremendous influence on terrorist incidents in the Middle East during the 1970s and 1980s. In theory, the long-term goal of all Arab states was to "liberate Palestine from Zionist imperialism." The declaration of this goal was originally made at the 1964 summit of the Arab League, an international organization of Arab states. But the actions of individual Arab governments frequently seemed to make it harder to achieve a liberated Palestine.

By the 1980s, both the PLO and much of the Arab world had adopted a more accommodationist approach to Israel, which was opposed by hard-line Islamist forces within Palestine. For the most part, Arab governments continued to back the PLO, especially as it was met with armed resistance from the Islamists.

PLO and Terrorist Groups

The PLO itself developed enormously during the 1970s and 1980s. Under the leadership of Yasir Arafat, and with his Fatah faction dominating decision-making bodies, it took on all the trappings of a government in exile. Many guerrilla and terrorist organizations took part in the formalities of running the PLO. There were eight main groups:

- Fatah, which normally sought a compromise peace.
- The Popular Front for the Liberation of Palestine (PFLP), which was dominated by Marxist leaders who also sought to unify the Arab states.
- The Democratic Front for the Liberation of Palestine, which was a Marxist splinter group that broke away from the PFLP in 1969.
- Saiqa (Arabic for "thunderbolt"), which was a Syrian-supported guerrilla force.
- The Arab Liberation Front, which was created by the Iraqi government in 1969 to represent its views in the PLO.
- The Popular Front for the Liberation of Palestine–General Command (PFLP-GC), the Palestine Liberation Front, and the Popular Struggle Front, which are smaller groups within the PLO. All three of these organizations have followed the twists and turns of Arab politics, sometimes putting them in opposition to, or, in the case of the PFLP-GC, in direct confrontation with, the PLO.

All of these groups were set up in the tradition of secular Arab nationalism. Islam and Muslim clerics had far less influence, unlike today, over Arab nationalism during the 1950s and 1960s, the era when these groups were established.

The most important decision-making body in the PLO during the 1970s and 1980s was the Palestinian National Council (PNC), which met irregularly. On it sat representatives of the various guerrilla and terrorist groups and other organizations the PLO set up. The PNC elected the fifteen members of the PLO's executive committee. Fatah could have used its political strength in the PNC to exclude other groups from the executive committee, but the creation of the forty-member PLO central council in 1973, which met every three months, ensured that minority views had a hearing.

Influences on PLO Strategy

There were four major elements in the PLO's attitude toward terrorism during the 1970s and 1980s. First, the organization sought international respect and so was willing to negotiate and compromise. Second, the PLO needed to keep a loyal following among the Arabs living in the occupied territories of the West Bank and Gaza Strip. Third, it had to deal with the attitude of the Israeli government toward a Middle East peace settlement. Fourth, it had to cooperate with the host states for its military bases and political administration.

Arafat gave priority to gaining diplomatic recognition for the PLO from the international community. At various times during the 1970s and 1980s, he pursued a policy of restraining PLO members seeking violent confrontations with Israel. These included the 1969–1970 period, when U.S. Secretary of State William Rogers sponsored a Middle East peace plan; the period from November 1973 to 1975, when negotiations took place between various parties in the aftermath of the 1973 Arab-Israeli War; and the period directly after the 1982 expulsion of the PLO from Lebanon.

In all three of these periods, however, groups inside the PLO, who adopted the name "rejectionist," defied Arafat and Fatah. In particular, some of the PFLP and Abu Nidal's Fatah: The Revolutionary Council (also known as the Abu Nidal Organization) tried to destroy attempts at compromise in the period from 1973 to 1975. Indeed, Arafat's appearances as a world statesman prepared to compromise may actually have provoked these rejectionists to terrorist acts.

Fatah, the most moderate group in the PLO, did not altogether reject terrorism either, and certainly encouraged it during 1974 and 1975. Fatah directed its strategy of violence against specifically Israeli targets in Israel and the occupied territories rather than attacking people and property around the globe. Terrorist attacks could take the shape of anything from a random grenade attack in Tel Aviv, to a bombardment of Galilee by Katyusha rockets, to the taking of civilian hostages. Fatah worked within the PNC to bring the rest of the PLO membership around to its viewpoint, and the number of PLO terrorist acts taking place outside Israel declined during the 1980s.

The PLO and Palestinians

The demand in the West Bank and Gaza Strip (the occupied territories) for an end to Israeli occupation encouraged a commitment to political compromise on the part of the PLO leadership. The seventh meeting of the PNC in April 1972 had instructed the PLO executive committee to concentrate its efforts on setting up a "national united front." This was in response to an initiative by King Hussein of Jordan, who suggested that the West Bank and Gaza Strip become part of a federated Jordanian-Palestinian state.

By August 1973, the Palestinian National Front (PNF) had been formed—in part the result of the PLO's decision, but as much out of the efforts of activists belonging to the Palestinian Communist Organization. The PLO had to decide whether to gain the support of those Palestinians in the occupied territories who supported the PNF's strategy of political mobilization to liberate territory occupied by Israel in 1967, or to side with those who wanted armed confrontation.

Israeli Responses to Terrorism

Another critical factor for the PLO's use of terrorism was the Israeli attitude. Israeli retaliation for Arab terrorist attacks varied according to the seriousness of the acts. There was no doubt that the right-wing Likud party, which came to power in Israel in 1977, was more willing to take military action. A more aggressive Israeli strategy, one associated with Ariel Sharon, resulted in the invasions of Lebanon in 1978 and, on a larger scale, in 1982. In particular, Palestinians were convinced that Israeli forces conspired with Christian Lebanese Phalangist militia in organizing the massacres of Palestinians at the Sabra and Shatila refugee camps in 1982. Such incidents were used by some Palestinians to justify their own retaliation. The artillery and aerial bombardment of Palestinian refugee camps in Lebanon served only to compound such attitudes.

The PLO and Its Hosts

The history of Middle Eastern terrorism between 1970 and 1987 can, to a large extent, be told in terms of the relationship between the PLO and the Arab states.

In 1970, the PLO was based in Jordan. From there, since 1969, the PFLP had carried out its campaign of hijacking that culminated in September 1970 with the incident at Dawson's Field, when three jetliners were blown up. Many within the Palestinian organizations, and especially the PFLP, believed it was necessary to overthrow Jordan's King Hussein to establish a safe base for terrorists and guerrillas. However, Hussein was a tough political operator, and he confronted the PLO eleven days after Dawson's Field. The well-trained Jordanian army eventually expelled the Palestinian fighters from Jordan, although the fighting went on until July 1971. Fatah radicals formed the terrorist Black September Organization, which organized many incidents during the early 1970s in reaction to the expulsion from Jordan.

The Palestinians now found themselves without any direct support from the other Arab states. Any Arab state that allowed the PLO to establish a large military force in its territory might experience what occurred in Jordan during the summer of 1970. If an Arab state offered itself as a terrorist base, then it could also expect Israeli retaliation.

The PLO moved its headquarters to Lebanon, whose government was too weak to keep Palestinian fighters out of the many refugee camps founded after the 1948–1949 Arab-Israeli War and reinforced by more refugees after the 1967 war. The rest of the organization simply followed in the footsteps of the fighters who had been expelled from Jordan.

Aftermath of the 1973 War

The Arab armies of Egypt and Syria fought well in the October 1973 Arab-Israeli War, although Israel won the conflict. In its aftermath, the possibility of a negotiated Middle East peace settlement looked its best since 1967. In this context, Fatah decided to abandon terrorism outside the immediate area of Israel, in the hope that the PLO would be invited to any general negotiated peace settlement. But Arafat's willingness to compromise was not matched by other members of the PLO, who formed a rejection front.

Rejectionist groups such as the PFLP carried on with terrorism and also attacked conservative Arab targets. Abu Nidal's Fatah: The Revolutionary Council was even more extreme in its rejectionism and attacked the PLO itself. The rejectionists relied heavily on support from Syria, Iraq, and Libya. Without this aid, rejectionist terrorists could never have had the impact they did. Syria, Iraq, and Libya were determined not to recognize Israel and encouraged the terrorists as proxies for their wider aims in the Middle East. Terrorist acts were timed to ensure maximum impact on any peace talks that took place.

The risk any Arab state took if it chose to act as the PLO's host was illustrated by events in Lebanon during

KEY DATES

1964 Under Egyptian aegis, Palestinian nationalists found the Palestine Liberation Organization (PLO).

1967 In the wake of the Arab-Israeli War, Yasir Arafat and the Fatah Party seize control of the PLO.

1988 Arafat and the PLO renounce terrorism and recognize Israel's right to exist.

1991 Many Arab states turn against the PLO after it backs Saddam Hussein in the Persian Gulf War.

1993 The PLO and Israel sign the Oslo Accords, calling for a Palestinian Authority (PA) in the West Bank and Gaza and negotiations leading to an independent Palestinian state.

2005 Israel unilaterally vacates Gaza.

2006 After winning PA elections and following bitter strife with Fatah, Hamas seizes control of Gaza.

2008 Israel launches an invasion of Gaza to prevent further rocket attacks by Hamas.

2010 The Barack Obama Administration attempts to restart peace talks between the PA and Israel, with strong backing from much of the Arab world, but these produce little results and are suspended after about a year.

2011 Leaders of Fatah and Hamas sign a reconciliation agreement brokered by Egypt that calls for a joint transitional government for Palestine and presidential and legislative elections in 2012.

PLO vs. Hamas

By the late 1980s and early 1990s, the Arab world, recognizing that Israel was not likely to be defeated in war, gradually adopted a new position—acceptance of Israel in exchange for the country's return to its borders prior to the 1967 war and the establishment of an independent Palestinian state in the West Bank and Gaza, with East Jerusalem as its capital.

That, too, became the position of the PLO, which denounced terrorism and recognized Israel's right to exist in the late 1980s. In 1993, Israel and the PLO signed an accord, calling for negotiations leading to a Palestinian state and the establishment of an autonomous Palestinian Authority (PA) in Gaza and the West Bank.

Ruled by Yasir Arafat's Fatah Party—part of the coalition of groups that constituted the PLO—the PA received enormous financial support from many Arab states, though its 1993 deal with Israel was objected to by several hard-line regimes, including Syria's. In addition, its support for Saddam Hussein in the Persian Gulf War of 1991 alienated many moderate Arab regimes, at least temporarily. Meanwhile, the PLO's accommodation with Israel was also met by strong resistance among radical Palestinian factions, some of whom coalesced into Islamist parties such as Islamic Jihad and Hamas.

Frustrated by PLO corruption and a lack of progress in establishing a Palestinian state and ending the Israeli occupation of the West Bank (Israel unilaterally vacated Gaza in 2005), Palestinians voters gave Hamas control of the PA parliament and prime minister's office in 2006 elections. This set off violent confrontations between the PLO and Hamas, which left the West Bank under the control of the former and Gaza under the control of the latter. Virtually the entire Arab world supported the PLO in this confrontation and continued to fund its operations in the West Bank, even as it cut off most of its funding and support for the Hamas-led regime in Gaza, especially after the latter launched numerous rocket attacks on Israel, prompting a devastating Israeli invasion of Gaza in late 2008. This left Hamas with only one major supporter, the non-Arab Islamist republic of Iran.

The lack of support for Hamas was a function of its refusal to acknowledge Israel's right to exist, which ran counter to the Arab consensus; its support for and participation in terrorist activity; and its Islamist principles, which were anathema to the secular and royal regimes in the region at a time when they were facing fundamentalist—and, as of 2011, popular democratic—challenges at home. The Hamas-Fatah merger signed in May 2011 offered hope of unified government for a consolidated Palestinian state, but Hamas's participation seemed to foreclose any possibility of a negotiated settlement with Israel.

Neil Partrick and James Ciment

the 1970s and 1980s. Palestinian raids from Lebanese bases into Israel attracted Israeli retaliation. The violence destabilized Lebanon, where tension between different religious groups heightened into a civil war in 1975, in which terrorism, including car bombs, assassination, and hostage taking, was prevalent. Factional fighting was followed by an Israeli invasion that forced the PLO to move its headquarters to Tunis in 1983.

During the civil war, an event the PLO considered a far greater disaster than the war itself took place when President Jimmy Carter brokered a peace agreement between President Anwar Sadat of Egypt and Israel's prime minister Menachem Begin in 1978. With Fatah's sponsor, Egypt, no longer at war with Israel, Camp David gave Syria and Iraq more control over the anti-Israeli coalition. Both countries were much closer to radical Palestinian terrorists than to Fatah.

The final political development that influenced terrorism lay in the success of the Ayatollah Khomeini in Iran (a non-Arab Muslim country) in 1979. His fundamentalist regime offered Muslims in Arab countries a strategy very different from the secular-nationalist path the PLO favored. Not only was it different; it was also successful. Suicide-bombing attacks by Iranian-backed Hezbollah fundamentalists in Lebanon effectively forced Western peacekeepers to leave Beirut in 1984.

See also: *Modern Terrorism*—Jordan: Palestinian Nationalism and Islamic Fundamentalism; Lebanon: Civil War; Palestine: Birth of Fatah and the Palestine Liberation Organization.

Further Reading

Jamal, Amal. *The Palestinian National Movement: Politics of Contention, 1967–2005.* Bloomington: Indiana University Press, 2005.

Meital, Yoram. *Peace in Tatters: Israel, Palestine, and the Middle East.* Boulder, CO: Lynne Rienner, 2006.

Schanzer, Jonathan. *Hamas vs. Fatah: The Struggle for Palestine.* New York: Palgrave Macmillan, 2008.

Palestinian Terrorism: Hijacking of the *Achille Lauro*, 1985

On October 1, 1985, Israeli aircraft attacked the headquarters of the Palestine Liberation Organization (PLO) in Tunis, Tunisia, killing fifty people, mostly PLO men. One week later, an Italian cruise liner, the *Achille Lauro*—en route from Genoa, Italy, to Ashdod, the main Mediterranean port in southern Israel—was captured by four young terrorist members (the oldest was just twenty) of the Palestine Liberation Front (PLF). The hijacking was interpreted internationally as an act of revenge, particularly since the PLF was associated with the PLO and Mohammad Abu Abbas, leader of the PLF and instigator of the operation, had a seat on the PLO executive committee.

Plan Discovered

The original intention of the PLF terrorists was not to hijack the *Achille Lauro* on its journey, but rather to wait until the liner reached Ashdod and to take Israelis hostage there. However, a member of the crew discovered the four men cleaning their weapons in their cabin. Forced into action, the terrorists seized control of the ship.

The liner was at that time sailing along the Egyptian coast, and the majority of passengers were away visiting the pyramids. However, there were still 427 passengers and 80 crew members on board. The terrorists demanded the release of 50 Palestinian prisoners in Israel and threatened to kill the hostages if their demands were not met.

In previous hijackings of aircraft, Middle Eastern terrorists had often specifically targeted and killed U.S. or Israeli officers or state officials. On the *Achille Lauro,* however, the terrorists went further. When Israel refused to agree to the PLF's demands, the terrorists shot and killed a sixty-nine-year-old wheelchair-bound Jewish American from New Jersey, Leon Klinghoffer, and dumped his body overboard.

The hijacking ended when Abu Abbas managed to negotiate an agreement with the Egyptian government. The Egyptians offered both the hijackers and Abu Abbas free passage in exchange for releasing the ship and the hostages. There was a further twist to the story, however. U.S. warplanes intercepted the aircraft flying the terrorists out of Egypt and forced it to fly to a NATO airbase in Sicily. Here, the Italian authorities took charge of the situation. The Italians, however, were hesitant about the best way to proceed, and began by releasing Abu Abbas, who was carrying an Iraqi diplomatic passport. The four terrorists, however, were tried and convicted for murder and conspiracy, and received sentences ranging from fifteen to thirty years. Abu Abbas was convicted only in absentia.

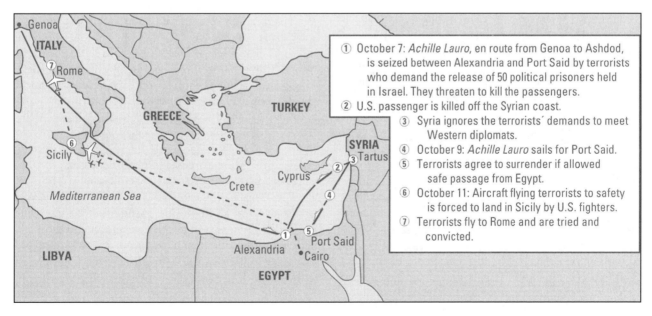

The route of the *Achille Lauro* after its hijacking by members of the Palestine Liberation Front on October 7, 1985.

The Italian cruise ship *Achille Lauro* docks in Egypt after Palestinian hijackers held its passengers and crew hostage for two days in October 1985. When Israel refused their demand to release Palestinian prisoners, the hijackers killed a Jewish American passenger. *(Mike Nelson/AFP/Getty Images)*

There were mutual recriminations over the affair. The United States was condemned by some for violating international law and for effectively hijacking an aircraft; the Italians were criticized for letting Abu Abbas slip through their fingers. There was a suspicion that the Italians had released him mainly because they feared reprisal terrorist raids if they did not let him go. Perhaps the most important result of the affair lay in its effects on the PLO. The peculiar horror of the murder of an elderly man in a wheelchair just because he was Jewish led to worldwide condemnation of the PLO.

Arafat Renounces Terrorism

Yasir Arafat's solution to the PLO's isolation was to revert to diplomacy. Encouraged by Egyptian president Hosni Mubarak, Arafat made the Cairo Declaration of November 1985, in which he officially condemned "all outside operations other than in Israel and the occupied territories and all forms of terrorism." In line with United Nations Security Council Resolution 3236, the PLO chairman also proclaimed the right of the Palestinian people to resist foreign occupation. The declaration simultaneously drew on UN resolutions that legitimized force in certain circumstances and affirmed support for

a peaceful political process by citing the UN charter on the "inadmissibility of settling disputes by force."

Arafat seemed to be on safe ground by differentiating between terrorism and armed resistance. The difficulty, as always, came in condemning attacks on "the innocent and defenseless wherever they may be," while legitimizing the right of self-defense, which presumably included the right of Palestinians to threaten the safety of Israeli settlers. However, without spelling it out, the Arafat statement clearly drew a distinction between actions in territories occupied by Israel in 1967 and actions against civilians "outside." The problem, of course, was that "outside" meant outside Palestine, and this suggested that such events as the Ma'alot massacre in northern Israel in 1974 were not included in Arafat's condemnation of terrorism.

The Cairo Declaration was a clear attempt by Arafat to distance himself from those members of the PLO who rejected any hint of compromise with Israel and the international community. Such hard-liners bitterly criticized Arafat, claiming that the Cairo Declaration was merely a stunt designed to please the United States. Nevertheless, the declaration was an important step toward peace in the Middle East.

Neil Partrick

```
┌─────────────────────────────────────────┐
│                                         │
│              KEY DATES                   │
│                                         │
│  October 1, 1985  Israeli aircraft attack the headquarters │
│  of the Palestine Liberation Organization in Tunis, Tunisia, │
│  killing fifty persons.                                     │
│  October 7  Four terrorists from the Palestine Liberation  │
│  Front seize the Italian passenger liner the Achille Lauro as it │
│  sails along the Mediterranean coast of Egypt, demanding the │
│  release of fifty Palestinian prisoners held by Israel.     │
│  October 8  The hijackers kill a wheelchair-bound Jewish   │
│  American passenger named Leon Klinghoffer and then toss   │
│  him overboard.                                            │
│  October 10  The hijackers negotiate a safe passage        │
│  off the ship; an Egyptian airliner carrying them to Tunis is │
│  intercepted by U.S. military jets and forced to land at a U.S. │
│  base in Italy.                                            │
│  July 10, 1986  The hijackers are convicted of various    │
│  crimes in Italian courts and are sentenced to fifteen to thirty │
│  years in prison.                                          │
│                                         │
└─────────────────────────────────────────┘
```

KEY DATES

October 1, 1985 Israeli aircraft attack the headquarters of the Palestine Liberation Organization in Tunis, Tunisia, killing fifty persons.

October 7 Four terrorists from the Palestine Liberation Front seize the Italian passenger liner the *Achille Lauro* as it sails along the Mediterranean coast of Egypt, demanding the release of fifty Palestinian prisoners held by Israel.

October 8 The hijackers kill a wheelchair-bound Jewish American passenger named Leon Klinghoffer and then toss him overboard.

October 10 The hijackers negotiate a safe passage off the ship; an Egyptian airliner carrying them to Tunis is intercepted by U.S. military jets and forced to land at a U.S. base in Italy.

July 10, 1986 The hijackers are convicted of various crimes in Italian courts and are sentenced to fifteen to thirty years in prison.

See also: Modern Terrorism—Israeli-Palestinian Conflict. *Tactics, Methods, Aims*—Hijacking.

Further Reading

Hart, Alan. *Arafat: A Political Biography*. Bloomington: Indiana University Press, 1984.

Livingstone, Neil, and David Halevy. *Inside the PLO: Covert Units, Secret Funds, and the War Against Israel and the United States*. New York: William Morrow, 1989.

Rubin, Barry. *From War to Peace: Arab-Israeli Relations, 1973–1993*. New York: New York University Press, 1994.

———. *Revolution Until Victory? The Politics and History of the PLO*. Cambridge, MA: Harvard University Press, 1994.

Palestinian Terrorism: Raids on Kiryat Shmona and Ma'alot, 1974

After the conclusion of the October 1973 Arab-Israeli War, U.S. Secretary of State Henry Kissinger began diplomatic efforts to establish a durable peace in the Middle East. Fatah, which was the leading Palestinian faction, wanted to ensure that the Palestinian Liberation Organization (PLO) would be party to any settlement. At the same time, other, often tiny, Palestinian groups were intent on undermining the peace negotiations and were prepared to carry out terror attacks on Israeli soil to do so.

While major groups such as the Popular Front for the Liberation of Palestine (PFLP) avoided terrorist attacks within Israel because of the risk of Israeli retaliation against their Arab hosts, some of the smaller groups had no such qualms. In 1974, groups opposed to a negotiated peace carried out two devastating and highly charged terrorist operations in Israel.

Kiryat Shmona

The first attack was carried out by the Popular Front for the Liberation of Palestine—General Command (PFLP-GC), which under Ahmad Jibril had split from the PFLP in 1968. On April 11, 1974, the PFLP-GC staged a hostage taking in the northern Israeli border town of Kiryat Shmona. Three members of the group raided a four-story apartment building, bursting into apartments and shooting the occupants. Israeli forces cornered the terrorists, who were finally killed when the explosives they were carrying blew up. The explosives may have been hit by Israeli gunfire, although some sources state that the terrorists detonated the bombs themselves. Altogether, eighteen Israelis, including eight children and five women, died in the attack, and a further sixteen were wounded.

A PFLP-GC spokesman described the operation as an example of "revolutionary violence within Israel that aimed at blocking an Arab-Israeli peace settlement." For the PLO, which was then seeking recognition as the legitimate representative of the Palestinian people in the peace talks, the attack was an embarrassment. Since the PFLP-GC was a member of the Palestine National Council (the Palestinian parliament in exile), the PLO was obliged to recognize the action at Kiryat Shmona as official. Two months later, in an attempt to control a tiny but, by virtue of its methods, influential group, the PLO gave the PFLP-GC a seat on its executive committee.

Ma'alot Massacre

When the Popular Democratic Front for the Liberation of Palestine (PDFLP) took ninety Israeli schoolchildren hostage in Ma'alot in northern Galilee on May 15, 1974, the PLO was once again obliged to give official recognition to an outrage that undermined its political initiatives. The PDFLP, led by Nayef Hawatmeh, was a resolutely left-wing group that believed in international revolution. It had left the PFLP in 1969.

The PDFLP was willing to use terror against Israel, and it was in this light that a three-man team took the Israeli schoolchildren hostage in Ma'alot, a village 5 miles (8 kilometers) from the border with Lebanon. The terrorists demanded the release of twenty-six prisoners, one for each year of Israel's existence. When the terrorists refused to extend a deadline they had set, Israeli soldiers stormed the school. The ensuing firefight resulted in carnage: sixteen children died at once, six were mortally wounded, and a further sixty-five were hit by bullets. Hawatmeh claimed that the raid had been specifically directed against U.S. Secretary of State Henry Kissinger's peace mission.

The PDFLP and the Israelis clashed again, on September 4, when an Israeli patrol thwarted a Palestinian terror squad at the village of Fasuta, 3 miles (5 kilometers) south of the Lebanese border. The terrorists, it seems, aimed to take hostages in order to bargain for the release of Hilarion Capucci, the Greek Catholic archbishop of East Jerusalem, who had been convicted of arms smuggling by the Israelis. On November 19, PDFLP terrorists struck against Israel again, raiding an apartment block in Beit Shean, in the north, killing four before being shot themselves.

Such terrorist activity triggered vigorous Israeli retaliation, especially raids into Lebanon, where most of

KEY DATES

April 11, 1974 Three terrorists of the Popular Front for the Liberation of Palestine—General Command (PFLP-GC) kill eighteen Israelis in the northern border town of Kiryat Shmona, taking others hostage; the terrorists are killed when Israeli security forces storm the apartment building where they are holed up.

May 15, 1974 Three terrorists from the Popular Democratic Front for the Liberation of Palestine (PDFLP) take ninety Israeli schoolchildren hostage in the northern Galilee town of Ma'alot, demanding the release of twenty-six Palestinian prisoners held by Israel; as Israeli security forces storm the school where they are held, the terrorists open fire, killing twenty-two students; the three terrorists are also killed.

the terrorists were based. By 1975, the pressure of Israeli retaliation had pushed Lebanon into civil war and into its own cycle of terrorism.

Neil Partrick

See also: *Modern Terrorism*—Israel: Response to Terrorism; Israeli-Palestinian Conflict; Palestine: Beginning of International Terrorism.

Further Reading

Cobban, Helena. *The Palestine Liberation Organization: People, Power and Politics.* New York: Cambridge University Press, 1983.

Kissinger, Henry. *White House Years.* Boston: Little, Brown, 1979.

Rubin, Barry. *Revolution Until Victory? The Politics and History of the PLO.* Cambridge, MA: Harvard University Press, 1994.

Palestinian-Israeli Conflict
See Israeli-Palestinian Conflict, 1960s–Present

Peru: Shining Path and Leftist Uprisings, 1970s–2000s

Shining Path (Sendero Luminoso) is a left-wing revolutionary movement that began a guerrilla campaign in Peru in 1980. The movement has used terrorism in pursuit of its aim—to overthrow the U.S.-backed government in Peru. Shining Path has a reputation for being the most brutal of the Latin American insurgencies and for making the most effective use of terrorism as part of its strategy.

Background and Origins

Although terrorist opposition had little success in the 1960s, it was obvious that these opposition movements easily gained popular support. The bulk of the population, mainly native Indians, were desperately poor, with negligible basic services such as education and health care. General Juan Velazco Alvarado, who came to power after a left-wing military coup in 1968, recognized their plight. He introduced land reform and made efforts to improve social welfare. If these policies had been developed, Shining Path would have gained less support. However, opposition from the wealthy landowners, combined with inflation at a time of world recession, meant that Velazco achieved little. At the start of the 1970s, several lecturers at the National University of San Cristóbal de Huamanga, in Ayacucho, a poor part of the southern Andes, founded what was to become a leading force in the communist revolution in Peru. Led by Abimael Guzmán Reynoso, the group, Shining Path,

based its ideology on Marxist theory. It believed that an armed struggle combined with the political education of Peru's peasantry and urban working class was the only way to achieve significant economic change in the country.

Guzmán and his like-minded colleagues, the intellectual nucleus of Shining Path, began operations by conducting a series of Marxist study groups at local universities. Guzmán believed that a transition to industrial capitalism in Peru could not involve an uprising of the capitalist class and its artisan and proletarian allies against the old regime, because they were too small and politically weak. However, its vast and land-hungry peasant class might join a revolution against the prevailing economic order. The challenge was how to meld these potentially revolutionary classes into a cohesive, progressive political force. In 1980, the military organized elections in order to hand over power to a civilian government. At the same time, Shining Path had emerged as a terrorist organization. Based chiefly in the province of Ayacucho, to the southeast of the capital, Lima, Shining Path gained support among the Indians, whose social deprivation had worsened in the late 1970s. Guzmán deliberately timed the beginning of Shining Path's terrorist operations to coincide with the 1980 elections, in an effort to undermine the new democracy. Peruvian intelligence failed to recognize the scale of the unrest, and the action took the government completely by surprise.

Children in a slum of Lima, Peru, rest near their school building, painted with propaganda slogans of the Shining Path leftist guerrilla movement. Shining Path's terrorist campaign since the 1980s has been called the deadliest in the Western Hemisphere. (Hector Mata/AFP/ Getty Images)

Revolution Through Education

To facilitate a successful uprising, Shining Path activists concentrated on educating the local peasantry and the urban working class in Marxist theory and armed struggle. Political education was needed because the peasantry did not yet appreciate how their economic interests converged and why the current economic order needed to be overthrown. Armed struggle was necessary, according to Shining Path, because Peru's landowning class, foreign investors, and government bureaucrats would never give up their wealth and political privileges without a bitter fight.

In 1979, Shining Path's national leadership established a school to train interested activists in guerrilla tactics and Marxist ideology. Some leaders dissented, arguing that guerrilla warfare would lead to repression and the movement's demise, and several of them were expelled by the advocates of military confrontation.

First Armed Action

On the eve of the 1980 presidential election, Shining Path carried out its first notable act of terrorism, though it was inauspicious compared to the violence that was to unfold over the following years. A few masked activists with malfunctioning pistols broke into an election office in the remote mountain town of Chuschi, then burned unmarked ballots and unused ballot boxes in a public plaza. The next day, the ballots were replaced and the election continued. By the end of 1980, however, between 300 and 400 violent "actions" had been committed by Shining Path members, including the destruction of local tax records, the bombing of administration offices, and the sabotage of power lines.

In 1981, Shining Path guerrillas began to appear regularly in remote villages in the southern Andes and gained popular support, partly by enforcing village laws and standards of behavior. The guerrillas caught and punished cattle rustlers, unfaithful husbands, and owners of small stores who were suspected of swindling costumers. They also stalked, verbally humiliated, whipped, and on occasion executed local government officials who were reputed to have abused their authority.

On the other hand, the guerrillas often antagonized villagers by imposing radical changes. Some guerrilla teams, for example, collectivized land, organized communal planting and harvesting, and prohibited peasants from selling produce at markets. Peasants seldom welcomed the revolutionaries' zealotry. Many peasants treasured their small, individualized plots, and many relied on cash crops to buy salt, matches, and other inexpensive comforts. Sometimes, if the guerrillas persisted in their attempts to reorder village life, peasants rebelled by stoning known guerrillas, turning them over to the police, or asking the police to build local stations.

Guerrillas Gathering Rural Support

In 1982 and 1983, the guerrillas entered remote localities in Peru's southern tip and central mountains, where they established "people's committees" (akin to democratic town meetings). The guerrillas organized popular land invasions, seized and redistributed cattle from haciendas, sabotaged machinery and pipelines, and ambushed police. In March 1982, around 150 guerrillas attacked a prison at Ayacucho, freeing 250 prisoners. Fourteen people died during the attack, and a thirty-day state of emergency for Ayacucho followed.

Having previously dismissed reports about Shining Path guerrillas as exaggerations about isolated criminals, the government dispatched a counterinsurgency force known as the Sinchis. Indiscriminate violence by the Sinchis prompted outcries from human rights organizations. Shining Path argued that the government was committing genocide against destitute Indians, and the movement escalated its attacks on the police, soldiers, and politicians. In one confrontation on August 22, 1982, 200 guerrillas engaged security forces in a five-hour gun battle in Vilcashumán, 75 miles (121 kilometers) south of Ayacucho.

Combating the Terrorists

During the early 1980s, the government set up the Directorate of Counter Terrorism to gather intelligence. Some army commanders copied Shining Path tactics by using Indian languages to appeal directly to the people. For example, General Adrián Huamán, a Quechua-speaking Indian, used this strategy in Ayacucho in 1984. However, this was the exception rather than the rule.

As Shining Path activities increased, Fernando Belaúnde, who had been elected president in 1980, allowed the military to operate in "emergency zones." There they used ruthless methods against the local populace, whether terrorist sympathizers or not. In November 1983, for example, thirty-one people were massacred at a wedding on the day of the municipal elections in the village of Soccos, 20 miles (32 kilometers) east of Ayacucho. The police alleged that guerrillas had been responsible for the slaughter, but in February of the following year, a judge in Ayacucho ordered the arrest of twenty-seven members of the civil guard on charges of murder. Stories of massacres and of suspects "disappearing" while in army detention served only to increase popular support for the terrorists.

Community Control and Protection

During the 1980s, many hundreds of peasants were killed as a result of government or Shining Path violence. Both sides denied responsibility for the majority of deaths. The police encouraged the peasants to form self-defense groups, or *rondas,* and brutally punished them if they resisted this encouragement. The *rondas* brought about their own problems, stirring up old hatreds within the communities. Internal fights broke out, threatening the guerrillas' control of the villages.

In response, the guerrillas killed scores of villagers each year. For example, in 1983, the guerrillas attacked two villages in Ayacucho, axing and shooting to death about eighty so-called traitor peasants, who tried to defend themselves with stones. The following year, they attacked a number of towns in the Ayacucho region, killing twenty-five citizens. At the same time, Shining Path guerrillas protected the small farmers in the eastern jungles of Peru, who cultivated coco plants and sold the leaves to cocaine producers in Bolivia. Shining Path guerrillas fought Bolivian toughs who tried to threaten farmers into selling coca leaves at below-market prices.

Shining Path activists also provided an impressive array of public services. They organized vigilante committees to control prostitution and drinking, coordinated litter cleanups, created local representative governments, and even supervised wedding ceremonies. In exchange, Shining Path took a share of the coca revenues to finance operations.

Power Behind Bars

By the mid-1980s, the armed forces believed they had defeated Shining Path, but Guzmán had various other targets up his sleeve, including the presidential election campaign of 1985, won by Alan García of the American Popular Revolutionary Alliance (ARPA). Shining Path guerrillas boycotted and sabotaged the election wherever they had the power to do so, virtually obliterating the polls altogether in some areas, including Ayacucho. A wave of car bombings, assassinations, and jail riots by Shining Path prisoners followed.

In 1985, Shining Path prisoners were granted special privileges and allowed to administer their own cell blocks. In October of that year, the Shining Path militants in Lurigancho jail set fire to their cell block, tying up and burning alive anyone who refused to participate in the riot. According to the prison authorities, around thirty inmates died, although no public investigation was carried out.

In 1986, Shining Path turned to Lima, bombing restaurants, shopping malls, government offices, and banks in the capital, and assassinating members of the police force. The group found an ally in a metropolitan labor newspaper, *El Diario,* which published favorable editorials about Shining Path. The guerrilla units in Lima also killed civilians, including the feminist and community organizer María Elena Moyano, who had urged less violent Shining Path members to end the terrorism.

New Government, Old Policies

President Alan García inherited this situation when he was elected in 1985. There was hope of reform, but the government soon found its policies frustrated by landowners and by the failing economy. Social welfare reform was too expensive to implement, thus denying the government a political weapon to combat terrorist subversion. A military solution seemed the only option. In May 1988, a military unit attacked the village of Cayara, in Ayacucho Province, in apparent retaliation for a Shining Path ambush. Most of the civilian population was massacred. At the same time, U.S. agencies became involved, providing training and equipment in an antidrug initiative throughout Latin America. The resultant destruction of coca plantations spelled ruin for the local peasants, who turned increasingly to Shining Path.

In 1986, more than 200 rebel prisoners were killed after they had organized mutinies in three separate prisons. Eventually Lima came under attack. A favorite Shining Path ploy was to blow up power lines, plunging the city into chaos. García declared a state of emergency, which allowed security forces to detain suspects and intensify repression. In June 1990, police raided six Shining Path safe houses in Lima, arresting 35 alleged guerrillas and seizing the plans for past and future missions and the identity cards of 176 rebels.

Militant Force in Action

While the group made its presence known in Lima, the power of Shining Path activists in Lurigancho, El Frontón, and Santa Barbara prisons, who were taking prison guards hostage until their demands were met, was making greater demands on the prison authorities. The armed forces, entrusted with the task of restoring order, conducted one of the biggest massacres in Peru. Around 120 prisoners were slaughtered, and hardly any of them were identified. The prison massacres immediately increased support for Shining Path.

As the 1980s drew to a close, Shining Path's capacity to take on the armed forces, not only in ambush but also in pitched battles, began to emerge. In July 1989, hundreds of guerrillas attacked the Madre Mía army barracks and, according to Shining Path, killed thirty-nine soldiers. Also in 1989, the group used its militant force to devastate the municipal elections in many areas of the Andes. The guerrillas assassinated around 60 mayors and mayoral candidates in the run-up to the municipal elections, and around 500 municipal candidates resigned in fear. Almost 60 percent of registered voters either destroyed their ballot papers or were absent on election day. In Ayacucho alone, absenteeism was around 85 percent.

In the run-up to the 1990 general elections, Shining Path launched a campaign of car bombings and industrial sabotage, assassinating several congressional candidates. The campaign had its desired impact: 35 percent of ballot papers were destroyed or left blank.

By 1991, between 3,000 and 5,000 armed Shining Path militants made up a sophisticated and highly organized network of support bases and battalions in the jungle areas along the east of the Andes and in the valley of the Erne River. Shining Path guerrillas were the dominating political force in 40 percent of Peru.

Meanwhile, around 400 rebel captives were being held at the high-security jail in Canto Grande, and once again Shining Path inmates had complete control of their cell blocks, including the keys. In prison, they held Sunday parades, performed plays, organized lectures for visitors, and even sold souvenirs to raise funds for the movement.

Mission Crushed by Massacre

Shining Path's guerrilla activity remained intensive in rural territory in the early 1990s. Another prime target for the group was the Cutivireni mission, the communal quarters of the Asháninkas. This Indian group—one of the largest remaining in the Peruvian Amazon—strongly resisted Shining Path's demands for recruits to their cause. In November 1989, sixty guerrillas armed with submachine guns and assault rifles pillaged and burned the mission, then shot three of the Indian mission leaders. One of them was the head schoolteacher, whom the guerrillas crucified, castrated, and disemboweled. Three months later, in February 1990, Shining Path massacred fifteen of the mission Indians in their camps. Although the Asháninkas retaliated with their own attacks, killing several Shining Path members, the guerrillas soon gained control over the mission, and their attacks on the Indian community continued. In August 1993, in several villages outside Satipo, 185 miles (298 kilometers) east of Lima, the guerrillas massacred fifty-five people. Many victims were mutilated beyond recognition— fourteen of them children.

Debate over Abandoning Violence

During the early 1990s, many Shining Path members argued over the continued use of violence against civilians. In 1992, the Peruvian president Alberto Fujimori declared himself a temporary dictator. Congress had been alarmed by Fujimori's election in 1990 and blocked his reforms. The president responded by suspending Congress and assuming special powers. He introduced counterinsurgency measures that included a penal code making it easier to convict terrorists. His Repentance Law allowed active insurgents to become government witnesses without fear of prosecution, which helped bring about the capture of Guzmán.

In September 1992, following an intelligence breakthrough, forces from the Directorate of Counter Terrorism raided a Shining Path safe house in the suburbs of Lima. They captured Guzmán with most of his command staff, as well as Shining Path archive material. Masked security forces exhibited Guzmán in a cage before he was prosecuted, found guilty of treason, and sentenced to life imprisonment.

Fujimori boasted that his strong leadership had defeated Shining Path terrorists. Shortly afterward, a wave of car bombings in Lima's wealthiest neighborhoods revealed that several guerrilla units remained intact. Pro–Shining Path banners in labor and neighborhood marches also indicated that some nonguerrilla cells were alive and well.

In 1993, from his prison cell, Guzmán urged Shining Path activists to abandon the armed struggle. Several subgroups ignored his instructions; others questioned more strongly than ever the wisdom of a guerrilla strategy. Nevertheless, the bombings and shootings continued through the 1990s.

A Diminishing Force

Unlike the violent years of the 1980s and early 1990s, the late 1990s and early 2000s saw a marked decline in the level of terrorist activity in Peru. By the mid-1990s, powerful leftist terrorist organizations had been largely defeated, and a relative level of calm returned to the country. Yet, during the period 1997–2002, terrorist activities continued in Peru. For example, in November 2001, Peruvian authorities captured two operatives of Shining Path who were involved in a planned attack on the U.S. embassy in Lima. Moreover, certain guerrilla groups attempted to regain the positions they had held in earlier decades, a goal that they tried to achieve through increased terrorist activities.

Ideologically nebulous, the current incarnation of Shining Path is much more involved in the drug trade than was its progenitor in the 1990s, especially in the cultivation of the highly lucrative poppy crop. Some analysts suspect that Colombian drug traffickers are supplying the group with poppy seeds and extending it financial credit in addition to supplying weapons. Shining Path is believed to have roughly 400 loyal fighters, and the group has increased its activities since the end of Alberto Fujimori's regime in 2000. In early December 2001, Shining Path attacked an army barracks in the jungle area of Nuevo Progreso. The Peruvian Army responded by announcing that it would open 100 new rural outposts. In March 2002, only days before President George W. Bush was scheduled to arrive for a meeting with Peruvian president Alejandro Toledo, a bomb exploded near the U.S. embassy in Lima, killing nine people. Many observers suspected that Shining Path was responsible.

For most of the 1980s and 1990s, the Tupac Amaru Revolutionary Movement (MRTA) was the second-largest guerrilla group in Peru, although it was significantly less threatening than Shining Path. In December 1996, fourteen MRTA guerrillas led by Nestor Cerpa Cartolini stormed a reception at the Japanese ambassador's residence in Lima and held seventy-three hostages for more than four months. The crisis ended in April 1997, when Peruvian president Alberto Fujimori ordered 140 elite troops to storm the compound. During the forty-minute operation, two government soldiers were killed while rescuing all of the hostages (one hostage later died of a heart attack). All of the MRTA gunmen were killed. The raid signaled the effective end of MRTA as a credible guerrilla threat in Peru.

Berenson Case

In February 2002, Peru's Supreme Court rejected an appeal by American Lori Berenson against her conviction for terrorism. Berenson had been arrested in late 1995, and a military tribunal ordered a life sentence for her activities with the MRTA. Berenson's conviction was overturned in 2000, and she was granted a new civilian trial. The civilian court also found Berenson guilty, but this time she received a twenty-year sentence. Berenson refused to serve out her sentence in a U.S. jail because she claimed to be innocent. After serving fifteen years, she was finally granted parole in 2010 but required to stay in Peru for another five years.

Fujimori Legacy

An important corollary to the terrorism issue in Peru occurred in early July 1999, when President Fujimori announced that Peru was withdrawing from the Inter-American Court of Human Rights. Fujimori made this decision after the court ruled that Peru needed to grant a new civilian trial to four Chilean MRTA members. This decision rekindled the controversy over the military tribunal system that Fujimori set up in the early 1990s in order to try convicted terrorists from Shining Path and MRTA. The Fujimori Administration implemented a "faceless-judges" system that shielded judges from the accused in order to protect the judiciary from reprisals for convicting terrorists. Although the faceless-judges system succeeded in reducing the number of judges who were targeted for retribution, its imperfections led to estimates that up to one-quarter of those convicted were in fact innocent. The Peruvian government responded to the mounting criticism by releasing thousands of people falsely convicted on terrorism charges. Many supposedly innocent citizens, however, remain in jail.

For most of the 1990s, Vladimiro Montesinos, President Alberto Fujimori's shady intelligence chief, was a reliable ally in the American-supported antidrug efforts in Peru. On June 23, 2001, a joint Peruvian-U.S. operation arrested Montesinos, who had fled Peru eight months earlier, in Venezuela. Montesinos was taken to

---

KEY DATES

Late 1970s Shining Path emerges as a revolutionary movement.

March 1982 Shining Path guerrillas lead an assault on a prison in Ayacucho, freeing 250.

1986 Shining Path terrorists unleash a bombing attack on civilian targets in Lima.

1990 In the run-up to the national elections, Shining Path launches a campaign of car bombings and industrial sabotage.

September 1992 Peruvian security forces capture Shining Path founder Abimael Guzmán and other leaders at a safe house in Lima.

December 1996 Guerrillas from the Tupac Amaru Revolutionary Movement seize the Japanese ambassador's residence in Lima, where a reception is being held, holding seventy-three hostages for more than four months.

April 1997 After a four-month standoff, 140 elite Peruvian troops storm the residence; 2 soldiers and all 14 guerrillas are killed; all hostages are led out safely, though one dies later of heart attack as a result of the operation.

Late 1990s Peruvian security forces decimate the Shining Path movement, killing or capturing many of its members and leaders.

November 2001 Peruvian authorities capture two Shining Path operatives.

February 2002 The Peruvian Supreme Court rejects an appeal by U.S. national Lori Berenson, convicted of aiding Tupac Amaru Revolutionary Movement guerrillas in terrorist activities. She remains in jail until 2010.

---

a high-security prison in Lima, a facility that he helped design in order to hold prisoners from Shining Path. Montesinos is thought to be the mastermind of up to 30,000 secretly recorded videotapes that show politicians and other public figures receiving bribes or engaging in other illicit activities. Montesinos used the tapes as blackmail. Nine hundred persons have already been identified on videotapes as accepting bribes. Montesinos is also suspected of selling weapons to the Revolutionary Armed Forces of Colombia, an insurgent group that the Colombian government now considers a terrorist organization. From behind bars, Montesinos continues to enjoy strong ties to certain elements of the Peruvian armed forces and government intelligence services. Observers have not ruled out the possibility that Montesinos would resort to terrorist activities in order to intimidate his opponents into not prosecuting him.

By 2003, Shining Path had seen its numbers lessen significantly, though a militant faction named Proseguir (Onward) continued to perpetrate terrorist attacks, including the kidnapping of sixty-eight employees of an Argentinean mining company in Ayacucho. Such actions led to further arrests of Shining Path militants and continued raids on the organization's bases and safe houses. Through the rest of the 2000s, Proseguir terrorists continued their sporadic attacks, largely against military targets, including the ambush and killing of thirteen government troops near the city of Ayacucho in April 2009 and the killing of a police officer and two civilians in the coca fields near Huanuco. Indeed, as in Colombia, these left-wing terrorists were believed to be increasing their involvement in the cocaine trade and using the proceeds to fund their activities. Still, most experts believed that the remnants of Shining Path had largely been neutralized by 2010, though they were clearly capable of launching occasional attacks.

Russell Crandall, John Pimlott, and Bertrande Roberts

See also: *Definitions, Types, Categories*—Ethnonationalist Terrorism; Left-Wing and Revolutionary Terrorism.

Further Reading

Bland, Gary, and Joseph S. Tulchin, eds. *Peru in Crisis: Dictatorship or Democracy?* Boulder, CO: Lynne Rienner, 1994.

Gorman, Stephen M., ed. *Post-Revolutionary Peru: The Politics of Transformation.* Boulder, CO: Westview, 1982.

Koppel, Martin. *Peru's Shining Path: Autonomy of a Reactionary Sect.* New York: Pathfinder, 1993.

McClintock, Cynthia. *Revolutionary Movements in Latin America: El Salvador's FMLN and Peru's Shining Path.* Washington, DC: United States Institute of Peace Press, 1998.

McGormick, Gordon H. *The Shining Path and the Future of Peru.* Santa Monica, CA: Rand Corporation, 1990.

Palmer, David Scott. *The Shining Path of Peru.* New York: St. Martin's, 1994.

Strong, Simon. *Shining Path: Terror and Revolution in Peru.* New York: Times Books, 1992.

Philippines: Marxist and Islamist Struggles, 1940s–2000s

As difficult as it is to distinguish between terrorism and revolution, in the Philippines it has been difficult to distinguish between terrorism and politics as usual. Politics in the Philippines goes beyond corruption. Political violence—including not only targeted assassinations, but also random acts of violence and bombings targeting innocent civilians—has become routine in the Philippines. It was not uncommon for as many as several hundred political murders, including innocent civilians, to occur within a single election season.

Background

From its very beginning, the Philippines has been a country divided. A complex archipelago with rugged mountains and thick rain forests divided the people into a multitude of tribes and linguistic groups. This isolation continued even as Hispanic culture permeated the northern and central islands, and Islamic culture established itself in the south. The Filipino revolutionary tradition began in the late nineteenth century against Spanish colonial rule and the Filipinos had all but won independence from Spain when the United States took the country as a spoil of the Spanish-American War. From 1899 to 1902, the United States conducted a bloody campaign against a Filipino guerrilla army, led by Emilio Aguinaldo, that left more than 200,000 dead, including 5,000 American troops. Notably, given the late twentieth- and early twenty-first-century struggles between the Filipino government and Muslim rebels in the south, Muslim Filipinos, or Moros, were the last to surrender to U.S. forces, fighting on until 1906.

International violence came to the Philippines with the Japanese invasion and occupation during World War II. The war left the Philippines devastated and disorganized, with a "military gun culture" and several disenfranchised guerrilla groups. During the "Japanese time," guerrillas, who were dependent on the goodwill of the rural population, became the heroes, and the invading Japanese, the terrorists. If terrorism was not a part of everyday life in the Philippines before the war, it certainly was afterward. As the Philippines gained a U.S.-supervised independence, those guerrillas that did not accept the new U.S.-sponsored government went to "the mountains" or into hiding.

The well-known Huk revolution of the 1940s and 1950s had its roots in the isolated peasant revolts of the 1920s and 1930s. Huks were less Marxist ideologues than peasants who just wanted to return to the days when the landlords were more attentive to their needs. The plight of the peasants did not change and could only worsen as the population increased and the available farmland diminished. Neither the government nor the revolution served the peasants. As time went on, the Huks grew weary, and, no longer able to sustain the uphill fight against government military operations and promised reforms, they turned increasingly to crime, reaping considerable profits from the illicit activities around the U.S. military bases.

By the late 1960s, Ferdinand E. Marcos had so corrupted the political system that several insurgency movements emerged to pose serious threats to the nation's stability. These movements can be classified into two major groups: the communists and the Muslims. The principal communist (Maoist) movement, the New People's Army (NPA), grew out of the old Huk movement in Central Luzon in 1969. In 1972, Marcos declared martial law and dismantled all of the instruments for legitimate protest. Many within the noncommunist, nationalist opposition had no other option but to go underground and join the revolution. Marcos, with his increasingly corrupt military, spurred NPA recruitment. For its first seventeen years, the NPA showed steady growth. It seemed that its operations were limited only by its lack of heavy weapons.

A classic act of political terrorism during the Marcos era was the Plaza Miranda incident. On August 21, 1971, two grenades exploded during the opposition party convention, killing 9 and wounding more than 100. Marcos used the bombing as an opportunity to conduct a dress rehearsal for his declaration of martial law thirteen months later. He suspended the writ of habeas corpus and had the military "round up the usual suspects." Although Marcos blamed the communists, a more commonly accepted hypothesis holds Marcos responsible. In either case, he did manage to use the event to his best political advantage.

The beginning of the end for Marcos came twelve years to the day after Plaza Miranda on August 21, 1983. The principal political threat to the Marcos regime, Ninoy Aquino, was assassinated by government troops as he deplaned at Manila International Airport. As Marcos continued to lose his grip on power, he became increasingly desperate and violent. Not only were political opponents targets of violence, but their families, friends, and poll workers were also marked for assassination. Marcos had no peer in the application of terrorism as politics. The Marcos regime ended in February 1986 with the "people's power"

Local officials in a town near Manila, the Philippines, examine a homemade flag of the Hukbalahaps (or "Huks"), a communist peasant insurgency who fought against Japanese occupiers during World War II and the Philippine government from 1946 to 1954. *(Associated Press)*

revolution, which was inspired by Marcos's blatant attempt to steal the presidential election. His replacement as president was Ninoy Aquino's widow, Corazon Aquino. There were fewer casualties in the revolution than there were in the election just weeks earlier.

Whereas the church and the middle class were instrumental in the election and Marcos's downfall, the communist movement decided to boycott the election and thereby missed the revolution. With Marcos out as the major recruitment vehicle, the NPA began to decline. Not only did its numbers decline, but also its territorial control was diminished as a result of more effective military operations. Whatever support the NPA enjoyed from its communist sponsors ended with the Cold War. Some members have remained in the mountains, enjoying pockets of support in small rural areas. They were occasionally credited with a murder or a bombing—including the off-base murders of U.S. servicemen and several bombings in metro Manila in the late 1980s. However, except for the possibility of a brutal invasion or the emergence of another ruthless dictator, such groups will have difficulty recruiting sufficient numbers to pose a significant threat to the government. The NPA did, however, pose a threat for a time to the economy as kidnappers, usually targeting

Chinese businessmen for profit. However, the kidnappings eventually dwindled as countermeasures became more effective.

Although no longer threatened by the communists, Corazon Aquino's administration was plagued by a series of attempted coups by the politicized military and former Marcos supporters who assumed they would receive U.S. support. This coup threat was all but eliminated when former general Fidel V. Ramos assumed the presidency in 1992. With the government secure in Manila, the Ramos administration was able to focus more of its attention on the Muslim conflict in the south. In the years since, the leftist guerrilla threat has remained a small but stubborn irritant. After peace talks between the government and the NPA failed in 2004 and again in 2008, the two sides engaged in occasional firefights. In March 2010, for example, NPA rebels slew eleven soldiers on the island of Mindoro.

Islamist Challenges

The longest ongoing conflict in the Philippines is the struggle for Muslim autonomy in the south. The conflict between the cultures subsided somewhat through the American colonial policy of guaranteeing the Muslims equal representation in national affairs. This policy continued under the 1935 constitution, based on the U.S. model. This relative peace was broken in the early 1970s when Marcos instituted a land-reform program, which relocated Christians from the north to the south. The terror inflicted in this religious conflict resulted in tens of thousands of deaths and millions of displaced refugees. Innocent men, women, and children became casualties as massacres and bombs tore through both churches and mosques.

However, the Muslims have not presented a unified voice. There were several different Muslim organizations that differed in their methods, objectives, and philosophies. While neither compromise nor appeasement could satisfy all the movements, some offered political possibilities. Nevertheless, in September 1996, Ramos concluded an agreement with the Moro National Liberation Front, ending the major insurgency. The largest remaining group, the Moro Islamic Liberation Front (MILF), was estimated to have a strength of more than 12,500 and had been credited with several attacks and bombings as they continued their fight for an autonomous region.

Meanwhile, despite continuing attacks by MILF guerrillas, including an assault on Mindanao that left thirty dead in February 2003, the government signed a cease-fire with the rebel movement in July, with formal peace talks planned for later in the year in Malaysia. But the talks yielded little progress, with both sides claiming the other was not negotiating in good faith. In January 2005, the year-and-a-half cease-fire collapsed, as the two sides engaged in some of the heaviest fighting of the war. The fighting, however, seemed to pave the way for a breakthrough, as the government agreed with MILF on the contentious issue of what territories would constitute a Muslim autonomous region in the south. Between April 2005 and July 2008, the two sides worked out a deal for expanding the Muslim autonomous area in the Jolo Islands, Basilan, and western Mindanao. When Christian communities in the region protested, however, the government began to back out, as new fighting on Mindanao left more than thirty people dead. This marked the beginning of a concerted military campaign against MILF that resulted in the capture of MILF leader Camarudin Hadji Ali in September 2009 and the resumption of talks in December. In March 2010, international monitors arrived in Mindanao to oversee peace talks between the government and MILF leaders. As of late 2010, no major breakthroughs had occurred in resolving the long-running dispute, though there was little fighting between MILF militants and Filipino security forces.

While MILF seeks an autonomous Muslim region in the south, others have wanted to establish an independent Muslim state there. A smaller, more radical spin-off of MILF was Abu Sayyaf, a Philippine veteran of the Afghan-Soviet war who met Osama bin Laden, and others, Abu Sayyaf grew to a top strength of more than 1,200. It became a significant political force in 1995 with the massacre of more than fifty civilians in a raid on a Christian town. With the death of Janjalani in a firefight in 1998, the group split, with one faction on Jolo Island and the other on Basilan Island. For the most part, Abu Sayyaf conducted conventional raids, bombings, and kidnappings. However, in April 2000 the Jolo group literally crossed the line when they raided a Malaysian resort and took more than twenty hostages—nineteen of whom were foreign tourists. Acting as interlocutor, Libya's Muammar Gadhafi paid several million dollars for the hostages' release. Abu Sayyaf spent the ransom on modern weapons and recruitment efforts. In June 2001, the Basilan faction snatched twenty captives, including three Americans, from a Philippine beach resort. One of

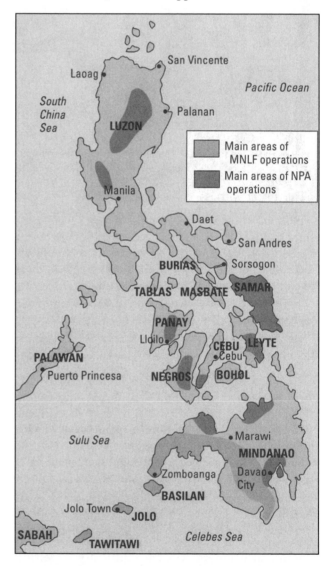

In the Philippines during the 1960s and 1970s, the New People's Army operated mainly out of the islands of Luzon, Mindanao, Samar, and Negros.

the Americans was beheaded, and most of the Filipinos were released upon the payment of ransom. Even after the terrorist attacks in the United States on September 11, 2001, they continued to hold three hostages, including two American missionaries. Meanwhile, terrorist attacks by Muslim separatists in the south continued through 2002. In October, two bombings at department stores in the city of Zamboanga left 7 dead and more than 150 injured. Filipinos quickly arrested members of Abu Sayyaf as suspects.

The kidnappings and bombings raised a serious question as to the motives of Abu Sayyaf. On the surface, they appeared to be more thugs than revolutionaries. Kidnappings and beheadings are too radical or un-Islamic for the larger Islamic groups in the Philippines, and, although there were rumored financial linkages, including alleged transfers of money from Osama bin Laden to MILF in the late 1990s and early 2000s, their links to al-Qaeda were questionable. It was not until March 2002 that they linked their hostage ransom demands to al-Qaeda objectives. For its part, MILF denies any direct connections with al-Qaeda, even while it sent more than 500 guerrillas to al-Qaeda camps in Afghanistan for training prior to the U.S. invasion of that country in October 2001. MILF also denies ties with the Indonesia-based Islamist terrorist group Jemaah Islamiyah (JI), though experts say JI has trained some MILF guerrillas. The connections between JI and Abu Sayyaf, on the other hand, are stronger, as numerous government raids on the latter's bases have uncovered evidence of links, including the presence of JI liaisons and trainers.

Abu Sayyaf has also proven to be a much more hardened foe than MILF. Thus, even as MILF guerrilla fighting in the south of the country died down after the middle years of the 2000s, the government's struggle with Abu Sayyaf intensified. In February 2004, Abu Sayyaf planted a bomb that destroyed a ferry in Manila Bay, killing 116 persons in the worst terrorist attack in Filipino history and the world's deadliest seagoing terrorist attack of modern times. The government responded with a major offensive against Abu Sayyaf bases in the south. In late 2005, dozens of persons were killed in fighting between government troops and Abu Sayyaf militants on the southern island Jolo. The next year, troops reportedly killed leader Janjalani, though it took until January 2007 for tests to confirm that the recovered body was his. Three months later, the government launched a major offensive against Abu Sayyaf on Jolo after the group beheaded seven of the Christian hostages it had seized earlier. Among the successes of the offensive, as well as efforts by security forces in other parts of the Philippines, were the arrest of Abu Sayyaf co-founder Abdul Basir Latip in December 2009; and, in February 2010, the capture of Mujibar Alih Amon, ringleader of the Malaysian kidnapping raid of 2000 and the killing

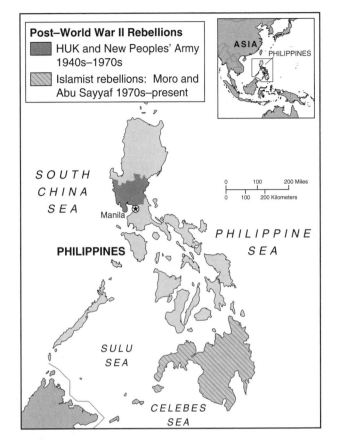

The Philippines, torn by the leftist uprisings from World War II to the 1970s, has been challenged more recently by Islamist separatists in the south. Since September 11, 2001, the country has received U.S. support in its war against Abu Sayyaf militants.

of Christian missionaries in 2001; and the killing of Abu Sayyaf military commander Albader Parad, who was on the top of the Filipino government's most-wanted-terrorist list. Despite such losses, Abu Sayyaf demonstrated its resiliency by conducting a raid on Basilan Island that left 11 civilians dead. Experts suspect it was in revenge for the killing of Parad.

U.S. Involvement

The global U.S. war on terrorism, according to many analysts, has caused problems with nationalists in the third world. The Bush doctrine that "any nation that continues to harbor terrorism will be regarded by the United States as a hostile regime" does not allow for nationalist sensitivities over sovereign neutrality. The next phase in the U.S. war on terrorism after Afghanistan was to support the Philippines in its hunt for Muslim rebels. In early 2002, an operation got under way that stretched the limits of the Philippine Constitution and the U.S.-Philippine Visiting Forces Agreement. U.S. Special Forces were sent to train the elite Philippine Scout Rangers on Basilan Island. Concluding on July

31 after its six-month mandate was up, this operation, say experts, achieved no clear results. Although Washington called it an advisory mission, the Filipinos called it a training exercise for constitutional reasons. Since the Philippine Constitution and the Visiting Forces Agreement do not allow foreign troops to engage in combat on Philippine soil, authorities assert that such U.S. operations do not constitute combat; rather, they are "counterterrorism" activities. This legal finesse may become a model for other nations such as Indonesia and Malaysia, who may want U.S. assistance but face similar domestic resistance.

Although there are some pockets of protest and political posturing and restrictions have been placed on U.S. operations, the general reaction to the U.S. involvement has been favorable. Philippine president Arroyo pledged the full cooperation of her administration. The fact that the Bush Administration promised $100 million in security assistance in 2002 provided considerable political cover. On the other hand, operations were encumbered by legal restrictions, and it is entirely possible that corruption within the Philippine military has allowed the Abu Sayyaf leadership to avoid capture. The hostage situation was resolved in June 2002 by U.S.-trained Filipino troops, with one U.S. hostage dead and another injured. Nonetheless, Abu Sayyaf remained a force, and in June 2002, U.S. Deputy Defense Secretary Paul Wolfowitz suggested that the U.S. contingent might remain in the Philippines indefinitely. Indeed, it remained there as of 2010, with a number of successes to its credit. In the years since 2002, the U.S. government has claimed that its assistance helped destroy 80 percent of Abu Sayyaf's military capacity on Basilan, and almost entirely eliminated the presence of JI militants there.

Yet analysts wonder whether the effort has been worth the danger of intensifying anti-American feelings in the area. A few kidnappers confined to a southern island, they say, could hardly be considered a serious threat to U.S. national interests; a more serious terrorism threat was establishing itself in Manila in the early 2000s. The threat itself was not just to the Philippines, but rather to the whole of Southeast Asia.

As an open society with a significant Muslim minority and a tradition of corruption, smuggling, and violence, the Philippines present an attractive haven for al-Qaeda groups, with cells throughout the region. Because of its long-standing relationship with the United States, the Philippines also offers a target-rich environment for those wishing to target U.S. interests. Furthermore, the Philippines has been a supply source and main transit point for weapons, explosives, and monetary support for terrorist groups.

In the mid-1990s, Manila hosted a veritable rogues' gallery of terrorists: Osama bin Laden's brother-in-law Mohammed Jamal Khalifa, who opened bank accounts

---

KEY DATES

September 1996   President Fidel Ramos concludes an agreement with the Moro National Liberation Front, an Islamic-nationalist guerrilla organization, ending its insurgency.

April 2000   The Jolo Island faction of the Islamic militant group Abu Sayyaf kidnaps twenty hostages at a Malaysian resort; the hostages are released after Libya's Muammar Gadhafi pays several million dollars in ransom.

June 2001   The Basilan Island faction of Abu Sayyaf kidnaps twenty hostages—including three Americans—from a Philippines beach resort; one of the Americans is beheaded.

January 2002   U.S. advisers join Filipino forces in attacks against Abu Sayyaf.

October 2002   Bombings in the southern city of Zamboanga leave seven dead; Abu Sayyaf members are arrested in connection with the attacks.

---

used to channel support to several Islamic terrorist activities; Abdul Hakim Murad, who was arrested in 1995 for plotting to kill Pope John Paul II and for planning, with roommate Ramzi Yousef, to blow up twelve U.S. airliners in one day; and Ramzi Yousef, who had his own claim to fame as the mastermind of the 1993 World Trade Center bombing. In 1995, Philippine intelligence uncovered a plot to fly a plane into U.S. Central Intelligence Agency Headquarters.

Of major regional concern was JI, a growing al-Qaeda–linked group with cells in Indonesia, Malaysia, and Singapore, as well as the Philippines; it seeks to create an Islamic state in the South China Sea. JI has been plotting strikes all over the region. Some of its members were caught in Singapore in 2001. In November 2001, Philippine police arrested a Jordanian and two Palestinians found to have explosives and false documents.

The U.S. war on terrorism requires international cooperation not only between governments and intelligence agencies, but also among the indigenous peoples. U.S. as well as Philippine intelligence agents have been engaged in sniffing out al-Qaeda cells. The Philippines has been on the front line in the war against terrorism in Southeast Asia. A key issue for regional counterterrorists is whether the Philippine model applies elsewhere. If the predominantly Christian Philippines cannot contain Muslim extremism, then what chance would the moderates have in those countries that are predominantly Muslim?

There are no ready answers to the issues of domestic terrorism in the Philippines. There is no adequate military solution, nor is it a matter of ideology. The Huks were not as Marxist as one might think, nor were the NPA as Maoist. Likewise, Abu Sayyaf was not as dedicated to al-Qaeda as commonly portrayed. Much of the violence in the Philippines is homegrown. The corruption that lies at the root of discontent remains unchanged. It is part of a vicious cycle: corruption breeds revolution, and the revolution becomes corrupted. Hope for a peaceful resolution lies in the unlikely prospect that those in power will surrender the very basis of that power. For all its involvement, the United States cannot realistically expect to change this cycle. It would be difficult enough to avoid getting involved or at least avoid giving the appearance of taking sides in domestic affairs.

Stewart S. Johnson and James Ciment

See also: *Definitions, Types, Categories*—Islamist Fundamentalist Terrorism; Left-Wing and Revolutionary Terrorism; Urban vs. Rural Terrorism. *Modern Terrorism*—Indonesia: Islamist Militancy.

Further Reading

Banlaoi, Rommel C. *Philippine Security in the Age of Terror: National, Regional, and Global Challenges in the Post-9/11 World.* Boca Raton, FL: CRC Press, 2010.

Barreveld, Dirk. *Terrorism in the Philippines: The Bloody Trail of Abu Sayyaf, Bin Laden's East Asian Connection.* Lincoln, NE: Writers Club Press, 2001.

Chapman, William. *Inside the Philippine Revolution.* New York: W.W. Norton, 1987.

Jones, Gregg R. *Red Revolution: Inside the Philippine Guerrilla Movement.* Boulder, CO: Westview, 1989.

Karnow, Stanley. *In Our Image: America's Empire in the Philippines.* New York: Random House, 1989.

Kerkvliet, Benedict J. *The Huk Rebellion: A Study of Peasant Revolt in the Philippines.* Berkeley: University of California Press, 1977.

Kessler, Richard J. *Rebellion and Repression in the Philippines.* New Haven, CT: Yale University Press, 1989.

Portuguese Africa (Angola, Cape Verde, Guinea-Bissau, Mozambique): Liberation Struggles, 1961–1975

Portugal was the first European colonial power to arrive in Africa and, with Spain, the last to withdraw. Portuguese navigators reached each of the three principal colonies of Angola, Portuguese Guinea (now Guinea-Bissau), and Mozambique by the end of the fifteenth century.

The Portuguese claimed that, uniquely, their imperialism was based not upon racial discrimination but upon educating the local people to take their place in Portuguese society. In 1951, they named the three colonies overseas provinces of Portugal, but in reality, the policy was exploitative. Back in 1878, the Portuguese had replaced slavery with a contract-labor system. They forced local farmers to grow cash crops for the government rather than food crops for themselves. As an added insult, education was not commonly made available.

Angolan Militants Attack Plantations

Initially, nationalist groups were content to pursue economic or social objectives, but by the late 1950s, meager social progress and the collapse of Belgian authority in the Congo (later the Democratic Republic of Congo) gave rise to a growing militancy. The trigger for violence came in 1961 in Angola. Militants attacked Portuguese cotton plantations in protest over laws forcing farmers to grow cash crops.

Meanwhile, an opponent of the then dictator of Portugal, Antonio Salazar, hijacked a Portuguese airliner and tried to bring it to Luanda, the Angolan capital. The world press hurried to Angola. On February 4, 1961, three bands of armed Angolans attacked a Luanda prison and two police barracks, possibly for the benefit of the press. The militants tried to free African prisoners detained for minor offenses. Security forces beat off the attackers, but many deaths resulted.

The next day, at the funeral of the seven slain policemen, shooting broke out. In all, thirty-six Africans and eight members of the security forces died.

Full-Scale Revolts in Angola

A month later, on March 15, terrorists armed with machetes and cutlasses hacked to death 300 farmers, shopkeepers, and their families in the northern cotton plantations. They attacked Portuguese farms, houses, crops, and government property. Refugees shuttled out by aircraft described how the terrorists had butchered the Portuguese without regard to age or sex.

The division was not as simple as native Angolans against the Portuguese. There was much rivalry among nationalist Angolan groups, based on tribal differences. Many refugees reported that the local African population had fought side by side with the Portuguese against the terrorists.

On April 13, 1961, terrorist violence went from bad to worse. Several thousand rebels launched an attack on Ucua village, 100 miles (161 kilometers) north of Luanda, killing thirteen Portuguese. A reporter described how the terrorists were armed with cutlasses inscribed with UPA—standing for the Union of Angolan Peoples—and how they attacked "as if demon-possessed, dancing and singing and shouting."

UPA (later the National Front for the Liberation of Angola, or FNLA) leader Holden Roberto said that

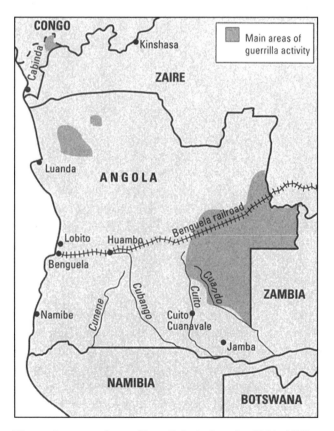

The main areas of guerrilla activity in Angola, 1961–1975.

the Angolan uprising was "an expression of desperation against Portuguese terrorism over the past 500 years." But he added, "We are deeply sorry that women and children have been killed." Holden Roberto stated that the attacks were the work of laborers rebelling against the Portuguese forced-labor system. He admitted that some of his members had taken part but insisted they had done so against orders. The revolt caught the Portuguese army by surprise, but it easily suppressed the rebels. Airpower was used ferociously, killing an estimated 50,000 Africans by September.

The uprising prompted the Portuguese to make concessions. They abolished compulsory cash-crop cultivation. They replaced the desire to "civilize" the natives with a declaration that all local people in overseas provinces were equal to Europeans as Portuguese citizens. But insurgency still spread to Portuguese Guinea in 1963 and to Mozambique in 1964.

Guinea Struggles to Break Free

The main insurgent group in Portuguese Guinea was the African Party for Independence for Guinea and Cape Verde (PAIGC). The group's targets were primarily the Portuguese military. On January 25, 1963, the terrorists attacked Portuguese barracks in the southeast of the country. They killed twenty army troops. On March 10, PAIGC units killed eight Portuguese troops and, on May 22, they shot down two aircraft. One pilot died in the crash; the terrorists captured the other.

The Portuguese answer to the insurgents was to put more and more troops on the ground. From 1,000 troops in 1961, government forces grew to 30,000 by 1967. The Portuguese intensified counterinsurgency efforts, centered on concentrating local populations in defended villages. When General Antonio de Spinola took over

the military command in Guinea in 1968, he initiated a coordinated "hearts and minds" strategy to win over the local people. Adopting the slogan "Better Guinea," Spinola focused his program on the villages and used the army to build 15,000 houses, 164 schools, 40 hospitals, 163 fire stations, and 86 water points.

Mozambique Steps Up Its Campaign

As in Guinea, the Mozambique Liberation Front (FRELIMO) started off in 1964 with military targets, including a rocket attack on the Cabora Bassa dam in Mozambique. During late 1973 and early 1974, however, FRELIMO terrorists shifted emphasis, mounting more than forty operations against civilian targets. Violent acts included mortar attacks on villages, hostage taking, and the downing of a private aircraft, killing six. According to the Portuguese, FRELIMO killed more than 300 civilians during 1973, wounded a further 554, and kidnapped 1,768 more. The Portuguese increased troop numbers from 16,000 in 1964 to more than 60,000 in 1974. They took a more active stand against the insurgents after 1968. In 1973, the army was accused of a massacre in which more than 400 African civilians were said to have died. This claim was denied, but some deaths almost certainly occurred.

In the face of an increasingly unpopular campaign at home and in Africa, the Portuguese granted independence to Portuguese Guinea (as Guinea-Bissau) in September 1974, to Mozambique in June 1975, and to Angola in November 1975. In military terms, neither the terrorists nor the authorities had won or lost. It was a 1974 left-wing military coup in Portugal that ended the country's "historic mission" in Africa.

Ian F.W. Beckett

See also: *Historical Roots*—European Colonial Expansion Conquests. *Modern Terrorism*—Angola: Civil and Separatist Wars.

Further Reading

Beckett, Ian F.W., and John Pimlott, eds. *Armed Forces and Modern Counterinsurgency.* New York: St. Martin's, 1985.

Bruce, Neil. *The Last Empire.* North Pomfret, VT: David and Charles, 1975.

Henriksen, Thomas H. *Revolution and Counter-Revolution: Mozambique's War of Independence, 1964–1974.* Westport, CT: Greenwood, 1983.

Porch, Douglas. *The Portuguese Armed Forces and the Revolution.* New York: St. Martin's, 1977.

KEY DATES

1956 Militants from the African Party for the Independence of Guinea and Cape Verde begin their armed campaign to oust Portugal from its West African colonies.

1961 Independence fighters launch their military campaign against Portuguese colonial authorities in Angola.

1964 Militants from the Mozambique Liberation Front (FRELIMO) begin their armed campaign against Portugal.

April 24, 1974 Left-wing military officers overthrow Marcello Caetano; they soon announce their intention to rid war-weary Portugal of its rebellious African colonies.

1974–1975 Lisbon grants independence to its four African colonies of Angola, Cape Verde, Guinea-Bissau, and Mozambique.

Russia/Soviet Union: Ethnic and Nationalist Conflict in the Transcaucasus Region and Ukraine, 1980s–2000s

The dissolution of the Soviet Union in 1990–1991 led inevitably to widespread terrorist activity, resulting mainly from nationalist insurgencies. Released from the tyranny of the state, ethnic enclaves sought self-identification and independence. When political solutions failed to materialize, extremists frequently turned to violence as a means to an end. Many such conflicts continue to this day.

State Terror Under Stalin

Terror was not new to the former Soviet Union, having been used by the state to impose its political will on the people. The Soviet Union stretched from Eastern Europe across Asia to the Bering Strait west of Alaska. It comprised vastly different peoples with nothing in common other than formerly being part of the Russian Empire. In a bid to stamp out national identity, whole peoples were forcibly relocated, many to the Soviet Far East, while others were brought in to take their place. Terrorist acts against the state occurred under Stalin but were put down with the utmost ferocity. For example, when Leningrad party boss Sergei Kirov was shot in December 1934 by dissident Leonid Nikolayev, Stalin ordered the execution of Nikolayev along with thirteen other "plotters"; sixty-six "White Guard terrorists" were convicted and shot in Moscow. Stalin also relocated members of groups suspected of collaboration with the Nazis.

When the last Soviet leader, Mikhail Gorbachev, brought in perestroika (restructuring) in 1985, many ethnic groups began to demand more political control over their affairs. After the Soviet Union was dissolved in 1991, millions of displaced people sought to redraw boundaries and recover their own territory, forcing out those who had been resettled there. Terror now became the weapon of the people.

Terror in Transcaucasia

In the late 1980s, as the government in Moscow lost control over the Soviet Union's smaller states, old enmities began to surface. Christian Armenians demanded the return of Nagorno-Karabakh, a landlocked Armenian enclave in neighboring Muslim Azerbaijan. They organized a riot in the Azeri city of Sumgait. Gorbachev responded by sending in the Red Army, but the fuse of ethnic conflict had been lit. A wave of nationalism swept through Azerbaijan, and Armenians bore the brunt of the violence. During a rally in the Azeri capital, Baku, in January 1990, Armenian homes were looted and set on fire, and hundreds were killed. Again, Soviet troops were sent in, killing sixty people as they smashed the uprising.

Terrorist acts were not confined within the borders of the warring states. In 1994, for example, Armenians murdered two Chechens in London for allegedly attempting to purchase arms for the Azeri government. Terrorism soon escalated into all-out civil war; although the war was terminated by a cease-fire in 1994, the wrangling over Nagorno-Karabakh continues.

The state of Georgia was also convulsed by terrorism leading up to independence from the crumbling Soviet Union in 1991. Georgia was one of the few territories in which the ethnic population remained largely intact. However, the small enclave of South Ossetia, of a different ethnic origin, declared itself a separate republic in 1990. The Georgian National Guard, made up of formerly illegal paramilitary troops, was mobilized to quell disturbances. It took the intervention of Russian troops, and a cease-fire in 1992, to halt brutal reprisals. Once again, war broke out between Russia and Georgia in the summer of 2008, as the former responded to pleas by South Ossetian separatists who claimed they were being repressed by the Georgian government. The war resulted in a devastating loss for Georgia and the virtual end of its authority in the breakaway province.

Georgia's northwestern province of Abkhazia suffered a similar fate in 1992, when nationalists sought separation from Georgia and alliance with Russia. Although supported by Russian military intelligence and soldiers, the Abkhazis suffered the loss of 3,000 lives before the 1994 cease-fire ended hostilities. During the 2008 war between Georgia and Russia, Abkhazian forces seized the disputed Kodori Gorge region from Georgia.

Terrorist Threat to Russia

Russia itself has not been immune to terrorist factions. In 1992, government sources estimated that there were fifteen groups with political aspirations in the Moscow region alone. These included Chechens, Azeris, and various northern Caucasian groups from Dagestan, Ossetia, Armenia, and Georgia.

Extremist groups in Russia represent further potential threats to the central government. Many of these

KEY DATES

1990 Violence breaks out between Armenians and Azeris in the Nagorno-Karabakh region of Azerbaijan, which is claimed by Armenia.

1991 Amid economic stagnation and growing political unrest, the Soviet Union collapses, unleashing pent-up national and ethnic passions in the Transcaucasian region of Russia and Ukraine.

1992 Georgian troops are dispatched to put down ethnic violence by South Ossetian separatists; the dispute is resolved by the intervention of Russian troops.

1993–1994 Terrorist acts and assassinations precede presidential elections in Crimea, a region governed by Ukraine but claimed by Russian nationalists.

2008 Violence between Georgian troops and South Ossetian separatists triggers a war between Georgia and Russia.

have openly developed paramilitary wings, are overtly fascist and anti-Semitic, and in some cases call for the overthrow of the state. Their public statements and documents often advocate terrorist actions, although they have perpetrated none so far. Strongholds of activity include St. Petersburg, Moscow, and Siberia. One such group, Russian National Unity, under former special forces officer Alexander Barkashov, is believed to have thousands of members, more than 350 regional branches, and a highly disciplined military arm. It has a Nazi-style agenda, seeking to keep Russia racially pure, and claims to have a surprise plan to take power.

Smaller and less focused groups led by former military officers include the Public Club Union of Officers, founded in 1991, which took part in the unsuccessful siege of the Russian parliament building in October 1993. The Congress of Russian Communities, which is committed to defending Russians in bordering states, has a paramilitary arm called the Russian Knights. They have been suspected of supporting Russian separatists in the Crimean part of the Ukraine.

Ethnic Clashes in the Ukraine

Apart from a brief period after the end of World War I, the vast land of Ukraine (nearly as large as Texas) had never been independent. In the twentieth century, Ukrainian nationalists have been responsible for a shocking catalog of terrorist atrocities.

As early as 1920, many thousands of Jews were massacred in a wave of anti-Semitism. During World War II, Ukrainian nationalists assisted the Nazis in implementing the Final Solution against the Jewish and Roma population. Since the breakup of the Soviet Union, political parties have sprung up, such as the Union in Support of Ukrainian State Independence, whose aims include

"ethnic cleansing." This xenophobia has been directed particularly against the Russian population, concentrated mainly in Crimea in the south. This region is 70 percent Russian, and many would prefer to be ruled from Moscow rather than from Kiev, the capital of Ukraine.

A series of terrorist acts and assassinations in late 1993 and early 1994 preceded the Crimean presidential elections. Extremist groups, such as the Ukrainian People's Self-Defense Force, were widely believed to be responsible for seeking to pervert the course of the election by terrorist means. Yuri Meshkov of the Republican Party of Crimea won the election on a platform advocating reunion with Russia.

Russian-Ukrainian antagonisms in Crimea have been further aggravated by the Muslims of Tatarstan. Since 1991, a quarter million Tatars have returned to their Crimean homeland. The majority are poor and have no vote; separatist groups, such as the All-Tatar Public Center under Marat Mulyukov, have threatened a terrorist campaign if their interests are ignored. They set up armed units in 1992, but these were banned after clashes with the Crimean authorities during October 1992. Several groups—the Majlis and Kurultai of the Crimean Tatar people, and the Crimean Tatars National Movement—have threatened violence against the Meshkov government.

Meanwhile, according to area experts, unstable conditions across the former Soviet Union continue to threaten to create a generation of "proto-terrorists." If economic conditions and cultural identities are not respected, groups that already use institutionalized violence may turn to guerrilla warfare and terrorism to achieve their objectives. The proto-terrorists of today may turn into the full-fledged terrorists of tomorrow.

Elaine M. Holoboff

See also: *Definitions, Types, Categories*—Ethnonationalist Terrorism. *Modern Terrorism*—Central Asian Republics: Islamist Terrorism; Russia: Chechnya Conflict.

Further Reading

Berberoglu, Berch, ed. *The National Question: Nationalism, Ethnic Conflict and Self-Determination in the Twentieth Century.* Philadelphia: Temple University Press, 1995.

Duncan, W. Raymond, and G. Paul Holman. *Ethnic Nationalism and Regional Conflict: The Former Soviet Union and Yugoslavia.* Boulder, CO: Westview, 1994.

Kaiser, Robert J. *The Geography of Nationalism in Russia and the U.S.S.R.* Princeton, NJ: Princeton University Press, 1994.

Slater, Wendy, and Andrew Wilson, eds. *The Legacy of the Soviet Union.* Houndmills, Basingstoke, Hampshire, UK: Palgrave Macmillan, 2004.

Szporluk, Roman. *National Ethnicity and Identity in Russia and the New States of Eurasia.* Armonk, NY: M.E. Sharpe, 1994.

Russia: Chechnya Conflict, 1994–Present

Chechnya (once part of the Soviet Chechen-Ingush Autonomous Republic) was generally unknown to foreigners before 1991. Within a few short years, however, Russia's military incompetence and mishandling of Chechen political issues brought the largely Muslim Chechen people and their issues into the international spotlight. Moscow's repeated claims that the Chechens are "terrorists" and therefore not soldiers has become more popularly accepted as the Chechens have struck targets in Russia and undertaken a closer alliance with terrorist organizations such as al-Qaeda.

Background

The Chechen lands of the Caucasus Mountains became part of imperial Russia in the early nineteenth century, after two generations of resistance. Chechen resistance to first Russian and then Soviet rule never really ceased, as Chechen bandits operated in the mountains until World War II. Some Chechens welcomed the German invaders in 1942–1943; in retaliation, Joseph Stalin ordered the entire Chechen population of 500,000 deported to Central Asia, along with other "disloyal" Caucasian peoples. More than one-third of the Chechen deportees perished during their first months in exile.

In the late 1950s, the Soviet government forgave the Chechens for their history of resistance, and many returned to find their cities, villages, and farms occupied by Russians. During the last decades of Soviet power, Chechnya simmered, and with the collapse of the Communist Party and the Soviet Union, Dzhokhar Dudayev, a Soviet Air Force general, declared Chechen independence in late 1991.

Chechnya Versus Russia, Round One

The government of President Boris Yeltsin, preoccupied with threats from hard-line communists, at first tended to ignore the Dudayev regime. Several issues, however, forced the Yeltsin government to turn its attention to this tiny breakaway regime. The role of Chechen criminal groups in Russia, Chechen involvement in illegal oil trading, and the threat of political succession all influenced Yeltsin's decision to intervene.

In 1993 and early 1994, Russia tried to defeat the Chechens by means of a low-cost secret war. A pro-Russian political regime was established, and Russian servicemen were recruited and impressed into a secret army to work in concert with the shadow regime in order to seize power. This effort by the Russian secret service turned into a debacle; the pro-Russian authorities had

Chechen rebels have been fighting to free their autonomous republic from Russian control since the collapse of the Soviet Union in the 1990s. In response, Russia has conducted a bitter war and occupation to keep the province.

no success in rallying support, and Chechen authorities easily rounded up clandestine liberation forces.

In the aftermath of this failure, Russian minister of defense Pavel Grachev reportedly told Yeltsin that he could seize the Chechen capital of Grozny with a single regiment. The December 1974 invasion of Chechnya showed more arrogance than planning: a three-pronged Russian invasion would seize the highly populated lowlands, while a motorized brigade would take the capital by a coup de main. The attacks were unmitigated disasters. The 131st Brigade was ambushed and all but annihilated in the center of Grozny: 225 of the brigades' 350 armored fighting vehicles were destroyed, and more than 1,000 Russian soldiers were killed, wounded, or captured.

Following this disaster, the Russians initiated a war of attrition. Grozny was largely demolished by air and artillery fire, as were other smaller settlements suspected of hiding rebels. To counter these tactics and take pressure off their homeland, the Chechens initiated a series of terrorist raids (*nabegs*) deep into Russian territory. Government offices and hospitals were occupied, and hostages were killed before the raiders negotiated their own safe retreat and escape.

In mid-1996, the Yeltsin government negotiated an armistice with the Chechen authorities. Moscow had lost considerable face in Europe and the Muslim world, and not even the successful assassination of Dudayev in 1996 could hide the fact that the performance of the army and security forces had been poor. Western academics believe that the Russian military suffered approximately 20,000 casualties, including almost 4,000 killed or missing. Chechen losses have been estimated at 80,000, with loss to the civilian infrastructure of over $100 billion.

New War, New Issues

During the war, the Chechen authorities had received millions of dollars in aid from Muslim organizations. Moreover, the regime accepted volunteers from fundamentalist Muslim organizations such as al-Qaeda, and some Chechen warriors received training in Afghanistan. Following the war, a low-key but violent struggle began between the older generation, who had conducted and won a partisan war, and the young volunteers and their foreign allies, who sought to turn Chechnya into a fundamentalist Islamic state. While Chechnya's nominal president, Aslan Maskhadov, sought to build a modern state, some younger, more radical veterans began a systematic campaign of kidnapping and terror in Chechen territory and southern Russian provinces. Russian civilians, journalists, and aid workers were abducted, held for ransom, and frequently murdered. Maskhadov's inability to halt this crime spree convinced many in Russia and the international community that Chechnya was little more than a terrorist enclave.

The First Chechen War, according to academic observers, radicalized Islam and gave fundamentalist Wahhabi beliefs, held by the Sunni sect predominant in Chechnya, greater authority. Moderates such as President Maskhadov had little impact on the spread of fundamentalist Islam; it was financed and preached by foreigners and some young veterans, who saw the first war as a major victory for militant Islam.

A major issue for fundamentalists has been to spread the message of Islamic renewal and resistance to the other Muslim people of the Caucasus. In 1998 and 1999, agents from Chechnya proselytized in Dagestan and other neighboring regions of the Russian republic, apparently with little measurable success. According to the Russian government, in the summer of 1999 a large armed group of Chechen and foreign Muslim soldiers slipped out of Chechnya into Dagestan. By mid-September 1999, these men were involved in skirmishes with local police and military troops.

Incursions from Chechnya coincided with several terrorist incidents in Moscow. Bombs exploded on September 30 in apartment buildings and an outdoor market. Although some Russian human rights observers blamed the security services for these attacks, seeing them as a provocation, most foreign observers believed the attacks were set to coincide with a major push into Dagestan. Within twenty-four hours of the bombings, the Yeltsin government moved troops to counter the fundamentalist movement into Dagestan and took steps to invade Chechnya for the second time.

The Russian experience in the Second Chechen War was more successful than that in the first. Russian troops used firepower to occupy Grozny and other major population centers, and they forced more than 150,000 Chechens from their country in a form of ethnic cleansing. Nevertheless, Russian patrols were frequently ambushed, and the Chechens maintained a base of support in the high mountains of southern Chechnya. Unlike in the first war, Chechen groups increased the use of terrorism to bring the war home to Russians; bombs exploded at public buildings, bus stops, and military parades, claiming civilian casualties. On May 9, 2002, a bomb exploded at a military parade in Dagestan, killing forty-six civilians.

Continuing War

Most foreign observers reported at the time that Russia fought a dirty war in both of its struggles against the Chechens, whom Russians continue to regard as rebels and terrorists to the present day. Chechen detainees have been tortured and executed without trial. A Russian reporter who reported on this aspect of the war in 2000 was kidnapped by Russian security forces and threatened with execution. Since the 1996 armistice, the Chechen authorities have had difficulty controlling their own armed bands, many of which are more and more willing to strike civilian targets deep inside Russia. Increasingly, the Chechens have embraced terrorism. According to Russian observers, Chechen terrorism reflects anger with Russian tactics against civilians; terrorist training in Afghanistan; and a growing belief that only by bringing the war home to Russia will Moscow realize the cost of the war.

Moscow's counterintelligence service, the Federal Security Service (FSB), was largely ineffectual against Chechen groups in the First Chechen War. Chechen commanders routinely bribed Russian military units to get weapons and to obtain safe passage from Chechnya into Russia, where they raided Russian towns. The FSB seems to have been more successful since 1999, probably because of Russian president Vladimir Putin, a former intelligence officer who served briefly as the FSB chief in the late 1990s. Putin was committed to the defeat of the Chechen rebels.

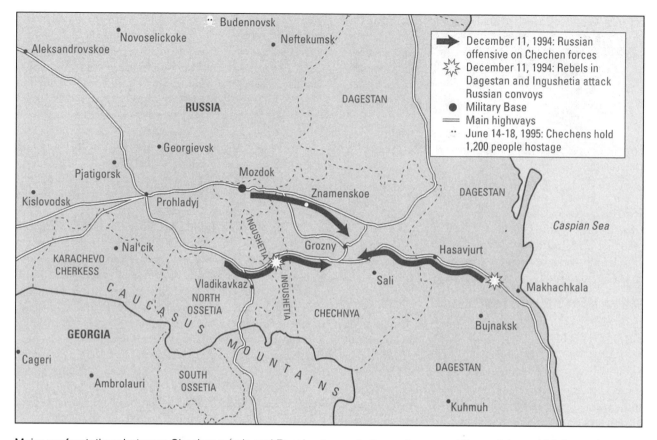

Major confrontations between Chechen rebels and Russian troops in the early years of the uprising, which began in 1991.

Putin unleashed the Russian armed forces and security services, which modified their tactics to eliminate guerrilla groups and kill their leaders. Military operations were more carefully coordinated, and FSB intelligence on insurgents was far better in the later struggle than in the 1994–1996 war. One vital sign of FSB success was that the Chechens were not able to conduct nabegs, as they had done in the First Chechen War. FSB covert actions also grew in sophistication and effectiveness. In the spring of 2002, Russian security forces killed the Saudi-born Samir bin Saleh al-Suwailem, known by his nom de guerre, Khattab, with a letter treated with poison. Khattab, who played a major role in Chechen terrorism, was the major link between Chechnya and the Taliban and al-Qaeda.

Nevertheless, the war would be hard to win, and for the Chechens time was their greatest ally. The Chechens had been at war seemingly for decades against Russia, and their family and clan networks could not be easily defeated. The Chechen memory is one of struggle against impossible odds, deportation, and genocide. Russian military sweeps produced civilian casualties and thousands of refugees. The war, in the words of one knowledgeable analyst, had become "Russia's Algeria," in which "a closed circle of violence" was formed between occupying troops and guerrillas, conditions similar to what France once faced in North Africa. Chechen

youth continued to volunteer for guerrilla bands and terrorist missions. For every man killed in a military sweep or a covert action, another emerged to take his place. The Chechens remained able to purchase arms, including U.S.-made M-16s, on the international arms market, and they could maintain supply lines through Georgia.

For Moscow, the greatest enemy was time. The war had cost Russia approximately 2,400 killed and 6,000 wounded in the late 1990s and early 2000s. The Russian military admitted that 80,000 combat troops were stationed in Chechnya, a territory only 75 by 112 miles (120 kilometers by 180 kilometers), which made it among the most heavily occupied of any land on earth. The war was a drain on the Russian population: political polls showed scant support for the war, and families resented having their sons sent to the war. President Putin had on several occasions declared victory over the Chechen terrorists. However, the Chechen terrorists remained able to strike Russian targets in Chechnya and bordering regions, as well as the Russian heartland. Moreover, while the Chechens had not received a great quantity of foreign funds, their cause had increasingly become an important issue for extremists. Meanwhile, Chechen-related issues had become a rallying cry for extremists throughout the Muslim world.

More Chechen Violence

The Chechen crisis once again exploded into the news in October 2002, when Chechen terrorists took hostage more than 700 audience and cast members at a Moscow theater. The Chechens threatened to shoot the hostages and set off bombs unless their demands for negotiations over the breakaway republic's political status were met. After sixty hours—and after hearing gunshots coming from inside the theater—Russian law enforcement and security officials attacked, leaving more than 100 of the hostages and all the hostage takers dead.

The violence continued later that year, when a suicide bomber set off a device at the Grozny base of the Russian-backed Chechen government, killing eighty persons. These violent acts, however, did not stop a March 2003 referendum, highly criticized by outside human rights observers, in which Chechen voters supported a new constitution declaring the province a part of the Russian Federation. Nor did the vote stop continuing acts of violence by rebels. Two months later, more than fifty were killed when a suicide bomber attacked a government building in north Chechnya. Meanwhile, militant attacks on neighboring Ingushetia killed dozens of persons in June 2004. But the most heinous attack of the Chechen rebels was the seizure of a school in Beslan, North Ossetia, in September 2004. As Russian security forces tried to retake the school, hundreds of children were killed. The violence continued. In February 2006, an explosion at a Russian military barracks near Grozny left thirteen persons dead.

Still, Russian forces scored some successes, most notably the killing of separatist leader Abdul-Khalim Saydullayev in June 2006, as well as Chechen warlord Shamil Besayev a month later. Less positive was the assassination of Russian reporter Anna Politkovskaya, a fierce critic of Russian tactics in Chechnya, in October. While it was never proved, many believed that her murder was ordered by the Russian government.

Ethnic Terror and Russian Counterterrorism

Penetrating Chechen political and military cells has been a formidable undertaking for Russian security services. The cells are based on clan loyalty; most members have had extensive military experience and are familiar with explosives and weapons. They were well financed from the Chechen diaspora inside Russia, and many had friends among foreign terrorist organizations. Many Chechens received military training in the Soviet army, and many of the younger generation were trained in Afghanistan. Another Chechen advantage was their ties to criminal groups throughout Russia. Some of the bombings in Moscow were apparently carried out by criminals and former military men who had been paid by Chechens.

Russian president Vladimir Putin placed counterterrorism issues on the front burner during his 2000 presidential campaign. He promised a robust Ministry of Internal Affairs and FSB, and in a controversial interview asserted that he intended to hunt Chechen terrorists, even

Escalating Chechen terrorism culminated in a tragic hostage crisis in Beslan, North Ossetia, in September 2004. Chechen rebels seized a school and held it for two days before Russian forces stormed the buildings. Over 330 people, half of them children, were killed. *(Associated Press)*

KEY DATES

1996 Dzhokhar Dudayev, the leader of the Chechen force, is assassinated.

1998 Chechen nationalists begin to push their cause in the neighboring Russian province of Dagestan.

1999 A large group of Chechen nationalists and foreign Muslims enter Dagestan and are soon engaged in skirmishes with local police and Russian troops there. Terrorists set off bombs throughout Russia, including in apartment buildings, killing more than 200 people in the Moscow area alone; authorities suspect Chechen nationalists.

2000 During the presidential campaign, Russian president Vladimir Putin vows to defeat Chechen rebels militarily.

2002 Chechen terrorists take more than 700 persons hostage at a Moscow theater; when Russian security forces attempt to retake the building, more than 100 hostages and hostage takers are killed.

2004 Hundreds of children are killed when Russian security forces try to retake a school seized by Chechen terrorists in Beslan, in northern Chechnya.

2006 Russian forces kill Chechen separatist leader Abdul-Khalim Saydullayev.

2009 Russian president Dimitri Medvedev declares an end to Russia's anti-Chechen operations.

2010 A suicide bombing by Chechen separatists in a Moscow metro station during the morning rush hour on March 29 leaves 40 people dead and more than 100 injured.

statistics went up significantly in the early 2000s, and the organization was responsible for the assassination of Khattab. Criticism of FSB operations also increased, however, as both Russian and Western human rights activists accused the security service of abductions, torture, and murders. The U.S.-based rights organization Human Rights Watch documented eighty-seven disappearances of Chechen citizens between September 2000 and January 2002 alone and believed that the overall total of "disappearances" attributable to the security services was far higher.

By 2009, violence had subsided significantly in Chechnya, to the point where the new administration of Russian president Dmitri Medvedev could declare an end to nearly ten years of counterterrorist operations. This success was belied by Chechen suicide attacks on the Moscow metro in March 2010, which left 40 people dead and more than 100 injured—suggesting that more acts of terrorism, and counterterrorist responses, lay in the future. In January 2011, a Chechen suicide bomber attacked Moscow's Domodedovo Airport, killing 36 persons.

Robert Pringle

See also: *Definitions, Types, Categories*—Ethnonationalist Terrorism. *Modern Terrorism*—Russia/Soviet Union: Ethnic and Nationalist Conflict in the Transcaucasus Region and Ukraine. *Tactics, Methods, Aims*—Suicide Attacks.

Further Reading

Gilligan, Emma. *Terror in Chechnya: Russia and the Tragedy of Civilians in War.* Princeton, NJ: Princeton University Press, 2010.

Hahn, Gordon M. *Russia's Islamic Threat.* New Haven, CT: Yale University Press, 2007.

Knezys, Stays, and Romanas Sedickas. *The War in Chechnya.* College Station: Texas A&M University Press, 1999.

Lieven, Anatol. *Chechnya: Tombstone of Russian Power.* New Haven, CT: Yale University Press, 1998.

Oliker, Olga. *Russia's Chechen Wars, 1994–2000.* Santa Monica, CA: Rand, 2001.

Sakwa, Richard, ed. *Chechnya: From Past to Future.* London: Anthem Press, 2005.

if they were found hiding in toilets. In the aftermath of the demise of the security services following the Cold War and the period under Boris Yeltsin, Putin revamped and strengthened the FSB. Former colleagues and friends from the KGB, the Soviet-era secret police, were appointed to leadership positions, and the service became more aggressive in its pursuit of terrorists.

The counterterrorism component of the FSB, called the Directorate for the Defense of the Constitution and the Struggle Against Terrorism, is divided into five major departments and managed by one of the service's deputy directors. According to the FSB, one of these departments is responsible for coordinating counterterrorism operations in the provinces, while another is charged with running counterterrorism operations in the Chechen region. FSB effectiveness is hard to measure, but arrest

Rwanda: Genocide, 1994–2000s

For three months in 1994, from April 6 to July 10, the interim government of Rwanda attempted to turn the entire population of that country into either killers or victims. It failed, yet hundreds of thousands of Rwandans died in one of history's most appalling reigns of terror.

Rwanda had no history of ethnic strife before or during the colonial period. The minority Tutsi tribe were interspersed among the majority Hutu. The process of decolonization began in 1959 as the Hutus asserted themselves against the Belgian colonial administration and against the economically stronger Tutsis. The early years of Hutu domination were marked by bouts of politically motivated violence. The Hutus drove Tutsi leaders out of the positions they had held under colonial rule. They killed thousands of Tutsis and forced many more to flee into exile.

An army of Tutsis exiled in Uganda, known by Hutus as the *inyenzi,* or cockroaches, invaded in 1963 in an attempt to take the capital, Kigali. The Rwandan army defeated them and took revenge on Tutsi civilians. About 10,000 died and still more went into exile.

In 1973, Major General Juvénal Habyarimana, a Hutu from northwestern Rwanda, staged a coup and established an army-backed, one-party regime. Habyarimana and his circle oversaw the development of a political machine for controlling every part of the state. This absolute control meant that the "Tutsi question" was not an issue during the 1970s and 1980s.

In the early 1990s, however, Habyarimana was forced to make a number of concessions to both Hutu opponents and Tutsi exiles. He responded to international pressure to introduce democratic reforms in exchange for desperately needed loans. The government began to lose its hold on power as new Hutu political parties emerged. Also, in 1990, a 20,000-strong army of the largely Tutsi Rwandan Patriotic Front (RPF) invaded from Uganda. The RPF forced the government to negotiate a settlement that would give them virtual control over the Rwandan army.

Preparations for Genocide

Hutu extremists rejected all the concessions outright. Determined to hold on to power at any cost, they strengthened their organization. With vital French training and financial assistance, Habyarimana reinforced the Rwandan armed forces. The elite Presidential Guard grew to 1,500, while overall military strength rose from 5,000 to 35,000. The Presidential Guard then turned the youth wing of the National Revolutionary Movement for Development (MRND) into a new militia. Known as the Intrahamwe (those with a common goal), this group had nearly 2,000 fighters by 1994, drawn from every part of the country. The Presidential Guard ran camps for these young men and prepared them for their central role in the coming genocide. The weapons needed for the killing were imported in huge quantities from South Africa and Egypt. They included small arms and ammunition, as well as vast numbers of machetes.

The extremists also developed a political ideology of Hutu supremacy to mobilize support. They exploited newspapers and even the state-run Radio Rwanda, calling on all Hutus to do their patriotic duty and defend so-called Hutu power. This required not only the extermination of the Tutsi, who, it was claimed, were all "RPF cockroaches," but also the elimination of their opponents among the Hutu themselves.

On April 6, President Habyarimana and the president of neighboring Burundi died when their plane crashed in suspicious circumstances near a Rwandan army base. The Presidential Guard took this as the signal to set their genocide machine in motion. The Hutu extremists

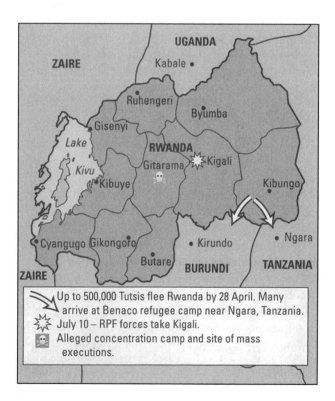

Up to 500,000 Tutsis flee Rwanda by 28 April. Many arrive at Benaco refugee camp near Ngara, Tanzania.
July 10 – RPF forces take Kigali.
Alleged concentration camp and site of mass executions.

Key events in the Rwandan civil war in 1994, and the exodus of refugees into Burundi, Tanzania, and Zaire.

had already drawn up lists of those who were to die at the hands of death squads, which included politicians, civil servants, and journalists. Prime Minister Agathe Uwilingiyimana, a moderate Hutu, was one of the first to die, and her family along with her. The Presidential Guard carried out a coup d'état, and two days later the new government, composed entirely of extremist Hutus, was announced.

Terror Intensifies

When the killing began, the Hutu radio and television station RTLMC called on Hutus to join with the Intrahamwe, asking publicly, "Who will fill up the half-empty graves?" In towns and villages across the country, extremist *bourgmestres* (mayors) instructed the police to lead Intrahamwe groups in seeking out all those suspected of being Tutsi, especially the prosperous and educated. The killers went from house to house. They killed known Tutsis immediately, hacking them to death with machetes. They forced other Hutus to murder their Tutsi neighbors and join the Intrahamwe. Those who refused died along with the Tutsis. Hutu husbands were forced to kill their Tutsi wives and children. Tutsis were rounded up and held in churches, schools, and sports facilities, while elsewhere they gathered together of their own accord, hoping vainly that there would be safety in numbers. In either case, they were butchered in such great numbers that the community buildings became death camps. Tutsis and moderate Hutus formed defense committees to resist the Intrahamwe, only to be disarmed by the Rwandan army and left to the mercy of ruthless killers. Faced with the prospect of brutal death by machete, many people paid their executioners to shoot them. Desperate mothers tried to hide their children in the piles of bodies. More than 500,000 fled the country.

As the killing intensified, however, the pro-Tutsi RPF military forces swept south, creating havens for hundreds of thousands of Tutsis. On July 10, the RPF took the capital, Kigali, and, for Tutsis, the reign of terror ended. Many Hutus, however, feared for their own lives, believing that it was now they who faced genocide. Many fled to a zone in the west protected by the French. When the French withdrew, they moved on to camps in Goma, Zaire (now Democratic Republic of the Congo), where the Hutu extremists tried to retain what little power they had left.

In fact, the struggle between the new Tutsi led government and Hutu extremists continued, albeit across the border in the Democratic Republic of the Congo. In 1995, the latter, assisted by the Congolese forces, launched attacks against the Banyamulenge, a population of Tutsis living in the Congo, with the goal of creating a haven to launch attacks against the new RPF government in Rwanda. Terror campaigns were launched against the

Banyamulenge, with the goal of pushing them out of the country. Many Congolese did not consider the Banyamulenge legitimate citizens of the country, even though many had resided there for generations.

In 1996, the RPF, aided by Ugandan forces, launched an attack into the Congo, with the goals of destroying the Hutu extremist military infrastructure and driving ordinary Hutus back into Rwanda. The RPF government, backed by many international observers, claimed that Hutu leaders were keeping ordinary Hutus hostage and threatening them with reprisals if they tried to leave the refugee camps. While some did indeed return, many fled deeper into the Congo, some voluntarily and others by force.

The Rwandan invasion helped trigger a general uprising against the corrupt Mobutu Sese Seko regime in Kinshasa, which ultimately fell to Congolese rebels in 1997. Meanwhile, tensions between Hutu rebels on the one side and Banyamulenge Tutsis, assisted by the Tutsi-led army of Rwanda, had sparked open conflict. By 1998, a multi-sided war had broken out in the Congo, which would draw in forces from a number of African nations. The war, which would continue until 2002, resulted in the death of more than 4 million, the worst tally of any war in African history and perhaps the bloodiest conflict anywhere in the world since World War II. While most of the deaths were the result of war-related famine and disease, tens of thousands of civilians were massacred, many of them Hutu refugees, killed at the hands of Banyamulenge and Rwandan Tutsi forces. Ultimately, peace treaties signed in 2002 between the Congo and other African states involved in the conflict ended much of the fighting, though sporadic outbursts continued through much of the rest of the decade.

As for Rwanda itself, the RPF government proved remarkably capable, helping the country recover economically. Indeed, in the years since the genocide, Rwanda has boasted some of the highest growth rates in Africa, albeit at the cost, say human rights observers, of an increasingly repressive one-party state. To deal with those guilty of the genocide, the International Criminal Tribunal for Rwanda was established under United Nations auspices. Hugely backlogged, the court has managed to bring down convictions against some of the most notorious leaders of the genocide.

Nick Hostettler

See also: *Definitions, Types, Categories*—Ethnonationalist Terrorism; State vs. Nonstate Terrorism.

Further Reading

Clark, John F. *The African Stakes in the Congo War.* New York: Palgrave Macmillan, 2002.

Clark, Phil, and Zachary D. Kaufman, eds. *After Genocide: Transitional Justice, Post-Conflict Reconstruction and Reconciliation in Rwanda and Beyond.* New York: Columbia University Press, 2009.

Destexhe, Alain. *Rwanda and Genocide in the Twentieth Century.* New York: New York University Press, 1995.

Dorsey, Learthen. *Historical Dictionary of Rwanda.* Metuchen, NJ: Scarecrow Press, 1994.

Gourevitch, Philip. *We Wish to Inform You that Tomorrow We Will Be Killed with Our Families: Stories from Rwanda.* New York: Picador/Farrar, Straus, and Giroux, 2004.

Hatzfeld, Jean. *The Antelope's Strategy.* Trans. Linda Coverdale. New York: Farrar, Straus, and Giroux, 2009.

Kinzer, Stephen. *A Thousand Hills: Rwanda's Rebirth and the Man Who Dreamed It.* Hoboken, NJ: John Wiley and Sons, 2008.

Malkki, Lisa H. *Purity and Exile: Violence, Memory, and National Cosmology Among Hutu Refugees in Tanzania.* Chicago: University of Chicago Press, 1995.

Prunier, Gérard. *The Rwanda Crisis: History of a Genocide, 1959–1994.* New York: Columbia University Press, 1995.

Vanderweff, Corrine. *Kill Thy Neighbor.* Boise, ID: Pacific Press, 1996.

Saudi Arabia: Domestic and International Terrorism, 1980s–2000s

The world's largest exporter of petroleum and one of the most important countries in the Arab world, Saudi Arabia is a kingdom of approximately 25 million people that covers much of the Arabian Peninsula. Home to Islam's holiest sites, Saudi Arabia is an extremely conservative and politically repressed country, where the royal family holds a virtual monopoly on political power and dissent is largely outlawed.

Iran and the Saudi Shiite Minority

During the 1980s, the kingdom of Saudi Arabia experienced a number of Iranian-sponsored attacks by indigenous Shiites and Iranian agents. The attacks came as part of the struggle for influence in the Muslim world between Iran and Saudi Arabia. Saudi Arabia's Shiite population, concentrated in the oil-rich Eastern Province, has long felt itself a victim of discrimination. Successive Saudi rulers, adhering to the strict Wahhabi form of Sunni Islam, have regarded Shiites as religiously misguided. Development spending and employment prospects in the Eastern Province have traditionally been lower than in the rest of the country.

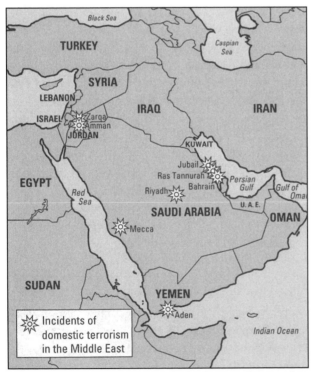

Homegrown terrorism by Islamic fundamentalists against conservative regimes in the Middle East increased dramatically between 1988 and 1996.

In 1987, a number of fires and explosions in the kingdom's oil fields were attributed by the government to accidents. However, they may have been the result of sabotage. In 1988, incidents multiplied as a result of rising Iranian-Saudi tensions, which had led to riots during 1987's hajj, or pilgrimage to Mecca.

In March and April, oil installations at Jubail and Ras Tannurah in the Eastern Province were bombed. Three suspects were arrested in August after a gun battle in which a policeman was killed. The three, along with an accomplice, were charged with sabotage, terrorism, and being Iranian agents; all three were convicted and executed.

The bulk of anti-Saudi activity, totaling some twenty-two incidents, happened abroad, though. A number of attacks were claimed by the Hezbollah of the Hijaz, a group made up of Saudi Shiites. They murdered a Saudi diplomat in Turkey in October 1988, ostensibly in revenge for the execution of the convicted Shiites. A group calling itself Soldiers of the Right attempted to kill a Saudi diplomat in Karachi, Pakistan, in December. Other attacks were carried out against three Saudi teachers in Nigeria and against offices of the national airline, Saudia.

Tensions remained high in 1989. During the hajj, two bombs were set off in Mecca by pro-Iranian pilgrims, killing one person. The Saudi authorities arrested sixteen Kuwaiti Shiites, accused them of working for Iran, and beheaded them. Iranian and Hezbollah leaders promised retaliation. On October 14, a Saudi office in Lahore, Pakistan, was blown up. Two days later a Saudi diplomat in Ankara, Turkey, was injured when his car exploded. On November 1, a Saudi diplomat in Beirut was assassinated by Islamic Jihad. On February 1, 1990, three Saudi diplomats were assassinated in Bangkok, Thailand, shortly after another diplomat had been injured in a bombing in Ankara.

Iraq and the First Gulf War

In late 1990 and 1991, Saudi concerns shifted to possible Iraqi terrorism. Iraq threatened retaliation against the Saudis and other members of the Gulf War coalition assembled against it, but tough security measures forestalled serious incidents. The Saudi government expelled Iraqi diplomats, closed its borders with Jordan and Yemen, and worked closely with its allies in restraining potential terrorists. Only a few incidents took place. On February 3, 1991, for example, two U.S. airmen and a Saudi guard were injured when a military bus in Jeddah was attacked. Four Palestinians were arrested for the attack.

After the Persian Gulf War (1990–1991), Saudi

Arabia sought to improve relations with Iran and to buy off its domestic Shiite opponents. Relations with Iran improved in the mid-1990s, and a deal was struck with exiled Shiite groups in 1993 that allowed their leaders to return home.

The Persian Gulf War also disrupted a long period of relative domestic stability, as bombings in Riyadh and Dhahran revealed that terrorism was again a grave threat to Saudi Arabia. Osama bin Laden, born and raised in Saudi Arabia and leader of the al-Qaeda terrorist network, focused even more attention on the country after the September 11, 2001, terrorist attacks in the United States. Even more important, fifteen of the nineteen suicide hijackers on 9/11 were Saudi citizens.

Sources of Terrorism in Saudi Arabia

Saudi Arabia has witnessed the increasing political alienation of its population vis-à-vis the ruling Saud family, especially among the younger, middle-class, and educated sector. Many Saudis believe that nepotism and the corruption of the ruling regime are the major factors in the declining social and economic conditions within the kingdom (such as deterioration of the welfare state). This belief has radicalized certain opposition elements. In addition, extreme demographic growth—the Saudi population, excluding the 6 million foreign workers living in Saudi Arabia, has doubled since the mid-1980s to 16 million—combined with waning economic conditions for the majority of the Saudi population as a result of the drop in oil prices and the underdeveloped non-oil sector of the Saudi economy, has intensified the political disaffection. Consequently, a very high rate of unemployment often exists, sometimes approaching 20–30 percent overall, and it is often proportionally higher among young university graduates.

Modernity and Western influence have brought reaction from Saudi society. It has been increasingly inclined to defend the Middle East's conservative social and religious traditions, which customarily underpinned the legitimacy of the ruling Saud family. This development, combined with an education system that encourages religious and cultural intolerance, has exacerbated the discontent among the general population, which was traditionally supportive of the king. Many have come to believe that the king and the ruling Sauds have "sold out" to the West and the United States for economic and security reasons, especially when Saudi Arabia turned to the U.S. military for protection against Iraq during the Persian Gulf War.

The Wahhabi tradition of the Hanbali school of jurisprudence in Sunni Islam has traditionally been a legitimizing factor for the Sauds, especially in building the Saudi state following the Ottoman exit from the Arabian Peninsula after World War I and the ousting of the traditional rulers of Mecca and Medina, Islam's two holiest places.

Wahhabism, therefore, came to serve as the basis of legitimacy to rule, and it underpinned the Saud custodianship of the holy sites. Given its significance of religious tradition to regime stability, the Saudi government has undertaken support of this religious tradition through, among other means, financing religious schools, or madrassas, in Saudi Arabia and abroad. Because Osama bin Laden and others have used Islamic—specifically Wahhabi—ideas to justify terrorism, many have charged in the wake of September 11 that the Saudi funding of such schools in places such as Pakistan has helped fuel the development of religious extremism and terrorism.

A less tangible, but no less important, factor has been the glorification of violence that developed among radical elements in Saudi Arabia, stemming in large part from the Afghan defeat of the Soviet Union in 1989. After nearly a decade of fighting, in which as many as tens of thousands of Saudi men participated with the encouragement of the Saudi regime as well as the United States and others, the mujahideen ("holy warriors") defeated a superpower. This legacy has made some radicals think that they can overcome even the most powerful enemy.

Categories of Opposition

There are generally three basic areas of opposition and potential terrorist activity in Saudi Arabia. First, Sunni domestic religious militants have stepped up their criticism of the Saudi regime, beginning with the Persian Gulf War. Religious leaders such as Safar al-Hawali and Salma al-Ouda have worked to galvanize opposition elements within the country. Members of their group include largely urban middle-class men who have been excluded from the state decision-making process and have no mechanism to publicly express their discontent.

Second, as noted earlier, the disgruntled Shiite minority in eastern Saudi Arabia continues to be a potential source of terrorist activities. The Shia Reform Movement, under the leadership of Sheikh Hassan al-Saffar, remains active in its opposition to the government. In the recent past, this group has focused on efforts to gain more international attention by decrying the poor human rights record as well as the lack of democracy and pluralism in Saudi Arabia. In response, the government has taken steps to appease the Shiite population, including the release of political prisoners and exiled leaders. Although the Saudi forces continue to monitor the Shias, this group has generally had a nonviolent agenda, after a brief outbreak of Iran-inspired attacks in the mid-1980s.

Finally, opposition groups operating from abroad—including the Committee for the Defense of Legitimate Rights (CDLR) under the leadership of Mohammed al-Masari; the Movement for Islamic Reform (MIRA), led by Saad al-Faqih, who split from al-Masari in 1996 over differences in ideology; and the more radical al-Qaeda network (an outgrowth of the Committee for Advice and

Reform that was created during the Afghan War), led by Osama bin Laden—represent threats to the regime. Both the CDLR and MIRA are based in London, while the U.S. military strikes on al-Qaeda camps in Afghanistan after the September 11 attacks forced the remaining members of the group, including its leaders, underground. Each of these groups has capitalized on modern technology, including the Internet, to organize and spread their ideas within Saudi Arabia and internationally. Of this category, however, those individuals and groups associated with al-Qaeda continue to pose the greatest terrorist threat.

Internal Threats

In 1995, however, the focus was on domestic terrorist threats sponsored by radical Sunni groups. Since the Persian Gulf War, the Saudi royal family had come under attack from conservative religious scholars and intellectuals, who complained of their excessive reliance on the West and their alleged corruption and economic mismanagement. These conservatives were suppressed and their supporters jailed or forced into exile. The foremost spokesman was al-Masari, who set up headquarters in London in 1994. His Committee for the Defense of Legitimate Rights carried out a massive and successful propaganda campaign against the royal family that embarrassed the kingdom. The CDLR and its sympathizers avoided violence but warned that government repression might provoke terrorism.

They were proved right in November 1995, when a car bomb went off outside a U.S.-manned training center for the Saudi National Guard in Riyadh. Five Americans and a Filipino were killed, and sixty people were injured. Three unknown groups claimed responsibility; ultimately, four men confessed to the Riyadh incident and were publicly beheaded in May 1996.

Bombing in Dhahran

On June 25, 1996, a massive truck bomb devastated a U.S. Air Force housing compound in Khobar, near the Dhahran airbase in Saudi Arabia. The bomb, a fuel truck packed with explosives, killed 19 U.S. servicemen and injured nearly 400 other people, mostly Americans.

The blasts aroused a storm of anger in the United States. Shortly after the Dhahran attack, President Bill Clinton spoke at the summit of the seven industrialized nations in Lyons, France. He vowed to make the fight against terrorism a top priority. He launched an urgent review of security at U.S. military installations worldwide, while an eighty-strong FBI team was sent to Saudi Arabia.

Although Clinton accused Iran of the attack and called on leaders of industrialized nations to isolate "rogue" states, it was widely assumed that the perpetrators hailed from a Saudi Islamic fundamentalist opposition group. The Riyadh bombers had confessed on television to opposing the presence of U.S. troops in Saudi Arabia. Although there were rumors that the men had been tortured—and FBI investigators were not allowed to interrogate them—few observers doubted the integrity of their confessions.

The only group that claimed responsibility for the Khobar bombing was the Legion of the Martyr Abdullah al-Huzaifi. The group demanded the removal of foreign troops from Saudi Arabia and warned that more attacks

A massive truck bombing at the U.S. airbase in Dhahran, Saudi Arabia, destroyed or damaged six buildings of the Khobar Towers housing complex on June 25, 1996. The U.S. government blamed Saudi Hezbollah and the Iranian regime. *(Associated Press)*

would follow. The group takes its name from a Saudi dissident who was executed after being convicted of throwing acid in the face of a secret policeman.

Protectors or Occupiers?

One purpose of both bombings was to highlight the growing American military presence in the kingdom. From the Persian Gulf War of 1990–1991 through August 2003, U.S. forces were based in the country. Although nominally present only as advisers and technicians, up to 20,000 U.S. troops were based in Saudi Arabia after 1991. Their presence became an increasing source of concern to hard-line Saudi fundamentalists, who regarded the U.S. troops as unwanted intruders.

The targeting of U.S. forces was, however, only the symbolic tip of the iceberg for Saudi Arabia's dissidents. The Saudi royal family has always sought to legitimize its rule by relying heavily on a combination of force and religion. This has brought it into opposition over the years with more conservative members of the ulema, the Islamic clergy. For instance, the introduction of television into the kingdom proved very difficult when the ulema opposed television as a morally corrupting force.

The Persian Gulf War sparked a round of conflict between the regime and its conservative critics. Although King Fahd justified the presence of foreign troops in the country on Islamic grounds, many members of the ulema regarded the king's reliance on "infidels" as sacrilegious.

After Iraq's defeat, religious leaders presented a series of petitions to the regime in which they demanded political and religious reforms, including the removal of foreign troops, the establishment of a consultative assembly, curbs on corruption, and a stricter application of Islamic law. King Fahd responded in part to the demands by establishing a *majlis al-shura* (consultative council), which began work in 1993. The council was seen as a powerless assembly by the dissidents, however. They complained that King Fahd would not acknowledge their other grievances. In response, the Saudi rulers arrested many people, including two outspoken young clerics, Sheikhs al-Ouda and al-Hawali; several dissidents escaped abroad.

As al-Masari consistently warned in the 1990s, if the Saudi government continued to repress dissent and refused to allow more power sharing, then radical dissidents who see force as the solution would emerge. The Riyadh and Khobar bombings demonstrated that this had happened. As noted earlier, there are some 20,000 Saudi veterans who fought with the mujahideen in Afghanistan, and the government's failure to accommodate these radical Muslims led to further terrorist violence.

Saudi Counterterrorist Measures

Overall, Saudi Arabia has had a mixed record with regard to combating terrorism. In 1991, the government persuaded (some say bribed) Osama bin Laden to leave the country and eventually revoked his citizenship in 1994, due to his extremist views and attempts to radicalize Muslims there and abroad. Critics have contended that the Saudi regime merely "exported" its terror problem. Furthermore, Riyadh's support of the Taliban regime in Afghanistan, which provided a safe haven to bin Laden and al-Qaeda, is well documented. Although tensions between the two governments were evident as early as 1998, Saudi Arabia officially rescinded its recognition of the Taliban regime only after the terrorist attacks of September 11. Riyadh claimed that it was trying to support stability in Afghanistan, but the result was that it indirectly supported bin Laden's terrorist camps. In addition, Saudi Arabia has reportedly financed Palestinian insurgent groups, including Hamas and Islamic Jihad, and it also allegedly assisted the families of Palestinian participants killed or wounded—including suicide bombers—in the Second Intifada (also called the al-Aqsa Intifada) against Israel through the Saudi Committee for Support of the al-Aqsa Intifada.

Until the terrorists attacks of September 11, 2001, domestic efforts to combat terrorism had been conducted largely by the heavy-handed internal security apparatus loyal to the Saudi king and the royal family, the 100,000-strong National Guard. Although mild criticism is tolerated in Saudi Arabia, strong opposition to the government remains suppressed. Human rights groups have charged the kingdom with unfair treatment and abuse of individuals who oppose the regime, including imprisonment, execution, and torture. In addition to these harsh measures, the government undertook constructive efforts after September 11 to enhance civil aviation safety, protect its long borders, disrupt terror financing, and promote peace between Palestinians and Israelis.

Riyadh refused to freeze suspected bank accounts at the request of the United States in November 2001 but eventually did so in response to UN resolutions in January 2002. This reluctance revealed the tension between the Saudi government and the United States, its desire to be viewed as an independent and proud political entity, and its concurrent desire to cooperate and prevent terror. Reportedly, the Saudi government was not initially inclined to provide full cooperation to the U.S. investigators of the Khobar Towers incident, withdrawing full access to the alleged culprits. Critics have suggested that the Saudi pattern is to conduct such investigations as quickly as possible, in order to belie or obfuscate rumors of complicity with members of the Saudi elite.

Support for the U.S. War on Terrorism

In response to the terrorist attacks of September 11 and under the leadership of Crown Prince Abdullah bin Abdulaziz, who became king upon the death of his half brother Fahd in 2005, the Saudi regime has made significant efforts to support the U.S.-led war on terrorism, including serving as the command base of U.S. air assaults against targets in Afghanistan. In addition, to exert positive Saudi leadership in the Middle East, Prince Abdullah initiated a plan to find a peaceful and final solution to the Israeli-Palestinian conflict, which Riyadh sees as a major cause of Arab frustrations.

Riyadh's perceived relationship with modernity and the West—above all the United States—and the resulting cultural and ideological imbalances associated with conservative institutions continue to be a crucial factor in the emergence of terrorism in Saudi Arabia. Another critical factor is a burgeoning population that is increasingly frustrated by an economy that is mired in corruption, nepotism, and a chronic inability to provide good jobs for an ever-increasing supply of relatively educated and alienated youth.

Perhaps fearing unrest at home if it too openly backs the United States in the latter's increasingly hostile approach to the Saddam Hussein regime in Iraq, Saudi officials consistently spoke out against any U.S.-led war against Iraq, going so far in August of 2002 as to deny the use of Saudi territory for any attack on Baghdad.

Nevertheless, the Saudi regime supported the United States, once the latter began combat operations in Iraq in March 2003, though it still did not allow its territory to be used to support those operations. This prohibition did little to quell the anger of Islamist extremists, who set off suicide bombs at Westerner housing compounds in Riyadh two months later, which resulted in the deaths of thirty-five persons. This was followed in September with another residential compound bombing that killed seventeen.

Saudi security forces were also targeted. Attacks near Riyadh in April 2004 killed four police officers, as did a bomb at the security headquarters in the capital. More violence quickly followed against foreigners, including three gun attacks in Riyadh that killed two Americans and a BBC cameraman and the kidnapping and beheading of a U.S. engineer in June. To deal with the unrest triggered by the Iraq War, the Saudi government used the carrot and stick against Islamist extremists, including the killing of a local al-Qaeda leader but also a general amnesty for militants, though the latter produced little tangible results, as more attacks hit the kingdom in December, including an attack on the U.S. consulate in Jeddah that killed five staff, and two car bombs in downtown Riyadh. More successful was the government's thwarting of a suicide bomb attack against a major oil refinery, planned for early 2006.

Still, Saudi security forces appeared to be gaining the upper hand in the second half of the decade, killing numerous militants and arresting dozens more. The government also launched a series of mild reforms, designed

KEY DATES

1989   Pro-Iranian Shiite pilgrims to Mecca set off two bombs there, killing one person during the hajj.

1990–1991   In the run-up to the Persian Gulf War, the Saudi government allows the United States to station troops in the kingdom, antagonizing Islamist radicals.

1995   A bomb placed in a van blows up outside the U.S.-manned training center for the Saudi National Guard, killing five, including four Americans.

1996   A large truck bomb explodes outside the U.S. Air Force compound in Khobar, killing nineteen service members and injuring hundreds more, mostly Americans.

2003   Widespread Saudi anger over the U.S. invasion of Iraq leads the George W. Bush Administration to withdraw virtually all troops from the kingdom.

2006   The Saudi government reports having thwarted a major Islamist militant assault on oil facilities.

to allow a modicum of peaceful protest and political discourse in the authoritarian kingdom, a major issue for Islamist activists. The measures appeared to be working, as Saudi Arabia has seen little in the way of Islamist violence since 2006. At the same time, however, it has reported thwarting a number of attacks, indicating that while its intelligence and security apparatus are becoming more effective, the problem of Islamist extremism remains very much alive.

Ashley Brown, Kimberly A. McCloud, and Andrew Rathmell

See also: *Definitions, Types, Categories*—Domestic vs. International Terrorism; Islamist Fundamentalist Terrorism. *September 11 Attacks*—Al-Qaeda.

Further Reading

Aburish, Saïd K. *The Rise, Corruption and Coming Fall of the House of Saud.* New York: St. Martin's, 1995.

Achcar, Gilbert. *The Clash of Barbarisms: September 11 and the Making of the New World Order.* New York: Monthly Review, 2002.

Al-Rasheed, Madawi. *A History of Saudi Arabia.* 2nd ed. New York: Cambridge University Press, 2010.

Bradley, John R. *Saudi Arabia Exposed: Inside a Kingdom in Crisis.* New York: Palgrave Macmillan, 2005.

Cordesman, Anthony H. *Saudi Arabia: Guarding the Desert Kingdom.* Boulder, CO: Westview, 1997.

Dekmejian, R. Hrair. *Islam in Revolution: Fundamentalism in the Arab World.* Syracuse, NY: Syracuse University Press, 1995.

———. "The Rise of Political Islamism in Saudi Arabia." *Middle East Journal* 48:4 (Autumn 1994): 627–44.

Fandy, Mamoun. *Saudi Arabia and the Politics of Dissent.* New York: St. Martin's, 1999.

Tollitz, Nino P., ed. *Saudi Arabia: Terrorism, U.S. Relations and Oil.* New York: Nova Science Publishers, 2005.

Serbia: Kosovo Conflict, 1990s

While tensions between ethnic Albanians and ethnic Serbs in Kosovo, along with disputes between Albanian Kosovars and the Yugoslav government in Belgrade, go back decades, the immediate cause of the Kosovo War of 1999 can be dated to 1990. In that year, Serbian president Slobodan Milošević, both egging on and responding to rising Serbian nationalism, revoked the autonomous status of Kosovo and imposed a pro-Serbian curriculum at the provinces' schools, a move rejected by the Albanian majority there, who then established a parallel school system. In the mid-1990s, a new force in the country had emerged, the Kosovo Liberation Army (KLA), to challenge Serbian repressive measures. In April 1996, it launched four simultaneous attacks on Serbian security forces. The KLA received much financing from Albanians abroad and took advantage of the growing chaos in neighboring Albania to secure a stockpile of weapons. Its frequent attacks on Serbian security forces led that country's government to declare it a terrorist organization, a move ratified briefly by the United States, which also added the KLA to its list of international terrorist organization.

But with tensions between Belgrade and Washington intensifying in the late 1990s, the Bill Clinton Administration removed the KLA from its list in 1998. Meanwhile, the Serbs refused to consider the Kosovo issue at the Peace Implementation Council, the international body established by the Dayton Peace Accords that ended the Bosnia war in 1995. The Serbs resisted such a move because they argued that Kosovo was an integral part of Serbia and home to sites revered by nationalists for their significance to Serbia's long history of resistance to outside powers. In addition, Kosovo was home to tens of thousands of ethnic Serbs, most of them living in an area alongside Serbia proper. In response to Serbian intransigence on considering autonomy or independence for Kosovo, the KLA began launching more attacks against Serbian security forces, which responded with an offensive against the organization. As 1998 turned into 1999, the fighting intensified, as did the refugee crisis that inevitably accompanies civil conflict.

NATO Peace Efforts

The North Atlantic Treaty Organization (NATO) led the effort to resolve the conflict, but a cease-fire arranged in late 1998 broke down, as bombings and murders struck urban areas throughout Kosovo, some perpetrated by the KLA and others by Serbian security forces. The worst such incident was the Serbian army massacre of forty-five Albanians in the town of Račak in January

Constituent republics and ethnic groups of the former Yugoslavia.

1999. The following month, NATO organized a conference at Rambouillet, France, to resolve the conflict. The agreement called for increasing autonomy for Kosovo but did not promise independence. Kosovar Albanian leaders signed the accord, but Serbs considered the deal too radical and rejected it.

With Serbian repression and military activities continuing in Kosovo, NATO opted for the military option it had been threatening all along, launching a sustained aerial assault on security and military targets in Serbia in late March 1999. Both the United States and its NATO allies were reluctant to send in ground troops, however, until a peace deal could be reached for them to enforce. Facing growing anger in Serbia over the bombing, Milošević finally succumbed on June 3, allowing for the introduction of KFOR troops (KFOR was the popular name for the Kosovo Force of NATO peacekeepers). The force was met by cheering Albanians and is largely considered to be one of NATO's great successes, having largely secured the peace with almost no troop losses of its own.

Overall the Kosovo War is believed to have resulted in about 10,000 deaths, the vast majority of them Albanian civilians killed by Serbian forces in Kosovo. While Serbia claimed that it had lost up to 5,000 civilians in the NATO assault, NATO itself put the figure at about

435

1,500. Meanwhile, the International Criminal Tribunal for the former Yugoslavia (ICTY) has conducted investigations into the deaths of thousands of Kosovar Albanians but has refused to say whether any were the result of war crimes.

In the years since the war ended, Kosovo has largely been at peace. In addition, Kosovo has been able to establish independent institutions and, as of August 2010, was recognized by 69 of 192 United Nations member states, including the United States and most of the other NATO states. Serbia and its main international ally, Russia, still refused to recognize it.

On March 24, 1999, as the first bombs began falling over Serbia and Kosovo, NATO member governments prepared their respective intelligence and security agencies for a wave of protests and violence. The spectrum of

NATO Bombing Targets, 1999

R	Refineries and warehouses storing liquid raw material and chemicals intended for the oil and chemical industry
A	Airports
I	Industries and factories
W	Water supply damaged
P	Power supply, power supply transmitter, power lines
C	Chemical
H	Hydroelectricpower supply
B	Bridges

Following Serbian efforts to "cleanse" the province of Kosovo of its Albanian ethnic majority, NATO launched air attacks in 1999, destroying much of the infrastructure of the country.

possible hostility ranged from street thuggery concurrent with peaceful protests to Serbian government-sponsored terrorist attacks against symbolic targets and persons. In the end, the actual worldwide violence toward the West was rather muted—with notable exceptions in Italy, Russia, China, and Greece. The United States, though a prime target because of its leadership role in NATO, received little more than vitriol. The threats within the United States did not go unnoticed, however, because of their potential use as indexes for antiterrorist operations.

Immediately following the initial NATO attack against Serb targets in Yugoslavia, anti-NATO and anti-U.S. violence erupted worldwide. This violence managed to sustain itself throughout the life of Operation Allied Force, NATO's code name for its last Balkan campaign of the twentieth century. Although the most damaging violence took place in Greece, Russia, and Italy, other European states and countries far from the military action, including China, Australia, and South Africa, saw serious protests and violence.

By any measure, the most persistent and violent anti-Western hostility during Operation Allied Force took place in NATO member Greece. Sharing cultural and religious affinities with the Serbs, the Greeks sparked serious, violent daily outbursts against targets symbolic of the West. Major world newspapers reported that on the day of the first wave of strikes, 15,000 protesters, waving Greek and Yugoslav flags, marched to the U.S. embassy shouting "Clinton, Fascist, Murderer." Greek police, positioned more out of prudence than concern, soon found themselves fighting protesters who were destroying stores and throwing rocks at the U.S. and British embassies.

Capitalizing on the civil unrest, on April 27, 1999, leftist insurgents detonated an improvised explosive outside of the Intercontinental Hotel in Athens, where final preparations for a trade fair highlighting U.S. products was under way. The explosion killed one Greek and injured another. Two days earlier, Greek police defused a bomb placed outside the Fulbright Center in Athens. In addition, the residences of Western diplomats were targets of violence. Protesters stoned the British and American ambassadors' homes, while the residences of Dutch and German diplomats came under fire from homemade rockets. No injuries occurred during these attacks. Softer targets, such as three Western banks in the port of Piraeus, were attacked in attempts to strike at Western business.

Although the most serious incidents occurred in Greece, other countries experienced violence as well. In Russia, the U.S. embassy in Moscow was the site of intense violence. Following four days of anti-U.S. protests, which saw Russian protesters hurling paint, beer, rocks, and eggs and the burning of U.S. flags, on March 28 a man sprayed automatic weapons fire into the embassy compound after his two grenade launchers failed to fire.

KEY DATES

1990   Serbian president Slobodan Milošević declares an end to Kosovo autonomy.

1996   Ethic Albanian militants organize the Kosovo Liberation Army and launch attacks on Serbian security forces.

March 18, 1999   Serbian and Russian representatives at the Rambouillet peace conference refuse to sign an agreement giving Kosovo autonomy within Serbia.

March 24, 1999   NATO begins attacking Serbia and Kosovo from the air.

April 15, 1999   The U.S. Justice Department reveals that letters had been sent to Serbian groups in the United States calling for attacks on U.S. military personnel and installations.

April 27, 1999   Pro-Serb leftists explode a bomb outside a hotel in Athens, killing a Greek national.

May 7, 1999   The U.S. bombing of the Chinese embassy in Belgrade leads to riots against the U.S. embassy in Beijing.

May 20, 1999   Several firebombs are hurled at the U.S. airbase at Aviano, Italy, by anti-imperialist activists.

June 3, 1999   Milošević accepts peace conditions.

Following the mistaken U.S. attack on the Chinese embassy in Belgrade on May 7, 1999, officially condoned violence against U.S., German, British, and other Western diplomatic facilities erupted in a half dozen Chinese cities. The mobs' actions, which included throwing stones, bottles, and firebombs at the U.S. ambassador's residence in Beijing, were so severe that the ambassador was unable to venture out for three full days. In Italy, leftists and anarchists capitalized on NATO's military action to begin violence anew. On May 20, 1999, the Red Brigades–Combatant Communist Party, a terrorist group with a long antigovernment history, gunned down Labor Minister Massimo d'Antona. The U.S. airbase at Aviano, which housed many of NATO's attack aircraft used in Operation Allied Force, saw several incendiary attacks directed against U.S. airmen stationed there. The leftist Territorial Anti-Imperialist Nuclei claimed responsibility for these actions. Moreover, demonstrations and violence were reported worldwide. Demonstrators in Sydney, Australia, hurled objects at police and smashed store windows. Reports of violence and demonstrations also came from Austria, South Africa, Germany, and France.

Potential for Violence in the United States

Two aspects of Operation Allied Force increased the likelihood of violent attacks within the United States. First, the 3 million people of southern Slav descent who reside in the United States provided an attractive target audience for anti-American propaganda. Second, some elements of U.S. combat forces engaged in the air campaign conducted operations directly from their home bases in the continental United States.

One particular incident highlighted these potential problems. On April 15, 1999, the U.S. Department of Justice revealed that on March 20, a letter calling for terrorist strikes against U.S. military personnel and installations had been faxed to a Serbian American social club and three Serbian Orthodox churches in Sacramento, California; Milwaukee, Wisconsin; Chicago, Illinois; and Indianapolis, Indiana. The message called for Serbian Americans to respond to NATO attacks with terror strikes against members of the U.S. armed forces "on the streets, in parks, in shopping malls, in movie theatres, in their homes, wherever they are." The Serbian churches in the United States did not comment on the faxes, and, equally significant, they also failed to condemn the ethnic cleansing in Kosovo. This threat, in addition to unspecified threats alluded to by the Justice Department, served to elevate the risk of terrorist violence within the United States.

In every U.S. military campaign there has been a latent terrorist threat to command and support elements. However, Operation Allied Force was unique in that, throughout the campaign, combat operations were launched daily from airbases *within* the United States. For example, the B-2 bombers, which combine a low radar profile with a high media profile, conducted all operations from Whiteman Air Force Base in Missouri. The existence of high-profile domestic targets and the well-publicized threat to military members and their families forced the U.S. military to dedicate valuable resources to ensuring tighter security at bases throughout the United States and greater operational security among U.S. pilots. Lieutenant General Ronald Marcotte, commander of the Eighth Air Force, emphasized that the press should avoid showing the names and faces of the men and women involved in Operation Allied Force, responding to a March 25 *USA Today* front-page newspaper article that provided a B-52 bomber crew's full names. Despite the potential for violence, no acts of terrorism occurred anywhere within the United States during Operation Allied Force.

Joseph L. Derdzinski, James Borders, and James Ciment

See also: *Definitions, Types, Categories*—Ethnonationalist Terrorism. *Modern Terrorism*—Bosnia: Civil Conflict.

Further Reading

Herscher, Andrew. *Violence Taking Place: The Architecture of the Kosovo Conflict*. Stanford, CA: Stanford University Press, 2010.

Ingrao, Charles, and Thomas A. Emmert, eds. *Confronting the Yugoslav Controversies: A Scholars' Initiative*. West Lafayette, IN: Purdue University Press, 2009.

Perritt, Henry H., Jr. *Kosovo Liberation Army: The Inside Story of an Insurgency*. Urbana: University of Illinois Press, 2008.

Weller, Marc. *Peace Lost: The Failure of Conflict Prevention in Kosovo*. Boston: Martinus Nijhoff, 2008.

Sierra Leone: Civil War, 1997–2002

The former British colony of Sierra Leone gained independence as a constitutional democracy on April 27, 1961. Since then, a long legacy of political instability, civil war, governmental corruption, and human rights abuses has relegated Sierra Leone to the status of a "failed state," especially with respect to the events and apparent trends in the period 1997–2002.

Background Profile

Sierra Leone, one of the poorest nations in the world, is bordered by Guinea and Liberia, which are inextricably bound to Sierra Leone vis-à-vis their participation in conflicts arising along those boundaries. Security along these borders is a source of continual strategic interest because transnational incursions by smugglers, adventurers, and terrorists have been historically common. The terrorism experienced in Sierra Leone is highly mobile and has moved easily across these national delineations, first, for purposes of obtaining safe haven, and second, to secure a platform for launching operations.

The area of Sierra Leone is slightly smaller than that of South Carolina, with a total bounded area of 27,700 square miles (71,740 square kilometers). Agriculture constitutes 43 percent of gross domestic product by sector. Further analysis would suggest that without significant improvement in the social and economic infrastructure, Sierra Leone's troubled past would weigh heavily on its future. It has natural resources, which may attract additional future global enterprise, although such endeavors are costly in risk-laden areas such as Sierra Leone. It has become common for global enterprises in Sierra Leone to enlist corporate "security consultants" to ensure their interests.

Diamonds are the leading export product of Sierra Leone; they are also the chief commodity used to finance terrorism within the country. Unconfirmed reports suggested that smuggled Sierra Leonean diamonds ended up in the hands of al-Qaeda, which used them to further its violent political agendas.

Sierra Leone, with twenty native African tribes, has a diverse ethnicity; 30 percent of these tribes are Temne, 30 percent Mende, and the remainder of various native African lineages. Tribal entities in Sierra Leone have a long history of documented animosity, which historically resulted in significant violence preceding even British colonial rule by centuries. English is the official language of Sierra Leone, but it is limited to the minority of citizens who are literate. Mende is the southern vernacular, whereas Temne is spoken in the north. Krio (creole) is understood by approximately 95 percent of the population, but only 10 percent use it regularly. Sierra Leone is 60 percent Muslim, 30 percent practitioners of animism (traditional beliefs), and 10 percent Christian.

Political parties, though numerous, are dominated by the Revolutionary United Front Party, led by Gbassay Kanu; the Sierra Leone People's Party, led by former Sierra Leone president Alhaji Ahmad Tejan Kabbah; and the United National People's Party, led by Abdul Kady Karim. Historically, political parties have been suspended in Sierra Leone according to the whims of the political incumbents and the perception that some parties might actually challenge the legitimacy of the regime in power. The constitution has been suspended on numerous occasions.

Insurgency

On February 26, 1996, presidential and parliamentary elections took place in Sierra Leone. In the course of these elections, in which thirteen political parties took part and monitored by international teams of observers, violence occurred in Freetown, the capital of Sierra Leone, at the hands of armed groups. The deaths of twenty-seven people were attributed to members of the Revolutionary United Front (RUF), whose objective was to thwart the electoral process. The election resulted in an outcome wherein no single party had the requisite 55 percent to seat a presidential candidate in office. Civil violence also occurred in other regions of the country, and, as a consequence, seven of the thirteen political parties competing in the presidential election requested that the outcome be annulled. In a second round of the presidential election, held on March 15, Ahmad Tejan Kabbah, of the Sierra Leone People's Party, was elected president with almost 60 percent of the vote.

On May 25, 1997, a military coup took place. Elements of the army led by Major Johnny Paul Koroma took control of the government and deposed Kabbah, who subsequently escaped to Guinea. Under the military junta, civil rights were immediately suspended; this arrogation of authority caused widespread violence throughout Sierra Leone. Nigeria demanded that the military junta step down and subsequently began to increase its troop level in Freetown. A subsequent Nigerian naval bombardment of Freetown took place in efforts to unseat the junta, but ensuing attacks upon Freetown by Nigerian troops were unsuccessful in their objective as elements of the RUF joined those of the junta in repelling the attacks. Reports listed 62 civilians killed in the fighting over Freetown. The taking of 300 Nigerian troops as hostages during the hostilities was attributed to the RUF. They were later released. Koroma then suspended the constitution and announced the formation of a twenty-member revolutionary council with himself at the head.

Nigeria again protested the move, stating that it would reinstate Kabbah as president with the support of the Economic Community of West African States (ECOWAS). During this time, widespread protests occurred in opposition to the military junta. Condemnation of the coup was widespread, ranging from Commonwealth partners to the United Nations Security Council. ECOWAS initiated an embargo of Sierra Leone, and a naval blockade and occupation of the Lungi Airport by Nigerian troops was also instituted. The results of these actions were significant shortages of food, petroleum, and essential commodities. The Kamajors, the traditional warriors of Sierra Leone, in support of deposed president Kabbah, clashed repeatedly with government forces. Eventually, the total weight of this multifaceted resistance caused the junta to declare an immediate cease-fire and to initiate peace negotiations at Abidjan between the junta's political wing, the Armed Forces Revolutionary Council (AFRC), and ECOWAS. However, hostilities between the disputing parties continued, and the escalation and intensification of the clashes increased with the use of aerial bombings against merchant vessels in the Freetown harbor and blockades of roads used for commerce into Freetown. The effect was to cut the capital off from the rest of the country and the world. The civilian population began to flee Freetown.

The pressure on the junta resulted in the AFRC's promising to relinquish control by April 22, 1998, and to begin disarmament. Still the violence persisted throughout wide areas of the country, often culminating in atrocities perpetrated by the RUF and those loyal to the junta. Refugees from the violence fled into neighboring provinces and into Liberia, as ECOMOG (Economic Community of West African States Monitoring Group) stepped up their attacks on the RUF throughout Sierra Leone. On March 10, 1998, President Kabbah returned to Freetown, assumed the presidency, and appointed a cabinet. The newly installed cabinet immediately began to level charges of treason upon arrested supporters of the deposed military junta. In July 1998, the United Nations Security Council adopted a resolution that provided a seventy-member observer force, the United Nations Mission in Sierra Leone (UNMISL), to monitor the poor internal security status of the country.

The release of rebel leader Foday Sankoh from Nigerian custody and his return to Sierra Leone to face charges stemming from the 1997 coup, which included treason and murder, precipitated a violent chain of events. Sankoh was subsequently found guilty of the charges and sentenced to death. Unfortunately, these verdicts caused widespread and intensified atrocities upon civilians by the RUF and the AFRC, both of which pledged to continue their campaign of violence upon civilians in the

event that the death penalty was carried out on Sankoh. Meanwhile, the violence escalated; reports increased of atrocities by Sankoh loyalists upon civilians on the one hand and by ECOMOG forces retaliating with summary executions. In January 1999, intense fighting broke out in Freetown between the RUF and ECOMOG forces in which more than 5,000 people were killed. This fighting prompted further escalation of atrocities upon civilians by the RUF.

Ultimately, Freetown was secured by ECOMOG in the months leading up to April 1999, when international pressure forced the warring factions to open negotiations in Lomé, Togo. In May 1999, the RUF and the Sierra Leonean government signed a cease-fire agreement. In early July 1999, a power-sharing agreement was reached between the RUF and the government of Sierra Leone whereby the government agreed to place Sankoh in control of the country's mineral resources. However, the Lomé agreement was quickly violated by the RUF, which continued committing atrocities directed at civilians.

Rebel Terrorism Before and After Lomé

In 1997, the RUF, the AFRC and forces loyal to exiled president Kabbah, and ECOWAS engaged in continual, large-scale confrontations that frequently resulted in civilian casualties. Estimates suggest that after 1992 the RUF insurgency displaced nearly 40 percent of the population. The chronology that follows illustrates the violence perpetrated not only by rebel factions but also by their opposition. The violence described herein includes an underlying political objective: the consolidation of power in this independent nation without an effective and functional social and economic infrastructure. Sierra Leone continued a significant rapid decline, which was due in part to the civil war and in part to the loss of political legitimacy attendant on the atrocities perpetrated upon civilians.

- On July 8, 1997, junta soldiers executed a woman for her public support of exiled president Kabbah.
- On August 18, 1997, eleven students, members of a "march for democracy" against the military junta, were killed in an AFRC attack. Another student was chopped into pieces by military junta forces.
- On September 1, 1997, Kamajoh and Kapra fighters decapitated four people for suspicion of belonging to the AFRC military. The RUF and AFRC continued their onslaught of terrorism throughout the year, using decapitation, maiming, rape, kidnappings, and torture to coerce and intimidate civilians for their political objectives. Children were frequently the objects of abduction, with boys forcibly conscripted as soldiers or guards, while girls became cooks or sex slaves.

- On March 22, 1998, it was reported that un-named assailants killed fifty civilians during their attempted escape from fighting in Kabala. The report went on to state that these deaths were "part of conflict fare, not just indiscipline on the part of fighters." Again, as in previous years, rape, torture, maiming, and abductions were common throughout 1998.
- On August 4, 1999, AFRC forces kidnapped more than two dozen UNMISL members along with numerous other foreign nationals, includ-ing aid workers and journalists, and demanded that the reinstated government of President Kabbah release imprisoned junta leader Johnny Paul Koroma from prison, where he awaited trial on charges of war crimes and murder. Those abducted were subsequently released unharmed over the next six days.
- On October 15, 1999, AFRC rebels reportedly kidnapped three clergymen, a Sierra Leonean and two Italians, who were subsequently released unharmed.
- On December 7, 1999, RUF rebels kidnapped two international members of the humanitarian agency Médecins Sans Frontières (Doctors With-out Borders). The rebels, who initially demanded a ransom for the release of the two men, finally freed them unharmed on December 16, 1999, after nine days of detention.
- On August 25, 2000, an eleven-man British patrol was taken hostage by an armed rebel group called the Westside Boys in the Occra Hills just outside the capital; on September 3, the rebels released five of the soldiers; the remaining six were rescued in a military operation a week later.

These examples of violence, whose persistent under-lying objective was to consolidate and secure power or to coerce capitulation from resistant factions or populations, underscore the kind of continued upheaval endemic to the sociopolitical and security environment of contemporary Sierra Leone.

Nevertheless, by the early 2000s, the war in Si-erra Leone was winding down, with the UN deploying troops in rebel-held territories in March 2001, followed by the beginning of the rebel disarmament process two months later. By July 2002, the country had become secure enough under UN peacekeepers to allow for the withdrawal of all British troops. Meanwhile, both Sierra Leoneans and the international community were demand-ing that the rebel leaders, and those who supported them, face punishment for their actions. The July 2003 death of Sankoh from natural causes prevented him from being put before a UN war crimes court, which had been approved

KEY DATES

1961 Sierra Leone wins its independence from Britain.

1996 Presidential and parliamentary elections are marred by violence from Revolutionary United Front (RUF) guerrillas and others; despite violence, Alhaji Ahmad Tejan Kabbah is elected president in a runoff in the following year.

1997 Major Johnny Paul Koroma takes power in a military coup.

1998 Alhaji Ahmad Tejan Kabbah returns to the presi-dency, backed up by Nigerian forces.

1999 The Sierra Leone government and RUF sign a power-sharing agreement; despite the agreement, fighting breaks out again.

2001 The war winds down as United Nations peacekeep-ers deploy and rebel disarmament commences.

2003 Rebel leader Foday Sankoh dies of natural causes.

2007 The Special Court for Sierra Leone in The Hague begins its trial of former Liberian president Charles Taylor, accused of war crimes and human rights violations for his support of the RUF.

to go into operation in January 2002. Still, in March 2004, a hybrid special tribunal in The Hague, affiliated with the International Criminal Court but under Sierra Leonean auspices, began to try senior rebel leaders.

The most notorious defendant at the Special Court for Sierra Leone, however, would not be a national, but a Liberian, specifically, former president Charles Taylor. Ousted from power by rebels in August 2003 and sent into Nigerian exile, Taylor was eventually extradited in March 2006 to the Netherlands to face trial for aiding and abetting the Sierra Leone rebels in the late 1990s and early 2000s, trading weapons for illegally smuggled diamonds. As of the spring of 2011, Taylor's trial re-mained ongoing.

Michael L. Largent

See also: *Definitions, Types, Categories*—Ethnonationalist Terrorism.

Further Reading

"Bleak Future for Kamajors." *Africa Research Bulletin* (July 1–31, 1998): 13156.

Dorff, Robert H. "Responding to the Failed State: What to Do and What to Expect." Paper presented at the International Programs, Failed States Conference, Purdue University, West Lafayette, IN, April 7–10, 1999.

"Foday Sankoh to Stand Trial." *Africa Research Bulletin* (August 1–31, 1998): 13228.

Gberie, Lansana. *A Dirty War in West Africa: The RUF and the Destruction of Sierra Leone.* Bloomington: Indiana University Press, 2005.

Somalia: Failed State Conflict and Rise of Islamist Militants, 1977–2000s

Somalia is a contemporary example of a failed state and, as such, represents an environment rich for the development of terrorism. After years of combat with Ethiopia over a disputed region known as the Ogaden, a decade-long civil war left the country with no central government from 1991 on. In its place lie three prominent political structures, as well as a radical Islamic fundamentalist movement with links to Osama bin Laden's al-Qaeda. Yet despite the poverty, proliferation of small arms, and fractured society, violence in Somalia, though pervasive, rarely meets the traditional conception of political terrorism. Rather, kidnappings and murders are usually the result of semiorganized crime or interclan or interfactional fighting. Nonetheless, a closer examination of Somalia's recent history demonstrates that its political vacuum has enticed both domestic and foreign actors to establish links to known terrorist groups as well as to participate in terrorist acts.

Independence and Ethnic Unrest

Previously colonized by Britain, France, and Italy in the nineteenth century, Somalia became independent in 1960. Nomadic Somalis in the Ogaden—an arid expanse of northeastern Ethiopia—agitated for inclusion in the Somali republic and in 1960 openly revolted, looking to Somalia for aid. Successive Somali governments tried to liberate the Ogaden. In 1961, the new Somali republic helped to organize and arm a guerrilla force that, by the early 1970s, was known as the Western Somalia Liberation Front (WSLF). Between 1960 and 1964, there were violent clashes and terrorist attacks in the Ogaden between Ethiopian troops and Somali-backed guerrillas.

Meanwhile, a dispute had arisen in the Northern Frontier District (NFD) of northeastern Kenya, where nomadic Somali tribes were resentful of Kenyan rule. During the late 1950s and early 1960s, Somalis of the NFD waged a terrorist campaign in the region. From hideouts in the desert, they attacked Kenyan police units. Although the NFD conflict escalated following Kenyan independence in 1963, the unrest was quelled the following year.

Open Conflict in the Ogaden

In May 1977, the guerrilla campaign for the Ogaden erupted into open warfare between the Ethiopian army and a 3,000–6,000-strong WSLF force. The WSLF aimed to regain for Somalia all the territory east of a line from Moyale on the Kenyan border to Lake Abbe, or roughly a third of Ethiopia. The WSLF took the initiative to attack without Somali approval. Faced with the reality of the attack, however, the Somali army rapidly joined in the fighting. Somali president Siad Barre had little choice but to permit his troops to "resign" and join the WSLF. The Somali troops and the WSLF easily overran the small Ethiopian garrisons in the Ogaden.

In July 1977, the WSLF cut off the Djibouti–Addis Ababa railroad, Ethiopia's only rail link to the sea. By September 12, 1977, Jijiga, the principal Ethiopian military headquarters in the Ogaden, had fallen to the WSLF. The Ethiopians only just managed to hold on to Harer and Dire Dawa, some 200 miles (322 kilometers) east of Addis Ababa. For their attack, the Somalis deployed some 35,000 regular troops and a substantial guerrilla force.

By the end of 1977, the WSLF and the Somali army had achieved a spectacular success: more than 90 percent of the disputed region was in their hands and the Ethiopian army had mutinied and retreated. The morale of the Ethiopian army had not been helped by a series of bloody purges before the war. The Ethiopian Third Division retreated from the key defensive position in the Gara Marda Pass by Jijiga, abandoning their equipment to the WSLF and leaving open the road to Harer. As the theater of conflict expanded, the WSLF enlisted the support of other clans, including the Oromo, and an Oromo guerrilla force, called the Somali Abo Liberation Front, was formed. However, Barre was now critically short of arms and requested Soviet aid.

The Soviets had been supporting Somalia in opposition to Haile Selassie's U.S.-backed Ethiopian empire. In 1974, however, Selassie was ousted, and a revolutionary council—the Dergue—set about removing the U.S. presence in Ethiopia. The Soviets welcomed these developments, but their position was complicated by the Somali conflict, and they were ultimately obliged to pick sides. In mid-1977, they withdrew support for Somalia in favor of Ethiopia. Accordingly, the Somalis ordered Soviet personnel from Somalia and renounced the Soviet-Somali treaty of friendship. These actions intensified Soviet support for the Ethopian Dergue.

Soviet support for Ethiopia gradually swung the balance of power away from Somalia, whose positions in the Ogaden were vulnerable. By August 1977, the Soviets halted military aid to Somalia. They began to supply arms to Ethiopia on a huge scale—far in excess of previous contributions to Somalia.

On February 3, 1978, the Ethiopians, now backed by the Cubans and Soviets, were finally in a position to launch a counterattack. The Somalis officially committed army troops to the Ogaden on February 12, 1978, having previously claimed that all the fighting was being done by the WSLF. On March 4, the Ethiopians attacked Jijiga in the Gara Marda Pass. The town fell after two days' fighting, in which about 10,000 Cuban troops and 1,500 Soviet advisers were involved on the Ethiopians' side. The Soviets also used South Yemeni soldiers and some East German advisers. The Soviets airlifted a Cuban armored column with sixty to seventy tanks behind Jijiga, trapping the Somalis and forcing them into headlong retreat. Somali relief units were strafed by MiG fighters before they could even reach the front.

Somalia announced its withdrawal from the Ogaden on March 9, 1978. Despite this declaration, the WSLF and the Somali army persisted in their campaign, exploiting the distraction caused by the escalating war between Ethiopia and Eritrea to the north, but were finally routed in 1980. In the aftermath of Somalia's defeat, about 1.5 million refugees fled to Somalia, and Barre executed a number of Somali generals. Other officers staged a failed coup in April 1978. Somalia's complained later that the United States had promised them aid if Barre ended his alliance with the Soviets but had ultimately failed to support them.

Continued Conflict

The conflict in the Ogaden continued after 1978, as the WSLF fought the Ethiopian government and their Cuban allies. In July 1982, clashes occurred near Belet Uen, involving the Somali Democratic Salvation Front. This Ethiopian-backed guerrilla movement intended to overthrow Barre. Other guerrilla groups active at the time included the United Somali Congress and the Somali National Movement. Operating at first from bases in Ethiopia, the Somali National Movement waged a terrorist campaign against the Somali government. In 1988, it invaded northern Somalia and the conflict escalated into open war. By 1989, when government forces regained the upper hand, some 10,000 people had been killed in the civil war.

Political History–Current Status

Meanwhile, beginning in the 1980s, insurgencies in the northeast and northwest began to significantly threaten Siad Barre's autocratic regime, then considered a defense partner of the United States, in the waning days of the Cold War. By 1990, the government's army began to factionalize along tribal and clan lines. This prompted Barre and his loyal forces to flee the capital in 1991, eventually leading to the declaration of an independent Republic of Somaliland in the northwest and in 1998 the autonomous State of Puntland in the northeast.

Finally, as a result of a conference held in late 2000 in neighboring Djibouti, a Transitional National Government was formed under the leadership of President Abdulkassim Salat Hassan, and it subsequently gained some authority in the south. Many countries (notably the United States) do not recognize the Transitional National Government, and its governance is contested by the Ethiopia-sponsored Somalia Reconciliation and Restoration Council. As a result, Somalia lacks effective law enforcement and is unable to monitor or regulate the financial sector. All told, some thirty factions vie for control of approximately eighteen historical administrative regions or states.

Somalia has become known as a cauldron of terrorism, largely because of the ethnic Somali regional diaspora, the failed political administration, and radicalized Islamic fundamentalism. First, as is true of much of postcolonial Africa, Somalia's international borders do not encompass all the major ethnic Somali groups or villages—significant populations live in both Kenya and Ethiopia. Somali nationalism sparked the 1977 offensive incursion into the Ogaden region in Ethiopia, which soundly defeated Somalia. Nonetheless the border territories continue to smolder. Second, the relative lawlessness of most of Somalia has allowed international terrorist groups to establish contacts, infrastructures, and training facilities within its borders. These two factors have in turn fostered the rise of the radical fundamentalist al-Ittihad al-Islami (AIAI)—meaning Islamic Unity—in the Puntland region, seeking to forge Islamic states in Somalia and Ethiopia.

Somalia and Terrorism

Despite an environment rife with potential for international terrorism, few such attacks were recorded in the country from 1995 to 2001. The U.S. Department of State reported only seven acts of international terrorism during that period. Suspected al-Ittihad al-Islami militants targeted foreign businessmen in single attacks in 1995 and 1996. In 1997, terrorist tactics switched to kidnapping aid workers and peacekeepers as militiamen of competing clans and warlords became the new perpetrators. In an attack in 1997 and again in 1998, clansmen kidnapped small groups of foreigners but released them all with ransoms not paid. Then, once in 2000 and twice in 2001, groups of aid workers were targeted in lethal attacks by competing warlords, resulting in at least fifteen deaths and more than forty injuries.

Though they were significant in their own context, it was not these events that brought Somalian terrorism to the American consciousness. Rather, it was Somalia's role as the setting for the failed 1993 U.S. humanitarian efforts (later described in the book and movie *Black Hawk Down*) as well as the staging area for the al-Qaeda's bombings of the U.S. embassies in Africa in 1998 and the subsequent U.S. retaliatory strike on a chemical plant in Sudan.

Terrorist Groups in Somalia

Led by the Unified Task Force and within the framework of Operation Restore Hope, U.S. forces landed in Somalia in 1992 to facilitate the distribution of foodstuffs and pave the way for the full-scale United Nations Operation in Somalia. As escort duties expanded to peacekeeping (employing military and security forces to maintain a minimal degree of civil order, particularly in the absence of, or after the destruction of, extant political institutions in war by either unilateral or multilateral intervention) and as peacekeeping broadened to peacemaking (imposing such civil order by foreign security forces), American troops eventually began engaging armed groups and Somali warlords. This escalation resulted in the death of eighteen U.S. servicemen in October 1993 in the capital city, Mogadishu.

Although definitive proof that bin Laden masterminded or had foreknowledge of that particular attack on U.S. military personnel has not been demonstrated, in 1998 and 1999 the United States indicted bin Laden for, among other things, training the Somalis involved in the 1993 attack. Later, in a CNN interview, bin Laden claimed to have trained Somalis in the tactics of targeting helicopters with rocket-propelled grenades—a skill acquired in Afghanistan against the Soviets in the 1980s.

The U.S. indictment sheds more light on bin Laden's interest in Somalia as well as al-Qaeda's activities there. It notes that al-Qaeda issued a fatwa describing the UN mission in Somalia as a cover for American aggression and called upon Muslims to attack those troops. The indictment also charged bin Laden with plotting and executing a 1992 bombing of a Yemeni hotel in which U.S. forces were staying en route to service in Somalia, as well as staging and coordinating the 1998 bombings of American embassies in neighboring Kenya and Tanzania from bases in Somalia. Though Somalia's collapsed political structure obviously provided an attractive vacuum in which to establish bases, burgeoning Islamic groups such as al-Ittihad al-Islami, which crosscut the clan-based political frontier of Somalia, provided both necessary and sufficient conditions for al-Qaeda cells to take root.

The most prominent Somali Islamic group to arise following the overthrow of Siad Barre's regime, AIAI was founded in the late 1980s. It became especially violent in the mid-1990s in Somalia, attacking foreigners and fomenting unrest among ethnic Somali Muslims across the border in neighboring Ethiopia, all in attempts to impose an Islamic regime in both countries. U.S. reports reveal that AIAI was more active in Ethiopia and was likely behind the 1996–1997 series of bombings in Addis Ababa. However, by 1998 as the southern Puntland region coalesced into a semiautonomous secular state, armed AIAI elements were driven out and the group was forced to revise its strategy. Numbering only about 2,000 members by 2001, AIAI focused on building physical infrastructure, such as Islamic schools and hospitals, as well as providing pockets of security as a means of building political support. Nonetheless, previously documented ties to bin Laden's al-Qaeda led to the group's inclusion on the USA Patriot Act's Terrorist Exclusion List, generated in response to the al-Qaeda attacks against America on September 11, 2001.

In addition to identifying AIAI as a terrorist organization in December 2001, the United States also froze the assets of the Somali financial company Al Barakaat, claiming that the institution laundered money for al-Qaeda and financially supported AIAI efforts. Upon further investigation, however, any Al Barakhat ties to al-Qaeda appeared to have diminished, if not ended, well before the September 11 attacks.

Rise of Radical Islamist Organizations

Meanwhile, the chaos and clan fighting in Somalia continued despite efforts by Somali leaders to forge a government of national unity. In 2004, a group of them met in Kenya to establish the Somali Transitional Federal Government (TFG) under Colonel Abdullah Yusuf Ahmed. But Ahmed was widely seen by Somalis as too closely allied with Ethiopia and so his claim to leadership of the TFG was widely disputed, leaving him unable to unite the clans of the country.

Of even greater concern to many in Somalia and the international community was the rise of radical Islamist groups. While these groups were able to use religion to unite Somalis across clans and demonstrated a greater capacity to provide a modicum of social services in the areas they controlled, they also threatened to impose rigid Islamist social customs on the country and draw it into the international war on terrorism. For these reasons, they were kept out of the general peace talks aimed at establishing a permanent government in Somalia.

Instead, the Islamic Courts Union (ICU), the leading Islamist faction in the country, chose to confront the Ethiopian-backed TFG militarily. In June 2006, militias allied with the ICU captured Mogadishu. The takeover concerned both Ethiopia and the international community, the former fearing that it would lose influence in the country and gain a bitter enemy on its border and the latter worrying that Somalia under the ICU would become a haven for international terrorist organizations such as al-Qaeda. In response to the ICU takeover, Ethiopia sent troops into the country and, with its allies in the TFG, drove the ICU from Mogadishu by the end of 2006 and from their last holdout, the port city of Kismayo in the south of the country, by early 2007. Renegade bands of Islamist fighters remained.

Despite the presence of peacekeepers from the African Union (AU), dispatched to the country in March 2007, fierce fighting continued between the Ethiopian-backed TFG and Islamist militias, among them al-Shabaab (Arabic for Youth Party). Al-Shabaab proved to be a resilient fighting force, capable of seizing control of Kismayo in August 2008 and, even as Ethiopia was withdrawing its troops under international pressure in January 2009, the strategic town of Baidoa as well. By summer 2010, al-Shabaab was in control of the southern outskirts of Mogadishu, poised to seize the entire capital from the TFG.

Al-Shabaab, which is on the U.S. State Department list of terrorist organizations, is a self-declared ally of al-Qaeda, having sworn allegiance to the latter's leader, Osama bin Laden, in September 2009 and then establishing a formal alliance in February 2010. The group has also declared its responsibility for a number of terrorist actions in Somalia, though only one abroad. In June 2009, it launched a suicide bombing attack at a hotel north of Mogadishu, where TFG officials were meeting, killing the security minister as well as more than twenty other persons. In July 2010, the group claimed responsibility for twin bombings in Uganda that left seventy-four persons, who had gathered to watch the World Cup final at a restaurant and rugby club in the capital Kampala, dead. Experts were baffled as to why the group would attack Uganda, since that country's involvement in Somalia derives only from its participation in the AU peacekeeping force, along with many other countries. Some argued that al-Shabaab was merely trying to flex its muscles with this first attack on foreign soil and Uganda presented a convenient target. To that end, in January 2010, the group declared its readiness to send fighters to help fellow Islamists in Yemen, just across the Gulf of Aden.

Security experts and policy makers in the West express extreme concern about al-Shabaab and the prospect of a Somalia ruled by this radical Islamist group, likening such a scenario to that of Afghanistan under the Taliban in the 1990s and early 2000s, where al-Qaeda was able to set up training camps and logistics networks, and plan numerous terrorist attacks overseas, including those of September 11, 2001. For that reason, the United States has actively targeted al-Shabaab leaders since 2008. In April of that year, it launched an air assault in Somalia, which killed insurgent leader Aden Hashi Ayro, the first in a series of Predator drone attacks against al-Shabaab leaders and bases ordered by Presidents George W. Bush and Barack Obama. Meanwhile, concerns grew over al-Shabaab's successful efforts to recruit disaffected youth among the Somali American population, concentrated in Minneapolis–St. Paul, Minnesota. In September 2009, one of these recruits drove a truck bomb into an AU base in Mogadishu, killing twenty peacekeepers. In August 2010, the Federal Bureau of Investigation announced that it had rounded up fourteen Somali Americans suspected of providing support for al-Shabaab. Back in Somalia, meanwhile, the organization was showing that it could still conduct dramatic and deadly raids, such as the one on a hotel favored by the Somali legislature on August 24, 2010, which killed more than thirty persons, including six parliamentarians.

Matthew Hughes, James T. Kirkhope, and James Ciment

See also: *Definitions, Types, Categories*—Islamist Fundamentalist Terrorism. *Modern Terrorism*—Eritrea: Anti-Ethiopian Struggle and Somali Civil War. *Tactics, Methods, Aims*—Safe Havens, Terrorist.

Further Reading

"Bombings in Uganda: Somalia Comes to Uganda." *The Economist,* July 15, 2010.

Cortright, David. *The Sanctions Decade: Assessing UN Strategies in the 1990s.* Boulder, CO: Lynne Rienner, 2000.

Kusow, Abdi M., and Stephanie R. Bjork, eds. *From Mogadishu to Dixon: The Somali Diaspora in a Global Context.* Trenton, NJ: Red Sea, 2007.

Menkhaus, Ken. *Somalia: State Collapse and the Threat of Terrorism.* New York: Oxford University Press for the International Institute for Strategic Studies, 2004.

Metz, Helen Chapin. *Somalia: A Country Study.* 4th ed. Baton Rouge, LA: Claitors, 1993.

Munck, Ronaldo, and Purnaka L. De Silva. *Postmodern Insurgencies: Political Violence, Identity Formation, and Peacemaking in Comparative Perspective.* New York: St. Martin's, 2000.

Phillips, James. *Somalia and al-Qaeda: Implications for the War on Terrorism.* Heritage Foundation Occasional Paper 1526. Washington, DC: Heritage Foundation, 2002.

"Somalia's Civil War: Jihadist's on the March." *The Economist,* February 25, 2010.

U.S. Department of State. *Patterns of Global Terrorism, 2001.* Washington, DC: U.S. Government Printing Office, 2002.

KEY DATES

1970s and 1980s Somalia fights a series of conflicts with Ethiopia over the Ogaden region.

1991 Dictator Siad Barre is overthrown and is forced to flee the country.

2000 Puntland declares itself independent of the rest of Somalia. Groups of aid workers are targeted in a lethal attack by competing warlords.

2001 Aid workers are again targeted in two lethal attacks by competing warlords. In December, the United States declares the Somali Islamic organization al-Ittihad al-Islami a terrorist organization and freezes U.S. assets of the Somali bank Al Barakaat.

2006 The radical Union of Islamic Courts seizes control of Mogadishu before being driven out by Ethiopian troops and their Somali allies in the Transitional Federal Government.

2009 The Islamist militia, al-Shabaab, launches a suicide attack on a hotel, killing Somalia's security minister and more than twenty others.

2010 Al-Shabaab declares an alliance with al-Qaeda and claims responsibility for twin bombings in Uganda that leave more than seventy persons dead.

South Africa: Antiapartheid Struggle, 1948–1994

Terrorism was used by opponents of racially segregated South Africa to achieve equal rights with the ruling white minority. The campaign for equality was spearheaded by the African National Congress (ANC).

The ANC was formed in South Africa in 1912 to further political reform and to protect the rights of blacks in South Africa. The founders advocated nonviolent political activity but achieved little in early years to disturb white rule. At the time of the ANC's formation, the South African population was made up of various racial groups: the black majority, the "Cape coloreds" (the authorities' description for those of mixed race), Asian communities, and whites of British or Dutch descent. Those of Dutch descent, known as Boers or Afrikaners, could often trace their families' residence in South Africa back to the time when English settlers were arriving in North America. The Dutch established themselves in Cape Town in 1652, thirty years before English Quakers arrived in Philadelphia.

In 1948, the right-wing National Party came to power. With its power base among the Afrikaners, the National Party legislated a rigid system of racial segregation: apartheid. In response, the ANC issued the 1955 "Freedom Charter," calling for human rights for all people in South Africa. In spite of the ANC's continued policy of nonviolence, the National government arrested and prosecuted for treason much of the ANC leadership. Upset by the failure of the nonviolent policy, a splinter group led by Robert Sobukwe broke away in 1959 and formed a new radical organization known as the Pan-Africanist Congress. The Pan-Africanists objected to the multicultural nature of the ANC and its closeness to white liberals.

A confrontation between the new organization and the authorities was not long in coming. On March 21, 1960, the Pan-Africanists organized a demonstration against the identity cards—referred to as passes—that the black population was required to carry. The police

Dead and wounded protesters lie in the streets of Sharpeville, South Africa, after police opened fire on a peaceful antiapartheid demonstration on March 21, 1960, killing sixty-seven. The massacre drew international condemnation and sparked rioting in black townships. *(Central Press/Stringer/Getty Images)*

opened fire, killing 67 blacks and wounding more than 200. Riots swept through the black townships, and 30,000 blacks marched on Cape Town. The government declared a state of emergency and banned the Pan-Africanists and the ANC. The Pan-Africanists were suppressed, but the ANC weathered the government's response even though its leaders were arrested or forced into hiding. Besides, ANC Youth League leader Nelson Mandela had prepared for the ANC to continue as an underground organization.

Beginning the Armed Struggle

The failure of the ANC policy of nonviolence caused a change in strategy, and in 1961 the organization opted for the selective use of violence—in other words, the use of terrorism. It was not easy to drop a fifty-year tradition of nonviolent activity, and a faction of the ANC leadership argued strongly that terrorism would damage the international prestige of the movement. Nonetheless, the ANC leaders voted to form a military wing, Umkhonto we Sizwe (Spear of the Nation). Deciding upon armed struggle was relatively simple, but implementing it was much more difficult. There was no weaponry or competent military leadership available; the underground network was far from secure; and there were no sympathetic neighboring countries to provide bases or infiltration routes. Every state in southern Africa was governed by European colonial powers or entrenched white minorities.

Umkhonto's opening terrorist campaign consisted mainly of sabotage operations against utilities, communications networks, and government buildings. This achieved limited results: the government claimed that the 194 operations launched between June 1961 and July 1963 caused an average of only $125 damage per incident, with the highest event reaching $10,000. The insurgents also attacked police informants and similar nonwhite targets, but most of these were mere random acts of terror. No effort was made to explain Umkhonto's aims and methods, and the operations did not have grassroots support. The government did not remain idle. Security police raided the Umkhonto headquarters in Johannesburg on July 11, 1963, capturing almost all the Umkhonto high command and valuable intelligence. A wave of arrests then jailed almost the entire ANC leadership, including Walter Sisulu, Govan Mbeki, and Nelson Mandela. The only leader to escape was Oliver Tambo, then living abroad.

Regrouping and Reorganizing

Umkhonto's amateurish terrorist campaign had failed, and the arrests of the leadership transformed Tambo into the effective head of the ANC. He controlled a demoralized domestic organization with a discredited strategy. Umkhonto needed a secure domestic underground net-

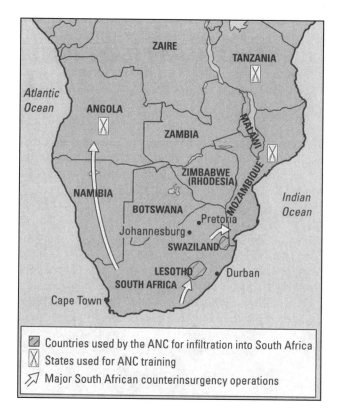

Countries used by the ANC for infiltration into South Africa

States used for ANC training

Major South African counterinsurgency operations

With the process of decolonization in southern Africa, neighboring countries eventually supported the antiapartheid campaign in South Africa.

work and a safe base for training and infiltration routes into South Africa. The ANC accomplished the necessary regrouping during fourteen years of comparative peace.

The complexion of South Africa's neighbors altered dramatically between 1963 and 1977. The Portuguese colonists left Angola and Mozambique in 1974, and the British colonies in the area had all gained independence in the 1960s. The only exception was the white renegade state of Rhodesia, which eventually came under black majority rule in 1980. As decolonization swept through Africa, sympathetic bases became available to the ANC in neighboring countries such as Zambia. In 1967, Umkhonto tried to infiltrate guerrillas through Rhodesia (now Zimbabwe), aided by the Zimbabwe African People's Union and using bases in Zambia. But Rhodesian security forces tracked them down. For the rest of the 1960s, Umkhonto conducted no further acts of insurgency against the South African government.

Within South Africa, black resentment grew, and a new force arose in internal politics. Stephen Biko's Black Consciousness movement intended to build self-reliance and pride within the black population—and Black Consciousness was resolutely nonviolent. Biko asserted, "We are not going into armed struggle. We'll leave it to the Pan-Africanists and ANC." However, the armed struggle came to them. On June 16, 1976, 20,000 schoolchildren marched into the black Johannesburg satellite township of Soweto. They were demonstrating against the introduction of compulsory Afrikaans (the language of the Afrikaners) courses into black schools. The demonstrators confronted large numbers of police. Scuffles broke out and by evening the township was ablaze. Within a week, 176 people had been killed. The violence spread across South Africa.

The death toll mounted and by the time the police regained control in 1977, as many as a thousand blacks were dead. The police beat and tortured Biko to death in September 1977. Black Consciousness could not control the rebellion and collapsed in its aftermath. Much of the township youth came to the conclusion that armed resistance was the only option left.

The failure of the Soweto uprising resulted in a large influx of recruits into the ANC training camps. Umkhonto launched a new guerrilla offensive beginning in the late 1970s to prove to the ANC domestic constituency that the armed struggle was feasible in South Africa. The Sasol oil-from-coal plant and South Africa's only nuclear power station were among the targets of several high-profile attacks. However, the South African army was ready to confront the challenge. South African leader P.W. Botha launched a deliberate policy of destabilization against neighboring states that were known to harbor ANC cadres. The South African army launched repeated commando raids against ANC targets within the "frontline states" (Angola, Zambia, Zimbabwe, Mozambique, and Tanzania) and invaded Angola. Attacks were launched as far north as the ANC headquarters in Lusaka, Zambia. A particularly violent attack on their offices in Lesotho in 1982 resulted in the deaths of forty-two people. The Umkhonto campaign flagged once again in the face of the security forces' massive retaliatory capabilities. As a result, the ANC dropped guerrilla warfare and turned again to terrorist tactics.

The 1984 Revolt

In 1984, the ANC stepped up their campaign, but again with little success. In May, for example, terrorists fired grenades at a U.S. oil refinery in Durban. But the police chased the terrorists and, in a shootout, killed them along with some innocent black workers. In July, a bomb intended for a military convoy exploded after the trucks had passed, killing more blacks.

On October 3, 1984, riots broke out in the townships of the Vaal Triangle, an industrial area containing Johannesburg and Pretoria. Forty thousand mine workers then went on strike. The police moved in and fighting between the police and residents became so fierce that the minister of law and order, Louis Le Grange, declared, "As far as we're concerned it is war, plain and simple." The violence spread across the Transvaal, and Prime Minister Botha sent the army into the black townships. It was the

first time the army had been used this way. On October 23, in Operation Palmiet, 7,000 police and troops poured into Sebokeng township, the heart of the revolt. After Palmiet, troops were regularly deployed in the townships but could not quell the tide of disturbance. In 1985, the trouble spread into the Cape Province. The police opened fire at a funeral procession in Uitenhage on March 21, 1985, the anniversary of the Sharpeville massacre, a 1960 police assault that left 69 peaceful protesters dead and 20 unarmed blacks died. On July 21, Botha declared a state of emergency, but this failed to halt the killing. By the end of 1985, 1,000 blacks had died and the authorities had detained more than 7,000 others, largely without trial. The state of emergency continued into 1986 and the military became increasingly aggressive.

Medical professionals cataloged the effects of state terror. A Port Elizabeth surgeon cited 153 cases in which injuries to detainees could not have been inflicted lawfully. A doctor in Soweto noticed a change in the cases he treated: there was a decrease in whip and bird-shot injuries and an increase in bullet wounds. It appeared also that the security forces had started to use high-velocity bullets. The same doctor explained, "A high-velocity bullet . . . is like a tornado—it just whips everything up inside you and you're finished. It's obviously a weapon designed to kill."

Bombs in Garbage Cans

The ANC was not slow in retaliating. Thirteen terrorist bombings in major downtown areas followed within twenty-three days of the declaration of a state of emergency. Sites for ANC attacks included a hamburger restaurant, the Anglo-American building, and the Holiday Inn in Johannesburg. In July 1986, an ANC grenade thrown in through a window injured a deputy cabinet minister of mixed race. But attacks went beyond establishment targets. The ANC also created an air of general terror with a series of bombs placed in garbage cans.

Other black African responses similarly became more violent. As well as the traditional methods of mass protest—strikes, boycotts, and demonstrations—militant black youths known as Comrades took the fight back to the security forces. Umkhonto guerrillas slipped into the townships to provide training. They dug trenches across roads to trap military vehicles and attacked the police and army with Molotov cocktails. Comrades obtained assault rifles. There was also much black-on-black violence between Comrades and progovernment vigilantes. Journalist Allister Sparks described how the vigilantes made their captives "walk barefoot over hot coals, and had them flogged naked in a room flooded with soapy water until they floundered about like stranded fish in the slippery, bloodied grime." The Comrades responded by car bombing vigilante leader Piet Ntuli and rampaging through the shantytowns. Extremist Comrades enforced discipline

KEY DATES

1948 White voters put the conservative, Afrikaner-dominated National Party in power; the new government institutes laws calling for the strict separation, or apartheid, of the various racial groups of South Africa.

1955 The African National Congress (ANC), the main antiapartheid organization, issues its "Freedom Charter," calling for, among other things, a non-racial democracy for South Africa.

1959 Radicals calling for a black-dominated government break from the ANC and form the Pan-Africanist Congress.

1960 Peaceful Pan-Africanist demonstrators are gunned down by security forces in the black township of Sharpeville; sixty-seven are killed.

1963 Police raids on the ANC and its armed wing, Umkhonto we Sizwe (Spear of the Nation), result in the arrests of Nelson Mandela and other anti-apartheid activists.

1976 Students begin nationwide protests against new laws calling for the teaching of Afrikaans in all schools.

1980s Umkhonto and the ANC step up their armed campaign against the government, planting bombs and attacking military forces; the campaign is brutally put down by security forces.

1989 Reformer F.W. de Klerk becomes head of the National Party and government, on a platform calling for a negotiated settlement with ANC.

1990 De Klerk releases Mandela and other ANC leaders from jail.

1994 In the nation's first democratic, non-racial elections, the ANC becomes the ruling party and Mandela is voted in as president.

1994 Farmers' Attack Troop, an Afrikaner group, sets off a bomb at a mosque in South Africa.

1998 In response to rising terrorist and other violence, President Nelson Mandela calls for a rural safety summit.

August 1998 The Muslims Against Global Oppression sets off a bomb at the Planet Hollywood restaurant in Cape Town, killing two and wounding twenty-eight; the group claims it is retaliation for the U.S. bombing of a pharmaceutical plant in the Sudan.

April 2010 Former apartheid defender Eugene Terre' Blanche is murdered by farm workers; some fear the killing was inspired by the racial rhetoric of the ruling ANC's youth leader.

in the townships through beatings and intimidation. They "necklaced" some who broke consumer boycotts—burned them to death by hanging a gasoline-filled tire around the victim's neck—and forced others to eat all their purchases, including soap and drain cleaner.

The revolt petered out after a crackdown on the remaining leadership. By the end of the year, 23,000 people, including about 9,000 children, had been jailed. Although the authorities controlled the townships, the balance of confidence had changed. Black Africans believed the ultimate revolution could not be far away. That the final bloody confrontation did not occur is credited to two men. Botha's discredited leadership came under pressure from within the National Party, and F.W. de Klerk maneuvered him out of office in 1989. De Klerk was aware that the situation as it stood could not continue. He released Mandela, removed the ban on the ANC, and dismantled apartheid. In the first multiracial elections, held in 1994, Mandela won the presidency with de Klerk as vice president. The two formed a partnership that navigated through an extremely hazardous transition with great skill. The legacy of the uses of terror in the struggle against apartheid, however, is a high rate of violent crime.

M. Christopher Mann

See also: *Definitions, Types, Categories*—Ethnonationalist Terrorism; State vs. Nonstate Terrorism. *Modern Terrorism*—Angola: Civil and Separatist Wars; Namibia: Anti–South African Struggle; South Africa: Postapartheid Violence.

Further Reading

Cock, Jacklyn, and Nathan Laurie. *War and Society: The Militarization of South Africa.* New York: St. Martin's, 1989.

Davis, Stephen M. *Apartheid's Rebels.* New Haven, CT: Yale University Press, 1987.

Edelstein, Jillian. *Truth and Lies: Stories from the Truth and Reconciliation Commission in South Africa.* New York: Free Press, 2002.

Jeffery, Anthea. *People's War: New Light on the Struggle for South Africa.* Johannesburg: Jonathan Ball, 2009.

Mandela, Nelson. *Long Walk to Freedom.* Boston: Little, Brown, 1994.

South Africa: Postapartheid Violence, 1994–2000s

South Africa was expected to experience some political violence in the transition from the repressive apartheid regime into an emerging fully enfranchised democracy. Some observers even predicted a long period of sustained terrorist campaigns, if not full civil war. Remarkably, however, following the nation's first elections in 1994, South Africa was fortunately spared from widespread violent upheaval. Nonetheless, as the former police state was dismantled, a few politicized factions resorted to violence—quite often bombings—to assert political dominance, protest certain policies, or communicate political messages. Adding to the political confusion of the era, significant economic transformations were implemented, which gave rise to both organized criminal violence and socioeconomic motives for attacks.

Much of the political violence from 1996 through mid-2002 fell within four broad categories: (1) conflicts between blacks and whites, (2) socioeconomic and political-criminal conflicts, (3) political party violence and assassinations, and (4) violent Islamic extremism.

Conflicts Between Blacks and Whites

Once negotiations to dismantle apartheid began in the early 1990s, many of the major South African urban centers, such as the predominantly English-speaking Cape Town and Durban, as well as Afrikaans-dominated Johannesburg, were legally desegregated quite quickly, and community acceptance soon followed. However, the racial lines in the rural farm areas traditionally dominated by the landowning Afrikaners remained more stagnant. Friction between the whites and blacks in these areas contributed to farm-based violence on three levels.

First, the white separatist movement gained notoriety when a faction called the Afrikaner Resistance Movement (Afrikaner Weerstandsbeweging—AWB) launched a bombing campaign leading to the first free elections in 1994. The attacks, including a car bomb at the Johannesburg International Airport, which killed 21 and injured at least 145, were attributed to the group's Iron Guard military wing, and subsequently some 30 individuals were arrested. In spite of the arrests, AWB leader Eugene Terre'Blanche remained free to continue his struggle for a white homeland separate from the black-dominated multiparty democracy of South Africa. Although Terre'Blanche appeared to have largely relinquished the sword, he remained a prominent figure in the overall separatist movement until his murder in 2010.

Second, a similar yet distinct group known as the Farmers' Attack Troop (Boers Aanvals Troepe—BAT) claimed responsibility for at least three bombings from December 1996 to January 1997, including one at a mosque. Suspects arrested in these attacks were directly linked to escaped prisoners awaiting sentencing for some of the 1994 bombings. However, the fact that a BAT spokesman proclaimed the need for white farmers to conduct retribution attacks in defense of farming communities suggests a motivation different from that of the AWB.

These perpetrators were reacting against a third component of racial violence—black workers attacking white farmers. Steadily increasing farm-attack fatalities, which had begun in 1991, prompted then-president Nelson Mandela to sponsor a rural safety summit in 1998 to coordinate community, police, and military preventive measures. Since these farm attacks occurred in isolation and were so rarely successfully investigated, motivational trends were difficult to determine. Robbery, opportunity, and retribution for previous ill treatment probably represented the most common motives. However, orchestrated efforts by the neighboring black government in Zimbabwe to drive out white landowners, combined with the South African government's failure to protect them, led many farmers to believe that the slayings represented implicit state acceptance of such terrorism, if not government sanctioning.

Socioeconomic and Political Violence Conflicts

Clearly, socioeconomic factors underpinned the farm attacks. Whether the crimes represented specific disputes on a given property, a wider amorphous collective consciousness by black farmworkers, or an explicit effort directed toward land redistribution, blacks suffered the greatest economic deprivation of all groups under apartheid, and the distribution of wealth remained—and continues to remain—extremely skewed. This economic environment, combined with a weak but transforming political environment, led to the use of terror in other parts of society, including, notably, cycles of taxi violence from 1996 to 2002 and a spate of armored car and armory attacks from 1997 to 1999. Although both phenomena are primarily criminal, they contained political motivations as well.

Taxi service expanded quickly with the dismantling of apartheid. With the elimination of travel restrictions, racial groups previously restricted to the townships flooded into urban centers and between communities, overwhelming the traditional bus and rail services. Fleets of minivan taxis emerged to satisfy commuter demand. Taxi wars were fought to secure and maintain lucrative routes. With access to large communities and money, however, came political power. Thus, fleet owners would order machine-gun attacks on competing taxis or at crowded taxi stands to scare customers toward a desired end. By 2000, however, increased legislation and improved taxi regulation had greatly reduced such attacks.

Another type of attack with ominous terror implications was a series of sophisticated special operations–type attacks on armored bank trucks and even a military armory between 1997 and 1999. Such attacks were often perpetrated by terrorist groups to fund and arm political attacks. Few perpetrators were caught, but police investigations concluded that many of the attackers had military or paramilitary training—perhaps dating back to the antiapartheid struggle. It was thought that the stolen arms were eventually smuggled out of the country for use in regional civil wars or perhaps stored for future use in South Africa. The sophistication of the operations led investigators to look beyond criminal motives to organized crime or political terrorism.

Political Party Violence and Assassinations

Ultimately, the transition of political power from white to black was peaceful, but the use of violence and terrorist tactics was an important factor in both forcing the apartheid regime to the negotiating table and hammering out representation and political control among the many black movements. African National Congress (ANC) forces battled the Inkatha Freedom Party from 1991 to 1993 for control of Richmond and its vicinity in what became part of the KwaZulu-Natal Province. Led by Sifiso Nkabinde, the ANC won political dominance through use of arms and subsequent intimidation. In 1997, Nkabinde was expelled from the ANC, resigned from the Richmond council, and was later charged (though acquitted) with plotting the execution of sixteen opponents from 1993 to 1997. Although Nkabinde joined another political party, the United Democratic Front, assassinations and reprisals continued in the region—prompting the federal government to deploy South Africa National Defense Forces on Richmond city streets and throughout the region. The wave of violence finally ended with Nkabinde's assassination in January 1999. However, the continuation of latent political hostilities, together with the relative youth of the decommissioned militia from the struggle against apartheid only ten years earlier, indicated that the potential for future political party violence remained significant.

Violent Islamic Extremism

South Africa has a significant, yet small, Muslim community located primarily in the Western Cape. It consists mostly of immigrants from pre-independence India and the Dutch East Indies. However, the end of apartheid made South Africa attractive for Muslims from all over Africa and the Middle East. As has been the case in Islamic communities worldwide, South Africa has seen a growth in radical Muslim fundamentalism—a portion of which has resorted to political violence and terrorist tactics. The prominence of People Against Gangsterism and Drugs (PAGAD), provocative proclamations by groups such as Muslims Against Global Oppression, and documented ties to Osama bin Laden's al-Qaeda network demonstrate that South Africa has already suffered at the hands of violent Islamic extremists.

PAGAD started out in 1996 benignly as a broad community-based effort to supplement a police force struggling to forge a new role in the postapartheid era. PAGAD soon became many things to many people, including a vigilante group, a political movement for Muslims, a haven for petty criminals and violence-prone individuals, and, to some, simply a cover for organized crime. Under the PAGAD banner, groups attacked known drug dealers and other enemies by firebombing homes and cars. Related perpetrators using a similar modus operandi detonated remote-control bombs targeting American and other Western targets under the names Qibla, Muslims Against Global Oppression, and Muslims Against Illegitimate Leaders. For example, Muslims Against Global Oppression claimed responsibility for the bombing of the Planet Hollywood restaurant in Cape Town, killing two and wounding twenty-eight in retaliation against the U.S. cruise-missile attack on a Sudan chemical plant in August 1998. Reports suggest that PAGAD was responsible for more than 200 bombings and related attacks from 1998 to 2000, almost entirely in the West Cape.

A review of the broad spectrum of print and electronic media (e.g., Radio 786 in the Western Cape) in South Africa reveals the existence of a small but vocal Muslim community supportive of extremist ideals in which bin Laden and his al-Qaeda network have found some support. Khalfan Khamis Mohamed was arrested in Cape Town for carrying false identity and passport papers and was ultimately extradited to the United States for his role in the bombings of the U.S. embassies in Kenya and Tanzania. Bangladesh officials arrested a South African who had received funding and training from bin Laden for his involvement in a plot to assassinate poet Shamsur Rahman. Other reports suggested individual South African Muslim ties to Hezbollah in Lebanon and to Algerian extremists, and with possible funding from Iran and training in Libya. Finally, one group, Tallai el

Fateh, based in the Eastern Cape, has had suspected links with al-Gama'a al-Islamiyya from Egypt, and elements of the group may have been trained in Sudan. Nonetheless, despite the numerous likely, yet limited, contacts with such groups, the majority of South African Muslims appear to have withdrawn their support from PAGAD and do not support violent extremist ideologies.

Meanwhile, old racial animosities continued to play themselves out, as in the April 2010 killing of Eugene Terre'Blanche, founder of the Afrikaner Resistance Movement. While the murderers turned out to be two disgruntled day laborers who worked for Terre'Blanche, some in the country, particularly in the minority white community, said the crime was inspired by the incendiary rhetoric of ANC Youth League leader Julius Malema, who had gained notoriety for singing in public an antiapartheid resistance song that had advocated killing white Afrikaners. Still, such incidents of racial violence were relatively rare, paling into insignificance compared to the nonpolitical violent crime that has ravaged the country since the end of apartheid, most of it perpetrated by members of the black majority against other blacks.

Counterterrorism Efforts

South Africa has pursued an aggressive multifaceted counterterrorism strategy, which has been successful on many, though not nearly all, levels. First, the atrocities of the apartheid regime provided ample motives for aggrieved parties to terrorize and exact justice in a society in transition. However, the establishment of the Truth and Reconciliation Commission provided a public platform on which to identify and condemn historical wrongs. Second, in both the political assassinations of Richmond and the bombing campaigns of the Western Cape, the South African government turned to its elite Directorate of Special Investigations, called the Scorpions, which led to a series of comprehensive and largely successful court cases.

Internationally, South Africa has played a significant and positive counterterrorism role. It has signed eight of the twelve international terrorism conventions as well as the Organization of African Unity Convention on the Prevention and Combating of Terrorism of 1999. Upon stepping down from the presidency in 1999, Nelson Mandela has fostered peace initiatives in various African conflicts and appears to have been instrumental in making great progress, if not having brokered, a final settlement between Libya and the families of Pan Am 103. South Africa quickly condemned the September 11, 2001, terrorist attacks on the United States and has cooperated in subsequent U.S.-led diplomatic counterterrorism efforts. Finally, its leadership position in the newly formed African Union will enable South Africa to extend its good offices toward resolving economic problems and political conflicts on the continent—the wellspring for much of contemporary international terrorism.

James T. Kirkhope

See also: *Definitions, Types, Categories*—Ethnonationalist Terrorism; Right-Wing and Reactionary Terrorism.

Further Reading

Bornman, Elirea, René van Eeden, and Marie Wentzel, eds. *Violence in South Africa: A Variety of Perspectives.* Pretoria: Human Sciences Research Council, 1998.

Boshoff, Henri, Anneli Botha, and Martin Schönteich. *Fear in the City: Urban Terrorism in South Africa.* Pretoria: Institute for Security Studies, 2001.

Byrnes, Rita M., ed. *South Africa: A Country Study.* 3rd ed. Washington, DC: U.S. Government Printing Office, 1997.

Crenshaw, Martha, ed. *Terrorism in Africa.* New York: G.K. Hall, 1994.

du Toit, Pierre. *South Africa's Brittle Peace: The Problem of Post-Settlement Violence.* Houndmills, UK: Palgrave, 2001.

Emmett, Tony, and Alex Butchart, eds. *Behind the Mask: Getting to Grips with Crime and Violence in South Africa.* Pretoria: Human Sciences Research Council, 2000.

Okumu, Wafula, and Anneli Botha, eds. *Understanding Terrorism in Africa: Building Bridges and Overcoming the Gaps.* Pretoria: Institute for Security Studies, 2008.

Schönteich, Martin, and Henri Boshoff. *"Volk," Faith and Fatherland: The Security Threat Posed by the White Right.* Pretoria: Institute for Security Studies, 2003.

U.S. Department of State. *Patterns of Global Terrorism, 2001.* Washington, DC: U.S. Government Printing Office, 2002.

Spain: Conflict with ETA, 1959–2000s

For thirty-seven years, Euskadi Ta Askatasuna (ETA, or Basque Homeland and Liberty) has waged a terrorist campaign that has killed hundreds. Its aim is to create an independent Basque state in northern Spain. The Basques, ETA argues, are an independent people with a history that stretches back to Roman times. They are noticeably different in appearance from the other peoples of Western Europe, and their language, Euskara, is unique.

Basques live around the western end of the Pyrenees, some 2 million on the Spanish side of the border and 200,000 on the French side. The French Basques have largely assimilated, while in Spain their ancient language survives. In the nineteenth century, the independence of the Spanish Basques, guaranteed by an ancient written code called the *furores*, was threatened by the encroaching Spanish state. The Basques reacted by supporting the cause of Don Carlos, a pretender to the throne. When the Carlist rebellion failed, the central government punished the Basques by revoking the *furores*.

The Basques found their identify further threatened by an influx of non-Basque workers looking for jobs in the rapidly industrializing cities of Bilbao and San Sebastián. In 1894, the Basque nationalist party, Partido Nacionalista Vasco (PNV), was set up. During the Spanish Civil War (1936–1939), the Republican government allowed the Basques to set up an independent government in Bilbao. In 1937, however, the Nationalists under General Francisco Franco responded with the brutal bombing of the ancient Basque city of Guernica, carried out by the Condor Legion, the German air squadron sent by Hitler to help the fascist cause.

Basque Terrorism Under Franco

With the establishment of the dictatorship of General Franco in 1939, Basque nationalism was ruthlessly suppressed, and Franco banned the use of the Basque language. Basque political leaders were either imprisoned or forced into exile. Usually they fled immediately across the border into the French Basque province, Pyrénées-Atlantiques. The PNV survived in exile in Paris, and Basque culture survived only in mountain-climbing and hiking clubs and other subterfuges. In 1959, however, a small group of university students in Bilbao decided to take a more revolutionary approach, and on July 31, the feast day of the patron saint of the Basque country, St. Ignatius Loyola, they set up the ETA as a terrorist organization.

For nearly a decade, ETA leaders debated their ide-

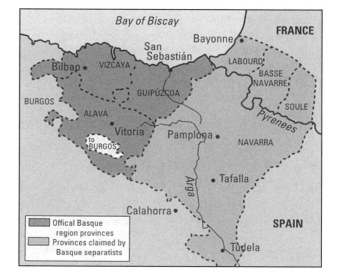

Spain recognizes only three provinces as constituting the autonomous Basque region, but ETA claims other provinces in Spain and France as part of the Basque homeland.

ology. Some were purely nationalists, while others were communist revolutionaries as well. The communists believed that disenchanted non-Basque immigrants, who congregated in the region's cities, could be convinced of the economic benefits of an independent Basque state and would join the struggle. Nationalists argued that this strategy was impractical, as workers' organizations such as trade unions were outlawed by the Franco regime. The nationalists said that only ethnic Basques should be recruited and argued instead for a spiral-of-violence strategy. They planned to attack the most oppressive symbols of the Spanish state—the police, the Civil Guard, and the military. Given Franco's record of brutal repression, ETA's leaders expected that their terrorist acts would provoke violent and indiscriminate countermeasures by government forces. This, they believed, would lead to a civil war, which would force the Spanish to give up on their costly occupation of the Basque "colony."

Armed Struggle

ETA's *lucha armada* (armed struggle) and *guerra revolucionaria* (revolutionary war) began in 1968, when the police killed a respected ETA leader in Guipúzcoa in a shoot-out at a roadblock. ETA responded by murdering the police chief of San Sebastián. As ETA activists predicted, the Franco government's response was immediate and indiscriminate. It involved the imprisonment, torture, and exile of thousands of Basques.

Sixteen ETA leaders were arrested and tried in Burgos in 1970. Six were sentenced to death. In December that year, however, ETA kidnapped Eugene Beihl, the West German honorary consul in San Sebastián. Franco was forced to commute the death sentences in exchange for his release.

The group barely survived this period of government repression. However, a charismatic leader named Eustatus Mendizabel and an unexpected new influx of disillusioned members of the youth wing of the PNV revitalized the organization. In 1972, ETA kidnapped a Spanish industrialist whose employees were on strike and, in return for his release, demanded he comply with the strikers' demands. The following year, ETA terrorists kidnapped another industrialist, this time to obtain a ransom.

A Dramatic Assassination

ETA's most audacious act took place in December 1973, when they assassinated the Spanish prime minister, Admiral Luis Carrero Blanco, the designated successor to the aged and ailing General Franco. Four amateur assassins dug a tunnel under the road in Madrid on which Carrero drove each day on his way to church. They packed it full of explosives and detonated them just as the admiral's car passed over it. The resulting explosion was enormous, throwing the car over an eight-story apartment building. It lodged on a balcony two stories up on the other side.

Such a bold terrorist strike kept ETA on the political map. At the same time, it sparked a new debate within the organization. A moderate faction challenged the militants' strategy of employing such risky terrorist acts, which not only precipitated a violent government response but also alienated supporters. They proposed to abandon the armed struggle and resurrect the strategy of joining forces with broad-based workers' organizations. The two factions split formally in 1974 after a bomb attack on a Madrid café. The resulting groups became known as ETA-militar (ETA-M), the militants who favored violent action, and ETA-político-militar (ETA-PM), the moderates who wanted to build up a political base first.

Post-Franco Era

After the death of Franco in 1975, and the rapid institution of democracy in Spain that followed, ETA found that it had lost international sympathy. It was no longer seen as a group of freedom fighters opposing a detested fascist regime, but a bona fide terrorist group attacking a fledgling democratic state. ETA's response was to accelerate its efforts to provoke a violent reaction from the Spanish military police and the Civil Guard by assassinating their members—and sometimes their wives and children. During the first year of Spain's democracy, 19 people were killed. In 1977, 30 people were murdered; in 1978, 66; and in 1979, 130.

By 1980, the total had reached 275—but the expected retaliation never came.

Democratic institutions and processes quickly took hold throughout Spain. The government gradually released political prisoners, and many Basque exiles, including ETA veterans, were permitted to return home. Moreover, the central government supported the gradual evolution of a more federal relationship with the Basque country and other Spanish regions such as Catalonia. The conciliatory attitude of the new government exposed splits within ETA. The leader of ETA-PM, Eduardo Moreno Bergareche, who had tried to combine communist theory with Basque nationalism, was murdered by unsympathetic colleagues in 1976. In 1978, José Miguel Beñaran Ordeñana, one of the ETA-M leaders who had participated in the assassination of Admiral Carrero, was himself assassinated in France on the fifth anniversary of the event.

With violence spreading across the border, the French government banished ETA militants from the Basque Pyrénées-Atlantiques Province. The militants moved to Paris, then to Brussels, where they were taken in by the Belgian communists. From there, they moved to Algiers, where the Algerian government gave them weapons and training. Meanwhile, the Spanish government proposed a new constitution—the Statute of Guernica—which established a Basque regional parliament with considerable powers. The majority of the Basque people were satisfied with the arrangement; only 4 percent voted against the statute when it was put to a referendum in the Basque country in 1979.

By the early 1980s, many from ETA-PM had negotiated an amnesty agreement with the Spanish government for its imprisoned and exiled members. In return, ETA-PM disbanded, with supporters joining various Basque socialist parties and coalitions.

Continuing Terror Campaign

Even ETA-M softened its hard line. As early as 1978, it had dropped its strategy of continuing violence until full independence was achieved. Terrorism, it conceded, would now be employed only to ensure that, first, the Spanish government agreed to six key demands and, second, these were properly implemented. Some of their demands included a general amnesty for all Basque prisoners; substitution of Basque police for Spanish police in Basque regions; Basque government control of the Spanish army in the Basque country; and the right to self-determination of the Basque people.

Nevertheless, terrorist action continued. On February 6, 1986, ETA assassinated Vice Admiral Cristobal Colon, a descendant of Christopher Columbus. In July of the same year, there was a flurry of attacks. A bomb on a Madrid bus killed ten members of the Civil Guard. A rocket attack on the Ministry of Defense building a week later wounded nine people. At the end of the month, a nine-year-old boy was injured in a bomb explosion in the tourist town of Marbella.

French Crackdown

Beginning in the mid-1980s, the French Socialist government led by President François Mitterrand finally took decisive action against ETA, in part because of its own fear of growing terrorism in French cities and the onset of a French Basque nationalist movement. The French police made several key arrests that struck at the core of ETA's decision-making structure, when its main military and political leaders were detained along with a major weapons expert. Virtually an entire generation of ETA leaders was imprisoned as a result of the joint French-Spanish operations. Some 500 ETA members, including most of its leaders, were then held in Spanish and French prisons. In 1988, the frequency of ETA's attacks dropped back to the lower levels of the mid-1970s, but the campaign continued. In 1995, the car bombing of an air force van killed 6 service people. By 1996, ETA attacks had claimed a total of approximately 700 lives.

ETA has a political front called Herri Batasuna (HB, now known as Batasuna), or "One People." The HB continues to insist on full independence for the Basque state, but it has never managed to win more than 20 percent of the votes in an election. However, at the height of its popularity, HB did win a seat in the European Parliament.

The HB has refused to oppose terrorism in all circumstances but has condemned specific ETA acts, such as the 1994 bombing of a store in a working-class area of Barcelona, which killed twenty-one people. This attack was admitted to be a mistake by the terrorists, whose warning to evacuate had not been effective. The result was a substantial drop in electoral support for the HB. Soon after, it lost its seat in the European Parliament.

ETA in 1990s and 2000s

Among the ETA's most spectacular actions in recent decades was the attempted car bombing of the opposition leader José María Aznar in 1995. Although he emerged with only minor injuries, the message was clear: major politicians, let alone local and regional officials in the Basque region, remain terrorist targets. This message was repeated to lethal effect during the 1996 national election campaign when, in February, terrorists shot dead the Basque regional leader of the Socialist Party. Shortly afterward, a former president of Spain's highest court, the Constitutional Court, was murdered.

Spain's Congress of Deputies elected Aznar prime minister in May 1996, after he formed a majority coalition with several regional parties. Under this arrangement, it was unlikely that Aznar would attempt to reverse the decentralization policies of the previous four Gonzalez administrations (1982–1996).

An important factor in Aznar's electoral success was the link between former Prime Minister Filipe Gonzalez and the secret government Antiterrorist Liberation Group (GAL). The group's death squads had been implicated in the killing of twenty-seven ETA members between 1983 and 1987. Given the continued popular fury against the GAL and its illegal counterterrorist activities, it is unlikely that the Aznar government would have resorted to a similar strategy.

ETA remains a viable organization that is clearly capable of being murderously effective in targeting high-profile politicians and police officials. Its durability is impressive, given that it has lost its strategic sanctuary in neighboring France, where, for most of its existence, the key leadership and operational structures had been based.

Estimates of ETA's core membership suggest that it has declined considerably since the early 1990s. On several occasions, the Gonzalez government and ETA representatives engaged in informal negotiations. Even though their talks were unsuccessful, they did reinforce the idea that nonviolent tactics might still advance the cause of Basque nationalism. In addition, the new generation of political ETA recruits, despite the crackdown between 1984 and 1987, have not been motivated by the crude totalitarian tactics of the Franco regime. Instead, they have lived in Basque provinces that are governed by moderate Basque nationalist politicians who openly acknowledge the importance of Basque culture. The public disgrace of the GAL was followed by the successful prosecution and sentencing of government and police officials to long terms in prison. This is further evidence that, in a multiparty democracy, nonviolent methods can ensure the continued existence of a Basque nation, even though it is not a fully independent state.

It seems extremely unlikely that any Spanish government would ever negotiate the dismemberment of Spain, even though there seems to be a general acceptance that regional parliaments do not threaten national integrity. However, moderate Basque nationalist parties and voters now feel they control their own destinies, within both Spain and the European Union. Nevertheless, ETA continues to represent the pure concept of Basque nationalism. Throughout its history, several attempts have been made to curtail its use of violence to gain an independent Basque homeland. All have failed. Each time, a new militant faction has formed, which has continued to wage a murderous terrorist campaign.

With Spain's continued integration into the European Union, the national government's devolution of power to the Basque region, and the growing number of ETA attacks, ETA's terrorist activities began to elicit increasing public condemnation. The turning point in public support for ETA came with their execution of councilman Miguel Ángel Blanco in 1997. In response to this murder, more than 1 million people marched in anti-ETA protests throughout Spain, and many of the political offices of HB were attacked and burned. In addition, Prime Minister Aznar called for the political isolation of HB, and all twenty-three members of the national committee of HB were charged and found guilty of collaborating with ETA. This resulted in each member being sentenced to seven years' imprisonment for their affiliation and collaboration with the terrorist organization. In 1999, however, in an 8–4 vote, the court overturned these sentences and released the prisoners. Perhaps in a move designed to avoid being outlawed as a political party and distancing itself from its violent past, in 1998, HB renamed itself Batasuna and joined a wider political coalition, Euskal Herritarrok (EH).

Recognizing that Spain would never agree to ETA's demand for Basque independence and hoping to advance its political agenda in the upcoming Basque parliamentary elections, ETA declared a cease-fire with Madrid on September 16, 1998. In the subsequent elections, the PNV remained the leading party in the region, and Aznar's Popular Party (PP) became the second-largest party in the regional legislative assembly. However, EH became part of the ruling coalition's regional government. With public support, political clout, and a popular cease-fire in place, ETA made several demands of Madrid. These demands included a Basque right to self-determination, a Basque referendum on independence, the withdrawal of all Spanish police from the Basque country, and the release of all ETA terrorists from Spanish prisons. Aznar's government countered that ETA had to disarm and dis-

avow the use of violence before any formal discussions could take place. Still, Aznar did make some conciliatory gestures, such as the release of 130 rebel prisoners and the transfer of dozens of other ETA prisoners to prisons closer to the Basque region. However, Aznar would not consider independence.

In late 1999, after fourteen months of a cease-fire that resulted in only one official meeting between ETA and Aznar's government, ETA declared that it was resuming its violent campaign for independence. The primary reason stated for its return to terrorism was that the national government had manipulated the cease-fire for its own political gain without considering the central issue of Basque independence. ETA's resumption of terrorism resulted in one of the bloodiest periods of violence in ETA's history. In the first two years after the abandonment of the cease-fire, ETA murdered thirty-five people and injured many more. However, as a strategy to achieve independence, terrorism remained unsuccessful, resulting in a significant reduction in popular and political support for ETA and Batasuna. In February 2000, the PNV formally severed all political ties with Batasuna. Moreover, EH saw its political support drop from 18 percent in 1998 to 10 percent in 2000. At the same time, EH's seats in the Basque parliament fell from fourteen to seven. In March 2000, Aznar's Popular Party was reelected with an absolute majority in the national elections, and PP increased its share of the vote in the Basque region. For the first time, Basque voters clearly said no to violence and terrorism.

Police in the northern Spanish town of Hernani prevent pro-ETA Basque separatists from entering the city hall in 2000. Except for a few ill-fated truces, the ETA has pressed its terrorist campaign for Basque independence since 1959. *(Associated Press)*

Still, the ETA killed more than twenty people in terrorist attacks in 2000. In response, there were mass public protests against ETA violence throughout Spain and the Basque region, and the government arrested dozens of ETA terrorists and members. In 2001, the carnage continued; ETA killed more than a dozen people in many attacks; politically motivated street violence, or *kale borroka*, increased; and youth participation in street violence and support for ETA grew significantly. The Spanish Newspaper *El Mundo* reported on August 6, 2001, that in July 2001, there were sixty-six acts of politically motivated street violence. However, rather than the violence advancing ETA's agenda, public and political protest against ETA increased. Even among those politicians who joined EH, there was a demand that Batasuna put direct pressure on ETA to enter into a cease-fire. The government's counterterrorism strategies achieved some dramatic results. For a variety of reasons, including better intelligence and information sharing, the autonomous Basque police, Ertzaintza, and the Civil Guard were very successful in arresting ETA commandos and leaders and in dismantling ETA's terror infrastructure. Dozens of terrorists and supporters were arrested, several key cell organizations were destroyed, and significant caches of weapons and munitions were discovered. By the summer of 2001, while still retaining the ability to carry out attacks, ETA was at its weakest point since before the cease-fire.

The terror attacks against targets in New York City and Washington, D.C., on September 11, 2001, had a major effect on the ETA and the government's and international community's response to it. Following the terror attacks in the United States, world opinion turned against the use of violence to achieve any political goals. In Europe and the United States, ETA was no longer considered a group of Basque separatists; rather, it was now defined as a terrorist organization. With the support of Spain's national government, on December 28, 2001, ETA was included on the European Union's list of terrorist groups and organizations. By their inclusion, ETA is subject to several significant consequences. This policy requires the 27 member states to freeze ETA's assets and to imprison any person within their borders whose name appears on any ETA membership list. On February 26, 2002, the United States put twenty-one members of ETA on its international terrorism blacklist, a list that includes Osama bin Laden.

ETA remains the only active ethnic nationalist antistate terrorist organization in the European Union. However, estimates of ETA membership suggest that its numbers and its ability to recruit new members continue to decline. This is due, in part, to the fact that since the end of the Franco regime, the national and regional governments have met many of ETA's demands. Spain's 1978 constitution provides explicit support and protec-tion for minority rights, and the Basque government has autonomous control over many key departments and services, such as education, health care, and the police force. Moreover, the Basque region collects its own taxes and continues to be governed by a Basque nationalist government, the PNV. Although many Basque people support greater autonomy, and even independence, fewer people are willing to support terrorism to achieve these objectives. Moreover, ETA does not enjoy any significant support outside its region. Unlike the Irish Republican Army, for example, ETA does not have an international network to raise funds and attract fresh recruits from outside the Basque region. Instead, ETA must rely on donations, a "revolutionary tax," and extortion to raise funds.

In the aftermath of September 11, the political pressure against ETA and its political wing continues to increase. In addition to the actions of the international community, the Spanish government reformed the Political Parties Law, allowing judges of a special court

KEY DATES

1959 Students in Bilbao set up ETA as a revolutionary group bent on Basque independence.
1968 ETA announces the beginning of its "revolutionary war."
1973 ETA militants assassinate Spanish prime minister Admiral Luis Carrero Blanco, who has been designated the successor to General Franco.
1995 ETA attacks opposition leader José María Aznar, with a car bomb; Aznar survives and goes on to become prime minister after his predecessor, socialist Felipe Gonzalez, is implicated in a scandal over terrorist hit squads.
1998 ETA declares a cease-fire with Spanish government in Madrid.
1999 With only one official meeting between ETA and the government of Prime Minister Aznar in fourteen months since the cease-fire, ETA announces it is resuming its campaign of violence.
2000 Support for Euskal Herritarrok, the Basque nationalist political coalition, falls to just 10 percent among Basque voters.
2001 The Spanish government successfully petitions the European Union to place ETA on its list of terrorist groups and organizations.
2002 The U.S. government places twenty-one ETA members on its international terrorism blacklist.
2003 The Spanish government bans Batasuna, the political wing of ETA.
2006 ETA announces a cease-fire, and the Spanish government announces peace talks with the group.
2007 ETA ends its cease-fire.
2009 Basque voters choose the first non-nationalist party to lead their region in thirty years.
2010 ETA declares a new cease-fire, but the move is dismissed by the Spanish government, which demands that the group renounce violence and disarm.

of the Supreme Court to prohibit a political party that does not respect democratic principles. The national government began the process of judicially outlawing Batasuna, groups that ally themselves with Batasuna or ETA, and ETA's youth wings, such as Segi. In addition, the PP denied Batasuna official subsidies under the Pact for Freedoms and Against Terrorism, which was designed to prevent public money from reaching political parties whose membership includes those convicted of terrorism or public officials who did not publicly and explicitly condemn the use of violence.

The government's and the international community's efforts to combat ETA notwithstanding, the national government's refusal to negotiate on the fundamental issue of Basque independence is likely to result in more ETA violence. After the turn of the twenty-first century, the situation remained mixed. While some observers were encouraged by the lack of an ETA counterresponse to the arrest of two top terrorists in France in September 2002, others noted ETA's continued propensity for violence, including an accident in which two terrorists blew themselves up in Bilbao that same month and the death the following day of a Civil Guardsman who was blown up trying to pull down a booby-trapped Batasuna banner in Bilbao. Finally, in 2003, the Spanish government acted upon the Supreme Court ruling and imposed an indefinite ban on Batasuna.

Despite the ban, in March 2006, ETA declared a cease-fire. Spanish prime minister José Luis Rodriguez Zapatero responded by announcing peace talks with the group. When an ETA car bomb went off at Madrid's airport in December, however, Zapatero called off the talks. Seven months later, ETA called off its cease-fire. ETA's effectiveness seemed diminished, though, as did support for its cause among the Basque people, who elected the region's first non-nationalist government in May 2009. This sign of evaporating support may have been a key reason for ETA's decision to renew its cease-fire in September 2010. The Spanish government was not so easily persuaded, however, discounting the overture and saying there could be no political settlement to the Basque question until ETA renounced violence and disarmed for good.

Irwin M. Cohen and Raymond R. Corrado

See also: *Definitions, Types, Categories*—Ethnonationalist Terrorism. *Modern Terrorism*—France: Ethnic, Nationalist, and Separatist Struggles.

Further Reading

Clark, Robert P. *The Basque Insurgents: ETA, 1952–1980.* Madison: University of Wisconsin Press, 1984.

———. *Negotiating with ETA: Obstacles to Peace in the Basque Country, 1975–1988.* Reno: University of Nevada Press. 1990.

Corrado, Raymond R., and Irwin M. Cohen. "A Future for the ETA?" In *Terrorist Victimization: Prevention, Control and Recovery*, ed. Dilip K. Das and Peter Kratcoski. Lanham, MD: Lexington Books, 2002.

Kurlansky, Mark. *The Basque History of the World.* New York: Walker, 1999.

Simonsen, Clifford E., and Jeremy R. Soindlove. *Terrorism Today: The Past, the Players, the Future*, 4th ed. Upper Saddle River, NJ: Pearson Prentice Hall, 2010.

Sullivan, John. *ETA and Basque Nationalism: The Fight for Euskadi, 1890–1986.* New York: Routledge, 1988.

———. "Forty Years of ETA." *History Today* 49:4 (1999): 34–36.

Watson, Cameron. *Basque Nationalism and Political Violence: The Ideological and Intellectual Origins of ETA.* Reno: Center for Basque Studies, University of Nevada, Reno, 2007.

Zirakzadeh, Cyrus Ernesto. *A Rebellious People: Basques, Protests, and Politics.* Reno: University of Nevada Press, 1991.

Spain: Islamist Terrorism, 2004

The center of Islamic culture in Europe in the Middle Ages, Spain in more recent times has become home to a significant population of Muslims, who were drawn to the country by a construction-led economic expansion between the 1980s and early 2000s. Among this population were a tiny minority of Islamist radicals, some having affiliations with terrorist organizations, particularly in North Africa, but largely operating out of independent cells within the country. On March 11, 2004, one of those cells perpetrated a series of bombings aboard commuter trains in Madrid that left nearly 200 persons dead, making it the worst terrorist attack in Europe since the downing of a Pan Am jet over Lockerbie, Scotland, in 1988.

Causes of Islamist Extremism

In the eighth century C.E., Spain was conquered by Muslim invaders from North Africa, who developed one of the most sophisticated cultures in the Islamic world. Over the next seven centuries, Christian kingdoms in the northern part of the Iberian Peninsula fought to evict the Muslims, finally succeeding in their *reconquista* of Spain with the capture of Granada of 1492. For many Muslims, this defeat represented the first of a series of humiliations perpetrated by Europeans, culminating in the imperialist conquest of much of the Islamic world in the nineteenth century. Bringing Catholic Spain back into the Islamic orbit remained a cherished, if unlikely, dream of Islamist militants in the twentieth and twenty-first centuries. In addition, many Moroccan Muslims remained angry that Spain held onto enclaves in their country, first captured from the Moors in the fifteenth century.

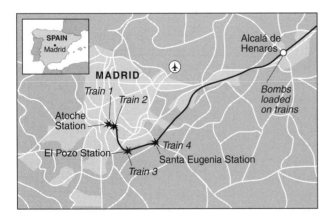

In March 2004, suicide bombers believed to be associated with local Islamic fundamentalist cells carried improvised explosive devices, hidden in backpacks, onto four trains along a single line of Madrid's commuter rail system. The ten explosions killed 191 passengers and injured hundreds more.

Far more important to contemporary Islamist radicals and their activities in Spain, however, have been more recent historical developments—specifically, the rapid growth of the country's Muslim population since the 1980s and Spanish foreign policy vis-à-vis the Islamic world. Under a dictatorship and an economically autarkic regime through 1975, Spain was gradually integrated into the larger European economy from the 1980s on, joining the European Community (now European Union) in 1986 and becoming a charter member of the euro zone in 1999. The Spanish economy boomed as a result, becoming one of the fastest growing in Europe. Leading the expansion was construction, a labor-intensive industry that drew in millions of unskilled immigrants, many of them Muslims from North Africa. From 1975 to 2010, Spain saw its Muslim population grow from just a few thousand to near 1 million, or about 1.5 percent of the population.

With little history of immigration and, among some elements of the population, a tradition of intolerance toward Islam, Spain was not the most welcoming place for incoming North Africans, many of whom found themselves segregated in poorly serviced communities on the outskirts of major cities, facing discrimination and even outright acts of hostility. Moreover, many of the immigrants were young, single men, separated from their families and communities, susceptible to radical ideologies. They were, say sociologists who study the subject, prime targets for recruitment by Islamist extremist organizations.

Adding to the anger and alienation of these people was the Spanish government's role in the U.S.-led war on terrorism, which intensified after the September 11, 2001, terrorist attacks. Since 1996, the country had been led by Prime Minister José María Aznar and his conservative Partido Popular (People's Party). A hard-liner on foreign affairs, Aznar strongly supported the George W. Bush administration's decision to invade Iraq in 2003, sending in some 1,300 troops in the early weeks of the war—one of the largest coalition contingents aside from the United States and Britain. The decision angered many Spaniards of all backgrounds, as huge demonstrations against the war and Spain's participation in it rocked the country. In addition, most Muslims in Spain viewed the country's participation in the war as an assault on Islam itself. Indeed, Spain was singled out in communiqués as a target for retaliation by various Islamist extremist groups, including al-Qaeda.

Madrid Bombings, 2004

There was little evidence, according to terrorism experts, that the perpetrators of the March 11, 2004, attacks were

In Spain's most lethal terrorist attack to date, Islamist radicals carried out a coordinated sequence of bombings aboard commuter trains in Madrid on the morning of March 11, 2004. A total of 191 people were killed and hundreds injured. *(Associated Press)*

planned or financed by al-Qaeda or North African terrorist organizations such as the Moroccan Islamic Combatant Group, an al-Qaeda–affiliated group. However, a few of those ultimately convicted of the bombings had once been members of the latter organization, and analysts agreed that the bombing, like other Islamist acts of terrorism, was certainly inspired by al-Qaeda ideology and methods.

In any event, the attacks were horrific. During the morning rush hour, ten bombs went off either in Madrid train stations or on commuter trains, killing 191 persons and injuring approximately 1,800 others. Three other bombs never went off and were disposed of by authorities. Unlike the London transit bombings of July 2005, these were not suicide attacks. The explosives had been concealed in backpacks left by the bombers.

At first, authorities announced that the Basque independence organization Euskadi Ta Askatasuna (ETA), which had been setting off bombs around Spain for decades and was angry at Aznar's hard-line approach to Basque issues, was responsible. But the attacks were brutal even by ETA standards, the organization usually giving authorities prior notice of bombings. Security officials quickly became convinced that Islamist extremists were responsible. Within weeks, after another explosive device was found on the tracks of one of Spain's high-speed trains, officials had identified an apartment in a

southern suburb of Madrid as the base of operations. On April 3, police moved in on the apartment, only to have three of the suspects kill themselves with explosives, taking the life of one officer as well. Many others were implicated, twenty-one of whom were found guilty of various roles in the attacks. Of the seven main suspects, six were of Moroccan origin (one was a Spanish national, a miner who had sold the group the explosives used in the attack). Seven other suspects were acquitted.

Although not suicide attacks, the Madrid bombings resembled other Islamist terrorist incidents of the time, such as the London bombings. Transport systems were targeted, with multiple devices going off simultaneously and meant to kill as many people as possible. Also, the perpetrators, though inspired by al-Qaeda, were not directly affiliated with it and operated out of independent cells based in the target country.

In outcome, however, the Madrid and London incidents could not have been more different. The London attacks only steeled the resolve of the Tony Blair government to stay the course in Iraq. For a variety of reasons, a very different chain of events occurred in Spain. While first rallying behind the nation's leaders, as is often the case after a major terrorist attack, Spaniards quickly turned against Aznar, whom they suspected of trying to use the bombings for political gain. By blaming ETA, he hoped to rally his countrymen to his hard-line position on the Basque organization and help his party retain power in elections that were scheduled for—and held—three days after the attack. (The timing was not coincidental, according to experts, as the perpetrators were hoping to undermine support for Aznar and his pro–Iraq War foreign policy.)

In the end, the terrorists got what they wanted. Voters gave the Partido Socialista Obrero Español, or Spanish Socialist Workers Party, a plurality in parliament and put José Luis Rodríguez Zapatero—who had made withdrawing Spanish troops from Iraq a key plank in his party's platform—in the prime minister's office. Within days, Zapatero announced that Spain would withdraw all its troops from the conflict within a year; the move was completed by April 2004, dealing a significant setback to the coalition effort.

James Ciment

See also: *Definitions, Types, Categories*—Islamist Fundamentalist Terrorism. *Modern Terrorism*—France: Islamist Terrorism; United Kingdom: Islamist Terrorism.

Further Reading

"Fighting Back: The Hunt for Terrorists in Spain and France." *The Economist,* April 7, 2004.

Jordan, Javier, and Nicola Horsburgh. "Mapping Jihadist Terrorism in Spain." *Studies in Conflict and Terrorism* 28:3 (May 2005): 169–91.

"Terror Before an Election." *The Economist,* March 11, 2004.

Zapata-Barrero, Richard, and Nynke de Witte. "Muslims in Spain: Blurring Past and Present Moors." In *Muslims in 21st Century Europe: Structural and Cultural Perspectives,* ed. Anna Triandafyllidou, pp. 160–180. New York: Routledge, 2010.

Sri Lanka: Tamil Tiger Uprising, Late 1970s–2009

The island nation of Sri Lanka (formerly Ceylon) was torn by civil war for some twenty-six years, from 1983 to 2009. In that conflict, the Liberation Tigers of Tamil Eelam (LTTE) battled with the government, dominated by the Sinhalese, to form the separate sovereign state of Tamil Eelam, comprising the northern and eastern parts of the country. The LTTE, also referred to as the Tiger Movement, was a formidable revolutionary organization; it was the only terrorist group to have assassinated two heads of government—Premier Rajiv Gandhi of India (1991) and President Ranasinghe Premadasa of Sri Lanka (1993)—as well as several prominent political and mili-

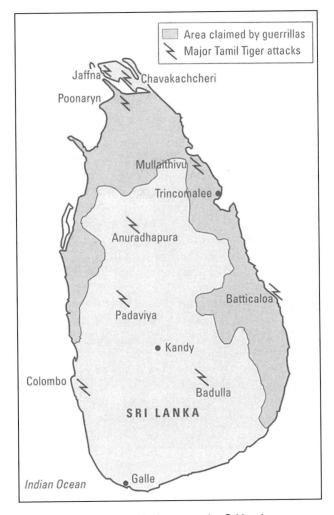

At the height of the conflict between the Sri Lankan government and Tamil Tigers in the 1990s, the latter controlled much of the coastal territory in the north and east. Government forces finally defeated the Tigers in 2009.

tary figures. During much of the 1990s and early 2000s, the international security community rated the Tamil Tigers as the world's most ruthless terrorist group.

Sri Lanka is an island 25,332 square miles in area, located 17 miles southeast of India across the Palk Strait in the Indian Ocean. The population totals more than 21 million and comprises the Sinhalese (74 percent), Sri Lanka Tamils (13 percent), Indian Tamils—migrant workers brought from India to work in coffee and tea plantations in the nineteenth century (5 percent), Muslims (7 percent), and others (Burghers, Malays, Parsis, and Vaddhas—1 percent). According to folklore, the Sinhalese and Tamils were migrants from India but have developed distinct ethnic identities with strongly held myths of origin. Social and economic development and the influence of the colonial Portuguese, Dutch, and British rulers helped establish strong ethnic boundaries in the country, backed by registration of title to land. Historically, a large number of the Sri Lankan Tamils tend to live mostly in the north and some in the east of the country. About one-third of the Tamil population has migrated toward the south of the country and are living among the Sinhalese.

History

Many of Sri Lanka's current ethnic problems have roots in the country's past political history. The British employed a divide-and-rule policy, which gave the minorities more opportunities to be employed as civil servants. English education, provided by the missionaries in the Jaffna Peninsula, enabled more Tamils to obtain a privileged position in the government. Tamils have generally looked to government jobs as a means of mobility, owing primarily to the lack of employment opportunities in the north, the prestige and security of government jobs, and the fact that this was the only way to move up in a society that had rigid caste barriers. The main avenue to government jobs was through a university education, and as a result, Tamils were disproportionately overrepresented in the civil service and in the universities. In 1946, the Tamils comprised 33 percent of the elite Ceylon civil service, 40 percent of the judicial service, and 31 percent of the university students, although they accounted for only 11 percent of the population at the time. Following independence from British rule in 1948, successive governments have introduced reforms, hoping to rectify the actual and perceived injustices suffered by the majority Sinhalese during British rule.

A root cause of the Tamil grievances was the introduction of the "Sinhala only" bill in 1956, which made Sinhala the only official language instead of English. As a result of this rule, by the late 1970s Tamils were underrepresented in government jobs relative to their proportion in the population. A second source of grievance was the introduction of a standardization scheme for university entrance, which was based on both merit and region. This method sharply limited the number of Tamil students entering the university. In 1988, the government ended the university admission program that favored the Sinhalese. At the same time, disproportionate resource allocation to Sinhala areas and Sinhala colonization of traditional Tamil areas were other factors that contributed to Tamil distrust.

From Politics to Terror

Initially, the Tamils sought to overcome discrimination against them through political means, and the Sinhalese political leaders were to some extent responsive to Tamil grievances. In 1958, Prime Minister S.W.R.D. Bandaranaike, and in 1967, Dudley Senannayake signed agreements with the leader of the Federal Party, S.J.V. Chelvanayakam, to give the Tamils regional autonomy, including the control of land settlement and recognition of Tamil as a minority language. However, under intense pressure from Sinhalese politicians and the general population, the pacts were abandoned.

The 1960s witnessed a series of bloody riots, and the Tamil youth sought a voice. This emerged in the form of the LTTE, which originated in 1972 along with other militant Tamil groups. The Tigers' charismatic leader and military commander, Velupillai Prabhakaran (also known as Karikalan), was a disciplined, dedicated leader and a self-taught military genius.

The formative phase of terrorism in Sri Lanka was marked by the assassination of Tamils who were associated with the government. Branded as traitors, the targets were Tamil politicians, police officers, government officials, and suspected informants. To establish greater security, the Tigers and other Tamil militant groups realized the importance of creating an exclusively Tamil northern province and began their campaign for the independence of Tamil Eelam in the northeastern part of the island. To this day, nationalism remains the driving force behind the Tiger Movement.

Trained to perform only ceremonial functions, Sri Lankan troops were incapable of meeting the terrorist threat during the early years of the struggle. By the time the military had become more professional, the terrorists were already masters of rural and urban guerrilla warfare. Trained in farms and jungle hideouts in northern Sri Lanka, and later in the Middle East, the Tamil groups operated out of the island's northern jungles and from bases in India. They weakened the government's author-

ity and restricted the movement of its troops by staging ambushes and mine attacks.

Demands for Independence

In 1976, the Tamil United Liberation Front, the major political party representing the Tamils at that time, campaigned for political independence on the basis of the Tamil nation's right to self-determination. Although the 1978 constitution recognized Tamil as an official language, said scholar N. DeVotta, "it was seen as too little too late by those alienated Tamils who had lost faith in the country's institutions and begun to mobilize." The call for independence by the Tamils and the state of Tamil Eelam "represented a shift from the struggle for equality to an assertion of freedom, from the demand for fundamental rights to the assertion of self-determination, from the acceptance of the pluralistic experiment to the surfacing of a new corporate identity," noted South Asian expert R.L. Hardgrave in 1994. The Tamil call for independence was met by resistance in the south. Several riots took place during this time against the Tamils—1956, 1958, 1977, 1981, and 1983. The 1983 riots were the most widespread and were sparked by the ambush and killing of thirteen soldiers of the Sri Lanka Army in Jaffna by Tamil terrorists. The riots caused a lot of damage to Tamil people's property, and many lost their lives.

The riots also polarized the two Sri Lankan communities and became a watershed in the history of the nation. Several hundred thousand Tamils left the Sinhala south for the northeastern provinces; almost all the Sinhalese left the north. Many young Tamils felt that they had no future in an island dominated by Sinhala politicians. Within five years, the Tamil independence movements had recruited, trained, and armed more than 20,000 soldiers. About 500,000 Tamils left for India and the West, seeking asylum. They became the economic backbone of the terrorist campaign, and in the years that followed, the Tigers established offices and cells throughout the world, building a network unsurpassed by any other terrorist group.

The call for Eelam helped mobilize many groups of Tamil youth by the early 1980s to fight the government to achieve their independence. The 1983 riots provided the opportunity for the terrorist groups to conduct large-scale recruitment of Tamil youth into the movement. In addition, the 1979 Prevention of Terrorism Act allowed security forces to arrest and imprison anyone suspected of conducting unlawful activity for eighteen months without a trial. This led to the torture and human rights abuse of many Tamil youth, which in turn spurred the Tamil youth to fight for an independent state. The LTTE manipulated and received unofficial support from India, such as training in the techniques of sabotage, intelligence gathering, and other guerrilla activities.

The LTTE and India's Involvement

Over time, the Tamil reaction to these incidents and other perceived injustices evolved toward abandonment of the political path and the adoption of force and terror as a means of winning their rights. In all, about thirty separate armed groups or factions arose, but the LTTE emerged as the dominant group after systematic elimination or marginalization of all other groups. The LTTE guerrilla campaign against the government began in 1983. The LTTE gained its clout from other sources as well. Between 1983 and 1987, the LTTE received help and support from the Indian intelligence agency the Research and Analysis Wing because India feared Sri Lankan support and growing friendship with the United States (by allowing broadcasting and naval facilities on Sri Lankan soil), Pakistan, and China.

With Indian military training and arms, the LTTE targeted the Sri Lankan transportation infrastructure, the security forces, and civilians, as evidenced by massacres of unarmed men, women, and children in border villages. However, the increasing dominance of the LTTE posed problems for India. The growing possibility of a separate Tamil state in close proximity to the southern Indian state of Tamil Nadu, which might seek a separate Tamil state of its own, finally compelled India to act decisively against its former protégé. The Indo-Lanka Accord signed by Indian prime minister Rajiv Gandhi and Sri Lankan president J. R. Jayawardene in 1987 made way for the 100,000 soldiers of the Indian Peacekeeping Force, or IPKF, to arrive in Sri Lanka to enforce the accord. However, within three months the accord collapsed and the LTTE turned against the Sri Lankan government and the Indian peacekeeping force. In April 1989 the Sri Lankan government and the LTTE agreed on a ceasefire. When New Delhi refused to withdraw the IPKF, the then Sri Lankan president Ranasinghe Premadasa sanctioned covert Sri Lankan military assistance to a militarily weakened LTTE. With the growing resistance, the IPKF withdrew in 1990, and within three months of the IPKF's departure the LTTE declared war against the Sri Lankan government.

Tiger Code and Strategy

The Tigers, unlike many other insurgent groups, kept rigid control over their growth, steadily improving control by investing in training and discipline, and using ideological indoctrination and psychological war conditioning. The Tiger code demanded that its rank and file—who ranged in age from fourteen to forty—abstain from liquor, smoking, and extramarital sex. The penalty for violation was instant death. The commitment of the Tamil Tigers was demonstrated by the fact that each carried a potassium cyanide capsule strung around the neck. Faced with capture, the warrior was likely to choose instant martyrdom by biting into the deadly capsule. The Tigers eulogized and venerated such suicide victims as if they were Hindu gods and goddesses.

Although the Tigers had a central committee, this functioned more as a forum for ideas. Nevertheless, all major decisions were taken by the leader, Prabhakaran, who was convinced that the success of the organization lay in his tight control and the excellent communication system that had been developed through the years.

The Tigers used bouts of peace to gain worldwide recognition, disseminate propaganda, generate funds, procure supplies, gather intelligence, regroup, retrain, and recruit. During periods of conflict, the Tigers examined every success or failure to improve the next strike. They built life-size sand models and trained on them, with the minutest details provided by intelligence operatives. With a capacity for innovation unequaled by any other terrorist group, the Tigers produced their own uniforms, antipersonnel and pressure mines, mortars, grenades, and other improvised explosive devices.

In battle, the Tigers did whatever was required to win. They fought like a professional military force when their strength was high, and less conventionally when their strength was low. When desperate, they hit vulnerable targets. Otherwise, they took on military targets. The Tigers' strikes, exploiting the element of surprise, became increasingly audacious over the years. In attack, they typically disoriented the enemy, often by ramming fortified camps with vehicles full of explosives. By overrunning several military camps, the Tigers had amassed large stocks of weapons.

The Tigers constructed two airfields in northern Sri Lanka and built a camp to train Air Tigers. However, the Sri Lankan air force bombed these bases in 1994. Suicide bombers, trained in France and Britain to fly miniature airplanes, which were invisible to radar, added a new dimension to the terrorist threat. The Tiger strategy was to use the explosive-laden airplanes to strike at military, political, and economic targets. The acquisition of gliders, gyrocopters, and minisubmarines in the mid-1990s also demonstrated their capacity for innovation.

Formidable Terrorist Organization

The military wing of the LTTE had several units: artillery, antitank, antiaircraft, medical corps, and a video and photography unit to document their activities and a transport and logistic division. The Sea Tigers, Air Tigers, Black Tigers, and the highly secretive intelligence unit formed the backbone of the military wing. "The Black Tigers are widely recognized to be the most lethal suicide unit anywhere in the world. They have carried out more suicide strikes than Hamas, Hizballah, and the

Kurdish PKK," noted scholar Peter Chalk in 2000. The LTTE forcibly recruited children, some as young as thirteen, and women. The LTTE had an elite women's force that carried out attacks against the Sri Lankan security forces. The political wing took the lead in propaganda and negotiations. The international operations were conducted by the international secretariat, which was responsible for the LTTE global network.

The weapons the LTTE acquired were often ultramodern and high-tech. "The Sri Lankan security forces have regularly acknowledged that the military weapons used by the LTTE were more sophisticated than theirs," noted one Sri Lankan newspaper during the conflict. They were also reported to have sea scooters, high-powered ships, and surface-to-air missiles. They regularly attacked Sri Lankan military camps and arms depots, and they seized long-range artillery from the Sri Lanka Army. They developed an indigenous weapons production program and a sophisticated short-range missile capability by 1990. Arms were purchased from Afghanistan, Pakistan, and India (before the 1987 Indo–Sri Lanka Peace Accord, after which the LTTE lost the benefit of Indian support). They acquired their weapons from a number of sources, as their agents were known to buy arms in Singapore, Rangoon, Bangkok, and Johannesburg. In addition, Chalk reported that arms procurement activity operated in Northeast and Southeast Asia, southwest Asia, the former Soviet Union (specifically Ukraine), southeastern Europe, the Middle East, and Africa.

The LTTE's external activities were divided into three main areas: publicity and propaganda; fundraising; and arms procurement and shipping. Publicity and propaganda activities were carried out throughout the world through offices in about fifty-four countries, with the largest and most important centers located in several Western countries: the United Kingdom, France, Germany, Switzerland, Canada, and Australia, where there was and is a large expatriate community. The group had an active Internet presence, with links to various humanitarian and development agencies. It also lobbied politicians and human rights activists and established numerous front organizations that acted as intermediaries. The LTTE conducted its international propaganda war at a highly sophisticated level, which the Sri Lanka government was often unable to match. It operated under the banner of "peace" and had been able to attract several international organizations to side with it, through its defeat by the Sri Lankan army in 2009.

"Trading in gold, laundering money and trafficking narcotics brought the LTTE substantial revenue . . . to procure sophisticated weaponry," wrote South Asia expert Rohan Gunaratna in the late 1990s. Similar to the propaganda campaign, international fund-raising activities were very sophisticated and came from six main areas: Switzerland, Canada, Australia, the United Kingdom, the United States, and the Scandinavian countries that have large Tamil communities. The older, first-generation immigrants from Sri Lanka contributed to the cause. There were reports that money was extorted from expatriates in many countries. It was also suggested that large amounts of money were raised through drug running, but positive proof was never found. In fact, estimates were that 80 to 90 percent of money for the organization came from overseas, largely from investments abroad and remittances from the Tamil diaspora. "Except for the PLO and the IRA, the LTTE is the only insurgent group that owns and operates a fleet of deep seagoing ships," wrote Gunaratna. The highly secretive shipping business, in operation since the 1980s with a fleet of at least ten freighters, equipped with sophisticated radar and communication technology, played a vital role in supplying explosives, arms, ammunition, and other war-related material.

The Sri Lankan government entered into cease-fire agreements and peace talks with the LTTE several times. Each time the peace talks collapsed, the LTTE was able to regroup and fight back, using the lull of the cease-fire to its advantage. In December 1995, the Sri Lanka Army captured the city of Jaffna after a fierce war with the LTTE. From 1995, the LTTE fought a guerrilla war with the Sri Lankan forces. It had its own military, judiciary, and postal and economic systems. By mid-1996, the Tigers controlled most of northern Sri Lanka with the exception of Jaffna, which was controlled by government forces.

The LTTE also assassinated two world leaders—Rajiv Gandhi of India in 1991 and Ranasinghe Premadasa of Sri Lanka in 1993—through suicide bombings. Tigers assassinated opponents to their struggle in India, France, Germany, Britain, and Canada. The first murder carried out by the LTTE is reported to have occurred in 1975—the killing of Alfred Duraiappah, the mayor of Jaffna, a representative of the government. Over the next thirty years, it carried out a large number of attacks, including the killing of politicians; massacres of civilians in border towns of northern and eastern Sri Lanka; attacks on places of worship, including driving an explosives-laden truck into the temple of the sacred tooth relic of Lord Buddha, where twelve people died; attacks on economic targets such as at the central bank building in Colombo in 1996, where eighty-six persons were killed and an attack on the international airport in 2001, where several airplanes were damaged; attacks on telecommunication centers and transformers. In all, it fought the Sri Lanka Army for almost two decades. The Sri Lanka Army fought an unconventional war with the LTTE in a conventional mode. By the time the conflict ended in 2009, it was estimated that between 80,000 and 100,000 persons were killed, most of them Tamil

KEY DATES

1997 The United States bans all activities of the Tamil separatist group Liberation Tigers of Tamil Eelam (LTTE).

August 1998 It is reported that Tamil separatist guerrillas have launched 155 suicide attacks.

2001 Several airplanes are destroyed in the Tamil attack on the international airport in the Sri Lanka capital of Colombo.

2002 A cease-fire between Tamil separatists and the Sri Lankan government goes into effect; in September the two sides meet in Thailand and tentatively agree on substantial autonomy for Tamil areas rather than full independence.

2008 The government pulls out of the 2002 cease-fire and launches a major offensive against LTTE.

2009 After a brutal siege that saw the deaths of hundreds of Tamil guerrillas and civilians, the LTTE is forced to surrender to government forces, ending the twenty-six-year-long conflict.

civilians, though thousands were killed far from the battlefields as a result of terrorist attacks.

Winds of Peace

Several countries banned the LTTE as a terrorist organization during the 1990s. In 1991, following the assassination of Rajiv Gandhi, Malaysia and India were the first to ban the organization, followed by the United States in 1997. Sri Lanka followed suit in 1998 after the attack on the Temple of the Tooth; the United Kingdom and Canada followed in 2001. As a result, some of the front organizations were also frozen, thereby making fundraising more difficult. With the change of government in 2001, LTTE leader Velupillai Prabhakaran and Prime Minister Ranil Wickramasinghe signed a memorandum of understanding to end the ethnic war in Sri Lanka. A cease-fire followed, and peace talks commenced in September 2002. The first round went well, as both sides tentatively agreed to settle for substantial autonomy in the Tamil regions rather than full independence. Committees were set up to deal with confidence-building measures such as de-mining operations, internal refugees, and ways to obtain foreign aid. In addition, and rather surprising to outside observers, a committee to deal with the more difficult political issues was also established. As a result of the talks and goodwill evinced by both sides, the prevailing mood on the island was one of cautious optimism.

The mood was dashed the following year when the Tigers pulled out of the peace talks, followed by a new rebel offensive in 2004, accompanied by a suicide bomb blast in the capital Colombo, the first since 2001. A temporary reprieve in the fighting followed the disas-

trous tsunami of December 2004, which killed upward of 30,000 people in Sri Lanka, many of them in the areas controlled by the LTTE. But disputes over aid money led to renewed fighting in 2005 and the assassination by Tamil Tigers of the country's foreign minister in August. By 2006, the Tamil areas of the north and east were once again embroiled in full-scale war. In January 2008, the government pulled out of the 2002 cease-fire, though the agreement had largely been a dead letter since fighting was renewed in 2006. The massive government offensive that followed would ultimately lead to the demise of the Tamil Tigers, which, by early 2009, had been isolated to a besieged zone in the northeast, holed up with thousands of Tamil civilians. Despite humanitarian pleas from the international community, the Sri Lankan military refused to ease the siege, finally forcing the heirs to Tiger leader Velupillai Prabhakaran, who was killed in the fighting that May, to sue for peace. In May, the group agreed to lay down their arms, ending the more than quarter-century-long conflict.

Priyantha Silva, Ajith Silva,
Rohan Gunaratna, and James Ciment

See also: *Definitions, Types, Categories*—Ethnonationalist Terrorism. *Tactics, Methods, Aims*—Suicide Attacks.

Further Reading

Bandarage, Asoka. *The Separatist Conflict in Sri Lanka: Terrorism, Ethnicity, Political Economy.* New York: Routledge, 2008.

Chalk, Peter. *Gray Area Phenomena in Southeast Asia: Piracy, Drug Trafficking and Political Terrorism.* Canberra, Australia: SDSC, 1997.

DeVotta, Neil. "Control Democracy, Institutional Decay, and the Quest for Eelam: Explaining Ethnic Conflict in Sri Lanka." *Pacific Affairs* 73:1 (Spring 2000): 55–76.

Gunaratna, Rohan. *International and Regional Implications of the Sri Lankan Tamil Insurgency.* Colombo, Sri Lanka: Alumni Association of the Bandaranaike Center for International Studies, 1997.

———. *Sri Lanka's Ethnic Crisis and National Security.* Colombo, Sri Lanka: South Asian Network on Conflict Research, 1998.

Hardgrave, Robert L., Jr. "India: The Dilemmas of Diversity." In *Nationalism, Ethnic Conflict and Democracy,* ed. Larry Diamond and Mark F. Planner. Baltimore: Johns Hopkins University Press, 1994.

Human Rights Watch. *Besieged, Displaced, and Detailed: The Plight of Civilians in Sri Lanka's Vanni Region.* New York: Human Rights Watch, 2008.

Swamy, M.R. Narayan. *The Tiger Vanquished: LTTE's Story.* Thousand Oaks, CA: Sage, 2010.

Sudan: Conflicts in South Sudan and Darfur, Late 1950s–2000s

For much of its history since independence in 1956, Sudan has been a nation at war with itself. Aside from a decadelong hiatus in the 1970s and early 1980s, the government fought with rebels in the southern part of the country from the late 1950s through the early 2000s, the longest ongoing conflict in post–World War II history. In addition, through much of the 2000s, government forces and government-backed militias have fought with rebels in western Sudan, a region known as Darfur. Each conflict has seen atrocities and massacres committed by both the government and rebels. Most international observers, however, have singled out the government and, in the case of Darfur, government-backed militias as having conducted campaigns intended to terrorize civilian populations. Such campaigns have been conducted, among other reasons, to undermine civilian support for rebel movements. At the same time, ethnic-based rebel groups—particularly those in the south—have launched attacks on civilian populations, especially those with differing ethnic backgrounds.

Southern Sudan Conflict

Part of the British Empire from the late nineteenth century to 1956—though technically under joint British and Egyptian rule—Sudan is Africa's largest country by area. Its huge expanses encompass a bewildering array of ethnic groups, as well as three separate religious traditions: Muslim in the northern two-thirds of the country and Christianity and animist faiths in the southern third. Racially, the country is divided into an Arab north and a black African South, though there has been much intermixing over the centuries. Traditionally, northerners exploited southerners, routinely raiding their lands for slaves, which engendered long-standing distrust among the latter. So bitter was the enmity that southerners insisted on a separate country upon independence, a request ignored by the British, who turned over power to the more-developed Arab north.

From the beginning, leaders in Khartoum, the nation's capital, sought to overcome resistance by southerners through military means, a policy that intensified with the coming to power of General Ibrahim Abboud in a 1958 coup. Abboud not only rolled back the autonomy southerners were supposedly guaranteed in the country's original constitution but began imposing Islamic law on the largely non-Muslim South. The goal was not only to end resistance to the regime in Khartoum but to "Arabize" the south culturally. In response to such policies, a group of southern exiles formed a rebel fighting force known as the Anya-Nya, meaning "viper venom" in one of the southern Sudanese languages. For the next decade, the Anya-Nya and government forces became locked in a brutal war, with the former massacring Arab civilians who had migrated to the south, often as part of the government's Arabization policies, and the latter attacking southern civilian populations allegedly supporting the rebels. In both cases, the aim was terror. The goal of the Anya-Nya was to drive northerners out of the south, while the government hoped to undermine civilian logistical and moral support for the rebels.

A 1969 coup by military officers tired of the war and the damage it was doing to the Sudanese economy led to lengthy peace talks with the Southern Sudan Liberation Movement, the political organization behind the Anya-Nya. The talks resulted in a 1972 agreement that allowed for more autonomy for the south. Altogether, a half million people are estimated to have been killed in what came to be known as the First Sudanese Civil War, four-fifths of them civilians.

The agreement kept the peace for eleven years. During this period, however, the country's Arab majority turned increasingly to Islamist politics. In 1983, the government imposed sharia (Muslim law) on the country, antagonizing non-Muslim southerners, and then sought to strip away some of the autonomy enjoyed by the south. The latter move, Khartoum said, was to shift power away from the Dinka, the dominant ethnic group in the region, and distribute it to other groups. To put down a mutiny by southern troops that year, Khartoum dispatched John Garang, a Dinka officer. But Garang switched sides and joined the mutineers, ultimately establishing a new rebel movement, the Sudanese People's Liberation Movement (SPLM) and its military wing, the Sudanese People's Liberation Army (SPLA).

The so-called Second Sudanese Civil War, which lasted from 1983 to 2002, both resembled and differed from the first. On the one hand, the issues dividing the two sides remained the same—northern attempts to Arabize and subjugate the southern third of the country and resistance on the part of the non-Muslim population of the regime to such efforts. Similarly, there were massacres and other atrocities on both sides, including mass rape on the part of government forces to terrorize civilians associated with or supporting the other side's armed combatants. Not surprisingly, given its much greater resources, most of the organized terrorist activities were perpetrated by government forces.

Three key differences, however, marked the second conflict. First, unlike the Anya-Nya, which had enjoyed wide support among all ethnic groups, the SPLM and SPLA were largely Dinka organizations. Other southern ethnic groups that resisted supporting these organizations often faced the same terroristic campaigns the SPLA perpetrated against Arab migrant populations in the south. Second was the late 1970s–1980s discovery of oil in southern Sudan, which raised the stakes of the conflict for both sides.

Finally, the second Sudanese conflict involved more foreign players. While the first conflict had drawn in neighboring regimes, some, like Egypt, backing the government, and others, such as the Congo, Uganda, and Ethiopia, siding with the rebels. The second drew in non-African parties, including the United States. Partly this had to do with oil, but the more important reason was international Islamist terrorism. Under the National Islamic Front government of Hassan al-Turabi and Omar al-Bashir, Sudan became a haven for al-Qaeda and other extremist organizations in the first half of the 1990s. But after a Sudan-based al-Qaeda plot to assassinate Egyptian president Hosni Mubarak was uncovered in 1995, pressure mounted on the Khartoum government to deport Osama bin Laden and other al-Qaeda leaders from the country, which it did in 1996. The decision to oust the terrorist organization and, after the September 11, 2001, terrorist attacks on the United States, to cooperate in antiterrorism efforts improved the Sudanese government's relationship with the United States and other Western countries.

By the early 2000s, the administration of U.S. president George W. Bush had made settling the southern Sudanese conflict a top priority, dispatching former senator John Danforth to act as an envoy to push Khartoum to open negotiations with Garang's organization. It did so in 2002, though only after nearly twenty years of fighting and the deaths of an estimated 2 million civilians in the south. Many of the deaths had been caused by famine, the result of an alleged government campaign to deny citizens food aid as a means of forcing them to accept Khartoum's authority. Two years after negotiations had begun, the two sides had reached an agreement calling for more autonomy for the south, a fifty-fifty split of regional oil revenues, a meshing of SPLA and government forces into a new military, and the right of southern Sudanese to opt out of sharia. In addition, it was stipulated that a local referendum on secession would be held within six years. In January 2011, the long-awaited referendum was held and, as expected, the overwhelming majority of south Sudanese opted for independence.

Darfur Conflict

The conflict in the western Sudanese region of Darfur is of newer vintage than the conflict in the south. Here

Sudan has been torn by civil war almost continuously since becoming independent in 1956. While the conflict in Darfur continues to the present day, the one in the south ended with a cease-fire in 2002. In January 2011, southerners voted overwhelmingly for independence in a special referendum.

the conflict did not have a religious element, since the rebel groups shared the Muslim faith of the majority of Sudanese. Instead, the conflict was based more on ethnicity and way of life—many of the people of Darfur spoke a different language and practiced a different culture than the Arab majority. Indeed, the region was divided between seminomadic herders who spoke Arabic and non-Arab farmers who were sedentary cattle owners, many of them of the Fur ethnic group (hence the name Darfur, "land of the Fur"). As drought intensified in the region through the 1970s and 1980s, the two groups began to come into increasing conflict over scarce water and pasturage. In addition, many people in the region resented what they regarded as neglect of Darfur by the central government, which provided few services there.

As disputes between the two sides intensified and older means of resolving conflict broke down, both pastoralists and farmers began to form militias and arm themselves against each other. By the early 2000s, the non-Arab militias had coalesced into two rebel movements, the SPLM and the Justice and Equality Movement (JEM), both with armed wings. As the rebel movements began to attack government forces, Khartoum turned

Sudanese refugees from the Darfur region settle at a UN refugee camp in eastern Chad after the Sudanese air force bombed their village in June 2009. The government-sponsored genocide against non-Arab peoples in Darfur caused a major humanitarian crisis. *(Marco Di Lauro/Getty Images)*

to traditional Arab militias in the region, known as the Janjaweed (Arabic for "devils on horseback"), which it had used against southern rebels.

By early 2003, Janjaweed forces backed by government troops were engaging in mass attacks against non-Arab villages. Khartoum maintained that its forces, along with the Janjaweed, were simply engaging in anti-rebel actions. Washington and much of the West, focused on solving the north-south conflict and trying to keep Khartoum as an ally in the war against terrorism, tended to ignore the fighting in Darfur. But as hundreds of thousands of civilians fled the region—telling stories of mass rapes, abduction of children, and slaughter of civilians—the war began to grab headlines around the world, sparking a global movement to aid the victims of the Janjaweed. More than mere terrorism aimed at forcing civilians to abandon their support of rebels, said critics of the government, Khartoum and the Janjaweed were actually engaging in genocide against the non-Arabs of the region, hoping to destroy them as a people. In 2004, after conducting an extensive investigation of the situation, the United States agreed that Khartoum was engaging in genocidal acts, while the United Nations Security Council followed up with a declaration that the Sudanese government had committed "crimes against humanity."

Meanwhile, in 2004 as well, the African Union (AU) deployed a peacekeeping force that eventually rose

to 7,000 in number. Most observers said that this was insufficient, especially as the force had little in the way of logistical support to police an area larger than California. In 2007, the United Nations formed a unique hybrid peacekeeping mission with the AU that proved more effective, with nearly 17,000 troops and nearly 5,000 police officers. At the same time, Khartoum and the various rebel movements engaged in desultory negotiations, while government forces and the Janjaweed continued to engage in their depredations against the non-Arab civilian population of Darfur. International sanctions against the Sudanese government failed to stop the attacks on civilians, largely because China, one of Khartoum's main trading partners, refused to abide by them. In 2008, JEM brought the conflict to the capital, with a large-scale attack on military targets in Khartoum's twin city of Omdurman, an attack the government labeled an act of terrorism.

Even as JEM took the fighting to the capital, the increased UN and AU presence helped stabilize the situation in Darfur itself, with the head of the joint mission declaring the war largely over by August 2009. Overall, casualty statistics have varied widely, with the government claiming that less than 30,000 died and international humanitarian organizations putting the figure as high as 500,000, virtually all of them Fur and other non-Arab civilians. The viciousness of the cam-

KEY DATES

1956 Sudan wins its independence from Britain and Egypt.

1962 Southerners form the Anya-Nya militia to resist government authority, including the imposition of Muslim law.

1972 Leaders of the southern rebel movement reach a peace agreement with the government, which includes a grant of more autonomy for the region.

1983 The 1972 peace agreement breaks down after the government imposes sharia law on the south and reduces the region's autonomous powers.

2002 A U.S.-mediated peace agreement brings the so-called Second Sudanese Civil War to an end, partly by promising southerners the chance to vote on secession.

2003 Government-backed Arab militias, known as the Janjaweed, launch attacks on non-Arab civilians in the Darfur region.

2004 The African Union (AU) deploys peacekeepers to the region.

2007 The United Nations forms a hybrid peacekeeping mission with the AU in Darfur.

2008 Sudanese president Omar al-Bashir is indicted by the International Criminal Court; among the charges are counts of genocide.

2009 The head of the UN-AU peacekeeping mission declares the war in Darfur over.

2011 Preliminary results from the plebiscite on independence for southern Sudan gives the separation vote an overwhelming majority.

paigns launched by the Janjaweed, with the government's backing, was underlined by the International Criminal Court, which issued indictments against two Janjaweed leaders in 2007, followed by one against al-Bashir a year later. The charges included genocide, marking the first time that a sitting leader of a country ever faced such an indictment. As of April 2011, the Sudanese government has refused to turn over any of the three to the International Criminal Court.

James Ciment

See also: *Definitions, Types, Categories*—Ethnonationalist Terrorism; State vs. Nonstate Terrorism. *Modern Terrorism*—Uganda: Lord's Resistance Army and Other Terrorist Groups.

Further Reading

Akol, Lam. *Southern Sudan: Colonialism, Resistance, and Autonomy.* Trenton, NJ: Red Sea, 2007.

Flint, Julie, and Alex de Waal. *Darfur: A New History of a Long War.* New York: Zed Books, 2008.

O'Ballance, Edgar. *Sudan Civil War and Terrorism, 1956–1999.* New York: St. Martin's, 2000.

Prunier, Gerard. *Darfur: The Ambiguous Genocide.* Ithaca, NY: Cornell University Press, 2005.

United Nations. *UN Commission of Inquiry: Darfur Conflict.* New York: United Nations, 2005.

U.S. Department of State. "Documenting Atrocities in Darfur." State Publication 11182. Washington, DC, September 9, 2004.

Sudan: Terrorist Haven, 1989–2000s

The National Islamic Front (NIF), led by Hassan al-Turabi and the military leader Brigadier Omar al-Bashir, came to power in Sudan in 1989. For the next seven years, Sudan became notorious as one of the world's seven state sponsors of terrorism. Of the many groups to which Sudan offered a safe haven, al-Qaeda emerged as the most dangerous.

The relations between the NIF and al-Qaeda were established after an NIF delegation from Khartoum visited Osama bin Laden in Peshawar, Pakistan, in 1989. The delegation, carrying a request from Sudan's spiritual leader and Islamist al-Turabi, invited bin Laden to visit Sudan. Al-Turabi and bin Laden had much in common. Like bin Laden, al-Turabi believed that the Americans also could be taken on, the same way the Islamists had defeated the Soviets in the preceding decade. Bin Laden subsequently visited Saudi Arabia and after a disagreement with the royal family returned to Pakistan in April 1991. As Saudi Arabia and Pakistan enjoyed close relations, bin Laden realized the danger of remaining in Pakistan, especially because he had planned to assassinate Prime Minister Benazir Bhutto and even funded Pakistani politicians to move a no-confidence motion against Bhutto in parliament. In the meantime, Sudan also asked bin Laden to provide Afghan veterans to train NIF members in guerrilla warfare to fight the Sudan People's Liberation Army, a largely Western-supported, predominantly Christian guerrilla group. Bin Laden accepted al-Turabi's invitation and visited Khartoum in late 1991. After meeting with al-Turabi, he transferred his infrastructure from Pakistan to Sudan. Bin Laden's intention was to foster the economic development of Sudan, which was one of the poorest countries in the world and in the throes of a long civil war. In many ways he wanted to do in Sudan what his father, a construction magnate, had done in Saudi Arabia.

The first company bin Laden established in Sudan was Wadi Al-Aqiq. Sudan's president, Omar al-Bashir, approved al-Qaeda requests to import and export goods without duty, and the nation's spiritual leader, Hassan al-Turabi, steadfastly supported al-Qaeda, even its efforts to open a bank. Among the construction projects bin Laden was involved in was the building of the Tahaddi Road, the so-called revolutionary highway, between Khartoum and Port Sudan. Al-Qaeda's Al Hijah Construction and Development Company built Sudan's newest airport in Port Sudan. Bin Laden, the first guest invited to attend the inauguration of the new airport, sat in the front row and was the ceremony's guest of honor. It was a group of bin Laden's companies that carried out the project for

the modern new airport, which cost a huge amount of money. During the airport inauguration ceremony, bin Laden donated $2.5 million to establish and operate the airport, the second largest international airport in Sudan after the one in Khartoum. Al-Qaeda used this airport extensively, especially to fly to Jeddah. Many al-Qaeda members flew to Port Sudan, Jeddah, Riyadh, and Europe—London and Germany mostly—or the United States, primarily New York. Bin Laden also used Khartoum International Airport, a fact made evident by the presence of bin Laden's private plane, purchased in Texas, in a corner of the airport.

When bin Laden provided funds for Sudan's military, the NIF reciprocated by providing him with land for training camps. After a while, al-Qaeda forged relations with Iran and Hezbollah, and about thirty camps were established throughout Sudan to train a dozen groups, including the Egyptian Islamic Jihad, Islamic Group of Egypt, Libyan Islamic Fighters Group, Armed Islamic Group of Algeria, Hamas, Palestinian Islamic Jihad, al Ansar Mujahideen, Islamic Army of Aden-Abyan, and Eritrean Jihad. While he was in Khartoum, the Saudi government urged bin Laden to return in 1993 and cease his organizing. After he refused, the Saudi government responded by withdrawing his citizenship and freezing his assets in February 1994. In March 1994, bin Laden's brother Bakr expressed through the Saudi media his family's "regret, denunciation and condemnation" of bin Laden's activities. Later bin Laden claimed that through the media the Saudi rulers had attempted to defame his character in Saudi Arabia and internationally. In retaliation, bin Laden formed an al-Qaeda front in the United Kingdom—the Advice and Reform Committee, in London. The Advice and Reform Committee, headed by Khalid al Fawwaz, issued several hundred press releases, pamphlets, and letters critical of the Saudi regime. Similarly, al-Qaeda was able to widen and deepen its influence in Africa because Sudan facilitated al-Qaeda's efforts to establish and operate a state-of-the-art terrorist operation in Africa and beyond.

The NIF under al-Turabi funded several Islamist political and terrorist groups around the world. He used nongovernmental organizations for this purpose, principally the Islamic Relief Agency (ISRA; also known as Iara, Yara, African Islamic Relief Agency), with its headquarters in Khartoum and offices in thirty countries. In addition to a presence in many cities in Germany, ISRA had offices in Sarajevo, Zagreb, Tirana, and Tuzla. It also operated in Kalesija, Banovici, Doboj East, and Zvornik. The ISRA office in Zagreb provided weapons to the Bosnian military. ISRA is linked to the Third World Relief Agency (TWRA), another nongovernmental organization headquartered in Sudan. TWRA had its offices in Turkey, Germany, Switzerland, as well as in Zagreb, Tuzla, Sarajevo, and Split. In retaliation for the arrest of a senior Egyptian Islamic Group member, an employee of TWRA, who was also a member of the Egyptian Islamic Group, an al-Qaeda associate group, conducted a suicide car bombing against a Croatian police station in Rijeka in mid-October 1995. The Croatian security forces killed the mastermind of that operation, Anwar Shaban, former mujahideen leader, in Zenica in December 1995. At the time of his death, Shaban, together with the Egyptian Islamic Group and al-Qaeda, was planning to attack North Atlantic Treaty Organization (NATO) forces expected in Bosnia. A TWRA senior official relocated his office from Zagreb after his weapons-smuggling operations were exposed. He also supported American Islamists, including the Taibah International, with offices in Zagreb, Split, and Sarajevo. Following raids by Italian police, the official intending to fund the rebuilding of the Egyptian Islamic Group and other Islamist networks in Rome and Milan sent his brother to assess the damage.

Sudan and Al-Qaeda

During the time Sudan was al-Qaeda's home (December 1991 to May 1996), al-Qaeda combined its forces with the NIF and spread Islam throughout Africa. After al-Qaeda mounted an operation from Sudan to kill visiting Egyptian president Hosni Mubarak in Addis Ababa, Ethiopia, in 1995, U.S., British, Saudi, and Egyptian pressure forced Sudan to persuade bin Laden to look for another home. Bin Laden did not wish to suffer the same fate as Carlos the Jackal, who had also been a guest in Sudan and was betrayed to the French by President al-Bashir in 1994. Although bin Laden and his entourage returned in a chartered C-130 from Khartoum to Afghanistan on May 18, 1996, the links between the Sudanese regime and bin Laden continued. Al-Turabi and his family were sad to see bin Laden leave Sudan. Al-Turabi's son Isam accused the military government of plotting bin Laden's departure with the

United States. After their guest left, the Sudanese government was still positively disposed to al-Qaeda for a number of years. As Sudan's information secretary Muhammad Al-Bashir Muhammad Al-Hady explained, al-Qaeda militants and other mujahideen were helping defend the country against incursions by neighboring Ethiopia and Eritrea.

The al-Qaeda infiltration of African states, using Sudan as a launching area, finally took its toll. In addition to countries to the north and the east, al-Qaeda established links with a dozen groups deep in the central and southern regions of Africa. Although some of the al-Qaeda links are with individuals, others are with political parties and terrorist groups in Somalia, Sudan, Republic of the Congo, the Democratic Republic of the Congo, and Guinea-Bissau. Al-Qaeda exploited these links to establish its presence. Initial preparation for al-Qaeda's landmark operation in East Africa was conducted from Sudan. The groundwork for al-Qaeda's coordinated attacks against U.S. embassies in Nairobi, Kenya, and Dar es Salaam, Tanzania, on August 7, 1998, was planned in Nairobi and Mombassa in 1994. In addition to the al-Qaeda suicide bombers, the attacks killed 232 Africans and 12 Americans and wounded 4,585 in Nairobi and Dar es Salaam. Thirteen days after the East Africa bombings, the United States responded by attacking the al-Qaeda infrastructure in Afghanistan and in Sudan. Before attacking the targets, U.S. satellites monitored an al-Qaeda complex of six camps with 600 trainees and trainers and an al-Qaeda–linked Shifa pharmaceutical industrial plant in Sudan. The Central Intelligence Agency (CIA) thwarted an al-Qaeda bombing of the U.S. embassy in Kampala, Uganda, on September 18, 1998. Twenty suspects, including Sheik Abdul Abdullah Amin, Omar Ahmed Mandela, and Mohamed Gulam Kabba, were arrested.

Al-Qaeda's funds were boosted by the illicit sale of diamonds from Sierra Leone. Dealings were supposedly done with the Revolutionary United Front, which denied any connection with al-Qaeda. The jewels, according to the *Washington Post* on November 2, 2001, were then sold at profit to European buyers.

Since the mid-1990s, the threat posed to Americans in Liberia has increased, finally forcing the evacuation of U.S. personnel from Liberia in 1996. Al-Qaeda influence also spread to South Africa, where it established links with Islamists and criminal organizations. Al-Qaeda's East Africa bomber, Khalfan Khamis Mohamed, was arrested in Cape Town, South Africa, on October 5, 1999.

In early 2001, the relationship between General Omar al-Bashir and al-Turabi began to deteriorate. Following intelligence that al-Turabi was planning to oust him, al-Bashir placed him under house arrest and, after the September 11 terrorist attacks on U.S. soil, decided

---

KEY DATES

May 1996 Osama bin Laden and the al-Qaeda leadership transfer their headquarters from Sudan to Afghanistan.
August 1998 The U.S. embassies in Kenya and Tanzania are bombed by al-Qaeda operatives, who planned the operations from Sudan.
September 1998 The Central Intelligence Agency thwarts an al-Qaeda plan to bomb the U.S. embassy in Uganda, an operation believed to have been planned in Sudan.

to fully cooperate with the United States. Since October 2001, al-Bashir has provided valuable information to the CIA and European intelligence agencies on al-Qaeda. The Americans helped Sudan to reach an agreement with the Sudan People's Liberation Army, led by John Garang, in early 2002, at least temporarily ending one of the most violent conflicts in Africa. Another broke out in the Darfur region of western Sudan in 2003, this time without religious overtones, pitting Muslim rebels against a Muslim government in Khartoum. Mass killings there prompted the International Criminal Court in The Hague to issue an arrest warrant for al-Bashir in 2009 on charges of war crimes and crimes against humanity. Not only did al-Bashir refuse to turn himself over, but he had al-Turabi arrested and put in jail for suggesting al-Bashir turn himself in to the Court.

The threat posed by the Islamists has not diminished in Sudan. As the Islamist support base is vast and deep, Islamic militancy is likely to resurface from time to time. Reflecting that, the United States has continued to maintain Sudan on its sponsors-of-terrorism list of countries, despite significant efforts by Sudan to disrupt terrorist training facilities in the country. Washington has applauded those efforts, at the same time recognizing that because of Sudan's vast size, weak government, and widespread popular support for al-Qaeda-style jihadism against the West, terrorist networks find it easy to operate under the radar there.

Rohan Gunaratna

See also: *Modern Terrorism*—Sudan: Conflicts in South Sudan and Darfur. *September 11 Attacks*—Al-Qaeda; Bin Laden, Osama. *Tactics, Methods, Aims*—Safe Havens, Terrorist; State-Sponsored Terrorism.

Further Reading

Deng, Francis Mading. *War of Visions: Conflict of Identities in the Sudan.* Washington, DC: Brookings Institution, 1995.

Farah, Douglas. "Al-Qaeda Cash Tied to Diamond Trade—Sale of Gems from Sierra Leone Rebels Raised Millions, Sources Say." *Washington Post,* November 2, 2001.

Jendia, Catherine. *The Sudanese Civil Conflict, 1969–1985.* New York: Peter Lang, 2000.

Majak, L. Lual. *Sudan: Events and Present Conflict.* Nairobi: L.L.M. Bol, 2000.

Petterson, Donald. *Inside Sudan: Political Islam, Conflict, and Catastrophe.* Rev. ed. Boulder, CO: Westview, 2003.

Shay, Shaul. *The Red Sea Terror Triangle: Sudan, Somalia, Yemen, and Islamic Terror.* Trans. Rachel Liberman. New Brunswick, NJ: Transaction, 2005.

Syria: State Sponsorship of Terrorism, 1979–2000s

The Syrian Arab Republic is a Middle Eastern country that shares land borders with Turkey, Iraq, Jordan, Israel, and Lebanon, and whose coastline is on the Mediterranean Sea. Syria is mostly desert, with hot, dry summers and mild, wet winters along the coast. The population of Syria is approximately 21 million, of whom 90 percent are Arab and 10 percent Kurdish, Armenian, and others. Religiously, Sunni Muslims represent 74 percent of the population; Alawites, Druze, and other Muslim groups about 16 percent; and various Christian sects 10 percent. There is also a numerically insignificant Jewish community. The Syrian economy is predominantly statist, which hampers economic growth. The primary industries are agriculture and petroleum, both of which are in need of reform. Syria's economic prospects are further clouded by the vulnerability of the agricultural sector to drought and water pollution, and a high rate of population growth (3.5 percent), which contributes to high levels of unemployment. The government has recognized the need for reform, but whether the autocratic regime will implement reform fast enough to ensure growth is uncertain. The primary impediment to change is the regime's fear of instability.

History

Syria was one of the ancient centers of civilization in the third millennium B.C.E. Over the centuries, it was occupied by Canaanites, Phoenicians, Hebrews, Armenians, Assyrians, Babylonians, Persians, Greeks, Romans, Nabataeans, Byzantines, Crusaders, and Muslim Arabs before coming under the rule of the Ottoman Turks in the early sixteenth century. Ottoman rule ended after World War I, and after a brief period as the independent Arab Kingdom of Syria, it became a French mandate. Pressure from nationalist groups forced the French to evacuate their troops in 1946. The period from independence to 1970 was marked by instability and a series of coups. In 1958, following the call to Arab nationalism after the 1956 Suez Crisis, Syria and Egypt merged to create the United Arab Republic. Following another military coup in 1961, however, Syria seceded and became the Syrian Arab Republic.

In 1963, the Arab Socialist Resurrection Party (Ba'ath Party) engineered a successful coup. In 1966, another coup resulted in a new Ba'ath-dominated leadership in Syria, and in 1970 the minister of defense, Hafiz al-Assad, assumed power in a bloodless military coup. In 1976, Syrian forces intervened in Lebanon, ostensibly as

a peacekeeping force, and sizable Syrian forces remained there until 2005. Assad consolidated his power and dealt ruthlessly with critics. Most notably, he clamped down on fundamentalist Sunni Muslims who objected to Ba'ath secular ideology and rule by the Alawites—the minority Muslim sect from which Assad and most of the regime's senior figures come. An attempted uprising by the Sunni Muslim Brotherhood in 1982 at the city of Hama was crushed by the Syrian army, leaving thousands dead. Since then, effective opposition to the regime has ceased. The collapse of the Soviet Union posed new challenges to Syria, particularly in the areas of economic and military assistance. Syria participated in the U.S.-led coalition against Iraq in the Persian Gulf War and in the aftermath attempted to reach agreement with Israel over the disputed Golan Heights area (captured by Israel during the 1967 Arab-Israeli War). These negotiations failed. Hafiz al-Assad died on June 10, 2000, and following some cosmetic amendments to the constitution, was succeeded by his son Bashar al-Assad. Assad the younger continued his father's authoritarian rule, with the trappings of democratic process.

Syria and the War on Terror

Syria has long been a safe haven for international terrorists, and since 1979, when the U.S. State Department drew up its list of state sponsors of terrorism, Syria has been on the list. As a result, Syria is subject to U.S. export sanctions (including all military equipment and "dual-use" technologies) and is ineligible for most forms of U.S. economic aid. The United States withdrew its ambassador in 1986 as a result of Syrian involvement with terrorism, but an ambassador returned to Damascus the following year in response to Syria's expelling the Palestinian Abu Nidal Organization and rendering its help in securing the release of an American hostage in Lebanon, where Syria maintained a peacekeeping force. According to the State Department, there has been no solid evidence that Syrian officials have been involved in planning or executing terrorist attacks since 1986.

Nevertheless, Syria has continued to offer safe haven and limited support to a number of terrorist organizations, including Hamas, Hezbollah, Palestinian Islamic Jihad, the Popular Front for the Liberation of Palestine (PFLP), the Popular Front for the Liberation of Palestine—General Command (PFLP-GC), and Abu Musa's Fatah-Intifada. Perhaps the most important aspect of this involvement is Syria's provision of secure training areas

Sheik Hassan Nasrallah (left), head of the militant Lebanese Shiite group Hezbollah, presents the gift of a rifle to Syrian military commanders in 2005. Syria withdrew its occupying forces from Lebanon but remained one of Hezbollah's leading supporters. *(Associated Press)*

and rest facilities. In particular, a safe base of operations outside the occupied territories (but close to Israel) is extremely useful for Palestinian terrorist organizations. Syria also granted basing privileges to international terrorist groups in the parts of Lebanon it controlled. Among other groups benefiting from the relative lawlessness of Lebanon is al-Qaeda, which has links to the Lebanese Hezbollah and other groups, and which has engaged in recruitment and indoctrination in Palestinian refugee camps in Lebanon. Syria is also the main transit point for terrorist personnel and weapons en route to Lebanon, particularly to Hezbollah. Syria does appear to have upheld assurances to Turkey that it will not support the Kurdistan Workers Party, allow terrorist groups in Syria to launch attacks from Syrian soil, or attack Western targets. Syria is important to Middle Eastern stability primarily because of its significant influence in Lebanon (particularly over Hezbollah) and because of its close proximity to Iraq. Similarly, Syria's importance to the war on terrorism is balanced on the one hand by its ideological conviction to support such groups, public sympathy for the Palestinian cause, and Arab/Muslim solidarity, and on the other by the need to avoid further U.S. sanctions and expand its markets.

Whatever moves Syria had made did not satisfy the George W. Bush Administration, which included Syria among the so-called "axis of evil" countries. In April 2003, just a month after the start of the Iraq War, which Syria opposed, Washington insisted that Syria stop its funding of terrorists, pursuit of chemical weapons, providing sanctuary for fugitive members of the Saddam Hussein regime, and maintaining troops in Lebanon. Syria denied all charges, but this did not stop the United States from imposing economic sanctions in May 2004.

Four months later, the UN Security Council issued a resolution calling on all foreign forces to leave Lebanon. International outrage over the killing of Lebanese prime minister Rafic Hariri in February 2005 finally forced

KEY DATES

June 10, 2000   Longtime Syrian dictator Hafiz al-Assad dies; his son Bashar takes power.

September 2001   Despite cool relations between Syria and the United States, Damascus issues an official condemnation of the attack and condolences to victims of the September 11 terrorist attacks.

April 2002   Syria expresses guarded support for an Arab League plan calling for recognition of Israel in exchange for Israeli withdrawal from all lands occupied in the June 1967 Arab-Israeli War.

May 2004   Claiming Syria is supporting terrorism and seeking weapons of mass destruction, the United States imposes economic sanctions on the country.

April 2005   Syria pulls its troops out of Lebanon in response to international outrage over the assassination of the country's prime minister, which it is suspected of orchestrating.

September 2007   Suspecting Syria of trying to develop nuclear weapons, Israel launches an air raid against a supposed nuclear facility under construction in the northern part of the country.

February 2010   The United States posts its first ambassador to Syria in five years.

May 2010   Claiming that Syria is aiding terrorists and attempting to develop weapons of mass destruction, the United States imposes new economic sanctions.

Early 2011   Popular uprisings calling for major economic and political reform—including the ouster of President Bashar Assad—sweep the country. Syrian security units respond with deadly force, killing hundreds of protesters. The demonstrations escalate.

Damascus, which was suspected of having a hand in the assassination, to pull its troops out of the country. Then, fearing Syria was developing nuclear weapons, Israel launched a raid in September 2007 against a site in the northern part of the country that it believed was a nuclear facility under construction. For its part, the United States insisted that Syria was supporting some of the terrorist groups in Iraq that were conducting attacks against coalition forces and civilian targets, leading the two countries to recall their envoys in August 2009.

With violence diminishing and a new administration in Washington, the two sides began a rapprochement in February 2010, with the United States posting its first ambassador there in five years. That did not prevent the Barack Obama Administration from imposing new sanctions in May 2010, claiming that Damascus was seeking weapons of mass destruction and providing its ally Hezbollah in Lebanon with ground-to-ground missiles, in violation of UN resolutions. The United States joined with the rest of the Western diplomatic community in condemning the Assad regime for its violent response to pro-democracy demonstrations in early 2011.

Angus Muir

See also: *Modern Terrorism*—Palestine: Islamist Fundamentalism; Palestine: PLO and the Arab States. *Tactics, Methods, Aims*—State-Sponsored Terrorism.

Further Reading

Hinnebusch, Raymond. *Authoritarian Power and State Formation in Ba'thist Syria: Army, Party and Peasant.* Boulder, CO: Westview, 1990.

Kazimi, Nibras. *Syria Through Jihadist Eyes: A Perfect Enemy.* Stanford, CA: Hoover Institution Press, 2010.

Ma'oz, Moshe, Joseph Ginat, and Onn Winckler, eds. *Modern Syria: From Ottoman Rule to Pivotal Role in the Middle East.* Brighton, UK: Sussex Academic, 1999.

Roberts, David. *The Ba'ath and the Creation of Modern Syria.* London: Croom Helm, 1987.

Tauber, Eliezer. *The Formation of Modern Syria and Iraq.* Portland, OR: Frank Cass, 1995.

U.S. Department of State. *Patterns of Global Terrorism, 2000.* Washington, DC: U.S. Government Printing Office, 2001.

Timor Leste (East Timor): Independence Struggle, 1975–2002

Timor Leste (formerly East Timor) is one of the world's newest independent states, having received independence on May 20, 2002. The emergence of an independent Timor Leste ended a twenty-eight-year period of turmoil for the island nation and its 800,000 people.

Portuguese Rule (1556–1975)

Europeans first settled Timor Leste in 1556, when Dominican friars from Portugal established a settlement in the present-day Oecussi enclave. The boundaries of the state were finalized in the 1859 Treaty of Lisbon, which divided the island of Timor into a Dutch-ruled western half (with the notable exception of Oecussi) and a Portuguese-ruled eastern half. During much of its colonial history, Portugal ruled Timor Leste indirectly through a system of local chiefs, who then reported to colonial agents in Dili, the capital. Direct control of the colony was achieved only in the 1920s. When Indonesia received independence in 1949, the regime of President Sukarno claimed the western side of Timor, but not Timor Leste, as part of the Republic of Indonesia.

The status of Timor Leste was undisputed until the Portuguese "Carnation Revolution" of April 25, 1974, when a bloodless revolution overthrew the dictatorship of Portugal and instituted a democratic regime. One of the principal policies of the new regime was decolonization. Political parties began to emerge in Timor Leste, and by the end of 1974, there were three main parties: the Timorese Democratic Union (UDT), which favored an independent Timor Leste "associated" with Portugal; the Popular Democratic Association of Timor (APODETI), which advocated that Timor Leste become the twenty-seventh province of Indonesia; and the Revolutionary Front for an Independent Timor Leste (FRETILIN), which advocated independence and became the most popular party in Timor Leste by the end of 1974. However, its advocacy of a Marxist-Leninist state frightened the Indonesian government, which previously, in the 1960s, had put down a communist revolt. Indonesia feared that an independent Timor Leste under FRETILIN could spread communism throughout the East Indies. This advocacy of communism plus FRETILIN's seizing the bulk of the colonial armory when Portugal started to withdraw from Timor Leste led Indonesia to clandestinely support APODETI and the UDT. (The UDT had changed its position from independence to integration with Indonesia by this time.)

Tensions in Timor Leste continued to rise in 1975 between FRETILIN and a UDT/APODETI alliance. In May 1975, Portugal attempted to broker a power-sharing regime between the two sides, but this attempt at a settlement failed. On August 11, 1975, the Indonesian-supported UDT/APODETI alliance launched an abortive coup d'état. This led to a brief civil war, which resulted in Portugal's withdrawal in late August 1975 from Timor Leste and a FRETILIN victory by early November 1975.

Indonesian Rule (1975–1999)

On November 28, 1975, FRETILIN proclaimed the Democratic Republic of Timor Leste (RDTL). This unilateral declaration of independence was not recognized by any state in the international community. The president of the new RDTL was Francisco Xavier do Amaral. Nine days later, on December 7, the Indonesian military invaded Timor Leste. About 35,000 troops participated in the operation. FRETILIN and its military wing, the National Armed Forces for the Liberation of Timor Leste (FALINTIL), were forced to flee Dili. The United Nations in Security Council Resolution 384 of December 22, 1975 condemned the Indonesian invasion and considered Timor Leste to still be a part of Portugal. On July 17, 1976, Indonesian president Suharto signed a bill formally annexing Timor Leste as the twenty-seventh province of Indonesia under the name Timor Timur. However, only Australia recognized the annexation. Three years of guerrilla warfare between FALINTIL and the Indonesian military (and its allied militias) ensued. By 1976, most of the regular forces of FALINTIL were defeated by the Indonesian military.

In September 1977, the Indonesian military adopted a new approach to suppressing nationalist resistance. The army launched attacks against guerrilla-held areas in the western, central, and southern areas of Timor Leste. Inhabited areas were subjected to saturation bombing accompanied by defoliation. Residents were pushed into increasingly confined areas. Deprived of food, they were forced down to the lower reaches of the mountainous interior, where Indonesian troops awaited them.

Throughout 1978, many massacres were reported. Those who escaped death were placed in newly created resettlement camps. Internees were prevented from traveling beyond camp boundaries. As a result, they could neither cultivate nor harvest crops and thus became dependent on the Indonesians for food as well as medical supplies. The East Timorese received little of either, and starvation became widespread.

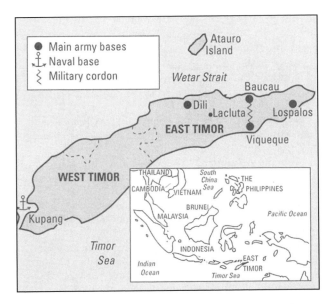

Prior to ceding independence to East Timor (now Timor Leste) in 1999, Indonesia maintained a massive military presence in the territory, including army and naval bases and a cordon to prevent the free movement of guerrillas and civilians.

FALINTIL guerrilla forces were defeated by December 1978, leading to the capture of RDTL president do Amaral and the execution of RDTL prime minister Nicolau Lobato. One minor official in the RDTL, Jose Alexandre "Xanana" Gusmao, took over the remnants of FRETILIN and FALINTIL shortly afterward, but Gusmao's forces numbered only around 200 men. According to the testimony of Assistant Secretary of State Stanley O. Roth in February 2000, between 50,000 and 200,000 East Timorese, with the latter figure being more probable, died during the early years of Indonesian rule.

The FRETILIN guerrillas, however, persisted with their struggle against the occupiers. The Indonesian army adopted a new tactic of using noncombatants to flush out resistance groups. Operation Final Cleansing involved taking men between the ages of sixteen and sixty from villages, organizing them into small groups, and forcing them to walk in front of soldiers searching the countryside for guerrillas. The latter had to choose between surrendering or firing on their own people. This tactic continued to be used into the mid-1990s.

The Indonesian government also created and perpetuated a climate of terror and intimidation in the areas it controlled, notably in the two main towns, Dili and Baucau. People would be arbitrarily detained on the streets or in their homes at night. They were then interrogated at the local subdistrict military command for days, weeks, or even months. Some suspects were released; others disappeared without trace. During the early years, the military focused on supporters of the nationalists and on educated people—academics, doctors, and engineers among them.

Particular sites were designated as killing grounds, where people would be murdered in groups.

The use of intimidation and torture is further evidence of the military's aim of terrorizing the population into submission. Imprisonment had been both arbitrary and indeterminate. There had been cases of imprisonment for refusal to give troops food or for straying too far from a resettlement village. At any time during detention, according to reports, prisoners could be taken out of their cells by troops and killed. Prisoners were often used as labor on military projects, and many were forced to become officers' servants.

The Indonesian authorities officially sanctioned the use of torture throughout Timor Leste. Army guidelines issued in July 1982 outlined a four-step program of procedures: preliminary interrogation, classification of suspects, main interrogation, and decision to execute, imprison, or release. Torture was systematic and extreme. Beginning with beatings, burning with cigarettes, and sexual abuse, the army and police progressed through electric-shock treatment, to systematic cutting of the skin, and even crucifixion with nails. While FRETILIN and FALINTIL conducted minor guerrilla operations in Timor Leste during the 1980s and 1990s, most of the operations against the Indonesian occupation took place on the political and diplomatic front. Several organizations supporting independence flourished in the West. At the same time, Gusmao personally abandoned Marxism and established the National Council of the Maubere (native term for the Timorese) Resistance (CNRM) in 1987 as an umbrella movement for all advocates of Timor Leste independence. Members of the UDT and APODETI joined the CNRM. (The CNRM was renamed the National Council of Timorese Resistance in April 1998, when the CNRM expanded to include more Timor Leste political organizations.)

During the 1980s, Indonesian rule concentrated on economically developing Timor Leste through various methods, including the immigration of non-Timorese. However, since Indonesian migrants dominated the economic life of Timor, discontent among the East Timorese youth emerged. Protests against the Indonesian regime were led by these youth, who were not affiliated with FRETILIN or FALINTIL. On November 12, 1991, one of these protests turned violent during a funeral procession in Dili, when Indonesian troops fired upon and clubbed the unarmed crowd. Between 70 and 180 people died in the Dili Massacre, which was filmed by the protesters and released to the international media. Under considerable international pressure, President Suharto was compelled to appoint a commission to investigate. The results of the investigation indicated that the army was indeed guilty of excessive force; a number of officers were court-martialed, but their punishments were lenient.

At the same time, in the early 1990s, Timor Leste began to experience ninja death squads. These men, dressed in black, masked, and armed with knives, attacked people on the street at night, stoned livestock, and burned houses. Although the military denied any involvement with these gangs, many of the Dili population saw them as linked to Indonesian special forces units. Most of the victims of these gangs were either pro-independence activists or relatives of known activists. Timor Leste independence advocates suffered another setback on November 20, 1992, when Indonesian forces captured Xanana Gusmao, the head of the CNRM and FALINTIL. Gusmao was convicted of subversion against the Republic of Indonesia and was sentenced to life in prison. His sentence was later commuted to twenty years. Four years later, in 1996, Timor Leste again emerged in the international spotlight when the Roman Catholic bishop of Dili, Carlos Belo, and the international spokesman for Timor Leste and FRETILIN (and current foreign minister), Jose Ramos-Horta, were both awarded the Nobel Peace Prize for their nonviolent campaign for an independent Timor Leste.

Referendum, Terror, and Independence (1999–2002)

The quest for an independent Timor Leste advanced one step in May 1998 when the thirty-two-year rule of Indonesian president Suharto ended as he was forced to resign under mass protests throughout the country. His vice president, B.J. Habibie, succeeded him as president of Indonesia. In January 27, 1999, Habibie announced that Timor Leste would be offered "special status" within the Indonesian republic, including wider autonomy over its affairs. If Timor Leste rejected autonomy in a referendum, independence could be considered. Shortly afterward, Xanana Gusmao was transferred from a prison to house arrest in Jakarta.

President Habibie's announcement led elements of the Indonesian military to form pro-autonomy militias under the control of the Indonesian military. Both the military and their allied militias launched a campaign of terror to force the East Timorese to accept autonomy within Indonesia. In February 1999, Indonesian troops fired upon an independence demonstration, killing three youths. The violence against independence-minded East Timorese continued into April 1999, when the Aitarak militia headed by Eurico Guterres attacked a church in the town of Liquica, killing forty. Later that month Aitarak attacked the home of former Timor Leste governor and Social Democratic Party leader Mario Carrascalao, who favored independence. More than a dozen people were killed in the attack, including Carrascalao's teenage son. In May 1999, the United Nations, Portugal, and Indonesia signed an accord scheduling the referendum on independence. Violence between independence and autonomy supporters continued until the referendum on August 30, 1999.

KEY DATES

May 1998 Indonesian president Suharto, responsible for the original invasion of East Timor in 1975, is forced to resign in the face of rising economic protests throughout Indonesia.

January 27, 1999 B.J. Habibie, the president who succeeds Suharto, announces that East Timor will be offered "special status" within Indonesia.

February–August 1999 Violence, perpetrated largely by anti-independence groups, breaks out as elections on independence approach.

August 30, 1999 A total of 95 percent of the eligible East Timor electorate cast ballots in an election that goes 78.5 percent for independence.

September 1999 Mass violence by Indonesian-supported, anti-independence militias leads to the deaths of more than 1,000 East Timorese and sends nearly 260,000 others, roughly one-fourth of the population, into West Timor; an international peacekeeping force, led by Australia, arrives, ending much of the violence.

October 1999 The United Nations establishes the Transitional Administration on East Timor (INTERFET) to help run the territory in preparation for independence; most anti-independence militia flee to West Timor.

August 2001 The Revolutionary Front for an Independent East Timor (FRETILIN) wins the elections for the post-independence government.

May 20, 2002 East Timor becomes an independent nation.

On August 30, 1999, 95 percent of the eligible electorate turned out to vote on the question of independence. On September 4, the results of the referendum were announced, with 78.5 percent of the electorate voting for independence. The pro-autonomy militias led by Aitarak started to burn the houses of and hunt down independence supporters. The militias were assisted by elements of the Indonesian military and effectively controlled the streets of Timor Leste. Throughout the next two weeks, the militias and the Indonesian military launched a campaign of terror throughout Timor Leste. The United Nations also became a target of the militias, as did the Catholic Church. The home of Nobel laureate Bishop Belo, who was providing shelter to victims of the terror, was attacked. More than 1,000 died in early September 1999 and nearly 260,000 East Timorese— more than one-fourth of the population—fled to refugee camps in West Timor. Another 240,000 East Timorese were internally displaced.

On September 12, 1999, President Habibie agreed to accept an international peacekeeping force to restore security. Three days later, the United Nations Security Council approved Resolution 1272, which established the International Force for Timor Leste (INTERFET), a multinational force commanded by Australia. INTERFET restored order and security throughout Timor

Leste, and the newly elected Indonesian president, Abdurrahman Wahid, turned over Timor Leste to the UN Transitional Administration on Timor Leste (UNTAET) on October 26.

Many of the militias' members and their leadership fled to Indonesia, including Guterres. Guterres was convicted in Jakarta of inciting violence in West Timor in April 2001 and sentenced to six months in jail. He served only twenty-three days. In February 2002, UNTAET indicted him for crimes against humanity, including murder for the September 1999 events.

Xanana Gusmao and Jose Ramos-Horta returned to Timor Leste and joined UNTAET in late 1999. UNTAET ruled Timor Leste and supervised parliamentary elections in August 2001 (won by FRETILIN, with Ramos-Horta appointed foreign minister) and presidential elections in April 2002 (won by Gusmao) and oversaw the return of most of the refugees (around 200,000) from West Timor. In addition, trials based on the September 1999 terror were held in both Indonesia and Timor Leste, and in January 2002 a truth and reconciliation commission was established.

As a new independent state in May 2002, Timor Leste hoped to put its recent turbulent history behind it through national reconciliation and to focus on developing its economy and democratic institutions. While the country has largely been at peace since, it continues to suffer from one of the highest poverty rates and lowest socioeconomic indices in Asia.

Vivek C. Narayanan and John G. Taylor

See also: *Definitions, Types, Categories*—Ethnonationalist Terrorism. *Modern Terrorism*—Indonesia: Islamist Militancy.

Further Reading

Cristalis, Irena. *East Timor: A Nation's Bitter Dawn.* New York: Zed Books, 2009.

Hainsworth, Paul, and Stephen McCloskey, eds. *The East Timor Question: Struggle for Independence from Indonesia.* New York: St. Martin's, 2000.

Molnar, Andrea Katalin. *Timor Leste: Politics, History, and Culture.* New York: Routledge, 2010.

Nevins, Joseph. *A Not-So-Distant Horror: Mass Violence in East Timor.* Ithaca, NY: Cornell University Press, 2005.

Parry, Richard Lloyd. *In the Time of Madness: Indonesia on the Edge of Chaos.* New York: Grove, 2005.

Tanter, Richard, Mark Selden, and Stephen R. Shalom, eds. *Bitter Flowers, Sweet Flowers: East Timor, Indonesia, and the World Community.* Lanham, MD: Rowman and Littlefield, 2001.

U.S. Congress. House International Relations Committee, Subcommittee on Asia and the Pacific, and Senate Foreign Relations Committee, Subcommittee on East Asian and Pacific Affairs. *East Timor: A New Beginning.* 106th Cong., 2nd sess., February 10, 2000.

———. House International Relations Committee, Subcommittee on International Operations and Human Rights. *The Humanitarian Crisis in East Timor.* 106th Cong., 1st sess., September 30, 1999.

Turkey: Kurdish Struggle, 1984–2000s

The modern Republic of Turkey was born in the ashes of the defeated multinational Ottoman Empire following World War I. During that war, the twelfth of U.S. president Woodrow Wilson's Fourteen Points declared that the non-Turkish minorities of the Ottoman Empire should be granted the right of "autonomous development." The stillborn Treaty of Sèvres, signed in August 1920, provided for "local autonomy for the predominantly Kurdish area" (Article 62) and in Article 64 even looked forward to the possibility that "the Kurdish peoples" might be granted "independence from Turkey." Turkey's quick revival under Ataturk—ironically enough with considerable Kurdish help, as the Turks played well on the theme of Islamic unity—altered the entire situation. The subsequent and definitive Treaty of Lausanne in July 1923 recognized the modern Republic of Turkey without any special provisions for the Turkish Kurds.

Ataturk's creation of a secular and purely Turkish state led to the first of three great Kurdish revolts: the rise in 1925 of Sheikh Said, the hereditary chief of the powerful Naqshbandi Sufi Islamic order. Sheikh Said's rebellion was both nationalistic and religious, as it also favored the reinstatement of the caliphate. After some initial successes, Sheikh Said was crushed and hanged. In 1927, Khoyboun (Independence), a transnational Kurdish party that had been founded that year in Lebanon, helped to launch another major uprising under General Ihsan Nuri Pasha in the Ararat area; it also was completely crushed, this time with Iranian cooperation. Finally, the Dersim (now called Tunceli) Rebellion, which lasted from 1936 to the end of 1938 and was led by Sheikh Sayyid Riza until his death in 1937, also ended in a total Kurdish defeat.

Although many Kurdish tribes either supported the Turkish government or were at least neutral in these rebellions, the Turkish authorities decided to eliminate anything that might suggest a separate Kurdish nation or culture. A broad array of social and constitutional devices was employed to achieve this goal. In some cases, what can only be termed "pseudotheoretical justifications" were offered to defend what was being done. For example, the so-called Sun Theory taught that all languages derived from a single, original Turkic language in Central Asia. Isolated in the mountains of eastern Anatolia, it was said, the Kurds simply forgot their mother tongue. Use of the new epithet "Mountain Turks" in reference to Turkish Kurds helped reinforce the language theory and the campaign to suppress Kurdish identity. Everything that recalled a separate Kurdish culture was to be abolished: language, names, clothing, and so on.

Population

The Kurds are a largely Sunni Muslim, Indo-European–speaking people. Thus, they are quite distinct ethnically from the Turks and Arabs but related to the Iranians, with whom they share the Newroz (New Year) holiday at the beginning of spring. Kurdistan, or the land of the Kurds, constitutes the geographical area in the Middle East where the states of Turkey, Iran, Iraq, and Syria converge and in which the vast majority of the people are ethnic Kurds. There are also significant enclaves of Kurds living in the Iranian province of Khurasan east of the Caspian Sea and in central Anatolia. Large numbers of Kurds also live in Turkey's three biggest cities, Istanbul, Ankara, and Izmir, as well as Iran's capital, Tehran. In addition, Kurds live in Armenia, Azerbaijan, and Turkmenistan, across the border from Khurasan.

No precise figures for the Kurdish population exist because most Kurds tend to exaggerate their numbers, while the states in which they live undercount them for political reasons. In addition, a significant number of Kurds have partially or fully assimilated into the larger Arab, Turkish, or Iranian populations surrounding them. Furthermore, debate continues over whether such groups as the Lurs, Bakhtiyaris, and others are Kurds or not. Thus, there is not even complete agreement on who is a Kurd.

Nevertheless, a reasonable estimate is that there may be as many as 12 to 15 million Kurds in Turkey (18 to 23 percent of the population), 6.5 million in Iran (11 percent), 4 to 4.5 million in Iraq (17 to 20 percent), and 1 million in Syria (9 percent). At least 200,000 Kurds also live in parts of the former Soviet Union (some claim as many as 1 million largely assimilated Kurds live there) and recently a Kurdish diaspora of more than 1 million has risen in Western Europe. More than half of this diaspora is concentrated in Germany. Some 25,000 Kurds live in the United States. Again, it must be noted that these figures are simply estimates given the lack of accurate demographic statistics.

Constitutional Issues

Turkey's present constitution, dating from 1982, contained a number of specific provisions that sought to limit even speaking or writing in Kurdish. Its preamble, for example, declared, "The determination that no protection shall be afforded to thoughts or opinions contrary to Turkish national interests, the principle of the existence of Turkey as an indivisible entity." Two articles banned the spoken and written use of the Kurdish language without specifically naming it.

Although restrictions on the use of the Kurdish language were eased following the Gulf War in 1991, Article 8 of the Anti-Terrorism Law that entered into force in April 1991 made it possible to consider academics, intellectuals, and journalists speaking up peacefully for Kurdish rights to be engaging in terrorist acts. Similarly, under Article 312 of the Turkish Penal Code, mere verbal or written support for Kurdish rights could lead one to be charged with "provoking hatred or animosity between groups of different race, religion, region, or social class." Despite harmonization efforts of the European Union (EU), a new Article 301 that took effect in June 2005 made it a crime to denigrate "Turkishness," a provision that made it possible for extreme nationalists and statists to accuse writers, scholars, and intellectuals, such as Nobel Prize–winning Orhan Pamuk, of treason and subversion. Article 301 was slightly rephrased in 2007 to make denigrating the "Turkish Nation" a crime, penalties reduced, and prosecution left up to the discretion of the prosecutor.

PKK Insurgency

Since the 1923 treaty, the Kurds have rebelled against the governments of Turkey (1925) and Iraq (1943–1946 and 1961–1975). The Kurds have engaged in guerrilla warfare and terrorism against both of these countries—as well as Iran—almost continuously since 1975.

Beginning in the 1970s, an increasingly significant portion of Turkey's population of ethnic Kurds has actively demanded cultural, linguistic, and political rights as Kurds. Until recently, however, the government ruthlessly suppressed these demands for fear they would lead to the breakup of the state itself. This reluctance toward genuine and full reform remains at the heart of the problem today. It has helped encourage extremism and spurred the creation of the Partiya Karkaren Kurdistan (PKK), or Kurdistan Workers Party, headed by Abdullah (Apo) Ocalan, on November 27, 1978. In August 1984, the PKK officially launched its insurgency, which by the middle of 2010 had resulted in more than 40,000 deaths, as many as 3,000 villages partially or completely destroyed, and some 3 million people internally displaced.

From 1978 to 1980, the PKK concentrated on killing Turkish landlords and obtaining funds from robberies, extortion, and narcotics. Moves against it, however, by the Turks in 1980, which led to the arrest of more than 2,000 alleged PKK members, forced the group's leadership to move abroad, initially to Syria.

The most striking PKK operation of those early years of the conflict was the takeover of several villages in Turkey in 1984, although the PKK abandoned its gains as soon as the Turkish army moved against it. This and other operations had little long-term effect, and the movement began an even more brutal campaign against Turkish villages. In the summer of 1987, the PKK murdered more than sixty villagers in Mardin Province, an atrocity that lost the group much support and forced it to resort to other methods, such as kidnapping.

In 1991, the PKK kidnapped but subsequently released a number of Westerners in Turkey. Then, in 1993, it launched a major offensive against the Turkish tourist industry and government. Beginning in May, the PKK bombed hotels, restaurants, and other tourist sites on the Turkish Mediterranean coast. In June, PKK activists attacked Turkish facilities in Europe. In November, the PKK firebombed Turkish targets in Europe, killing one person in Germany.

Banning the PKK

In response to these attacks, European governments took action. France and Germany banned the PKK. French police arrested twenty suspects, and German police raided PKK offices. The PKK then escalated its campaign in Turkey in 1994. Three attacks in Istanbul killed two foreign tourists in May. In June, the PKK bombed Turkish coastal resorts, killing a British woman and injuring more than ten tourists. In August, two Finnish tourists were seized but were released three weeks later. Confrontations with European governments escalated. In October, British police arrested Faysal Dunlayici, a senior PKK official.

The PKK's military bases are located in Turkey and in northern Iraq. Since the 1991 Gulf War and the creation of a UN-protected zone for Kurds in northern Iraq, the Turks have launched several armed incursions into Iraq with the purpose of destroying the PKK's infrastructure. In March 1994, after the PKK had killed 18 soldiers in an ambush in Turkey, 35,000 Turkish troops moved into northern Iraq and attacked about 20 alleged PKK camps. Two further incursions followed in 1995, and Turkey threatened to create a self-protection zone in northern Iraq in September 1996, after fighting broke out between Kurdish nationalist factions.

Syria allowed the PKK to maintain training bases in the Bekaa Valley in Lebanon, which was under the control of Damascus's army, despite repeated protests from Turkey. The PKK's leader, Abdullah Ocalan, reportedly resides in Syria, and the small Kurdish community there supports the movement. Syrian aid has been given in retaliation for a Turkish irrigation project, which threatens Syria's water supplies.

Counter-PKK Offensives

For a short period in the early 1990s, Ocalan actually seemed close to achieving a certain degree of military success. In the end, however, he overextended himself, while the Turkish military spared no excesses in containing him. Slowly but steadily, the Turks marginalized the PKK's military threat. Ocalan's ill-advised decision in August 1995 to also attack Massoud Barzani's

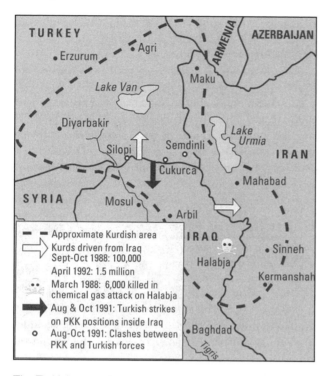

The Turkish army, like its counterpart in Iraq under Saddam Hussein, frequently attacked Kurdish terrorist camps. This map indicates Turkish offensives undertaken before, during, and after the Persian Gulf War of 1991.

Kurdistan Democratic Party in northern Iraq because of its support for Turkey further sapped his strength. The final blow came when Turkey threatened to go to war against Syria in October 1998 unless Damascus expelled Ocalan from his longtime sanctuary in that country.

Ocalan fled to Italy, and U.S. influence on behalf of its NATO ally Turkey pressured Italy and others to reject Ocalan as a terrorist undeserving of political asylum or negotiation. Indeed, for years the United States had given Turkey intelligence training and weapons to battle what it saw as the "bad" Kurds of Turkey, while ironically supporting the "good" Kurds of Iraq against Saddam Hussein. With U.S. and possibly Israeli aid, Ocalan was finally captured in Kenya on February 16, 1999, flown back to Turkey for a sensational trial, and sentenced to death for treason.

Instead of making a hard-line appeal for renewed struggle during his trial, however, Ocalan issued a remarkable statement that called for the implementation of true democracy to solve the Kurdish problem within the existing borders of a unitary Turkey. He also ordered his guerrillas to evacuate Turkey to demonstrate his sincerity. Thus, far from ending Turkey's Kurdish problem, Ocalan's capture began a process of implicit bargaining between the state and many of its citizens of Kurdish ethnic heritage as represented by the PKK and the People's Democracy Party (HADEP). HADEP had been founded in 1994 as a legal Kurdish party and had elected numerous mayors in the Kurdish areas during the local elections held shortly after Ocalan's capture.

At this point, Turkey's potential candidacy for membership in the European Union entered the picture. If implemented, EU membership would fulfill Ataturk's ultimate hope for a strong, united, and democratic Turkey joined to the West. Until Turkey successfully implemented the Copenhagen Criteria of minority rights for its Kurdish ethnic population and suspended Ocalan's death sentence to conform with EU standards, which banned capital punishment, however, it was clear that Turkey's long-treasured candidacy would be only a pipe dream. As some have noted, Turkey's road to the European Union lies through Diyarbakir, the unofficial capital of Turkish Kurdistan.

There were unfortunately still powerful forces in Turkey that did not want further democratization because they feared it would threaten their privileged positions as well as Turkey's territorial integrity. The military's favored position in Turkey has been a prime example of this continuing situation. Thus, Turkey's passage of reform legislation beginning in August 2002 to harmonize its laws with EU norms and allow significant Kurdish cultural rights in theory, as well as the commutation of Ocalan's death sentence to life imprisonment in October 2002, did not solve the continuing Kurdish problem in practice. Nevertheless, the European Union finally began what promised to be long, open-ended accession negotiations with Turkey on October 3, 2005.

Arguing that Turkey had not implemented the necessary reforms, the PKK ended the cease-fire it had implemented after Ocalan's capture and renewed low-level fighting in June 2004. In addition, opposition to Turkish membership in the European Union began to grow in such EU members as France, Germany, and Austria, among others. New EU members must be approved unanimously, so any one member of the European Union could veto Turkey's membership, which many now saw as not possible until sometime in the distant future. Nevertheless, the promise of eventual EU membership and the process it entailed still offered a realistic solution to the Kurdish problem in Turkey.

EU Membership

As part of Turkey's drive to win a date for EU accession talks to begin, a series of harmonization laws began to be passed in an attempt to meet the EU *acquis communautaire,* or body of economic, social, administrative, and environmental legislation that all EU member states were required to implement. Turkey's sudden economic collapse in February 2001 and the resulting unpopularity of the Bulent Ecevit coalition government, eventually led to the overwhelming victory of Recep Tayyip Erdogan's AK Party, with its roots in Islamic politics, in November 2002 as Turkey's first majority government since the victory of Turgut Ozal's ANAP Party in 1987.

In a confused attempt to reflect supposed moves toward peaceful politics (and possibly earn itself omission from various lists of terrorist organizations), the PKK changed its name first to KADEK (Kurdistan Freedom and Democracy Congress), then to Kongra Gel (People's Congress), and then back to the PKK. Beginning in 2009, the name Kurdistan Topluluklar Birligi (KCK), or Kurdistan Communities Union, began to be used. The PKK was said to be included within the KCK, while Kongra Gel was said to be the thirty-one-member executive council of the KCK. Murat Karayilan, a longtime associate of Abdullah Ocalan, served as the chairman of the KCK's executive council, but most observers still referred to the overall organization as the PKK. Ocalan was said to still hold the highest position despite his continuing imprisonment. Indeed, more than 3 million Turkish Kurds signed a petition in 2006 calling for his release.

Although Ocalan continued to be recognized as the leader of the PKK, his statements from prison often seemed perplexing. One such declaration called for the Kurds to live under a system of "democratic confederalism," in which the Kurds somehow would rule themselves within a Turkish state, with their rights protected by EU-style laws. In 2005, Ocalan's younger brother Osman Ocalan and several hundred followers tried to establish another group called the Patriotic Democratic Front, near Mosul in northern Iraq, but failed. Under the leadership of Murat Karayilan, however, some 5,000 PKK guerrillas remained entrenched in the Kandil Mountains straddling the border between northern Iraq and Iran. A militant new PKK Iranian offshoot called PJAK (Free Life Party of Kurdistan) joined it there. Frustrated by the lack of progress, the PKK began low-level military operations again in June 2004, only to announce another cease-fire in October 2006, which quickly broke down. During 2006, the TAK (Kurdistan Freedom Hawks, or Falcons) began to set off bombs in several Turkish cities. It remained unclear whether the TAK was connected to the PKK or was a rival breakaway organization. In Europe, the Kongra Gel under the leadership of Zubeyir Aydar continued to act as a peaceful political wing of the PKK.

In Turkey, HADEP was finally closed down in 2003. Its place was taken first by the Democratic People's Party (DEHAP), which then merged into the Democratic Society Party (DTP), which was created in November 2005. Osman Baydemir was elected mayor of Diyarbakir in 2004 and quickly emerged as one of the most successful young ethnic Kurdish politicians in Turkey. Baydemir also carried his message of achieving Kurdish rights peacefully in his travels to Europe and the United States but was constantly in danger of being arrested for his activities. The off-again, on-again Ilisu Dam project on the Tigris River was touted by the government as a way to help modernize the southeast's agriculture, while opponents denounced the project as a way literally to drown the Kurdish historical presence in the area. ROJ TV, a Kurdish television station in Denmark connected to the PKK, stoked Kurdish self-awareness throughout Turkey, the Middle East, and Europe. Leyla Zana—a Kurdish leader elected to the Turkish parliament in 1991 but imprisoned in 1994 for her nonviolent support of the Kurdish cause—was finally released in 2004 after her case had become a cause célèbre for Kurdish human rights. However, Zana was sentenced to a new prison term in December 2008 for comments she made about Abdullah Ocalan being one of the Kurdish leaders. She remained free pending appeals, however, as of August 2010.

Recep Tayyip Erdogan's AK Party, with its roots in Islamic politics, first swept to victory in November 2002 on the promise of economic achievement, honest government, and pursuit of EU membership. This, of course, implied a solution to Turkey's long-standing Kurdish problem as well as further democratization of the state. In August 2005, Prime Minister Erdogan declared that Turkey had a "Kurdish problem," had made "grave mistakes" in the past, and now needed "more democracy to solve the problem." Never before had a Turkish leader made so explicit a statement regarding the Kurdish problem. As progressive Islamists, however, the AK Party was increasingly opposed by the reactionary Kemalist establishment, which included Turkey's influential military, fearful of losing their long held privileged positions.

This situation eventually led to the crisis of 2007 over the election of the AK Party's Abdullah Gul as Turkey's new president. Although the AK Party seemingly triumphed in this struggle by winning an enormous electoral victory on July 22, 2007 (even slightly outpolling the pro-Kurdish DTP in the southeast), and then electing Gul as president, the party was soon put on the defensive by a nearly successful attempt in the Constitutional Court to ban it as a threat to Turkey's secular order. Having survived this threat to its very existence by a mere one vote, the AK Party seemingly lost its reformist zeal and became a party of the status quo that had forsaken reform and the Kurdish issue. Turkey's secretive Deep State seemingly continued to oppose Turkey's democratization and Kurdish rights.

Nevertheless, in 2009, Turkey's AK Party government again began to institute reforms. On January 1, 2009, the state initiated a new twenty-four-hour, seven-day-per-week Kurdish-language television channel known as TRT 6. In addition, the new Turkish president, Abdullah Gul, declared in May 2009 that the Kurdish problem was Turkey's "most pressing" and that there was now a "historic opportunity" to solve it. Even the Milli Guvenlik Kurulu, or National Security Council, gave its cautious approval to proceed. Thus, as of September 2009, the AK Party government had begun a new promising

Kurdish Opening, or Democratic Initiative, with the announced intention of helping to solve the Kurdish problem. However, the opposition parties, including the DTP, refused to support the vague proposals for reforms. On December 11, 2009, the Turkish Constitutional Court banned the DTP on the grounds that it supported the PKK, and many of its supporters were arrested. Ahmet Turk, the DTP leader, was banned from politics for five years. The DTP was the sixth pro-Kurdish party to be banned, but its position was quickly taken by the Baris ve Demokrasi Partisi (Peace and Democracy Party), led by Nurettin Demirtas. Turkey sunk into new uncertainty; the PKK stepped up its military attacks in June 2010, and the entire country was soon seething with unrest and violence. The AK Party's Kurdish Opening had clearly failed due to Turkish unwillingness to accept genuine reform for its ethnic Kurdish population.

Michael M. Gunter and Andrew Rathmell

See also: *Definitions, Types, Categories*—Ethnonationalist Terrorism. *Historical Roots*—Ottoman Empire (Turkey): Armenian Massacres and Genocide. *Modern Terrorism*—Iraq: State Terrorism Against the Kurds.

Further Reading

Ahmed, Mohammed M.A., and Michael M. Gunter. *The Evolution of Kurdish Nationalism.* Costa Mesa, CA: Mazda, 2008.

Bulloch, John, and Harvey Morris. *No Friends but the Mountains: The Tragic History of the Kurds.* New York: Oxford University Press, 1992.

Ciment, James. *The Kurds: State and Minority in Turkey, Iraq, and Iran.* New York: Facts on File, 1996.

Entessar, Nader. *Kurdish Politics in the Middle East.* Lanham, MD: Lexington Books, 2010.

Gunter, Michael M. *The Kurds Ascending: The Evolving Solution to the Kurdish Problem in Iraq and Turkey.* New York: Palgrave Macmillan, 2008.

Houston, Christopher. *Kurdistan: Crafting of National Selves.* Bloomington: Indiana University Press, 2008.

Marcus, Aliza. *Blood and Belief: The PKK and the Kurdish Fight for Independence.* New York: New York University Press, 2007.

Natali, Denise. *The Kurds and the State: Evolving National Identity in Iraq, Turkey, and Iran.* Syracuse, NY: Syracuse University Press, 2005.

Olson, Robert. *Blood, Beliefs and Ballots: The Management of Kurdish Nationalism in Turkey, 2007–2009.* Costa Mesa, CA: Mazda, 2009.

Ozcan, Ali Kemal. *Turkey's Kurds: A Theoretical Analysis of the PKK and Abdullah Ocalan.* New York: Routledge, 2006.

Ozoglu, Hakan. *Kurdish Notables and the Ottoman State: Evolving Identities, Competing Loyalties, and Shifting Boundaries.* Albany: State University of New York Press, 2004.

Romano, David. *The Kurdish Nationalist Movement: Opportunity, Mobilization and Identity.* Cambridge: Cambridge University Press, 2006.

Yavuz, M. Hakan. *Secularism and Muslim Democracy in Turkey.* Cambridge: Cambridge University Press, 2009.

Yildiz, Kerim. *The Kurds in Turkey: EU Accession and Human Rights.* London: Pluto, 2005.

Yildiz, Kerim, and Susan Breau. *The Kurdish Conflict: International Humanitarian Law and Post-Conflict Mechanisms.* New York: Routledge, 2010.

Uganda: Lord's Resistance Army and Other Terrorist Groups, 1996–2001

In 1962, Uganda, the former British colony located in east-central Africa, gained political independence. Since that time, the security of the nation has been largely overshadowed by acts of violence, political corruption, and Ugandan state support for rebels in neighboring countries. Clearly, in Uganda's case, political stability is no guarantee that extremist forces will not try to attack the bastions of power and that terrorist groups will not threaten any semblance of public discourse with extraordinary acts designed to engender fear and intimidation.

Since 1986, President Yoweri Museveni, has provided a modicum of stability, sorely needed in the wake of dictator Idi Amin Dada and his political successors. Museveni has remained in power since 1986, which is remarkable when viewed against the short-lived regimes of his predecessors, many deposed by military coups. In other areas, Museveni's success in economic policy and privatization has been lauded by the World Bank and the European Commission. However, such plaudits largely overlook the reality of Ugandan democracy—where political parties exist but are constitutionally prohibited under the one party "Movement" system, which defines Ugandan politics.

In spite of the authoritarian tenor of the regime, small groups of armed individuals in many areas of the country make their presence felt with acts of violence, greatly adding to an already tenuous level of security. Various insurgent groups have forced many marginalized citizens to live in guarded camps, where they are sustained only by aid from nongovernmental organizations (NGOs) and private international donations. These marginalized citizens and the groups to which they belong are generally without adequate protection from rebels seeking to impose their political will via terrorism.

Contributing to this insecurity is the proliferation of small arms on the African continent. A significant number of small arms of various types are imported or smuggled into Uganda from other African nations, the former Soviet Union, Germany, and the United States: automatic rifles, handguns, underbarrel grenade launchers, and the traditional farming tool, the machete, abound in Uganda. In this environment, easily obtained automatic weapons can be bought with little cash or by bartering foods. The implication of this flood of small arms is that significant political instability on both local and national levels could perhaps depend on the transshipment of a few loads of automatic weapons.

Ugandan security has further been destabilized by the influx of Rwandan refugees fleeing the genocide in 1994. This immigration exacerbated an already delicate balance in which intertribal violence long preceded British colonial rule. Uganda's northern Muslim minorities continue to receive the brunt of internal domestic violence, perpetrated by the majority Ugandans of different faiths and ethnicity. Some 66 percent of Ugandans are Christian, 16 percent are Muslim, and the remainder practice traditional religions. Taken as a whole, an independent Uganda of the late 1990s through the present, while making marked economic progress through increased exports, a variety of national programs, and significant international funds from the World Bank and the International Monetary Fund, suffers from persistent sociopolitical and national instability.

Acts of terrorism in Uganda may appear to be primarily criminal rather than political. For example, kidnapping girls in order to exploit them as sex slaves appears to be void of obvious political content. However, such acts by various groups are part of a larger political motivation: the creation of fear or intimidation in the target populations.

Lord's Resistance Army

The Lord's Resistance Army (LRA) is led by Joseph Kony, a self-proclaimed Christian prophet. The LRA espouses the religious tenets of the biblical Ten Commandments and has vowed to return Uganda to their adherence. Since 1986, Joseph Kony's LRA has been fighting a guerrilla-style war against Ugandan government forces, with the primary objective of overthrowing the government and imposing the LRA's espoused religious-based political agenda. The LRA is decidedly selective in its application of terrorism, choosing civilians as victims and avoiding confrontations with the Ugandan People's Defense Force (UPDF), a substantial opponent. The LRA's preferred method of attack is to strike poorly defended targets and retreat across national borders into the jungles.

The LRA is most active in the north of Uganda near the borders of southern Sudan and the Democratic Republic of the Congo (DRC). The LRA's reputation for child abduction equals its notoriety for violent killings and maiming of noncombatants. In the past two decades, the LRA has kidnapped between 6,000 and 10,000 children. Examples of LRA kidnappings include the abduction of 100 girls from St. Mary's School in Aboke, Lira District, in October 1996 and the June 1998 kidnapping of 39

Although Uganda ended two decades of dictatorship and returned to civilian rule in the 1990s, the country remains torn by rebel uprisings in the north and southwest. This map shows the extent of rebel control at its peak in the early 2000s.

girls from St. Charles Lwanga School in Kalongo, Kitgum District. Kidnapped boys are forced to become fighters or guards; girls become the sex slaves of higher-ranking leaders, often acquiring sexually transmitted diseases, including AIDS. Civilians are routinely targeted for attack and are often maimed by land mines placed on roadways by the LRA. During the second week of January 1997, the LRA killed 412 civilians, beating and clubbing them to death in villages throughout Kitgum. Reports of LRA maiming include severing the lips from the faces of their victims, ostensibly to prevent them from communicating with UPDF forces or the police.

In addition to its attacks on civilians, the LRA often targets NGOs. In 1998, the LRA issued a warning to NGOs, stating that they would become targets if they continued to assist the Ugandan government in relief efforts for refugees living in internally displaced protection camps. The warning forced the suspension of aid from some NGOs in May and June 1998 and again in December 1998. The outcome of these aid suspensions caused malnutrition, particularly among children in some of the camps.

Criminal acts, such as kidnapping, often intermesh with LRA political issues. On June 29, 1998, one of twenty-nine schoolgirls released from LRA captivity carried a letter addressed to Alphonse Dollo, President Yoweri's cabinet minister, which described Kony's plan for an LRA nation in northern Uganda to be known as

the Nile Republic. Subsequently, in September 1998, reports surfaced that Sudanese forces had linked up with LRA contingents in Khartoum to wage an insurgency in northern Uganda. The reports caused widespread panic among civilians in the northern districts, who called upon the government to immediately hold peace talks with the LRA. A prominent argument of the civilians was that more tribal-ethnic violence would cause a de facto split of Uganda into the have-nots in the north and the haves in the south.

Although the LRA's actions could be interpreted as criminal brutality, virtually all their activity has a political objective: to frighten the civilian population, disrupt civil order, and destroy the lines of communication and commerce vital to the economy. Although the Ugandan government, in January 2001, announced a general amnesty for insurgents who renounced rebellion and surrendered to Ugandan authorities, LRA violence has continued.

Civilian Terror by State Agents

The UPDF is charged with the protection of civilians in internally displaced protection camps in Uganda. Ironically, however, seeking to consolidate their political power, they are often reported to be the perpetrators of terror against the very people they are mandated to defend. As a result, because of its human rights abuses, this agency has earned the distrust of much of the population. Reports abound of UPDF forces beating and torturing camp civilians in efforts to elicit confessions of rebel collaboration. UPDF mobile units are also known to loot and burn the abandoned compounds of displaced civilians, and reports of deaths at the hands of these mobile units are not uncommon.

State and local police and security forces in Uganda frequently oppress the population and occasionally impose harsh treatment, including incarcerating, beating, torturing, and executing individuals who come under scrutiny as members of an insurgent group. Animosity between UPDF forces and civilians in the northern districts is well documented. In November 1996, the UPDF began placing the population of the northern districts in internally displaced protected camps. The strategic intent was to prevent LRA rebels from gaining access to supplies, protect the civilian population from further LRA abuses, and restrict LRA access to potential sources of civilian support. UPDF forces were particularly brutal in their treatment of civilians who refused to relocate, reportedly beating them and threatening to burn their homes. In addition to its abuses of those who refused to relocate, the UPDF also targeted suspected rebel sympathizers.

From 1997 through 2002, though lacking any legal mandate, Uganda's Local Defense Units continued to arrest, detain, and in many cases torture civilians suspected of rebel sympathies. These alleged practices added to many reported deaths at the hands of the Local Defense Units. In 1997, the Internal Security Organization was reported to have killed three Muslims in the Kasese District. The subsequent year it was reported that the Internal Security Organization had beaten, tortured, and used electric shock on detainees. Although various human rights reports from 1997 through 2002 indicate some improvement with respect to human rights, these state and quasi-state security forces and police are still committing serious abuses of citizens who resist government policies.

Allied Democratic Forces

The Allied Democratic Forces (ADF) is a rebel group of Islamic fundamentalists waging terror in western Uganda. The ADF is comprised of rebels from the Tabliq Muslim sect and former members of the National Army for the Liberation of Uganda. In June 1997, more than fifty-eight civilians were murdered by the ADF following their repulsed attack upon the Bundibugyo District. An additional fifty civilians were murdered in ADF attacks in the Kasese District. In April 1998, a series of bombings in Kampala were attributed to the ADF, and a wave of similar ADF terrorism in the form of grenade attacks and bombings is reported to have killed up to forty-nine people between April and November 1998. Sudan refuted accusations by President Museveni that it had armed and aided the ADF.

On November 13, 1999, the ADF attacked UPDF forces and villages from their bases in the former Zaire, now the Democratic Republic of the Congo (DRC). These ADF attacks reportedly displaced thousands of villagers in an area within 200 miles (322 kilometers) of Kampala. In 2000, local press reports attributed 210 killings to the ADF. Many of these victims were children. Between 1986 and 2000, the ADF and the LRA were responsible for 8,000 to 10,000 civilian kidnappings. These figures include children who were forced into fighting or used as sex slaves. Civilian abductions by the ADF continued into 2001—but at a reduced rate. Both the ADF and the LRA continue their operations in an attempt to destabilize and undermine the Ugandan government.

Interahamwe Terrorists

On March 1, 1999, the Bwindi Impenetrable Forest National Park was the scene of the massacre of foreign tourists at the hands of Rwandan Hutu rebels striking from bases inside the DRC. The insurgents, who demanded money and valuables, held thirty-one people hostage and segregated them by nationality and language. The Ugandan game warden, John Wagaba, was tied up and burned alive. French deputy ambassador to Uganda Anne Peltier was among those kidnapped. She successfully negotiated the release of the French and Australian tourists in exchange for her promise

to convey to the world the Hutu extremist Interahamwe terrorists' protestations over what they viewed as American and British support of Tutsi minorities. The remaining tourists were again split up and led on foot toward the DRC. Six of the remaining hostages were released, but eight others were hacked and beaten to death with machetes and clubs. A pregnant woman was raped before she was killed. A note pinned to one of the bodies stated that the objective of the massacre was the collapse of the Ugandan government and infrastructure. Ugandan president Museveni apologized for the deaths and promised to apprehend the terrorists and increase security for tourists in the region. Ugandan and Rwandan counterterrorist forces ambushed and killed fifteen of the Interahamwe terrorists on March 4, 1999, in the DRC. Another ten Interahamwe terrorists were killed on March 5, 1999, by Ugandan and Rwandan counterterrorist forces. U.S. Federal Bureau of Investigation agents and officials from Scotland Yard were sent to Uganda to aid in the investigation.

West Nile Bank Front

Formed in May 1995, the West Nile Bank Front (WNBF) supported the return to power of former Ugandan dictator Idi Amin Dada. The WNBF comprises mostly Ugandan Muslims seeking an autonomous Islamic state in northern Uganda. The WNBF reportedly deployed land mines extensively along major roads used for relief and commercial transport. These mines are said to have caused scores of deaths and injuries. In Sudan, in March 1997, fighting between UPDF forces and the WNBF left hundreds of rebels killed, and more than 1,000 others surrendered to Ugandan forces. By the end of that year, clashes between the WNBF and the UPDF caused the WNBF to curtail its terrorist activities. However, in August 1998, the WNBF was reportedly responsible for more than 100 civilian abductions in Aringa County and various episodes of looting and livestock raids. Various press reports in 2002 indicated that the WNBF resurfaced in efforts to recruit citizens of Nebbi District to serve as rebel fighters, but little violence resulted.

Even as the fight against the WNBF wound down, the LRA came increasingly under siege later in the decade. In 2005, the International Criminal Court in The Hague issued arrest warrants for Kony and four other organization leaders for crimes against humanity. With peace coming to southern Sudan, the LRA lost the support of the government in Khartoum, which had backed it as a means of countering Ugandan support for southern Sudanese rebels. This forced Kony to sign a temporary cease-fire with Kampala in 2006 and a permanent one in February 2008. But when Kony failed to show up for the signing of the final peace agreement, Uganda, southern Sudanese forces, and the armed forces of the DRC launched a common offensive against LRA bases

KEY DATES

October 1996 The Lord's Resistance Army (LRA) kidnaps 100 girls from St. Mary's School in Aboke.

January 1997 Guerrillas from the LRA kill 412 villagers in the Kitgum District.

June 1997 Guerrillas from the Allied Democratic Forces kill fifty-eight civilians in the Bundibugyo District.

August 1998 The West Nile Bank Front abducts more than 100 civilians in Aringa County.

December 1998 Some nongovernmental organizations suspend aid operations after threats against their personnel by the LRA.

March 1999 Hutu rebels kill foreign tourists in the Bwindi Forest National Park.

November 1999 The Allied Democratic Forces attack Ugandan government forces from bases in the Democratic Republic of the Congo.

January 2001 The Ugandan government offers a general amnesty for members of the LRA who surrender to authorities.

2005 The International Criminal Court indicts LRA leader Joseph Kony and four others for crimes against humanity.

2008 After Kony fails to show up to sign a peace agreement, Uganda, joined by the forces of the southern Sudanese and the Democratic Republic of the Congo, launch an offensive against LRA rebels.

2010 Al-Shabaab militants from Somalia set off bombs in Kampala that kill seventy-four civilians.

off two bombs—at a restaurant and a rugby club in Kampala, where people had gathered to watch the World Cup soccer final—killing seventy-four persons.

The Future

The history of Ugandan terrorism should be viewed in relation to the security status of the state as well as that of the whole of sub-Saharan Africa. It is to be expected that the Ugandan government will be compelled to assimilate a diverse and conflicted population into the Movement system of government, while simultaneously balancing its national security priorities with those of its neighbors. Therefore, the threat of extremist violence will continue. But Uganda's success or failure in impeding the terrorists will depend primarily on its efforts to integrate the various disparate tribal-ethnic forces into coherent national political organizations and its ability to deal successfully with pervasive socioeconomic issues, especially the reduction of widespread poverty and the amelioration of the conditions of marginalized groups. Another aspiration is the potential future development of a functionally organized, security-focused Pan-African association that is both dedicated to combating terrorism and capable of garnering the international resources required for the task.

Michael L. Largent and James Ciment

See also: *Definitions, Types, Categories*—Religious (Non-Islamist) Terrorism. *Modern Terrorism*—Sudan: Conflicts in South Sudan and Darfur.

Further Reading

"Arrest Warrant." *Africa Research Bulletin* (April 1999).

"Bombings in Uganda: Somalia Comes to Uganda." *The Economist,* July 15, 2010.

Dolan, Chris. *Social Torture: The Case of Northern Uganda, 1986–2006.* New York: Berghahn, 2009.

Green, Matthew. *Wizard of the Nile: The Hunt for Africa's Most Wanted.* Northampton, MA: Olive Branch, 2009.

Hara, Fabienne. "Unseen Wars: Worldview Special." *Observer,* July 7, 2002.

Human Rights Watch. *Hostile to Democracy: The Movement System and Political Repression in Uganda.* Washington, DC: Human Rights Watch, August 1999.

Toft, Monica Duffy. *Securing the Peace: The Durable Settlement of Civil Wars.* Princeton, NJ: Princeton University Press, 2010.

in their three countries, including a Ugandan incursion into the DRC. Facing an increasingly effective Ugandan counterinsurgency, the LRA had largely relocated to the DRC by the mid-2000s. Under this onslaught, the LRA once again agreed to a cease-fire in 2009. The government of Uganda remained wary, especially after a massacre in December left more than 300 persons dead in the DRC and another in February 2010 that saw more than 100 civilians killed.

Uganda also faced an increasing threat from an unlikely quarter in the latter part of the decade—Somalia. As part of the African Union peacekeeping force in that country since early 2007, Uganda was declared an enemy by Islamist militants, including the al-Shabaab militia, following an incident in which Uganda's troops killed several Somali citizens in October 2009. Nine months later, in July 2010, al-Shabaab militants struck, setting

Uganda: State Terrorism Under Idi Amin, 1971–1979

General Idi Amin Dada's bloody reign of terror in Uganda began in 1971 and lasted eight years. Only a few years earlier, in 1962, the country had gained its independence after sixty-two years of British rule. Although exact numbers are hard to verify, it has been estimated that more than 300,000 Ugandans were killed during Amin's dictatorship. Most were victims of terror. People were imprisoned, tortured, and murdered, often on the personal orders of Amin himself. He used the army as an instrument of terror to intimidate his own citizens, especially those who belonged to tribes other than his own. Tribal warfare has characterized the recent history of many African states—Zimbabwe and the Central African Republic, for example—but Amin's regime stands out for the sheer scale of its brutality.

Amin Comes to Power

Major General Idi Amin Dada, commander in chief of the Ugandan army, and once a sergeant in the British army's King's African Rifles, overthrew President Milton Obote on January 25, 1971, while Obote was out of the country. The former army boxing champion accused Obote of corruption, tribalism, and lining the pockets of his favorites at the expense of the largely poor population. Amin promised free elections, an end to Obote's martial law, and the release of political prisoners jailed on trumped-up or flimsy charges.

Unsurprisingly, Amin's coup was popular with many Ugandans. Fewer than 100 casualties were reported during sporadic fighting in the capital, Kampala. The coup was equally popular with many Western nations suspicious of Obote's recent left-wing economic reforms. Amin, a member of the small Muslim Kakwa tribal group of northern Uganda, swiftly moved to guarantee the future of his regime. Pro-Obote officers, mostly from the Lango and Acholi tribes, were purged. An estimated 1,000 soldiers, many badly beaten, were seen being transported to Kampala's notorious Luzira prison. Less than a month later, Amin promoted himself to general, proclaimed himself president, and put off the promised elections for five years until the country was "calm." He then drafted into the army supporters on whose loyalty he could rely, particularly Sudanese, Palestinians, and Nubians. Amin then tripled the strength of his army by forcing the poor to enlist.

250,000 Dead in Three Years

Although Amin released fifty-five political prisoners on coming to power, hundreds of thousands met a grisly death instead—250,000 by June 1974. Many were members of rival tribes. The Asian minority also came in for persecution, although they escaped with their lives, if not much else. Accusing the 50,000 prosperous Ugandan Asians of "sabotaging the economy," Amin expelled them all to Britain in the fall of 1972. Soldiers assaulted them and confiscated their possessions even as they mounted the aircraft steps.

Initially, Amin curried favor with several Western or pro-Western powers to equip his forces. Weapons worth several million dollars were imported from Britain and Israel, following Amin's visits to both countries in July 1971. The international community tended to regard Amin as something of a buffoon. Stunts such as launching a Save Britain fund in 1973, to help Britain out of an economic crisis, persuaded some governments that he posed no threat.

However, Amin was forging links with anti-Western groups, such as the Palestine Liberation Organization. Then, as relations with the West deteriorated during 1973–1975, Amin turned to the Soviet Union for arms. Amin's pro-Palestinian stance led terrorists from the extremist Popular Front for the Liberation of Palestine, aided by the German Baader-Meinhof Gang, to land a hijacked El Al Airbus at Kampala's Entebbe airport on June 29, 1976. When Israeli commandos flew in to free the hostages on July 4, Amin deployed his troops to defend the terrorists. In response to the Israeli action, Amin's troops murdered one of the hostages, Dora Bloch, in an Entebbe hospital.

Meanwhile, Amin's grip on Uganda was strengthened by the formation of the State Research Bureau and the Public Safety Unit. These outfits used intimidation,

---

KEY DATES

January 25, 1971 General Idi Amin seizes power in Uganda in a coup, ousting president Milton Obote.

June 1974 Human rights experts say Amin's government has executed an estimated 250,000 political prisoners since coming to power.

July 1976 Israeli commandos retake an aircraft hijacked by Palestinian terrorists at Uganda's Entebbe airport.

February 1977 Amin orders the murder of Kampala's Anglican bishop, Janana Luwun, a regime critic.

April 1979 Amin is overthrown by Ugandan rebels and an invading force of Tanzanian troops; Amin flees the country, ultimately settling in Saudi Arabia.

torture, and murder to cow the population and liquidate opponents. Informers throughout the society reported to their superiors, who acted with extreme ruthlessness on the least evidence. Bodies of victims were found almost daily dumped in Lake Victoria or in the Namanve Forest.

Amin also replaced the independent judiciary with military tribunals, which sat in judgment on all major violations of the law. Policing was dominated by army officers, who controlled day-to-day police activities. By controlling the army, destroying the independence of the courts, and creating a brutal apparatus of internal state security, Amin limited organized dissent. He also took economic measures, such as nationalizing more than forty foreign-owned businesses, ostensibly to gain the support of the people. In reality, the "reforms" were just a smokescreen behind which Amin and his supporters were able to line their pockets. Embezzlement and inefficiency crippled the Ugandan economy: the output of raw materials, principally copper, fell dramatically, and inflation rocketed.

The Tide Turns

By 1977, the economy went into free fall and what little popular support Amin enjoyed evaporated. There was also discontent within the armed forces. A group of noncommissioned officers protested at all positions of power being held by members of Amin's Kakwa tribe. Retribution was swift. Bodies of dissenters were soon seen floating down the Malaba River on the border with Kenya. About 130 people were massacred, and the period of unrest led to the notorious political murder of Kampala's Anglican bishop, Janana Luwum, on February 16, 1977.

Amin's regime came to an end in April 1979, following a failed attempt to invade neighboring Tanzania. The Tanzanian armed forces, supported by exiles of the Uganda Liberation Front, counterattacked. Amin's troops deserted or surrendered in droves, despite last-minute support from 2,000 Libyan troops.

Amin pursued no ideological goals and supported no known cause during his reign of terror. Neither was he called to account for his crimes. On fleeing Uganda, he was sheltered by sympathetic countries, including Saudi Arabia, where he died in 2003.

Ian Westwell

See also: *Definitions, Types, Categories*—State vs. Nonstate Terrorism. *Modern Terrorism*—Israel: Raid on Entebbe.

Further Reading

Avirgan, Tony, and Martha Honey. *War in Uganda: The Legacy of Idi Amin.* Westport, CT: Lawrence Hill, 1982.

Kyemba, Henry. *State of Blood: The Inside Story of Idi Amin.* New York: Ace Books, 1977.

Pirouet, Louise M. *Historical Dictionary of Uganda.* Metuchen, NY: Scarecrow, 1995.

United Kingdom: Decolonization and Post-Decolonization Struggles, 1945–1970s

The British enjoy a reputation for success in what is known as "counterinsurgency" (COIN), a form of warfare in which terrorism has played a major part. After the end of World War II, as the empire dwindled, British political and military authorities faced widespread armed opposition, much of it under the guise of insurgency. Their COIN methods, while not always successful, included valid responses, particularly compared with those used by other Western powers. Most terrorism since 1945 has been in the context of nationalist and Marxist insurgencies, so the British experience is critical in the West's response to terrorism.

The British Army defines insurgency as "the actions of a minority group within the state, intent on forcing political change by means of a mixture of subversion, propaganda, and military pressure, aiming to persuade or intimidate the broad mass of the people to support such change." Here, "military pressure" is taken to include both guerrilla warfare and terrorism, the latter being seen as an integral part of insurgency and not a separate phenomenon. Once this premise is accepted, a broad definition of counterinsurgency is relatively straightforward: "the actions of an existing government and its security forces to combat insurgency and prevent its resurgence." Two interrelated points are worth noting. First, there is a recognition that insurgency is essentially a political problem, and, second, there can be no such thing as a purely military solution.

Range of Terrorist Campaigns

The period after 1945 saw the British involved in a long round of counterinsurgency campaigns. When World War II ended, there was already trouble in Palestine, where Jewish nationalist groups were intent on ousting the British from the mandate of the League of Nations established in 1920. That campaign ended in British withdrawal and the creation of an independent state of Israel in May 1948.

Less than a month later, a state of emergency was declared in Malaya, where communist terrorists, following the pattern of revolt advocated by Mao Zedong in China, tried to overthrow colonial rule. The Malayan Emergency ended in British-Malayan victory in 1960. The British waged campaigns in Kenya against the Mau Mau in 1952–1960, and in Cyprus against EOKA (National Organization of Cypriot Fighters) in 1955–1959. The former may be termed a success, in that the Mau Mau failed to gain political power when Britain granted independence to the country in the early 1960s. The latter ended in compromise: EOKA failed to achieve its aim of union with Greece, while the British failed to retain political control of the island, which received its independence in late 1959.

Meanwhile, an Irish Republican Army (IRA) campaign had been going on in Northern Ireland since 1956,

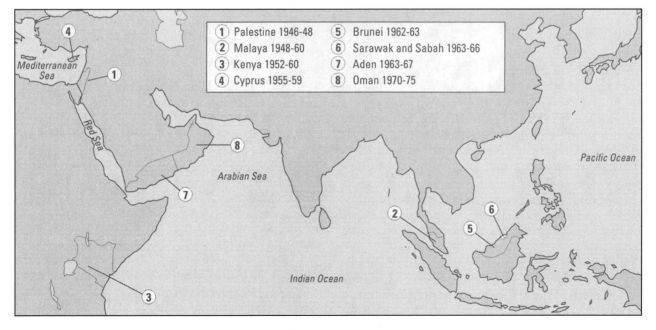

① Palestine 1946-48		⑤ Brunei 1962-63	
② Malaya 1948-60		⑥ Sarawak and Sabah 1963-66	
③ Kenya 1952-60		⑦ Aden 1963-67	
④ Cyprus 1955-59		⑧ Oman 1970-75	

British military responses to terrorism in post–World War II counterinsurgency campaigns.

characterized by armed raids on military establishments and attacks on Royal Ulster Constabulary (RUC) bases in the province. By 1963, the IRA campaign had lost all momentum and come to a halt. By then, however, British forces had become involved in Brunei, where they put down a revolt against the sultan. In neighboring Borneo, the British faced Indonesian-backed rebels (and later regular Indonesian troops) in operations that, although not strictly counterinsurgency, incorporated and refined many of its techniques. The Borneo Confrontation concluded in Indonesia backing down in 1966, by which time further revolts against British rule had broken out in Aden in the Middle East. The Aden campaign ended in a British withdrawal in late 1967, after which Marxist insurgents seized power in what was to become the People's Democratic Republic of Yemen.

Thompson Principles

Of all the campaigns discussed above, that in Malaya between 1948 and 1960 seems to offer the best example of British success—at least until the 1970s—and much of what we now know as British counterinsurgency had its origins there. The relevant lessons of the campaign were summarized by Sir Robert Thompson, a colonial administrator who had served in Malaya throughout the emergency. Thompson drew five principles from his experiences in Malaya: (1) that the government must have a clear political aim; (2) that the government and its security forces must function in accordance with the law; (3) that the government, its agencies, and its forces must have an overall plan; (4) that the government must give priority to defeating political subversion, not guerrilla action; and (5) that the government must make sure it secures its own base areas first, before moving into the insurgent-affected locations.

Clear Political Aim

That the government needs a clear political aim seems to be an obvious principle to lay down. Thompson defined this aim, when describing the situation in Malaya, as "to establish and maintain a free, independent, and united country which is politically and economically stable and viable." The British have always viewed insurgency essentially as a political process, designed to "force political change," and so any counterinsurgency campaign must also be essentially political in nature.

But the government must also ensure that the political aim is realistic and attainable. In this respect, the British in Malaya adopted a sensible approach by promising independence to the country by 1957 and ensured that this was carried out, regardless of the persistence of insurgency. If the other aspects of counterinsurgency had not worked effectively by 1957, the offer would probably have been withdrawn. As it was, the offer acted as a powerful incentive to the ordinary people to accept government authority; having attracted this support from the middle ground, the British policy left the insurgents isolated.

Elsewhere, the viability of such a straightforward political aim could not be assumed. No one on the British side was prepared, for example, to contemplate full withdrawal from Cyprus, because of the island's key strategic importance in the eastern Mediterranean.

Keeping Within the Law

The government and its security forces have an obligation to uphold the authority they represent in the face of rebellion from those who wish to overturn it. This "minority group within the state" is, by definition, opposing the rule of law, and if the government or its agencies go beyond that law themselves, they are no better than the rebels they are confronting. Of course, the government can change the law to suit the circumstances of the campaign. During colonial policing activities before 1939, for example, it was normal for British authorities to declare local versions of martial law, introducing packages of emergency legislation that were, in retrospect, repressive. However, soldiers and policemen have always remained subject to the law of the land since 1945. As long as such a democratic system prevails, the middle ground should not be alienated by government actions, although it must be admitted that the dividing line between acceptability and alienation can be extremely thin.

Overall Plan

The principle that the government, its agencies, and its forces must have an overall plan ties in closely with the first principle of a clear political aim. If such an aim is laid down, it is only sensible to ensure that all government agencies and forces are aware of it and are prepared to work toward it in a unified manner. If this does not happen, energies will be wasted and gaps in government policy will be created that may be exploited by the insurgents.

In Malaya, Thompson helped to set up a unifying structure based on committees at various levels within society, so that policy made at the top by the high commissioner filtered down the pyramid to state, district, and even village locations. This meant that once an overall plan, incorporating political and military efforts, had been created, there was no excuse for anyone to deviate from it. Moreover, as that plan was essentially political in nature, designed to gain the loyalty of the middle ground by offering independence on government terms, there was less chance of military action getting out of hand.

Defeat of Political Subversion

Thompson's fourth principle, that the government must give priority to defeating political subversion, was based very much on a British interpretation of

Maoist-style insurgency. Once it had been recognized that guerrilla action was only a method of obtaining political change, the focus of counterinsurgency could be directed toward ensuring the loyalty of the middle ground to the prevailing regime, thereby denying rebel groups popular support.

This did not mean that antiterrorist action was ignored, but antiterrorist action was seen as only a part of the overall threat. If a government ordered its security forces merely to seek out and destroy guerrillas, not only would this be intensely difficult, but it would also stand a good chance of alienating the ordinary people. By its very nature, guerrilla warfare is secretive and clandestine, with activists hiding among the people. If the government does not prepare the way politically, but sends its security forces among civilians to flush out insurgents, it runs a very high risk of killing innocent people and losing support for using strong-arm tactics. In Malaya, that had been the case during the early years, leading to counterproductive incidents. Once the nature of the problem became clear, however, and attempts were made specifically to counter political subversion, security forces focused on guerrillas who found it difficult to retain support. This principle represented a key feature of the British view of insurgency.

Protecting the Base Areas

The final principle put forward by Thompson represents the closest he came to acknowledging the role of the security forces. This was to protect areas loyal to the government from terrorist attack or infiltration first, before moving into insurgent-affected areas. Clearly, it would be foolish for a government affected by insurgency to devote all its efforts to confronting the activists in areas they control, while leaving its own base unprotected. In such circumstances, the guerrillas would merely bypass the main government effort and infiltrate that base, undermining what remained of government control.

Again, Thompson was aware of the importance of this principle from his experience in Malaya. Some areas were obviously under close communist control, temporarily outside the influence of the colonial government, while others were in the process of being subverted. However, quite substantial areas were not yet involved, and they represented the government's safe base, within which it was essential to ensure continued loyalty. If the British had concentrated all available forces and policies in the communist-controlled areas of Malaya after about 1952, they would have left the unaffected areas vulnerable to infiltration. Instead, they ensured that security forces were available to protect the safe bases, while regular army troops fought campaigns elsewhere.

An important aspect was to separate the terrorists from the population they were trying to subvert. Tangible action to split active insurgents from their supporters sometimes took the simple, but nonetheless effective,

form of creating physical barriers to movement. For example, in Kenya, security forces constructed a huge ditch along the border of the forests, leading into an area of cleared ground, so that any Mau Mau who ventured out had difficult and exposed terrain to cross in order to reach the people. The aim was to make movement into populated areas difficult for the terrorists. This policy was followed elsewhere in British counterinsurgency campaigns. It depended on the ability of security forces to recognize and target guerrilla-affected areas. If this could be done, the policy went a long way toward undermining terrorist strategy.

Every one of Thompson's five principles is sound, and, taken together, the five provide a valuable insight into British counterinsurgency methods. However, they are not perfect. For example, the principles are not complete. Two vitally important factors are not specified: the need to gather information and turn it into usable tactical intelligence, and the use of the policy of "hearts and minds"—winning over the loyalty of the ordinary people. Fortunately, other theorists filled in the gaps. Sir Frank Kitson, a British Army officer with wide counterinsurgency experience, advocated a closer emphasis on low-level intelligence. British campaigns since 1966, when Thompson published his principles, clearly employed the hearts-and-minds approach.

Counterterror Methods after Decolonization

British forces have been actively engaged in warfare almost continuously since 1945. In most of these years they have been engaged in campaigns in which terrorism played a greater or lesser role. The year 1968 marked something of a watershed, however. Before 1968, British forces were engaged chiefly in campaigns of decolonization, while after 1968, the campaigns they engaged in were more varied.

The British Army examined its counterinsurgency campaigns since 1945 and identified several common denominators. From these, it outlined six principles designed to provide an analysis of counterinsurgency success. The six principles were as follows: (1) political primacy and political aim; (2) coordination of government machinery; (3) obtaining intelligence and information; (4) separating insurgents from their support by means of propaganda, a hearts-and-minds campaign, and physical barriers; (5) neutralizing insurgents; and (6) long-term post-insurgency planning. These principles were refined in the early 1990s.

Campaign in Dhofar

The codification of the army's principles grew largely out of the counterinsurgency campaign in Dhofar, southeastern Arabia. Between 1970 and 1975, British soldiers and administrators helped the sultan of Oman

1948 Facing rising Arab-Jewish violence, Britain gives up its mandate over Palestine; a communist insurgency against British colonial rule breaks out in Malaya; it continues through 1960.

1952 The Mau Mau rebellion in Kenya begins; it continues through 1960.

1956 Britain faces an independence struggle in its colony of Cyprus.

1966 Colonial administrator Sir Robert Thompson lays out his formula for defeating guerrilla insurgencies, based on his successful experience in Malaya.

1967 In the wake of a growing Marxist insurgency, British forces leave Aden, later called Yemen.

1970–1975 In its first major post-decolonization counterinsurgency effort, British forces help the sultan of Oman defeat Marxist insurgents in the province of Dhofar.

to gain victory against Marxist rebels in Oman's western province of Dhofar.

In Dhofar, the first two principles—of a political aim and a coordination of government machinery—were established as soon as Sultan Qaboos bin Said seized power in July 1970 and were strictly adhered to thereafter. There was, for example, an overall plan to prepare the province for "civil development" that would appeal to the populace. The third principle played out as an effective flow of intelligence and information was set up, partly by offering generous bounties to members of the insurgent groups who crossed to the government side.

The separation of the insurgents from their popular support—the fourth principle—was an area in which British troops played a key role, putting the government message across to the people and letting them know the terms and conditions of any change. In Dhofar, the Twenty-second Special Air Service (SAS) Regiment took charge of government propaganda in late 1970, dropping leaflets over the rebel-affected areas to inform the people that the new sultan was intent on modernization efforts that would benefit those who remained loyal to his rule.

At the same time, Radio Dhofar was set up to beam out progovernment information in direct opposition to the communist-controlled Radio Aden. In an effort to ensure that people listened to Radio Dhofar, the SAS purchased cheap transistor radios, fixed the dials so they were permanently tuned to Radio Dhofar, and gave them away to people in the affected areas when they came down to the markets. Unfortunately, the rebels realized the danger and destroyed any radios they found—a loss that had little impact, as the people did not value radios that were free. Once they realized this, the SAS then began to *sell* the radios, so that when the sets were destroyed, people resented the loss. In time, people began to listen regularly to Radio Dhofar.

A second method of splitting insurgents from their supporters involved a hearts-and-minds policy. In Dhofar, Sultan Qaboos's promises of civil development always had the potential to attract support, but he needed to be seen as carrying them out. This was done by means of Civil Action Teams comprising engineers, teachers, and medical personnel, and set up under military protection from 1972 onward. The teams would, for instance, dig a well in the mountains, attracting essentially nomadic people with the prospect of running water even during the dry period. Then they would set up a clinic and school to keep the people in one place, away from rebel influence. Finally, physical barriers—large-scale defended lines—were built to keep the insurgents in set areas.

The fifth principle, that of neutralizing the insurgents, could then come into play. At this level, with the previous principles having been implemented, the relative strength of government firepower quickly overpowered the rebels. Finally, the long-term planning for a more modern nation ensured that, once defeated, the insurgency did not come back.

No two insurgencies are ever the same, so responses always have to be adapted to suit the circumstances. The British enjoyed proven counterinsurgency success, implying that the principles they adopted and refined contained some measure of relevance applicable across the board. However, neither the Thompson nor Kitson principles provided the British Army with a comprehensive strategy for counterterrorism. It was not until the 1980s that a set of principles was codified into an army order that could be followed in all campaigns.

John Pimlott and Ashley Brown

See also: *Definitions, Types, Categories*—State vs. Nonstate Terrorism. *Historical Roots*—European Colonial Expansion Conquests; Palestine, British. *Modern Terrorism*—Cyprus: Anti-British Struggle; India: Kashmir Struggle; Kenya: Mau Mau Uprising; Malaysia (Malaya): Anti-British Conflict; United Kingdom: Northern Ireland Troubles.

Further Reading

Beckett, Ian F.W., and John Pimlott. "The British Army: The Dhofar Campaign, 1970–1975." In *Armed Forces and Modern Counterinsurgency*, ed. Ian F.W. Beckett and John Pimlott, pp. 16–19. New York: St. Martin's, 1985.

Carruthers, Susan L. *Winning Hearts and Minds: British Governments, the Media, and Colonial Counter-Insurgency.* New York: Cassell Mansell, 1995.

Elkins, Caroline. *Imperial Reckoning: The Untold Story of Britain's Gulag in Kenya.* New York: Henry Holt, 2005.

Lawrence, James. *Imperial Rearguard: Wars of Empire, 1919–1985.* Elmsford, NY: Pergamon, 1988.

Pimlott, John. *British Military Operations, 1945–1984.* New York: Military Press, 1984.

———, ed. *War in Peace.* New York: Marshall Cavendish, 1987.

United Kingdom: Islamist Terrorism, 2000s

With its long history of imperialism in heavily Islamic South Asia, which led to mass emigration from that region after World War II, and its more recent history of involvement in the wars in Afghanistan and Iraq, Great Britain has been both the birthplace of a number of prominent Islamist terrorists and the target of terrorist attacks in recent years. Of the latter, the most spectacular was the July 7, 2005, attack on London's transportation system, a series of coordinated suicide bombings perpetrated by British-born or British-raised Islamist terrorists that killed more than fifty persons.

Britain's Muslim Radicals

Like much of Western Europe, Britain experienced a major inflow of Muslim peoples after World War II, many of them lured to the country by the opportunities of the postwar economic boom. Given Britain's long occupation of South Asia, most of these immigrants came from Islamic-majority Pakistan and Bangladesh (until 1971, East Pakistan), as well as India. By the early 2000s, it was estimated that there were roughly 2.5 million Muslims, most of them of South Asian descent, living in the United Kingdom, representing about 4 percent of the country's total population.

While improving their economic condition, most South Asian immigrants and their offspring faced lives of poverty and discrimination. Censuses over the past few decades have routinely found that they experience higher unemployment, school dropout, crime, and mortality rates than the British population as a whole. In addition, they have faced prejudice, both violent and subtle, frequent racial slurs, occasional act of racist violence, and routine, albeit de facto, housing and employment discrimination. Many South Asians have found themselves culturally isolated and living in communities apart, often in large public-housing projects.

According to sociologists, the older generation of Muslim immigrants generally accepted their situation, focusing, as first-generation immigrants often do, on economic betterment for themselves and their families. While devout, most eschewed the politicized Islam that was gaining acceptance both in their South Asian homeland and in Muslim communities in Britain itself. Not so some of their offspring.

While the vast majority of mosques and Islamic community centers in Britain have always offered the traditional solaces and services of religious institutions everywhere—faith, community, social welfare—a few

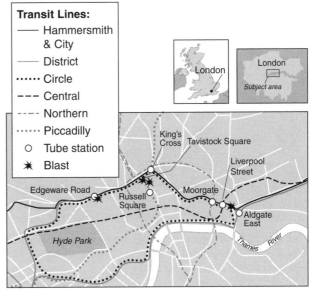

For many Britons, the most disturbing aspect of the transport suicide bombings that rocked London in 2005 and killed fifty-two persons was that most of the Islamist extremist perpetrators had been born and raised in the United Kingdom.

were very different, having been founded by radical clerics who preached a strict and politicized form of Islam, usually with an anti-Western and anti-Jewish bias. Clerics such as Abu Hamza al-Masri, who was convicted in 2006 of inciting violent acts against non-Muslims, preached a message of violent jihad, or holy war in defense of Islam.

Their message of resisting the corrupting temptations of modern British life and committing oneself to a higher cause—defending Islam and the Islamic world against Western attack, both real and perceived—appealed to a minority of alienated British Muslim youths, many of them with middle-class backgrounds and university educations. Not only did the message of jihad appeal to these youths ideologically, according to experts who have studied the phenomenon of homegrown Islamist terrorism in the United Kingdom, but it gave them a sense of mission and belonging, a way to imbue their lives with meaning.

In addition, many of these youths were influenced by radical Islam during routine trips back to South Asia, Pakistan in particular, to visit family. Some traveled to militant Islamist training camps in the frontier regions of the country, where al-Qaeda and the Pakistani Taliban operated bases, while others received indoctrination in

Four Islamic terrorists with ties to al-Qaeda carried out suicide bombings on three London Underground trains and one double-decker municipal bus on the morning of July 7, 2005. Fifty-two people were killed, and the city's transport system was shut down. *(Associated Press)*

jihad at madrassas, or religious schools. Wherever they learned about radical Islam, many of Britain's alienated Muslim youths began to see Islamist terrorist organizations such as al-Qaeda as heroic and righteous, not only offering resistance to Western invaders in Afghanistan and Iraq but also standing up to corrupt and apostate regimes in the Muslim world as well.

July 2005 London Bombings

Among these youths were Mohammed Sidique Khan, Shehzad Tanweer, Hasib Hussein, and Germaine Lindsay, perpetrators of the July 7, 2005, London transport attacks, known colloquially in Britain as 7/7. With the exception of Lindsay, a Jamaican-born convert to Islam, the 7/7 perpetrators were born in the north of England to parents who had immigrated from Pakistan. Little was unusual about the four, other than Lindsay's conversion to Islam at the age of fifteen.

With the exception of Khan, who was thirty at the time of the bombings, all were young, in their early twenties or late teens, and both Khan and Tanweer had some university training. Hussein was just eighteen but on track to go to university. All four were later identified by security officials as "cleanskins," a term signifying that none had had any previous run-in with the law, aside from such minor offenses as shoplifting as youths. At the same time, relatives and friends later told police that all four of the bombers had evinced increasingly radical Islamist views as they grew into their late teens and twenties, praising al-Qaeda and talking of the need for

violent jihad against the West. Both Khan and Tanweer had traveled to Pakistan, where they trained in militant camps. In videotaped confessions released on the Arabic language news station Al Jazeera after the attacks, both Khan and Tanweer spoke of having become "soldiers" in the cause of holy war.

Others were implicated in the attacks as well, having set up safe houses and manufactured the explosives used in the bombings. Among these were a group known as the Luton cell, named after a town in Bedfordshire, England, where they operated. Police later noted that the peroxide-based explosives were of a primitive sort that did not require much expertise in manufacturing or deploying; the perpetrators carried the explosives in backpacks.

The coordinated timing of the attack—three of the bombs on the London Underground (subway) occurred within a minute of each other during morning rush hour, at three different points on the system—suggested a certain level of sophistication and, perhaps, an effort to mimic al-Qaeda's signature style of near simultaneous attacks on different targets, as in the 1998 U.S. embassy bombings in East Africa and the 9/11 attacks in the United States. A fourth bomb went off about an hour late, aboard one of London's double-decker public buses. Altogether, 56 persons were killed in the attacks, including the four hijackers, while another roughly 700 persons were injured.

Two years later, another Muslim of British birth was convicted of conspiracy to commit murder after he drove an explosive-packed SUV into a terminal at Glasgow Airport in Scotland on June 30, 2007; his coconspirator was a Saudi Arabian–reared Indian national. The attack failed to kill or injure anyone, aside from the attackers, one of whom eventually died of his burns. Both men were highly educated; the British-born Bilal Abdullah was a medical doctor, while his accomplice, Kafeel Ahmed, was working on his PhD in computer technology at Cambridge's Anglia Ruskin University.

Future Responses

What both of these attacks illustrated, according to terrorism officials, was the growing danger of homegrown terrorism perpetrated by nationals of the target country—whether Great Britain, another European country, or even the United States—where the Muslim community tends to be better educated, wealthier, and more integrated into the larger society than those in Europe. Such terrorists can more easily evade the scrutiny of authorities, especially if they stay within the law. In addition, conducting surveillance on them raises ticklish civil liberty and privacy questions not relevant when dealing with foreigners abroad.

On the other hand, the law-abiding, nonradical Muslim communities in both the United Kingdom and the United States have proved themselves more than willing to cooperate with authorities in rooting out potentially violent extremists in their midst, especially when the right outreach is done by police. Thus, say security experts and officials, thwarting what are probably inevitable acts of homegrown terrorism by a few alienated and politicized actors will require a delicate balancing act between increased scrutiny and heightened awareness of the sensitivities of a community that often sees itself as maligned by society at large.

James Ciment

See also: *Definitions, Types, Categories*—Islamist Fundamentalist Terrorism. *Modern Terrorism*—France: Islamist Terrorism; Spain: Islamist Terrorism.

Further Reading

"Britain Under Threat." *The Economist,* July 3, 2007.

Hewitt, Steve. *The British War on Terror: Terrorism and Counter-Terrorism on the Home Front Since 9/11.* New York: Continuum, 2008.

London Assembly. Report of the July 7 Review Committee. London: London Greater Authority, 2006. http://www.london.gov.uk/who-runs-london/the-london-assembly/publications/safety-policing/report-7-july-review-committee.

"Murder in the Rush Hour." *The Economist,* July 7, 2005.

Seidler, Victor Jeleniewski. *Urban Fears and Global Terrors: Citizenship, Multicultures, and Belongings After 7/7.* New York: Routledge, 2007.

United Kingdom: Northern Ireland Troubles, 1968–2000s

The origins of the Irish Republican Army (IRA) and the struggles of Irish partisans seeking independence have for some acquired a kind of romantic glamour. In the latter third of the twentieth century, however, the Provisional IRA was one of the world's deadliest and most efficient terrorist organizations, involved in a whole gamut of gangster-style activities, from racketeering to kneecapping. Its campaign to force the British government to withdraw its forces from Northern Ireland, and to bring about a united Ireland, was prolonged and bloody. From the late 1960s, when the Troubles began, to the early 2000s, when they largely came to an end, more than 3,000 people died in Northern Ireland, almost two-thirds of these murdered by the IRA. Although the IRA announced a cease-fire in August 1994, it resumed its bombing campaign in February 1996, amid recriminations from all sides about the lack of a real commitment to the peace talks.

The "Irish Problem"

Britain has ruled Ireland since the twelfth century, and the vast majority of the Irish have never accepted the union with England. Since the English Reformation in the sixteenth century, resistance to control from London has been colored by the fact that the Irish remained Catholic while the English embraced Protestantism. Moreover, in the sixteenth and seventeenth centuries, successive English monarchs settled the northern provinces of Ireland with Protestant immigrants from England and Scotland, thereby fomenting religious conflict within the country.

There has been a long tradition of armed rebellion against British rule in Ireland, as well as brutal repression by the British authorities. In the 1640s, for example, there was a massive Catholic revolt in Ireland, which was eventually crushed by the troops of Oliver Cromwell. In 1801, a complete political union between Ireland and Britain was enacted.

In 1858, a group of Irish emigrants living in New York formed the Fenians, a revolutionary society whose aim was to win Irish independence from Britain. At first, the Fenians struck at Britain by making raids from the United States into Canada—at the time a British colony. The Fenian movement spread to Ireland itself and to England, where, during the 1880s, it carried out a bombing campaign that included an attack on the Houses of Parliament in London. In 1885, the Fenians declared that "this dynamite work will go on till Ireland is free, or till London is laid in ashes."

At the beginning of the twentieth century, the question of Ireland could no longer be ignored. While the British Parliament debated Home Rule, meaning partial independence, Irish extremists demanded full independence. At Easter in 1916, there were violent uprisings in Dublin, the largest city in Ireland. In the general elections of 1918, the pro-independence party Sinn Féin won a slight majority of the Irish vote. The following year, Irish activists led by Michael Collins formed the Irish Republican Army (IRA), which began a guerrilla war against the British.

In 1921, the British offered the nationalists a treaty. Under the agreement, an Irish Free State would be created in the predominantly Catholic south, while six counties of an area in the north (which formed the bulk of the traditional province of Ulster) would remain under British control. In these provinces, the Protestant loyalist majority wished to remain in the United Kingdom. Ulster was to have its own parliament at Stormont Castle, near Belfast, the north's largest city, and would maintain a certain amount of autonomy. While the moderate nationalists accepted the settlement, the IRA, led by Eamon de Valera, vehemently opposed it. The treaty was signed in London on December 6, 1921. However, the split in the nationalist movement provoked a bitter civil war, during which the Irish Free State crushed the dissident IRA. More than 12,000 IRA members were imprisoned and 77 were executed. By the time a cease-fire was called in May 1923, the IRA had been decimated.

In the late 1920s, de Valera led the majority of the IRA in renouncing violence and entering Irish democratic politics as the Fianna Fáil party. A splinter group under the leadership of Sean Russell, however, continued the armed struggle against the partition. In 1939, Russell developed a strategy for an audacious, but indiscriminate, bombing campaign on mainland Britain. During World War II, six people were killed in more than 250 attacks. The Irish government, to avert a possible British invasion, vigorously pursued IRA suspects. Internment, or imprisonment of suspects without trial, was introduced, and some 2,000 IRA activists were incarcerated for the duration of the war. Unable to function in Ireland or on the mainland, the IRA's campaign and organization fell apart.

After the release of the detainees at the end of World War II, the IRA regrouped and pursued a new strategy of attacking British targets in Northern Ireland. A number of raids in Ireland and Britain helped build up supplies of

The six counties of Northern Ireland, also known as Ulster, include a Protestant majority and remained part of the United Kingdom after the Republic of Ireland became independent in the 1920s. The Sinn Féin party has sought an end to British rule in Northern Ireland and unification of Ulster and the Republic of Ireland ever since.

weapons, but all attacks from the what had now become the Irish Republic into Northern Ireland (the so-called Border War) failed. In 1957, the Republic reintroduced internment, and the campaign collapsed. In 1962, the IRA called a cease-fire. A debate followed within the organization concerning the direction it should take. Under the leadership of Cathal Goulding in the 1960s, the IRA moved away from violence and associated itself with the growing civil rights movement. The Catholics of Northern Ireland were beginning to agitate for political and social rights. The Northern Ireland Civil Rights Association campaigned for an end to discrimination in employment and to voting abuses that kept Protestants in power on local councils.

Provisionals and Officials

In July 1969, Protestant paramilitary police (known as the "B-Specials") brutally broke up a peaceful civil rights demonstration in Derry, the second-largest city in Northern Ireland, and anti-Catholic violence spread through the country. In August, the British government sent in troops, initially to defend Catholic communities from Protestant mobs. The Catholics defended themselves, establishing no-go areas in the Catholic sections of both Derry (known as the Bogside) and Belfast. The

Catholics erected barricades and prevented the British forces from crossing them.

The IRA, meanwhile, was stirred into action by the events of 1969. Economic recession, in which Catholics tended to be the hardest hit, helped to ensure that hundreds of new recruits were attracted into the movement. Almost simultaneously, however, the organization split. Goulding and the so-called Official IRA continued to espouse civil rights, while Sean MacStiofain, a member of the leadership, formed the Provisional Army Council, which soon became the militant Provisional IRA—sometimes known as the "Provisionals." By the 1970s, the Official IRA had drastically declined in importance, and the Provisionals were generally referred as the IRA. In 1970, the Provisionals were divided into three main brigades, based in Derry, Belfast, and the border counties of Tyrone and Armagh. The Belfast Brigade alone, under the command of first Billy McKee and then Joe Cahill, comprised over 1,000 active members by 1971.

Despite a shortage of both funds and weapons, both Provisionals and Officials were prepared to use terrorism as a means to achieve their political ends. The Provisionals frequently took on Protestant groups in gun battles, particularly in Belfast, and in 1970, they started a campaign of bombing aimed principally at economic targets. In 1971, terrorists targeted British security forces for the first time. For the first time, too, the Provisionals began using a devastating new weapon: the car bomb.

Bloody Sunday and Bloody Friday

The British government responded to the violence by flooding the province with troops. The army tore down the barricades and entered the no-go areas. Internment of terrorist suspects was reintroduced. Unfortunately, this high-handed response alienated the Catholic community. The violence reached a climax on January 30, 1972, when, in what became known as Bloody Sunday, British paratroopers fired on Catholic civilians rioting in Derry, killing 13. The deaths unleashed a wave of Catholic violence. In one of the earliest IRA attacks on the British mainland, the Officials killed five cleaning women, an army chaplain, and a gardener in a bomb blast at the Parachute Regiment's headquarters in Aldershot, in southern England. In 1972, deaths in the violence in Northern Ireland peaked at 474, of whom 255 were killed at the hands of the IRA.

In July 1972, there was a brief cease-fire. The British government held secret talks in London with the Provisional IRA. The Provisionals' delegation included Martin McGuinness of the Derry brigade and Gerry Adams. The talks proved fruitless, however, and the Provisionals returned to violence. Only by an escalation of terror, they believed, would they achieve their objective. On July 21, 1972, in what was quickly dubbed Bloody Friday, the Provisional IRA unleashed an unprecedented series of atrocities against civilians in Northern Ireland. Twenty-two bombs exploded in Belfast city center, killing nine people and causing widespread panic among shoppers.

Terror on the Mainland

After Bloody Sunday, IRA terrorism entered a new phase. Under increasing threats from the security forces in the province, the Provisionals saw the mainland as a tempting, and relatively easy, means to strike at the heart of British resolve. In March 1973, a series of attacks that was to last until 1975 began on the mainland. The Provisionals attacked prestige and tourist targets in London, including the Tower of London. In 1973, a bomb exploded in a pub in Birmingham, in central England, killing 21 and injuring 164; in 1974, a pub in Guildford, a small town in the southeast of England, was targeted, killing 5 and injuring 54. The pub bombings caused widespread outrage in Britain.

One of the most successful Provisional IRA units was the Balcombe Street gang, which operated on the British mainland from 1974 to 1975. It carried out a series of bomb and gun attacks on hotels and restaurants, and attempted to assassinate the former British prime minister, Edward Heath. The gang was eventually caught in December 1975, after attempting a drive-by shooting into a restaurant. Police trapped the gang in an apartment in Balcombe Street, in central London, where it took an elderly couple hostage for six days before surrendering. At their trial the gang members were charged with ten murders and twenty bombings, and each received thirty years' imprisonment.

A result of the 1973–1974 London bombings, the British government revived contacts with the Provisionals. Secret negotiations began at the end of 1974, and in February 1975, the Provisional IRA agreed to an indefinite cease-fire, which lasted until the spring of 1976. After the collapse of the cease-fire in spring 1976, the Provisionals would radically change their organization and tactics, and a new phase in the terrorist war in Northern Ireland would begin.

During the cease-fire of 1975–1976, the various nationalist groups broke apart. Members of the former Official IRA formed the Irish National Liberation Army (INLA), which adopted an avowedly socialist philosophy and carried out many terrorist atrocities over the next two decades. The most notorious of these was the March 1979 murder of Airey Neave, the British Conservative party spokesman on Northern Ireland affairs; INLA members placed a bomb underneath his car in the House of Commons parking lot. In 1994, members also carried out a number of attacks on Protestant organizations, including the murder of three members of the Protestant paramilitary group the Ulster Volunteer Force. The INLA never achieved the importance of the Provisional IRA, partly because it was riven with internal feuds, often over ob-

scure matters of political doctrine. From December 1986 to March 1987, for example, twelve INLA terrorists died during one such feud. In the mid-1990s, there was further internal strife in which two rival chiefs of staff died: Gino Gallagher in January 1996 and Hugh Torney in August 1996.

IRA Restructures

Meanwhile, the Provisional IRA was reorganizing. Its structure had remained unchanged since the 1920s: each active IRA unit sent delegates to an Army Convention, which appointed a twelve-person Army Executive Committee, from which was elected a seven-person Army Council. The council then appointed one of its members as chief of staff with complete operational command.

In the mid-1970s, however, the Army Council disbanded the old companies and battalions in favor of smaller, cell-like structures known as active service units (ASUs).

These contained between six and twelve active members, grouped in geographic "brigades," such as the Belfast, Derry, and East Tyrone brigades. Recruits were from predominantly working-class backgrounds. Numbers were deliberately limited because of the danger of infiltration by the security forces, with brigades normally having no more than sixty members. Active service units in Britain usually reported to the chief of staff or the Army Council. In the autumn of 1976, however, after the end of the cease-fire, the Army Council approved the establishment of a semi-independent Northern Command. This decision gave the more aggressive units, who were active in Northern Ireland, a much greater degree of autonomy.

The Provisionals simultaneously took a more aggressive stance with regard to controlling (or what they described as "policing") the Catholic population. In 1977, they carried out 126 kneecappings—a gruesome punishment for such antisocial behavior as drug trafficking that involved breaking knees by dropping concrete blocks on them or by shooting. In one incident alone, 23 youths were assaulted in a street that was soon nicknamed Kneecap Alley.

Assassinations, the "Dirty Protest," and Hunger Strikes

During the late 1970s, the Provisionals attacked the security forces and Protestant paramilitary groups in Northern Ireland. There was also a halfhearted attempt to attack economic targets by assassinating businessmen, but this was short-lived. Some high-profile incidents also occurred. In August 1979, Earl Mountbatten, a prominent former admiral and politician, and the last British viceroy of India, was murdered by a bomb while sailing on a lake in the Irish Republic. On the same day, eighteen British soldiers died in an ambush involving two bombs at Warrenpoint, County Down, the single biggest loss suffered by the British Army in Northern Ireland.

More significant in the long term, however, were events that took place in the prisons of Northern Ireland. Until 1976, IRA activists in jail had effectively enjoyed prisoner-of-war status. In that year, however, the British government decided they should be treated as common criminals. The IRA prisoners protested. From the fall of 1976, they refused to wear prison uniforms and the so-called dirty protest began, in which prisoners wore only blankets and smeared their cells with excrement. By the summer of 1978, almost 300 republican prisoners had joined the "dirty protest."

By 1980, the fourth year of protest, the prisoners turned to hunger strikes to keep up the pressure on the British government. Prime Minister Margaret Thatcher took a tough stance and refused to give in to the hunger strikers' demands. Rioting returned to the streets of Belfast and Derry on a scale not seen since the early 1970s. One of the hunger strikers, Bobby Sands, ran as a candidate in a parliamentary election and won. As a prisoner, however, he was unable to take his seat in the House of Commons. On May 5, 1981, Sands died. More than 100,000 people attended his funeral. Nine more hunger strikers died before the protest was called off in October 1981.

At the beginning of the 1980s, the pattern of violence in Northern Ireland was also changing. Since 1976, the British Army had scaled down its presence, acting mainly as support for the police, known as the Royal Ulster Constabulary (RUC), in the province's cities. Consequently, the Provisional IRA took its campaign to the countryside, assassinating Protestants in rural areas where army presence was minimal and intelligence gathering was weak. The IRA also targeted off-duty policemen and army reservists. In 1981, the total number of security force members murdered reached forty-four.

From this peak, however, the number of killings dropped sharply. The security forces appeared to have changed their tactics. In 1982, following the shooting of two IRA activists by the Special Air Service, many believed that the army and the RUC were pursuing an assassination policy against Provisional IRA suspects. Under increasing pressure from the security forces in Northern Ireland, the Provisionals again shifted their campaign to mainland Britain.

Spectacular Targets

The new mainland campaign included a series of attacks on military and prestige targets. On July 20, 1982, eight soldiers were killed and forty-one civilians were injured when bombs exploded in Hyde Park and Regent's Park in London. Three more people later died of their injuries. On December 17, 1983, a bomb exploded

In an assassination attempt against British prime minister Margaret Thatcher, the IRA planted a bomb at the Grand Hotel in Brighton, England, during the annual Conservative Party convention on October 12, 1984. Thatcher was uninjured; five others were killed. *(Associated Press)*

outside the famous London department store, Harrods. In October 1984, the IRA mounted its most spectacular attack when it almost managed to assassinate Prime Minister Margaret Thatcher by planting a bomb at the Brighton hotel in which she was staying while attending the Conservative Party's annual convention. When the bomb went off during the night, Thatcher was herself unhurt, but her room was badly damaged. Five people were killed, including one MP and the wife of a cabinet minister; another thirty people were injured.

Ballots and Bombs

Because of the clandestine nature of the IRA, it is difficult to make accurate estimates of the size of its membership. Unlike terrorist groups elsewhere in the world, however, the Provisional IRA's level of support could be tested through democratic politics. By the early 1980s, Sinn Féin had long been recognized as the political wing of the Provisional IRA, despite repeated denials from the party.

Sinn Féin leaders Martin McGuiness and Gerry

Adams publicly distanced themselves from the IRA. Sinn Féin's peak of 102,000 votes in the 1983 election in Northern Ireland, or 13.4 percent of the nationalist vote, demonstrated the level of support for the Provisional IRA in the province. Electoral success enabled Sinn Féin to distance itself from the IRA's military campaign against the British in Ireland.

Financially, the organization was growing, too. For many years it had resorted to robbery and extortion for much of its finances, but in the 1980s this changed. Legitimate businesses, such as real estate and restaurants, both in Northern Ireland and among the Irish community on the British mainland, also appeared to account for a significant proportion of the IRA's income. At the same time, money flowed in from the Irish Northern Aid Committee (Noraid), which had been set up in the United States by Irish emigrants. On the face of it, Noraid was a charitable organization raising funds for the poor and needy in Ireland. The FBI, however, believed that the contributions were being used to purchase arms, and several members of the committee were convicted for refusing to reveal how funds were distributed. With the Provisional IRA's increased wealth, weapons were acquired in gunrunning operations and were also supplied by countries such as Libya and Iran.

During the mid-1980s, the Provisionals suffered setbacks. In November 1985, for example, Britain and the Irish Republic signed the Anglo-Irish Agreement, which led to increased security cooperation between the two governments. Moreover, although Provisional IRA assassinations continued in the province, with regular attacks on police stations in rural border areas, a considerable number of terrorists died during operations. In the 1987 general election, Sinn Féin's vote dropped to 11.3 percent. Further atrocities drew condemnation from all sides. On Remembrance Sunday (Veterans' Day) in 1987, a bomb attack in Enniskillen, a town in Northern Ireland, killed eleven and injured sixty-three, almost all of them civilians. In Dublin, thousands marched to protest against the atrocity.

Return to the British Mainland

The groundswell of opinion against the Provisional IRA in Northern Ireland encouraged the group to turn its attention to the British mainland. The first damaging attack of the new campaign came in September 1989, when the Provisional IRA detonated a bomb at a military base at Deal, on the south coast of England. Ten band members of the Royal Marines School of Music died in the blast. Then, in July 1990, Ian Gow, a Conservative member of parliament, was murdered. In February 1991, the Provisionals again came very close to killing a British prime minister. Provisional IRA members launched a mortar attack on John Major's official London residence, 10 Downing Street, just missing the entire British cabinet. The Provisional IRA had shown that it could penetrate the tightest security.

During 1991, the organization returned to its policy of hitting economic targets, aware of the precarious state of the British economy at that time. In Northern Ireland, there had been a shift toward a traditional war against the army and the RUC, but by the start of the 1990s it was apparent that the security forces were not going to be defeated over the long term. In this context, it was natural for the Provisional IRA to resort to economic pressure. In late 1991, four large bombs were detonated in Belfast city center. The Provisional IRA knew the economic cost that such bombs imposed: from the 1970s until the early 1990s, the British government had paid more than $1 billion to repair damage caused by almost 10,000 explosions. The Provisional IRA campaign against commercial property reached a new level in April 1992, when a device hidden in a van exploded outside the Baltic Exchange in London's financial district, killing three. In April 1993, an explosion devastated the Bishopsgate area of London. The cost of the damage from this one bomb alone was estimated at $1 billion. On March 20, 1993, two children died after two bombs exploded in succession in Warrington, in northern England.

Politically, it was not clear that Provisional IRA tactics were paying off, at least in the short term. Economically, however, a possible crisis of confidence among foreign banks and institutions, which might seek to relocate to alternative centers such as Frankfurt, Germany, now loomed. Insurance premiums were escalating. Policy makers in the City of London Corporation, the governing body of the City (London's financial center), felt they had to react.

The City was by no means the most frequently attacked part of London, but it was the size of the bombs (homemade devices mounted in commercial vehicles) used against the City, rather than their frequency, that gave rise to concern. Furthermore, it was not the ruined buildings that mattered so much, but the activities conducted inside them—notably, foreign exchange trading. The challenge for the City was to prevent another major explosion and to ensure that its disaster recovery systems minimized the dislocation of business activity if its defenses were breached. The problem for the City's planners was that the greater the effort to prevent another attack, the more attractive the challenge for the Provisional IRA to breach any security measures.

New Security Measures

In mid-1993, the City ratified a series of measures to reassure residents and prevent another bomb attack. A Traffic Management Scheme monitored all traffic entering the square mile of the City. Officially designed to meet traffic and environmental needs, the plan dramatically reduced the number of entry points into the City by sealing off streets and establishing police checkpoints. All vehicles entering the City passed police cordons, where random searches took place, mainly of larger commercial vehicles. Closed-circuit TV cameras were placed at strategic sites around the City. Private companies were encouraged to join a Camera Watch plan, whereby existing security cameras were positioned to cover the streets. Backing up the static security measures were mobile, armed City of London police units, which established checkpoints at random, checking vehicles and occasionally pedestrians.

Disaster recovery measures were taken at all levels. The Corporation introduced a pager alert system to keep businesses informed about potential and actual threats. It encouraged companies to develop disaster recovery plans, establishing backup facilities where, for example, foreign exchange trading rooms could be relocated. By 1994, the majority of all firms operating in the City had some form of contingency plan.

There were objections to the traffic management plan from nearby boroughs and automobile organizations, which feared an increase in traffic and pollution—and even terrorism—in their districts. Politicians expressed concern that the measures gave a propaganda victory to the Provisional IRA, encouraging it to target the City. Such concerns were not without force. In July 1993, a Provisional IRA operative was arrested at a bus stop; he had a bag of explosives and may have been traveling to the City. For the Corporation, however, the plan proved effective: no major bombings struck the City following its implementation. When the Provisional IRA broke its cease-fire, in February 1996, with a 1,000-pound bomb, it targeted London's Docklands, a satellite business district.

In implementing its security measures, the City benefited from a number of unique circumstances that set it apart from other London districts. Perhaps most significantly, it possessed its own police force, the City of London Police. Furthermore, the unusual structure of the Corporation, which included representatives from the business community, allowed for rapid consensus on developments. Public support increased when it emerged that the security measures greatly reduced the level of crime in the City. Public approval had been aided by the low population of City residents (only 5,000, swelling to 280,000 on workdays). Commuting workers and large businesses were found to be less likely to object to tight security, on civil liberty grounds, than would residents of the district.

The Way Forward

Given the City's unique circumstances, the extent to which lessons can be drawn from its experience is questionable. Clearly, the threat of bomb attacks remained, but the danger of large, vehicle-borne devices was much reduced. The major problem in implementing the security measures was the drain of police manpower away from other duties, and the long-term sustainability of such a plan remained in doubt. In terms of disaster contingency planning, however, the City pointed the way forward for modern business districts—and specifically financial centers—where the dislocation of business needs to be counted in hours, not days, before the costs become prohibitive. Only through coordinated planning between public and private authorities could contingencies be effectively met and beaten. The experience of Provisional IRA terrorism gave the City greater confidence in its security capabilities, and no significant relocation of foreign institutions from London occurred.

Loyalist Terror in Northern Ireland

Although the best-known form of terrorist violence in Northern Ireland and the United Kingdom mainland had been the campaign carried out by such groups as the Provisional IRA, there was another set of terrorists at work in this troubled part of the world. These terrorists were the Loyalists, who were fighting to keep Northern Ireland as an integral part of the United Kingdom, as opposed to the nationalists, or republicans, who were fighting for a united Ireland.

While nationalist terrorists relied on support from the Catholic minority of Northern Ireland, the Loyalist terrorists were from the majority Protestant community. Within Ireland as a whole, the majority of the population was always Catholic. In the seventeenth century, however, the English encouraged Protestants from Scotland to settle in the north of Ireland, in the province known as Ulster. During the period just before World War I, when independence for all Ireland seemed likely, Ulster Protestants formed the formidable Ulster Volunteer Force, which threatened open revolt if a Catholic-dominated government was given control over them. In the settlement of 1922, six northern counties of Ireland became Northern Ireland, a constituent part of the United Kingdom. Within Northern Ireland, Protestants formed a majority, and there were attempts to minimize Catholic political influence, partly by gerrymandering but also by intimidation. In 1966, Protestant activists formed a new Ulster Volunteer Force (UVF), which received covert support from the British Army. The UVF murdered two Catholics before being outlawed.

Anti-Catholic Violence

In the late 1960s, the Northern Ireland Civil Rights Association began organizing demonstrations to protest against the effective disenfranchisement of many Catholics and received support from the British government of the time. Protestants responded once again with violence directed against the Catholic community. In particular, a Protestant-dominated auxiliary police force, the B-Specials, used brute force to break up civil rights marches.

The British government disbanded the B-Specials in 1972. Even before then, however, Protestants were turning to other paramilitary forces. The Ulster Defence Association (UDA) was formed in 1971, and the Ulster Vanguard Movement in 1972. These groups paraded in public in military style and were connected to mainstream political parties. Nevertheless, members from both organizations participated in sectarian killings. The first bomb attack on Catholics took place in December 1971, when the well-known McGurk's bar was destroyed, killing fifteen. In 1972, UDA men set up no-go areas from which they excluded the British Army, and from March to July 1972, some forty Catholics were killed. UDA leader Andy Tyrie defended his organization's use of terror: "We're a counterterrorist organization. The only way we'll get peace here is to terrorize the terrorists." Groups such as the Ulster Freedom Fighters (UFF) and the Red Hand Commandos claimed responsibility for the killing of Catholics during the 1970s. These groups, however, were almost certainly not independent organizations but occasional combinations of UDA members.

There also have been numerous assassination campaigns directed against prominent nationalists. In June 1980, UDA members shot and killed John Turnley, a nationalist member of the British Parliament. In March 1984, the UFF attempted to assassinate Sinn Féin president Gerry Adams as he was being driven through Belfast. In February 1989, UFF terrorists broke into the home of a prominent Catholic lawyer and murdered him in front of his family.

Links with Security Forces

There was strong Catholic concern about the pro-Protestant stance of the British security forces. Until 1973, no member of any Protestant paramilitary organization had been interned by the security forces, although there had been large-scale internment of Catholics and nationalist sympathizers since 1971. Such suspicions seemed to be confirmed when, in 1970, the British government formed the Ulster Defence Regiment (UDR), an official military body of part-time soldiers, designed to back up the army and the police force of Northern Ireland—the RUC. There was widespread belief among Catholics that members of the mainly Protestant UDR took part in killings, and in March 1979, the RUC publicly admitted that UDR members had been involved in at least thirty known cases of murder.

By the 1980s, the Protestant terrorist groups had become a permanent part of the Northern Irish scene.

KEY DATES

1921 After a bitter struggle, the British government grants independence to Ireland but maintains control over the six northern provinces, which are known as Ulster, or Northern Ireland.

1968 Long seeing themselves as second-class citizens, the Catholics of Ulster begin civil rights demonstrations.

1969 Protestant paramilitaries break up Catholic demonstrations, launching the so-called Troubles that would engulf Northern Ireland for nearly thirty years.

1972 British troops open fire on rioting Catholic civilians in Derry, killing thirteen, in an incident that comes to be known as Bloody Sunday.

1973 The IRA begins its two-decade-long bombing campaign on the British mainland.

1979 IRA terrorists set off a bomb, killing Lord Mountbatten, a prominent British politician.

1984 An IRA bomb explodes at the Conservative Party convention in the south of England, though its primary target, Prime Minister Margaret Thatcher, is unhurt.

1992 The IRA sets off a huge bomb in the City of London, Britain's financial center, causing damages estimated at $1 billion.

1998 The various parties to the conflict—the nationalists, loyalists, and British and Irish governments—sign the Good Friday Accords, creating a blueprint for peace in Ulster.

2006 A new power-sharing agreement goes into place, as loyalists and unionists sit down together in a new Northern Ireland parliament.

The groups established their own political front organizations and, like the IRA, used protection rackets and gangsterism to provide funds. Some of their activities were astonishingly brutal: the Shankhill Butchers murdered at least twelve Catholics, torturing their victims before they killed them. Protestant terrorist activities were mainly confined to Northern Ireland, although in 1974 bombs exploded in the Irish Republic that were almost certainly the work of Protestant terrorists. Again, like Republican terrorists, the Protestant terrorists had their internal feuds: two leaders of the UDA, Tommy Heron and Ernie Elliott, were killed for "going soft" on republicanism.

Protestant terrorists took part in the cease-fire of 1994 and kept to it, despite the strains of the protracted 1996 peace talks. Ultimately, the Protestants Loyalists and the Catholic nationalists agreed to the Good Friday Peace Accords of 1998, which called for a new power-sharing arrangement in a new parliament for Northern Ireland. After many disputes, particularly over the question of the disarming of the IRA, the parliament was elected by Northern Ireland voters in March 2006, and peace returned to the long-tortured six provinces of Northern Ireland.

Bertrande Roberts, Ashley Brown, and John Gearson

See also: Definitions, Types, Categories—Ethnonationalist Terrorism. *Historical Roots*—Ireland: Independence Struggle.

Further Reading

Bruce, Steve. "The Problem of Pro-State Terrorism: Loyalist Paramilitaries in Northern Ireland." *Terrorism and Political Violence* 14:1 (Spring 1992): 67–88.

Davis, Richard. *Mirror Hate: The Convergent Ideology of Northern Ireland Paramilitaries, 1966–1992.* Dartmouth, VT: Aldershot and Brookfield, 1994.

Dixon, Paul. *Northern Ireland: The Politics of War and Peace.* New York: Palgrave Macmillan, 2008.

Doumitt, Donald P. *Conflict in Northern Ireland: The History, the Problem, and the Challenge.* New York: Lang, 1985.

Dunn, Seamus, ed. *Facets of the Conflicts in Northern Ireland.* New York: St. Martin's, 1995.

Ellison, Graham, and Jim Smyth. *The Crowned Harp: Policing Northern Ireland.* London: Pluto, 2000.

Hennessey, Thomas. *A History of Northern Ireland, 1920–1996.* London: Macmillan, 1997.

Jackson, Alvin. *Ireland, 1798–1998.* Oxford: Blackwell, 1999.

O'Day, Alan, ed. *Dimensions of Irish Terrorism.* New York: G.K. Hall, 1994.

O'Leary, Brendan, and John McGarry. *The Politics of Antagonism: Understanding Northern Ireland.* Atlantic Highlands, NJ: Athlone, 1993.

Talbot, R.M. "The Balancing Act: Counter-terrorism and Civil Liberties in British Anti-terrorism Law." In *Law After Ground Zero,* ed. John Strawson. London: Glasshouse, 2002.

United States: Animal Rights, 1970s–2000s

Since the nineteenth century, the animal welfare movement in the United States has acknowledged the suffering of all nonhumans and made attempts to reduce or eliminate that suffering through "humane" treatment. The movement is represented by organizations such as the Society for the Prevention of Cruelty to Animals and the American Veterinary Medical Association, which defines animal welfare as "a human responsibility that encompasses all aspects of well-being, including proper housing, management, disease prevention and treatment, responsible care, humane handling, and, when necessary, euthanasia."

Beginning in the mid-1970s, the arguments for the better treatment of animals underwent a dramatic change. The publication of *Animal Liberation* (1975), by Peter Singer, and *Animal Rights and Human Obligations* (1976), edited by Peter Singer and Tom Regan, challenged the prevailing philosophy of animal welfare and espoused the view that animals have rights. The philosophy behind the animal welfare movement is that all animals have interests but that these interests may be traded away as long as there are expected results that are thought to justify the sacrifice. Under animal rights philosophy, however, the interests of animals cannot be traded away simply because good consequences will result. According to members of the animal rights movement, the law does not protect animals, because it regards them as the property of human beings—a condition that leaves them vulnerable to human exploitation. Thus, for example, while persons committed to animal welfare might be concerned that cows get enough space and proper food, those same persons might have no qualms about killing cows or eating their meat, as long as the rearing and slaughter are humane. Animal rights proponents have varied beliefs, but most support laws and regulations that would prohibit rodeos, circuses, horse racing, hunting, and the use of animals in research.

The methods used by various animal rights groups differ. Some try to work within the legal and political system by making changes in the law. The Chimpanzee Collaboratory, a partnership of concerned lawyers, scientists, and policy advocates, maintains that chimpanzees are so close to humans that they deserve the same kind of legal representation as children. This would permit animal rights activists to act as legal guardians for the chimps and file lawsuits against researchers who mistreat them. People for the Ethical Treatment of Animals (PETA) is the largest and best-known animal rights group. Its motto is "animals are not ours to eat, wear, experiment on, or use for entertainment." PETA is a nonprofit organization that publicizes the plight of animals and has had significant success in stirring up public opinion against using animals in ways that do not meet their guidelines.

A third type of animal rights activist is more radical and destructive. The Animal Liberation Front (ALF) was formed in Great Britain in 1976. There, the ALF has not hesitated to use terrorism against those who, in its opinion, mistreat animals. In January 1981, the homes of several Oxford University scientists were attacked by ALF activists. The activists daubed slogans on walls and damaged a garage and cars. In March 1984, the group issued a warning that it had contaminated bottles of shampoo in stores in London, Leeds, and Southampton, claiming the manufacturers tested the product on animals. Bottles spiked with bleach were discovered in Leeds and Southampton.

On October 24, 1984, a group of ALF activists attacked a dog kennel in southern England, assaulting three people. Simultaneously, other ALF supporters attacked buildings at two research laboratories with sledgehammers. A fourth group visited the home of a laboratory research director, who was beaten with an iron bar. In December 1987, the ALF targeted the fur trade, firebombing stores selling furs in Manchester, Liverpool, and Cardiff.

The ALF consists of small autonomous groups of people in more than a dozen countries who carry out direct action. This direct action takes two forms: (1) the rescue or liberation of animals from laboratories or pet shops; (2) damage to property connected to animal abuse. Both types of action usually occur during the same raid. ALF policy does not advocate violence against people, despite some incidents to the contrary.

Other animal rights extremist groups, however, will use and threaten violence. Groups calling themselves the Justice Department and the Animal Rights Militia have put pipe bombs in storefronts and razor blades in letters.

KEY DATES

1976 Animal rights activists in Great Britain form the Animal Liberation Front (ALF), globally launching the militant animal rights movement.

1985 Sixteen members of the ALF attack the Riverside Life Buildings at the University of California, taking hundreds of animals.

2006–2009 ALF members are involved in nearly a dozen sabotage and harassment incidents against animal research facilities and researchers at the University of California, Los Angeles.

Booby-trapped letters have been received by fur farmers and by researchers at several universities. In England, letter bombs were sent to an agricultural auctioneer and a pest control firm. When conventional legal action and direct action do not achieve their goals, some animal rights extremists will likely use more violence.

In April 1985, sixteen members of the ALF raided the Riverside Life Sciences Building of the University of California, taking hundreds of animals. ALF spokespeople claimed that the institution caused the animals to suffer in isolation and sight-deprivation experiments. While the U.S. version of the Animal Liberation Front has a policy of avoiding injuries to people, sabotage makes research more expensive, so the movement hopes its actions will encourage animal-friendly methods; the attack at Riverside caused hundreds of thousands of dollars' worth of damage.

Perhaps the most publicized case involving animal rights militants has been the sustained sabotage conducted at the University of California, Los Angeles (UCLA), where, from 2006 to 2009, activists conducted attacks against laboratories and the property of researchers, along with harassment of researchers and their families. To counter such violence, President George W. Bush signed the Animal Enterprise Terrorism Act in 2006, which expanded federal jurisdiction over crimes against animal-testing institutions and their employees. UCLA is not alone, says the FBI, which reported nearly fifty such actions in 2008 and 2009, roughly doubling the figure for the period 2006–2007. Meanwhile, antifur activists engaged in a number of actions in the 1990s and 2000s, including the throwing of animal blood on persons publicly wearing furs. The activists claim that the trapping of animals for furs is inhumane, as are the conditions at fur farms.

Gary Perlstein

See also: *Definitions, Types, Categories*—Left-Wing and Revolutionary Terrorism. *Modern Terrorism*—United States: Ecoterrorism.

Further Reading

Gaarder, Emily. *Women and the Animal Rights Movement.* New Brunswick, NJ: Rutgers University Press, 2011.

Newkirk, Ingrid, and Chrissie Hynde. *Free the Animals: The Story of the Animal Liberation Front.* New York: Lantern Books, 2000.

Singer, Peter. *Animal Liberation.* New York: Random House, 1975.

Singer, Peter, and Tom Regan, eds. *Animal Rights and Human Obligations.* Englewood Cliffs, NJ: Prentice Hall, 1976.

United States: Anthrax Attacks, 2001

"Bioterrorism" was not a household word in the United States until the twenty-first century. A sequence of events beginning in October 2001, however, made people keenly aware of the term. Bioterrorism is the intentional use of any living organisms, such as bacteria or viruses, as a weapon. One of the main goals of using such a weapon is to create widespread fear. Anthrax, one of the most feared and discussed of these disease threats, is caused by a type of bacteria called *Bacillus anthracis,* which is found naturally in soil, as well as in some animals and humans. There are three types of anthrax infections.

1. Skin infection: The most common type and the least serious. It can develop when a cut or scrape on the skin comes in direct contact with anthrax spores.
2. Gastrointestinal infection: Can be contracted by eating undercooked meat that contains anthrax bacteria.
3. Inhalational infection: The most serious type of anthrax; can be caught by inhaling large amounts of anthrax spores from the air. Inhalational anthrax is not contagious but is often fatal.

On October 2, 2001, Bob Stevens, a photo editor at American Media, Inc., in Florida, arrived at a hospital. He had a 102-degree fever and presented a confused mental state. By the following day, doctors confirmed that Stevens had contracted anthrax. He was treated with antibiotics and placed on a respirator, but he died on October 5. Stevens was the first anthrax fatality in the United States since 1976. On October 7 an employee of American Media who delivered mail tested positive for anthrax exposure, and anthrax spores were subsequently found on Stevens's computer keyboard.

At first, authorities assumed the Florida case was an isolated incident. On October 9, however, letters containing anthrax addressed to Senate Majority Leader Tom Daschle and Senator Patrick Leahy were found in Washington, D.C. Investigators from the Federal Bureau of Investigation (FBI) and health authorities began to realize that someone or some group was attacking the United States using anthrax as a weapon. Within a few days, employees of media networks NBC, CBS, and ABC were found to have been exposed to anthrax. Postal workers were also being hospitalized, and on October 21 a postal worker died of inhalation anthrax. On November

Hazardous materials workers clean up after searching for anthrax at the Dirksen Senate Office Building in Washington, D.C., in November 2001. The spread of deadly anthrax spores by mail—never criminally prosecuted—caused twenty-two cases of the disease, five fatal. *(Alex Wong/Getty Images)*

21, the fifth and final fatality occurred. Anthrax, mainly a disease of grazing animals, has been a part of every known bio-arsenal in the world. However, this attack that killed five people and infected thirteen others represented the first known use of the toxin.

Domestic U.S. Terrorism

Inasmuch as it came within a month of the September 11 terrorist attacks on New York and Washington, the anthrax incidents were believed to be linked to the same perpetrators and cause. The FBI and other investigators, however, soon came to believe that the anthrax attacker was an American who was probably acting out of anger at some government agency; the individual, it was believed, had worked or maybe was still working in the U.S. biodefense program.

In August 2002, the U.S. Justice Department announced that it was considering Stephen J. Hatfill a "person of interest" in the ongoing anthrax investigation. A forty-eight-year-old scientific researcher who had worked on biological weapons research for the government and private companies under government contract, Hatfill vigorously maintained his innocence. Authorities eventually dropped Hatfill as a suspect, however, and in 2005 the FBI had focused on a new candidate for the attacks—a senior researcher for the U.S. Army Medical Research Institute of Infectious Diseases at Fort Detrick, Maryland, named Bruce Ivins. Two years later, the FBI put him under periodic surveillance, claiming he was a possible suspect. By June 2008, it was becoming clear to Ivins that he was to be formally charged with the attacks and, on July 27, 2008, he committed suicide. A month later the FBI officially declared Ivins the lone perpetrator of the attacks, though some experts disagreed. The FBI based its conclusions on a number of suspicious actions he had taken after it learned of a history of anthrax contamination at his laboratory. As for motives, the FBI offered little; some suspect that Ivins may have been seeking publicity—even though he had not claimed responsibility or allowed himself to be caught for seven years.

Gary Perlstein

See also: Tactics, Methods, Aims—Freelance, Contract, and Lone Zealot Terrorists; Weapons, Chemical and Biological.

Further Reading

Jones, Susan D. *Death in a Small Package: A Short History of Anthrax.* Baltimore: Johns Hopkins University Press, 2010.

Miller, Judith, Stephen Engelberg, and William J. Broad. *Germs: Biological Weapons and America's Secret War.* New York: Simon and Schuster, 2001.

Parents' Committee for Public Awareness. *Anthrax: A Practical Guide for Citizens—What You Should Know, What You Can Do, and How It Came to This.* Cambridge, MA: Harvard Perspectives Press, 2001.

United States: Antiabortion Violence, 1973–Present

Violent antiabortion groups are the undemocratic face of a movement for legal reform. Frustrated by the inability to overturn the Supreme Court's 1973 decision in *Roe v. Wade,* which held that laws forbidding abortion are an unconstitutional infringement of a citizen's rights, antiabortionists have formed a number of groups to campaign against abortion providers. Defensive Action, Operation Rescue, the American Family Association, Lambs of Christ, and similar organizations have demonstrated outside clinics, even establishing blockades to prevent people from entering or leaving.

Some antiabortionists have turned to firebombing clinics and murdering medical staff. The Reverend Paul Hill, director of Defensive Action, was convicted of murder in the slayings of abortion doctor John Britton and his security escort, James Barratt, who were shot outside a clinic in Pensacola, Florida, in June 1994; in 2003, Hill was executed by lethal injection in a Florida state prison. In December 30, 1994, John C. Salvi III walked into the Planned Parenthood clinic in Brookline, Massachusetts, and opened fire with a rifle, killing the receptionist and wounding three other people. Salvi then drove to the Preterm Health Services clinic, where he killed a second person and injured two more. The next day, he fired twenty-three shots at an abortion clinic in Norfolk, Virginia, before police apprehended him. Although Salvi's defense lawyers protested that their defendant was insane at the time of the killings, Salvi was sentenced to two consecutive life terms in prison.

Twenty years earlier, in the early 1970s, protests against abortion had been relatively peaceful events. Even when *Roe v. Wade* gave American women the constitutionally protected right to abortion, the reactions were initially mild. Two years after the ruling, for example, the National Conference of Catholic Bishops merely issued a "pastoral plan for pro-life activities." It was not until 1979 that conservative lobbyists and fund-raisers started working in earnest to defeat politicians who were known to support abortion rights. Although there were a few bomb and death threats, almost all antiabortion activists were confident that the *Roe v. Wade* ruling could be reversed through the legitimate political process. By the late 1970s, that belief began to fade.

Path to Direct Action

Groups such as the National Right to Life Committee (NRLC), which had formed after the 1973 ruling, were beginning to exert political pressure on the govern-

Flowers of condolence lie on the steps of the Planned Parenthood Clinic in Brookline, Massachusetts, where antiabortion campaigner John Salvi opened fire on December 30, 1994. He did the same at another abortion clinic in town, killing two people and injuring five in all. *(Associated Press)*

ment. Some members, frustrated by the lack of progress in changing abortion law, formed more activist organizations. They resorted to such direct-action tactics as picketing clinics and physicians' offices and homes, and filling the locks of clinic doors with glue. Another tactic was "sidewalk counseling," in which an activist would approach a woman entering a clinic and try to persuade her not to have an abortion.

In 1986, Randall Terry, together with Joseph Scheidler, founder of the Pro-Life Action League, formed Operation Rescue, which resorted to more radical acts. Members of the organization demonstrated outside clinics and lay down in clinic doorways to prevent abortion patients from entering. When the police inevitably arrived to break up the blockade, the activists simply relaxed their bodies so they had to be physically removed from the premises. In 1991, members of Operation Rescue staged a three-week blockade of local abortion clinics in Wichita, Kansas, where the police arrested 1,900 protesters.

Antiabortion Terrorism

In addition to forming physical blockades, antiabortionists began resorting to arson, bombings, and shootings. According to the National Abortion Federation, activists committed 161 bombings and acts of arson against abortion clinics between 1977 and 1992. In 1984, violence erupted in Pensacola, Florida, where activists bombed a women's clinic, and several other terrorist incidents followed. One group linked with the attacks in Pensacola was Rescue America, a militant organization that advocated the use of violence. In March 1993, Michael Griffin, then a new recruit to Rescue America, shot and killed Dr. David Gunn outside a Pensacola clinic. The violence also spread across the border into Canada. In May 1992, a firebombing destroyed a clinic in Toronto. In November 1994, an activist shot and wounded an abortion doctor at his Vancouver home. On May 31, 2009, a mentally unbalanced antiabortion activist named Scott Roeder murdered George Tiller, the only late-term abortion provider in Kansas, while the latter was attending church services in Wichita.

U.S. authorities have become increasingly concerned that some radical antiabortionists may be linking up with right-wing militia groups. They fear antiabortionists plan not only to use existing paramilitary training camps, but also to develop their own armed militia. Moreover, the Ku Klux Klan also began taking a stance against abortion rights—for Caucasian women, if not for other races. In August 1994, the KKK demonstrated outside a Florida abortion clinic, protesting against the protection offered to clinics by federal marshals.

Most antiabortion organizations in the United States have condemned extremist violence, pointing out that the bombers and arsonists are terrorist individuals on the fringes of the movement. However, not all such organizations are unequivocal in their condemnation. Some antiabortionists blame bombings on the very existence of abortion clinics, while others defend the terrorist killings as justifiable homicide.

Legislation Against Activists

In the 1990s, the U.S. Congress began to react to the escalation of violence among the more radical elements of the antiabortion movement. In May 1994, President Clinton signed into law the Freedom of Access to Clinic Entrances Act, which restricts antiabortion groups from interfering with or intimidating someone who is obtaining or providing any form of "reproductive health services." First-time offenders face fines of up to $100,000, with far stiffer fines and three-year prison sentences for subsequent offenses.

Pro-choice groups and government prosecutors also explored the possibility of employing the Racketeer Influenced Corrupt Organizations Law (RICO) against perpetrators of crime in the name of antiabortionism. Congress enacted RICO in 1970 primarily to stop organized crime from taking over legitimate businesses, but federal courts began upholding broader applications of the law. In 1986, the National Organization for Women used RICO to initiate a case against two pro-life groups and their directors for blockading abortion clinics, threatening clinic staff and patients, and causing physical damage. The defendants were found guilty, but the case was appealed through the federal courts system. In 2003, the U.S. Supreme Court finally ruled that RICO could not be used against abortion clinic protesters.

In spite of the efforts made in legislation and law enforcement, the tactics of antiabortion groups have been effective in making abortions more difficult to secure. Fear of harassment—or even death—is one reason for a decline in the number of doctors seeking training or becoming approved abortion providers. Some landlords have refused to renew leases for abortion clinics through fear that their property might be damaged, and many insurance companies now place prohibitively expensive premiums on policies for abortion clinics.

Army of God and Atlanta Olympics Bombing

In 1984, a caller claiming responsibility for several clinic bombings said he was a member of the Army of God. That same year, at the site of a bombing in Norfolk, Virginia, a sign was found with the letters "AOG." Whether the Army of God is a concept or a loosely organized underground group is still not known. However, many experts on domestic terrorism are beginning to believe that it is a real terrorist group. One of the main reasons for this new thinking has been the Army of God manual that was found in 1993 during a search of the home of an antiabortionist indicted for arson attacks on several abortion clinics. The manual provides instructions on how to build ammonium nitrate bombs and the best ways to maim abortion doctors. Neal Horsley, an antiabortion militant, has a Web site where he has posted an article entitled "Understanding the Army of God." He states that "the Army of God not only will not be stopped until legalized abortion is repealed, but the Army of God will continue to grow in direct proportion to the energy this society exerts in trying to stop the growth of the Army of God."

Eric Rudolph, the man convicted in 2003 of the 1996 Olympic Park bombing, was also found guilty

KEY DATES

1973 In its *Roe v. Wade* decision, the U.S. Supreme Court legalizes abortion.

1986 Randall Terry forms the militant antiabortion group Operation Rescue.

1993 Abortion provider David Gunn is murdered at his clinic in Pensacola, Florida.

1994 President Bill Clinton signs the Freedom of Access to Clinic Entrances Act, restricting the right of antiabortion activists to intimidate abortion seekers and providers.

1996 White supremacist and antiabortion militant Eric Rudolph sets off a bomb at Olympic Park in Atlanta, killing two persons.

1998 Abortion provider Barnett Slepian is murdered at his home in Amherst, New York.

2009 George Tiller, the only late-term abortion provider in Kansas, is killed at his church in Wichita, Kansas.

of involvement in two bombings of abortion clinics in Atlanta for which the Army of God claimed responsibility. In December 2001, Clayton Lee Wagner was arrested for sending hundreds of anthrax hoax letters to abortion clinics. Many of the letters sent to the clinics were signed "Army of God." These militant activists who claim to be affiliated with the Army of God see themselves as fighting a holy war and believe they are doing God's work.

Antiabortion activists have also used the Internet to attack abortion providers. A Web site called the Nuremberg Files has been a major source of concern. The site contains wanted-style posters depicting physicians who performed abortions. It also includes detailed dossiers on many abortion providers, and doctors who were killed in antiabortion violence have a line struck through their names. Planned Parenthood, the Portland (Oregon) Feminist Women's Health Center, and four doctors sued the activists, stating that the site and posters encouraged violence against doctors and others who help provide abortions. On February 2, 1999, a federal jury ordered the antiabortion activists to pay more than $100 million in fines. The case was appealed, and on March 28, 2001, a three-judge panel of the Ninth Circuit Court of Appeals threw out the 1999 verdict and award. The appeals court ruled that offensive speech does not equal threatening speech and that the Web site was protected by the Constitution.

As for lethal violence against abortion providers, there has been a continuing spate of murders. Altogether, according to authorities, as many as eight persons connected with facilities performing abortions between 1993 and 2009—including four doctors, two clinic employees, a clinic escort, and a security guard—may have been murdered by antiabortion activists. The doctors include David Gunn of Pensacola, Florida; George Patterson of Mobile, Alabama; Barnett Slepian of Amherst, New York; and George Tiller of Wichita, Kansas, though Patterson's death may have been the result of a common robbery.

There is no way of predicting the outcome of the confrontation between the antiabortion and pro-choice forces. The commitment displayed by activists on both sides of the issue remains intense. Meanwhile, abortion rights activists warn that the continuing demonization of abortion providers—along with the publicizing of names and addresses of abortion providers by militant antiabortion rights groups—is likely to prompt individuals, especially mentally unstable ones, to commit acts of violence.

Gary Perlstein

See also: *Definitions, Types, Categories*—Right-Wing and Reactionary Terrorism. *Tactics, Methods, Aims*—Freelance, Contract, and Lone Zealot Terrorists.

Further Reading

Blanchard, Dallas A., and Terry J. Prewitt. *Religious Violence and Abortion.* Gainesville: University Press of Florida, 1993.

Doan, Alesha E. *Opposition and Intimidation: The Abortion Wars and Strategies of Political Harassment.* Ann Arbor: University of Michigan Press, 2007.

McKeegan, Michele. *Abortion Politics: Mutiny in the Ranks of the Right.* New York: Free Press, 1992.

Munson, Ziad W. *The Making of Pro-Life Activists: How Social Movement Mobilization Works.* Chicago: University of Chicago Press, 2008.

Staggenborg, Suzanne. *The Pro-Choice Movement.* New York: Oxford University Press, 1991.

Wilson, Michele, and John Lynxwiler. "Abortion Clinic Violence as Terrorism." *Terrorism* 11:4 (1988): 263–73.

United States: Aryan Nations and White Supremacists, 1970s–2000s

Some time in the 1970s, an aerospace engineer and neo-Nazi named Richard Girnt Butler founded Aryan Nations, a white supremacist hate group, in Hayden Lake, Idaho. Aryan Nations was established as the political arm of Butler's Church of Jesus Christ–Christian, a Christian Identity ministry. According to Christian Identity doctrine, white Anglo-Saxons, not Jews, are the real biblical "chosen people"; Jews are the descendants of a union between Eve and Satan, and blacks and other nonwhites are "mud people," on the same level as animals. In short, it is a belief system that provides a religious foundation for racism and anti-Semitism.

As the head of Aryan Nations, Butler advocated paramilitary training and had members wear military-style uniforms. Members of various Ku Klux Klan organizations, the Posse Comitatus, other Identity churches, and several neo-Nazi groups also became affiliated with Aryan Nations, which Butler hoped would unify the various Far Right racist groups in America.

Beginning in 1979, Aryan Nations maintained an active prison outreach program. It published a newsletter, called *The Way,* designed to maintain a connection between Aryan Nations and the prison gang Aryan Brotherhood. During the 1980s, several members of Aryan Nations formed a secret spin-off group known as the Order, or the Silent Brotherhood. Led by Robert Mathews, they tried to follow the plans for revolution described in the white supremacist novel *The Turner Diaries* (1978). The Order robbed banks and armored cars and, in 1984, murdered the Jewish talk show host and Denver attorney Alan Berg. The group's end came in December 1984, when Mathews was killed in a shootout with FBI agents and other members were imprisoned. Shortly thereafter, Aryan Nations began holding summer festivals at Hayden Lake to recruit new members. In the late 1980s and early 1990s, the World Congress of Aryan Nations offered classes on guerrilla warfare and urban terrorism and presented prominent leaders of right-wing groups as speakers.

In the late 1990s, Butler began talking about stepping down. Pastors of various other Christian Identity churches were seen as possible successors. However, a lawsuit brought by the Southern Poverty Law Center and civil rights attorney Norm Gissel on behalf of Victoria and Jason Keenan, who were assaulted by Aryan Nations security guards when they stopped their car outside the Aryan Nations compound to look for a missing wallet, forced Butler to modify his plans. The jury awarded the

---

KEY DATES

1970s White supremacist Richard Butler founds Aryan Nations as a political arm of the Church of Jesus Christ–Christian.

1979 Aryan Nations founds its prison outreach program.

1980s Members of Aryan Nations found the Order, or the Silent Brotherhood.

1984 Outspoken Denver-based Jewish radio talk show host Alan Berg is murdered by members of the Order; Richard Mathews, founder and leader of the Order, is killed in a shootout with the FBI.

2004 Butler dies, as Aryan Nations splits into three factions.

2005 John Juba, a leader of one of the Aryan Nations factions, calls for an alliance with al-Qaeda.

---

woman and her son $6.3 million. Butler filed for bankruptcy protection and designated Harold Ray Redfeairn as his successor. Redfeairn and Butler died of natural causes in 2003 and 2004, respectively.

Even before Butler's death, the Aryan Nations was in decline, as the organization split into three factions. By 2010, according to authorities, these factions had only several dozen members each and posed little threat of violence, though the leader of one faction, John Juba, gained a degree of media notoriety when he called for an al-Qaeda–Aryan Nations alliance in 2005.

Gary Perlstein

See also: *Definitions, Types, Categories*—Religious (Non-Islamist) Terrorism; Right-Wing and Reactionary Terrorism. *Modern Terrorism*—United States: Ku Klux Klan Violence; United States: Oklahoma City Bombing and the Militia Movement, 1990s; United States: Response to Terrorism Before September 11; United States: Tax Protesters.

Further Reading

Berlet, Chip, and Matthew N. Lyons. *Right-Wing Populism in America.* New York: Guilford, 2000.

Hall, Dave, Tym Burkey, and Katherine M. Ramsland. *Into the Devil's Den: How an FBI Informant Got Inside the Aryan Nations and a Special Agent Got Him out Alive.* New York: Ballantine Books, 2008.

Neiwert, David A. *In God's Country: The Patriot Movement and the Pacific Northwest.* Pullman: Washington State University Press, 1999.

United States: Black Panther Violence, 1966–1971

Two young black men, Huey P. Newton and Bobby Seale, founded the Black Panther Party in Oakland, California, in October 1966. Their ostensible aim was to protect the black community from police persecution, but by deliberately assuming an aggressive stance, their organization drifted into provocative and violent confrontation. At the height of its powers, the Black Panther Party became the leading black nationalist organization of the late 1960s. In the opinion of J. Edgar Hoover, head of the Federal Bureau of Investigation, the Panthers were "the greatest threat to the internal security of the country."

Ideals and Objectives

Newton chose the group's name because "the panther never strikes first, but when backed into a corner, he will strike back viciously." However, the Panthers' initial ten-point program went far beyond the limited objective of communal defense. In addition to adequate education, housing, and standards of justice for the African American community, they demanded black self-determination and the establishment of a black separatist state. To achieve these goals, the Black Panthers were willing to enlist the support of predominantly white groups, such as the communists. They also formed an alliance until 1969 with the radical student Weathermen organization.

Although the Panthers' eventual goal was political revolution, they did not embark on terrorist or guerrilla operations. They intended to stay within the bounds of legality until the conditions were right for revolution. However, their recruiting methods, rhetoric, and actions made confrontation inevitable. Dressed in black berets and black leather jackets and openly carrying guns, Panther members presented an aggressive and appealing image to young African Americans. They were not the first black group to take up firearms in "self-defense." In the 1950s and 1960s, armed blacks had banded together to protect themselves from the Ku Klux Klan and other white supremacists. However, most of the Panthers' recruits came from the street gangs of the urban ghettos, and this created some problems for the group. Seale, the chairman, complained of "problems with a lot of people who came in and used the Party as a base for criminal activity which the Party never endorsed or had anything to do with."

The Panthers also employed highly inflammatory language. The party newspaper, *Black Panther,* was full of provocative statements and incitements to violence, for example: "America, you will be cleansed with fire, by blood, by death. We . . . will trample your . . . ashes beneath our naked black feet; we must step up our sniping—until the last pig is dead, shot to death with his own gun and the bullets in his guts that he had meant for the people." The Panthers' chief of staff, David Hilliard, attempted to justify such statements when brought to trial on charges of advocating the assassination of President Richard Nixon. He had said, "We will kill Richard Nixon. We kill anyone . . . who stands in the way of our freedom." Hilliard maintained this was "political rhetoric. We can call it a metaphor. It is the language of the ghetto."

Violent Confrontation

The Black Panthers' policy of overtly "patrolling" the police out on the streets, while openly carrying guns, led to hazardous situations, which Newton described in his autobiography: "At times [the police] drew their guns and we drew ours, until we reached a sort of standoff. . . . I often felt that some day one of the police would go crazy and pull the trigger." Even though Newton, a university student, was well versed in the law—particularly in regard to freedom of speech—and was careful to stay within it, the atmosphere was dangerously confrontational.

From the beginning, the authorities watched the Panthers closely. Police infiltrated the organization, a task made considerably easier by the Panthers' haphazard recruiting methods. The inevitable crackdown began when local police and federal officials raided Panther offices. The Panther's use of violence also helped justify stronger measures by authorities to crack down on the organization. In 1968, Newton was involved in a shootout with the police and was wounded in the stomach; a

KEY DATES

1966 Huey Newton and Bobby Seale found the Black Panther Party in Oakland, California.

1969 Following civil unrest, police arrest nearly 750 Black Panther members across the country, killing 27 in the process, including Chicago leaders Mark Clark and Fred Hampton.

1971 Seale is arrested for inciting riots at the 1968 Democratic Convention in Chicago; his arrest effectively destroys the Panthers as a viable political organization.

policeman was killed in the exchange of fire. Newton was accused of murder but was jailed for three years for voluntary manslaughter.

By 1969, all the Black Panthers' leadership had been imprisoned or—like Eldridge Cleaver, the Panthers' minister of information—had fled the United States. The most controversial case involved the death of two Chicago Panthers, Mark Clark and Fred Hampton, killed in a police raid on their apartment on December 4, 1969. A federal grand jury heard that the Panthers had been asleep, and that during the raid, in which another seven Panthers were arrested, the police fired eighty-three shots into the apartment, while only one shot was fired at the police.

In 1971, Seale was tried for inciting a riot in Chicago, and by mid-1971, the Black Panthers had effectively fallen apart. The party was split between the exiled Cleaver, who advocated bloody revolution and guerrilla warfare, and the increasingly law-abiding Newton. Newton later admitted his policy of confrontation with the police had been ill conceived: "All we got was war and bloodshed." He said that the Panthers in the future would be ready "to operate within the system to see whether we can change it. It is wrong to say the system cannot give you anything because it is just not true."

M. Christopher Mann

See also: Definitions, Types, Categories—Left-Wing and Revolutionary Terrorism. *Modern Terrorism*—United States: Response to Terrorism Before September 11; United States: Symbionese Liberation Army Violence; United States: Weathermen Violence.

Further Reading

Andrews, Lor B. *Black Power, White Blood.* New York: Pantheon Books, 1996.

Foner, Philip S., ed. *Black Panthers Speak.* New York: Da Capo, 1995.

Newton, Huey. *War Against the Panthers: A Study of Repression in America.* New York: Writers and Readers, 1996.

United States: Ecoterrorism, 1980s–2000s

The Federal Bureau of Investigation (FBI) defines ecoterrorism "as the use or threatened use of violence of a criminal nature against victims or property by an environmentally oriented, sub-national group for environmental-political reasons, or aimed at an audience beyond the target, often of a symbolic nature." Ecoterrorism is part of what is called single-issue terrorism. It differs from traditional right-wing and left-wing terrorism in that extremist special-interest groups seek to resolve specific issues rather than effect widespread political change. Special-interest extremists continue to conduct acts of politically motivated violence to force segments of society, including the general public, to change attitudes about issues considered important to their causes.

Many mainstream environmental organizations, including the Wilderness Society, the Sierra Club, and Greenpeace, work through the established political process to protect the environment. In 1980, a new environmental group formed with a different philosophy. Founded by David Foreman, Chris Manes, Howie Wolke, and Mike Roselle, Earth First!, the best-known organization in the radical environmental movement, was born. Foreman and his colleagues had tried to work within the system but became frustrated by the lack of success by traditional conservation groups in halting nature's destruction.

The battle cry of Earth First!'s founders was "No Compromise in Defense of Mother Earth," and their tactics combined civil disobedience with direct action. Direct action, or "monkey wrenching," became their trademark. The driving of spikes into a tree in such a manner that they shatter a saw on impact and vandalizing and disabling logging equipment were the main methods. Foreman became the chief spokesperson for the group. He believed that nations could be influenced democratically, and he was strongly influenced by eco-activist Edward Abbey's *The Monkey Wrench Gang* (1975). During the late 1980s, some members who joined the movement did not share Foreman's philosophy, instead espousing a left-wing, countercultural, anarchistic philosophy.

Uncomfortable with what he saw becoming a major part of Earth First!, Foreman left the group, which became increasingly radical. Some of its members went so far as to defend Ted Kaczynski, the Unabomber, who was sentenced in 1998 to four life terms in prison for a series of mail bombings perpetrated against the "evils" of technology.

In May, two Earth First! activists were injured when the car they were driving blew up in Oakland, California. At first, the FBI and Oakland police arrested the activists themselves, claiming they were carrying the bomb to carry out a terrorist action and that it went off prematurely. But the activists were never prosecuted, and many in Earth First! and the environmental movement believed that the bomb had been planted by persons connected

The ecoterrorist group Earth Liberation Front claimed responsibility for fires causing $12 million in damage at a busy ski resort in Vail, Colorado, in October 1998. "Putting profits ahead of Colorado's wildlife will not be tolerated," said an ELF press release. *(Associated Press)*

KEY DATES

1975 Edward Abbey publishes the novel *The Monkey Wrench Gang*, inspiring environmental activists.
1980 Radical environmental activists found Earth First!.
1992 The group Earth Liberation Front (ELF) is founded in Great Britain.
1996 The American branch of the ELF commits its first act of sabotage, when it sets fire to a U.S. Forest Service truck and ranger station in Oregon.
1998 Two Earth First! activists are injured when a bomb goes off in their car in Oakland, California; the FBI says the activists were transporting the device but this is later proved to be false.
2002 The Earth First! activists injured in the 1998 Oakland car bombing are rewarded $4.4 million in a lawsuit against the FBI on civil rights violations.
2006 The FBI launches Operation Backfire to arrest and convict violent animal and environmental activists on charges of domestic terrorism.

to the timber industry, against which Earth First! was struggling to preserve old-growth forests in California. Eventually, the activists sued the FBI for violating their civil rights, and, in June 2002, a jury reached a verdict in their favor, awarding the activists $4.4 million.

Meanwhile, other radical environmental groups were forming in the 1990s. The most active of them, the Earth Liberation Front (ELF), was started in Great Britain in 1992. In 1996, the ELF announced its presence in the United States by burning a U.S. Forest Service truck and perpetrating an arson attack against the U.S. Forest Service Oakridge Ranger Station in Oregon. The ELF is organized in a decentralized manner, being made up of small cells that remain unaware of other cells' identities or plans. Since 1976, according to FBI estimates, the ELF has committed well over 100 criminal acts, resulting in

damages in the tens of millions of dollars. The group still claims that it is trying to protect life and points out that it has never killed anyone.

Ongoing FBI investigations into the activities of ecoterrorist groups have led to indictments against at least thirty individuals since 2005. In 2006, the FBI launched Operation Backfire, an attempt to put ecoterrorists connected with the Animal Liberation Front and the ELF in jail. As a result, eleven members of the groups were arrested on charges of domestic terrorism. Two years later, activist Eric McDavid was convicted of perpetrating attacks on a fish hatchery, dam, power station, and cell phone towers, and received a twenty-year prison sentence. Despite stepped-up efforts by law enforcement, experts say, more violence on the part of ecoterrorist groups is expected. Continued development and environmental degradation, it is suggested, will almost inevitably spur to violence those who believe extreme measures are necessary and justified to save the planet from human impact.

Gary Perlstein

See also: *Definitions, Types, Categories*—Left-Wing and Revolutionary Terrorism. *Modern Terrorism*—United States: Animal Rights; United States: Response to Terrorism Before September 11.

Further Reading

Abbey, Edward. *The Monkey Wrench Gang.* Philadelphia: Lippincott, 1975.

Foreman, Dave. *Confessions of an Eco-Warrior.* Nevada City, CA: Harmony Books, 1991.

Liddick, Donald R. *Eco-Terrorism: Radical Environmental and Animal Liberation Movements.* Westport, CT: Praeger, 2006.

Manes, Christopher. *Green Rage.* Boston: Little, Brown, 1990.

Miller, Joseph A., and R.M. Miller. *Eco-Terrorism, Eco-Extremism Against Agriculture.* Chicago: Joseph A. Miller, 2000.

United States: Ku Klux Klan Violence, 1860s–1990s

Founded in Pulaski, Tennessee, in 1865, the Ku Klux Klan (KKK) began as a secret society for former Confederate officers but soon became a widely feared terrorist organization. Although its membership and influence have experienced repeated rises and falls, the Klan survives to this day as one of the most extreme exponents of American racism, though it is no longer a centralized organization but a collection of individual groups sharing a common name.

First Wave of Terrorism

The term "Ku Klux" derives from the Greek kyklos—drinking cup—suggesting that the Klan founders were both educated and intent on having a good time. But the post–Civil War South that spawned this secret club was populated by impoverished laborers and landless cotton planters. The Thirteenth Amendment, ratified in 1865, abolished plentiful and cheap slave labor, and the freedmen, or ex-slaves, were to bear the brunt of white southern recriminations.

The KKK took violent action against government officials and freedmen, who together threatened the supreme status of whites in the southern states. Killings, beatings, lynchings, arson, and other terrorist attacks became common. By 1871, the KKK had attained considerable power in the South, attracting middle-class whites whom the Civil War had left poor and powerless. Riding at night, Klan members bedecked in white robes, masks, and hats intimidated juries, freed prisoners, and attacked officials who encouraged freedmen to vote.

The outrages compelled Congress to intervene. In 1870 and 1871, it passed a series of Force Acts, giving the president power to quash civil disturbances and to prosecute terrorist groups. Indictments under the Force Acts disrupted the formal KKK organization. After 1872, however, new legislation at the state level institutionalized southern white supremacy. The KKK was quiet for the next forty years, its aims satisfied.

In 1915, however, D.W. Griffith's epic motion picture *Birth of a Nation* was released. Glorifying the Old South and the Klan, it revived southerners' fears of black equality and aroused northerners' anxieties over large-scale black migration northward. The film helped trigger a massive revival of the KKK.

After 1920, Klan membership soared as white Protestants reacted against the effects of Jewish and Catholic, especially Slavic, immigration. Economic factors played a part. The immigrants would work for lower wages, and wealthy factory owners such as Henry Ford eagerly hired the cheaper labor. The Klan became a legitimate pressure group with a peak membership of 5 million by 1925. Its appeal to the traditional values of patriotism, morality, and virtue brought it political success. The KKK helped elect eleven state governors and ten congressmen, and in 1924 it split the Democratic presidential convention, mainly because the Catholic Al Smith was a strong contender.

In addition to this legal activity, KKK terrorism continued in the southern states. Klansmen tarred and feathered, tortured, and lynched blacks suspected of being involved with white women. Prosperous African Americans and immigrants who jeopardized white economic power found their businesses burned and their possessions stolen. The KKK's administration tacitly supported such acts of vigilantism, maintaining that they embodied the popular will of the citizens.

This second period of KKK activity came to an abrupt end in 1925 with the imprisonment of Indiana Grand Dragon D.C. Stephenson, who was convicted of second-degree murder. Revelations regarding the Klan's fostering of terrorism and corruption surfaced during and after the trial. The nation was so appalled that this incarnation of the KKK was effectively finished as a political force by 1927.

The KKK experienced a renaissance after World War II, when African Americans migrated to the North in search of work. Federal civil rights legislation, coupled with renewed fears of communist subversion, helped fuel white paranoia and hatred. In the 1960s, the Klan's popularity grew in response to efforts by the government, the Supreme Court, and civil rights workers to attack decades of legal segregation in the South. Many bombings and murders were attributed to the KKK during this period. Mississippi was the focus of renewed Klan violence as civil rights groups targeted the state in their voting rights drives of the midsixties. Between 1964 and 1969, led by Grand Wizard Samuel Holloway Bowers, the Mississippi KKK was allegedly responsible for 9 murders, 75 bombings of black churches, and 300 beatings. The most infamous event in Mississippi occurred in 1964, when three student civil rights workers were murdered. Although the FBI investigated Klan activities, the collusion of the local police with the KKK hindered the bureau's progress.

The KKK murder of Viola Luzzo, a white civil rights worker, in Alabama in 1965 finally prompted a government crackdown. Investigations by Congress exposed gross misappropriation of KKK funds by Klan leaders.

The revelations helped reduce the influence of the KKK leadership and, in concert with heightened FBI surveillance, its ability to pursue terrorist activities.

New Extremists

The KKK burst back onto the scene in the 1970s under the charismatic leadership of David Duke. However, the reborn KKK was factious, and by 1975, a new leader had emerged in the shape of Bill Wilkinson, the most influential KKK leader for the next decade. Adopting a policy of inflaming racial tension wherever there was a spark of friction, Wilkinson pursued an increasingly militant stance by organizing KKK chapters in the American armed services and by recruiting retired servicemen.

In North Carolina in November 1979, two carloads of white men ambushed a "Death to the Klan" march. They shot dead four demonstrators and wounded eight. Klan members were later arrested and charged but were acquitted by a local all-white jury. Also acquitted was a Tennessee KKK member who shot and wounded four African Americans in 1980.

In 1982, it was revealed that the KKK was operating a paramilitary camp in Texas. Vietnam War veterans and other retired servicemen were instructing Klansmen in guerrilla warfare and the use of explosives and sophisticated weapons. A judge closed the camp down after trainees threatened to turn their weapons on nearby immigrant communities. Other such camps, however, are known to exist.

By the late 1980s, the KKK had begun to work in earnest on its public image. It needed to garner public sympathy for its cause, yet avoid surveillance by federal authorities. To evade prosecution, the KKK leadership have taken pains to deny involvement in terrorist activities. However, the rhetoric of its leaders has remained violent and inflammatory. Furthermore, KKK members have been linked directly to a number of violent terrorist acts that, it is believed, could never have occurred without the approval of Klan leaders.

The KKK's membership dwindled to a few thousand during the early 1990s, and its violent acts became less frequent. Public condemnation and ubiquitous media coverage have made it difficult for extremist groups to sustain a national infrastructure. As an alternative, many Klan members have been drawn to the white supremacist Aryan Nations, to right-wing militias, and to neo-Nazi activists.

However, the outbreak of arson attacks on African American churches in southern states in 1996 showed that the capacity of racist terrorists for violence was still as strong as ever. The FBI failed to identify an organized conspiracy behind the attacks, with alleged culprits ranging from teenage delinquents to pyromaniacs. Nonetheless, it attributed some of the attacks to Aryan Nations and to the Christian Knights, a KKK subgroup founded in 1985.

The challenge to the authorities may lie not so much in indicting the racist groups themselves as in a more insidious threat. In the words of Jesse Jackson, "The Klan is the extreme expression of a deeper trend, of a white America that is targeting blacks as scapegoats." Therefore, the Ku Klux Klan and other pro-white groups are still greatly feared and continue to be monitored by the government and by various civil rights groups.

Still, while feared, the Klan has been much diminished since the 1990s and the government crackdown against right-wing extremist groups in the wake of the 1995 Oklahoma City bombing. Further crippling the group was a lawsuit, settled in 2008, brought by a black man beaten by Klansmen in Kentucky. In that case, the jury awarded the plaintiff $2.5 million in damages against the Imperial Klans of America, an offshoot group of the KKK. By 2010, the KKK had effectively ceased to exist as a centralized organization, though experts say there are more than 100 independent chapters around the United States, with a collective membership of perhaps 5,000–10,000.

Allison J. Gough

See also: *Definitions, Types, Categories*—Right-Wing and Reactionary Terrorism. *Modern Terrorism*—United States: Aryan Nations and White Supremacists; United States: Response to Terrorism Before September 11.

Further Reading

Chalmers, David M. *Hooded Americanism: A History of the Ku Klux Klan.* Rev. ed. New York: Franklin Watts, 1981.

Maclean, Nancy. *Behind the Mask of Chivalry: The Making of the Second Ku Klux Klan.* New York: Oxford University Press, 1994.

Rice, Arnold S. *The Ku Klux Klan in American Politics.* Washington, DC: Public Affairs, 1962.

Wade, Wyn Craig. *The Fiery Cross: The Ku Klux Klan in America.* New York: Simon and Schuster, 1987.

United States: Millennium Bomb Plot, 1999

On December 14, 1999, Ahmed Ressam, an Algerian, arrived in Port Angeles, Washington, by ferry from Victoria, British Columbia. As he was going through customs, an alert customs agent became suspicious and began to search his car. Ressam tried to run away, but he was caught after a short chase. The search uncovered explosives and bomb-making materials hidden in the trunk of his car. He was placed under arrest.

Investigators soon realized that they had uncovered a conspiracy. Ressam was not working alone. He, along with several coconspirators, was planning to bomb buildings and facilities on both coasts of the United States and disrupt the 2000 millennium celebrations. The investigation led to the arrests of Mokhtar Haouari and Abdelghani Meskini, who had close ties to Ressam. Abdelmajid Dahoumane was also indicted for assisting Ressam in the assembly of some explosive material. He escaped to Algeria and was arrested by Algerian security forces in March 2001. He was convicted of terrorism-related charges there. Ressam's targets were supposed to be Seattle's Space Needle and the crowded Los Angeles International Airport. The Philadelphia Mint was a target of the East Coast co-conspirators.

The well-planned plot was linked to several major international terrorist groups. Ahmed Ressam had been trained by the Algerian Armed Islamic Group, an Islamic fundamentalist organization that has claimed responsibility for a series of bombings in France over the years. In 1996, they attempted to bomb the G7 ministers' meeting in Belgium. According to Ressam's testimony, he received training in Afghanistan at a terrorist camp run by Osama bin Laden's al-Qaeda organization. He stated that the planning for the millennium bombings began at this camp. Apparently, bin Laden was involved in the planning of this attempted act of terrorism in the United States. Ressam also testified that there were other terrorist

groups planning to attack U.S. interests in Europe. These plots were also timed to the millennium rollover.

Ressam was convicted and sentenced to 130 years in prison. However, he then agreed that, in exchange for a recommendation of leniency, he would testify in any trial to which the government calls him as a witness, and his sentence was reduced to 22 years. Prosecutors plan to use him when captured leaders of al-Qaeda are put on trial.

Gary Perlstein

See also: *Definitions, Types, Categories*—Islamist Fundamentalist Terrorism. *Modern Terrorism*—Canada: International Terrorism; United States: Response to Terrorism Before September 11.

Further Reading

Bergen, Peter L. *Holy War, Inc.: Inside the Secret World of Osama Bin Laden.* New York: Free Press, 2001.
Rashid, Ahmed. *Militant Islam in Central Asia.* New Haven, CT: Yale University Press, 2002.

KEY DATES

December 14, 1999   U.S. Customs officials arrest Algerian national Ahmed Ressam in Port Angeles, Washington, after they find explosives and bomb-making materials in the trunk of his car; Ressam is alleged to have conspired to set off bombs at Los Angeles International Airport on January 1, 2000.

April 6, 2001   Ressam is convicted in federal court of terrorism, weapons, and other charges.

July 27, 2005   After cooperating with federal authorities in their investigation of other Islamist terrorists, Ressam is sentenced to twenty-two years in prison.

United States: Oklahoma City Bombing and the Militia Movement, 1990s

At 9:02 A.M. on April 19, 1995, a rented truck parked outside the Alfred P. Murrah federal building in Oklahoma City exploded with the force of 4,800 pounds of explosives. The blast ripped into the federal building, bringing down several floors and burying hundreds of victims beneath tons of rubble. Rescue workers spent days sifting through the debris in search of victims who may have been trapped. The bombing killed 169 people and injured more than 500. The horror grew worse when it was realized that many of the victims were children who had been in the day-care center on the second floor of the building. This incident was the deadliest terrorist attack to be perpetrated on U.S. soil and the first such incident to occur in America's heartland. The nation was shocked and horrified.

Less than two hours after the explosion, a highway patrolman stopped a speeding 1977 Mercury near Perry, Oklahoma. The driver had a concealed weapon and was taken into custody. Police were about to release him when an eyewitness description of the man who rented the truck used in the bombing reached the highway patrol station. The police discovered that they held the leading suspect in the Oklahoma City bombing. Contrary to immediate assumptions, the chief suspect was not an emissary of a Middle Eastern terrorist group but instead was an American citizen. His name was Timothy McVeigh, and the authorities later charged him with the bombing. They also charged Terry Nichols, a longtime friend of McVeigh's, with helping mix fertilizer with fuel oil to make the bomb. Michael Fortier, another of McVeigh's friends, pleaded guilty to charges of transporting stolen guns, lying to the FBI, and failing to warn authorities about the bomb plot. Prosecutors used his testimony against McVeigh.

McVeigh's and Nichols's actions added to a lengthy, but often overlooked, tradition of American terrorism originating on its own shores. It has included the activities of the Molly Maguires in the 1870s and the Black Panther Party, the Weathermen, and the Symbionese Liberation Army during the 1960s and 1970s.

Timothy McVeigh

McVeigh's background was quite ordinary. He was born on April 23, 1968, in Pendleton, New York, completed high school, and attended a community college for a short time before dropping out. He enlisted in the U.S. Army in 1988, served in the Persian Gulf War, was awarded the Bronze Star, and was honorably discharged

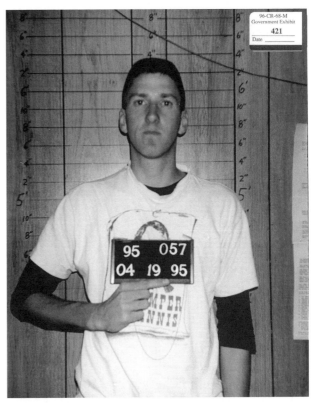

Timothy McVeigh, convicted and executed for the truck bombing of the Alfred P. Murrah Federal Building in Oklahoma City on April 19, 1995—the deadliest act of domestic terrorism in U.S. history—had strong ties with the right-wing militia movement. *(Associated Press)*

in 1991. After the war, he went back to Pendleton and worked as a security guard. In 1993 he began to travel. He visited with two army buddies, Terry Nichols in Michigan and Michael Fortier in Arizona. He also traveled to Waco, Texas, during the standoff between the Branch Davidians and federal authorities. He had no affiliations with any extremist groups.

When police arrested McVeigh, their investigation revealed him to be a twenty-seven-year-old drifter with an honorable military background. However, as police accumulated more information about him and his friends and associates, a different picture began to emerge. McVeigh was an individual who had been outraged by the federal government siege of the Branch Davidian compound at Waco, Texas, which ended on April 19, 1993. He believed this to be just one more example of U.S. government interference in the lives of its citizens. He also appeared to have an association with the Michigan Militia, an organization with loose ties to other militias around the United States, as well as other groups that can be placed in a category called the radical right wing.

Paranoid Right

The militias have existed for more than twenty-five years and have a heritage that goes back to the anti-immigrant, or nativist, movements of the middle of the nineteenth century and the Populist Party political campaigns of the 1880s and 1890s. The militias are just the most recent manifestation. The groups have various names, such as the Klan; Posse Comitatus (Latin for "power of a county"); the American Nazi Party; the Covenant, the Sword, and the Arm of the Lord; Aryan Nations; the Church of Jesus Christ–Christian; the Minutemen; and the Order. The groups are not united, and members sometimes move from one organization to another. However, the groups usually share similar beliefs about religion and about a government conspiracy against the citizens of the United States.

The unifying religious force behind these paramilitary antigovernment groups is the Christian Identity movement. Founded by Richard G. Butler in the 1970s, Christian Identity did not receive much attention until the 1980s, when representatives of several right-wing, extremist groups began having annual meetings at Hayden Lake, Idaho. Christian Identity is a mixture of anticommunism, anti-Semitism, and racism. These are combined with an eccentric school of thought known as British Israelism, which holds that Anglo-Saxons are God's true chosen people. Members of Christian Identity believe that Jews are the children of Satan, that Jesus was not Jewish but an Aryan, and that the majority of true Israelites migrated from the Middle East to Western Europe in the sixth century B.C.E. The United States, to members of Christian Identity, is the promised land.

There are many Christian Identity churches in various parts of the United States, but the most well-known is the Church of Jesus Christ–Christian of Aryan Nations located near Hayden Lake. The theology of Christian Identity also drives the political behavior of many right-wing groups.

Such organizations often believe in economic conspiracy theories. One example is the belief that national and international forces, led by Jewish financiers, are responsible for the hardship and economic depression in rural America. Radical right-wingers also reject the policies and authority of the federal government. They refer to it as the Zionist Occupational Government and see it as controlled by Jews, African Americans, or the United Nations. Many right-wingers also emphasize survivalism, the idea of living self-sufficiently after some breakdown of society such as the aftermath of a nuclear war. This will ensure that they are prepared for the race war they expect to occur and that they are protected against the international conspiracy.

While it is true that many members of the militias and other members of radical right-wing organizations do not advocate the use of violence against the government, the 1980s witnessed several incidents in which members of paramilitary groups had confrontations with federal law enforcement agencies.

Violence and the Radical Right Wing

The first incident concerned Gordon Kahl, a North Dakota farmer, who was a Christian Identity believer and a member of the Posse Comitatus movement. Posse Comitatus was founded in 1969 by Henry L. Beach, who in the 1930s was a member of a pro-Nazi movement. It held that the only legitimate government was at the county level and that the county sheriff should be the highest government official. Beach also proposed punishing any official who committed criminal acts or violated his or her oath of office with a public hanging at a busy intersection.

Posse Comitatus's main objection has always been to income tax and the Federal Reserve Bank. Its members have had many conflicts with the federal government over taxes and weapons. Kahl had stopped paying taxes in 1967 and later organized a Posse chapter. He was involved in setting up a shadow government composed of heavily armed men who would preserve order when the U.S. government collapsed. In 1983, federal marshals came to his home. He shot them dead and fled to Arkansas, where, later that same year, FBI agents tracked him down. In the ensuing shootout, Kahl was killed.

The next incident also began in 1983, when Robert Mathews founded the organization most commonly referred to as the Order. The Order was formed to overthrow the so-called Zionist conspiracy in the United States. Members financed the Order through counterfeiting and armored-car robberies during the 1980s. They also murdered Alan Berg, a Jewish radio talk show host known for his liberal politics and hostility to right-wing views, in Denver on June 18, 1984.

With the help of informants, the FBI located Mathews on Whidbey Island, Washington, and killed him in the ensuing shootout on December 8, 1984. The authorities also arrested other members of the Order, convicting those who refused plea bargains. There is evidence that Mathews read and used information from the novel *The Turner Diaries,* written by William Pierce, using the pseudonym Andrew Macdonald, as a terrorist blueprint.

The last major confrontation of the 1980s occurred on April 20, 1985, when agents of the Bureau of Alcohol, Tobacco, and Firearms (ATF) raided the paramilitary compound of the Covenant, the Sword, and the Arm of the Lord located in northern Arkansas. The members of this group believed that a race war was soon to come, and they had trained their members and other right-wingers in guerrilla warfare. After two days of negotiations, the Covenant, the Sword, and the Arm of the Lord members surrendered to the federal authorities. Police arrested their leader, James Ellison, and secured his conviction for arson and the manufacture of automatic weapons.

Ruby Ridge

Friends and associates of Timothy McVeigh told reporters and government investigators that two confrontations between federal law enforcement agents and extremist paramilitaries, in 1992 and 1993, put him on the path to terrorism. The first incident, in August 1992, occurred when U.S. marshals attempted to serve a warrant on Randy Weaver for illegally trying to sell sawed-off shotguns to federal agents. Weaver and his family were followers of Christian Identity and lived at Ruby Ridge in rural Idaho. Since the federal marshals knew that Weaver was heavily armed, they arrived in force. A standoff developed, and during the first two days a deputy federal marshal and Weaver's wife and son were killed. The standoff ended after eleven days when the FBI permitted former Green Beret Lieutenant-Colonel James "Bo" Gritz to mediate. Right-wingers respected Gritz because of his record during the Vietnam War. Weaver and a friend surrendered after Gritz's intervention. A federal case was brought against them for the murder of the federal marshals and the original firearms violation. The jury convicted them of the firearms charge but acquitted them of murder.

Weaver's acquittal did not end the case. The Department of Justice and the Senate both investigated the FBI agents' tactics during the siege. The reports directed severe criticism at the behavior of the FBI Hostage Rescue Unit and the rules of engagement used by agents. Right-wingers saw the Weaver incident as another example of the continuing invasion of their private lives by the federal government.

Waco Siege

The second incident occurred on February 28, 1993, in Waco, Texas. ATF agents attempted to serve search and arrest warrants on the Branch Davidian leader, David Koresh. The Davidians, forewarned of the raid, opened fire, killing four agents and wounding twenty, while suffering seven casualties of their own, three fatal. The FBI took control of the situation on March 1 after the ATF requested their assistance. Negotiations that ensued during the fifty-one-day standoff resulted in thirty-five people leaving the compound. On April 19, 1993, however, the FBI decided that the siege should end and fired CS gas (a riot control agent) into the compound. It was the start of an assault that included tanks. The explod-ing gas canisters started a fire that destroyed the buildings and killed almost eighty people, including David Koresh and many children.

The violence of the Waco incident, and the fact that millions of people around the world saw film of it on television, led to two separate investigations into the handling of the confrontation. Both the Department of the Treasury and the Department of Justice issued reports. These, and various statements by the authorities about millenarian beliefs, provide some understanding of what happened. Apparently, the authorities regarded the Branch Davidians as a cult holding hostages, who needed rescuing. There is little evidence that they believed that Koresh and his followers genuinely thought themselves to be fighting against an evil regime.

While the Branch Davidians were not a Christian Identity group, right-wingers regarded the actions of federal law enforcement agencies as just another example of the government's tyrannical trampling over the liberties of American citizens. That the event took place on April 19, the date on which the American Revolution began in an exchange of fire between Redcoats and Minutemen in Lexington, Massachusetts, in 1775, gave it even greater significance in the minds of these extremists.

At some point after Waco, the planning of the Oklahoma City bombing began. McVeigh traveled to Kansas and Michigan and also made a trip to the ruins of the Branch Davidian compound at Waco. On April 14, 1995, McVeigh checked into a motel in Junction City, Kansas. On April 16, he called Terry Nichols from Oklahoma City and asked him to pick him up. Nichols drove down from Herington, Kansas, and collected McVeigh. The next day, McVeigh rented a truck from a Ryder lot in Junction City. The last sighting of McVeigh before the bombing was at 4 A.M. on the morning of April 18, sitting in the Ryder truck.

Trial of McVeigh and Nichols

In March 1996, U.S. District Court Judge Richard Matsch moved the trial of McVeigh and Nichols to Denver, ruling that the constitutional rights of the defendants to a fair trial could not be observed in Oklahoma. Attorneys for both the government and the accused filed numerous motions, and these delayed the proceedings. Once the trial started, Matsch kept court proceedings under tight control. He banned cameras from the courtroom and narrowly limited the scope of comments by attorneys outside the courtroom. The evidence against McVeigh was circumstantial, but when added up, there was enough to convict him. Among the most damaging bits of testimony presented at the trial was the fact that he had made a fake driver's license in the name of Bob Kling, the same name used to rent the Ryder truck that destroyed the Murrah Federal Building. McVeigh's fingerprints were also found on the receipt for 2,000 pounds of ammonium nitrate, an ingredient used in the bomb. In addition, his sister testified about his hatred for the government following the 1993 siege of the Branch Davidians and the deaths of eighty of its members. Finally, his former army buddy Michael Fortier testified about how McVeigh had made a model of the bomb.

On June 13, 1997, the jury found him guilty and sentenced him to death by lethal injection. Matsch formally sentenced him on August 14. Terry Nichols was convicted of being a coconspirator and sentenced to life in prison. Michael Fortier, who testified for the government, was given a twelve-year sentence for having prior knowledge of the bombing plot.

While awaiting execution, McVeigh said he was sorry the people had to lose their lives, but the blame rested on the U.S. government and the way it bullies its citizens. The bombing, he said, was revenge for the government raids at Ruby Ridge, Idaho, and Waco, Texas. McVeigh was executed on June 11, 2001.

Consequences of the Bombing

After the World Trade Center bombing in 1993, the Clinton Administration proposed an Omnibus Counterterrorism bill. It was only after Oklahoma City, however, that the bill started getting serious attention from legislators. The bill increased penalties for terrorist crimes, including a mandatory death penalty for terrorist murders. The FBI has kept a closer watch on militias and other right-wing groups, but there is disagreement about the guidelines under which the bureau must operate. Criticism of the FBI's harassment of civil rights groups during the 1960s and early 1970s has left the bureau cautious in its political surveillance.

Meanwhile, the Far Right did not go into hiding after Oklahoma City. A standoff between federal law enforcement agents and a group called the Freemen at a compound near the town of Jordan, Montana, began in March 1996. The Freemen, like other similar groups, believe that the federal government is illegal. The authorities have charged the group with writing fraudulent checks and money orders in a federal grand jury indictment. Law enforcement officials, mindful of the fateful consequences of the confrontations at Ruby Ridge and Waco, avoided an assault on the Freemen compound, which was occupied by heavily armed defenders. While tensions between right-wingers and the federal government remained high for several years, they began to ease in the early 2000s, a development experts attribute to increased government surveillance and prosecution of movement members, the inauguration of conservative president George W. Bush in January 2001, and the terrorist bombings of September 11, which undermined support for violent antigovernment actions. Later in the

---

KEY DATES

April 1985   Agents of the Bureau of Alcohol, Tobacco, and Firearms (ATF) raid the paramilitary compound of the Covenant, the Sword, and the Arm of the Lord in Arkansas.

August 1992   U.S. Marshals attempt to serve a warrant on right-wing extremist Randy Weaver at Ruby Ridge, Idaho, triggering a standoff and the deaths of Weaver's son and wife.

April 19, 1993   After a fifty-one-day standoff, ATF agents attempt to storm the Branch Davidian compound in Waco, Texas, setting off a fire that kills nearly eighty persons inside.

April 19, 1995   A bomb-laden truck detonates outside the Alfred P. Murrah Federal Building in Oklahoma City, killing 169 persons and injuring more than 500 others.

July 13, 1997   Army veteran and right-wing militia member Timothy McVeigh is convicted of carrying out the Oklahoma City bombing of 1995 and sentenced to death.

December 24, 1997   Militia member Terry Nichols is convicted of conspiring with McVeigh to use a weapon of mass destruction; he is eventually sentenced to life imprisonment without the possibility of parole.

June 11, 2001   McVeigh is executed at the Federal Prison in Terre Haute, Indiana.

---

decade, however, with the financial crisis and economic recession of 2006–2009 and the inauguration of a black president, membership in radical right-wing organizations was reported to be increasing rapidly.

Gary R. Perlstein

See also: *Definitions, Types, Categories*—Right-Wing and Reactionary Terrorism. *Modern Terrorism*—United States: Aryan Nations and White Supremacists; United States: Response to Terrorism Before September 11. *Tactics, Methods, Aims*—Weapons, Conventional.

Further Reading

Aho, James A. *The Politics of Righteousness: Idaho Christian Patriotism.* Seattle: University of Washington Press, 1990.

Barkun, Michael. "Millenarian Groups and Law Enforcement Agencies: The Lessons of Waco." *Terrorism and Political Violence* 6:1 (Spring 1994): 75–95.

Corcoran, James. *Bitter Harvest: Gordon Kahl and the Posse Comitatus—Murder in the Heartland.* New York: Viking, 1990.

Flynn, Kevin, and Gary Gerhardt. *The Silent Brotherhood: Inside America's Racist Underground.* New York: Free Press, 1989.

Jones, Stephen, and Peter Israel. *Others Unknown: Timothy McVeigh and the Oklahoma City Bombing Conspiracy.* Washington, DC: Public Affairs, 2001.

Michel, Lou, and Dan Herbeck. *American Terrorist: Timothy McVeigh and the Oklahoma City Bombing.* New York: Regan Books, 2001.

United States: Puerto Rican Separatism, 1950s–1980s

The United States invaded the Caribbean island of Puerto Rico in 1898, during the Spanish-American War, and established a colony there. Since 1952, Puerto Rico has been an associated free state of the United States. While many Puerto Ricans welcome the fact that their country is a possession of the United States, there is a powerful movement for independent status. A minority engages in sporadic acts of terrorism, both on the island itself and on the U.S. mainland, in order to achieve their goal of independence.

"Free Puerto Rico"

There has always been a nationalist resistance to the U.S. presence in Puerto Rico, and occasionally this has exploded into violence. In 1954, the nationalists staged an uprising that was put down by troops, tanks, and aircraft. The town of Jayuya, held briefly by the nationalists, was bombed, and there were allegations of massacres in the streets of Utuando. At the same time, seeking to bring the plight of Puerto Rico to world attention, two Puerto Rican nationalists, Oscar Collazo and Griselio Torresola, attempted to assassinate President Harry S. Truman. Torresola and a presidential guard were killed. Collazo was jailed for twenty-nine years.

Many nationalists saw the establishment of the associated free state in 1952 as a disguise for the continuing colonization of the island. In 1954, four Puerto Rican nationalists, shouting "Free Puerto Rico," sprayed bullets from the gallery of the U.S. House of Representatives, injuring five congressmen. Although no one was killed, Rafael Cancel Miranda, Andres Figueroa Cordero, and Irvin Flores received sentences totaling seventy-five years, while Lolita Lebron was sentenced to fifty years. All four were released in 1979.

A new wave of nationalist terrorism erupted during the late 1960s, with bombings aimed at U.S. businesses and military installations across the island. These were the work of a group called Armed Freedom Fighters, which was backed by Cuba. In 1975, two people were killed and eleven were injured when a bomb exploded in the town of Mayaguez, just minutes before the start of a socialist party rally. Two weeks later, terrorism spread to mainland America, when a bomb exploded at New York's historic Fraunces Tavern. Four were killed and forty-five were injured.

A new organization called the Armed Forces of National Liberation (FALN) claimed responsibility for this attack. Founded in 1974, the group was headed by Chicago-born

Puerto Ricans William Morales and Luis Rosado Ayala. The group has claimed responsibility for more than 100 bombings, including 30 in New York and others in Chicago, San Francisco, and Washington, DC. These attacks have claimed the lives of six people, injured many more, and caused more than $3.5 million in damages.

In 1979, Morales lost an eye, one hand, and all but two of his fingers on the other in an explosion at the FALN's bomb factory in Queens, New York. He was imprisoned but escaped while being treated in a hospital. Eleven other members of the FALN were indicted for bombings in Chicago, including the group's leader, Carlos Torres, who was on the Federal Bureau of Investigation's (FBI's) most-wanted list.

Other groups, however, continued the struggle. In 1978, a nonviolent protester named Angel Rodriguez was murdered while serving time in a federal prison in Tallahassee, Florida. The guards were suspected, but no one was arrested. In response, on December 9, 1979, a group calling themselves Los Macheteros (the Cane Cutters or Machete Wielders) attacked a navy bus, killing two sailors.

During the 1980 U.S. presidential elections, Puerto Rican nationalists seized the headquarters of the Carter and Bush campaigns in several U.S. cities, holding staff hostage. On December 21, 1980, a group calling itself the Puerto Rican Armed Resistance set off two pipe bombs in Penn Station, New York City. No one was injured.

On January 12, 1981, Los Macheteros blew up nine military jet fighters and damaged two more at the Muñiz air base on Puerto Rico. On November 28, they blew up a power station in the Puerto Rican capital, San Juan, blacking out part of the island. On May 16, 1982, terrorists attacked American sailors returning to the ship after a night of shore liberty in San Juan, killing one and badly injuring three others. The FALN, inactive for two years, set off a bomb on Wall Street on February 28, 1982.

On September 16, 1983, Los Macheteros stole $7.2 million from the Wells Fargo terminal in Hartford, Connecticut. The raid, although a lucrative venture for Los Macheteros, gave the FBI enough evidence to arrest a number of the terrorist group's leaders. In August 1985, the authorities also arrested several prominent members of the FALN; since then, both groups have been relatively quiet.

Periodically, there are moves within Congress to hold referenda in Puerto Rico on its future status, whether as the fifty-first state of the United States or as a fully independent country. It remains to be seen whether the outcome of such a referendum will finally put to rest the specter of terrorism that has haunted this island.

Nigel Cawthorne

See also: *Definitions, Types, Categories*—Ethnonationalist Terrorism; Left-Wing and Revolutionary Terrorism. *Modern Terrorism*—United States: Response to Terrorism Before September 11.

Further Reading

Fernandez, Ronald. *Puerto Rico: The Disenchanted Island.* New York: Praeger, 1992.
Jiménez de Wagenheim, Olga. *Puerto Rico's Revolt for Independence.* Boulder, CO: Westview, 1985.

United States: Response to Terrorism Before September 11: 1960s–2001

Like other modern industrialized nations, the United States was forced in the latter part of the twentieth century to confront terrorist threats with a combination of tactics. These included a legal framework defining terrorism, as well as diplomacy, intelligence gathering, intensified security measures, and the use of force.

An estimated two-thirds of all victims of terrorist actions worldwide at that time were Americans, and most of them were attacked outside the United States. According to the State Department, 162 lethal attacks occurred abroad between 1973 and 1986, claiming 440 American lives.

During the Cold War, the U.S. preoccupation with international terrorism focused primarily on radical left-wing insurgent groups that sought to overthrow anticommunist regimes friendly to the United States. Beginning with the Kennedy Administration in 1961, the United States developed counterinsurgency policies to combat communist or communist-inspired guerrillas. However, the U.S. interest in the terrorist aspect of such campaigns was limited. In Vietnam, for example, successive U.S. administrations expected the South Vietnamese government to undertake police actions to deal with terrorist incidents.

The same was true in Latin America, where U.S. support for friendly regimes in the 1960s and 1970s involved help and training. The U.S. forces themselves were rarely involved in specific antiterrorist activity.

New Terror Groups

The U.S. perception of a terrorist threat as distinct from an insurgency threat began to emerge in the late 1960s. A major background factor was the worldwide spate of anti–Vietnam War demonstrations and the emergence of anticapitalist terrorist organizations such as Germany's Baader-Meinhof Gang. At about the same time, radical Palestinian groups began to undertake terrorist activities.

The violent tactics of these militant groups differed from guerrilla and insurgency tactics mainly in that they had no military or paramilitary objectives. Their aim was purely psychological—to intimidate governing authorities and their constituencies through the use of terror. The United States, faced with what it defined as nonmilitary political violence that was international in scope, radical in ideology, and carried out by groups organized in small cells, had to develop its antiterrorist methods almost from scratch.

In this period, numerous terrorist incidents did occur within the United States. The anti-establishment Weathermen (later known as the Weather Underground), founded in 1969, carried out some thirty bombings. Nationalist groups such as the Armed Forces of National Liberation (Puerto Rico) and the anti-Castro Cuban group Omega 7 were still bombing and murdering on U.S. soil in the 1980s. These attacks, however, were generally viewed not as terrorism, but instead as straightforward criminal behavior, which U.S. federal, state, and local law enforcement agencies had the primary responsibility for tackling. As a result, the prevalent view in the United States was that terrorism as such was an international, not a domestic, threat.

In contrast, most other countries were primarily concerned about terrorism as a domestic problem, rather than as an international one, regardless of the nationality of the victim. An attack on American citizens in a third country, for example, while considered an international incident in the United States, would be considered an internal problem in the country in which it occurred. This difference of perspective constituted the greatest challenge to U.S. diplomacy in seeking a multinational, cooperative approach to countering international terrorism.

Facing Up to the Problem

The creation of modern U.S. counterterrorism policy stemmed neither from the Cold War nor even from an incident involving Americans or American property. Instead, it was a result of the kidnapping and massacre of Israeli athletes at the Munich Olympics by Palestinian terrorists in September 1972. The terrorists were members of the Black September Organization, the paramilitary wing of Yasir Arafat's Fatah organization. The West Germans badly bungled the rescue operations, and as the entire world watched in horror on television, nine Israelis were killed, another two having been killed earlier.

Not only did the incident leave the world in shock—a major triumph from the terrorists' point of view—but it caused the major world powers to review their capabilities and the organizational structures available to cope with similar situations. Following the attack, President Nixon established a cabinet-level committee chaired by the secretary of state to coordinate U.S. efforts in countering terrorism. The president delegated responsibility for coordinating responses to incidents occurring within the United States to the Federal Bureau of Investigation (FBI). Responsibility for incidents aboard aircraft over which the United States exercised jurisdiction was assigned to the Federal Aviation Administration.

One of the greatest impediments to an effective counterterrorism policy is interagency rivalry. For the politician, terrorism is primarily a political problem. From a law enforcement viewpoint, it is a matter of criminal justice. From a military point of view, it is at the lowest end of the scale of low-intensity conflict. From security and intelligence points of view, it is a matter of keeping one step ahead of adversaries through accurate intelligence and perpetual vigilance. All these viewpoints are reflected in U.S. policy.

Political Analysis

The U.S. approach to counterterrorism at the time gave the highest priority to the political aspects of terrorism. Deciding who is or is not a terrorist, and how to respond to terrorist acts, are essentially political decisions. The political nature of terrorism is expressed in that often-heard expression "The only difference between terrorists and freedom fighters is what side they are on." This is not mere cynicism. No country, including the United States, would be willing to base its response to terrorism merely on a set of definitions.

The U.S. government's list of state supporters of terrorism is a good case in point. As of June 1996, the list included Libya, Sudan, North Korea, Cuba, and Syria. Although the State Department testified to Congress in June 1995 that there had been no evidence of direct Syrian involvement in terrorism since 1986, Syria remains on the list, presumably until peace terms are worked out between it and Israel.

By contrast, Serbia, which in the early 1990s did support large-scale acts of terrorism by Bosnian Serbs against Bosnian Muslims, was never placed on the list. Nor were the terrorist acts committed by both sides in Bosnia generally included in the State Department's annual report of incidents. Presumably it was thought that to have done so would make the task of working out a peaceful settlement in Bosnia more difficult.

The vigor with which the United States pursues counterterrorist policies abroad has always reflected broader U.S. foreign policy priorities. Energetic diplomatic efforts against terrorism in the 1980s were spurred on, in part, by the U.S. global confrontation with the Soviet Union, and in part because much Middle Eastern terrorism was aimed not merely at the United States, but also at its close ally Israel. Renewed U.S. emphasis on Iraq and particularly on Iran as state supporters of terrorism in the 1990s was also motivated to a great degree by broader political considerations than terrorism.

The political dimension aside, U.S. concern over terrorism is also a response to specific attacks on American citizens and property. The major focus of U.S. diplomacy in countering terrorism, therefore, has been multina-

tional. The United States realizes that attacks against Americans abroad cannot be stopped without international cooperation. The U.S. diplomatic message is that terrorism is everybody's problem.

Security Fighting the Hijackers

In September 1970, the Popular Front for the Liberation of Palestine carried out a spectacular multiaircraft hijacking to Dawson's Field in Jordan, involving more than 300 hostages. In the aftermath of this event, President Nixon appointed a director of aviation security to coordinate antihijacking measures. Eventually, some 1,500 customs security officers were recruited to travel alongside passengers. Also, in 1973, passenger searches became compulsory. The searches proved to be valuable: in 1973 and 1974 alone, security staff discovered 4,400 firearms and thousands of pounds of high explosives.

In the late twentieth century, American officials were often singled out as terrorist targets. Between 1979 and 1993, there were 460 attacks on U.S. diplomatic personnel, buildings, and vehicles. Twenty-five diplomats were killed and 55 were wounded. Military personnel have also been targeted, as in the suicide bomb attack by Hezbollah at the marine barracks in Beirut, Lebanon, on October 23, 1983, which killed 241 U.S. Marines and 58 French soldiers.

In 1986, the State Department moved to enhance physical security abroad by creating the Bureau of Diplomatic Security. In addition to protecting U.S. personnel and missions abroad, the Bureau of Diplomatic Security is responsible for investigative work and collecting intelligence. The bureau also works closely with private U.S. firms and nongovernmental organizations in foreign countries through its Overseas Security Advisory Council. This body maintains an electronic bulletin board for exchanging security-related and terrorist information internationally. The State Department, as a matter of public policy, also regularly issues warnings to citizens traveling to countries considered dangerous because of terrorist threats.

The rule of law is a basic tenet of U.S. constitutionalism and a major goal of U.S. foreign policy. In legislative terms, the rule of law is all the more accentuated by the large number of lawyers in Congress who tend naturally to look for legal solutions to what are often essentially political problems—such as terrorism. There is also a practical element involved. The more highly politicized terrorism is, the more difficult it is for the U.S. government to reach an international consensus on concerted action. It has been a major strategy of the United States, therefore, to depoliticize terrorism as much as possible and to justify collective counterterrorism measures in terms of simply bringing criminals to justice.

Despite the absence of an acceptable legal definition of terrorism, virtually all terrorist activity is criminal in nature, not only in the United States but also in most countries. Within U.S. borders, the Justice Department and the FBI have the primary responsibility for terrorist incidents. Cooperation against terrorism with national law enforcement agencies abroad, as well as with international organizations such as Interpol, is a major policy goal. FBI agents and State Department regional security officers abroad maintain close liaisons with law enforcement agencies in host countries, sharing intelligence and cooperating on investigations.

Learning to Share

Institutionally, U.S. law enforcement had to adjust to a new environment as it assumed its responsibilities in counterterrorism policy during this period. For example, the FBI had never before had to share its mission to any great degree with other U.S. agencies, particularly at the state and local levels. An example of how counterterrorist law enforcement broke new ground was shown in the creation of a joint FBI–Los Angeles Police Department antiterrorism task force to provide security for the 1984 Los Angeles Olympics. Since then, similar joint task forces have been created in major cities throughout the country.

The FBI had an even greater adjustment abroad. By law, its jurisdiction ended at the water's edge, just as the Central Intelligence Agency (CIA) could not operate inside the United States. Moreover, crimes such as murder were subject to state law but not federal law in the United States. When Americans were killed in terrorist attacks at Rome and Vienna airports in 1985, the FBI could not intervene. Therefore, Congress passed legislation designating various criminal acts, including murder committed in a terrorist context abroad, as federal crimes, empowering the FBI to investigate. Even then, however, the FBI had no legal jurisdiction in a foreign country and could proceed only with the permission of the host governments.

International law was another area of emphasis in U.S. counterterrorism policy during this period. The United States has extradition treaties with most countries but generally insists on a political exclusion clause exempting the extradition of those wanted for "political crimes." Where terrorism was involved, the problem was not always clear-cut. On the one hand, the United States opposed political trials as contrary to the rule of law. On the other hand, preventing exploitation of this position proved difficult. Terrorists from Northern Ireland for years regularly fled to the United States, claiming the crimes for which they were wanted by the British were political in nature, and thus exempted under a political exclusion clause of the Anglo-American extradition treaty. To close this loophole, the British and Americans negotiated a supplementary extradition treaty in the 1980s, which stated that political exclusion clauses should not impede extradition for violent crimes to democratic countries that respect due process of law and provide a fair trial.

International Treaties on Terrorism

Gaining support for multinational treaties to combat terrorism was then and continued to be now a major goal of U.S. policy. There remains no single convention or treaty proscribing terrorism. Instead, over the years, specific categories such as airline and maritime sabotage, hijackings, hostage taking, and protection of diplomats and of nuclear materials have been singled out for treaties. By mid-1995, there were eleven major international treaties and conventions against various forms of terrorist acts.

Gathering intelligence on the structure, organization, tactics, and plans of terrorist groups is one of the most important components of counterterrorism policy, but Americans have historically had a strong aversion to spying in peacetime. In 1929, Secretary of State Henry Stimson, who believed that "gentlemen do not read other gentlemen's mail," closed the State Department's Black Chamber, where codes were broken, and banned the reading of other nations' coded messages.

With the advent of the Cold War, intelligence operations came to be considered a necessary evil. Such operations have continued to have strong domestic critics, however, which in some respects has reduced their efficiency. The amended Freedom of Information Act was one of a series of restrictions placed on the intelligence-gathering activities of the CIA and the FBI in the 1970s, following a public reaction to overzealous surveillance and other tactics. For a while, these restrictions hampered cooperation between the CIA and intelligence organizations in Israel and Europe. However, with the end of the Cold War, U.S. intelligence agencies had to restructure their priorities. Nevertheless, terrorism has remained a major threat to the United States, and as such an important information-collection target—one reason why counterterrorism policies have been relatively successful in recent years.

In recent decades, the electronic revolution has sharpened the surveillance capacities of intelligence agencies. There is no longer such a thing as a private telephone conversation. In addition, coded information can be transmitted between agencies and countries at high speed, encouraging national governments to collaborate in antiterrorist operations.

Coercive Force

Just as diplomatic and law enforcement perceptions of terrorism differ, military perceptions differ again. From a military point of view, armed conflict can be placed on a linear scale from global nuclear war to localized low-intensity conflict. The latter includes insurgencies and guerrilla warfare, with terrorism at the lowest end of the scale. Because most terrorism involves civilians, and because the most suitable responses to it could be through law enforcement or diplomatic means rather than the use of military force, terrorism cannot be placed wholly within the concept of warfare. Nevertheless, the fact that it is a form of low-intensity conflict means that, in certain circumstances, the use of force is the preferred response.

The highest-priority military response to terrorism is hostage rescue. The United States was not the first country to develop a covert military force with a hostage-rescue capability. Following the rescue of a hijacked Lufthansa jet by German special operations forces in Mogadishu, Somalia, in 1977, the Pentagon authorized the creation of such a specialized force. The so-called Delta Force was originally led by Colonel Charlie Beckwith, who for years had advocated the creation of a unit similar to the British Special Air Service.

Despite its superb training and capabilities, the Delta Force is best known for its failure to rescue the American hostages in Tehran in 1980. The operation turned out to be far too complicated for the margin of error built into it and was aborted at the last minute. Nevertheless, as an integral component of U.S. counterterrorism policy, Delta Force fulfills a vital role.

The Delta Force and its maritime equivalent, SEAL Team Six, eventually came under the Special Operations Command, with unconventional combat responsibilities far beyond hostage rescue. The Special Operations Command's capabilities fell and continues to fall into the dim category where terrorism, insurgencies, and guerrilla warfare overlap. In this period and today, in a hostage crisis situation, an Emergency Support Team, led by a State Department officer, is generally sent to the country where the incident is taking place. Composed of intelligence, special operations, and communications specialists, as well as a senior diplomat, the team serves in an advisory role with the U.S. ambassador, as well as with the host country. It is in constant communication with crisis managers in Washington.

Since the end of the Cold War, regional and local conflicts have replaced global confrontation as the major cause of terrorism. The Iranian revolution in 1978–1979 demonstrated that religious fundamentalism was far more appealing as a justification for terrorist tactics than was an ideology such as communism.

With small-scale conflicts posing only marginal threats to U.S. strategic interests in the pre 9/11 period, the United States was far more reluctant to become involved abroad than it was during the Cold War, even when U.S. lives and property were at stake. As before, however, broader foreign policy considerations continued to shape U.S. counterterrorist priorities.

New Threats at Home and Abroad

In the Middle East, where the Arab-Israeli peace process is a foreign policy priority, the United States now considers militant Islamic terrorism a major threat, particularly from

---

KEY DATES

Late 1960s Widespread terrorist activities in Europe and the Middle East force the United States to recognize that terrorism is an international threat to all democracies.

1972 The Nixon Administration sets up an antiterrorist committee under the secretary of state after the murder of Israeli athletes at the Munich Olympics.

1977 In an era of hijackings, the Pentagon authorizes the creation of the Delta Force, an unconventional military body with a hostage-rescue capability.

1980s Terrorists target U.S. diplomatic and military personnel, particularly in the Middle East. The State Department sets up the Bureau of Diplomatic Security.

1990s Terrorists, both foreign and domestic, set off major bombs within the United States, with great loss of life.

---

those groups opposed to the Arab-Israeli peace process, such as Hamas and Hezbollah. Nevertheless, the United States repeatedly stressed that the enemy was terrorism, not Islam, a position maintained to the present day.

The greatest change in attitudes toward terrorism in the 1990s, however, was on the home front. The New York World Trade Center bombing in February 1993 and the Oklahoma City bombing in April 1995 added a new dimension to U.S. perceptions of the terrorist threat. The New York attack shattered the myth of U.S. domestic immunity to terrorist attacks. The Oklahoma City bombing further refuted the perception that no American groups or individuals would ever carry out a large-scale terrorist attack.

The two attacks did not lessen U.S. preoccupation with international terrorism, but they did boost efforts to upgrade local counterterrorism measures, particularly in law enforcement and intelligence gathering. Security measures were put in effect for the 1996 Summer Olympics when it was announced they would be held in Atlanta. This did not prevent the detonation of a bomb in Centennial Park on July 27, however.

Prior to the various al-Qaeda attacks of the late 1990s and early 2000s, it appeared that the U.S. approach to terrorism was not likely to change greatly in the near future. It was expected that the government would continue to focus primarily on international terrorism, while evolving a greater sensitivity to the threat of domestic terrorism. The main focus at home and abroad, it seemed, was likely to continue to be on targeting the criminal nature of terrorism and disassociating it from legitimate political activity. But with the 9/11 assault, all of that changed, as the administration of U.S. president George W. Bush opted to go onto the offensive against al-Qaeda, launching an invasion of Afghanistan, where it had its headquarters, and Iraq, where claims of al-Qaeda penetration proved false.

David E. Long

See also: *Modern Terrorism*—United States: Antiabortion Violence; United States: Black Panther Violence; United States: Ecoterrorism; United States: Ku Klux Klan Violence; United States: Oklahoma City Bombing and the Militia Movement, 1990s; United States: Millennium Bomb Plot; United States: Puerto Rican Separatism.

Further Reading

Adams, James. Secret *Armies: Inside the American, Soviet and European Special Forces.* New York: Atlantic Monthly, 1987.

Clarke, Richard A. *Against All Enemies: Inside America's War on Terror.* New York: Free Press, 2004.

Johnson, Haynes. *The Age of Anxiety: McCarthyism to Terrorism.* Orlando: Harcourt, 2005.

Long, David E. *The Anatomy of Terrorism.* New York: Free Press, 1990.

Martin, David C., and John Walcott. *Best Laid Plans: The Inside Story of America's War Against Terrorism.* New York: Harper and Row, 1988.

Sterling, Claire. *The Terror Network: The Secret War of International Terrorism.* New York: Holt, Rinehart and Winston, 1981.

U.S. Department of State. *Patterns of Global Terrorism.* Washington, DC: U.S. Government Printing Office, August 1988.

United States: Symbionese Liberation Army Violence, 1970s

The Symbionese Liberation Army (SLA), a leftover of 1960s radicalism, achieved notoriety in 1974 when its members kidnapped Patricia Hearst, granddaughter of U.S. newspaper tycoon William Randolph Hearst. The product of an affluent and conventional upbringing, Hearst, in turn, achieved notoriety when she was pictured by security cameras taking part in a bank robbery carried out by the SLA.

The group originated in Berkeley at the end of 1972. Its founders included Berkeley graduate Nancy Ling, her partner, Chris Thompson, and Willy Wolfe, a prison welfare visitor involved with the Black Cultural Association. Various others, most from comfortable middle-class backgrounds, gradually joined this circle.

One of the prisoners Wolfe visited was Donald DeFreeze, who led a group called Unisight. Although Unisight was ostensibly tackling African American social issues, it was in fact preparing for an armed urban insurrection. When DeFreeze escaped from prison in March 1973, he went to Berkeley, and slowly this circle of friends consolidated into an active political group.

The SLA took its name from the concept of symbiosis—the mutual interdependence of organisms—because of its belief that the revolution would come about only through oppressed blacks and whites, and men and women, working together in a symbiotic relationship. Ideologically, the SLA were muddled, uneasily linking outlandish notions with orthodox socialist beliefs.

The SLA viewed people in terms of nationality and race rather than class and wanted a system of sovereign nations of racial types. Declaring a revolutionary war against "the Fascist Capitalist Class," it offered its help to all liberation movements. However, only the Black Guerrilla Family—a splinter group of the Black Panthers—proved sympathetic, providing help when the SLA was later on the run.

Murder and Kidnapping

The SLAs first action was the murder of Oakland's African American superintendent of schools, Dr. Marcus Foster, on November 6, 1973. The SLA chose him because of his controversial decision that pupils in local black schools should carry identity cards in the interests of their safety. As a number of black activists opposed this, the SLA thought the issue would provide a popular local cause to justify violent action. In fact, the terrorist act brought condemnation from all quarters, including Black Panther leader Huey Newton.

KEY DATES

1973 African American militant Donald DeFreeze escapes from prison and forms a political group, soon to be called the Symbionese Liberation Army (SLA), dedicated to addressing social problems and preparing for armed urban insurrection.

November 6, 1973 SLA militants murder Marcus Foster, school superintendent of Oakland, California.

February 4, 1974 Three SLA members kidnap newspaper heiress Patricia Hearst from her apartment in Berkeley, California.

April 15, 1974 Patricia Hearst is filmed, along with other SLA members, participating in the armed robbery of a San Francisco Bay Area bank.

May 17, 1974 Los Angeles police fire on an SLA safe house, killing DeFreeze and other SLA leaders, effectively destroying the organization.

September 18, 1974 Hearst is captured by police in San Francisco.

The next planned move was the kidnapping of Patricia Hearst. The SLA selected her because she was from a wealthy family and presented an easy target, as she was living unprotected in Berkeley. On February 4, 1974, three SLA members entered Hearst's apartment and forced her into the trunk of a car. Three days later, the SLA released a taped message in which it threatened to kill Hearst if any attempts were made to free her or if any action was taken against SLA elements. The next message demanded that a system of free food distribution to the poor be set up and funded by Hearst's father, Randolph Hearst. He agreed to the demand. A further taped message, however, lent an unusual twist to the story. Patty Hearst insisted that it was the Federal Bureau of Investigation (FBI) that was trying to kill her and that all the SLA wanted was to feed the people and get justice for two imprisoned members.

When Hearst's father promised $2 million at once and another $2 million in January 1975 for the food plan, the SLA promised to arrange his daughter's release. But to her parents' astonishment, Hearst decided to stay with the SLA. Following the bank raid in which Hearst took part, and during which she was caught on film, a warrant was issued for her arrest by the FBI.

Fugitives from Justice

Now on the run, the SLA headed to Los Angeles. DeFreeze, Wolfe, and four others took refuge in an apartment in Compton. From previous incidents, the authorities knew the vehicles they were using. On May 17, 1974, 150 members of the Los Angeles Police Department, 11 FBI agents, and 100 sheriff's officers fired on the apartment, and the fugitives were killed.

Patty Hearst disappeared but was finally captured on September 18. She was found guilty of armed robbery and sentenced to seven years, although the sentence was commuted and she walked free in February 1979. To this day, Hearst insists that she was brainwashed by the SLA.

For many, the SLA was merely a postscript to 1960s radicalism. But if the group left any legacy, it was in helping to reinforce the mistaken belief that terrorist acts in the United States would come only from the left.

John Finlayson

See also: *Definitions, Types, Categories*—Left-Wing and Revolutionary Terrorism. *Modern Terrorism*—United States: Black Panther Violence. *Tactics, Methods, Aims*—Kidnapping and Extortion.

Further Reading

Hearst, Patricia. *Patty Hearst: Her Own Story.* New York: Avon Books, 1988.

Kinney, Jean. *An American Journey: The Short Life of Willy Wolfe.* New York: Simon and Schuster, 1979.

Weed, Steven, with Scott Stanton. *My Search for Patty Hearst.* New York: Crown, 1976.

United States: Tax Protesters, 1970s–Present

Citizens of the United States have been protesting against taxes since the founding of the country. In 1791, the federal government imposed an excise tax on whiskey. Farmers in the western counties of Pennsylvania, protesting that the tax destroyed their profits, assaulted and tarred and feathered excise agents. Attacks on tax collectors increased, and by July 1794 the rioting by the farmers was being called an insurrection, and so the Whiskey Rebellion began. A federal marshal was assaulted in Allegheny County, Pennsylvania, and several hundred men attacked the home of the regional inspector. His home and barn were burned. On August 7, 1794, President George Washington issued an order mobilizing an army of 13,000 and demanded that the farmers return to their homes. The uprising was suppressed; a few men were arrested, tried, and later pardoned.

Another tax, a federal property tax levied in 1798 because of a possible war with France, caused another uprising. When people among the German-speaking population of Pennsylvania resisted the new tax, several were arrested. John Fries, representing this population, led 140 men and freed the prisoners. President John Adams accused the insurgents of treason, and Fries was arrested, found guilty, and sentenced to death. However, President Adams pardoned him in 1802.

Few, if any, people enjoy paying taxes, and many try to avoid them through legal and illegal means. However, tax protesters are not to be confused with tax evaders. Whereas a tax evader uses illegal methods to avoid paying taxes, tax protesters may evade paying, but they believe that they have a moral, ethical, and even a legal right to refuse to pay taxes. The tax protest is an ideological commitment.

Since the end of World War II, there have been two major tax protest movements. The first is left-wing in orientation and gained popularity during the Vietnam War. Pacifists argued that it was immoral to pay income tax that would go to support the military and the war. After the end of the war, however, resistance organizations lost members. They still exist today, and their membership began growing again when the wars in Afghanistan and Iraq broke out. The largest group in the antiwar tax protest movement is the National War Tax Resistance Coordinating Committee, which publishes several booklets on how to resist war taxes.

The other tax protest movement is an extreme right-wing movement that had its origins in organized opposition to the Sixteenth Amendment to the Constitution, which created the income tax. Early opposition was nonviolent. The most significant campaigns were attempts to pass the "Liberty Amendment." First introduced in 1952, this amendment tried to strengthen states' rights. In 1957, a revised version was introduced that mandated the abolition of the income tax. After all attempts at ratification failed, the tax protest movement began to change. Tax protesters started to develop theories that offered alternative interpretations of the Sixteenth Amendment. They wrote books and lectured around the country to various groups. During the 1970s, the movement became more radical. The most infamous radical tax protest group, known as the Posse Comitatus, urges the use of vigilante justice to fight a tyrannical government. By the 1980s, group members were harassing and intimidating law enforcement and other public officials by putting phony liens on their property.

The movement turned deadly in 1983 when Gordon Kahl, a Posse member and a convert to Christian Identity, killed two U.S. Marshals who had come to arrest him for a probation violation and tax charges. Kahl fled to Arkansas, where he died in a shootout. Other tax protesters have used violence and have been members of domestic terrorist groups such as the Order. Most tax protesters, however, are not involved in violent criminal activity. Nonetheless, some see themselves as part of the so-called Patriot movement of antigovernment activists and will use violence to fight what they believe is an unjust government.

On February 18, 2010, Joseph Stack, a software engineer, flew his plane into the Internal Revenue Service

---

KEY DATES

1794 Farmers angry over the federal whiskey tax rebel in the nation's first antitax violence.

1913 The Sixteenth Amendment to the U.S. Constitution is ratified, allowing for an income tax.

1970s The right-wing Posse Comitatus is formed, protesting, among other things, government tax policy.

1983 Posse Comitatus organizer Gordon Kahl kills two U.S. Marshals sent to arrest him in Texas on probation and tax charges.

2010 Joseph Stack, a software engineer with tax problems, flies his airplane into the Internal Revenue Service building in Austin, Texas, killing himself and an IRS employee; Stack has no connection to organized antitax groups.

building in Austin, Texas, killing an IRS employee and committing suicide in the act. While Stack was not connected to any antitax protest group, he was reportedly despondent and angry that his software firm had been shut down for nonpayment of state taxes nearly half a dozen years earlier, and that he had continuing delinquent tax problems. In his suicide note, he lashed out at the government, not only for its tax policy, but also for the bank bailout of 2008 and 2009, among other things.

Gary Perlstein

See also: *Definitions, Types, Categories*—Right-Wing and Reactionary Terrorism. *Modern Terrorism*—United States: Aryan Nations and White Supremacists; United States: Response to Terrorism Before September 11.

Further Reading

George, John, and Laird Wilcox. *American Extremists.* Amherst, NY: Prometheus Books, 1996.

Stock, Catherine McNicol. *Rural Radicals: From Bacon's Rebellion to the Oklahoma City Bombing.* New York: Penguin USA, 1997.

United States: Weathermen Violence, 1960s–1970s

The Weathermen—who later referred to themselves as the Weather Underground—were an anarchic splinter group made up of various left-wing student factions in the late 1960s. They first declared their goal to be "the destruction of American imperialism and the achievement of a classless world." Through the 1970s, the Weathermen waged a campaign of bombings and other terrorist attacks and included many high-profile institutions among their targets.

Campus Origins

One of America's most influential left-wing groups of the 1960s was Students for a Democratic Society (SDS), which aimed at revitalizing American democracy by shaking up existing institutions. By the late 1960s, however, the SDS was so frustrated with its lack of achievement that some of its members began waging a terrorist campaign.

In the spring of 1969, a number of SDS leaders in Chicago re-formed into a national collective. They issued a manifesto entitled "You Don't Need a Weatherman to Tell You Which Way the Wind Blows." The manifesto spelled out the group's aims, which were essentially to subvert the government and bring about a mass revolution by the working proletariat.

The Weathermen formed collectives of between five and twenty-five members in a number of cities, all under the strict control of the so-called Chicago Weather Bureau. In these collectives, members gave up their possessions, their bank accounts, their privacy, and any monogamous relationships—all seen as undesirable sentimental ties. In effect, they had to surrender their individuality to serve the cause. Some of the Weathermen's first actions took place in the summer of 1969, when they carried out "jail breaks" in schools, taking over classrooms to deliver their revolutionary message to the pupils, and in the process sometimes becoming involved in violent scuffles with the police.

In the fall of 1969, the Weathermen began their so-called Days of Rage campaign. On October 8, the second anniversary of Che Guevara's death, eighty Weathermen marched into Lincoln Park in Chicago. Wearing black helmets and shouting slogans, they made speeches in front of a few hundred youths who had gathered there. The crowd of youths rushed out into the streets and rioted. Vastly outnumbered by the police, most of the rioters were beaten and arrested.

By the time the Weathermen conducted their National Council meeting in Flint, Michigan, in December 1969, the group was disillusioned—not only with the student left, but also with the working class. The Weathermen now saw themselves as the only revolutionary group in America and were increasingly committed to violent insurgency.

Bombing Campaigns

Early in 1970, about a hundred members of the Weathermen went underground to escape the law, and started a campaign of violence. Although it is difficult to establish the number of bombings they carried out, it is known that, between September 1969 and May 1970, various radicals were responsible for about 250 bomb-

Three members of the radical left-wing Weathermen, who advocated the violent overthrow of the U.S. government, accidentally blew up a townhouse in Greenwich Village, New York City, where they were assembling explosives on March 6, 1970. *(Associated Press)*

<table>
<tr><td colspan="2">

KEY DATES

1969 A number of leaders of the radical student group Students for a Democratic Society form a splinter group, which is soon known as the Weathermen, the name derived from the lyrics of a popular Bob Dylan song; the group organizes the Days of Rage campaign of demonstrations across America.

1969–1970 Group members set off roughly 250 bombs across America, including one at the University of Wisconsin that kills a student.

1970 Hundreds of Weathermen go underground to escape a police crackdown, pledging themselves to a revolutionary campaign of violence; three Weatherman are killed while manufacturing bombs in a New York City townhouse.

1976–1977 As a result of police activity and changing political values, many of the members leave the organization, leading to its demise.

</td></tr>
</table>

Breakup

In 1971, the collective renamed itself the Weather Underground, both to appease growing concern about feminist issues and to reflect the fugitive nature of its core command. At about this time the activists began to disagree over diverging aims and ideals. Although the Weather Underground continued to commit terrorist acts, even bombing the Pentagon in 1975, the collective eventually broke up during 1976–1977. Some of the more hard-line members went on to found new extremist groups. A number of founding members eventually surrendered to the authorities: Mark Rudd turned himself in, in 1977, followed in 1981 by Bernadine Dohrn and William Ayers. The final fugitive from justice, Jeffrey Powell, gave himself up in January 1994.

John Finlayson

See also: *Definitions, Types, Categories*—Left-Wing and Revolutionary Terrorism. *Modern Terrorism*—United States: Black Panther Violence; United States: Response to Terrorism Before September 11; United States: Symbionese Liberation Army Violence.

ings, mainly against government buildings with Vietnam War connections, such as draft board offices.

Terrorists bombed a department at the University of Wisconsin where work on an army math research project was taking place, and killed a graduate student. Not only did the bombing campaign fail to achieve anything; it was also self-defeating: in March 1970, three members of the Weathermen blew themselves up while constructing a bomb in Greenwich Village.

Nevertheless, the Weathermen continued with their terrorist campaigns. In August 1970, they bombed the Bank of Brazil in New York; on September 13, they helped LSD guru Timothy Leary escape from prison; and on March 1, 1971, they bombed the U.S. Senate offices in the Capitol building in Washington, D.C.

Further Reading

Gitlin, Todd. *The Sixties: Years of Hope, Days of Rage.* New York: Bantam Books, 1987.

Hoffman, Abbie. *Soon to Be a Major Motion Picture.* New York: Putnam, 1980.

Zaroulis, Nancy, and Gerald Sullivan. *Who Spoke Up? American Protest Against the War in Vietnam.* New York: Doubleday, 1984.

United States: World Trade Center Bombing, 1993

On February 26, 1993, a truck laden with 1,200 pounds (544 kilograms) of dynamite exploded in the basement parking lot of one of the Twin Towers of the World Trade Center, in New York's downtown business district. The blast carved a 200-foot (61-meter) crater in the parking lot, tore a hole in the ceiling, and poured rubble onto the subway station below. The explosion killed six people and injured more than a thousand. Fortunately, the structure of the 110-story tower remained unshaken; otherwise, the death toll would have been enormous. In the aftermath of one of the worst terrorist incidents in the United States to date, police and FBI agents set to work finding out who was responsible.

Just two hours after the explosion, a man named Mohammed Salameh entered a truck rental office in New Jersey. He claimed the truck he had rented had been stolen and demanded the return of his $400 deposit. Five days later, FBI agents at the bomb site found the serial number of the van used in the attack. The FBI quickly traced the van to the truck rental company, and then arrested Salameh.

Links with Islamic Fundamentalism

The FBI next exposed a network of Muslim fundamentalists, some with terrorist links, centered around Sheikh Omar Abdel-Rahman, the spiritual leader of the Islamic Group (al-Gamaa al-Islamiyya), a splinter group of the extremist al-Jihad ("Holy War") movement in Egypt. In 1981, Abdel-Rahman had been implicated in the assassination of Egyptian president Anwar Sadat. Eventually acquitted, Abdel-Rahman came to the United States in 1990. From a mosque in New Jersey, he broadcast his anti-Western sermons to militant Muslims in Egypt.

The presence of Islamic fundamentalists in the United States largely stemmed from the Soviet occupation of Af-

Police officers assist an evacuee of the World Trade Center after the bombing attack of February 26, 1993. The explosion in the underground parking lot—for which Islamic fundamentalists were later convicted—failed to topple the building but caused six fatalities. *(Associated Press)*

KEY DATES

February 26, 1993 A bomb-laden truck detonates in the subterranean garage of the World Trade Center, killing 6 persons and injuring more than 1,000 others.

March 1994 Egyptian cleric Sheik Omar Abdel-Rahman and three other suspects are convicted in federal court of planning and carrying out the bombing.

October 1995 Abdel-Rahman and nine others are convicted of planning a spate of urban terrorist attacks.

November 1997 Al-Qaeda-affiliated terrorist Ramzi Ahmed Yousef is convicted of masterminding the bombing.

ghanistan (1979–1989). In the 1980s, the United States supported fundamentalists based in Pakistan, who fought alongside Afghan mujahideen (holy warriors) against the Soviets. Mahmud Abouhalima, one of those implicated in the World Trade Center bombing, had fought in Afghanistan, and Sheikh Abdel-Rahman had visited the mujahideen bases in northern Pakistan. Initially, the CIA supported Abdel-Rahman, but with the Soviet withdrawal from Afghanistan in 1989, many mujahideen joined Islamic fundamentalist organizations, which were increasingly anti-American and anti-Western.

Plot Exposed

Following investigations into the bombing, the FBI set a trap for mujahideen suspects. They sent into the group an undercover agent, who posed as a former Egyptian military officer with access to explosives. He drew in various fundamentalists, including Abdel-Rahman, who were determined to avenge the arrests following the New York City explosion. During the course of meetings in May 1993, recorded secretly by the FBI, the fundamentalists hatched an extraordinary plot.

In a single day, the terrorists planned to assassinate UN secretary-general Boutros Boutros-Ghali; blow up the UN headquarters; and destroy an office building with 10,000 workers, along with two New York City traffic tunnels under the Hudson River that allow access to the island of Manhattan from New Jersey. Had the plot succeeded, it would have brought immeasurable bloodshed

and chaos to New York City—certainly more than the 1993 World Trade Center bombing.

In June 1993, FBI agents arrested the terrorists as they mixed explosives in a safe house in Jersey City. In August, Abdel-Rahman and three others were charged with participation in the World Trade Center bombing and with the additional plots uncovered by the FBI. In March 1994, the four were found guilty on all charges and sentenced to life imprisonment. In a second ruling in October 1995, Abdel-Rahman and nine others were found guilty of planning a campaign of urban terrorism. Another suspect, Ramzi Ahmed Yousef, an al-Qaeda–affiliated terrorist, was extradited from Pakistan to New York in February 1995 to face charges of buying and mixing the explosives used in the 1993 bombing.

Although these terrorists were brought to justice, a question remained concerning the motives behind the bombing. Throughout the late 1990s and up until the terrorist attacks of September 11, 2001, which destroyed the World Trade Center and killed nearly 3,000 persons, U.S. authorities remained convinced that the 1993 bombing was not an isolated incident, but part of a wider Islamic plot to destabilize the U.S. government and weaken its friendly ties with Israel and Egypt. That thesis was further confirmed in 1998, when Yousef was convicted in federal court of masterminding the bombing and sentenced to life imprisonment without the possibility of parole.

Matthew Hughes

See also: *Definitions, Types, Categories*—Islamist Fundamentalist Terrorism. *Modern Terrorism*—United States: Response to Terrorism Before September 11.

Further Reading

Jeffrey, Simon. *Terrorist Trap: America's Experience with Terrorism.* Bloomington: Indiana University Press, 1994.

Nacos, Brigitte L. *Terrorism and the Media.* New York: Columbia University Press, 1996.

Precht, Robert E. *Defending Mohammad: Justice on Trial.* Ithaca, NY: Cornell University Press, 2003.

Smith, Brent L. *Terrorism in America: Pipebombs and Pipedreams.* New York: State University of New York Press, 1994.

Uruguay: Tupamaro Uprising, 1960s–1985

The National Liberation Movement—or Tupamaros—operated in Uruguay from the early 1960s, specializing in the kidnapping of diplomats. Its aim was to achieve a fairer society, and it became the blueprint for urban guerrilla movements in Latin America. In its early years, the Tupamaros grabbed headlines with publicity stunts such as hijacking truckloads of food on Christmas Eve 1963, and distributing festive snacks in the slums of the capital, Montevideo. In another public relations gesture, a terrorist paused to administer first aid to a bystander who fainted when caught up in a Tupamaros bank raid. But the Tupamaros' Robin Hood image faded as they found themselves with more and more blood on their hands.

Economic Crisis

In a series of liberalizing reforms in the first half of the century in Uruguay, the ruling Colorado Party had checked the powers of the military and set up a welfare state. The constitution was also restructured, initially to limit the powers of the executive presidency, and then in 1952 to replace it by a council of state. By the 1960s, however, Uruguay was in economic decline. Lacking industrial or mineral resources, its economy was based almost entirely on the export of grain and beef. While the prices of its exports had been falling steadily, inflation within the country was rampant. The council of state seemed unable to make decisions, while the declining economy created more and more difficulties in maintaining the welfare state.

By referendum, the executive presidency was restored in 1967, but the first president, the popular General Óscar Gestido, died soon afterward. Gestido was succeeded by his vice president, General Jorge Pacheco Areco, a former boxer with authoritarian tendencies. It was his government that had to deal with the first phase of the Tupamaros terrorist campaign.

Marxist Beginnings

The Tupamaros were formed in Uruguay in 1962 as part of the continent-wide reaction to the Cuban Revolution in 1959. Although they began operating in the countryside among impoverished cane cutters in the rural north of Uruguay, the Tupamaros soon became an urban, middle-class movement. Their purpose was first to discredit and ultimately to overthrow the existing political order. The movement was led by Raúl Sendic Antonaccio, who had trained as a lawyer. Sendic began his political career acting as legal adviser to the cane cutters he led in a march to Montevideo in 1962. The march was a decisive

event since it marked his break with the Socialist Party, which he considered guilty of inaction. The Tupamaros movement recruited former socialists as well as people with more radical beliefs.

Ideologically, the Tupamaros were fervently nationalist, arguing in their few public statements for the creation of an independent national community based on socialism. They sought to drive out foreign interests, since they felt that the Uruguayan economy was dominated by the United States and Brazil. Specific Tupamaros policies included the nationalization of banks and export houses, as well as a full land reform program.

The Tupamaros concluded that the only way to reform the system was through violence, in order to highlight the faults of the regime and to make the public conscious of the need for change. Many members found justification that force could be used to redress the evils of society in Catholic liberation theology. Ironically, a large number of Tupamaros came from privileged positions, which gave them access to high-grade intelligence about government intentions. The information proved useful in organizing the daring mass jailbreaks that became one of the trademarks of the movement.

The Tupamaros had a well-deserved reputation for tight security and were organized in cells. Each cell had between five and ten members and was self-sufficient. By decentralizing operations, the Tupamaros sought to guarantee security against infiltration.

Beginnings of Terrorism

The Tupamaros came to prominence in July 1963, with a raid on a gun club. The group then targeted U.S. and Brazilian diplomatic vehicles, and the homes of important politicians and businessmen, with bomb attacks and armed robberies. In January 1966, Sendic called the first national Tupamaros convention, in which he broke with the Latin American traditions of rural guerrilla warfare established in Cuba. Instead, Sendic chose to concentrate Tupamaros operations in Uruguay's cities. In December 1966, the terrorists suffered their first casualties in shoot-outs, when police discovered a Tupamaros training center, a shooting range, and two safe houses. The Tupamaros were unable to carry out any attacks for a year.

A second phase began with the publication of its manifesto, "An Open Letter to the Police," on December 7, 1967. The letter stated: "For these reasons, we have placed ourselves outside the law. This is the only honest action when the law is not equal for all; when the law exists to defend the spurious interests of a minority in detriment to the majority; when the law works against the country's progress; when even those who have created it place themselves outside it, with impunity, whenever it is convenient for them."

Clashes with the Government

In this second phase, between 1967 and 1970, the strategy was to concentrate on exposing the corrupt political and economic system and dramatizing the movement. Pacheco declared a state of siege in 1968 and sent in troops to break up strikes organized as a protest against the government's austerity measures.

Pacheco's actions alienated public opinion, and the Tupamaros stepped up their action. In January 1968, after stealing more than 1,000 pounds of explosives, Tupamaros terrorists conducted a campaign of bomb attacks throughout the year. They also carried out nine major bank raids. In three years, through the ingenuity of prominent members such as Jorge Amílcar Manera Lluveras, the Tupamaros movement had established itself as a powerful and impenetrable terrorist network.

There was a great deal of sympathy among ordinary citizens for the young rebels of the Tupamaros. Some of the episodes of this period had a decidedly prankish quality, such as publishing the president's income tax returns and circulating a photograph of him in the nude. His leading adviser was kidnapped but released unharmed after four days. In another notorious raid, Tupamaros members stole money from a casino and distributed it among the poor. They even advertised on radio stations they occupied for brief periods.

This phase of psychological warfare culminated in the temporary occupation of the town of Pando for a day in September 1969. On the way back to Montevideo, however, things went badly wrong. The participants, many of them students, were met by large forces of military and police. The security forces overreacted and killed three Tupamaros members. Hundreds more were arrested, beaten, and tortured.

Spate of Kidnappings

The Tupamaros chose activities that could not be concealed from the press and so were certain to bring them attention. This led the Tupamaros to more overt acts of terrorism. The most striking was a spectacular sequence of kidnappings.

As with other Latin American terrorist groups at the time, victims were selected by occupation. Uruguayan hostages included a prominent banker, released after the payment of $60,000 to a Montevideo hospital, and the head of the National Energy Corporation.

The Tupamaros also targeted foreign nationals for kidnapping. U.S. citizen Dan Mitrione, an employee of the CIA, was kidnapped on July 31, 1970. He was an obvious target because he reputedly knew more than anyone

else about the Tupamaros. He had also been instructing the police in methods of interrogation. At the time, the Tupamaros were outraged by the authorities' use of torture, including beatings, rape, submersion, suspension, and shocks with electric cattle prods. Earlier that year, the Tupamaros assassinated one of the most notorious torturers, police inspector Héctor Morán Charquero, in broad daylight on the streets of the capital.

In return for Mitrione's release, the Tupamaros demanded the freedom of 150 jailed colleagues. They also stated that they had given Mitrione medical treatment, as he had been wounded. Soon afterward, police arrested many of the Tupamaro leadership, including Sendic and the second-in-command, Raúl Bidegain Greissing. In response, the Tupamaros gave Mitrione a summary "trial" and shot him.

On August 8, the Tupamaros announced that they had shot Mitrione because the government had failed to meet their demands. They stated that a similar fate awaited Días Gomide and the U.S. agronomist Claude Fly, both of whom they had captured on the previous day. However, they released both men early in 1971. Días Gomide's wife had to pay a large ransom, and Fly was released in March, after he had suffered a mild heart attack. The Tupamaros targeted him merely because he was American and presumably of importance to the U.S. government.

Prize Diplomatic Target

The British ambassador, Geoffrey Jackson, on the other hand, was a first-rate target. He had been under surveillance from the moment he arrived in the country and was regarded as an especially valuable prize. The Tupamaros kidnapped him on January 8, 1971, and held him for eight months. Jackson, an experienced diplomat and devout Catholic, established a rapport with his captors. He made it clear that British policy was neither to make deals with terrorists nor to pay ransoms. The extensive security operation to find Jackson in his makeshift "people's prison" included a house-to-house search of Montevideo.

Meanwhile, the Tupamaros had organized dramatic mass jailbreaks. Some 106 Tupamaros men, including Sendic and several of his key officers, broke out of jail or were freed by their colleagues in a spectacular mass escape from Punta Carretas prison. Soon afterward, 38 inmates escaped from the women's prison. These successes provided the Tupamaros with a convenient excuse to release Geoffrey Jackson.

The kidnappings of Jackson and Mitrione each had two purposes: to pressure the government and to secure publicity for the Tupamaros cause. The breach of the well-established principle of diplomatic inviolability increased the notoriety of the terrorists. But despite the emphasis in the movement on good organization and a commitment to

542 | Modern Terrorism

securing the release of its jailed members to maintain support, the Tupamaros lost momentum when they suspended hostilities for the presidential elections in 1971.

Tupamaros in Decline

The Tupamaros had achieved success as a secretive organization, but to achieve their ultimate objective of gaining power, they needed to cultivate a following among the masses. For the elections of November 1971, the Tupamaros gave their support to a new left-wing coalition, the Broad Front. However, in the elections, the Broad Front candidate, retired General Liber Seregni, got only 18 percent of the popular vote.

When the Tupamaros started their activities, they opposed a police force in a society that had been at peace for sixty years. Following the mass breakout from Punta Carretas prison in 1971, President Pacheco placed the armed forces in charge of the counterinsurgency campaign. By this stage, the military were deploying death squads to hunt down Tupamaros members and other left-wing opposition. The armed forces responded with a substantial escalation of violence. They used torture and drugs to break down suspects arrested in mass sweeps. In May 1972, the security forces located the movement's "people's prison" and freed two members of the former government who had been imprisoned there. By June, more than 1,200 people had been arrested without significant response from the Tupamaros. With the capture of Tupamaros leader Antonaccio in September 1972, the armed forces made it clear to the insurgents that he and other senior Tupamaros in detention would be shot if the violence did not stop. Then, on April 14, 1972, Pacheco was succeeded by the right-wing minister of agriculture, Juan María Bordaberry, who publicly proclaimed his sympathy with the dictatorial military regime in Brazil.

Consequently, the Tupamaros resumed operations with the simultaneous assassination of a number of government officials. These, according to the Tupamaros, were responsible for the death squads that were killing an increasing number of civilians. The new president immediately asked Congress for and obtained a "state of internal war," and with this came the suspension of constitutional guarantees. The regime had time to regroup, and so the advantage shifted back to the government. At the beginning of 1972, Héctor Amodio Pérez, one of the Tupamaros movement's key figures, defected and gave the government a large quantity of information about the movement and its leaders.

In less than three months, the movement collapsed. After a series of successes, the security forces recaptured Sendic in September 1972, after a shoot-out in which he suffered serious facial wounds. He and eight other Tupamaros leaders were held hostage, and the military warned their organization that they would be killed if hostilities resumed. The Tupamaros were seriously weakened,

but the movement did not abandon its commitment to violent struggle.

By December 1972, some 2,600 Tupamaros had been imprisoned and 42 killed. Police uncovered more than 200 safe houses and hideouts. Police also found an electronics laboratory, a weapons factory with a furnace, a laboratory for forging documents, and many other printing and information facilities. The Tupamaros also had a hospital, complete with operating tables and X-ray equipment. When Sendic was recaptured in September 1972, the authorities discovered that he had undergone plastic surgery to avoid recognition.

Military Coup

On June 27, 1973, a military coup supported by Brazil enabled President Bordaberry to eliminate rival centers of power. He closed Congress, forbade the operation of political parties, banned trade unions and other organizations, and acted without constitutional restraints.

By this time, Sendic had been tried and condemned to death, a sentence later commuted to forty-five years in prison. He was held captive, often in solitary confinement, until civilian government returned. The Broad Front Party leader, General Seregni, was also arrested for a second time in 1976. He was deprived of his military rank and sentenced to fourteen years in jail for "conspiring against the constitution."

Military rule continued with civilian figurehead presidents throughout the 1970s. In 1976, Bordaberry was overthrown when he proposed a fascist-style regime, with himself at its head. After a succession of problems finding acceptable civilian leaders, military leader General Gregorio Álvarez Armelino assumed the presidency himself in 1981.

End of Military Rule and the Tupamaros

Over the next four years, Álvarez tried to gain popular consensus by referendum on constitutional amendments that would safeguard the power of the military. However, the Uruguayan people, despite ominous warnings from the armed forces, twice refused to ratify the constitutional changes. The government was thus forced to make further concessions. In the latter part of 1983, massive spontaneous demonstrations began to take place. Contrary to expectations, the government did not respond with massive repression, and as a result the demonstrations remained peaceful.

In the end, the armed forces proved unwilling or unable to withstand pressure for the restoration of democratic government. Instead, the military was finally able to negotiate a path to elections in November 1984 that was acceptable to the main political parties. Uruguay returned to civilian government in 1985, and its political prisoners received a general amnesty. Among those pardoned in March 1985 were Sendic, who called on the Tupamaros to abandon the armed struggle for peaceful political action, and Seregni, whose military rank as general was restored at the same time.

By 1988, the Tupamaros had totally abandoned the armed struggle, preferring instead to reenter democratic politics by means of the Broad Front Party. The founder of the Tupamaros, Raúl Sendic Antonaccio, died in Paris on April 28, 1989, from injuries sustained during his torture by the Uruguayan authorities. One observer said of the Tupamaros that they "dug the grave of democracy and fell into it themselves."

Peter Calvert

See also: *Definitions, Types, Categories*—Left-Wing and Revolutionary Terrorism; State vs. Nonstate Terrorism.

Further Reading

Kaufan, Edy. *Uruguay in Transition: From Civilian to Military Rule.* New Brunswick, NJ: Transaction Press, 1979.

Porzecanski, Arturo C. *Uruguay's Tupamaros: The Urban Guerrilla.* New York: Praeger, 1973.

Rial, Juan. "Makers and Guardians of Fear: Controlled Terror in Uruguay." In *Fear at the Edge: State Terror and Resistance in Latin America,* ed. Juan Corradi, Patricia Fagen, and Manuel A. Garreton Merino. Berkeley: University of California Press, 1992.

Sosnowski, Saul, and Louise B. Popkin. *Repression, Exile and Democracy: Uruguayan Culture.* Durham, NC: Duke University Press, 1993.

Weinstein, Martin. *Uruguay: Democracy at the Crossroads.* Boulder, CO: Westview, 1988.

Venezuela: Guerrilla Uprising, 1962–1979

Terrorism occurred in Venezuela as part of a guerrilla campaign in the early 1960s. Left-wing militants formed the Armed Forces of National Liberation (FALN) to wage a campaign of urban terrorism in order to prevent the presidential elections of 1963. When this failed, militants turned to a program of rural revolution, which also proved unsuccessful. By 1970, violent opposition of any significance had ceased.

In the early 1960s, Venezuela was regarded by many on the left as one of the most favorable areas in Latin America for successful armed struggle. It had been under dictatorship until a revolt in 1958 toppled the last dictator. The revolt originated among the armed forces and gained strength from an alliance with a patriotic junta of left-wing elements led by a twenty-nine-year-old journalist, Fabricio Ojeda. A democratic government, led by Rómulo Betancourt, took office.

Meanwhile, democracy remained a fragile flower in Venezuela. Rómulo Betancourt, the country's first democratically elected president, had led a long underground campaign against the dictatorship of Peréz Jiménez, who was ousted in 1958. Betancourt was elected in 1959. However, although a Marxist in his youth, Betancourt found himself facing opposition groups who felt that he was simply not left-wing enough. Castro's communist revolution in Cuba in 1959 had inspired uprisings in Latin America. Many Venezuelans also wanted a communist revolution in their country and felt that terrorism was the only way to make it happen.

The government came under fire from other quarters as well, with unsuccessful right-wing military insurrections in San Cristóbal in April 1960 and in the Venezuelan city of Barcelona in June 1961.

Rural Guerrillas

Ojeda's Venezuelan Communist Party (PCV) opposed the new government and set up a militant wing to prepare for armed struggle. Led by Douglas Bravo, the PCV set up a *foco,* a small force of revolutionary guerrillas operating in the countryside. Meanwhile, a group called the Movement of the Revolutionary Left (MIR) had emerged in May 1960, after splitting from the ruling Democratic Action Party. The government moved speedily to arrest its leaders. As a result, there was fighting on the streets and at the university campus of Venezuela's capital, Caracas, from October to December 1960, along with a series of strikes called by the MIR. Betancourt's personal standing had already been elevated when he survived an assassination attempt on June 24, 1960. At a mass rally at El Silencio on December 1, 1960, Betancourt successfully defended his decision to deploy troops to secure the capital. That same month, the MIR unsuccessfully called for the resignation of the government, but MIR opposition leader Domingo Alberto Rangel later admitted that these moves came too late. The government had already established a broad base of support through realistic social reforms. This helped government security forces remain loyal.

When the disturbances of late 1960 were suppressed, the MIR, with support from communist Cuba, also sought to establish guerrilla bases in the countryside. But before the MIR could begin operations, the army discovered a base in January 1962. As a result of this failure of security, the army began a series of small-scale ambushes in March. The ambushes were over such a wide area that many of the twenty groups set up were soon destroyed. The movement suffered excessive losses.

The guerrillas were inadequately trained and organization was poor. However, in isolated incidents during the same year, rebellions led by junior officers within the armed forces raised the scale of insurgencies. In one incident, on May 4, 1962, 450 marines seized the naval base at Puerto Cabello, 250 miles (402 kilometers) east of Caracas, and held it for twenty-four hours. Rebel forces took over the radio station and broadcast appeals for support against the government. But they surrendered when the air force bombed and strafed the radio tower and airport. Two rebels died and ten were injured.

Ojeda himself joined the MIR in July, but he was captured on October 12, 1962. He was sentenced to eighteen years' imprisonment, but he escaped in September 1963 with two companions to continue agitation underground. By that time, President Betancourt was taking a strong anticommunist line. Although he was from a Marxist background and initially had been sympathetic to the Cuban Revolution, Cuba's support for insurrection in his country had alienated him. The anticommunist drive brought new recruits to the MIR.

FALN Terrorism Begins

On February 24, 1963, members of the PCV and the MIR joined with rebels from the military to form the FALN in Caracas. Its first head was Captain Manuel Ponte Rodríguez, one of the leaders of the Puerto Cabello rebellion. On communist insistence, a political wing, the National Liberation Front (FLN), also was formed by the insurgents. Both attempted to assassinate Betancourt on June 13, 1963. In response, Betancourt ordered the arrest of all known communists. In October, Congress again lifted parliamentary immunity so that suspected sympathizers could be detained.

The FALN also set out to attack U.S. interests. Terrorists sabotaged power stations and blew up pipelines owned by U.S. companies. In February 1963, armed FALN stowaways captured the *Anzoategui,* a 3,000-ton (2,722-metric ton) ship on its way to New Orleans, and took it to Brazil.

The FALN was intent on gaining publicity, and it selected targets accordingly. In August 1963, guerrillas disguised as police officers abducted Argentine soccer superstar Alfredo di Stefano and held him for two days. In November, four terrorists seized a Venezuelan airliner with seventeen people on board. After scattering communist leaflets over the city of Ciudad Bolívar, the hijackers demanded to go to Trinidad. On November 27, terrorists kidnapped U.S. army attaché Colonel James Chenault. They released him after the government freed several left-wing radicals. The same year, terrorists stole French paintings from an important exhibition, only to return them three days later.

The insurgents then tried a variety of terrorist methods to disrupt the presidential elections of December 1963. Their failure to achieve this was a blow to their credibility. The PCV accepted the amnesty offered to them by the new president, Raúl Leoni. This ended the possibility of mass insurrection. Although substantial elements of the FALN remained in the field through 1967, they did not pose a significant threat to the fledgling democracy.

Armed Struggle Wanes

Raúl Leoni succeeded Betancourt as president in March 1964. He offered to lift the ban on the operation of the PCV on condition that the armed struggle was abandoned. The PCV accepted the offer and withdrew its support for guerrilla activity.

Bravo became leader of the FALN and issued a manifesto in March 1966. The FALN embarked on a campaign of urban terrorism in 1966, including the systematic assassination of police officers. This campaign alienated support in the cities, but the FALN remained popular in the countryside.

On March 1, 1967, FALN members abducted former director of social security Julio Iribarren Borges, the foreign minister's brother. On March 2, his body was found with gunshot wounds and signs of torture. The terrorists also left the message, "For each member of the FALN killed, we kill three of our enemies." But by the end of 1967, the FALN was no longer a serious threat. Ojeda had died in police custody in July 1966 and the PCV had expelled Bravo.

The FALN continued to receive Cuban backing, however, until 1969, when the Christian Democrats took power in Venezuela. The Soviet Union, wishing to establish relations with the new government, pressured Cuba into withdrawing support for the guerrillas. The Christian Democrats offered an amnesty, which most of the guerrillas accepted, and FALN activity ceased. Bravo resisted and left the country. He returned in 1975 to help release his colleagues in a dramatic jailbreak. Finally, in 1979, after eighteen years of militant opposition, Bravo accepted an amnesty deal from the government.

In the end, the terrorists were neutralized largely by the government's political strategy. Both Betancourt and his successor showed themselves ready to act against the insurgent threat without trying to create a dictatorship. They were helped both by the mistakes of the insurgents, especially in the unpopular use of terrorism in the cities, and by Venezuela's growing economic strength, which officials used to reward their supporters and so isolate the guerrillas. Deprived of popular support, the terrorist movements were unable to survive.

Peter Calvert

See also: *Definitions, Types, Categories*—Left-Wing and Revolutionary Terrorism.

Further Reading

Blank, David Eugene. *Venezuela: Politics in a Petroleum Republic.* New York: Praeger, 1984.

KEY DATES

1958 Left-wing officers in the military lead a revolt overthrowing Venezuelan dictator Marcos Peréz Jiménez.

1960 Left-wing revolutionaries form the Movement of the Revolutionary Left (MIR).

1963 MIR rebels join with members of the Venezuelan Communist Party (PCV) to form the Armed Forces of National Liberation (FALN) and its political wing, the National Liberation Front (FLN); FALN militants kidnap Argentine soccer star Alfredo di Stefano, blow up pipelines and power stations owned by U.S. companies, hijack a Venezuelan freighter, and attempt to violently disrupt presidential elections.

1964 An offer of amnesty gets the PCV to abandon the rebel movement.

1967 FALN members kidnap the former director of social security and then kill him.

1969 Under pressure from the Soviet Union, the Cuban government abandons its support for the FALN; the new Christian Democratic government in Venezuela offers a general amnesty, which is accepted by most guerrillas; the rebel movement all but comes to a halt.

1975 FALN leader Douglas Bravo returns to the country and leads a jailbreak of his colleagues.

1979 Bravo accepts amnesty from the government, officially bringing the rebellion to an end.

Ellner, Steve. *Venezuela's Movimiento al Socialismo: From Guerrilla Defeat to Innovative Politics.* Durham, NC: Duke University Press, 1988.

Hernandez, Tosca. "Extraordinary Police Operations in Venezuela." In *Vigilantism and the State in Modern Latin America,* ed. Martha Kinsley Huggins. New York: Praeger, 1991.

Hillman, Richard S. *Democracy for the Privileged: Crisis and Transition in Venezuela.* Boulder, CO: Lynne Rienner, 1994.

Lombardi, John V. *Venezuela: The Search for Order, the Dream of Progress.* New York: Oxford University Press, 1982.

McCoy, Jennifer. *Venezuelan Democracy Under Stress.* Miami, FL: University of Miami North-South Center, 1995.

Vietnam: American War, 1959–1975

Of all the conflicts fought to contain communism during the Cold War, none has provoked so much debate as the Vietnam War. Commentators have questioned not only the validity of the U.S. forces' involvement, but also their methods of combat. Three major areas of terror were used by the various combatants. The first was formal terrorism by the communist Vietcong; the second was the search-and-destroy missions of the U.S. ground forces; and the third was the extensive bombing campaigns carried out by the U.S. Air Force.

Vietnam was once a colony of the French Empire. It gained its independence in 1954, after communist-led revolutionaries, the Vietminh, defeated the French Far East Expeditionary Corps in a decisive battle at Dien Bien Phu in the north of the country. The resulting peace accord, signed in Geneva, partitioned Vietnam at the seventeenth parallel into two states, North Vietnam and South Vietnam. The communists, headed by Ho Chi Minh, took over the administration of North Vietnam, with the capital at Hanoi. In South Vietnam, an American-backed regime was set up under premier Ngo Dinh Diem.

Both regimes immediately set about consolidating their power. The communist regime, the Democratic Republic of Vietnam, as North Vietnam became known, used methods that can only be described as state terror. As General Vo Nguyen Giap, creator of the Vietminh military organization that fought the French, admitted, "We attacked on too large a front, and, seeing enemies everywhere, resorted to terror . . . disciplinary punishments, expulsions from the party, executions. . . . Worse still, torture came to be regarded as normal practice." Similarly, Diem's regime, the Government of (South) Vietnam, launched a drive against those Vietminh supporters who remained in South Vietnam. So-called security committees tried and convicted many South Vietnamese, regularly using torture, execution, and incarceration in prison camps. Hence, the people of Vietnam, both North and South, became used to living under conditions of oppression and terror.

Vietcong Assassination Campaign

Starting in 1959, North Vietnam encouraged and supported insurgency in their rival state, South Vietnam. This was designed to spread communist doctrine, reduce support for the government there, and, ultimately, "liberate" South Vietnam. Using the guerrilla tactics pioneered by China's Mao Zedong, communist cadres—known collectively as the National Liberation Front, or Vietcong—began a program of armed revolt backed by political and logistical support from the North.

In indoctrination leaflets, the Vietcong's military organization claimed members of the Liberation Front would "perform armed propaganda, liquidate tyrants in the area, and subvert in all ways the enemy's hold on the people." Secret guerrilla and special activity cells, each one usually comprising three fighters, undertook this subversion.

Between 1959 and 1965, assassination teams drawn from the special activity cells killed thousands of village and district officials of the South Vietnamese government. Many more were kidnapped or beaten. The purpose of this violence was to intimidate the general population. A 1962 Vietcong declaration specified this use of terror: "It is the duty of all to support the Revolution. If you obey orders you will be forgiven by the people and the Liberation Army. . . . If you work for the enemy you will be punished according to the law." Assassination was not indiscriminate, and great care was taken to make sure there were no unexplained killings. For example, leaflets were issued denouncing certain killings as being the work of bandits masquerading as Vietcong soldiers.

After 1965, the Liberation Front's assassination program tailed off. However, the terror continued in concerted attempts to undermine support for South Vietnam. The methods of terrorism were less discriminating than the assassination program. The dynamiting of trains was commonplace. Despite warning leaflets stuck to train seats, many civilians were killed as a result of these attacks.

In urban areas, Vietcong death squads operated on a regular basis. Such was the terror that they instilled in people that, often, the mere threat of violence was enough for Vietcong subversion to be swiftly successful. Attacks against American personnel in Vietnam were not particularly widespread. The Hanoi leadership discouraged an all-out terror campaign against American forces as being tactically unjustified. The Vietcong terror campaigns were targeted mainly at the people of South Vietnam, to eliminate opposition forces and provoke an authoritarian response from South Vietnamese forces. However, the methods first used by the Vietcong against their own people were employed extensively in the ground war against the United States after 1965. Grenade traps, mines, trip wires, and spiked booby traps all contributed to the dangerous and terrifying conditions faced by American soldiers.

Conflict of Theory and Practice

In any fight against an enemy using guerrilla tactics, the main weapons in the arsenal of the defenders are psychological. Guerrillas use the civilian population to shield their operations. Their strength comes from their ability to melt into the countryside and disperse. A defense force must therefore isolate the guerrillas from the civilians, cutting them off from their source of protection. The defense must generate sympathy for the antiguerrilla cause with the local inhabitants.

The Americans used this well-established principle in Vietnam. A card entitled "The Nine Rules" was given to every U.S. soldier in Vietnam. It began, "The Vietnamese have paid a heavy price in suffering for their long fight against the communists. We military men are in Vietnam because their government have [*sic*] asked us to help their soldiers and people in winning their struggle. The Vietcong will attempt to turn the Vietnamese against you. You can defeat them at every turn by the strength, understanding, and generosity you display with the people."

It was counterproductive for the American forces in Vietnam to use any form of terror as a tactic against the population of South Vietnam. Hence, a pacification program was introduced to separate the population from the Vietcong. Military operations could then be undertaken without endangering civilians, whose support was needed if the Vietcong were to be defeated. The villagers were to be moved to pacification camps, where they would be safe from military actions. Such was the theory; the reality was different.

Much of the civilian population remained outside the pacification camps. In August 1967, under Operation Benton, the camps became so full that the army was ordered not to drive any more civilians from their farms. As former chairman of the Joint Chiefs of Staff Admiral Thomas H. Sharp explained, "We should have fought in the north, where everyone was the enemy, where you didn't have to worry whether or not you were shooting friendly civilians. In the south, we had to cope with women concealing grenades in their brassieres, or in their baby's diapers."

To prevent such chaos, American troops were expected to operate under certain rules while on patrol. Any village could be bombed or shelled if American troops had received fire from within it. Any village known to be hostile could be bombed or shelled if its inhabitants were warned in advance by leaflet drop or loudspeaker from helicopter. Once the civilian population had been moved out, a free-fire zone could be declared and the villages and surrounding countryside could be attacked at will. In practice, these restraining rules were flexibly applied or ignored completely. Warnings of impending bombardment by leaflet or loudspeaker were often useless to peasants who could not read or understand English.

Free-fire zones were often designated in areas that were not fully "pacified." This resulted in the death of many civilians for whom there was no room in the overcrowded pacification camps. Many villagers had no

control over, nor the ability to influence, the Vietcong cadres operating in their area. They were just as terrified of the punishments meted out by the Vietcong's special activity cells as they were of American firepower.

The Americans employed a search-and-destroy strategy that relied on killing as many of the enemy as possible. According to the commander of U.S. combat forces, General William Westmoreland, the aim was to "find, fix in place, fight, and destroy (or neutralize) enemy forces and their base areas and supply caches." The object was not to hold ground.

The emphasis in mission reports was on body counts. Officers were promoted and recreation passes granted to enlisted men for meeting body-count quotas. As a result, at times, all pretense of following the rules of engagement was dropped. In some cases, because only body counts mattered, prisoners were in danger of on-the-spot execution. An unofficial history by "Cincinnatus," an alias used by a member of the U.S. army reserve, claimed that some units' policy was to "kill them if they try to surrender—we need the body count."

Helicopter gunship pilot David Bressum testified that air cavalry units frequently followed unwritten rules. Individuals were often killed without proper clearance: "If we received clearance, we would report it as a kill. If we did not receive clearance, we would just forget about it. This happened all the time." This was, in part, a reaction to the hazardous nature of patrolling. Booby traps, snipers, and ambushes were the most frequent form of engagement and, with few clear targets except villages that might or might not be hostile, many American soldiers saw such an attitude as the only guarantee of survival.

While these factors do not add up to the use of terror as explicit policy, the real result was a population caught between punishment by the Vietcong for collaboration and attack by American or South Vietnamese ground and air forces. As in a situation of state-sponsored terrorism, villagers were killed for supporting either side or simply for being in the wrong place at the wrong time. As one soldier put it, "If a village is not VC [Vietcong] when we go into it, it's VC when we leave."

From 1968, U.S. Navy special forces and South Vietnamese forces undertook counterterror operations under the auspices of the Civil Operations and Revolutionary Development Support—an organization that aimed to coordinate pacification. The organization's chief, William Colby, believed that the only possible path was to rebuild village society in South Vietnam, as a stronghold of progovernment influence.

At the core of pacification was the Phoenix operation, designed to smash the Vietcong cadres. According to Colby, Phoenix operatives were not authorized to engage in assassination or "other violations of the rules of land warfare." Evidence suggests, however, that between 1968 and 1971, some 28,000 Vietcong insurgents were captured and approximately 20,000 killed. U.S. Navy officer Mike Beamon reported that assassinations were devised to make it appear that the Vietcong had done the killing. North Vietnam claims that, in some provinces, 95 percent of communist cadres were neutralized by Phoenix.

Air War

Between 1965 and 1973, at least 8 million tons of munitions were dropped on Vietnam, Laos, and Cambodia. The intentions of strategic bombing under the so-called Rolling Thunder (1965–1968) and Linebacker (1972–1973) campaigns were roughly the same as those of the 1940s. The United States aimed to destroy the enemy's war-making capability and weaken morale, inflicting enough damage to persuade the leadership to sue for peace.

President Lyndon B. Johnson, explaining the objectives of Rolling Thunder in March 1967, claimed that bombing North Vietnam had three objectives. It aimed to deny the enemy a sanctuary, to exact a penalty against North Vietnam for violations of the Geneva Convention, and to limit the flow of materials and increase the cost of logistical support and infiltration from North to South Vietnam. The unstated objective, however, was to demonstrate the superiority of American technology and resources.

Civilian morale was not viewed as a primary target of the air campaign. In 1966, a paper by Assistant Secretary of Defense John McNaughton stated that "strikes at population targets are likely . . . to create a counterproductive wave of revulsion abroad and at home." The bombing was directed primarily at breaking the will of the Hanoi leadership to continue its support of the insurgency in South Vietnam.

As a measure of U.S. determination to minimize civilian casualties and deflect any accusations of terror bombing, geographical restrictions were placed on all bombing raids. The so-called Hanoi Do-not, an area around Hanoi where much of the North Vietnamese population resided, was declared off-limits. The self-imposed restrictions left few legitimate military targets for the air force to hit. Lacking any heavy industry and arms factories, North Vietnam acted as a staging area for Soviet and Chinese material passing to the battlefields of the south. A Central Intelligence Agency report of 1966 claimed that the geographical restriction meant that "almost 80 percent of North Vietnam's limited modern, industrial economy and 75 percent of the nation's population . . . have been effectively insulated from air attack." The Joint Chiefs of Staff argued in March 1968 that there were no real civilians left in the cities of Hanoi and Haiphong: "Air strikes in and around these cities endanger personnel primarily engaged, directly or indirectly, in support of the war effort." As a result, restricted areas were gradually reduced as militarily viable targets became harder to find.

The bombing campaigns, despite their intensity, did not achieve their objectives. Logistical support to the Vietcong transported down the Ho Chi Minh Trail, a supply route through Laos to South Vietnam, continued to operate with increasing efficiency. The 1967 Jason Study (a U.S. Senate scientific investigation) reported that Operation Rolling Thunder had no measurable effect on North Vietnamese military support to the southern insurgents. Furthermore, they concluded that "the bombing clearly strengthened popular support of the regime by engendering patriotic and nationalistic enthusiasm to resist attacks."

It is clear that Rolling Thunder did not target civilians intentionally. However, numerous reports from foreign observers collected in 1971 maintained that a number of raids using antipersonnel weapons destroyed many schools, churches, and hospitals, resulting in significant civilian casualties. U.S. General William W. Momyer claimed that many civilian casualties were self-inflicted by the North Vietnamese defense forces through indiscriminate firing of antiaircraft rounds and surface-to-air missiles. "Never in the course of the war," he stated, "was a target selected for any reason other than its military significance." However, in a report by General Westmoreland on the bombing campaign of 1966–1968, more than 10,000 objectives identified simply as "buildings" were listed as damaged or destroyed. It is inconceivable that these were all viable military targets, given that military installations were listed separately. A Defense Department study of 1966 calculated that 65 percent of the total tonnage of bombs and artillery rounds was expended against places where the enemy "might" have been. In other words, there was no reliable intelligence that the enemy was there.

Under the administration of President Richard M. Nixon, all geographical restrictions were lifted for the Linebacker Two campaign of 1972–1973. With the objective of coercing the North Vietnamese into a cease-fire arrangement, 40,000 tons of bombs were dropped on the corridor between Hanoi and Haiphong. Although encouraged to exaggerate their statistics by American antiwar campaigners, the North Vietnamese set civilian deaths at approximately 1,600. These raids should be considered as terror bombing because their aim was simply to "communicate" rather than destroy military capabilities. President Nixon himself described the action as an application of his "madman" theory. The intention was to convince North Vietnam that he would go to any lengths to reach a settlement, including massive urban air attacks and ultimately a nuclear strike.

Drawing Conclusions

Throughout the war in Vietnam, the Vietcong employed terrorism as a specific tactic. It was designed to coerce the population of South Vietnam into supporting the insurgents. At the very least, the terrorism was intended to compel the South Vietnamese to stop supporting their government's efforts at controlling the insurgency. The explicit purpose of the assassination campaign was to wipe out any civilian opposition to the communist cadres operating in the villages. Similarly, the urban campaigns relied heavily on terror attacks. Assaults against American personnel cannot, however, be described as acts of terrorism. As combatants involved in or supporting the war effort, they should be considered legitimate military targets.

It was not the policy of American forces to engender a feeling of terror among the Vietnamese civilians. But the lax application of the rules of engagement created an atmosphere of terror, despite the fact that it ran counter to America's antiguerrilla strategy. Indeed, the atmosphere of terror served only to legitimize the Vietcong's efforts. In addition, the strategy of attrition, which laid such emphasis on body counts, resulted in serious infringements of the self-imposed restrictions. Civilians were permanently at risk from attack by one side or the other. On the other hand, the difficulties faced by American ground forces should not be underestimated. Vietcong tactics increased the terror faced by U.S. combat personnel and led to the indiscriminate methods used in some search-and-destroy missions.

The American bombing campaigns, especially Rolling Thunder, were not, as a matter of policy, terror attacks in the mold of the widespread bombing of civilian targets during World War II. President Johnson described Rolling Thunder as "the most careful, self-limiting air war in history." However, the gradual lifting of geographical restrictions as the conflict progressed and the sheer tonnage of munitions dropped on North Vietnam caused significant numbers of civilian deaths.

In the end, the temptation to strike at urban targets in an attempt to break the will of the North Vietnamese government led to Operation Linebacker Two. In terms of results, this could be described as a terror bombing campaign even though the civilian population was not a specific target of the raids.

During the Vietnam War, the citizens of both the north and the south suffered as a result of the strategies employed by both sides. The Vietcong created an atmosphere of terror as matter of policy. American forces contributed to this terror by default.

Gregory Simpson

See also: *Definitions, Types, Categories*—Left-Wing and Revolutionary Terrorism; State vs. Nonstate Terrorism. *Modern Terrorism*—France: Response to Anti-Colonial Struggles; Indochina (Cambodia, Laos, Vietnam): Anti-French Conflict.

Further Reading

Fitzgerald, Frances. *Fire in the Lake: The Vietnamese and the Americans in Vietnam.* Boston: Little, Brown, 2002.

Gallucci, Robert L. *Neither Peace nor Honor.* Baltimore: Johns Hopkins University Press, 1975.

Gibson, James W. *The Perfect War.* New York: Vintage, 1986.

Karnow, Stanley. *Vietnam: A History.* New York: Penguin Books, 1997.

Walzer, Michael. *Just and Unjust Wars.* New York: Basic Books, 1992.

Yemen: Civil War and Islamist Terrorism, 1990s–2000s

The Republic of Yemen, a Middle Eastern country on the Arabian Peninsula, shares land borders with Saudi Arabia to the north and the Sultanate of Oman to the northeast, and its coastline touches the Arabian Sea, the Gulf of Aden, and the Red Sea. Yemen has a mountainous interior surrounded by desert, with a flat, sandy coastal plain. The climate is temperate in the mountainous regions in the western part of the country and extremely hot, with minimal rainfall, in the rest of the country. The population of Yemen is about 24 million, mostly Arab in ethnicity. The predominant religion is Islam (although there are small numbers of Jews, Christians, and Hindus), divided between Shafi'i (Sunni) and Zaydi (Shia) schools of thought.

Yemen has long been one of the poorest countries in the Arab world, a situation that began to change with the beginning of oil production in the mid-1990s. Since then, the International Monetary Fund has been active in Yemen, helping to institute a structural adjustment program designed to modernize the economy. The World Bank has also been active, providing loans. Yemen's dependence on petroleum production means that its economy is vulnerable to fluctuations in oil prices. This vulnerability may be alleviated somewhat when Yemen's reserves of liquid natural gas begin to be exploited on a large scale. The country's first liquefied natural gas plant went online in late 2009. A high population growth rate (estimated at 2.7 percent in 2010) complicates the task of economic reform and is a contributing factor to relatively high levels of unemployment.

History

Yemen is one of the older centers of civilization in the Middle East, a position created in large part by the ancient spice trade. Following the emergence of Islam in the seventh century, Yemen came under the influence of the first Arab caliphates. Following this, indigenous Islamic religious dynasties (or imamates) emerged in the north of the country, which established a theocratic political structure that survived into the twentieth century. By the sixteenth century, the Ottoman Empire had established a presence in northern Yemen, although control was centered on the cities, with the imam's control of tribal areas formally acknowledged by the Ottomans. In 1839, the British captured the port of Aden and the surrounding southern districts (southern Yemen), which were administered as part of the Indian Empire until 1937, when Aden became a crown colony and the

surrounding areas (East and West Aden) became British protectorates. By 1965 most of the tribal entities within Aden and the protectorates had come together to form the British-sponsored Federation of South Arabia. Northern Yemen was abandoned by the Ottomans in 1918, after which the imamate assumed control. The imam was deposed in 1962 by revolutionary forces, and the Yemen Arab Republic was formed. Egypt assisted the Yemen Arab Republic, while Saudi Arabia and Jordan supported the royalist forces of the imam. Fighting continued sporadically until 1967, when Egyptian troops were withdrawn.

In 1967, the British withdrew from southern Yemen following an intensive two-year guerrilla and terrorist campaign. The south became the People's Republic of South Yemen following the British withdrawal and in 1970 adopted a Marxist system of government, becoming the People's Democratic Republic of Yemen (PDRY). The PDRY established close relations with the Eastern bloc countries as well as radical Palestinian groups. The PDRY enjoyed difficult relations with its neighbors, engaging in military clashes with Saudi Arabia in 1969 and 1973 and providing support for the Dhofar Rebellion against the Sultanate of Oman. Diplomatic relations were further strained when the PDRY became the only Arab state to vote against admitting new Arab states from the Gulf area to either the United Nations or the Arab League. Although there was talk of reunification, relations between the two states were strained, and in 1979 these tensions erupted briefly into open fighting. In 1986, political tensions within the PDRY led to intense fighting in Aden and a leadership change. In 1988, the two countries agreed to renew talks on unification, and in 1990 the two states merged to form the Republic of Yemen.

Shortly afterward, during the Gulf Crisis and subsequent Persian Gulf War, Yemen supported Iraq (Yemen was at the time a member of the UN Security Council), a stance that led to Western and Gulf states suspending aid programs and diplomatic ties. Nearly 1 million Yemeni workers were also repatriated from Saudi Arabia and the Gulf. Integration continued, however. A "unity constitution" was ratified by the population of Yemen in May 1991, and the former northern capital, Sanaa, became the capital of united Yemen, though the seaport of Aden remains the country's commercial center. Despite these moves toward stability, a secessionist movement broke out in the south of the country in 1994, gaining the support of many of Yemen's neighbors. The secessionists did not receive international recognition, and the movement was quickly defeated. Since the end of this conflict, progress has been made in restoring relations with Yemen's neighbors. Yemen's fifty-year border dispute with Saudi Arabia has been settled with an international border treaty, and the border with Oman has been officially demarcated. Yemen held its first direct presidential election in 1999, electing Ali Abdullah Saleh (former president of North Yemen) in relatively free and fair elections. A constitutional amendment in 2000 extended the president's tenure by two years, moving the date of the next presidential elections to 2006, which Saleh won by an overwhelming margin in a contest that international observers once again verified as "open and genuine." Yemen is a member of the United Nations, the Arab League, and the Organization of the Islamic Conference.

Yemen and the War on Terror

Yemen's connection with terrorist organizations is a long one. As early as 1967, the PDRY was placed on the U.S. list of nations that support terrorist activity for providing sanctuary and material support to a variety of international terrorist groups, particularly those related to the Palestinian struggle. Although the United States has maintained diplomatic relations with the united Yemen since 1990, many terrorist groups have had a presence in the country since then. These include Hamas, Palestinian Islamic Jihad, Egyptian Islamic Jihad, al-Gama'a al-Islamiyya, Libyan opposition groups, the Algerian Groupe Islamique Armé, al-Qaeda, and a variety of other Islamic organizations. Other indigenous terrorist groups also exist, such as the Islamic Army of Aden (one of the three groups that claimed responsibility for the USS *Cole* bombing) and Shabaab al-Muomineen (Believing Youth).

In October 2000, Islamic terrorists, allegedly associated with al-Qaeda, attacked the USS *Cole* in the port of Aden, killing seventeen U.S. servicemen. Relations between Yemen and the United States plummeted amid accusations that Sanaa was unwilling or unable to help in the investigation. The United States has publicly stated that the current Yemeni government is neither directly nor indirectly involved in support for terrorism. Rather, the government is hampered by its inability to control its own borders and some of its own territory and by the inadequacy of Yemeni travel documentation—in 2000 the government tightened the passport application process, but terrorists still have access to passable forgeries. Support is bolstered for Islamic terrorist groups by the long tradition of conservative Islam as exemplified by the Yemeni imamate (particularly in the northwest), by the absence of central control in many regions of the country, and by the proximity to the southwestern

Wahhabi areas of Saudi Arabia. Islam is also represented at the political level by the Islamic Reform Grouping, or Islah Party (a junior partner in the current coalition government). Islah leaders derive their support base from conservative Islamic tribesmen, and the party leadership has repeatedly objected to a U.S. presence in the country. The country's role in supplying terrorists to organizations such as al-Qaeda can be noted in the fact that roughly 40 percent of the hard-core detainees at Guantánamo in 2010 were Yemeni nationals.

Still, since September 11, 2001, and the onset of the war on terrorism, relations between the two countries have improved dramatically. Shortly after, the U.S State Department described Yemen as "an important partner in the campaign against terrorism." Yemen and its immediate surroundings represent an important theater of operations in the war against terrorism and for maintaining U.S. security interests in the Gulf region. In April 2002, the Yemeni and U.S. governments signed an agreement allowing U.S. warships to once more use Aden and allowing U.S. Marines to provide security in cooperation with Yemeni forces. In November 2002, the Yemeni government gave the go-ahead for a successful U.S. Predator drone attack on an automobile in its territory, which was carrying half a dozen alleged terrorists, including al-Qaeda in Yemen leader and USS *Cole* attack mastermind Qaed Salim Sinan al-Harethi. A year later, Yemeni security forces arrested his replacement, utilizing U.S. intelligence.

Yemen has also received significant monetary and technical aid in its efforts to combat terrorists operating on its territory. To beef up the country's coastal defenses and to prevent infiltration by Islamist extremists from Somalia (Yemen is home to tens of thousands of Somali refugees, as well as an older population of several hundred thousand ethnic Somalis), the United States helped Yemen develop a coast guard force. In addition, the United States continues to equip and train a variety of Yemeni security forces, including the Anti-Terrorism Unit of its Central Security Agency.

Despite President Ali Abdullah Saleh's efforts to cooperate with Washington on the war on terrorism, many experts argue that Yemen—and particularly its tribal areas in the north—offered sanctuary to al-Qaeda operatives and that the operatives of the terrorist organization infiltrated the country's security services. An attack against the French tanker *Limburg* in October 2002, in which one crewmember was killed and 90,000 gallons (340,687 liters) of oil were spilled into the Gulf of Aden, was launched from Yemen. More recently, on September 17, 2008, the U.S. embassy was attacked. In that assault—for which the al-Qaeda affiliate Islamic Jihad of Yemen claimed responsibility—attackers dressed as policemen used car bombs, automatic weapons, and rocket-propelled grenades to try to storm the embassy. While the attack was

KEY DATES

1999   Yemen holds its first direct presidential poll, electing Ali Abdullah Saleh, the former president of North Yemen.

October 2000   Islamic terrorists, allegedly associated with al-Qaeda, attack the American warship USS *Cole* in the harbor of Aden, Yemen's main port, killing seventeen servicemen.

April 2002   Yemen and the United States sign an agreement allowing U.S. warships to once more use Aden harbor and to allow U.S. Marines to provide security in cooperation with Yemeni forces.

October 2002   Terrorists launch an attack against the French tanker *Limburg* from Yemeni territory.

November 2002   An unmanned CIA aircraft fires a missile at a car, killing al-Qaeda operative Qaed Salim Sinan al-Harethi and five others.

September 2008   Militants, allegedly part of the terrorist organization Islamic Jihad in Yemen, an al-Qaeda affiliate, launch an armed attack on the U.S. embassy in Sanaa that leaves nineteen Yemeni nationals dead, including seven of the perpetrators.

December 2009   A Nigerian national with close connections to Yemeni cleric Anwar al-Awlaki unsuccessfully attempts to blow up a jetliner bound from Amsterdam to Detroit on Christmas Day.

Early 2011   Pro-democracy demonstrations sweep the country, forcing President Ali Abdullah Saleh to step down.

ultimately unsuccessful and the assailants were fought off by embassy and Yemeni security forces, it led to the deaths of six civilians and six Yemeni police, along with seven of the attackers; no Americans were killed in the attack. A day later, Yemeni authorities rounded up thirty suspects with varying ties to the group.

Anwar al-Awlaki

Another concern of Washington has been the activities of Anwar al-Awlaki. An American-born Islamic cleric of Yemeni origins, al-Awlaki is believed by U.S. authorities to have met with a number of terrorists while working in the United States as an imam and an official for an Islamic charity in the 1990s and early 2000s, including persons connected to the 1993 World Trade Center bombing and two of the nineteen 9/11 hijackers. He also provided religious and political instruction to Nidal Malik Hasan, the Muslim U.S. Army major allegedly responsible for the Fort Hood, Texas, massacre in November 2009 in which twelve soldiers and a civilian Defense Department employee were killed. After a two-year stint in the United Kingdom from 2002 to 2004, where he preached a violent jihadist message to Muslim youth, al-Awlaki returned to Yemen, where he settled in his family's ancestral town. In August 2006, he was arrested by Yemeni authorities, allegedly upon the urging of U.S. Federal Bureau of Investigation agents, but was released at the end of 2007.

Al-Awlaki has been a major concern to both U.S. and Yemeni officials ever since. A member of a powerful tribe in the south of the country, he has offered the sanctuary provided by fellow tribesmen for al-Qaeda operatives in the country. At the same time that he allegedly provides this traditional form of help to Islamist terrorists, al-Awlaki has also embraced modern technology, providing videoconferencing lectures on jihad and Islamist politics to mosques in the United Kingdom. British authorities say he offered religious and political instruction to the terrorists who perpetrated the July 2005 bombings of the London transportation system, which killed fifty-two persons. Al-Awlaki's facility with social media has earned him the moniker "the bin Laden of the Internet."

Al-Awlaki came to the attention of the American public after the attempted Christmas Day 2009 bombing of a Northwest Airlines jet bound from Amsterdam to Detroit. The alleged perpetrator of the plot, a young Nigerian national named Umar Farouk Abdulmutallab is said to have received ideological training from al-Awlaki when he traveled to Yemen in the mid-2000s. Abdulmutallab continued to receive indoctrination in extremist Islamist thought right up to the attacks, via al-Awlaki's presence on the Internet. The Barack Obama Administration considered al-Awlaki's influence so dangerous that it included him among the international terrorists slated for government assassination by Predator drone or missile.

Meanwhile, the Saudi and Yemeni branches of al-Qaeda joined forces in 2009 to form Al-Qaeda in the Arabian Peninsula (AQAP). Initially dedicated to the overthrow of what it considered apostate regimes in the two countries, AQAP was influenced by al-Awlaki to go after international targets. To that end, it claimed responsibility for sending package bombs from Yemen to targets in the United States via UPS in late October 2010; among the targets was a Chicago synagogue. The packages, which never exploded, were found by authorities during layovers in Dubai and the United Kingdom. Days later, a female Yemeni engineering student was arrested for sending the packages. In response to the spread of AQAP, the Obama Administration accelerated drone attacks against suspected members, while aiding the Saleh regime in fighting the organization on the ground.

In early 2011, however, Saleh's authoritarian rule faced an outbreak of mass protests inspired by the pro-democracy demonstrations in Tunisia and Egypt. When the protests grew larger and more widespread, national security forces responded with tear gas and finally bullets. The United States and other Western powers expressed "concern" at the devolving situation but, according to analysts, feared antagonizing a key ally in the struggle against Islamist terrorism. Saleh finally announced that he would step down in late May, and the United States expressed its intention to lend social, economic, and political assistance while striving to preserve the counter-terrorism campaign. Al-Awlaki remained at large in southern Yemen and AQAP very much alive.

Angus Muir

See also: *Definitions, Types, Categories*—Islamist Fundamentalist Terrorism. *September 11 Attacks*—Al-Qaeda.

Further Reading

Burrowes, Robert. *Historical Dictionary of Yemen.* Lanham, MD: Scarecrow, 1995.

Dresch, Paul. *A History of Modern Yemen.* New York: Cambridge University Press, 2000.

———. *Tribal Government and History in Yemen.* Oxford: Clarendon Press, 1989.

Dumont, Gabriel A., ed. *Yemen: Background, Issues, and Al Qaeda Role.* Hauppauge, NY: Nova Sciences, 2010.

Peterson, John. *Yemen: The Search for a Modern State.* London: Croom Helm, 1982.

U.S. Department of State. *Background Note: Yemen.* Washington, DC: U.S. Government Printing Office, January 2002.

———. *Patterns of Global Terrorism, 2000.* Washington, DC: U.S. Government Printing Office, 2001.

U.S. Senate. *Al Qaeda in Yemen and Somalia: A Ticking Time Bomb.* A Report to the Committee on Foreign Relations, United States Senate, 111th Congress, 2nd sess., January 21, 2010. Washington, DC: U.S. Government Printing Office, 2010.

Zimbabwe (Rhodesia): Liberation Struggle and Postliberation Violence, 1965–2000s

On November 11, 1965, the British colony of Rhodesia (now Zimbabwe), led by a white minority, declared itself independent. Prime Minister Ian Smith declared that "never in a thousand years" would he accept black majority rule, although only 5 percent of Rhodesia's population was white. As a result, African nationalists set up two terrorist groups to oppose white rule. The Zimbabwe People's Revolutionary Army (ZIPRA), based in Zambia, drew strength from the small but powerful Ndebele community. The Zimbabwe African National Liberation Army (ZANLA), based in Mozambique, drew from the larger Shona tribe.

Differences between the two forces soon became apparent, although their targets were initially similar. China armed and influenced ZANLA. The Soviet Union armed and trained ZIPRA. Both groups launched guerrilla attacks on white-owned farms and police bases between 1966 and 1969 but were all but annihilated by the Rhodesian security forces.

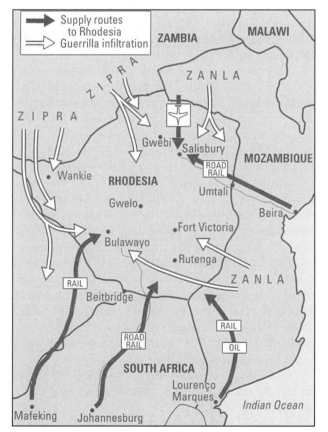

The terrorist group ZIPRA was based in Zambia; ZANLA operated from Mozambique.

After peace talks failed in 1971, ZANLA hit white targets again. They attacked a farm on December 21, 1972, wounding a three-year-old girl. The Rhodesians countered by launching Operation Hurricane and, by September 1975, claimed 651 guerrilla deaths at a cost of 73 fatalities among their own troops. In June 1975, when neighboring Mozambique became independent, ZANLA gained safe bases from which to attack eastern Rhodesia. By 1978, an estimated 4,645 ZANLA and 953 ZIPRA recruits were active in Rhodesia.

Whites were not the only targets of ZANLA. The terrorists also wished to control the Shona population and began a campaign to intimidate villagers. For example, on August 13, 1973, in the Kandeya area, a headman was shot dead in front of his assembled villagers. The terrorists also committed other atrocities, including bayoneting, stabbing, or beating villagers to death, shooting parents in front of their children, blowing up country buses, hacking off fingers and lips, severing feet, and inflicting burns.

Using Torture to Enforce Support

ZANLA lectured people on nationalist aims at compulsory rallies called *pungwes,* reinforcing speeches with calculated terror. They tortured or killed suspected progovernment black Africans. In the Mount Darwin District in 1973, for example, terrorists beat two wives of an alleged informer and shot his third wife. Terrorists shot another headman, killed his cattle—the wealth of the village—and burned down every hut. On April 18, 1974, in the Madziwa area, terrorists entered a beer hall. They had a "death list" of those sentenced to die for helping the security forces. Two men answered when their names were called out. Their hands were tied and they were beaten to death before the crowd of 150 people.

The terrorists also attacked rival nationalists, passing strangers, and even people using skin-lightening cosmetics. The police registered 2,751 such killings by 1979. Most people executed at *pungwes* were denounced by *mujibas,* local youths who helped the guerrillas. Many *mujibas* abused their authority by raping, stealing, or killing. The terrorists also killed missionaries and teachers and abducted thousands of pupils for guerrilla training. At night the terrorists forced people to demolish bridges, dig up roads, and cut telephone and electricity lines. Through terror, ZANLA came to dominate the countryside.

From their bases, ZANLA guerrillas regularly raided the 6,000 economically crucial white-owned farms that covered nearly half the country. The terrorists ambushed white farming families, attacked their homes, burned their barns, and stole their cattle. They intimidated or killed black farmworkers and burned down their huts. As a result, people abandoned hundreds of the most exposed white farms.

The guerrillas ambushed roads and railroads and mortared the city of Umtali, but police intelligence made urban terrorism rare. One exception was a bomb that killed eleven black Africans in the capital, Salisbury. The most serious blow to white morale occurred when ZIPRA SAM-7 missiles downed two airliners in September 1978 and February 1979. In the first crash, terrorists shot ten women and children who survived.

Government Countermeasures

In May 1973, the Rhodesian security forces declared a no-go zone 190 miles (306 kilometers) inside the northeastern border and laid widespread minefields. From late 1973, they forcibly removed to protected villages people living in the areas most affected by terrorism in order to deny the guerrillas food, intelligence, and recruits.

In June 1974, the Rhodesians introduced fire forces. A fire force consisted of several helicopters, each carrying four people, who would be dropped around a guerrilla sighting. Backed up by helicopter gunships, they would close in on the guerrillas and destroy them.

Rhodesian special forces also resorted to unconventional countermeasures. One unit, the Selous Scouts, instigated clashes between ZANLA and ZIPRA. The Grey's Scouts, a mounted unit, bred killer dogs to hunt down terrorists. Rhodesia's Central Intelligence Organization assassinated nationalist leaders in exile. Rhodesia's Special Air Service laid mines in neighboring countries. By 1976, the conflict was too expensive for any side to maintain. South Africa put pressure on the Rhodesian regime to come to a political settlement, and countries helping the guerrillas began to insist on a compromise.

A conference in Geneva between groups broke down in January 1977, however, and war continued. More guerrillas entered Rhodesia from neighboring states, forcing white farmers to build security fences around

---

KEY DATES

1965 Rhodesian whites unilaterally declare independence from Great Britain.

1966 Guerrillas representing the black majority of the country launch their first attacks against government targets.

1980 After years of struggle and lengthy negotiations, black liberation fighters take control of the country.

1980s–2000s The government of Robert Mugabe seizes white-owned farms and attacks opposition-party members.

2008 A coalition government is formed between the ruling party and the main opposition party.

---

their homes and to armor their vehicles. The whites also formed local self-defense militias. But the cost of these measures was immense, which pushed Prime Minister Smith to concede majority rule to moderate Africans in Rhodesia. Neither ZANLA nor ZIPRA leaders accepted this deal and continued their attacks.

In 1979, Britain sponsored a cease-fire, and elections followed in 1980. The new constitution included majority rule and safeguards for the white minority. Most of the black population voted along tribal lines. As the Shona was the largest tribe, ZANLA leader Robert Mugabe became president of Zimbabwe.

Postliberation Violence and Repression

In the years following liberation from white minority rule, Mugabe and his Zimbabwe African National Union (ZANU) government became increasingly repressive, launching pacification campaigns in Matabeleland against members of the Patriotic Front–Zimbabwe People's Union (PF-ZAPU), once allies in the struggle against white minority rule and now rivals for national power. Mugabe belonged to the dominant Shona ethnic group, while most PF-ZAPU members were part of the Ndebele minority. The government also launched a campaign to liberate the economy from the tiny white minority, which still owned much of the land and capital assets of the country. This included terror campaigns to drive farmers from their land without compensation and violent seizures of white-owned farms. The lands were supposed to be distributed to landless black peasants but often ended up in the hands of Mugabe supporters, most of whom had little experience or interest in running large commercial farms. In a number of instances, the seizures resulted in the beatings and deaths of farmers and their black laborers who resisted takeover.

As a result of these seizures, Zimbabwe's commercial agricultural sector—critical to the country's exports—went into steep decline, creating an economic crisis marked by hyperinflation, high unemployment, and the exodus of hundreds of thousands of Zimbabweans, mostly to neighboring South Africa. With the countryside increasingly impoverished, tens of thousands of Zimbabweans also moved to the capital, Harare. In 2005, the Mugabe government launched a brutal campaign to drive out these economic refugees, under the chilling rubric Operation Muranbatsvina (Shona for "Sweep out the Trash"). More than 22,000 persons were arrested and had their possessions seized.

In response to the economic crisis and the growing repression, a resistance movement formed under the leadership of Morgan Tsvangirai, a former Mugabe ally in ZANU. The Movement for Democratic Change (MDC), as the opposition party was called, tried to challenge Mugabe's leadership, but some of their leaders, including Tsvangirai himself, were repeatedly arrested, harassed, and even beaten by security forces and thugs working for Mugabe's ruling ZANU party. After a number of fraudulent elections, which kept Mugabe and ZANU in power, international pressure and popular resistance mounted against the regime, forcing it into a power-sharing agreement with Tsvangirai and the MDC in 2008. While the economy improved somewhat under the new coalition government, and the MDC called for the lifting of international sanctions against the country, the harassment of white commercial farmers continued. In addition, the government is said to be responsible for the deaths of dozens of freelance diamond miners during an eviction campaign in 2009 and 2010.

Bertrande Roberts and James Ciment

See also: *Definitions, Types, Categories*—Ethnonationalist Terrorism; State vs. Nonstate Terrorism. *Modern Terrorism*—South Africa: Antiapartheid Struggle.

Further Reading

Auret, Michael. *From Liberator to Dictator: An Insider's Account of Robert Mugabe's Descent into Tyranny.* London: Global, 2009.

Charlton, Michael. *The Last Colony in Africa.* Cambridge, MA: Blackwell, 1990.

Cilliers, J.K. *Counterinsurgency in Rhodesia.* Dover, NH: Croom Helm, 1985.

Godwin, Peter, and Ian Hancock. *'Rhodesians Never Die': The Impact of War and Political Change on Water Rhodesia, c. 1970–1980.* New York: Oxford University Press, 1993.

Holland, Heidi. *Dinner with Mugabe. The Untold Story of a Freedom Fighter Who Became a Tyrant.* New York: Penguin, 2008.

SEPTEMBER 11, 2001—ATTACKS AND RESPONSE

September 11, 2001–Attacks and Response: Introduction

On the morning of September 11, 2001, the United States was attacked by the al-Qaeda terrorist group, which hijacked four transcontinental jetliners and flew three of them into targets in New York and Washington, while a fourth crashed into rural Pennsylvania after passengers confronted the hijackers. The worst terrorist attack in modern world history and the deadliest day in U.S. history since the Civil War, September 11 cost nearly 3,000 American lives and billions of dollars in property and economic damage, and utterly transformed U.S. security and foreign policy.

New York City

The first attack began when al-Qaeda terrorists hijacked American Airlines flight 11, a B-767 carrying ninety-two people, including nine flight attendants and two pilots, shortly after it left Boston's Logan International Airport at 7:59 A.M. for Los Angeles International Airport. The terrorists, using box cutters, knives, and martial arts techniques, took over the plane over New York City. Flight attendant Betty Ann Ong was permitted to phone her supervisor to say that three hijackers had stabbed more than one person on board and planned to crash the plane into New York City. Soon after this initial act, a second plane was hijacked. Al-Qaeda terrorists used box cutters, knives, and martial arts to take over the cockpit of United Airlines flight 175, a B-767, which had taken off at 7:58 A.M. from Boston's Logan International Airport en route to Los Angeles International Airport with sixty-five people on board.

Flight 11 diverted from its scheduled flight path over New York and crashed into New York City's 110-story World Trade Center (WTC) North Tower near the ninety-sixth floor at 8:45 A.M., killing all on board. A fireball engulfed the tower as millions watched on television, hoping that it was a horrible accident. Dozens of people jumped out of the North Tower windows to a certain death in order to escape the flames. Police and firefighters ran into the burning building, set up a command center, and began climbing the stairs in an effort to evacuate people from the smoke-filled building. As rescue attempts were under way in the North Tower, flight 175 flew across New Jersey, took a sharp left turn, and barely missed hitting a Delta flight and a U.S. Airways aircraft. The doomed plane flew at maximum speed into the World Trade Center South Tower near the eightieth floor at 9:03 A.M. as millions in the television audience were watching flames shooting out of the North Tower. First responders in the North Tower sent a new team to

Flames engulf the South Tower of the World Trade Center (left) as hijacked United Airlines Flight 175 from Boston crashes into the building at 9:03 A.M. on September 11, 2001. The North Tower had been struck by another hijacked airliner 18 minutes earlier. *(Spencer Platt/Getty Images)*

the crippled South Tower, again in an attempt to evacuate the building.

Structural Damage and Collapse

Although the WTC towers were built to withstand a crash by an airliner, they were not designed for the high temperatures that resulted following impact. The heat from the burning jet fuel, approximately 2,000 degrees Fahrenheit (1,093 Celcius), melted the steel columns in the upper floors, which eventually collapsed nearly straight down onto the lower floors. The fires burned for weeks and were not officially declared extinguished until December 19 (although hot spots were still being found).

The South Tower collapsed at 10:05 A.M., killing thousands, including hundreds of police officers and firefighters. Uncontrolled fire and major structural damage caused by falling debris from the Twin Towers caused the collapse of 7 World Trade Center later that afternoon. Nu-

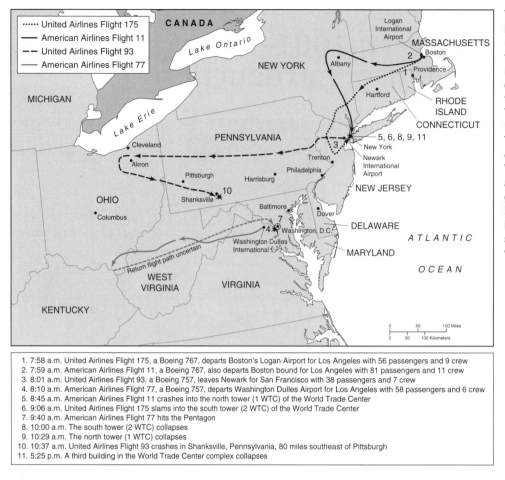

The four planes hijacked by the September 11 terrorists were all transcontinental jets carrying the maximum payloads of combustible fuel. The two that flew into the World Trade Center took off from Boston's Logan Airport. The jet en route from Dulles Airport returned to the Washington, D.C., area and flew into the Pentagon, while the plane from Newark crashed into a field in Pennsylvania after passengers and crew fought with the hijackers.

1. 7:58 a.m. United Airlines Flight 175, a Boeing 767, departs Boston's Logan Airport for Los Angeles with 56 passengers and 9 crew
2. 7:59 a.m. American Airlines Flight 11, a Boeing 767, also departs Boston bound for Los Angeles with 81 passengers and 11 crew
3. 8:01 a.m. United Airlines Flight 93, a Boeing 757, leaves Newark for San Francisco with 38 passengers and 7 crew
4. 8:10 a.m. American Airlines Flight 77, a Boeing 757, departs Washington Dulles Airport for Los Angeles with 58 passengers and 6 crew
5. 8:45 a.m. American Airlines Flight 11 crashes into the north tower (1 WTC) of the World Trade Center
6. 9:06 a.m. United Airlines Flight 175 slams into the south tower (2 WTC) of the World Trade Center
7. 9:40 a.m. American Airlines Flight 77 hits the Pentagon
8. 10:00 a.m. The south tower (2 WTC) collapses
9. 10:29 a.m. The north tower (1 WTC) collapses
10. 10:37 a.m. United Airlines Flight 93 crashes in Shanksville, Pennsylvania, 80 miles southeast of Pittsburgh
11. 5:25 p.m. A third building in the World Trade Center complex collapses

merous nearby buildings were also damaged. The rubble reached six stories and covered sixteen acres that came to be known as Ground Zero. The dust clouds from the collapsed buildings raced down major New York avenues, overcoming many victims with smoke and dust.

Although the structural damage to the North Tower was massive, thousands of survivors were able to find their way out before it collapsed at 10:28 A.M., sending a huge cloud of smoke and ash throughout Manhattan. The 1,353-foot (412-meter) World Trade Center Towers contained 200,000 tons (181,437 metric tons) of steel, 950,000 tons (861,821 metric tons) of concrete, 600,000 square feet (55,742 square meters) of glass window area, 239 elevators, but only 3 stairwells. All of this material had to be carefully sifted for human remains before it was carted away.

Survivors and Victims

Very few survivors were pulled from the wreckage. Genelle Guzman, who worked for the Port Authority on the sixty-fourth floor, was an exception. She was pulled out from under two pillars that pinned her legs. Rescuers searched for days for survivors and combed the rubble for months, still finding the bodies of victims and the first responders who attempted to save them.

At least 20,000 people were inside the WTC Towers at the time of the attacks. The number of missing and confirmed dead initially hit 6,700 but ultimately settled around 2,820. Relatives and friends posted photos of the missing on walls, mailboxes, and telephone poles throughout the city in hopes that someone had seen them in hospitals or wandering the streets, dazed. But few "good news" stories emerged, and authorities asked the relatives for toothbrushes, shavers, and unwashed clothing so that they could obtain DNA samples to help identify remains.

At least 265 firefighters and 78 police officers were initially reported to have died on the first day.

The largest tenant was the Morgan Stanley investment firm, whose 3,500 workers occupied twenty-five floors between the forty-third and seventieth floors; 2,500 of them worked in the South Tower. All but forty of them were reported safe. Not so fortunate were the London-based Cantor Fitzgerald International and eSpeed International, Cantor's electronic trading spinoff, which employed 1,000 people on the 101st and 103rd to 105th floors. At least 700 of them were believed to have died. Cantor did $50 trillion in bonds business in 2000; eSpeed did $11 trillion during the previous quarter. ABM Industries employed more than 800 engineers, janitors, and lighting technicians at the WTC. Insurance firm Marsh and McLennan lost 600 employees.

By early evening, St. Vincent's Medical Center had treated 319 patients, and 50 of them were listed in critical condition. Three of them died, two from smoke inhalation and one who was crushed. Seven New Jersey hospitals treated 600 people who fled the city on tugs, ferries, and police boats. By midafternoon, Mayor Rudolph W. Giuliani (named *Time* magazine's Person of the Year 2001) said there were about 2,100 injuries—1,500 "walking wounded" and another 750 who were taken to New York's 200 hospitals, 150 of them in critical condition.

The casualties were greater than those tallied from all international terrorist attacks recorded during the previous decade; it is likely that the direct damage and secondary losses will also dwarf the previous decade's losses.

Economic Costs

The monetary costs of 9/11 were staggering. The New York Stock Exchange closed at 9:40 A.M. and remained closed until Monday, September 17, the longest shutdown since the Great Depression. At 9:49 A.M. the Federal Aviation Administration grounded the American commercial airline system for the first time in U.S. history. No plane was allowed to take off, and all in-flight aircraft were ordered to land at the closest available airport. At 11:00 A.M. New York City mayor Giuliani called for the evacuation of lower Manhattan, and Governor George Pataki ordered all state government offices in New York closed. In Manhattan 20 percent of downtown office space was damaged or destroyed, and preliminary estimates for the cleanup and repair of Ground Zero hit $105 billion. An insurance industry official said that claims would probably reach $70 billion. The stock market, which closed during the week of the attacks, lost $1.3 trillion in paper assets during the first week it was reopened.

The immediate economic impact of the WTC disaster includes the tragic loss of life and property, the disruption of activities immediately following the attack, and the costs of returning the city and its support services agencies to their pre-attack state. The longer-term costs include but are not limited to the disruption to specific service industries (e.g., airline and travel) and higher business operating costs resulting from increased expenditures for security and the potential rise in the costs of insurance.

Media Coverage

The media extensively covered the attack, with many television and radio stations providing twenty-four-hour coverage of the incidents for several days. The events dominated the front pages of newspapers and news magazines around the world. The worldwide outpouring of public sympathy can be attributed in part to the media coverage. Billions of dollars were donated from around the world to assist the victims and their families.

Perpetrators: Background and Timeline

Law enforcement and intelligence officers around the world began the world's most extensive terrorist investigation in history and soon developed evidence of the involvement of Osama bin Laden's al-Qaeda organization. Bin Laden had earlier been linked to the February 26, 1993, bombing of the World Trade Center and had staunchly refused to accept defeat in his meticulously planned operations. The flight 11 hijackers were identified as Mohamed Atta, thirty-three, believed to be the leader of all nineteen hijackers involved in the four incidents of that day; Waleed M. Alshehri, aged between twenty-two and twenty-eight; Wail M. Alshehri, twenty-eight, possibly Waleed's brother; Satam M.A. Al Suqami, twenty-five; and Abdulaziz Alomari. The flight 175 hijackers were Mar-wan Al-Shehhi, twenty-three, of the United Arab Emirates; Fayez Rashid Ahmed Hassan Al Qadi Banihammad, twenty-four, a Saudi; Ahmed Alghamdi; Hamza Alghamdi, twenty; and Mohand Alshehri. Among the nineteen hijackers, one group studied piloting techniques in the United States and elsewhere for several months, blending into their local communities. Those who provided the "muscle" for the operations (foot soldiers) arrived in the United States much later, devoting themselves to studying martial arts techniques and working out at the local gym.

In October 1992, Mohamed Atta traveled to Hamburg, Germany, to study urban planning as a graduate student at Germany's Technical University of Hamburg-Harburg. He had previously studied architectural engineering at Cairo University. In the late 1990s, Atta began writing his master's thesis, which focused on the clash between Islam and modernity as reflected in city planning. His thesis, which won high marks from his advisers, was eventually completed in late 1999. That year he also obtained permission from the university to establish a religious student group. It was through this Islamic study group in Hamburg that he formalized his relationships with fellow hijackers Marwan Al-Shehhi (possibly Atta's cousin) and Ziad Jarrah. Marwan Al-Shehhi had arrived in Germany from the United Arab Emirates in 1997 to attend classes at the University of Bonn; he moved to Hamburg in 1999. Jarrah arrived in Hamburg from Greifswald, Germany, in 1997; he arrived in Greifswald from Lebanon in 1996 to study German at the University of Greifswald. It is in Hamburg, Germany, where Atta, Jarrah, Al-Shehhi, and Ramzi Bin al-Shibh (a Yemeni suspected of providing logistical support for the Hamburg group that entered the United States) are suspected of forming an al-Qaeda terrorist cell and planning the attacks of September 11, 2001.

During the writing of his thesis, Atta reportedly made trips to Aleppo, Syria; Turkey; and al-Qaeda training camps in Afghanistan, presumably during a study hiatus from mid-1997 to October 1998. According to those who knew him, Atta was a different man when he returned to Hamburg, more serious and much more religious. In late 1999, Atta, Al-Shehhi, and Jarrah claimed that their passports had been stolen. They were subsequently issued new passports, thereby erasing all evidence of their previous travels. In Hamburg, Atta and Al-Shehhi lived lives ostensibly committed to Islamic practice and community in a 780-square-foot (72.5 square meter) apartment in a working-class district. They had frequent visitors, sometimes in groups of twenty at a time. Visitors took their shoes off and could be heard reciting the Koran. Sometimes they wore traditional Islamic garb, and most of them spoke good German. Once a neighbor complained about the loud music.

Al-Shehhi arrived in the United States in late May 2000 on a tourist visa issued in Berlin. Atta initially entered the United States on a tourist visa he had received in Berlin in May. He arrived in Newark on June 3, 2000, from Prague, in the Czech Republic, and then rented rooms with another hijacker in Brooklyn and the Bronx. In late June, Ziad Jarrah took a commercial flight from Munich, Germany, arriving in Atlanta, Georgia, on June 27. In July 2000, Atta and UA 175 hijacker Al-Shehhi visited the Airman Flight School in Norman, Oklahoma, but did not enroll. Al-Shehhi had previously taken two test flights at the Albatross Air flight school near Bonn, Germany, in 1999.

The group eventually made their way to Florida, where Atta and Al-Shehhi began pilot training at Huffman Aviation International in Venice, Florida, in July 2000. By November 2000, Ziad Jarrah had begun taking flight lessons at the Florida Flight Training Center, also in Venice, Florida. The terrorists learned the importance of blending in with American society and attempted to avoid appearing too devout as Muslims. In late November 2000, Atta purchased flight deck videos for Boeing 747 and 757 aircraft and other items from a Pilot Store in Ohio. In late December 2000, Atta and Al-Shehhi were confident enough in their flight skills to take two three-hour jet simulator lessons at SimCenter, Inc., a flight school near Miami.

On January 4, 2001, Mohamed Atta flew from Miami to Madrid, Spain, on a U.S. commercial flight. He returned to Miami six days later and was briefly detained by immigration officials for having an expired visa. He was subsequently granted an eight-month extension. In February 2001, Atta and Al-Shehhi rented a Piper Cherokee in Atlanta. That month, Atta inquired about crop dusters at Belle Glade State Municipal Airport in Belle Glade, Florida. Also in February, Jarrah returned

to Lebanon to visit his father, who was undergoing heart surgery. He returned to Hollywood, Florida, in April and in June moved to Fort Lauderdale to share an apartment with Ahmed al-Haznawi (UA flight 93). Between April and June 2001, other accused hijackers entered the United States from various locations throughout the world. Once in the United States, the hijackers began obtaining U.S. identities, residences, vehicles, gym memberships, and flight memberships using the Internet, credit cards, and cash, while honing their flying skills. Atta and Jarrah obtained Florida driver's licenses on May 2; Waleed M. Alshehri (AA flight 11) obtained a Florida driver's license two days later. In April 2001, Atta traveled to the Czech Republic, where he met with Khalil Ibrahim Samir al-Ani, an Iraqi intelligence officer. Al-Ani was subsequently expelled from Prague after being seen casing the building housing Radio Free Europe and Radio Liberty, two possible terrorist targets.

In late May, Atta skipped his Broward County court appearance for a citation he previously received for driving without a license; a bench warrant was issued for his arrest. On June 13, 2001, Atta and Al-Shehhi moved into the Hamlet Country Club, a gated community in Delray Beach, Florida. The hijackers stayed only a few weeks in any location. Residences included locations in Boynton Beach, Las Vegas, and Delray Beach. Although initially they paid $17 a night for a room in the home of a Huffman Aviation bookkeeper, Charlie Voss, that arrangement ended when Charlie's wife, Drew, objected to the presence of the roomers out of a dislike for the distant and surly Atta, and they were both asked to leave. Subsequently, they moved to Coral Springs, Florida. In late June, Atta and Al-Shehhi took a trip to Las Vegas, Nevada, where they stayed in an Econo Lodge motel. Several other individuals showed up, and investigators believe this may have been an important planning site. On July 9, 2001, Atta flew commercially from Miami to Madrid's Barajas Airport and then flew from Madrid back to Miami on a business visa on July 19. During his ten days in Spain, he stayed at the Montsant Hostel in Salouand and ran up 1,250 miles (2,012 kilometers) on his rental car. Upon his return, Atta made two brief trips to Las Vegas, presumably to finalize planning for the attack. Also, according to the criminal indictment against Zacarias Moussaoui (the presumed twentieth hijacker), issued in the Eastern District of Virginia, Jarrah traveled to Germany on July 25 and returned to the United States on August 4. In the latter part of August, Jarrah purchased Global Positioning System equipment in Miami, Florida.

During the first week in September 2001, some of the hijackers arrived in Boston. Credit card transactions have led investigators to believe that Atta was in New York on September 10, probably to obtain the coordinates of the Twin Towers for the Global Positioning

System previously purchased by the hijackers. Sometime on September 10, Atta traveled to Boston. Atta and Abdulaziz Alomari (AA flight 11) left Boston in a rented Nissan Altima and drove to Portland, Maine, where they visited two bank ATMs and a Wal-Mart and stayed overnight at the Comfort Inn in South Portland. On the morning of September 11, shortly after 6 A.M., both men took a commuter flight to Boston to board the doomed plane.

Mohamed Atta left behind a will, dated April 11, 1996, when he was a student in Hamburg, Germany. The will was in a suitcase checked for the flight but was not loaded onto the plane. It listed eighteen instructions for a strict Islamic burial. He referred to himself as Mohamed bin Mohamed El-Amir Awad El-Sayed, and said, "I don't want anyone to weep and cry or to rip their clothes or slap their face, because this is an ignorant thing to do." He wanted no women to attend the funeral or visit his grave. Also in the suitcase were instructions on how the hijackers should prepare for their last day of life, a Koran, and pilot-training materials, including a handheld electronic flight computer and a simulator-procedures manual for B-757s and B-767s.

Pentagon Attack

On September 11, 2001, as the world was transfixed by the live televised reporting of the aftermath of the attacks on the World Trade Center, other al-Qaeda terrorists were taking over American Airlines flight 77, a B-757 that had left Washington's Dulles International Airport at 8:10 A.M. en route to Los Angeles with sixty-four people on board, including four flight attendants and two pilots. The terrorists, armed with box cutters, knives, and martial arts techniques, ran into the cockpit and bludgeoned to death Captain Charles Burlingame, and then forced their victims to the back of the plane. They told Barbara K. Olson, a former federal prosecutor and prominent television commentator who was married to Solicitor General Theodore Olson, a Senate staffer, three teachers on an educational field trip, and a family headed to Australia to call relatives to say they were about to die. The plane made a sharp turn over Ohio and Kentucky. The pilot then turned off the transponder, which made tracking it on its flight back to Washington impossible. The plane aimed at the White House at full speed but made a 270-degree turn at the last minute and instead slammed into a helicopter-landing pad before ramming the west face of the Pentagon in northern Virginia at 9:40 A.M. That section of the Pentagon had recently been refurbished with structural improvements; otherwise, the devastation would have been far worse.

Structural and Economic Damage

The Pentagon, the command headquarters for the U.S. Department of Defense and workplace for over 24,000

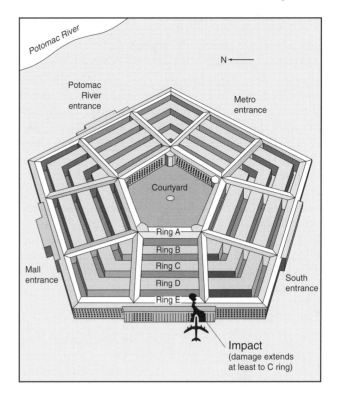

Only a small section of the massive Pentagon building, the newly refurbished west side, was damaged by the impact of American Airlines flight 77, but the devastation left 189 persons dead.

military and civilian personnel, lost 4 million square feet (371,612 square meters) of office space when the hijacked plane cut a 35-foot (10.5-meter) wedge through the building's E, D, C, and B rings between corridors 4 and 5. A huge fireball erupted when 30,000 pounds (13,608 kilograms) of jet fuel ignited, making rescue efforts nearly impossible. Construction teams worked around the clock in an effort to rebuild the felled section of the building before September 11, 2002, the one-year anniversary of the attacks. The region's economy lost $1.8 billion and experienced a sharp increase in unemployment, including the loss of 18,700 jobs from the temporary closing of Reagan National Airport. The federal government shut down within the hour amid reports that other planes had been hijacked and were screaming toward other targets in the Washington area. Hundreds of local schools also closed. The D.C. mayor and governors of Virginia and Maryland declared states of emergency, which prompted many businesses and government offices to close.

As was the case in the WTC attacks, public donations to assist in the support of the victims and their families were overwhelming, with a huge warehouse for the Salvation Army being filled with foodstuffs, medicines, clothing, and other items destined for first responders and victims' families.

Survivors and Victims

All 64 people aboard the aircraft and 125 Pentagon occupants perished. At least 94 Pentagon employees and first responders from local and state jurisdictions were treated in local hospitals, many for severe burns. Others underwent numerous surgeries. Tales of heroism abounded, as wounded Pentagon employees dragged their colleagues to safety. Lieutenant Colonel Paul T. Anderson saved more than 50 lives. Lieutenant Commander David A. Tarantino ran into the burning part of the building and rescued Jerry Henson, who was trapped in the wreckage. Pentagon police officer Isaac Hoopii carried out 8 people and talked out several more. On December 17, 85 soldiers, sailors, and civilians were honored for their bravery. Captain Leigh Newman, U.S. Army Reserve, was also cited with the soldier's medal.

Perpetrators: Background and Timeline

The AA flight 77 hijackers used the names Hani Hanjour, twenty-nine; Majed Moqed, twenty-two; Nawaf al-Hazmi, twenty-five; Salem M.S. al-Hazmi, twenty; and Khalid al-Midhar, twenty-six. Hanjour, who grew up in Taif, Saudi Arabia, was just one of two hijackers with a student visa and the only pilot who was not part of an al-Qaeda cell in Europe.

The investigation into the background of the hijackers has shown that Hani Hanjour received a commercial pilot's license from the Federal Aviation Administration in April 1999. Also, records from the CRM Aviation Training Center in Scottsdale, Arizona, confirm that Hanjour was a student there in the fall of 1996 and again in December of 1997. In January 2000, Nawaf al-Hazmi and Khalid al-Midhar were videotaped meeting with operatives of the Osama bin Laden organization al-Qaeda in Malaysia. Nawaf al-Hazmi is believed to have entered the United States at least twice since 1999, most recently on a tourist visa in January 2000 in Los Angeles, where he purchased a Toyota truck with al-Midhar and rented an apartment in San Diego. Nawaf al-Hazmi and al-Midhar became friendly with numerous people in San Diego, unlike their fellow terrorists, who tended to remain aloof. Authorities later detained several of their contacts, including Mohdar Abdallah and Omar Bakarbashat, Yemenis who both worked with Nawaf al-Hazmi at a Texaco station; Omar al-Bayoumi, a Saudi who had given a welcoming party for the duo and may have paid their rent; Yazeed al-Salmi, a Saudi who shared a car insurance policy with Nawaf al-Hazmi to save money; and Osama Awadallah, a Jordanian whose phone number was found in the hijackers' Toyota, which was left at Dulles. In May 2000, Nawaf al-Hazmi and al-Midhar took flying lessons at Sorbi Flying Club in San Diego.

In December 2000, Hani Hanjour arrived in Cincinnati from Paris on a student visa and in February or March 2001 rented an apartment with Majed Moqed in Paterson, New Jersey. Records show that they moved out of this apartment in August 2001. Hanjour, the most accomplished pilot in the group, practiced on a flight simulator at Sawyer Aviation in Phoenix, Arizona, in June 2001. On July 4, 2001, Nawaf al-Hazmi and al-Midhar arrived at JFK International Airport from Saudi Arabia. In August 2001, Hanjour took flight lessons at Freeway Airport in Bowie, Maryland, and flew, with an instructor, over the Washington, D.C., area several times in a small private plane.

On August 23, 2001, the Central Intelligence Agency (CIA) put Nawaf al-Hazmi and al-Midhar on a watch list, but the Immigration and Naturalization Service (INS) and the Federal Bureau of Investigation (FBI) were unable to find them. Moqed and Nawaf al-Hazmi booked plane tickets through the Internet on August 25; all other hijackers did so between August 25 and September 5. The hijackers moved around between Florida, New Jersey, and Maryland, taking flight lessons, setting up frequent flyer accounts, working out in Gold's Gym, and even renting adult videos. In late August, all of the hijackers on this team eventually stayed at the Valencia Hotel in Laurel, Maryland, met at the Pizza Time restaurant, and worked out at a Gold's Gym nearby. Nawaf al-Hazmi also stayed for a time at the Pin-Del Motel in Laurel, Maryland, where one of the hijackers on Flight 93 had stayed.

Pennsylvania Crash

On September 11, 2001, at 9:31 A.M., al-Qaeda terrorists, by this point, using a modus operandi all too familiar, seized United Airlines flight 93, a B-757-200 that had left Newark International Airport at 8:01 A.M. on its way to San Francisco International Airport with forty-five people aboard, including five flight attendants and two pilots. Two terrorists broke into the cabin as an American voice was heard screaming, "Get out of here." The terrorists, armed with box cutters and knives, cut the throats of at least two people, probably Captain Jason Dahl and flight attendant Deborah Welsh.

A hijacker, probably Ziad Jarrah, grabbed the controls, got on the microphone, and told the passengers, "Ladies and gentlemen, it's the captain. Please sit down. Keep remaining sitting. We have a bomb aboard." He later reiterated, "Hi, this is the captain. We'd like you all to remain seated. There is a bomb aboard. And we are going to return to the airport. And they have our demands, so please remain quiet." One hijacker with a bomb strapped to his waist forced most of the passengers to the back of the plane; others were moved forward into first class.

The hijackers forced several passengers to phone their relatives to say they were about to die. One man locked in a lavatory screamed into his cell phone, "We are being hijacked!" Passenger Jeremy Glick, a national judo champ, told his wife that the passengers were planning to fight three Middle Eastern–looking men with knives and a red box they claimed was a bomb. Glick's wife told her husband that the WTC had already been hit. Business executive Thomas Burnett, Jr., told his wife that a passenger or pilot had died and that "a group of us are going to do something." The passenger team may have included 6' 5" (198 centimeter) former University of California rugby player Mark Bingham and Louis Nacke, a 200-pound (91-kilogram) executive who wore a Superman tattoo on his left shoulder. Oracle software executive Todd Beamer, a former star athlete at Illinois's Wheaton College, told GTE operator Lisa Jefferson that the passengers were about to fight the terrorists, ending his conversation with "Are you guys ready? Let's roll," which became the battle cry for an angry nation.

The plane turned over Cleveland and aimed at Washington; many believed it was on its way to the White House or Capitol. Air Force fighter pilots were ordered to shoot the plane down if it came near Washington. During the battle between the passengers and the terrorists, the plane took several sharp turns, an explosion was heard, and the plane crashed near Shanksville in Stonycreek Township, Pennsylvania, 80 miles (129 kilometers) southeast of Pittsburgh, at 10:06 A.M., killing all on board.

Perpetrators: Background and Timeline

The hijackers were identified as Ziad Samir Jarrah, twenty-six; Ahmed Alnami, twenty-three; Ahmed Ibrahim A. Al-Haznawi, twenty; and Saeed Alghamdi, twenty-one. Jarrah, part of the terrorist cell in Hamburg, Germany, which included Atta (AA flight 11) and Al-Shehhi (UA flight 175), is believed to have been the pilot on UA flight 93. Jarrah trained at US 1 Fitness in Dani Beach, Florida, in "close-quarter grappling" and in how to use knives and sticks in combat. Apart from Jarrah, little is known about the other three men. Alnami was a mosque prayer leader in the city of Abha in Saudi Arabia and former student at the King Khaled University Islamic law school. He entered the United States in May 2001 and rented an apartment with Alghamdi in Delray Beach, Florida. Al-Haznawi entered the United States, arriving in Miami in June 2001. The terrorists rented apartments and cars, met with some of the other hijackers, and used their time to blend into the U.S. landscape. Alnami and Alghamdi purchased one-way airline tickets from Mile High Travel in Lauderdale-by-the-Sea on September 5, and on September 7 they took a commercial airline flight (Spirit Airlines flight 1460) from Fort Lauderdale, Florida, to Newark, New Jersey. On November 17, police found a suicide note Jarrah sent to his girlfriend in Germany on September 10; it had been returned to the United States because of an incorrect address.

All nineteen hijackers, fifteen of them with Saudi ties, had legally entered the United States and obtained identification through loopholes in the system. Financing for the operations, which many believed required between $500,000 and $1 million, was laundered through the *hawala,* or informal underground banking system, and legitimate banks in Dubai, United Arab Emirates.

The other groups of terrorists had five hijackers, leading many to suspect that this group should also have had a team of five. The missing hijacker was alleged to be Zacarias Moussaoui, a French Moroccan who had been arrested on August 11 in Minnesota and was possibly a replacement for Ramzi Bin al-Shibh, a Yemeni fugitive in Hamburg who was unable to enter the United States from Europe on repeated tries. Moussaoui had attempted to train as a pilot but was heard to say that he only wanted to learn how to steer the large plane, not to take off or land it. He also inquired about crop dusters. On December 11, 2001, Moussaoui became the first person indicted in the attacks when a federal grand jury in Alexandria, Virginia, charged him on six counts of criminal conspiracy, including involvement in the murder of federal employees and committing terrorist acts; four charges carry the death penalty.

America's Response

In his address to the American people on the evening of the attacks, President George W. Bush announced, "We will make no distinction between the terrorists who committed these acts and those who harbor them." In his address to a joint session of Congress on September 20, 2001, the president declared war on international terrorists, vowing, "We will not tire, we will not falter, and we will not fail."

An international coalition went after the terrorists on a broad scale. Authorities in more than 40 countries had arrested 230 people associated with al-Qaeda or other terrorist networks by mid-October. They also froze the accounts of numerous organizations believed to be involved with terrorist financing, and they freely shared intelligence information with the United States. Several countries also joined the U.S.-led coalition against the Taliban supporters of al-Qaeda in Afghanistan. The United States detained hundreds of suspects, many on the fringes of radical Islam, several of whom had some connection with the terrorists domestically or overseas. Several were convicted on minor charges related to assisting the hijackers. Plotting had been conducted in Germany, Malaysia, the United Arab Emirates, Afghanistan, and Pakistan. In several tapes released by bin Laden or found in al-Qaeda hideouts, bin Laden praised the attacks and indicated that he had foreknowledge of them.

Edward Mickolus

Further Reading

Bernstein, Richard, and the Staff of the *New York Times. Out of the Blue: The Story of September 11, 2001, from Jihad to Ground Zero.* New York: Times Books, 2002.

Mickolus, Edward F., with Susan Simmons. *International Terrorism: A Chronology of Events, 1996–2001.* 3 vols. Westport, CT: Greenwood, 2002.

The 9-11 Commission Report: Final Report of the National Commission on Terrorist Attacks upon the United States, Official Government Edition. Washington, DC: U.S. Government Printing Office, 2004.

Al-Qaeda

The emergence of al-Qaeda Central as the leading global terrorist organization, with the advanced operational capabilities to successfully attack the territory of the world's only superpower, the United States, on September 11, 2001, is a dangerous development. To provide an understanding of al-Qaeda's rise and development, its origins, structure, training camps, and long-range military strategy are discussed. Moreover, the organizational and ideological growth and evolution of al-Qaeda Central's strategic culture, which provide it with the ability to plan strategically on issues of war and peace, and the continued adaptation of its senior leadership core and lead operational commands and affiliates worldwide to U.S. and allied counterterrorism policies are also examined in a review of al-Qaeda Central from September 2001 to October 2010.

Origins

The spiritual debate among 1.2 billion Muslims on the Prophet's call for holy jihad, or the striving on the path of Allah, which can sometimes mean armed struggle against non-Muslims or Muslims who have been deemed to have lost their faith, is centered on whether it should be a peaceful striving or an armed striving against the enemies of Islam. In the late twentieth century, jihad, defined as armed striving on the path of Allah, gave birth to a radical militant Islamism, which is anti-Western, anti-Eastern, and anti-international in its fundamentalist ideology. The baptism of the radical militant Islamist terrorist organization al-Qaeda (the Base) can be traced directly to the brutal mujahideen war (1979–1984) against the Soviet Union in Afghanistan. The war brought together the National Islamic Front of Sudan, Egypt's al-Gamaa al-Islamiyya, al-Jihad, and the Palestinian Muslim Brotherhood to create the International Islamic Front for Jihad Against Crusaders and Jews under the leadership of Osama bin Laden, Mohammed Atef, Abdullah Azzam, and Abu Ubaidah al-Banshiri. It was bin Laden who provided the financial backing for the transportation, training, and support of Arab fighters to fight the Russians in Afghanistan.

In 1984, the senior leadership group of al-Qaeda had consolidated. It included Osama bin Laden, Ayman al-Zawahiri, Abu Ubaidah al-Banshiri (now deceased), Mohammed Atef (now deceased), and Abu Zubaydah (recently captured; his real name is Zain al-Abidin Mohammed Husain). Their collective goal was to pursue an unrelenting armed jihad against the enemies of Islam to restore the true faith of Islam to Muslim countries and eject the United States from Saudi Arabia and other holy Islamic sites. In 1988, al-Qaeda emerged, a battle-tested and extremely dedicated organizational product of the Mekhtab al Khidemat, or Afghanistan's Mujahideen Services Office, which had provided both the trained manpower and the massive funding for the successful holy war against the Soviet occupation army in Afghanistan. By 1996, bin Laden and al-Qaeda had fortified their position in Afghanistan in alliance with the Taliban and prepared for the war against the United States and the Western alliance. Since the 9/11 al-Qaeda attack against the United States and the massive retaliation of the United States in the Middle East and internationally, al-Qaeda Central has been firmly entrenched throughout Pakistan's urban and rural areas, in the Middle East, Africa, Europe, and Southeast Asia, and on the Internet. It continues to launch global, regional, and country-sensitive operations against the United States, NATO members, and other nations through its global militant Islamic affiliate units. The death of Osama bin Laden at the hands of U.S. special forces in May 2011 renewed debate in the West over as to whether or how al-Qaeda had been weakened by drone missile attacks and other operations against middle-level and senior al-Qaeda commanders, ideologues, strategists, and trainers in Afghanistan, Pakistan, and elsewhere in the Middle East. Few experts believed that the ground operations of al-Qaeda Central—ever amorphous and resilient—had been brought to an end.

Structure

Before the September 11 strikes against the United States, al-Qaeda was a loose global network of hierarchically based cell systems and affiliated terrorist groups linked to a robust and flexible terrorist command-and-control structure. As members of a global-reach terrorist organization, al-Qaeda's strategic policy makers were highly efficient in tasking out well-planned, resource-adequate, and time-sensitive terrorist missions to their middle-management operatives and secondarily to their global field operatives and sleeper jihadists. The highly trained middle managers of al-Qaeda in more than sixty countries became the organization's field managers, who provide logistical resources either to terrorist operatives in cells engaged in strategic and tactical missions or to sleeper jihadists blended into foreign societies and

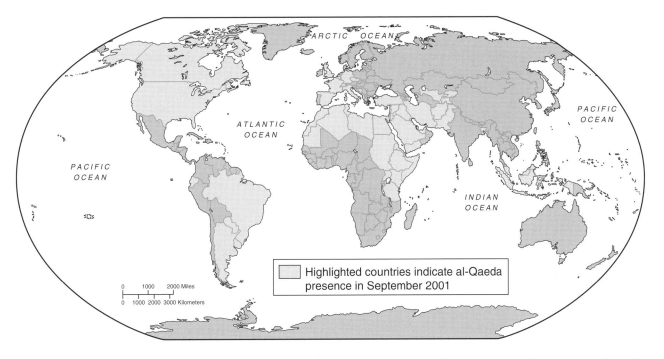

Highlighted countries indicate al-Qaeda presence in September 2001

In the months leading up to the September 11 attacks, al-Qaeda maintained a worldwide network of operations, with cells operating in countries throughout the world.

tasked to strike when ordered. The middle managers provide the following resources to terrorist operatives and sleeper jihadists: (1) false identification documents (e.g., identity cards, social security cards, driver's licenses, fake passports); (2) untraceable currency in all foreign denominations, including gold and diamonds; (3) shelter, food, and transportation; and (4) other tangible and intangible resources necessary to carry out their strategic and tactical terrorist missions against the United States and Western nations.

In this context, the careful planning, efficient resource allocation, and advanced deception skills of al-Qaeda's middle managers were clearly demonstrated in the September 11 multitasked global terrorist attacks against American targets. The ring of middle-management al-Qaeda operatives directly and indirectly responsible for the successful U.S. attacks has never been fully and definitively identified, despite a massive intelligence effort by the U.S. Federal Bureau of Investigation, the Central Intelligence Agency, and other lead organizations in the U.S. intelligence community.

Tactically, the al-Qaeda organization has three layers: the terrorist cell system, the sleeper jihadists, and supporters. Before joining, potential members of the terrorist cells and sleeper jihadists are asked to adhere to the *bayat,* or give allegiance to bin Laden and al-Qaeda. Once allegiance is given, they must do whatever they are asked by al-Qaeda. The terrorist cell system typically has five members, with an *emir,* or leader. In addition, the cell system usually has four distinct sections: administration,

intelligence, planning and preparation, and execution. The terrorist emir of the intelligence section assigns tasks to the other cell members on a need-to-know basis, and there is very tight discipline. There is no information on the number of al-Qaeda cell systems in foreign countries, but it is clear that, for the sake of security, they do not have knowledge of the cell systems beyond themselves. In this context, al-Qaeda's cell system is linked to a sophisticated global and regional command structure that is ever changing to meet the demands of a highly threatening environment and capable of adapting to both external and internal infiltration. It is noted both for its sophistication and for its simplicity in the utilization of advanced technology, strict financial discipline, and expert use of clandestine methods.

Second, there is an underlying and reinforcing substructure of sleeper jihadists, independent and rootless operatives throughout the international system. They have avoided the security problems of cell organization and the attendant surveillance and detection regimes of U.S. and European intelligence services. The sleeper jihadists hold no allegiance to or have any communication links with rival terrorist groups. They have been trained to completely immerse themselves in the foreign society they are living in and are capable of doing great damage once unleashed. There is no information as to how many sleeper jihadists are operating in foreign countries and what targets they are assigned to attack once awakened. However, the phenomenon of sleeper jihadists reflects the long-term dynamic adaptation, organizational innovation, and strategic capabilities of the rapidly morphing al-Qaeda organization. Moreover, the communication linkages between al-Qaeda's middle management and its sleeper jihadists in foreign societies are minimal due to security and surveillance concerns.

Finally, there are the supporters or sympathizers of al-Qaeda Central (or the al-Qaeda brand), and they number literally in the hundreds of thousands if not in the millions in the Middle East and internationally. They provide a wide range of financial and other material resources to al-Qaeda Central. Their extreme dedication to bin Laden reflected the success of al-Qaeda Central's propaganda, ideological, and psychological warfare campaigns against the United States and the Western alliance, and the inherent political difficulties of the global war against international terrorism. Nonetheless, between 2001 and 2010, al-Qaeda Central was structurally downsized by U.S. and allied special military operations and Predator/Reaper missile strikes. As a direct result, al-Qaeda Central became a much leaner, "invisible" secret terror organization. It adopted a high level of clandestine cover to cloak the presence of its strategic leadership core, including the protection of its most critical intellectual, spiritual, and ideological managers, advanced thinkers, and senior trainers; to conserve and hold in battle reserve its most hardened special forces formations; and to protect the members' large number of close family and friends. Senior, midlevel, and field operatives perform their duties without knowing the location of al-Qaeda's strategic leadership, realizing that they are the targeted martyrs in the field for both American missile strikes and special forces attacks, promising them a quicker death and path to paradise.

Training Camps

It is estimated that more than 70,000 Islamic militants from fifty different countries were trained in al-Qaeda's terrorist camps to fight a sustained global war against the enemies of Islam. The high level of military training and religious discipline of al-Qaeda's fighting force is unparalleled in the history of modern terrorism and guerrilla warfare. The advanced military and ideological training of tens of thousands of radical Islamic militants from the Muslim world, speaking different languages and hailing from different cultures, is based on a long-term strategic fighting doctrine defined by a well-rounded and well-organized training curriculum that teaches kidnapping, assassination, suicide attacks, hijacking, bombing, small and large infantry tactics, advanced guerrilla warfare, and terrorist practices. The trainers in the al-Qaeda camps use both language-specific training books sensitive to language diversity and translated U.S. and allied special forces and army warfare manuals. Recently captured in Pakistan, Abu Zubaydah was the commander of all al-Qaeda training

camps worldwide. His duties included personnel screening, recruitment, training, evaluation, and assignment of al-Qaeda, Taliban, and affiliated terrorist members. He also had direct responsibility for al-Qaeda's long-range planning of strategic and tactical terrorist strikes against American and allied targets.

In recent years, al-Qaeda Central has moved its advanced training camps and secret command installations into Pakistan's rugged tribal and sprawling urban areas, into other rural and urban Middle Eastern, African, and Asian countries, and into the Internet community. The newest training camps are hidden in the vast mountains and wooded valleys of Pakistan and elsewhere internationally, where al-Qaeda Central has trained thousands of jihadists, suicide bombers, regular ground fighters, and special forces formations. Al-Qaeda Central has also implemented the same rigorous training programs in cyberspace, where faceless jihadist men are recruited, trained, indoctrinated, financed, and directed to their targets as suicide bombers or as members of military guerrilla units or special forces formations. In all of these strategic dimensions, al-Qaeda Central's trainers, ideologists, and guerilla strategists have worked out and operationalized an overarching strategic culture at the global noncountry group level to plan, launch, adjust, and sustain operations to defeat the United States, the West, and the East far into the future, laying the strategic long-term foundation for the global Islamic Sunni caliphate.

Long-Range Military Strategy

The long-range military strategy of al-Qaeda Central includes the following: maximizing cyberwarfare capabilities to create chaos in U.S. information and financial systems; killing large numbers of Americans; destroying U.S. strategic industrial and economic infrastructure nodes; destroying famous U.S. historical landmarks; destroying high-profile government facilities; killing key U.S. and foreign personnel; and launching punishing attacks on American targets in Europe, the Middle East, central, South, and Southeast Asia, and sub-Saharan Africa. Moreover, al-Qaeda Central's long-range military strategy approves of sustained worldwide tactical attacks by low-level and nonaligned mujahideen operatives against the United States and allied targets. It is clear that al-Qaeda Central has the strategic leadership capabilities, robust religious doctrine, financial assets, highly trained terrorist operatives, sleeper jihadists, and strategic and tactical planning skills required to wage a dedicated guerrilla war against the United States. Al-Qaeda Central's search for nuclear, chemical, biological, and other weapons of mass destruction increases the lethality of the strategic threat. While it is clear that the United States has degraded al-Qaeda Central's capabilities with its recent military and intelligence successes, the war will be very difficult to win.

Nevertheless, the United States and its allies in the war against terrorism can claim significant progress in disrupting the operational functionality of al-Qaeda Central. On the first anniversary of the September 11 attacks, U.S. and Pakistani authorities arrested Ramzi bin al-Shibh, the alleged German-based liaison between the al-Qaeda leadership in Afghanistan and the September 11 hijackers in the United States. Then, in early November, an unmanned CIA aircraft launched a missile that killed Qaed Salim Sinan al-Harethi, allegedly one of bin Laden's top operatives, in Yemen. The big coup came on May 2, 2011 (May 1 in the United States), with the killing of Osama bin Laden in a helicopter raid by U.S. special forces on his residential compound in Abbottabad, Pakistan.

According to U.S. and European intelligence sources, the war in Afghanistan and the international effort to disrupt al-Qaeda have forced changes in leadership, with six new names topping the most-wanted lists of Western security agencies: Saif al-Adel and Abdullah Ahmed Abdullah of Egypt; Rahim al-Nasihri of Saudi Arabia and Yemen; Abu Musab al-Zarqawi, a Jordanian; Riduan Isamuddin, also known as Hambali, from Indonesia; and Tawfiq bin Attash, who may be either a Saudi or a Yemeni national.

Intelligence officials say that these six are experienced terrorists who have worked extensively with one another on attacks dating back to at least 1993, when at least some of them were involved in the shooting down of a U.S. helicopter in Mogadishu, Somalia, that led to the death of eighteen American Rangers. Others were involved in the U.S. embassy bombings in Kenya and Tanzania in 1998 and the attack on the USS *Cole* in Aden harbor in 2000. It is suspected that these individuals were at least partly responsible for the April 2002 bombing of a Tunisian synagogue that left twenty-one dead and the October 2002 bombing of a Bali discotheque.

In the period from 2002 to 2011, al-Qaeda Central's long-range military strategy also made alliances and coalitions with like-minded and independent militant Islamic terrorist organizations such as al-Qaeda in the Islamic Maghreb (Algeria), al-Qaeda in Iraq, Lashkar-e-Taiba (Pakistan), al-Qaeda in the Arabian Peninsula (Yemen), the Libyan Islamic Fighting Group (Libya), Jemaah Islamiah (Southeast Asia), and al-Shabaab (Somalia), among other affiliates and franchises, providing al-Qaeda Central with the operational strike capabilities and ideological means and maneuverability to strike directly at the United States and its allies worldwide and regionally. Because of al-Qaeda Central's logistical, financial, weapons, and other levels of support to these jihadist organizations in the past, and vice versa in recent transactions, these jihadist organizations are empowered and have been encouraged to develop an independent level of action that complements rather than

inhibits al-Qaeda Central's overall strategic planning and tactical military and intelligence operations against the United States and its allies. Its varying levels of financial and nonfinancial support for their independent-acting franchises and affiliates (and al-Qaeda Central's recent requests for like financial support from these same jihadist organizations) are consistent with its newly developed strategic culture paradigm, which allows al-Qaeda Central to exhibit both the policy flexibility and organizational adaptability to "bend like a reed" in responding to the enormous and unrelenting global financial, military, intelligence, and technological pressures exerted by the United States and its closest allies. In a permanent condition of war, al-Qaeda Central, even in a strategically weakened condition, is able to react spontaneously and rapidly to U.S. and allied pressures without collapsing (or it would have already collapsed because of the continued heavy weight of these global pressures). In addition, al-Qaeda Central's recruitment, training, and support of internally developed jihadists from the United States, Europe, Asia, Africa, Australia, Latin America, and other regions provide the global terrorist organization with more decision options in planning and executing (or threatening to execute) attacks against its enemies worldwide to relieve some of these global pressures. For example, young Somali Americans provide al-Shabaab's (and al-Qaeda Central's) strategic planners with a critical source of informed manpower for launching potentially destructive terrorist strike operations in Somalia, the Eastern Africa region, and the heart of the United States and Europe. It is clear from very recent events that the development and movements of American and European jihadist terrorists greatly complicates U.S. and European counterterrorism and intelligence policy-planning initiatives because of their relative freedom to travel, their intimate knowledge of U.S. and Western cultures and vulnerabilities, and their fierce ideological commitment to implementing their tasks.

Nonetheless, the record of battlefield losses of the jihadists and intelligence successes of the United States and its allies against al-Qaeda Central and its global franchises and affiliates has improved considerably. The evidence indicates that senior commanders of al-Qaeda Central have been forced to go deep underground in Pakistan and to disperse to other secret locations around the world to escape U.S. missile strikes and special forces attacks. Meanwhile, the human personnel strategy used by al-Qaeda Central to mitigate against the high level of manpower losses is based on a robust corporate recruitment regime with generous salary, benefits, and vacation leave as well as on a jihadist radicalization program for new recruits. It appears that the jihadist radicalization program for new recruits (and some veterans) is embedded within a dynamic strategic culture paradigm created by al-Qaeda Central whose central elements synthesize and integrate classical Arab military text and recent guerrilla insurgency history, a profound immersion in Sunni Islamic teachings and sharia law, a standing operational strategy for achieving victory over the "infidels" in the West and the East, a robustly adaptive global and regional military guerrilla strategy to "win" against the United States and its allies, and a financial and economic strategic plan to severely cripple the economies of the United States and its allies through planned military engagements in global, regional, and in-country military actions.

Strategic Culture

The December 2001 escape of bin Laden and al-Qaeda Central's senior leadership from U.S. forces and their Afghan allies during the Battle of Tora Bora had enduring consequences. It has allowed the organization to recover, rebuild, and rethink how it would confront the United States and its allies at all levels of engagement. In particular, it allowed bin Laden, Ayman al-Zawahiri, and the senior leadership to engage in long-range strategic thinking about how al-Qaeda Central could survive once the present senior leadership core disappeared from the scene through either natural death or martyrdom. The Tora Bora episode was therefore a major wake-up call for al-Qaeda Central's senior leadership core (in terms of their mortality) and, of course, a fundamental strategic mistake by senior U.S. political and military decision makers.

From 2002 to 2010, the U.S. and Western debate on the regeneration or decline of al-Qaeda Central often ignored a fundamental reality of the group's insurgent existence: that al-Qaeda Central thrives in a relatively secured environment, nurturing among its strategic and operational leadership formations both theoretical analysis and practical-scenario problem solving on how and when to attack the United States and the West, with the long-term meta-objective of establishing a united global Islamic state. Al-Qaeda Central is one of the few global terrorist organizations in modern insurgent history (along with Hezbollah) to both nurture and encourage the generation of empirical in-house analyses and studies of the United States and of its major allies using its internal think tank capabilities (including the Center of Mujahideen Services) and their advanced thinkers to generate internal policy and ideological debates. Topics include politics, guerrilla warfare, economics, ideology, intelligence, strategic affairs, espionage and counterespionage, media affairs, cyberwarfare and cyberpower, weapons of mass destruction, U.S. and West European studies, and other important issues to both strengthen and solidify the development of its strategic culture paradigm to address issues of war and peace as well as long-term organizational and ideological survival and advancement. For example,

in the domain of developing cyberwarfare and cyberpower capabilities, al-Qaeda Central has had time to explore what the new fifth dimension of warfare means in terms of conducting cyberwarfare campaigns against the U.S. economy and industrial infrastructure within the matrix of its strategic culture paradigm. Its early utilization of the Internet and the World Wide Web for information warfare, recruitment, fund-raising, logistics, and other purposes clearly demonstrated al-Qaeda Central's interest in the mastery of advanced scientific and technological capabilities to wage global cyberwar against the United States and its closest allies. Another important issue area is weapons of mass destruction. In this domain, al-Qaeda Central has redoubled its efforts to acquire weapons of mass destruction, including nuclear weapons (even engaging in secret discussions with Dr. Abdul Qadeer Khan, the father of Pakistan's nuclear weapons program, and members of his research team), biological and chemical weapons, and related mass destructive systems, as well as the means to deliver these weapons. The technological acquisition of these advanced weapons systems dates back to al-Qaeda's occupation of Afghanistan, where it had the time and the resources to study these systems and explore how to use them, and indicated al-Qaeda Central's long-standing search to add these systems to its advanced weapons arsenal.

The question of interest is the extent to which al-Qaeda Central has developed an ideologically centered militant strategic culture that provides the functional actionable blueprint for creating theoretical analysis and practical operational scenarios to satisfy its long-term objectives. Based on the evidence, al-Qaeda Central has in fact developed an ideologically centered militant strategic culture, principally drawn from classical Arabic military culture and recent guerrilla warfare events, a radical Islamic spiritual interpretation of Islam and sharia law, a documented history of successful and failed military insurgency activities and guerrilla and intelligence operations worldwide against U.S. and Western targets, and the experience and dedication of a strategic leadership group dedicated to global jihad. The ideologically centered strategic culture of al-Qaeda Central is reenergizing its analytical and policy-making systems and senior leadership formations and reconfirming the organization's central mission, preventing both internal bureaucratic decline and deterioration of its military, psychological warfare, propaganda, and anticounterinsurgency operations, capabilities that some Western counterinsurgency circles long predicted would decline. In summary, al-Qaeda Central's long-term survival is based on its ability to regenerate a resilient strategic culture that is spiritually, politically, and strategically acceptable to the global *ummah* of Muslims, potentially the future insurgent foot soldiers, operational commanders, and strategic leadership cadres of al-Qaeda Central and of its proliferating and morphing affiliates and franchises worldwide.

Michael J. Siler

See also: *Definitions, Types, Categories*—Islamist Fundamentalist Terrorism. *Modern Terrorism*—Afghanistan: Terrorist Haven Under the Taliban; Sudan: Terrorist Haven. *September 11 Attacks*—Bin Laden, Osama; Pursuit and Death of Osama bin Laden. *Tactics, Methods, Aims*—Suicide Attacks.

Further Reading

Alexander, Yonah, and Michael S. Swetnam. *Usama bin Laden's al-Qaida: Profile of a Terrorist Network.* Ardsley, NY: Transnational, 2001.

Berntsen, Gary, and Ralph Pezzullo. *Jawbreaker: The Attack on Bin Laden and Al-Qaeda.* New York: Three Rivers, 2005.

Bjelopera, Jerome P., and Mark A. Randol. *American Jihadist Terrorism: Combating a Complex Threat.* Washington, DC: Congressional Research Service, 2010.

Gunaratna, Rohan. *Inside Al Qaeda: Global Network of Terror.* New York: Berkley, 2003.

Hoffman, Bruce. *Combating Al Qaeda and the Militant Islamic Threat.* Santa Monica, CA: Rand, 2006.

———. *Islam and the West: Searching for Common Ground, The Terrorist Threat and the Counter-Terrorism Effort.* Santa Monica, CA: Rand, 2006.

Jenkins, Brian Michael. *Building an Army of Believers: Jihadist Radicalization and Recruitment.* Santa Monica, CA: Rand, 2007.

———. *Terrorists Can Think Strategically: Lessons Learned from the Mumbai Attacks.* Santa Monica, CA: Rand, 2009.

Johnston, Alastair. "Thinking About Strategic Culture." *International Security* (Spring 1995): 33–64.

Long, Jerry Mark. *Strategic Culture, Al-Qaida, and Weapons of Mass Destruction.* McLean, VA: SAIC, 2006.

Ross-Gartenstein, Daveed, and Kyle Dabruzzi. "Is Al-Qaeda's Central Leadership Still Relevant?" *Middle East Quarterly* (Spring 2008): 27–36.

Thomas, Timothy C. "Al-Qaeda and the Internet: The Dangers of Cyperplanning." *Parameters* (Spring 2003): 112–23.

Trabelsi, Habib. "Al-Qaeda Wages Cyber War Against the United States." *Middle East Times* (June 27, 2002).

Bin Laden, Osama

Osama bin Laden was born in Saudi Arabia in 1957, the seventeenth son of fifty-one children of Muhammad bin Laden. The bin Laden family grew extremely wealthy from construction and related businesses helping to build the infrastructure—palaces, highways, mosques, and more—of Saudi Arabia, providing bin Laden and the other bin Laden children with the best that Saudi Arabia had to offer. He graduated from King Abdul Aziz University in 1979 at the top of his class with a bachelor of science degree in civil engineering, and he went to work for his father's firm (the Bin Laden Group, the largest private construction company in the world at the time, which endeared Muhammad bin Laden to the Saudi royal family), where he learned the intricacies of civil engineering and construction practices, as well as the very complex economics of the Saudi construction industry. In 1968, his father died and bin Laden inherited a considerable fortune that made him a multimillionaire. During this formative period, bin Laden was extremely dedicated to the study of Islam, and he would develop religious views consistent with militant radical Islamism.

The Afghanistan Conflict

In 1979, the Soviet Union invaded Afghanistan, and bin Laden, a very charismatic and devoted Islamist, began traveling to Afghanistan and Pakistan to talk with prominent mullahs, scholars, and leaders who had regularly visited his family home in Saudi Arabia in earlier years. These early policy discussions in the late 1970s and early 1980s on how to deal with the menacing Soviet military threat in Central Asia increased bin Laden's determination to materially assist the mujahideen (or holy warriors) in their jihad. Along with Abdallah Azzam, bin Laden built the Mekhtab al Khidemat (the Mujahideen Services Office, or MAK), a global and regional organizational mechanism to recruit, evaluate, train, and support Arab and Muslim personnel to conduct the jihad against the Russians. In 1986, the MAK allowed bin Laden to develop and implement a comprehensive strategy to build toward global terrorist capabilities drawing on his Afghani veterans, providing advanced military training and material support for Arab and Muslim personnel from around the world. By 1989, with the Russians defeated, bin Laden had built a robust infrastructure of roads, tunnels, bunkers, hospitals, and at least six military training camps in Afghanistan. When he left Afghanistan in 1989 to return to Saudi Arabia, after surviving a number of assassination attempts, he, along with Ayman al-Zawahiri, Abu Ubaidah al-Banshiri, Mohammed Atef, and Abu Zubaydah, the original senior leadership core, established al-Qaeda (the Base) terrorist organization, with its strategic headquarters in Peshawar, Pakistan, and Afghanistan.

Al-Qaeda in the Sudan

In the early 1990s, Iraq's invasion of Kuwait and the start of the Persian Gulf War brought massive U.S. and allied military forces into Saudi Arabia and the Middle Eastern region. Bin Laden's fierce religious objections to U.S. military forces in Saudi Arabia and his energetic efforts to organize religious leaders and scholars to protest against the Saudi government finally forced him to leave his home country for the Sudan. In the Sudan, he worked closely with Hassan al-Turabi, the spiritual leader of Sudan and head of the National Islamic Front, both to financially strengthen al-Qaeda as a global terrorist organization and to build the strategic industrial and transportation infrastructure of the Sudan for the coming global jihad with the United States and the West. At the same time, bin Laden developed a sophisticated financial system to support al-Qaeda and its strategic leadership, middle-management operatives, terrorist cell networks, sleeper jihadists, and regional supporters, while making elaborate preparations to provide al-Qaeda with the advanced military training, sophisticated military weapons, military logistics, and military infrastructure required to engage in sustained global terrorist operations.

Declaration of War Against the United States

In 1992, civil war broke out in Afghanistan and bin Laden issued orders for al-Qaeda to redeploy to Afghanistan and begin the advanced training of top commanders and terrorist and nonterrorist operatives in preparation for jihad with the United States and the West. In 1996, bin Laden declared war against the United States and Israel, and in 1998 called for a jihad against both countries by issuing a fatwa. In the ensuing months, a series of strategic and tactical attacks by al-Qaeda against U.S. and allied territories took place. During this critical period, the most prominent bin Laden–inspired al-Qaeda attacks on U.S. territory included the 1983 Islamic extremists' strike at the U.S. embassy complex in Beirut, Lebanon; the 1983 Hezbollah-launched coordinated truck-bomb attacks against the U.S. Marine compound and French paratroop headquarters in Lebanon, which killed 241 U.S. marines and resulted in U.S. withdrawal; the 1993 World Trade Center bombing, which killed six people and wounded hundreds; the 1994 bombing of the U.S. embassy complex in Kuwait; the attempted assassination of Egyptian president Hosni Mubarak in 1995; the 1995 and 1996 bombings that killed 22 U.S. soldiers in Saudi Arabia; the 1998 attacks on U.S. embassy complexes in Kenya and Tanzania, in which 224 people died; the October 2000 suicide explosion that nearly sunk the USS *Cole* in Yemen, which killed 17 Americans and wounded many more; and the September 11, 2001, strikes against U.S. territory. In these cases, bin Laden has never taken direct responsibility but has always given full support to those who have carried out the strikes.

The Search for Bin Laden and Senior Al-Qaeda Leadership

In 2001, the military destruction of the Taliban regime and al-Qaeda formations in Afghanistan by U.S. and

Exiled Saudi dissident and al-Qaeda leader Osama bin Laden speaks from an unknown location in Afghanistan in 1998. In February of that year, bin Laden declared jihad (holy war) against the United States and Israel. "Strikes will continue from everywhere," he wrote. *(AFP/Getty Images)*

allied forces forced the senior leadership of the former Taliban government and al-Qaeda to flee into remote regions of Afghanistan and Pakistan. Some Western intelligence sources suggest that Mullah Mohammed Omar and senior Taliban officials, as well as bin Laden and senior al-Qaeda lieutenants, hid in undisclosed locations in Afghanistan and in Pakistan, especially in the untamed tribal regions, and in particular the North Waziristan region. There is some evidence to suggest that bin Laden and senior al-Qaeda and Taliban leadership were communicating among themselves and with middle-management operatives and affiliated terrorist networks worldwide through Pakistani-based Web site communications, numerous unregulated Internet cafés, Web-based e-mail addresses, and Internet access in more than 500 Pakistani cities.

During this period, the problem with the U.S. search for bin Laden and the senior al-Qaeda and Taliban leadership cadres was that it was based on flawed intelligence supplied either by local Afghani warlords and Pakistani chieftains who had their own strategic political agendas, or by Afghani and Pakistani tribesmen who were motivated by the American dollar or by ideological and religious objectives. In both cases, the raw intelligence data given to U.S. policy makers initially led to ill-advised bombing runs on innocent Afghani villages, resulting in increased ill feelings toward Americans. In November 2002, an audiotape was made available to Al Jazeera, the Qatar-based Arab TV news network, which supposedly included a speech by bin Laden praising the bombing in Bali and the Chechen hostage taking at a Moscow theater and warning the West against attacking Iraq. There were questions about the authenticity of the voice on the tape.

Al-Qaeda Central, 2002–2011

In late 2001 and 2002, reeling from the U.S. invasion of Afghanistan, bin Laden, al-Qaeda, and Taliban leadership formations and elite military forces were forced to disperse throughout Afghanistan and escape into Pakistan to bypass unrelenting U.S. military air and ground attacks. Bin Laden, the senior Al-Qaeda leadership core, and special forces brigades fled to the Tora Bora mountain range to exit into Pakistan's North Waziristan region. The CIA commander on the ground ordered the full weight of U.S. airpower to pound the locations of bin Laden and al-Qaeda. He also ordered a limited contingent of U.S. special forces and Afghan allies to attack the al-Qaeda position, though he was prevented by senior government leadership in Washington from placing a larger number of U.S. special forces to seal bin Laden and the senior al-Qaeda leadership group from escape. Nonetheless, after fierce firefights with American elite forces and feigned negotiations with the Afghan general who ordered a temporary cease-fire over the objections of the CIA commander, bin Laden, the senior leadership core of al-Qaeda Central, and the remaining elite special forces brigades escaped with their lives from the vast Tora Bora mountain range into Pakistan's ungovernable Northern Waziristan region. The traumatic experience with mortality (or potential martyrdom) at Tora Bora gave bin Laden and the senior leadership core of al-Qaeda the proverbial second chance, and they quickly renewed their commitment to defeat the United States and its closest allies with a holy jihad raged worldwide.

First, bin Laden and the senior leadership devoted their time, intellectual resources, and ideological energy toward developing a unique strategic culture that would guide future generations of Sunni Muslim jihadists long after they were gone. From the evidence, al-Qaeda Central developed an ideologically centered militant strategic culture principally drawn from classical Arabic military culture and recent guerrilla warfare events, a radical Islamic spiritual interpretation of Islam and sharia law, a documented history of successful and failed military insurgency activities, guerrilla and intelligence operations worldwide against U.S. and Western targets, and the experience and dedication of a strategic leadership group dedicated to global jihad.

Second, bin Laden and the senior leadership decided to accelerate terrorist attacks against U.S. and Western targets worldwide, including providing full operational support for Jemaah Islamiah's planning and execution of the bloody nightclub bombing in Bali, Indonesia, on October 12, 2002; for Chechen terrorists' seizure of a packed Moscow theater on October 23, 2002; for the failed assassination of Pakistan's president, Pervez Musharraf, twice in the month of December 2003; for the attack on commuter trains in Madrid, Spain, on March 11, 2004; for Chechen terrorists' seizure of the southern Russian town of Beslan on September 2004; and for the attack of British-born Pakistani Muslim suicide bombers on London's public transit system in 2005. In addition, it negotiated through intermediaries with Pakistan's president, Perez Musharraf, the South Waziristan Accords and North Waziristan Accords, allowing al-Qaeda Central a permanent safe haven, as well as additional accords solidifying al-Qaeda Central, the Taliban, the Haqqani network, and other militant Islamic terrorist groups' safe haven in the Federally Administered Tribal Areas.

Third, bin Laden and the senior al-Qaeda leadership group increased relations with like-minded and independent militant Islamic terrorist organizations such as al-Qaeda in the Islamic Maghreb (Algeria), al-Qaeda in Iraq, Lashkar-e-Taiba (Pakistan), al-Qaeda in the Arabian Peninsula (Yemen), the Libyan Islamic Fighting Group (Libya), Jemaah Islamiah (Southeast Asia), and al-Shabaab (Somalia), among other affiliates and franchises. These relationships provided al-Qaeda Central with additional operational strike capabilities and the ideological means and logistical maneuverability to strike directly at the United States and its allies regionally and worldwide.

Fourth, bin Laden and the senior al-Qaeda Central leadership core encouraged the long-term recruitment, training, and support of internally developed jihadists from the United States, Europe, Asia, Africa, Australia, Latin America, and other regions, providing the global terrorist organization with more decision options in planning and executing (or threatening to execute) attacks against its enemies worldwide. Evidence of al-Qaeda Central's threats to attack urban cities in Western Europe to cause mass casualties and great economic damage along the Mumbai model was a direct result of the planning and logistical flexibility provided by the internally developed jihadists phenomena.

Fifth, bin Laden and the senior al-Qaeda Central leadership core sought to develop both cyberwarfare capabilities and weapons of mass destruction assets to provide both the freedom of decision and a deterrence posture (if possible) as the global jihad with the United States and its closest allies reaches a strategic watershed. These developments were consistent with the strategic culture paradigm developed to allow al-Qaeda Central to deal with critical issues of war and peace at the global noncountry group level.

In all of these instances, bin Laden's guiding influence and that of the senior leadership core of al-Qaeda Central were strategically important in rebuilding its strength levels, developing a strategic culture paradigm for the future, creating new alliances and coalitions with fellow jihadist organizations worldwide, and establishing the freedom of action, time, and space to plan. Before the September 11 attacks on the United States, al-Qaeda was not the lethal terrorist it would become in the years that followed.

U.S. missile attacks and special-forces counteroffensives have succeeded in reducing the number of al-Qaeda Central's senior and subsenior commanders and operatives in Pakistan's tribal areas and elsewhere. The demise of Osama bin Laden came at the hands of U.S. special forces in a helicopter raid on the night of May 2, 2011 (May 1 in the United States) at the residential compound in Abbottabad, Pakistan—far from the mountains of the Pakistan-Afghanistan frontier—where U.S. intelligence had tracked the al-Qaeda leader and his family. Although information gathered from the site indicated more active participation in al-Qaeda operations on bin Laden's part than many experts had believed, his death put the West on terrorist alert precisely because the leadership of al-Qaeda Central was known to have been dispersed, decentralized, and reenergized by his personal charisma and organizational efforts over nearly a decade.

The Navy SEALs who killed Osama bin Laden removed his body from the Abbottabad compound for positive identification and for burial at sea within 24 hours, according to Islamic custom. The news of his death inevitably triggered memories of the events of September 11, 2001, but no one was ready to write the obituary of the terrorist organization he founded.

Michael J. Siler

See also: *Definitions, Types, Categories*—Islamist Fundamentalist Terrorism. *September 11 Attacks*—Al-Qaeda; Hunt for al-Qaeda and Terrorist Networks; Pursuit and Death of Osama bin Laden. *Tactics, Methods, Aims*—Ideological Orientations: Anti-Western and Anti-U.S.; Media Coverage and Manipulation; Recruitment and Training.

Further Reading

Alexander, Yonah, and Michael S. Swetnam. *Usama bin Laden's al-Qaida: Profile of a Terrorist Network.* Ardsley, NY: Transnational, 2001.

Bergen, Peter. *Holy War, Inc.: Inside the Secret World of Osama bin Laden.* New York: Free Press, 2001.

Berntsen, Gary, and Ralph Pezzullo. *Jawbreaker: The Attack on Bin Laden and Al-Qaeda.* New York: Three Rivers, 2005.

Bodansky, Yossef. *Bin Laden: The Man Who Declared War on America.* Roseville, CA: Prima, 2001.

Cooley, John. *Unholy Wars: Afghanistan, America and International Terrorism.* London: Pluto, 1999.

Gunaratna, Rohan. *Inside Al Qaeda: Global Network of Terror.* New York: Berkley, 2003.

Hoffman, Bruce. *Combating Al Qaeda and the Militant Islamic Threat.* Santa Monica, CA: Rand, 2006.

———. *Islam and the West: Searching for Common Ground, The Terrorist Threat and the Counter-Terrorism Effort.* Santa Monica, CA: Rand, 2006.

Jenkins, Brian Michael. *Terrorists Can Think Strategically: Lessons Learned from the Mumbai Attacks.* Santa Monica, CA: Rand, 2009.

Long, Jerry Mark. *Strategic Culture, Al-Qaida, and Weapons of Mass Destruction.* McLean, VA: SAIC, 2006.

Ross-Gartenstein, Daveed, and Kyle Dabruzzi. "Is Al-Qaeda's Central Leadership Still Relevant?" *Middle East Quarterly* (Spring 2008): 27–36.

Trabelsi, Habib. "Al-Qaeda Wages Cyber War Against the United States." *Middle East Times,* June 27, 2002, p. 573.

Emergency Response: Police, Firefighters, and Medical Personnel

Although terrorism, by its very nature, has always presented a threat to life and property, the September 11, 2001, attacks targeting innocent civilians thrust American emergency response personnel into action on American soil and into a new crisis environment involving weapons of mass destruction and the consequences of their use. At the start of the twenty-first century, emergency response, which at times is also called emergency management, disaster services, or domestic preparedness, could be seen for the first time as a critical component of a larger concept called "homeland security." Following terrorist attacks involving the detonation or release of a weapon of mass destruction, emergency response personnel are the first line of defense and protection. Therefore, they must be exceptionally well trained and ready to respond quickly to a variety of situations, including chemical, biological, radiological, nuclear, or high-yield explosive attacks. Emergency response involves various capabilities, different levels of government, and various types of equipment and technology.

Key Capabilities

The four key capabilities are *firefighting, emergency rescue operations, emergency medical services,* and *policing and public protection.* On September 11, al-Qaeda terrorists stunned the world when they hijacked four U.S. commercial airliners. Two crashed into and destroyed the World Trade Center towers, killing 2,823 people (the official death toll reported at the end of the recovery operation on May 28, 2002), including 343 New York City firefighters while they were helping to evacuate people from the burning skyscrapers. (For perspective, consider that 99 firefighters died in the entire year 2000 in all of the United States.) First the South Tower collapsed at 9:59 A.M., and then the North Tower collapsed at 10:28 A.M., both producing a massive cloud of dust, smoke, and debris. Ground Zero, known as "the Pile" among the firefighters, became a ten-story pile of burning rubble. At least ten fire trucks were buried in the rubble. In addition, 72 police officers were killed in the line of duty on September 11 (37 of whom were Port Authority police)—the largest recorded loss of law enforcement officers in the United States in a single day. The third airliner crashed into the Pentagon in Arlington, Virginia, at 9:37 A.M., and the fourth, believed en route to Washington, D.C., plummeted to the ground in Somerset County, Pennsylvania, around 10:03 A.M. In all three localities, it was local emergency response personnel who arrived on the scene first, personnel who are often referred to as "first responders." In the case of New York City specifically, it was first responders who either heroically sacrificed their lives to save others or became unintentional victims themselves owing to the scale of the disaster.

Unfortunately, the New York City Police and Fire Departments did not work together effectively on September 11. Neither could agree who was in charge because there was no incident command system in place. Each department had a separate command post that resulted in command, control, and communication breakdowns throughout the rescue operation. All this must be considered within a context of chaos, jet fuel–fed flames, and the smell of burning metal—creating an incredible crucible of destruction. Problems with communications along with a flood of too many rescue workers also

occurred at the Pentagon, but no first responders were killed or seriously injured there.

New York City was at times overwhelmed, as demonstrated by the backlog of some 400 emergency calls requesting an ambulance. More than 100 ambulances were at the World Trade Center, representing almost a third of the Emergency Medical Service's fleet at one location. Hospitals were standing by, but very few casualties arrived.

With regard to different levels of government, the United States conducts its public business within a federal system in which power and responsibilities are shared both within the federal government and with state and local governments. As a result, emergency response is a shared responsibility. In addition to local fire and police departments, there are state emergency management agencies and the Federal Emergency Management Agency (FEMA). At the federal level, FEMA has written the *Federal Response Plan*, a signed agreement among twenty-seven federal departments and agencies, including the American Red Cross. The *Federal Response Plan* provides a framework for coordinating the delivery of federal assistance and resources to augment the efforts of state and local governments overwhelmed by a major disaster or emergency. It can be implemented either in anticipation of a significant event that is likely to result in a need for federal assistance or in response to an actual event that requires federal assistance under a presidential declaration of a major disaster or emergency. The *Federal*

New York City firefighters pull survivors from the rubble of the World Trade Center on September 11, 2001. More than 400 firefighters and police lost their lives in rescue efforts that day; thousands of other first responders suffered long-term health effects. *(New York Daily News/ Getty Images)*

Response Plan, released in April 1999, included for the first time a Terrorism Incident Annex, signed by the Departments of Defense, Energy, Health and Human Services, and Justice, plus the Federal Bureau of Investigation (FBI), the Environmental Protection Agency, and FEMA. The Terrorism Incident Annex delineates the roles and responsibilities of the signatory agencies and distinguishes between "crisis management" and "consequence management." Both are managerial constructs designed to help frame a problem.

At the beginning and end of a terrorist incident, each type of management is mutually exclusive—crisis management at the beginning and consequence management at the end—but during an ongoing incident they operate concurrently.

The Department of Justice assigns the FBI the lead responsibility for crisis management involving the prevention, preemption, and resolution of a threat or act of terrorism, including the apprehension and prosecution of perpetrators. State and local governments provide assistance as required. Crisis management is predominantly a law enforcement response. Consequence management, on the other hand, involves measures to protect public health and safety, restore essential government services, and provide emergency relief to governments, businesses, and individuals affected by the consequences of terrorism. State and local governments exercise primary authority to respond to the consequences of terrorism. The federal government provides assistance as required, with FEMA designated as the lead agency for consequence management within U.S. territory. To ensure unity of command, FEMA supports the Department of Justice and the FBI until the attorney general transfers the overall responsibility to FEMA. Consequence management is generally a multifunction response coordinated by emergency management that also includes the private sector, voluntary organizations, and international assistance.

Equipment and Communications

The last area of importance is equipment. There are three major types of emergency response equipment: detection, protection, and communications. Detection equipment includes such items as biological and chemical detection kits and alarms. Beyond the traditional firefighter's personal protective equipment and police officer's uniform, the wearing of hazmat (hazardous materials) or MOPP (Mission Orientated Protective Posture) suits provides emergency response personnel with protection against all known chemical agents, live biological agents, and toxins. MOPP gear generally consists of an overgarment (chemical suit), a pair of overboots, a gas mask with hood, and gloves.

When it comes to communications and emergency response, "Our effectiveness is only as good as our ability to communicate," states an assistant chief of the New York City Fire Department. Communications equipment is the keystone to emergency response and to a successful resolution of an emergency incident. Cheap and low-tech communications equipment can cost lives. A case in point involved New York police officials surveying the North Tower by helicopter and issuing a warning twenty-one minutes before the building fell that those inside should evacuate immediately. That warning reached the police but apparently not the firefighters, based on internal reviews following the attack. The lack of a common radio channel—an adequate communication system—probably led to an increase in firefighter fatalities.

Compensation

Shortly after the 9/11 terrorist attacks, Congress established the September 11th Victim Compensation Fund, a more than $7 billion fund to compensate the families of persons who had died on 9/11, including emergency responders. The fund, which settled its last case by the end of 2003, offered roughly $1.8 million to the families of each person killed in the attack. Ultimately, more than 97 percent of families accepted this compensation. But the September 11th Victim Compensation Fund did not provide help to those responders, as well as members of cleanup crews, who became ill because of their exposure to toxic substances in the wreckage of the World Trade Center. To compensate them, Congress established the World Trade Center Captive Insurance Company, which was endowed with more than $1 billion in federal funds to insure the city of New York and the more than 100 contractors engaged in the cleanup. Around the same time, a process was established to determine who was eligible. In November 2010, more than 10,000 emergency responders and construction workers whose health was impacted agreed to a settlement of $625 million from the insurance company, with individual victims being awarded up to $1 million for serious health effects. The families of those whose deaths could be attributed to the disaster were entitled to up to $1.5 million.

Many of the illnesses suffered by the emergency responders and cleanup crew members were long-term ones, such as asthma and emphysema, caused by their exposure to environmental toxins. But as with all long-term illnesses, it is difficult to determine causes definitively. A victim may have smoked, been exposed to toxins in other places, or had a genetic predisposition for the condition. In 2006, Representative Carolyn Maloney (D-NY) and Senator Robert Menendez (R-NJ) sponsored the James Zadroga 9/11 Health and Compensation Act after a policeman died of a respiratory illness that may have been caused by his exposure to toxins when responding to the World Trade Center attack. The law called for $7 billion in compensation for those suffering long-term illnesses because of exposure to 9/11-related toxins, as well as medical monitoring of those exposed to such toxins among cleanup crews and emergency responders. Although responder advocacy groups lobbied heavily for the bill, House Republicans defeated the measure in 2006. A new version of the bill finally passed the House in September 2010 and, amid bipartisan wrangling over the extension of Bush-era tax cuts, passed the Senate in December 2010. President Barack Obama signed it into law on January 2, 2011.

Mark S. Bittinger and James Ciment

See also: *September 11 Attacks*—Shock and Mourning; Victims and Survivors; Victim Relief.

Further Reading

Arlington County. *Arlington County: After-Action Report on the Response to the September 11 Terrorist Attack on the Pentagon.* Reston, VA: Titan, 2002.

DePalma, Anthony. *City of Dust: Illness, Arrogance and 9/11.* Upper Saddle River, NJ: FT Press, 2010.

Federal Emergency Management Agency. *Federal Response Plan, 9230.1-PL.* Washington, DC: FEMA, 1999.

———. *Federal Response Plan, 9230.1-PL, Terrorism Incident Annex.* Washington, DC: FEMA, 1999.

Langewiesche, William. "American Ground: Unbuilding the World Trade Center." *Atlantic Monthly* (July–August 2002): 44–79.

Lioy, Paul J. *Dust: The Inside Story of Its Role in the September 11th Aftermath.* Lanham, MD: Rowman and Littlefield, 2010.

The Hijackers

The nineteen hijackers who executed the attacks of September 11, 2001, were all young Muslim men between the ages of twenty-one and thirty-four. Some of these individuals had lived in the West for years and had well-documented biographies; little is known about some of the others.

The nineteen suspects are listed by airline flight.

American Airlines Flight 11: Mohamed Atta (probable pilot and ringleader), Satam M.A. Al Suqami, Waleed M. Alshehri, Wail M. Alshehri, Abdulaziz Alomari

United Airlines Flight 93: Ziad Samir Jarrah (probable pilot), Saeed Alghamdi, Ahmed Ibrahim A. Al-Haznawi, Ahmed Alnami

American Airlines Flight 77: Hani Hanjour (probable pilot), Khalid al-Midhar, Majed Moqed, Nawaf al-Hazmi, Salem al-Hazmi

United Airlines Flight 175: Marwan Al-Shehhi (probable pilot), Ahmed Alghamdi, Fayez Rashid Ahmed Hassan Al Qadi Banihammad, Mohand Alshehri, Hamza Alghamdi

American Airlines Flight 11 was hijacked out of Boston and hit the North Tower of the World Trade Center (WTC) at 8:45 A.M. in the first attack. Mohamed Atta, the apparent ringleader of the September 11 attacks, is assumed to have taken over the pilot's role; with him were Satam M.A. Al Suqami, Abdulaziz Alomari, and Waleed M. Alshehri and his brother, Wail M. Alshehri. Except for Atta, all of these individuals were Saudi nationals who had entered the United States on visas sometime in 2000 or 2001.

United Airlines Flight 175 was also hijacked out of Boston. It hit the South Tower of the WTC a few minutes after Flight 11 hit the North Tower. The hijackers aboard this aircraft were Marwan Al-Shehhi (acting as pilot), Ahmed Alghamdi, Fayez Rashid Ahmed Hassan Al Qadi Banihammad, Hamza Alghamdi, and Mohand Alshehri. Al-Shehhi and Banihammad were from the United Arab Emirates; the others were Saudi nationals who had entered the United States in 2000 or 2001 on visitor or tourist visas.

Flight 77 was hijacked out of Washington's Dulles International Airport. It hit one face of the Pentagon at 9:40 A.M. Majed Moqed, Nawaf al-Hazmi, Khalid al-Midhar, Salem al-Hazmi, and Hani Hanjour were the hijackers on board. All were Saudi nationals, and most had entered the United States in 2000–2001 on tourist visas.

United Flight 93, out of Newark, crashed in a field outside of Pittsburgh as the passengers attempted to regain control of the aircraft—which probably prevented another suicide attack in Washington, D.C. There were only four hijackers on this aircraft: Saeed Alghamdi, Ahmed Ibrahim A. Al-Haznawi, Ahmed Alnami, and Ziad Samir Jarrah (acting as pilot). U.S. authorities believed Zacarias Moussaoui, arrested shortly before the September 11 attacks, was supposed to be the fifth hijacker aboard this aircraft. Despite his own admission of guilt, however, a jury was never convinced of this, concluding that he was, at most, a peripheral player in the plot. Jarrah was a Lebanese national; the remainder were Saudis who had entered the United States in 2000 or 2001 on tourist visas.

Mohamed Atta

Osama bin Laden, the leader of the al-Qaeda network, described Mohamed al-Amir Awad al-Sayed Atta as the leader of the September 11 attacks in a videotape released by U.S. authorities in December 2001. The son of a Cairo lawyer, Atta traveled to Germany in 1992 for graduate study in architecture and urban planning. He spent seven years in a five-year course of study at the prestigious Technical University in Hamburg, frequently traveling for extended periods during this time. He also secured a part-time job with a design firm in Hamburg.

Hijacking Letter Found at Three Locations

American Airlines #11
Boeing 767
7:45 am **Departed Boston** for Los Angeles
8:45 am **Crashed** into North Tower of World Trade Center

Mohamed Atta

Found in Atta's Suitcase

American Airlines #77
Boeing 757
8:10 am **Departed Dulles** for Los Angeles
9:39 am **Crashed** into Penatgon

Nawaf Alhazmi

Found in Vehicle
at Dulles International Airport

United Airlines #93
Boeing 757
8:42 am **Departed Newark** for San Francisco
10:03 am **Crashed** in Stony Creek Township

Found at Crime Scene

The U.S. Justice Department discovered photos, written instructions, and other evidence in the left-behind luggage of Mohammed Atta, one of the nineteen terrorists involved in the September 11 hijackings, and at various other locations. *(Luke Frazza/AFP/Getty Images)*

Atta was in Afghanistan for several months in 1996, and bin Laden later implied (in the same videotape) that he was a member of the Egyptian group al-Gamaa al-Islamiyya. Atta was in Egypt in 1997 when members of this organization massacred a number of tourists at Luxor. Upon returning to Hamburg in 1998 to finish his studies, Atta founded Islam AG, a special room in the university where Muslim students could meet. He also attended the nearby Al-Quds Mosque, which had a strong fundamentalist following. It was here that he met and seemingly dominated other young fundamentalists, including fellow hijackers Marwan Al-Shehhi and Ziad Samir Jarrah. Atta was considered to be the leader of a Hamburg al-Qaeda cell.

After graduating in August 1999, Atta traveled throughout Europe and America, presumably preparing for the September 11 attacks. He visited a number of suspected al-Qaeda members. According to one report (subsequently discounted by the United States), Atta had met on three occasions with Ahmed Khalil Ibrahim Samir al-Ani, Saddam Hussein's chief consul and spy chief in the Czech Republic. Al-Ani also met with Khalid al-Midhar.

Reportedly, it was after the first meeting with al-Ani that Atta developed an interest in crop-dusting techniques—possibly as a means of delivering chemical or biological agents. Atta and Al-Shehhi received flight training at Huffman Aviation International in Venice, Florida, and received their pilot licenses in December 2000.

Zacarias Moussaoui

Like both of his parents, Zacarias Moussaoui was born in France. His mother, a divorced woman, was not religious at all. Zacarias barely practiced Islam until he went to London in 1992 to study for his master's degree. There he came under the influence of the radical Muslim cleric Abu Qatada. French authorities began a file on Moussaoui in 1994 when they found his name in an address book seized in an investigation of the murder of three French consular officials in Algeria.

Moussaoui went to Afghanistan several times. He also prayed in the same Brixton mosque as the future "shoe bomber," Richard Reid. The British Intelligence Agency MI6 intercepted several phone calls between the two men in 2000. In February 2001, Moussaoui flew to the United

States to take flying lessons. He received funds from the same al-Qaeda sources in Germany and the Middle East that financed the other hijackers. He also purchased the same kind of knives that the September 11 hijackers used and developed a similar interest in crop dusting. When he was arrested on August 16, police found two knives, flight manuals for the Boeing 747 Model 400, a flight-simulator computer program, and a computer disk containing information related to the aerial application of pesticides in his residence.

After four years of investigations and trial, Moussaoui became the only person convicted of participation in the 9/11 plot. In 2005, Moussaoui pleaded guilty to involvement in the attack, leading to his conviction the following year on six conspiracy charges connected to 9/11. However, the jury, believing he was not a critical part of the plot and was never supposed to be the so-called twentieth hijacker, opted to sentence the French-born terrorist to life in prison, without parole, rather than death, as the government had been seeking. In 2010, a U.S. Court of Appeals upheld the conviction and sentence.

Other Hijackers

Marwan Al-Shehhi arrived in Germany in April 1996. He came from the United Arab Emirates, where his father was a successful businessman. He first went to Bonn to study German, and later he enrolled at Bonn University under the name Marwan Lekrab. In September 1998, he moved to Hamburg to study electronics at the Technical University, where Mohammed Atta was also studying; later he moved into Atta's apartment. In 1999, Al-Shehhi showed a sudden interest in flying. He attended a German flight school and asked his instructor to fly over chemical plants.

Ziad Samir Jarrah came from Lebanon to study in Griefswald, Germany, in April 1996. The affluent Jarrah family came from the village of Al-Marj in the Bekaa Valley in eastern Lebanon. Since he was a good student, his father, a liberal Muslim, and his mother, a teacher, had sent him to a Christian high school in Beirut. Attractive, friendly, and spontaneous, young Ziad was said to be popular with women.

While studying in Germany, Ziad befriended local radical Muslims from the pro-Hamas organization Al Aqsa e.V. In September 1998, Jarrah moved to Hamburg and enrolled at the University of Applied Science, where he studied aircraft construction and aeronautics and became associated with Al-Shehhi and Atta. His girlfriend reported him missing in November 1999, although he returned (possibly from Afghanistan) early in 2000. A little over a year later, he began flight training in the United States.

According to U.S. law enforcement and intelligence officials, Ramzi Binalshibh, a Yemeni national, was intimately involved in the planning and financing of the terrorist attacks against the World Trade Center and the Pentagon. A roommate of Mohammed Atta's in Hamburg, Binalshibh planned to be one of the four pilots on the terrorist mission but was forced to give up those plans when he was repeatedly denied a visa by U.S. immigration authorities. Ultimately, Moussaoui was sent in his place. In an interview with an Al Jazeera reporter in November 2002, Binalshibh declared that he helped coordinate and finance the mission and served as a go-between for al-Qaeda leadership in Afghanistan and the hijackers based in the United States.

John Thompson

See also: *September 11 Attacks*—Al-Qaeda. *Tactics, Methods, Aims*—Psychology of Terrorists; Recruitment and Training.

Further Reading
McDermott, Terry. *Perfect Soldiers: The Hijackers: Who They Were, Why They Did It.* New York: HarperCollins, 2005.
National Commission on Terrorist Attacks upon the United States. *The 9/11 Commission Report: Final Report of the National Commission on Terrorist Attacks upon the United States.* New York: Norton, 2004.

Media Coverage

Communications media perform four key functions in modern society; three of these functions generally increase in value in times of crisis. In the aftermath of 9/11, the public media functioned to provide information about the unfolding events and their implications for the public's security and welfare. A second key role was to provide a vehicle for reassurance, from both political and private sources, to the public on critical issues such as encouraging civil order in the immediate aftermath of the disaster; establishing appropriate expectations for the resolution of the crisis (i.e., in terms of a decisive political and military victory and justice for the perpetrators), and discussing what steps needed to be taken to deal with the immediate, midterm, and long-term consequences of the event. A third role of the media was to serve as a "transmission belt," or a propaganda instrument for the dissemination and emulation of appropriate behavioral role models (i.e., responses, values, beliefs, and opinions that were determined by political elites to be appropriate responses to the act) by facilitating interaction between the public and opinion leaders and subject-matter experts, including civil authorities. Finally, the terrorists deliberately and temporarily appropriated the media in order to sustain the act of terrorism itself, because the central purpose of a terrorist act is typically to convey a message of fear and intimidation to a targeted audience.

After September 11, the communications media continued to serve as the main source of information on all aspects of the crisis. Primary news outlets such as newspapers and national network television and radio conveyed information to the public at all levels from a variety of perspectives, including political, public safety and security, criminal-investigative, and journalistic orientations. In addition, because of the scale of the tragedy, other sources of information, whether media focused or not, also provided information. Official media provided the public with ongoing evaluations of casualty figures, assessments of the implications for public security in the immediately affected areas, and updates with respect to national security issues. Private and nongovernment media such as the telephone and Internet were also important sources of information on the events of 9/11; the Internet was virtually unprecedented in its ability to convey news information on demand to individuals and to serve as a focal point for public opinion in chat rooms and other online media. In many ways, because of the centrality of the targets attacked—the media centers of New York City and metropolitan Washington, D.C.—the role and impact of the communications media were without serious precedent.

Without question, September 11 caught everybody's attention, much as major national crises had done before. People everywhere reported that they would always remember what they were doing at the exact moment when they heard the news of the event and that, as President George W. Bush asserted in a subsequent speech, life would never be the same. The national media appeared to rise to the occasion with appropriate coverage, gravitas, and competence. Most of the television news anchors spent more than one work shift harnessed to microphones, and support staffs rotated in and out of twenty-four-hour, seven-days-a-week coverage for more than a week after the attack. Much of the attention in the early hours focused on the horrible violence of the tragedy, including the mounting death and casualty figures. The media were also able to make full use of an array of technical marvels, such as minicameras and satellite dishes that allowed reporters to provide in-close action shots from every conceivable angle from virtually any location and time.

On the other hand, the focus was on an event that had already occurred, and the need for action footage was not typically apparent. Much of the television coverage was reduced to highly redundant shots of the immediate aftermath of the attacks, of the towers collapsing and subsequent interviews with first-responder personnel and political authorities and experts on emergency response issues and terrorism. Initially, there was almost no criticism of the way the government was handling the crisis or any question of official responsibility for failing to warn the public of the attack. But the abundant coverage did serve to inform people, and the American propensity for obsessing on the details of a national tragedy was obvious within a short time after the disaster began to dominate the airwaves. The majority of the public media discussions focused on the nature and scale of the tragedy, the emerging investigation of the criminal perpetrators, and the eventual cleanup, not on substantive political issues that might involve significant contention.

The potential for controversy became apparent as the government began to roll back some of the protections and privileges of the press, such as access to officials in a crisis, which Americans have traditionally held as precious prerogatives. Although many in the media were not pleased by the stifling of press access and initiative, most were nevertheless not prepared to take on a president who, in the aftermath of 9/11, appeared to enjoy the overwhelming support of the American people. Indeed, some members of the journalism establishment, such as CBS's fabled anchorman, Dan Rather, in an uncharacteristic emotional lapse, expressed an extraordinarily fervid support of the war effort.

Media Functions

After 9/11, the primary message emanating from the government and transmitted by the media was a statement of outrage, followed immediately by political reassurances. These reassurances came in various forms: that the country would survive and thrive; that justice would ultimately prevail; and that the effort to strike back at the perpetrators would call for much public patience. Another message was an explicit request for national unity and support. The public responded with a surge of patriotism that was reminiscent of the early days of World War II. This wave of national pride was largely defined by the events of 9/11, but it was constantly fed and exploited by the media. In the postevent honoring of the victims and the subsequent glorification of firefighters and police, the media focused on both the scale of the tragedy and the personal losses to the victims' families and friends. Because of this consistent media focus, virtually the whole country felt that 9/11 had directly and physically affected their local communities.

Part of the public's response to the attacks was patriotism, with a sensitivity that bordered, in some cases, on paranoia and xenophobia. Some of that sensitivity was expressed in terms of a readiness to impose heavy pressure on certain media outlets to refrain from insensitive productions. Thus, several Hollywood movies were scrubbed or postponed or significantly altered in content (e.g., Arnold Schwarzenegger's action film *Collateral Damage* and Dave Barry's comedy *Big Trouble*), and the debut of a terrorism-focused, Central Intelligence Agency (CIA)–oriented television series called *The Agency* was temporarily postponed because of the perceived possibility of adverse public reaction. On the official side, Condoleezza Rice, national security advisor, requested that five media networks "exercise judgment"—political jargon to henceforth refrain from rebroadcasting videotapes emanating from Al Jazeera, the Qatar-based television outlet that has millions of viewers in the Arab world, on the grounds that taped statements by Osama bin Laden might include hidden messages in code to his followers and operatives in the United States.

The third function of the "established" media, whether a conscious activity or an unintended consequence, is to serve as a "transmission belt" for the reinforcement of positive social values across the various social classes and divisions and between the political elites and the public masses. Most observers agree that, in the aftermath of 9/11, the public was more supportive of politicians in general and less inclined to tolerate substantive dissent from President Bush's approach to national security on either domestic or international fronts. However, six months after 9/11, some of this original patriotism-derived unity had dissipated as a result of the continually disappointing economy and the growing inclination of the public to investigate perceived intelligence failures associated with 9/11—especially in the wake of new revelations about what was known before the event by the Federal Bureau of Investigation (FBI) and the CIA and the perceived failures of those agencies to take effective action to redress it. According to the Pew Research Center, the media's handling of 9/11 and its general status as a public watchdog went from a high of 73 percent in November 2001 (indicating in poll responses that the media had done a highly professional job on the 9/11 issue) to a lesser score of 43 percent in August 2002 for the same category. In November 2001, 69 percent of the American people believed that the media stood up for America; only 49 percent maintained that opinion in August 2002. On the other hand, 57 percent said that the influence of the media was growing.

A fourth function of the media, its role as a deliberately and temporarily appropriated communications channel in the terrorist incident, is covered in the article titled "Media Coverage and Manipulation," later in this volume. Suffice it here to say that "the medium is the message," as the media theorist Marshall McLuhan famously asserted, and terrorists are generally very sensitive to the way their message is being played in the media and adept at effectively manipulating it to their own ends. Terrorism from this perspective is an act of communication between perpetrators who want to intimidate and scare a target audience and their elites into policy changes. Osama bin Laden's taped messages broadcast on Al Jazeera appear to have convinced the American people of his culpability for the incident, but they also demonstrated his cunning, forthright resolve, and abject hatred for America—something many Americans, and by his own admission, former president George W. Bush, have difficulty understanding and accepting. In any case, the decision makers of target countries must carefully calculate how to inform the public about such acts without letting the terrorist's message of fear and malice serve to accomplish one of their major objectives: civil disruption and public discord.

Mark S. Bittinger

See also: *September 11 Attacks*—National Political Response; International Reaction. *Counterterrorism*—Media and Propaganda in Counterterrorism.

Further Reading

Izard, Ralph, and Jay Perkins, eds. *Lessons from Ground Zero: Media Response to Terror.* New Brunswick, NJ: Transaction, 2010.

Livingston, Steven. *The Terrorism Spectacle.* Boulder, CO: Westview, 1993.

Monahan, Brian A. *The Shock of the News: Media Coverage and the Making of 9/11.* New York: New York University Press, 2010.

Weimann, Gabriel, and Conrad Winn. *The Theater of Terror: Mass Media and International Terrorism.* New York: Longman, 1994.

Wilkinson, Paul. *Terrorism Versus Democracy: The Liberal State Response.* London: Frank Cass, 2000.

National Political Response

Before the events of September 11, 2001, many questioned whether or not President George W. Bush was up to the job. Although perceived by many to be a court-appointed president of arguable legitimacy, he nevertheless pursued policies as though he had a mandate. He issued a series of executive orders reversing those issued by his predecessor, including popular policies such as those raising workplace ergonomic standards and minimizing the level of arsenic in drinking water. Bush also provoked controversy with a few "flagship" issues, such as a proposed tax cut and an energy policy that contained a provision to drill in the protected Arctic National Wildlife Refuge. During the first few months of his administration, it appeared that Bush's most prized programs would be successfully implemented, inasmuch as they had the support of a Republican majority in both houses of Congress. However, moderate Republicans had begun to feel marginalized by the White House, so much so that Senator Jim Jeffords of Vermont left the party to become an independent, thereby shifting control of the Senate to the Democrats.

One of the last legislative acts passed before the Republicans lost the Senate was the centerpiece of the president's policy agenda—a budget bill that gave the country a tax cut, albeit a temporary one. The tax relief did not spur the economy, and the Democrats were ready to reshape the issue. By early September, they were pressing the president to explain how he would balance the budget and continue a tax cut without creating a shortfall.

The Democrats were optimistic about their chances to gain control of Congress in 2002, and several potential candidates were lined up to challenge Bush in 2004. Al Gore, who had won the popular vote in 2000, was poised to launch his return to politics with a speech, scheduled for September 29. The events of September 11 would change the political calculus, like so much else. Rather than launch an attack on the administration, Gore called for support of the president in a time of unusual crisis.

Impact of 9/11

The national emotional reaction to the events of 9/11 was complex. Along with grief, there was anger combined with a desire to lash out, as well as frustration over not knowing who, what, or where to fight. Some conservatives were quick to assign blame. The most inflamatory of these comments came from the televangelist Jerry Falwell, who, on his *700 Club* broadcast of September 13, 2001, blamed pagans, abortionists, feminists, gays, lesbians, the American Civil Liberties Union, and People for the American Way. Some citizens viciously lashed out on their own, leading to an increase in hate crimes against persons of apparent Middle Eastern ethnicity. For the most part, however, it was a time for America to unite, show the flag, and look to its leader.

Initially, America did not know where its leaders were. Shortly after the attacks, the president was flown from Florida on Air Force One and then taken on a circuitous route—via Barksdale Air Force Base in Louisiana and Offutt Air Force Base in Nebraska—to Washington, D.C. Vice President Dick Cheney, meanwhile, was taken to an undisclosed location. Later that day, at 8:30 P.M., President Bush addressed the nation in a televised speech, declaring, "We will make no distinction between the terrorists who committed these acts and those who harbor them."

Nine days later, on September 20, Bush gave what has been characterized as the best speech of his life, issuing a call to arms and a call for patience before a joint session of Congress. His request for special antiterrorism legislation was quickly taken up by Congress and passed through both houses with minimal resistance. Special funding was made available not only to pursue the war in Afghanistan, but also to bail out the airline industry and other victims of 9/11. The USA PATRIOT Act, which was signed into law by President Bush on October 26, 2001, expanded the powers of intelligence and law enforcement agencies; it also raised serious civil liberties issues pertaining to, among other things, the right to privacy, the right to counsel, and the right to due process. While Congress was supporting the president's programs, a series of probusiness executive orders and administrative policy announcements managed to be implemented without challenge.

Few people—not political leaders, the media, or the general citizenry—were second-guessing the president for fear of being accused of being unpatriotic. Shortly after military operations began in Afghanistan in early October,

the president's approval ratings soared above 90 percent. Initially, even fair criticism of the administration was off limits, especially in matters of war. The popularity of the president allowed Bush to pursue his conservative agenda as well as to dodge several political icebergs, most notably the first salvo in the Enron accounting scandal.

Revelation of Failures

As time went on, a series of revelations exposed a litany of analytic and communications failures prior to September 11, which subjected the intelligence community to severe criticism from both the Left and the Right. In response, Washington undertook the largest government reorganization in the United States since the end of World War II. On June 6, 2002, President Bush called for the formation of a new cabinet department dedicated to homeland security. His plan would bring under one roof a multitude of agencies and functions, which until then had been held by other agencies.

The climate was such that the conservative leadership in the House believed that they could push much of their legislative agenda through Congress if it were linked to the desires of the popular president. Bush, however, was hesitant to spend political capital by embracing high-profile conservative issues. As a result, one of the key provisions of his energy bill was soundly defeated in the Senate. In addition, the president allowed the House economic stimulus plan to be watered down in the Senate, and he reluctantly signed a campaign finance reform bill. Because he did not go out on a limb for his friends in Congress, neither would Congress surrender its turf to the White House. The central area of contention focused on White House stonewalling congressional efforts to obtain data pursuant to its oversight function.

While the continuing war against al-Qaeda progressed during the spring and summer of 2002, the Bush Administration broadened the focus of the war on terrorism to countries that it claimed were developing weapons of mass destruction, specifically Iraq under Saddam Hussein. By fall 2002 the United States had reached agreement with key UN Security Council nations allowing for the passage of a UN resolution that called for the return of UN weapons inspectors to Iraq in November 2002 or, if Iraq did not comply, the threat of military action.

Elections

In the fall of 2002 the president asked Congress to pass a resolution authorizing him to ". . . use the armed forces of the United States as he determines to be necessary and appropriate in order to defend the national security of the United States against the continuing threat posed by Iraq." Few wanted to challenge the president just three weeks before the mid-term election. Debate was limited at best, and the resolution easily passed in both houses.

With the control of Congress at stake, Democratic leaders believed that they could simultaneously support the president in his pursuit of the war and challenge his policies in areas such as education, employment, equal rights, health care, social security, and the budget. No matter how the Democrats voted on the war resolution, they were attacked on national security grounds. Among those Democrats was Senator Max Cleland of Georgia, a seriously wounded, decorated veteran, who voted in favor of the resolution, was attacked as a supporter of Osama bin Laden and was defeated by Saxby Chambliss. The midterm elections in November 2002 were overwhelmingly carried by the Republicans, who were successful at gaining control of both houses of Congress. This, according to political commentators, reflected the lasting impact of the 9/11 attacks, as it is rare for the party of a sitting president to make gains in midterm elections. Republicans had positioned themselves as tougher on terrorism than Democrats were, and voters seemed to concur.

Again, two years later, Bush won reelection by emphasizing his record in the war on terrorism, beating out a Democratic candidate with a sterling combat record in Vietnam—Massachusetts senator John Kerry—by emphasizing his credentials as an effective commander in chief during the 2004 campaign. Only with the 2006 midterm congressional elections—in part, a referendum on the Iraq War, which many Americans saw as an unnecessary diversion in the war on terrorism—did Democrats begin to make substantial gains.

The events of 9/11 and the war on terror played more in the primaries than the general election of 2008. "America's Mayor" Rudolph Giuliani mentioned 9/11 and the war on terrorism at every opportunity. On the other hand, it is generally accepted that New York senator Hillary Clinton's vote to support the war hurt her with the Democratic base. In general the Republicans wanted to keep national security as the foremost issue in the general presidential election. By so doing, as the economy was in decline, they appeared to be out of touch. Their misjudging the issue was but one of several missteps in what was one of the most inept presidential campaigns in modern history.

With the exception of the artificial issue of the proposed construction of a Muslim community center near ground zero, the events of 9/11 were all but forgotten in the 2010 midterm elections.

Stewart S. Johnson

See also: *September 11 Attacks*—Media Coverage; New York City and State Political Response.

Further Reading

Bruni, Frank. *Ambling into History: The Unlikely Odyssey of George W. Bush.* New York: HarperCollins, 2002.

Geraghty, Jim. *Voting to Kill: How 9/11 Launched the Era of Republican Leadership.* New York: Simon and Schuster, 2006.

Jacobson, Gary C. *A Divider, Not a Uniter: George W. Bush and the American People.* New York: Pearson Longman, 2011.

New York City and State Political Response

The response of the New York City and New York State governments to the attacks of September 11, 2001, focused primarily on new security measures, aid to victims, and economic revitalization. Most of these efforts, which would rely to some measure on federal assistance, began immediately after the attacks and were led by New York City mayor Rudolph Giuliani and New York State governor George E. Pataki.

Immediately following the attacks, both Giuliani and Pataki urged calm and promised assistance for affected residents of the city and state. In street appearances, numerous press conferences, and a message to the United Nations General Assembly on October 1, Giuliani called for decisive action and encouraged New Yorkers to band together for immediate relief efforts, often appearing to be coordinating those efforts himself. His symbolically important appearance on NBC's *Saturday Night Live* on September 29 typified his role throughout the crisis. Pataki, through the broader authority of his office, assembled the New York State National Guard to assist in relief efforts and authorized state agencies to take any necessary actions to help those in New York City. Canceling the mayoral primaries, which were scheduled to occur on the day of the terrorist attacks, Pataki also initiated full activation of the State Emergency Operations Center in Albany, which would coordinate disaster response for all state agencies and work simultaneously with the state's Disaster Preparedness Plan.

Long-Term Response

In October 2001, as part of the state's long-term response, Governor Pataki created the Office of Public Security, headed by James Kallstrom, a former assistant director of the FBI. This new office was charged with coordinating virtually all aspects of New York's future antiterrorist protection plans, including those pertaining to communication and transportation centers, as well as monitoring the safety of the state's water supplies, bridges, and tunnels. Other responses included creation of the Lower Manhattan Development Corporation, a joint city and state venture to oversee and facilitate rebuilding efforts in the area, and the New York State World Trade Center Relief Fund, a program created to assist victims of the World Trade Center attack. Smaller-scale efforts included specific economic incentives for tourists, such as Playbill coupons for theater events, and Gubernatorial Executive Order 113.21, which strongly encouraged the creation of academic scholarships to the city and state universities of New York for survivors of the September 11 attacks and for the spouses and children of victims.

In his 2002 State of the State address, Governor Pataki proposed a number of other programs, pending legislative and budgetary assistance. First was an Empire Opportunity Fund that would, over time, spend between $750 million and $2 billion to support economic development in upstate New York and Long Island. Also proposed was a Security Through Advanced Research and Technology (START) program, which would help state institutions of higher learning procure funding for the research and development of programs and technologies for the growing homeland security industry. In addition, a doubling of funding was requested for the Excelsior Linked Deposit Program, whose goal was to provide low-cost loans to New York's small businesses. Further proposals involved automatic life sentences for those found in possession of biological or chemical weapons and a removal of the statute of limitations on all terrorist crimes.

As a result of their effective response to 9/11, both Governor Pataki and Mayor Giuliani gained national prominence. While Giuliani was term-limited out of office in 2001, Pataki went on to win a third term for governor and was then talked about as a possible contender for the presidency in 2008—a prospect he did not seriously pursue.

Still, Pataki's reputation on 9/11 was eclipsed by that of Giuliani. Many New Yorkers and Americans came to admire his capacity to strike the right tone of calmness and firmness in the days and weeks immediately following the attack. Giuliani was lauded in the national media as "America's mayor" and featured as *Time* magazine's person of the year for 2001. There was much talk of his bright political future, which might lead as far as the White House—talk that Giuliani did little to squelch. During the six years between his leaving the mayor's office and the 2008 Republican primaries, Giuliani toured the country, speaking about 9/11, leadership, and the war on terrorism. He positioned himself as an expert on terrorism, with a hawkish stance on foreign policy—qualities that made him the front-runner for the GOP nomination for a time. However, Giuliani's popularity began to wane as memories of 9/11 faded and the ongoing war in Iraq, which Giuliani wholeheartedly supported, became increasingly unpopular. After finishing poorly in the early primaries, Giuliani dropped out of the race on January 30, 2008, having won exactly one delegate. His aura of leadership on 9/11 proved insufficient to win over voters nearly seven years after the attack. Indeed, the Republicans, who had positioned themselves as the party that would be tougher on terror, were overwhelmingly defeated in 2008.

Mark C. Milewicz

See also: *September 11 Attacks*—Media Coverage; National Political Response.

Further Reading

Foner, Nancy, ed. *Wounded City: The Social Impact of 9/11.* New York: Russell Sage Foundation, 2005.

Geraghty, Jim. *Voting to Kill: How 9/11 Launched the Era of Republican Leadership.* New York: Simon and Schuster, 2006.

Marlin, George J. *Squandered Opportunities: New York's Pataki Years.* South Bend, IN: St. Augustine's, 2006.

Newfield, Jack. *The Full Rudy: The Man, the Myth, the Mania.* New York: Nation Books, 2007.

Shock and Mourning

Terrorism undermines both individuals' and communities' sense of peace and tranquility. Terrorist attacks on innocent civilians challenge human beings' natural tendency to want the world to be a predictable and orderly place. The attacks on September 11, 2001, changed the collective conscience of America. Millions of people in America and around the world watched in horror the shocking, unimaginable images of two jet airliners being flown into the World Trade Center's Twin Towers. Everyone watched in stunned disbelief the unbelievable carnage and devastation as the towers collapsed and the damaged section of the Pentagon burned. The vivid images were all the more shocking since viewers knew that thousands of innocent lives were being lost before their eyes. Although reactions to such an event are individual and personal, there is a shared visceral horror to the experience of extreme inhumanity.

The behavioral and psychological responses to disasters and trauma are varied. For many, the post-trauma symptoms are transitory. For others, the effects of a disaster or trauma linger long after its occurrence. Studies of emotional reactions to disasters can be seen as far back as the Civil War, when casualties were sometimes described as suffering from "nostalgia," a type of melancholy or depression. After World War I, some combat veterans were described as suffering from "shell shock" or "combat fatigue." However, it was not until 1980 that the American Psychiatric Association acknowledged posttraumatic stress disorder (PTSD) in the third edition of its *Diagnostic and Statistical Manual of Mental Disorders* (DSM-III) as an emotional response to disaster or trauma. PTSD is only one of several psychological disorders associated with responses to trauma. Major depression, generalized anxiety disorder, alcohol and drug abuse, and adjustment disorder have also been noted in reactions among persons exposed to traumas and disasters. DSM-IV contains a new disaster-related diagnosis, acute stress disorder.

According to DSM-IV, a person who experienced, witnessed, or was confronted with an event that involved actual or threatened death or serious injury, or a threat to the physical integrity of self or others, may exhibit the major symptoms of PTSD. In addition, such a person's response involves intense fear, helplessness, or horror. The victim of PTSD persistently reexperiences the traumatic event through recurrent, intrusive, and distressing recollections or dreams of the event, or feeling as if the traumatic event were recurring. There is a persistent avoidance of stimuli associated with the trauma and a general numbing of responsiveness through, for example, efforts to avoid thoughts, feelings, conversations, activities, or people associated with the trauma. In addition to the primary symptoms, a person must experience at least two of the following to be diagnosed with PTSD: (1) difficulty falling or staying asleep, (2) irritability or outbursts of anger, (3) difficulty in concentrating, (4) hypervigilance, or (5) exaggerated startle response. For PTSD, the duration of the disturbance can last for months and even years.

Traumas caused by human actions, such as the terrorist attacks on the World Trade Center and the Pentagon, and the crash of United Airlines Flight 93 in Pennsylvania, are more likely to precipitate more severe psychological reactions than natural disasters such as floods or tornadoes. Those people most directly exposed to terrorist attacks are at the highest risk of developing PTSD. Predictors of PTSD include being closer to the attacks, being injured, or knowing someone who was killed or injured. Among groups of people exposed to traumatic events, the incidence of PTSD has been estimated to be between one-third and one-half. Almost half of the survivors directly exposed to the Oklahoma City bombing (1995) reported problems with anxiety, depression, and alcohol abuse, and more than one-third reported PTSD symptoms. In response to the September 11 terrorist attacks on the World Trade Center and the Pentagon, rescue workers, police officers, firefighters, emergency medical personnel, and volunteers faced danger of death or physical injury and the loss of coworkers, families, and friends. This special population of first responders is especially at risk for behavioral and psychological readjustment problems, including increased likelihood of PTSD.

The general public was exposed to nonstop, twenty-four-hour, seven-days-a-week media coverage showing the shocking images of the horrific September 11 attacks in the privacy of their own homes. Those who watched more media coverage were at higher risk for PTSD and other associated psychological problems. Young schoolchildren who saw these images were also at risk. One study of 8,266 New York public schoolchildren reported that six months after the attacks, these students still frequently thought about the terrorist attacks on the World Trade Center. Researchers found higher rates of PTSD, depression, and other psychological problems among them.

The first anniversary of the attacks saw major memorial services conducted at the disaster sites in New York City and Washington, as well as smaller ones around the country. Tens of thousands of mourners descended on Ground Zero—site of the former World Trade Center—for a ceremony that began at 8:46 A.M., the exact time the first plane hit the towers a year earlier. Meanwhile, in Washington, President George W. Bush led ceremonies for upwards of 13,000 persons in front of the refinished west side of the Pentagon. While the Defense Department headquarters was largely rebuilt before the anniversary, reconstruction plans for the World Trade Center site remained in dispute

for some time, as various groups, including victims' families, contended over the appropriate replacement for the Twin Towers. Some felt no building should replace them, that the land should be used instead as a memorial.

In 2002, the Lower Manhattan Development Corporation hosted an international competition for a design to replace the World Trade Center. In 2005, a final plan by architect Daniel Libeskind was approved, featuring several buildings, the most important of which was the Freedom Tower—since renamed One World Trade Center. At 1,776 feet (541 meters) in height, the glass-sheathed tower—with its sculpted broadcasting antenna on top—will be the highest building in the United States and among the tallest in the world upon its expected completion in 2013. Included in the project will be the National September 11 Memorial Museum, which will include two square pools of water in the exact footprints of the former Twin Towers.

Douglas G. McKenzie and James Ciment

See also: *September 11 Attacks*—Emergency Response: Police, Firefighters, and Medical Personnel; Victims and Survivors; Victim Relief.

Further Reading

DiGiovanni, C. "Domestic Terrorism with Chemical or Biological Agents: Psychiatric Aspects." *American Journal of Psychiatry* 156 (1999): 1500–1505.

Faludi, Susan. *The Terror Dream: Fear and Fantasy in Post-9/11 America.* New York: Metropolitan, 2007.

North, C., et al. "Psychiatric Disorders Among Survivors of the Oklahoma City Bombing." *Journal of the American Medical Association* 282 (1999): 755–62.

Victims and Survivors

More than 3,000 persons were killed in the September 11 attacks, a total that far exceeded the number killed in any previous single act of terrorism anywhere in the world. In addition to the 226 passengers on the four planes (including the 19 hijackers), an estimated 2,823 individuals lost their lives at the World Trade Center, while 125 perished at the Pentagon. The number killed at the World Trade Center was originally estimated at more than 6,000 as officials were inundated with missing-person reports. However, the number fell steadily as many of those feared dead were found to be safe. In addition, many victims were double counted because they were reported missing by more than one relative or friend, or listed under different spellings of their names. The total was lower than it might have been because the attack came early in the morning, before some workers and many visitors had arrived at the site. However, as then mayor Rudolph Giuliani said immediately af-

In the days after 9/11, friends and family members posted flyers across New York City hoping for word of missing loved ones. Of the more than 2,800 who lost their lives in the Twin Towers, about three-quarters were male and two-thirds were in their thirties or forties. *(Thomas Nilsson/Getty Images)*

ter the attack, whatever the casualty count, it would be "more than any of us could bear."

The New York City Health Department issued a preliminary report on the demographics of the World Trade Center victims, based on death certificates filed through January 25—which covered more than 90 percent of the estimated total fatalities at that site. The victims ranged in age from two to eighty-five years of age, and three-quarters were males. Most were in the prime of their lives. Two-thirds of those killed were in their thirties and forties, many of them recently married with young children. The diversity of New York City is reflected in the fact that almost a fifth of the victims were foreign-born, coming from at least 115 different

countries. Of these, the United Kingdom was the birthplace of the largest number, with fifty-three, followed by India with thirty-four and the Dominican Republic with twenty-five.

The overwhelming majority of the victims worked in the World Trade Center complex, although the death toll also included scores of firefighters, emergency rescue workers, and police officers. Three hundred and forty-three firefighters perished as well as fifty-eight members of the New York Police Department and Port Authority police force. Consequently, most of those killed were residents of New York City or the surrounding suburbs. Forty-three percent lived in New York City, another 21 percent elsewhere in New York State, and 25 percent in New Jersey. Ultimately, less than half of the World Trade Center victims were positively identified, but a streamlined process was developed so that death certificates could be issued in the absence of a body.

In a sense, the victims of the September 11 attacks include not only those killed, but also their families, relatives, and friends. Indeed, the attack led to widespread fear and a heightened state of anxiety throughout the country. According to a survey reported in the *New England Journal of Medicine,* nine out of ten of those sampled showed clinical signs of stress, with almost half reporting at least one symptom of substantial stress, such as insomnia or outbursts of anger and crying.

Christopher Hewitt

See also: *September 11 Attacks*—Emergency Response: Police, Firefighters, and Medical Personnel; Victim Relief.

Further Reading

Bernstein, Richard, and the Staff of the *New York Times. Out of the Blue: The Story of September 11, 2001, from Jihad to Ground Zero.* New York: Times Books, 2002.

Lipton, Eric. "In Cold Numbers, a Census of the September 11 Victims." *New York Times,* April 19, 2002, A12.

Murphy, Dean. *September 11: An Oral History.* New York: Doubleday, 2002.

International Reaction

The September 11, 2001, terrorist attacks on the United States generated nearly universal condemnation of the strikes and aroused genuine sympathy for the United States and those who perished. Condolence letters, telephone calls pledging support and cooperation, street marches, and moments of silence marked the days following September 11. Even longtime U.S. adversaries condemned the attacks, including North Korea, Iran, and Cuba. Within the Muslim world there was widespread sympathy for those innocent Americans and foreign nationals who were killed, though leaders of nations with large or majority Muslim populations had a more cautious response. Malaysia's Mahathir Mohamad and Indonesia's Megawati Sukarnoputri condemned the terrorist attacks but urged a measured response.

Arab Reaction

Reactions among foreign citizens, and to a lesser degree their leaders, tended to reflect the state of relations between the United States and individual nations. Responses ranged from unwavering support from U.S. allies and friends to unfriendly comments by some people from nations with recent or long-standing grievances against the United States, such as Yugoslavia, China, and some Muslim nations. Several of the countries in the Persian Gulf have populations that opposed the strong and high-profile presence of U.S. troops stationed there following the 1990–1991 war with Iraq. Commonly referred to as the "Arab street," this general population is resentful of the perceived U.S. tilt toward Israel in its conflict with the Palestinians. Saudi Arabians were among those who demanded proof of Muslim culpability in the September 11 attacks, no doubt embarrassed by the revelation that fifteen of the nineteen hijackers were from Saudi Arabia. This compelled many leaders to walk a fine line between supporting the United States and remaining loyal to their restive populations.

International Solidarity

Chinese feelings were still raw over the accidental U.S. bombing of their Belgrade embassy in 1999 and the very recent April 2001 fatal collision between a Chinese fighter and a U.S. Navy reconnaissance plane. Even so, China condemned the attacks and cleared anti-American statements from Internet chat rooms.

It was evident to most nations that even before President George W. Bush's warning "you're either with us, or you're with the terrorists," lines were being quickly drawn by the United States. Nations pledged to deny refuge and harbor for terrorists or their finances, while the United Nations Security Council, on September 29, adopted a resolution requiring members to clamp down on terrorists and to cooperate in any antiterrorist campaign, military or otherwise. Nations as diverse as Ghana, Venezuela, Thailand, and the Palestinian Authority voiced offers of cooperation. In all, almost thirty nations pledged full military support, while many more made offers of cooperation.

With more than seventy-eight nationalities represented among the dead, there was good reason for widespread sympathy and solidarity. Many nations condemned the tragedy as an attack on all civilized peoples and emphasized that those killed in Washington, D.C., New York, and Pennsylvania were clearly innocent. U.S. embassies worldwide saw host-nation citizens and officials call on them with messages of sympathy and concern. Numerous U.S. embassy gates overflowed with flowers, wreaths, and candles, as well as very heavy security. German Navy ships that passed U.S. Navy ships in British harbors that same week flew the American flag and saluted the U.S. sailors. Several nations also held huge rallies to show solidarity with the United States, while parliaments the world over observed a moment of silence in honor of those killed.

America's friends and allies signaled varying levels of support and cooperation to pursue the terrorists and cut off their lines of support. On October 2, the North Atlantic Treaty Organization (NATO) invoked article 5 of its binding mutual defense treaty, requiring the armed defense of any member that suffers an attack, eventually deploying five Airborne Warning and Control System planes to help monitor the North American airspace. Canada, some European allies, Australia, New Zealand, Israel, the Philippines, Uzbekistan, and Kyrgyzstan all pledged full support, including military aid. Meanwhile, Russian president Vladimir Putin placed the first condolence call to the White House and played a central role by first allowing and then prodding Central Asian nations to open their bases to U.S. needs in preparation for an eventual attack on Afghanistan. Russia also opened its airspace to the U.S. Air Force, which eventually flew millions of rations to drought-stricken Afghanistan from bases in Germany.

India and China equated the U.S. effort with their own problems with terrorism and gave the United States commensurate levels of intelligence support, while Japan provided logistical support, sending naval supply and escort vessels into action. In an announcement that surprised many, Iran pledged to aid U.S. pilots and Special Operations Forces in distress during action in Afghanistan, although it indicated that it would not be part of any U.S.-led strikes. As the focus of U.S. and British retaliation quickly became Afghanistan's Taliban rulers and their al-Qaeda tenants, Pakistan emerged as the pivotal nation for these plans. Given little choice after intense U.S. and allied pressure, Pakistan quickly supported these efforts under the leadership of General Pervez Musharraf. Arab states also pledged support but cautioned that Israel's participation in the retaliation would prevent them from fully backing the United States.

Questions Raised

Some individuals in the Middle East and other predominantly Muslim nations, as well as in non-Muslim quarters (including U.S. allies), gave early voice to the notion of partial U.S. responsibility in creating the conditions that lead to terrorism. Still others immediately questioned whether Islamic terrorists were even responsible for the strikes on Washington and New York, asserting instead that this was the work of American terrorists or even a conspiracy by Israel to create a vicious backlash against Muslims. In some instances, there was some celebration on the streets of Palestinian territories, but Yasir Arafat harshly rebuked those individuals. For many in the Muslim world, there was quick denial of Islamic extremist culpability, while a few admitted the high likelihood that al-Qaeda or a similar group had carried out the brazen, well-planned hijackings. Many Muslim and non-Muslim nations felt that momentum was building toward a clash with Muslim culture, and not merely against the terrorists alone. Early reprisals against Muslims living in the United States added to this fear.

Caution and Coalition

The outpouring of sympathy was genuine and widespread, but many nations also realized that a robust U.S. retaliation was imminent. Numerous leaders, such as Egyptian president Hosni Mubarak, urged the United States to use caution and patience; other leaders immediately asked for proof of al-Qaeda's culpability before striking facilities in Afghanistan. Many also urged that any retaliation be carried out under the UN flag. The United States immediately concluded that Osama bin Laden and his network of terrorists, known as al-Qaeda ("the Base" in Arabic) were responsible for the attack. U.S. intelligence had been pursuing al-Qaeda for some time and had disparate pieces of a puzzle that demonstrated a years-long campaign of attacking U.S. interests, including the 1998 Kenya and Tanzania bombings of American embassies.

Many countries were quick to point out that the United States should consider the reasons that terrorists would strike America. Several clearly wanted the United States to address the issue of terrorism with more than just weapons. A Swiss poll by Isopublic found that the majority of people in thirty-one countries preferred extradition and trials of terrorists to military action. The European Union gave full support to the United States but asked for clear evidence of culpability for those to be attacked, while at the same time voicing great concern about alienating Muslims worldwide. Virtually all world leaders recommended that the United States "take a deep breath" before striking any target and that it then pursue a precisely targeted, proportionate retaliation.

Sympathy for the United States and concern about the al-Qaeda threat emanating from Afghanistan produced strong support for the October 2001 American-led effort to topple the Taliban regime in that country, from both allies, such as members of NATO, and former foes, such as Russia. The subsequent war in Iraq, begun in March 2003, was another matter. While the Bush Administration tried to justify it by claiming the Saddam Hussein regime had both weapons of mass destruction and links to al-Qaeda, many in the international community were skeptical. Critics of the Bush Administration's foreign policy, both in the United States and abroad, claim that the Iraq War did much to undermine international support for America in the wake of the September 11 terrorist attacks, particularly in the Arab and Muslim worlds. Further eroding that support were the measures the administration took to detain suspected terrorists and glean information from them. Detention camps, notably the one at the U.S. base in Guantánamo, Cuba; controversial interrogation techniques, such as water boarding, or simulated drowning; and extraordinary rendition, in which suspected terrorists captured on the battlefield were sent to countries where torture was routine, offended many in the international community. Many Americans were also upset about both the war and the detention policies.

Indeed, one of the foreign policy appeals of Barack Obama's successful presidential candidacy in 2008 was a call to heal America's strained relations with much of the international community. And, indeed, upon becoming president, Obama made a major effort to reach out to alienated allies, particularly in the Muslim world, through both rhetoric and action, including ending America's combat mission in Iraq and declaring a no-torture policy for detainees. Efforts to close the detention facilities at Guantánamo, however, have proved more difficult and, as of early 2011, they remained open. In March 2011, Obama announced that military tribunals would resume at Guantánamo.

Thomas M. Sanderson and James Ciment

See also: *September 11 Attacks*—Media Coverage. *Counterterrorism*—International Cooperation Against Terrorism; International Law and the War on Terrorism.

Further Reading

Kepel, Gilles. *Bad News Rising: A Chronicle of the Middle East Today.* London: Saqi, 2003.

Pludowski, Tomasz, ed. *How the World's News Media Reacted to 9/11: Essays from Around the Globe.* Spokane: Marquette, 2007.

Wolfe, Wojtek Mackiewicz. *Winning the War of Words: Selling the War on Terror from Afghanistan to Iraq.* Westport, CT: Praeger Security International, 2008.

Global Economic Impact

Without question, the terrorist attacks that were unleashed on the United States on September 11, 2001, had a substantial impact on the global economy. Because of the timing of the attacks, which came in the midst of a global recession following the boom of the 1990s, it was difficult to assess the long-term effects on the U.S. and other world economies. The immediate direct effect on the U.S. economy was easier to measure.

Because of the economic linkage between the United States and other nations, global economic activity weakened in the aftermath of 9/11. The global economy relied at the time on the U.S. consumer to import goods and services from other nations. When a slow fiscal environment in the United States caused consumers to tighten their spending habits, this directly impacted international trade and financial markets across the globe. The attacks on 9/11, then, had a domino effect on the global economy.

The question of what 9/11 added to the recession which began in March of the previous year requires some background. Prior to 9/11, economic weaknesses first appeared in profits and investments rather than in consumption. Poor profit margins compelled companies to immediately slash investments in inventories of products and equipment. The next step was to lay off segments of the workforce. In 2001, profit margins were further squeezed by increases in labor, energy, and interest costs.

Immediate Effects

The attacks had a profound destabilizing effect on a number of Western economies, particularly those of the United States, Japan, and European countries. Many global economic sectors were already in a weakened condition as a result of the recession. Both the U.S. service sector and the index of manufacturing contracted sharply in October 2001, declining to a twelve-year low. Of course, some industries benefited from these tragic events—as governments and corporations worldwide prepared for a much riskier environment amidst public demands for the effective restoration of civil order.

The obvious immediate effects of the terrorist attacks on 9/11 were the tragic loss of thousands of lives, the injury costs, and the property destruction. Other impacts were the temporary disruption of economic activity and the negative effect on certain industries (e.g., airline, travel, and leisure). In the United States, the shutdown of the air traffic control system immediately following the attacks resulted in a $4.72 billion loss in September 2001 alone. Employment in these service industries was also affected. The closing of U.S. airports had a negative effect not only on airports in America, but on airlines and related industries (e.g., travel and tourism) throughout the world.

Within a month of the attacks, as a result of the sharp reduction in domestic and transatlantic flights, airlines around the world moved to trim schedules and shrink costs. Capacity was reduced by 11 percent, and 96,800 layoffs were announced: British Airways cut 7,000 jobs, United Airlines eliminated 20,000 jobs, American Airlines 20,000 jobs, and Delta Airlines 12,000. Other carriers have gone bankrupt (e.g., the Belgian airline Sabena) or have sought government assistance to avoid bankruptcy. Airline manufacturers also announced job cuts in anticipation of lost or canceled airplane orders. Boeing cut tens of thousands of jobs over a fifteen-month period following the attacks.

The insurance industry faced the biggest loss in its history. In the remaining months of 2001, insurers lost an estimated $10 billion in claims, costs directly due to the attacks. According to the Insurance Services Office and the National Association of Independent Insurers, it was the industry's largest loss since the figures were first recorded almost 100 years ago. Overall, losses were placed in the $40 to $70 billion range. However, not all was bad for the insurance industry. The average increase for property/casualty insurance policy renewals in 2002 was 20 percent. In addition, a cottage industry of terrorism insurance emerged because many insurance companies had previously excluded terrorism coverage (losses due to acts of war or terrorism) from their policies and policy renewals.

Investment companies and securities brokerage firms also felt the direct impact as the financial markets were shut down for the remainder of the week following the attacks. This action, which had not occurred since the Great Depression, decreased revenues from transactions and other investment-related activity. Wall Street also suffered a huge loss of investment talent, as many of the tenants of the World Trade Center were in the investment industry. The costs associated with the loss of investment expertise and knowledge were substantial. However, one thing is clear: the recession was largely about diminished business investment, not consumer spending. Americans appeared to be willing to buy homes under any but the most adverse conditions on the theory that real property can at least be held on to—for good times and bad. Such a view held sway until the collapse in housing prices in the latter years of the decade.

Short-Term Effects

In 2002, the situation grew even worse for the major affected industries: airlines, insurers, and supporting industries such as tourism, hotels, and car rental companies. US Airways, for one, filed for Chapter 11 bankruptcy protection. American Airlines announced additional layoffs and a restructuring in an attempt to save $1 billion annually by moving away from the hub-and-spoke system, which was established after the U.S. government deregulated the airlines in 1978. The ANC Rental Corporation (the parent company of National and Alamo Car Rental) and Budget Car Rental filed for Chapter 11, blaming 9/11. Six months after the attacks, the car rental industry's revenues were 25 percent below the previous year's numbers. Car rental companies, whose businesses were more highly coordinated with airport traffic, bore the brunt of the decline.

The tourism industry was particularly hard hit following the events of 9/11, as tourism decreased in all parts of the world, especially in the Caribbean and parts of Asia and the Middle East. In the United States, the downturn in tourism, particularly in New York, hurt businesses, especially hotels, restaurants, leisure activity companies, and tour companies, which cater to foreign visitors. According to NYC & Company (the city's official Web site), foreign visitors typically made up only 18 percent of tourists but yielded 42 percent of tourism revenues. Thus, the decrease in foreign visitors had an almost 2.5-fold effect on tourism revenues.

The peace dividend (the notion that fewer resources are needed for military preparedness and therefore those resources can be allocated away from defense and military spending to the private sector economy) also evaporated as the United States and other countries began restoring and enhancing national security programs. The peace dividend was expected to lower the cost of capital and ignite creativity, investment, and productivity and increase business efficiency. This would have enabled the global economy to achieve more robust earnings and growth while at the same time reducing the price of goods and services. Having lost the peace dividend, the United States has been forced to once again accept budget deficits instead of budget surpluses, a situation that continued through the deep recession of 2007 and 2009, then spiraled as a result of the economic downturn and stimulus measures taken to overcome it. Defense and military expenditures accounted for 3.9 percent of U.S. economic spending in 2000, down from more than 7 percent at the end of the Cold War and the Persian Gulf War. But the predictions of many economists that this would significantly lower GDP growth proved unfounded, at least until the global recession began in 2007.

In the short term, the U.S.-led war on terrorism had a positive impact on certain industries. The Bush Administration's proposed budget for 2003 increased defense spending by $45 billion, or 14 percent, and doubled homeland security spending to $36 billion (including increased border security and combating of bioterrorism). Production of weapons skyrocketed. The manufacture and output of laser-guided bombs doubled, and many ammunition factories are operating at their highest production levels in fifteen years. Moreover, an entirely new sector, the development of unmanned aircraft, came into being, as the government sought new ways to attack terrorist outposts around the world.

Long-Term Effects

Since the attacks were premeditated and could occur again, certain economic ramifications have become inevitable. In short, the cost of doing business has increased, and this cost has been passed on to the end consumer. Investors have demanded a higher risk premium, which has been passed on to companies in the form of a higher cost for capital. Businesses have needed to absorb higher insurance costs as insurance premiums increased, particularly property/casualty insurance premiums. The costs of doing business have also increased owing to the need for companies to expend resources to ensure heightened security measures for employees, facilities, and intellectual property. The security issues of cyberterrorism have also required serious consideration and planning. Some of the benefits of globalization have been dampened as countries' borders and immigration laws have become more restrictive—inhibiting and limiting the flow of goods and people. In addition, international financial transactions have taken longer to process because they require more "transparency" of financial documents, and they are more heavily scrutinized for both security and terrorist investigations purposes. Undoubtedly, defense spending has become an increasingly important component of the economic landscape in the United States and many countries around the world. Between 2001 and 2010, for example, defense spending in the United States climbed from $300 billion to $700 billion.

Other ramifications of 9/11 have been lower levels of foreign investment in states whose stability appears to be directly threatened by existing terrorism, social or political unrest, or areas characterized by long-held irredentist ethnonationalist claims. Clearly, in the wake of 9/11, foreign investors began to take a more serious look at security needs associated with foreign infrastructure and investment capital; this affected their willingness to get involved in marginal areas. This lack of investment not only has inhibited the flow of capital into the areas that need it most, but has also lent credence to the terrorist objective of intimidating potential investors and other business interests.

While all of the global economic effects discussed indeed have been felt in the decade following the September 11 terrorist attacks—consequences magnified by subsequent high-profile terrorist incidents, such as those in Madrid and London in 2004 and 2005—the economic juggernaut of globalization has continued apace, as the forces for economic integration have proven strong enough to overcome fears of violence and the additional costs of security and security-related delays in trade. Indeed, the global financial crisis and recession of 2007 to 2009 did far more to disturb and hinder the flow of trade and economic integration than did the September 11 terrorist attacks.

Nasser Ali

See also: *September 11 Attacks*—U.S. Aid and Relief; U.S. Economic Impact. *Tactics, Methods, Aims*—Money: Raising, Laundering, and Transfer. *Counterterrorism*—Financial Counterterrorism.

Further Reading

Beusa, Mikel, and Thomas Baumert, eds. *The Economic Repercussions of Terrorism.* New York: Oxford University Press, 2010.

Morgan, Matthew J., ed. *The Impact of 9/11 on Business and Economics: The Business of Terror.* New York: Palgrave Macmillan, 2009.

Napoleoni, Loretta. *Terrorism and the Economy: How the War on Terror Is Bankrupting the World.* New York: Seven Stories, 2010.

Richardson, Harry W., Peter Gordon, and James E. Moore II, eds. *Global Business and the Terrorist Threat.* Northampton, MA: Edward Elgar, 2009.

U.S. Aid and Relief

In the wake of the attacks of September 11, 2001, the United States launched an international war on terrorism, including an invasion of Afghanistan in October 2001, which toppled the Taliban government, and an invasion of Iraq in March 2003, which led to the destruction of the Saddam Hussein regime.

While the exact costs of the war are in some dispute, it is estimated that by fiscal year 2009–2010 the United States had spent about 1 trillion dollars on these military efforts, about three-quarters of which went for the Iraq conflict. At the same time, the United States embarked on a major program of foreign aid to both countries, as well as continuing and expanding foreign aid to other developing countries prone to terrorism. This came in the form of both military and economic aid. While the latter can consist of any number of services, goods, and financial credits, the former is divided largely between training and hardware.

Between 2000 and 2007, U.S. foreign aid around the world climbed from just over $17.5 billion to nearly $42 billion. Of this amount, roughly one-third was military aid and two-thirds was in the form of economic aid. For Afghanistan and Iraq, the increases were even more dramatic. In 2000, Afghanistan received just $54 million in aid. Of course, this was when the Taliban—a regime that was seen as hostile to the United States and that provided sanctuary to the al-Qaeda terrorist network—was in control of the country. With the United States fully engaged in the War in Afghanistan and a major ally of the government in Kabul by 2004, aid had climbed to just over $2 billion. For 2007, the last year for which the government offers definitive figures, Afghanistan received roughly $5.8 billion, of which about $2.2 billion was in the form of economic assistance and about $3.6 billion was in the form of military assistance. Similarly, Iraq—then under Saddam Hussein and subject to strict U.S. and international sanctions—received virtually no U.S. aid. By 2004, of course, the United States had committed more than 100,000 troops to fighting a stubborn insurgency in the country and was strongly supporting a democratically elected government in Baghdad. That year, it provided Iraq with more than $8.6 billion. In 2007, the United States was providing Iraq with a roughly similar amount—$8.2 billion—of which about half went to military assistance and half to economic assistance. (These figures dwarfed the aid the United States provided to Israel—$2.5 billion in 2007, of which $2.3 was in the form of military assistance—which until the wars in Afghanistan and Iraq had been the leading recipient of U.S. aid.)

At the same time, assistance to other governments viewed by the United States as critical in the international war on terror also saw huge jumps between 2000 and 2007. The Philippines, which was battling Moro separatists and the al-Qaeda linked terrorist organization Abu Sayyaf, saw its aid increase from $82 million in 2000 to $168 million in 2007, the latter including $43 million in military assistance. Pakistan, which became a major front in the war on terrorism when al-Qaeda relocated there after the U.S. invasion of Afghanistan, saw its aid increase from $24 million in 2000 to $441 million in 2004 to nearly 1 billion in 2007, of which more than $300 million was in the form of military assistance.

While all of these sums are large, they represent a relatively tiny portion of overall gross domestic product (GDP) or even government spending. Indeed, the United States ranks last among major industrialized countries in the proportion of its GDP devoted to foreign aid. Even in absolute terms, while the United States remains the largest economy in the world, doubling that of runner-ups China and Japan, it is only second in foreign aid, lagging behind Japan.

While the argument for increasing military assistance

to countries that are critical to the war on terrorism is easy to make, increasing general economic assistance is fraught with controversy. Supporters of the argument that economic aid can help in the war against terrorists point out that people who are angry and frustrated over their economic circumstances would seem to be more likely to engage in terror. And, as 9/11 and subsequent large-scale bombings in Europe made abundantly clear, in the age of global transportation and communication, it is easy for people from distant and impoverished lands to strike out against the heartland of the industrialized West. Moreover, countries that lack effective governance and internal security, such as pre-invasion Afghanistan or contemporary Yemen, often provide the kinds of safe havens where terrorist organizations can flourish.

Skeptics of the idea of foreign aid as a tool in fighting terrorism point out that the perpetrators of some of the most horrendous acts of international terrorism either do not come from the poorest or most lawless of countries or are members of the middle and upper classes of those countries. The nineteen 9/11 hijackers, for instance, all came from countries in the oil-rich Persian Gulf and were well educated, while the London transport suicide bombers had been raised in Britain itself.

More fundamentally, the debate about the usefulness of foreign aid in the fight against terrorism gets tied up in the overall debate about the efficacy of foreign aid itself, not only in terms of whether it can actually help lift countries out of poverty but also in terms of what effect it has on a country's basic social structure. That is to say, economic assistance can fail in several ways pertinent to the terrorist-breeding issue. First, if economic assistance does not actually lift a country out of poverty, then money from a donor country interested in fighting terrorism might be better spent in other ways. Second, as anyone who studies foreign aid can attest, much of the money is often squandered or stolen by elites, raising the level of frustration and antagonizing populations against their leaders and the Western governments that support them. Finally, say experts, even if economic assistance does work, the process of economic improvement can exacerbate social conditions, since growth is often accompanied by increasing inequality, exactly the kind of situation that breeds frustration and anger.

In sum, then, while most experts agree that economic assistance to impoverished countries remains an important foreign policy tool for any number of geopolitical reasons, they caution policy makers to avoid the easy assumption that the economic growth it can contribute to provides a ready means for fighting terrorism, since economic change can often create the conditions in which terrorism flourishes far more readily than does economic stagnation.

James Ciment

See also: *September 11 Attacks*—Global Economic Impact; U.S. Foreign Policy; U.S. Foreign Relations.

Further Reading
Chickering, A. Lawrence, Isobel Coleman, P. Edward Haley, and Emily Vargas-Baron. *Strategic Foreign Assistance: Civil Society in International Security.* Stanford, CA: Hoover Institution Press, 2006.
Graham, Carol. "Can Foreign Aid Help Stop Terrorism?" Brookings Institution, 2002. http://www.brookings.edu/articles/2002/summer_terrorism_graham.aspx.
Howell, Jude, and Jeremy Lind. *Counter-terrorism, Aid and Civil Society: Before and After the War on Terror.* New York: Palgrave Macmillan, 2009.

U.S. Foreign Policy

The challenge in addressing the changes in U.S. foreign policy after 9/11 lay in the difficulty of defining the Bush Administration's foreign policy in general. The Bush White House operated in a "permanent campaign" mode, wherein political considerations weighed as much as, if not more than, policy outcomes. The president seldom spoke on foreign issues, and his foreign policy team did not speak with a unified voice. Major differences in worldview within the administration quickly surfaced: Secretary of State Colin Powell represented one side, and a group of hard-line neoconservatives, or neocons, from the former Reagan and Bush Administrations led the other. The most notable hard-liners were Vice President Richard Cheney, Secretary of Defense Donald Rumsfeld, Deputy Secretary of Defense Paul Wolfowitz, and National Security Advisor Condoleezza Rice. Where Powell was considered a consensus builder in the international community, the hard-liners were inclined toward more unilateral policies. By postulating American exceptionalism, the neocons maintained that the United States could and should pursue its interests without undue deference to international opinion.

Bush vs. Clinton Foreign Policy

The central theme in the George W. Bush Administration's foreign policy could be succinctly summed up as ABC+I (Anything But Clinton plus Iraq). In general terms, ABC implied the rejection of Clinton's globalism. Where Clinton was engaged, the Bush team wanted to withdraw. In terms of policy, ABC translated into the rejection of several international agreements, including the Kyoto Accords on global warming and the 1972 ABM Treaty. Powell, however, wanted to pursue several policies that coincided with Clinton Administration orientations. This desire eventually brought him into conflict with the administration on several issues. For example, while Powell saw merit in the U.S. troop presence in Europe, the hard-liners did not. Indeed, they wanted to reduce, if not eliminate altogether, any such presence in the Balkans. Powell wanted to remain engaged in the Middle East, but the administration maintained that Clinton's aggressive engagement was not productive; therefore, they adopted a hands-off policy.

This is not to say that there were no recognizable policies other than general disengagement. The administration's first foreign policy efforts involved Mexico, with the promise of a Latin American focus, an area where the former governor of Texas could feel most comfortable. Such a focus also played well politically because the Latino vote had become rather significant. Domestic politics also played a crucial role when Bush went against his free-trade values. His decision to impose tariffs on European steel as an appeal to an important voting bloc contributed to the worst relationship that the United States had had with Europe in years.

Many overseas observers of the United States came to the not unprecedented conclusion that the United States had a double standard: the United States would not necessarily follow the rules of multilateral diplomacy and free trade that it prescribed for the rest of the world. In that context, when the United States was voted off the UN Human Rights Commission, the international community could be seen as reacting in kind.

Every new administration must eventually learn that it has few options in foreign policy. Having already come to this realization, Secretary of State Powell found himself increasingly isolated. His differences with the administration were often public and occasionally humiliating. In March 2001, he was quoted as saying that the Bush Administration would "pick up where the Clinton Administration left off" in negotiating a nuclear nonproliferation deal with North Korea. In a move that also proved embarrassing to the president of South Korea, the White House had Powell retract his position the next day. When pressured by the international community as to when there would be an American alternative to the Kyoto Accord, Powell responded that it should be produced by October 2001. Shortly thereafter, Rice retracted both the plan and the date. The supposed icon of American foreign policy appeared to be out of the loop—so much so that the cover story of the September 10, 2001, issue of *Time* asked "Where Have You Gone, Colin Powell?"

Foreign Policy Post-9/11

Appearances changed in the wake of the events of 9/11, when Powell "took the point" as the administration's most respected statesman to muster international support. The administration realized that it could not proceed alone without exorbitant costs and political risks.

For all its military capabilities, the United States required intelligence data and financial sanctions from the international community. In response to the dramatic destruction of 9/11, many countries rallied to support the United States, providing everything from troops and bases to intelligence cooperation and overflight permission. This response included not only traditional allies such as the NATO countries, but also erstwhile opponents such as Russia and China. In addition, other countries grew more aggressive with counterterrorism efforts of their own, resulting in several overseas terrorist arrests.

It was not as though the nations of the world were offered a wide range of options. In his speech of September 20, the president laid out what has become known as the Bush Doctrine: "Every nation in every region now has a decision to make. From this day forward, any nation that continues to harbor or support terrorism will be regarded by the United States as a hostile regime." Sovereign neutrality was no longer an option. The Bush Doctrine was further defined in his June 2002 speech at West Point: "We must take the battle to the enemy, disrupt his plans, and confront the worst threats before they emerge. In the world we have entered, the only path to safety is the path of action. And this nation will act." Many in the academic and international communities, however, saw this as stretching the concept of "just war" to the breaking point.

The Middle East and Texas-Style Diplomacy

Although sympathy for the United States was almost universal, there was also a measure of resentment over the administration's lack of consultation with the international community. The change that had taken place in U.S. policy had been rather subtle: It had shifted from disengaged unilateralism to engaged unilateralism. Although there appeared to be an international consensus supporting military action in Afghanistan, the prospect of such support for pursuing Saddam Hussein was not assured.

Before 9/11, the hard-liners had consistently argued that a regime change in Iraq was a major foreign policy objective. After the events of 9/11, the hard-liners began looking hard for an al-Qaeda link to Iraq. Although they could not successfully identify a direct and concrete link to that terrorist act, Iraq's acquisition of weapons of mass destruction was nevertheless touted as a major concern. In spite of the administration's hands-off policy in the Middle East, the situation in the region nevertheless appeared to be worsening—the violent dialectic between Palestinian suicide bombers and Israeli army reprisals was a constant reminder of America's diplomatic impotence and failure in the region. Since the cooperation of the Arab states was central to conducting combat operations in the region, the administration went on a full-court press to gain support in the region. Both Vice President Cheney and Colin Powell went on separate multination missions to the Middle East to obtain regional support for an action against Iraq. Neither trip produced the desired result. The Arab nations were united in the position that the United States should reengage in the Middle East, the Israelis must withdraw from the West Bank, and Yasir Arafat must be accepted as the legitimate Palestinian leader. In the week that followed Cheney's tour, the Arab League met and issued a communiqué that included a warning notice: any attack against Iraq would be an attack against each of them.

In late April 2002, the president invited Saudi Arabia's crown prince Abdullah to his ranch in Crawford, Texas, for some Texas-style diplomacy. Rather than obtaining a promise of support, he was given a lecture on the Middle East, which again stressed the necessity of the United States reigning in Israel.

When Bush made a public call for Israel to withdraw from the West Bank, Israel would not do so. Then, on June 24, 2002, the president effectively called for Arafat's removal when he announced a Middle East policy in the Rose Garden that day. The policy itself called for an independent Palestinian state and differed little from the plan previously endorsed by Clinton. However, the call for Arafat's "effective" removal as a necessary condition rendered the "Clinton" part of the policy dead in the water. Rumsfeld and Wolfowitz were strong supporters of Israel, and a common perception developed that they had effectively undercut Powell's efforts to get Arab support. Although Powell was, arguably, the most respected member of the Bush cabinet both at home and abroad, he appeared to remain the odd man out. Nonetheless, Powell was called upon, again, to take the point and put his personal credibility on the line when he presented the administration's argument before the UN Security Council in February 2003.

Selling the War

Whereas the invasion of Afghanistan had international support as the legitimate pursuit of an international fugitive who declared war on and attacked the United States, the invasion of Iraq marked a fundamental shift in American foreign policy. The intelligence presented in support of such action was, at best, cherry-picked, if not fabricated. Nonetheless, the United States had, for the first time in modern history, set out to become an aggressor nation.

The alliance that supported the hunt for Osama bin Laden in Afghanistan had whittled down to Great Britain and a few minor commitments from secondary powers to form a "coalition of the willing" in Iraq. Other powers were put off by what they perceived as America's unwillingness to consult or share intel-

ligence. The Bush Administration's reaction to the lack of support from Western Europe was less than diplomatic. Rumsfeld dismissed longtime U.S. allies as "Old Europe," and Congress renamed its popular side dish "freedom fries."

Selling the war at home required another full-court press. Deputy Secretary of Defense Paul Wolfowitz went before the Senate and testified that U.S. troops would be welcomed with open arms and the war would be paid for with liberated Iraqi oil. In an effort to create a sense of urgency, administration officials were sent on the media circuit to suggest that Saddam Hussein was about to use weapons of mass destruction against the United States, an effort best categorized by Rice's statement "we don't want the smoking gun to be a mushroom cloud." It was further suggested, principally by Cheney, that Saddam was involved in the 9/11 attacks. In the 2003 State of the Union address, Bush stated, "The British government has learned that Saddam Hussein recently sought significant quantities of uranium from Africa." His words, like most of the administration's arguments, were later proven false. Nonetheless, the offensive served its purpose. The administration would stifle debate by impugning the very patriotism of those who questioned the policy, political opponents were accused of comforting the enemy in time of war, and national security was threatened by the outing of a CIA operative for political cover. In the end, fear trumped reason.

In Afghanistan, the military had pushed al-Qaeda to the point where they thought they had bin Laden holed up in the rugged mountain region of Tora Bora. However, before the operation was complete, resources were diverted to Iraq and bin Laden made his escape. The war did not go well in Iraq. Not only were the troops on the ground unable to find any evidence to support the rationale for the invasion, but they were totally unprepared for the civil unrest that followed. Moreover, there was no definitive exit strategy, only a slogan: "When they stand up we will stand down." In Washington, Bush seemed detached from the realities of the war. On May 1, 2003, in what could have been one of the best photo-ops in history, Bush declared combat operations over from the deck of an aircraft carrier. He followed up by awarding Medals of Freedom to three of the major players in the Iraq invasion; CIA director George Tenet, General Tommy Franks, and the head of the Coalition Provisional Authority in Iraq, Paul Bremer. Unfortunately, the political theater was not supported by the images from the front.

Politics and Foreign Policy

When journalist Bob Woodward asked Bush if he had consulted his father in planning the invasion of Iraq, he replied that he had consulted a higher authority, presumably meaning God. Indeed, faith played a large part in the younger Bush's foreign policy. Bush's faith also led him to understand that his narrow victory in the 2004 election was a mandate and an endorsement of his policies, including the war. With Powell's resignation at the end of the first term, the moderate counterweight to Cheney and Rumsfeld was gone. His replacement, Condoleezza Rice, was considered more cooperative with the neocons. The hard-line policies of the first administration continued until significant losses in the midterm election of 2006 caused Bush to change his perspective.

After the 2006 election, there was a noticeable shift in Iraq policy. By the end of the second term, Bush relied less on Cheney's council, Rumsfeld and most of the nonelected neocons were out of the administration, and Bush had attempted to find a way out of Iraq. To that end, he relied on what became known as the surge. Proposed and implemented by General David Petraeus, the surge combined a stepped-up military and diplomatic push to produce a stable environment and allow the reform of the political system. By the time Bush left office, the surge had shown a measure of success, which made it easier for his successor to fulfill his campaign promises to end America's combat mission in Iraq in relatively short order.

Obama and the Bush Legacy

The Obama Administration ushered in a return to the internationalism of the Clinton Administration. Obama put together a foreign policy team of veterans and high-profile officials that included his vice president Joe Biden, Rumsfeld's replacement, Robert Gates, Hillary Clinton as secretary of state, and Ambassador Richard Holbrooke. He also continued to maintain a measure of continuity with General Petraeus in command. As promised, he pulled all combat troops out of Iraq and refocused on Afghanistan with his own troop surge in late 2009 and early 2010, though with a flexible withdrawal date of mid-2011.

Stewart S. Johnson

See also: *September 11 Attacks*—U.S. Aid and Relief; U.S. Foreign Relations. *Counterterrorism*—International Cooperation Against Terrorism.

Further Reading

Anonymous. *Imperial Hubris: Why the West Is Losing the War on Terror.* Washington, DC: Brassey's, 2004.
Bush, George W. *Decision Points.* New York: Crown, 2010.
Clarke, Richard A. *Against All Enemies: Inside America's War on Terror.* New York: Free Press, 2004.
———. *Your Government Failed You: Breaking the Cycle of National Security Disasters.* New York: HarperCollins, 2008.
McClellan, Scott. *What Happened: Inside the Bush White House and Washington's Culture of Deception.* New York: PublicAffairs, 2008.
Ricks, Thomas E. *Fiasco: The American Military Adventure in Iraq.* New York: Penguin, 2006.
Suskind, Ron. *The One Percent Doctrine: Deep Inside America's Pursuit of Its Enemies Since 9/11.* New York: Simon and Schuster, 2006.
Wilson, Joseph. *The Politics of Truth: Inside the Lies That Led to War and Betrayed My Wife's CIA Identity.* New York: Carroll and Graf, 2004.
Wilson, Valerie Plame. *Fair Game: My Life as a Spy, My Betrayal by the White House.* New York: Simon and Schuster, 2007.
Woodward, Bob. *Bush at War.* New York: Simon and Schuster, 2002.
———. *Plan of Attack.* New York: Simon and Schuster, 2004.
———. *State of Denial: Bush at War, Part III.* New York: Simon and Schuster, 2006.
———. *The War Within: A Secret White House History, 2006–2008.* New York: Simon and Schuster, 2008.
Zakaria, Fareed. *The Post-American World.* New York: W.W. Norton, 2009.

U.S. Foreign Relations

The events of September 11, 2001, had a dramatic effect on the foreign relations of the United States. The attacks altered America's foreign policy priorities and led to the deployment of tens of thousands of U.S. troops across Afghanistan, Iraq, Pakistan, the Philippines, Georgia, and other nations. In other ways, however, much of America's foreign relations continued unchanged. For most countries in Africa and the Americas, for example, relations before and after the attacks remained the same. The varied impact of 9/11 is reflected in two elements of America's foreign relations: (1) the definition of interests and threats and (2) the character of bilateral relations.

Interests, Threats, and Shifting Relationships

In international politics, governments are expected to define a set of vital interests, identify the threats to those interests, and pursue a foreign policy to protect them. Over the decades, American foreign policy has recognized a number of vital interests, including protecting the U.S. homeland, safeguarding U.S. personnel and assets abroad, and preventing any one country from dominating Eurasia (e.g., Germany during World War II, the Soviet Union during the Cold War).

The September 11 attacks did not change America's core interests, but they substantially altered the U.S.

government's view of the likely threats to those interests and, in particular, the identity and methods of the attackers. In the months leading up to 9/11, discussions of threat focused on ballistic missiles and so-called rogue states. Terrorism was considered one item in a long list of potential threats to American national security. After 9/11, combating terrorism became the dominant U.S. foreign policy goal.

As America's perception of threats changed, so did its bilateral relationships. Washington's relations with some countries improved. For example, sympathetic allies rallied to the side of the United States and refrained from their earlier criticism of American foreign policy. Other countries, such as Pakistan and Uzbekistan, were able to dramatically upgrade their ties to the United States because America needed their help to fight the Taliban. Even past adversaries offered to assist American antiterrorist efforts, perhaps, as some analysts speculated, because they wanted to avoid confrontation with a riled superpower. In other instances, however, bilateral relations deteriorated. Such was the case with Iran, for example. Finally, for many nations, U.S. foreign relations continued as before. For many countries in this group, relations with Washington remained the same, but their relative standing declined, especially compared to countries directly involved in the campaign against terrorism. September 11 resulted in a new focus on Central Asia, South Asia, and the Middle East, and that left fewer resources and less time for the Americas and other parts of the globe.

Central Asia

The most direct and immediate effects of 9/11 were on U.S. foreign relations with Central Asia. Prior to September 11, Central Asia was not a foreign policy priority. The attention it did receive was limited to interest in oil and complaints about political repression.

After 9/11, all that changed, particularly for Afghanistan, Uzbekistan, Tajikistan, and Turkmenistan. First, there was a U.S. decision to topple the Taliban government in Afghanistan. To accomplish that goal, Washington needed air and land access from Kabul's northern neighbors. Uzbekistan and Tajikistan had actively opposed the Taliban government and were battling their own Islamist rebel groups. Relations with Washington were dramatically upgraded, as both American troops and financial aid were rushed to the region.

Bilateral relations with the other major player in the region, Iran, were more complicated. Although both the United States and Iran opposed the Taliban, the relationship between the two nations had been cool since the 1979 Islamic Revolution. Further complicating relations was the ongoing domestic political struggle in Iran between hard-liners opposed to better relations with the United States and reformers eager to improve

relations with Washington. Following 9/11, there was an outpouring of sympathy for the United States, and the Iranians offered to allow search-and-rescue missions from Iran. Over the next several months, however, U.S.-Iranian relations deteriorated. Iran worried about the presence of U.S. forces on its border and a U.S.-backed government in Kabul. For its part, the United States accused Iran of supporting terrorism against Israel and trying to destabilize Afghanistan's interim government. By January 2002, President Bush had declared that Iran was part of the "axis of evil." In short, although officials on both sides had hoped that the terrorist attacks would provide an opportunity for stronger U.S.-Iranian ties, the relationship instead took a turn for the worse.

By the mid-2000s, despite a continuing convergence of interests in keeping the Afghan Taliban from returning to power, antagonism between Washington and Tehran had intensified further with the victory of hard-liner Mahmoud Ahmadinejad as president. This was especially so after he committed Iran to an accelerated development of a domestic capacity for enriching uranium. Ahmadinejad insisted such enrichment was for peaceful purposes, but Washington, and much of the Western world, charged Iran with pursuing nuclear-weapons-grade material. As a result, Washington led the international effort to impose tighter sanctions on the Tehran government.

South Asia

The events of September 11 had a major impact on U.S. foreign relations in South Asia. For much of the Cold War, America's strongest ties in the region were with Pakistan. Pakistan had, for example, been particularly helpful to the United States after the Soviet invasion of Afghanistan in 1979. After the fall of the Soviet Union, however, relations began to change. America put increasing value on its relationship with India, which was viewed as a future economic partner and as a potential check on future Chinese inroads in the region. The Bush Administration came to office hoping to strengthen economic relations with India and to downplay the issue of nuclear weapons. By contrast, U.S.-Pakistan relations suffered, particularly after the 1999 Kargil offensive in Kashmir and the subsequent coup that brought General Pervez Musharraf to power.

The 9/11 attacks altered the South Asian equation. The United States still desired better relations with India, but the importance of Pakistan reasserted itself. The United States needed Pakistan's help to remove the Taliban and suppress al-Qaeda.

Further complicating the picture was the fact that Pakistani-based militants were simultaneously engaged in a terror campaign against India, most notably in a December 2001 assault on the Indian parliament in New Delhi. The attack brought the two nuclear rivals close to conflict and further complicated American foreign policy in the region. In short, the events of September 11 gave South Asia a higher priority in U.S. foreign relations, but it required the United States to balance three competing goals: working with Pakistan to defeat al-Qaeda, improving U.S.-Indian relations, and preventing the outbreak of nuclear war on the subcontinent. This multitrack approach to the subcontinent could be seen in both the rising level of economic and military aid to Pakistan—from $24 million in 2000 to nearly $1 billion in 2007—and a nuclear arms deal with India, signed into law by Bush, in 2008.

Middle East

In the weeks immediately following the 9/11 attacks, many nations in the Middle East offered assistance to the United States in its fight against terrorism. These countries included longtime allies, including Turkey and Oman, as well as countries that had previously been associated with terrorism, such as Syria and Yemen. Yemen, for example, agreed to the deployment of U.S. troops to train Yemeni antiterrorist forces.

Over time, however, U.S. relations in the region became increasingly strained. This was particularly the case with Saudi Arabia. The U.S.-Saudi relationship is firmly anchored in oil and security, but the terrorist attacks served to highlight the cultural and political differences between the two countries. Not since the Organization of Petroleum Exporting Countries oil embargo of the 1970s had the U.S.-Saudi relationship been so openly questioned.

Indeed, the U.S. position in most of the Arab world declined—even among American allies such as Egypt and Jordan. The chief cause of the strain in U.S-Arab relations was the increasing violence of the Israeli-Palestinian conflict. The upward spiral of Palestinian-Israeli violence had begun well before the September 11 attacks. The violence had increased in September 2000, following a visit by then prime ministerial candidate Ariel Sharon to the al-Aqsa Mosque compound and again after the Israeli election in February 2001. This had led to the Second Intifada, a wave of Islamist terrorist bombings in Israel, and Israel's invasion of Gaza and the West Bank in 2002.

Following 9/11, then prime minister Sharon invoked President Bush's campaign against terrorism to justify Israeli military operations against Palestinian targets. These operations often won the public backing of President Bush. For many in the Arab world, the linking of the United States and Israel at a time of rising bloodshed contributed to a level of anti-American sentiment unseen since the Arab-Israeli Wars of 1967 and 1973.

U.S.-Israeli relations in this period were both closer and more difficult. Israel received strong support from the Bush Administration for its response to suicide bombings, but the administration was unhappy with the conflict, which hampered the campaign against terrorism and complicated plans for intervention against Iraq. Even before the 9/11 attacks, the Bush Administration had hinted that one of its foreign policy goals was the removal of the Saddam Hussein regime in Iraq. After the terrorist attacks of 2001, the administration moved inexorably toward war, despite the expressed misgivings of many Arab regimes. The U.S. invasion of Iraq in March 2003—justified by the Bush Administration as a way to prevent Iraq from developing weapons of mass destruction—met with protests from much of the Arab world, but, with few exceptions, not particularly vociferous ones, as many saw the Hussein regime as a threat to the region's stability. But as Iraq collapsed into chaos in the years following the invasion—and as Iran gained influence in the country—many Arab regimes became more torn in their attitude toward America's Iraqi policy. Publicly, they condemned this breach of an Arab nation's sovereignty, but most feared that a precipitous American withdrawal could destabilize the region further. In the end, the Bush Administration increased its presence in the country with a troop surge in 2007 that helped quell the civil war–like conditions in the country.

With the onset of the Barack Obama Administration in Washington in 2009, the United States committed itself to withdrawing combat troops from Iraq by August 2010, which it did. At the same time, Obama personally set a goal of improving relations with the Arab Middle East by engaging in a dialogue with the region, starting with a major speech in Cairo in which he expressed the sentiment that America was at war with Islamist extremism, not Islam itself. The message was not all that different from that delivered by the Bush Administration. But the messenger was. Free of the baggage of having invaded Iraq—indeed, Obama had long opposed the war—and being seen as more culturally sympathetic to the developing world, the new president was able to reach out to the so-called Arab Street in a way Bush had not been able to. However, the initial rapport Obama had achieved with ordinary Arab people was gradually undermined by his administration's continuing strong support for Israel and his decision to intensify the U.S. war in Afghanistan.

Asia-Pacific

In the Asia-Pacific region, America's new emphasis on terrorism had a varied but mostly limited effect. Relations with a majority of countries in the region—Japan, South Korea, Australia, and Vietnam—were unaffected by the terrorist attacks. North Korea was included in President Bush's "axis of evil," but there was little change in policy. In Indonesia, protesters took to the streets to voice opposition to the conflict in Afghanistan, but government-to-government relations continued as before. The impact of 9/11 was felt most by three countries in the Asia-Pacific region: China, Malaysia, and the Philippines.

Before 9/11, Sino-American relations had entered a difficult phase. The new administration had come to office with a more adversarial view of China than previous administrations held, describing Beijing as a strategic competitor and highlighting America's commitment to Taiwan. Relations between the two countries were further aggravated by the "spy plane" incident in April 2001, when an American reconnaissance aircraft collided with a Chinese jet fighter. Immediately following the 9/11 terrorist attacks, these issues were set aside, and both sides emphasized a new spirit of cooperation. Beijing and Washington found common ground in their opposition to Islamist terrorism and the Taliban government. Over the subsequent decade, new strains have developed in U.S.-Chinese relations, not just over economic issues, but also over China's unwillingness to cooperate fully with U.S. sanctions against Iran and its more accommodating stance toward a now nuclear-armed North Korea.

Before the September 11 attacks, U.S.-Malaysian relations were chilly. Malaysia was a vocal critic of the United States, and American officials objected to Prime Minister Mohamad Mahathir's human rights record, in particular the jailing of his former deputy prime minister. After 9/11, however, relations quickly improved, culminating in a visit by Prime Minister Mahathir to the White House in May 2002. The United States and Malaysia now shared a common interest—battling Islamist terrorist groups.

Perhaps the Asia-Pacific country most impacted by the 9/11 attacks was the Philippines, a longtime U.S. ally. The Philippines was the first country outside Central Asia to receive American troops for terrorist-related operations, and the deployment of U.S. military forces to the southern Philippines represented a dramatic change in policy for both governments.

Europe

In Europe, the terrorist attacks did not substantially alter American foreign relations, but they had an effect nonetheless. Prior to 9/11, European officials had begun to complain that American foreign policy was increasingly unilateralist. Following 9/11, European capitals rallied around Washington, and criticisms were muted. European support also took the form of a precedent-setting decision by the North Atlantic Treaty Organization (NATO) to invoke article 5 of the defense treaty, thus defining the September 11 attacks as an attack on all NATO members. As the campaign moved to Afghanistan, more than a dozen NATO countries sent forces.

Still, not all countries in Europe were equally enthusiastic about the campaign against terrorism. Britain provided the most public support for U.S. initiatives, but other American allies such as France and Germany became increasingly uncomfortable with American plans to strike against terrorists and countries suspected of supporting them. Nor did the European capitals react favorably to President Bush's speech labeling Iran, Iraq, and North Korea as the "axis of evil." Later, when the United States invaded Iraq, Europe became divided. Of the three largest material powers in Western Europe—France, Germany, and the United Kingdom—only the latter fully supported it. However, many of the newer members of NATO from the former Eastern bloc supported the United States and sent troops, leading some in the Bush Administration to talk of a new orientation in U.S.-European relations.

Meanwhile, the September 11 attacks gave a boost to U.S.-Russian relations. Early in his administration, President Bush expressed a fondness for President Putin and a willingness to develop a new Russian-American relationship. He stressed, however, that the U.S. government would not alter its objectives, especially regarding missile defense. After the terrorist attacks, the United States needed Russia's support to conduct military operations in the region—operations that included the staging of American troops on soil that was formerly part of the Soviet Union. Russia responded with an extraordinary level of cooperation, hoping that the result would be stronger ties to the West and less criticism of its policies in Chechnya. Over the following decade, however, relations between the two nations cooled, though this had less to do with differences in their approach to the war on terrorism than it had to do with Putin's increasingly antidemocratic tendencies.

Africa

For most countries in Africa, particularly nations in southern and western Africa, the U.S. campaign against terrorism had little consequence. The exceptions included countries such as Somalia, Sudan, and Libya—countries that had poor relations with the United States and had previously been accused of involvement with terrorism. Indeed, all three of these countries had previously been hit with American military strikes following terrorist attacks against U.S. targets. Following 9/11, however, Libya condemned the attacks, offered to share its intelligence on bin Laden, and took other moves to distance itself from its reputation as a state sponsor of terrorism. As for the rest of Africa, it has gained more attention from the U.S. foreign policy establishment, which fears that failed states on the continent could provide safe havens for terrorist groups.

The Americas

U.S. foreign relations with the Americas did not change substantially following 9/11. There were some alterations (e.g., efforts to integrate border and port security with Canada and Mexico), but fundamentally, U.S. foreign policy remained the same. Perhaps the largest change in bilateral relations involved Colombia, where Washington became increasingly active in Bogotá's military campaign against rebel groups. But this move predated the 9/11 attacks.

Overall, the effect of September 11 on U.S. foreign relations was something of a paradox: both change and constancy. The U.S. government gave unprecedented priority to fighting terrorism, and the new emphasis on terrorism created unexpected opportunities for cooperation with Russia, China, and nations that had suffered poor relations with Washington. In other parts of the globe, however, the impact of 9/11 hardly registered, and over time, increasing complaints about American unilateralism were reminiscent of the period prior to September 11.

James Walsh and James Ciment

See also: *September 11 Attacks*—U.S. Aid and Relief; U.S. Foreign Policy. *Counterterrorism*—International Cooperation Against Terrorism; International Law and the War on Terrorism.

Further Reading

Banuazizi, Ali, and Myron Weiner, eds. *The New Geopolitics of Central Asia and Its Borderlands.* Bloomington: Indiana University Press, 1994.

Barnett, Thomas P.M. *Great Powers: America and the World After Bush.* New York: G.P. Putnam's Sons, 2009.

Blitz, Amy. *The Contested State: American Foreign Policy and Regime Change in the Philippines.* Lanham, MD: Rowman and Littlefield, 2000.

Brands, H.W. *Bound to Empire: The United States and the Philippines.* New York: Oxford University Press, 1992.

Cohen, Warren I. *America's Response to China: A History of Sino-American Relations.* 4th ed. New York: Columbia University Press, 2000.

Hart, Parker T. *Saudi Arabia and the United States: Birth of a Security Partnership.* Bloomington: Indiana University Press, 1998.

Kux, Dennis. *The United States and Pakistan, 1947–2000: Disenchanted Allies.* Baltimore: Johns Hopkins University Press, 2001.

Lampton, David M. *Same Bed, Different Dreams: Managing U.S.-China Relations, 1989–2000.* Berkeley: University of California Press, 2001.

Malik, Hafeez, ed. *Central Asia: Its Strategic Importance and Future Prospects.* New York: St. Martin's, 1994.

McMahon, Robert J. *The Cold War on the Periphery: The United States, India, and Pakistan.* New York: Columbia University Press, 1994.

Sanger, David E. *Inheritance: The World Obama Confronts and the Challenges to American Power.* New York: Three Rivers, 2009.

Zakaria, Fareed. *The Post-American World.* New York: W.W. Norton, 2009.

Political, Legal, and Social Issues

Aside from their national security implications, the September 11, 2001, terrorist attacks and the heightened concern about extremist attacks from abroad that they engendered have had a profound affect on virtually every aspect of American life—political, legal, economic, and social.

With the collapse of the Soviet Union and the end of the Cold War at the beginning of the 1990s, foreign policy and national security concerns had lost much of their political urgency. As the world's sole superpower, without a global ideological enemy, the United States appeared to be reaping a peace dividend, not only in terms of lowered defense budgets but also in a more open view of the outside world. The September 11, 2001, terrorist attacks once again put national security at the top of the nation's political agenda. As the party that had traditionally been viewed by voters as stronger on national security, Republicans reaped a political windfall from 9/11, helping them gain congressional seats in 2002—a rare

accomplishment in a midterm election when the party also holds the White House—and win George W. Bush, who ran largely on antiterrorism and national security, a second presidential term. Ironically, it would be the Bush Administration's bellicose response to 9/11—especially its invasion of Iraq in 2003—that would cost the Republicans control of Congress in 2006 and the White House in 2008, though the financial collapse and recession were probably larger factors in the latter election.

On another front in the war on terrorism that the 9/11 attacks triggered, the Bush Administration responded to the 9/11 disaster with a series of legally and constitutionally dubious measures, concerning both domestic surveillance and the treatment of enemy combatants, both linked to the al-Qaeda terrorist organization that perpetrated the attacks and the Taliban regime that harbored them in Afghanistan, following America's invasion of that country in October 2001. The USA PATRIOT Act, passed with the overwhelming support of both parties that

Opponents of the USA PATRIOT Act protest surveillance measures in the antiterrorist legislation that they regard as infringements of essential civil liberties. The law was passed in October 2001 and reauthorized and amended several times thereafter. *(Spencer Platt/Getty Images)*

same month, gave law enforcement enhanced powers to search people's homes without their knowledge, obtain wiretaps on their communications, and obtain documents revealing how they lived their lives, including the books they checked out of libraries. Supporters of such measures defended them as necessary to track down and stop a devious enemy that operated from within our midst, but critics said it gave government far too great power to pry into the private lives of citizens, a fear confirmed in 2005 when it was learned the Bush Administration had illegally accessed thousands upon thousands of Internet-facilitated communications without warrants.

The Bush Administration also set up a shadow legal system that effectively denied foreign detainees at the U.S naval base at Guantánamo Bay, Cuba, the right of habeas corpus guaranteed to them under the constitution—a system that the Supreme Court would rule illegal in several decisions in the mid-2000s. In addition, the administration authorized interrogation techniques that seemed to violate both U.S. laws and international conventions to which the United States was a signatory. These measures, said critics, not only undermined American ideals of justice but diminished the country's standing in the world as a defender of human rights and civil liberties.

Economically, the 9/11 attacks had a more mixed impact. While experts and the public generally feared that they would deal the U.S. economy a devastating blow, just as it was emerging from the post-dot-com recession of 2001, in fact, the drop was rather slight, given the overall size of the U.S. economy: no more than perhaps half a percent of gross domestic product, say most economists. Even New York City seemed to recover quickly, as it entered a period of sustained growth, though much of it was fueled by a bubble in real estate prices. On the other hand, the 9/11 terrorist attacks directly led to much higher defense budgets, as well as wars in Afghanistan and Iraq, all of which contributed to huge federal deficits that threatened the country's long-term economic health.

Finally, the 9/11 attacks have had a profound effect on U.S. society. Americans now live in a state of heightened fear, though nothing like what gripped the country during the height of the Cold War, and while the fear of new attacks has eased somewhat as 9/11 fades into the past, the heightened security measures they led to have made everyone's daily existence that much more exasperating in big and little ways, whether it be in the form of long lines at the airport or the inability to put large packages into the local mailbox.

Americans rightfully prided themselves on the relative lack of vitriol that greeted foreigners in general and Muslims in particular in the wake of terrorist attacks that killed nearly 3,000 people and which were perpetrated by terrorists acting in the name of a perverted form of Islam. Nevertheless, 9/11 has contributed to a lingering intolerance and fear of Muslims, as witnessed by the 2010 uproar over the construction of an Islamic cultural center near the World Trade Center site in lower Manhattan.

How long these various political, social, and economic effects of 9/11 will last is unknown. While Pearl Harbor was the defining moment for a generation back in 1941 and led to much greater political, economic, and social changes than 9/11—not least of which was the incarceration of more than 100,000 American citizens and resident aliens of Japanese descent—it soon became little more than a day to commemorate the loss of victims and celebrate American resolve in the face of enemy attack. Then again, World War II was over in four years, with a decisive victory over Japan. The war on terrorism has already lasted more than twice as long, with no end in sight. It is anybody's guess what the effects of a lingering war—with such a shadowy enemy—will have on the institutions we live by and the values we cherish.

James Ciment

See also: *September 11 Attacks*—National Political Response; New York City and State Political Response; Anti-Muslim Sentiment; Civil Liberties, Civil Rights, and National Security; Government Spying and Privacy Issues; Imprisonment and Legal Status of Detainees; Torture.

Further Reading

Abdo, Geneive. *Mecca and Main Street: Muslim Life in America After 9/11.* New York: Oxford University Press, 2006.

Cole, David, and James H. Dempsey. *Terrorism and the Constitution: Sacrificing Civil Liberties in the Name of National Security.* New York: New Press, 2005.

Engle, Karen. *Seeing Ghosts: 9/11 and the Visual Imagination.* Montreal: McGill-Queen's University Press, 2009.

Hafetz, Jonathan. *Habeas Corpus After 9/11: Confronting America's New Global Detention System.* New York: New York University Press, 2010.

Honigsberg, Peter Jan. *Our Nation Unhinged: The Human Consequences of the War on Terror.* Berkeley: University of California Press, 2009.

Morgan, Matthew J., ed. *The Impact of 9/11 on Business and Economics: The Business of Terror.* New York: Palgrave Macmillan, 2009.

Anti-Muslim Sentiment

Many people have described the events of 9/11 as the single worst terrorist attack in history. It is therefore understandable that one of the first reactions many Americans felt was outrage and anger at those who would perpetrate such disaster on innocent people. It is also not uncommon for that anger to be projected by stereotyping all those who resemble or belong to the particular ethnic group of those perceived to be responsible for the carnage. However, when generalizations and prejudiced attitudes evolve into verbal and physical abuse of the targeted minority, these actions run counter to American principles and laws. There are 6 to 7 million Muslims in the United States, the vast majority of whom are patriotic, hardworking, and productive members of society.

Aftermath of the Attacks

Violence and threats of violence against Arab Americans and Muslims escalated dramatically following the events of September 11, 2001. According to the Council on American-Islamic Relations, headquartered in Washington, D.C., more than 540 incidents ranging in severity from verbal threats to, in some cases, murder were reported in the first ten days after the September 11 attacks. The Federal Bureau of Investigation also reported a dramatic increase in the number of hate crimes targeting Arab and Muslim Americans. Attacks on South Asian immigrants also increased. Under the banner of patriotism, hundreds of incidents of harassment, intimidation, and violence were perpetrated against people of Middle Eastern descent and other minority ethnic groups who are somehow culturally similar to the perpetrators of the 9/11 attacks. Acting primarily out of fear, those who instigated or engaged in attacks against this segment of society responded irrationally to the events of 9/11 by collectively blaming an entire ethnic group or religion for the actions of a fringe element.

This rising tide of post-9/11 harassment and violence took many forms: Businesses were vandalized, mosques defaced, and people of Middle Eastern descent victimized by racist violence, both verbally and physically. Some of these violent encounters resulted in fatalities. One of the worst incidents occurred on September 15 in Mesa, Arizona, when an Indian American Sikh was shot and killed outside his owner-operated Chevron gas station. He was attacked because he wore a turban, had a beard, and looked Muslim. On the same day, in Dallas, Texas, a Pakistani grocery store owner was killed.

In addition to verbal and physical assaults, many Americans of Middle Eastern and South Asian heritage were singled out for discrimination in the workplace and racial profiling at America's airports. In many instances, people perceived to be members of a certain ethnic group were prevented from boarding aircraft because the passengers or crew did not like the way they looked, or, if they were allowed to board, airport security officials often subjected them to selective and rigid screening measures. In some cases, passengers were removed from the aircraft after having already endured rigorous security checks. Many Muslim schools across the country closed in the wake of the attacks because a large number of parents decided to keep their children home rather than risk having them victimized on the streets. Anti-Arab and anti-Muslim sentiments also filled Internet chat rooms with racial hatred, in the form of verbal threats and disparaging comments.

The causes of terrorism are complex and do not lend themselves to easy solutions. The notion that Islam is behind the atrocities of 9/11 provides a quasi-logical rationale but not a morally acceptable basis for the systematic persecution of those who practice that faith. Some people seem to forget that Arab Americans and other minorities were among the nearly 3,000 victims of 9/11.

Although President George W. Bush, U.S. attorney general John Ashcroft, and many congressional leaders on both sides of the aisle issued public statements denouncing threats and actions that target specific ethnic groups, numerous incidents ranging from death threats to vandalism and in some cases murder continued to occur. Although most Americans responded to the attacks with true patriotism and a sense of grief and sadness for those victimized by these senseless acts, a fringe element decided to take out their frustrations on those whose religion and appearance were different from their own. Prejudicial stereotypes and ethnic targeting are not unprecedented in American history, but they are certainly a phenomenon that we need to consistently condemn if we want to continue to view America as above the hatred and xenophobia commonly exhibited in societies that give birth to terrorism.

Ground Zero Mosque Controversy

As time passed and America experienced no subsequent direct attack by Islamist extremists, anti-Muslim rhetoric and incidents lessened somewhat. According to the Federal Bureau of Investigation, anti-Islamic hate crimes in the United States dropped from 481 in 2001 to 105 in 2008, though the latter figure was still substantially higher than the 28 in the last full pre-9/11 year of 2000.

Anti-Muslim sentiment revived somewhat in 2010, however, as New Yorkers and Americans reacted to the announcement that a Muslim group was planning on building an Islamic cultural center three blocks from the former site of the World Trade Center. The so-called Ground Zero mosque, as detractors referred to it, was challenged on several grounds. Some 9/11 victims' families said the location of the center so close to where their loved ones had died at the hands of Islamist extremists was insensitive. Other opponents went further, some calling the center a "victory mosque" built by Muslims to show their triumph over the United States. American Muslims and their supporters contended that the cultural center was simply meant to serve the large working Muslim population of lower Manhattan and that it would serve as a bridge between cultures. Indeed, the imam of the cultural center was a man the

Plans to build an Islamic center three blocks from "Ground Zero," former site of the World Trade Center, sparked emotional protest—some of it Islamophobic—on September 11, 2010. Nearby, others demonstrated for religious tolerance. *(Associated Press)*

U.S. government had sent abroad on missions to create closer ties between the United States and predominantly Muslim cultures.

The anti-Muslim rhetoric grew even more heated when a Florida pastor announced plans to burn the Koran on September 11, 2010. While the pastor was ultimately persuaded not to do so by high-level U.S. government and military officials, other persons around the country tried to block the building of mosques in their communities, all of which drew national and international media attention. Fueling the controversy was the heated political season—the midterm elections of 2010—in which it occurred. Once the elections were over, attention from the issue faded from view, leading some commentators to argue that much of the furor was drummed up by opportunistic politicians seeking an advantage by stirring up anti-Muslim prejudice.

Frank Shanty and James Ciment

See also: *September 11 Attacks*—Political, Legal, and Social Issues; Civil Liberties, Civil Rights, and National Security; Immigration Policy and Border Defense.

Further Reading

Abdo, Geneive. *Mecca and Main Street: Muslim Life in America After 9/11*. New York: Oxford University Press, 2006.

Human Rights Watch. *USA: "We Are Not the Enemy": Hate Crimes Against Arabs, Muslims, and Those Perceived to be Arab or Muslim after September 11*. November 14, 2002, G1406. Available at http://www.unhcr.org/refworld/docid/45db101e2.html. Accessed 29 March 2011.

Peek, Lori. *Behind the Backlash: Muslim Americans After 9/11*. Philadelphia: Temple University Press, 2010.

Civil Liberties, Civil Rights, and National Security

Civil rights and civil liberties are categories of human action arising from limits on government. Rights, such as religious preference and trial by jury, guaranteed by the U.S. Bill of Rights of 1791, are immunities from government's operations that the Constitution obligates it to provide its citizens, whereas liberties are options of personal behavior within those operations. One arguable distinction between the two is that government observance is mandatory for rights but optional for liberties, which are only revocable gratuities. In practice, civil rights and liberties overlap and interpenetrate.

The incompatibility of terrorism with rights and liberties is not only inherent but historically manifest. On one hand, the terrorist's bomb extinguishes life and liberty without due process or trial of any sort. On the other hand, incumbent regimes have typically responded to terrorist outrages by constricting liberties of expression and the rights of the criminally accused in the name of national security.

At the very root of the word "terrorism" is the terror of the French Revolution, which climaxed in 1794 with the ironic execution of Maximilien Robespierre, mastermind of that terror. The assassination of Czar Alexander II in 1881, on the very day that he had approved the first steps toward a representative assembly, instigated a ruthless crackdown on dissent by Alexander III (1881–1894) that flooded Siberia with political and religious prisoners. Popular revulsion provoked by the Haymarket Affair of 1886 in Chicago, in which seven policemen were killed, centered on not only the anarchist perpetrators but also the leadership of America's nascent organized labor movement. In 1919 and 1920, several U.S. terrorist bombings occurred, one of which, on September 16, 1920, targeted the Wall Street headquarters of financier J.P. Morgan and killed thirty-four persons. In the resulting Palmer Raids, which Attorney General A. Mitchell Palmer supervised, hundreds of Americans were illegally arrested and searched without warrants, held incommunicado, denied legal counsel, and encouraged to incriminate themselves.

Among the first to lament terrorism's impact on civil rights was none other than Leon Trotsky, "Father of the Red Army," who had himself employed terrorism lavishly to overthrow the Romanov dynasty (1613–1917) during the Bolshevik Revolution of 1917. Expelled from the Soviet Union after losing a power struggle in 1929, Trotsky had written Terrorism and Communism in 1921 to justify his extreme methods. Afterward, however, he turned on Vladimir Lenin and Joseph Stalin, his former comrades, accusing them of betraying the revolution by adopting the same methods as the czars.

American Law and Terrorism

The developing American law of terrorism and its impact on civil rights and liberties extends from earlier laws governing military-civilian relations. In Ex parte Milligan (1866), a case decided after the Civil War for activities during the war, the Supreme Court limited military trials of civilians to narrow circumstances combining hostilities with concurrent closures of the civilian courts. The Court of Chief Justice Salmon Chase held, in effect, that the military could try a civilian only when wartime exigencies foreclosed all other options.

Perhaps the first federal litigation on the reality, but not the terminology, of terrorism arose during World War II in Ex parte Quirin (1942). After infiltrating the United States to sabotage its munitions and armaments factories, a would-be German commando got cold feet and turned in his compatriots, who were tried before a military commission by presidential fiat and received death sentences. Supreme Court Chief Justice Harlan Fiske Stone upheld the convictions, perhaps because the defense counsel had argued the implausible fiction that his clients were de facto refugees from Nazi oppression. By a single vote, however, the Stone Court in Cramer v. United States (1945) also refused to sustain the collateral execution of a German immigrant and Nazi sympathizer who admitted concealing the saboteurs' equipment but denied knowledge of its purpose.

A year later, in 1946, the Stone Court upheld the Milligan immunity of civilians from military tribunals but elsewhere extended the Milligan precedent from American servicemen to enemy combatants. Although the imposition of martial law after December 7, 1941, had suspended all civilian courts in Hawaii, Stone and his brethren, in Duncan v. Kahanamoku (1946), overturned the use of military courts, the only surviving tribunals, to try Hawaiian civilians. Simultaneously, however, in In re Yamashita (1946), the same Court upheld the military trial and death sentence for war crimes of the Japanese commandant of the occupied Philippines.

During the remaining half of the twentieth century, American law confronted an escalating terrorist threat without significantly abbreviating rights or liberties. In 1950 and 1954, Puerto Rican nationalists shot up the residence of President Truman and the House of Representatives, respectively, killing and wounding scores of civilians. The Vietnam War spawned numerous protest groups (such as the Weathermen, Symbionese Liberation Army, and Black Panthers), some of which used assassination, bombings, kidnappings, and other tactics to influence public policy and opinion. The constitutional hallmark of the 1960s and 1970s, however, was not the contraction of civil rights but their dilation under the chief justiceship of Earl Warren and his like-minded, pro–civil liberties brethren of the Supreme Court.

Although the Senate had instituted a subcommittee on terrorism by 1981, Congress did not enact legislation to address and define international terrorism until November 5, 1990. That legislation, introduced by Senator Charles Grassley (R-IA) with Joseph Lieberman (D-CT), Joseph Biden (D-DE), Orrin Hatch (R-UT), and seven other senators as cosponsors, originated as a mere rider to a routine military appropriations bill and occupies only eight sections and two pages of the voluminous U.S. Code.

September 11 and Civil Liberties

The September 11, 2001, assaults on the World Trade Center and Pentagon prompted the almost immediate redefinition and proliferation of federal antiterrorist law. On October 26, 2002, President George W. Bush signed into law the USA PATRIOT Act of 2001, which established "roving wiretaps." Since its origin in 1791, the Fourth Amendment to the federal Constitution has required "particularity" in warrants of search and arrest. When a warrant is the vehicle of search or seizure, it must limit the resulting search to a single location and the arrest or seizure to the exact persons or objects that it names or specifies. Also, ever since the Warren Court decision in *Katz v. United States* (1967), the "reasonable expectation of privacy" at the amendment's core has applied to electronic as well as physical searches. Section 221 of the Patriot Act, however, seems inconsistent with these traditional guarantees because the "roving wiretaps" that it creates target a particular individual, not, as before, a single location. In effect, the wiretapped person becomes subject to a de facto general search warrant, exposing to electronic oversight his or her conversation with every person whom he or she addresses or telephones in every room of every building that he or she enters.

On November 13, 2001, and March 21, 2002, a military order by Bush and an affiliated decree by the Department of Defense instituted military commissions to judicially try members of the Taliban and al-Qaeda, 363 of whom the United States had imprisoned at Guantánamo Bay, Cuba, by May 4, 2002. Based on military law, these commissions lack not only juries but other libertarian features of civilian jurisprudence.

Although *Duncan v. Louisiana* (1968), the leading federal case, mandates a unanimous jury, the military commissions at Guantánamo, as in other military trials, needed merely a two-thirds vote for conviction, with only capital cases requiring unanimity. Furthermore, under two leading Fourth Amendment cases, *Weeks v. United States* (1914) and *Mapp v. Ohio* (1961), evidence seized unconstitutionally cannot be introduced against the accused at trial. By contrast, the admissibility of future evidence before the Guantánamo commission hinged only on its probity, not the constitutionality of its acquisition. The "exclusionary rule," a keystone of the Fourth Amendment for nearly a century, did not apply.

In fact, the Guantánamo detainees forfeited not only their civilian status but also many of the rights that the Uniform Code of Military Justice (UCMJ) affords U.S. servicemen at trial. For example, under the UCMJ, prosecutors must disclose whatever exculpatory evidence they uncover to the civilian attorneys defending military defendants, but the court can withhold evidence sensitive to national security from the civilian attorney of an al-Qaeda defendant and disclose it only to the two military attorneys assigned him, emasculating the Sixth Amendment right to effective counsel. Also, enlisted servicemen can demand the inclusion of peers of similar rank on the court, which votes guilt or innocence in ascending order of rank to avoid the intimidation of low-ranking members by higher ones. No such features applyed to the Guantánamo commission, on which only officers sit.

These efforts of the Bush Administration to enhance government powers in the wake of the 9/11 terrorist attacks generated intense resistance as well as counterefforts to sustain and expand them. Virtually every aspect of the Patriot Act has ignited firestorms of criticism and defense.

Critical Court Cases

In *United States v. Lindh* (2002), a federal court initially accepted the administration's assumption that the scope of the 9/11 assault justified unprecedented curtailments of civil liberties. John Walker Lindh, an American Taliban supporter, fell captive to U.S. forces that had invaded Afghanistan, where the Taliban government had given refuge to Osama bin Laden, the 9/11 instigator. Lindh's case raised obvious questions about the constitutionality of the new draconian federal powers because he was a U.S. citizen, and the Patriot Act expanding those powers was not yet law. On October 4, 2002, however, Lindh and Judge T.S. Ellis III of the U.S. District Court for Eastern Virginia sidestepped the issue with a plea bargain. In return for a twenty-year sentence with no possibility of the death penalty, Lindh pleaded guilty to serving as a Taliban soldier and to bearing arms illegally.

The liberal Ninth Circuit federal Court of Appeals in San Francisco provided a far less accommodating reception to the government's vast powers to detain terrorists as "illegal combatants." After other courts and the administration had ignored repeated pleas for a judicial hearing by Guantánamo detainees, Justice Stephen Reinhardt and two of his Ninth Circuit brethren listened with more sympathetic ears in *Falen Gherebi v. Bush* (2003). Although they ignored the larger constitutional issues of the Guantánamo detentions, Reinhardt et al. invited confrontation of them by denying that "the courts of the United States are entirely closed to detainees held at Guantánamo indefinitely."

Both the war on terror and the responses to it intensified in 2004. On March 10, a secretive, warrantless surveillance of domestic communications by American citizens produced a major confrontation within the Bush Administration when James Comey, the acting attorney general, refused to sanction continuance of that surveillance. Alberto Gonzalez, the White House counsel, and Andrew Card, its chief of staff, tried and failed to obtain the necessary signature from Comey's boss, Attorney General John Ashcroft, who was then sedated after surgery in George Washington University Hospital. A few months later, Seymour Hersh, the Pulitzer Prize–winning journalist who had disclosed the My Lai Massacre during the Vietnam War, wrote three exposes in *The New Yorker*, illuminating torture by the U.S. military of detainees at Abu Ghraib Prison in Baghdad, Iraq.

The presidential authority to detain U.S. citizens in military custody reached the Supreme Court in two cases decided on June 28, 2004, *Rumsfeld v. Padilla* and *Hamdi v. Rumsfeld*. José Padilla, an American citizen, had been apprehended as a terrorist when deplaning at O'Hare Airport in Chicago. American allies, the Northern Alliance, had captured Yaser Hamdi, also an American citizen, in Afghanistan. Although a congressional resolution had given the president vast powers to detain and arrest a week after 9/11, the administration argued that Article 2 of the Constitution inherently furnished wartime presidents with practically limitless authority to detain, without recourse to trial or counsel, anyone whom they chose to designate as an "illegal combatant." Chief Justice William Rehnquist dismissed the appeal of Padilla, in military custody in Charleston, on the jurisdictional grounds that his counsel had misfiled his plea of habeas corpus. With Justice Sandra Day O'Connor speaking for a six-judge majority, however, the Court reached a different result in *Hamdi*. In *Hamdi*, O'Connor et al. concluded that a citizen detained as an enemy combatant deserved not only "notice of the factual basis for his classification," but also "a neutral decision-maker" before whom to factually refute the charges against him.

On December 31, 2005, the Bush Administration answered with the Detainee Treatment Act, which categorically deprived U.S. courts and judges of jurisdiction to hear any habeas corpus plea by any Guantánamo Bay Prisoner. Moreover, the USA Patriot and Terrorism Prevention Reauthorization Act of March 9, 2006, expanded the death penalty for terrorists apprehended in air piracy and strengthened the legal machinery against terrorist money laundering.

The Supreme Court pushed back. Speaking for the new Roberts Court on June 29, 2006, Justice John Paul Stevens, in *Hamdan v. Rumsfeld*, not only denied that the administration could construct extrastatutory military commissions, but also held that such commissions violated both the UCMJ and four Geneva Conventions governing the treatment of prisoners of war. As recently as June 12, 2008, Justice Anthony Kennedy sustained the habeas corpus rights of Guantánamo detainees in Boumediene v. Bush.

A pivotal section of the Patriot Act amended earlier legislation by expanding federal power to issue "national security letters," that is, subpoena-like commands that require an Internet service provider or telephone company to produce incriminating records of clients suspected of international terrorism or clandestine espionage. Not only do NSLs facilitate "fishing expeditions" into the privacy of suspects, say civil libertarians, but the ISP or telephone company is forbidden to inform those whose records have been accessed of the intrusion. On September 6, 2007, federal judge Victor Marrero of the Southern District of New York delivered an abrupt check to the Patriot Act by holding that NSLs violated both the First and Fourth Amendments to the federal Constitution. Compulsory nondisclosure, he concluded, flouted the First Amendment's guarantee of freedom of speech while the vagueness of NSLs infringed Fourth Amendment guarantees relating to judicial oversight and the generality of warrants.

The foregoing tensions of the Bush Administration endured into that of his successor, Barack Obama. Judge Milan Smith of the Ninth Circuit held on September 7, 2009, that Muslims arrested as material witnesses by the former attorney general, Ashcroft, could sue him if his actual motive had been to investigate their possible links to terrorism. Guantánamo Bay remains operational. On February 27, 2010, President Obama signed a reauthorization of the Patriot Act, albeit with the stipulation of enhanced judicial oversight of roving wiretaps.

William Cuddihy

See also: September 11 Attacks—Political, Legal, and Social Issues; Government Spying and Privacy Issues; Imprisonment and Legal Status of Detainees; Torture; Security and Defense.

Further Reading

Cole, David, and James H. Dempsey. *Terrorism and the Constitution: Sacrificing Civil Liberties in the Name of National Security*. New York: New Press, 2005.

Foerstel, Herbert N. *The Patriot Act: A Documentary and Reference Guide*. Westport, CT: Greenwood, 2008.

Hersh, Seymour. "Chain of Command." *The New Yorker*, May 17, 2004.

———. "The Grey Zone." *The New Yorker*, May 24, 2004.

———. "Torture at Abu Ghraib." *The New Yorker*, May 10, 2004.

Laqueur, Walter. *A History of Terrorism*. New Brunswick, NJ: Transaction, 2001.

Michaels, C. William. *No Greater Threat: America Since September 11, and the Rise of the National Security State*. 2nd ed. New York: Algora, 2005.

Cleanup and Rebuilding

The task of cleaning up after the September 11, 2001, terrorist attacks and the issue of rebuilding the buildings damaged by the attacks have involved a myriad of considerations for local police and firefighters, state politicians, and the federal government, since the overall scope of the attacks was enormous and the total social, cultural, and economic effects are still being determined. As symbols of America, the World Trade Center and the Pentagon represented—and still represent—more than just buildings; they were and are more than rebuilding projects. Their resurrection from the rubble represents a cultural defiance of the violence that was the cause of their destruction.

The extent of the devastation at the World Trade Center suggests that the task of removing the debris and the decisions regarding the rebuilding process should be part of a national effort to address the effects of terrorism. The scope of the problem that this work site represented was enormous. The Twin Towers stood 110 stories tall and were constructed with a steel frame, had concrete slabs attached to steel trusses, and were faced with walls of glass. They were part of a seven-building complex that covered sixteen acres of prime real estate in the financial district of Manhattan, and they contained 200,000 tons (181,436 metric tons) of steel and huge quantities of concrete, building materials, piping, electrical wiring, office furniture, and the other materials that would be expected in a modern office complex. The Federal Emergency Management Agency estimated the actual weight of the debris at 115,000 tons (104,326 metric tons), but the final total may well have been significantly higher. In addition, their destruction heightened the area's levels of dust and potentially toxic substances such as asbestos fibers, silica, fiberglass, gypsum, and lead. In addition to the immediate damage to the World Trade Center office complex, there was extensive collateral damage to adjacent buildings, underground utilities, the subway system, and many other vital urban services. The cleanup alone was originally estimated to take up to one year but was largely completed within about eight months. The time needed for complete rebuilding or replacement of this complex and these services proved to last more than a decade, as the replacement Freedom Tower was still under construction as the tenth anniversary approached.

The Pentagon was also a large-scale disaster site that posed challenges to rescuers and emergency responders. This enormous building was dedicated on September 11, 1941, exactly sixty years before the attack. The building covers thirty-four acres, twenty-nine of which are under roofing. It is five stories, or seventy-one feet (22 meters), tall, has five concentric rings of corridors, and has five sides that each measure 921 feet (291 meters) in length. Inside this structure lie 6.5 million square feet (600,000 square meters) of space, with 3.7 million (350,000 square meters) set aside for offices. The structure is a combination of reinforced concrete, steel, and wood framing, and it has slate roofing. Because the Pentagon is the center of American military operations and a symbol of the nation's military might, the decision to rebuild was tied to a national effort to counteract the violence that the acts

of terrorism represent. The construction effort was geared to completion of the outer structure prior to the one-year anniversary of the attack and was largely completed by September 11, 2002. Additional work continued on the interior portions of the project for several more years and included a memorial for the 9/11 victims.

Given the scope of the disaster and the fact that various governmental entities had authority over the site, rebuilding on the World Trade Center site has proved much more expensive and contentious. There were many—notably victims' families—who felt that the site should remain free of all construction, beyond a memorial, as a way of honoring the fallen. That view was always in the minority, however, for both practical and symbolic reasons. Lower Manhattan real estate is simply too valuable to leave such an extensive area largely idle. In addition, many felt that rebuilding a major structure on the site would be a way of demonstrating American resolve in the face of terror.

In the end, those factors won out and the question emerged about what exactly should be constructed on the site. A competition was established in 2002 by the Lower Manhattan Development Corporation, the New York City–New York State entity created to coordinate the rebuilding of lower Manhattan. Three years later, the design of celebrated architect Daniel Libeskind, who built the well-received Jewish Museum in Berlin, was selected. The most notable elements of the design were a 1,776-foot-high, glass-sheathed tower, initially called the Freedom Tower but later renamed One World Trade Center. Construction on the tower began in April 2006, with an expected completion date sometime in 2013.

Meanwhile, Israeli American architect Michael Arad won the competition to build the National September 11 Memorial and Museum. Bowing to the wishes of 9/11 victims' families, the design avoided structures on the actual footprints of the old towers; instead, those two squares would be marked by reflection pools. Groundbreaking for the memorial occurred in March 2006, with an opening planned for the tenth anniversary of the attacks, on September 11, 2011.

James David Ballard and James Ciment

See also: *September 11 Attacks*—U.S. Economic Impact; Victim Relief.

Further Reading

Engle, Karen. *Seeing Ghosts: 9/11 and the Visual Imagination.* Montreal: McGill-Queen's University Press, 2009.
Lower Manhattan Development Corporation. http://www.renewnyc.com/.
Ward, Chris. *World Trade Center Report: A Roadmap Forward.* New York: Port Authority of New York, 2008.

Government Spying and Privacy Issues

Since the terrorist attacks of September 11, 2001, and the USA PATRIOT Act of October 2001, government spying and national security concerns have expanded dramatically while at the same time contracting the compass of individual privacy.

National Security

The 9/11 terrorist attacks have refocused national security from threats by nation-states to transnational terrorism. In response to 9/11, legislation backed by the Bush Administration enhanced government powers of surveillance and detention. The Patriot Act of 2001 greatly extended both the scope and the methods of government surveillance. The Homeland Security Act of 2002 not only invigorated many powers of existing agencies, such as the customs department and Secret Service, but also consolidated them and others in a new Department of Homeland Security.

Moreover, the government has incarcerated hundreds of "illegal combatants" from Iraq and Afghanistan at the U.S. naval base at Guantánamo Bay, Cuba, and created military commissions to try them without the full panoply of traditional civil rights. In *Hamdan v. Rumsfeld* (2006), however, Justice John Paul Stevens of the Supreme Court struck down these extrastatutory military commissions and held that they violated both the Uniform Code of Military Justice and several Geneva Conventions regarding prisoners of war. In 2008, in *Boumediene v. Bush*, the same court sustained the habeas corpus rights of Guantánamo detainees.

Government Spying

The Patriot Act elevated government powers of surveillance to unprecedented heights. For example, one provision of the act permits nationwide search warrants to obtain electronic evidence, all in the name of combating terrorism. Other sections enable the interception of wire, oral, and electronic communications to combat computer fraud as well as terrorism. Pen registers and trap-and-trace procedures facilitate the global identification of e-mail users.

Moreover, sneak-and-peek warrants authorize government agents to clandestinely enter a residence or business, observe and photograph everything present, and depart without immediate notification. Yet another provision compels suspects to physically provide the Federal Bureau of Investigation (FBI) with business, medical, and educational records without divulging to others either the demand for the records or their identity.

National security letters, however, also afford the government access to many of these same records without judicial resort or oversight. FBI field supervisors can is-

sue such letters simply by certifying their relevance to investigations into international terrorism or "clandestine intelligence activities." The law does not require approval by a prosecutor, judge, or grand jury; nor does it impose probable cause to believe or even suspect that the documentation sought relates to a specific crime. The person receiving the letter may inform no one beyond his or her attorney.

Perhaps most notably, section 206 of the Patriot Act authorizes roving wiretaps, which closely resemble the general search warrants that the Fourth Amendment forbids. A key provision of the act requires that each warrant particularize the place, persons, and objects that it targets for arrest, search, or seizure. Roving wiretaps, however, enable all conversations of targeted individuals to be overheard regardless of the structures they inhabit or the persons with whom they converse. The person monitored by such a wiretap becomes, in effect, an electronic general warrant who involuntarily broadcasts all of his or her conversations regardless of where or with whom they occur.

Legislation in 2005 and 2006 extended the Patriot Act with slight modifications. Henceforth, recipients of national security letters may judicially challenge both them and the command of nondisclosure. Only top FBI officials can now compel librarians to disclose the reading lists of their patrons. Judges now decide if reasonable grounds exist for FBI orders to produce records, which orders must also particularize the object sought. On the other hand, under some circumstances, the government can now take ninety days, not thirty as before, to divulge the service of a sneak-and-peek warrant to the person on whom it was served.

The new focus on terrorism's threat to national security, however, has supplemented rather than displaced ongoing challenges to that security by nation-states. Thus, in 2001, Robert Hanssen was unmasked as an FBI mole who had revealed to the Soviets and Russians the identities of key American agents, thereby causing their executions. Jonathan Jay Pollard remains in federal prison for disclosing massive quantities of American naval intelligence to Israel despite vigorous, continuing agitation by his supporters to free him.

Privacy

In a seminal, concurring opinion in the pivotal case of *Katz v. U.S.* (1967), Justice John Marshall Harlan had posited a "reasonable expectation of privacy" as the cornerstone to cases involving electronic surveillance. Under Chief Justices William Rehnquist and John Roberts, however, the Supreme Court has accelerated a trend that Professor Silas Wasserstrom described in 1984 as the "Incredible Shrinking Fourth Amendment." Thus, national security and spying have enlarged since 9/11 in part because contemporary case law has compromised privacy as a barrier to their growth.

Privacy rights contracted substantially during the last half decade, 2000–2005, of the William Rehnquist Court. In fact, the contractions accumulated almost annually. These include decisions allowing for more invasive searches of paroled prisoners and border crossers (*Illinois v. Wardlow*, 2000) as well as cars subject to routine traffic stops (*Maryland v. Pringle*, 2003, and *Illinois v. Caballes*, 2005) and consensual searches of bus passengers' luggage (*U.S. v. Drayton*, 2002).

Further limitations on privacy rights have occurred under the John Roberts Court since 2005. These include the admissibility of evidence from a search where the knock-and-announce rule had been ignored by police (*Hudson v. Michigan*, 2006) and a decision, *U.S. v. Grubbs* (2006) that sustained the constitutionality of "anticipatory" search warrants, where law enforcement expects future illegality to occur rather than a reported past occurrence of illegality. While this case involved child pornography, its implications for antiterrorism are significant, given the general consensus that terrorist acts of violence are so heinous as to justify broad measures to prevent them.

Foreign Intelligence Surveillance Act and Warrantless Wiretap Controversy

Most civil libertarians agree that warrantless wiretaps, however, remain the paramount threat to privacy in the age of terrorism. In the wake of revelations about government spying on citizens in the Cold War era, Congress passed the Foreign Intelligence Surveillance Act (FISA) in 1978. This set up a three-judge court, which issued warrants in situations where national security issues were at stake and where one of the parties was a U.S. citizen or permanent resident operating on U.S. territory. The court quickly gained a reputation for approving virtually all of the government's requests. According to the Foreign Intelligence Surveillance Court's (FISC) Web site, the federal government submitted 1,329 wiretap requests under FISA in 2009, a typical year since the war on terrorism began. Of these requests, 14 were modified, 1 was withdrawn, and 1 was partially granted. Not one was fully denied. But such a record of getting wiretaps easily approved by FISA was deemed insufficient for the Bush Administration in the early years of the war on terrorism.

In late 2005, it came to light in a *New York Times* exposé that the National Security Administration (NSA) had been provided total access by major telecom companies, without any FISC warrants, to fiber-optic communications within the United States. Critics of the administration said that such massive sweeps of electronics communications involving a citizen or resident on U.S. soil—including voice calls, e-mails, Web browsing, and even traffic on private corporate networks—required FISC warrants. The Bush Administration agreed that it had allowed for warrantless wiretaps on communications

originating in or coming to the United States but that FISA allowed for exceptions based on future legislation. Moreover, according to the Bush Administration, both the USA PATRIOT Act and the Authorization for Use of Military Force against those perpetrating the September 11 terrorist attacks, both from 2001, allowed for such exceptions. Because of the intense secrecy surrounding the wiretaps, it has been difficult for civil libertarians and others opposed to the Bush Administration's warrantless wiretaps to sue on behalf of those whose privacy rights may or may not have been violated.

William S. Cuddihy and James Ciment

See also: *September 11 Attacks*—Political, Legal, and Social Issues; Civil Liberties, Civil Rights, and National Security; Intelligence Community: Pre-9/11 Failures and Successes; Intelligence Community: Response to 9/11. *Counterterrorism*—Intelligence, Counterterrorist.

Further Reading
Kreimer, Seth. "Watching the Watchers: Surveillance, Transparency, and Political Freedom in the War on Terrorism." *University of Pennsylvania Journal of Constitutional Law* 7 (2004): 157.

McInnis, Thomas. *The Evolution of the Fourth Amendment.* Lanham, MD: Lexington, 2009.

Schulhofer, Stephen. *Rethinking the Patriot Act: Keeping America Safe and Free.* New York: Century Foundations, 2005.

Wasserstrom, Silas. "The Incredible Shrinking Fourth Amendment." *American Criminal Law Review* 21 (1984): 257–401.

Imprisonment and Legal Status of Detainees

In response to the attacks of September 11, 2001, the United States identified Osama bin Laden's terrorist group, al-Qaeda, as the perpetrators and sent American forces to Afghanistan, where al-Qaeda had been operating. Many combatants affiliated with both al-Qaeda and the Taliban government of Afghanistan, which had given them sanctuary, were subsequently captured by U.S. troops and eventually transferred to the U.S. military base at Guantánamo Bay, Cuba. However, since such a large-scale military operation in response to a terrorist attack was unprecedented, many significant questions arose regarding the treatment, prosecution, and sentencing of the prisoners.

Al-Qaeda and the Taliban

Initially, al-Qaeda and Taliban forces were separate entities. Members of al-Qaeda were militants under the leadership of Osama bin Laden, originally drawn from international Muslim recruits who had served in the Afghan mujahideen against the Soviet occupation of Afghanistan in the 1980s. Most had followed bin Laden to Somalia from 1991 to 1996 before returning to Afghanistan. Al-Qaeda established camps for recruiting and training terrorists in both Somalia and Afghanistan, and it is this group that allegedly provided training and logistical support for the September 11 attackers. The Taliban was one of the factions fighting against the Soviet occupation of Afghanistan. It continued battling against other Afghan groups and eventually took control of the capital, Kabul, in 1995, whereupon it implemented strict fundamentalist Islamic rule. Sharing many philosophical tenets with bin Laden, the Taliban invited al-Qaeda to reestablish its bases in Afghanistan upon its expulsion from Somalia. Throughout its roughly six-year rule, the Taliban never held effective political control over all of Afghanistan and had diplomatic recognition from only one country; thus, it was generally considered an outlaw regime. Although the Taliban did not likely play a direct role in the September 11 attacks, the United States opted to treat both sets of combatants similarly since the Taliban aided and abetted al-Qaeda terrorism efforts.

Status of Detainees

Soldiers and countries that take prisoners from battle are obliged by laws of treaty and common practice to ensure their humane treatment. However, the status of the detainees determines what rights and privileges they should receive. Lawful combatants held as prisoners receive pay and some freedoms and cannot be tried for murder and other lawful acts conducted in combat. However, unlawful combatants lose many protections of their citizenship, can expect greater restrictions while imprisoned, and may face charges of improperly waging war. Terrorism is not adequately defined in international law, but certain acts are. Hijacking, hostage taking, and wanton targeting and destruction of civilian life and property are outlawed in most countries domestically as well as internationally, and thus, prisoners could be tried in criminal courts for these and similar acts. As such, defendants in U.S. courts would receive the widest range of humanitarian protections among the three status options presented here.

The George W. Bush Administration, however, decided to treat al-Qaeda and Taliban detainees as unlawful combatants. The choice of Guantánamo as the venue for holding the prisoners was carefully thought through, as the Bush Administration argued that habeas corpus—or the right to legal redress for unlawful imprisonment—did not apply to non-U.S. enemy combatants held on foreign territory, which Guantánamo legally was. The Bush Administration then established special military tribunals for the purpose of determining whether such persons were, indeed, enemy combatants and so could be held

without habeas corpus rights. In several decisions, including *Hamdi v. Rumsfeld* (2004) and *Hamdan v. Rumsfeld* (2006), the Supreme Court ruled in the defendants' favor, saying that such tribunals violated the U.S. Constitution and the Geneva Conventions on the rights of prisoners of war, of which the United States was a signatory. The Bush Administration and Congress responded with the Military Commissions Act of 2006, which defined enemy combatants more broadly than in the past, to include noncitizens, whether living legally in the United States or abroad, as determined by criteria established by the president or the secretary of defense. In addition, rather than receiving regular habeas proceedings, such prisoners could only challenge their imprisonment through special military tribunals. Two years later, in *Boumedienne v. Bush*, the Supreme Court overturned much of the Military Commissions Act, arguing that prisoners held at Guantánamo have a right to constitutionally challenge their detention in federal court.

In the first few years of the War in Afghanistan, roughly 800 prisoners were brought to the facility from Afghanistan; by December 2010, approximately 240 remained in custody at Guantánamo, of which some 50 to 60 were scheduled for release, pending U.S. authorities' finding a country that would take them. Of the more than 500 persons who have been released from Guantánamo, most were remanded to national governments, to face imprisonment and trial in those countries, while the rest were released and allowed to go free in other countries. The precise number of how many prisoners remain incarcerated in other countries is not known. During his campaign for the presidency, and after his inauguration in January 2009, President Barack Obama declared his intention to close Guantánamo within a year of taking office, either releasing the detainees to other countries or placing them in stateside prisons, to await trial in federal court. An inability to find host countries to take them, along with political resistance in the United States to having the prisoners relocated here, has stymied those efforts, and a final date for the closing of the prison camp remained undetermined as of early 2011.

Conditions at Guantánamo

Aside from the number of prisoners and their right to trial, conditions at the Guantánamo camp have been an issue of controversy. Many detainees were subject to coercive interrogation techniques, which the Bush Administration declared legal but most experts in the field held to be torture, and thus illegal under U.S. and international law. Among the techniques, the most controversial were water boarding, or simulated drowning, and sensory and sleep deprivation, all of which are considered torture under international law, including treaties and conventions to which the United States is a signatory. In addition, the United States tried Japanese military leaders as

Military Police guard Taliban and al-Qaeda prisoners at the Guantánamo Bay Military Detention Center in Cuba. By presidential military order in September 2001, suspected terrorists were to be held as "illegal enemy combatants" rather than prisoners of war. *(Shane McCoy/WireImage/ Getty Images)*

war criminals for using such techniques during World War II. In 2005, Congress passed the Detainee Treatment Act, banning inhumane treatment of prisoners at Guantánamo. A year later, the Military Commissions Act barred the admission of evidence obtained through inhumane or cruel methods, though it did allow it if the evidence was obtained prior to passage of the Detainee Treatment Act in December 2005. After that date, the only evidence that could be admitted was that obtained in conformity with the *U.S. Army Field Manual*.

Torture was not the only complaint voiced by Guantánamo prisoners and their representatives. Prisoners released from the camp spoke of cruel and degrading conditions, including desecration of the Koran, sleep deprivation, extended periods of sensory deprivation, isolation, and forced feeding during prisoner protest fasts. Over the past eight years, prisoner representatives and released prisoners say there have been hundreds of suicide attempts, though officials put the number at just forty-three. Moreover, both the Bush Administration and camp officials contended that conditions at the camp are humane and in full accord with U.S. and international law. Indeed, they have even argued that some prisoners'

health improved as a result of having access to proper diet and medical attention, unavailable to them in the spartan conditions of terrorist camps and Taliban outposts in Afghanistan.

Military Tribunals

Military tribunals are unusual in American history but not unique in times of war. During World War II, President Franklin D. Roosevelt called a military tribunal to try eight German saboteurs captured in New York and Florida. Earlier in U.S. history, President Abraham Lincoln utilized military tribunals to try captured Confederate soldiers, including one accused of attempting to commit large-scale arson in New York City during the American Civil War. Indeed, the U.S. Supreme Court has upheld the president's right to enact this particular wartime power at least three times, most notably in its *Ex Parte Quirin* decision (1942). In addition, both the Nuremberg and Tokyo trials after World War II were military tribunals, which tried soldiers, government officials, and civilians alike for violating the laws of war and crimes against peace and humanity.

The rationale for implementing such tribunals after 9/11 was supported by a number of facts, according to Bush Administration legal experiments, including bin Laden's 1998 fatwa declaring war against the United States and its allies, as well as al-Qaeda's suspected support and involvement in previous terrorist attacks against American interests, such as the 1993 World Trade Center bombing, the 1996 Khobar Towers truck bombing in Saudi Arabia, the 1998 African embassy bombings, the 2000 attack on the USS *Cole*, and the September 11, 2001, attacks. In addition, President George W. Bush declared war against the Taliban and the al-Qaeda terrorist network, and on September 14, 2001, the U.S. Congress passed a joint resolution authorizing the president to use force against those determined to be involved in the September 11 attacks (though the resolution fell short of a formal declaration of war per se). As for Taliban prisoners, the Bush Administration argued that they should be treated in a similar manner because the Taliban regime harbored the al-Qaeda terrorist network, which thereby links the two as co-combatants. Al-Qaeda violated laws of war by targeting civilians and conducting operations against military targets utilizing legally unrecognized combatants. Finally, the United States established its precedent for declaring war on nonstate actors in two separate campaigns against pirates in the late 1700s and again in the early 1800s.

As noted earlier, however, the Supreme Court ruled in several key decisions that military tribunals to determine the status of Guantánamo detainees and thereby their right to habeas corpus were unconstitutional and in violation of international treaties and conventions that the United States had signed; under the Constitution, such treaties are the law of the land. However, the decisions did not outlaw military tribunals per se to determine whether a combatant had violated U.S. law or had committed war crimes, as determined by the Geneva Conventions.

Under the Bush Administration, no al-Qaeda or Taliban detainees taken in the Afghanistan conflict were tried, either in special military tribunals for the detainees, or in federal court, or through the military justice system. While campaigning for office, Obama argued that detainees should be tried either in federal court or through the military justice system, which tries members of the armed forces and guarantees the accused roughly the same rights accorded to defendants in civilian courts. As president, Obama said that some detainees—particularly those whose cases involved classified material, which might make it difficult to try them in civilian federal court—might by tried by special military tribunals, but these would allow for greater defendant rights, including prohibitions on evidence obtained through cruel or unusual means and hearsay evidence. In addition, detainees would have wider latitude in choosing their lawyers. Critics with a civil liberties bent charged that the additional rights were not sufficient and would face numerous legal challenges that could delay justice for years. At the same time, more conservative critics challenged Attorney General Eric Holder's decision in November 2009 to try Khalid Sheikh Mohammed, suspected of being the leading planner for the September 11 al-Qaeda terrorist attacks, in federal court in New York, arguing that under evidentiary and other rules accorded to suspects in such venues Mohammed might very well go free or not receive the death penalty, which the administration sought. For their part, Holder and Obama argued that past terrorism suspects—including the so-called twentieth (9/11) hijacker, Zacarias Moussaoui—had been found guilty in federal court and that trying detainees there would show the world that the United States lived up to its own high standards of justice.

James Ciment and James T. Kirkhope

See also: *September 11 Attacks*—Political, Legal, and Social Issues; Civil Liberties, Civil Rights, and National Security; Torture.

Further Readings

Claeys, Noah M. *Closing Guantanamo: Issues and Legal Matters Surrounding the Detention Centers End.* Hauppauge, NY: Nova Science, 2009.

Hafetz, Jonathan. *Habeas Corpus After 9/11: Confronting America's New Global Detention System.* New York: New York University Press, 2010.

Honigsberg, Peter Jan. *Our Nation Unhinged: The Human Consequences of the War on Terror.* Berkeley: University of California Press, 2009.

Rotunda, Kyndra Miller. *Honor Bound: Inside the Guantanamo Trials.* Durham, NC: Carolina Academic Press, 2008.

Worthington, Andy. *The Guantánamo Files: The Stories of the 774 Detainees in America's Illegal Prison.* Ann Arbor, MI: Pluto, 2007.

Torture

Torture, generally defined as the infliction of physical pain or extreme mental distress, is illegal in most countries and forbidden by numerous international conventions and the United Nations. In the United States, the Eighth Amendment's protection against cruel and unusual punishment guards against torture, and the federal statute 18 U.S.C. § 2340 extends the ban on torture beyond the country's borders. The latter defines torture broadly, covering physical and psychological variants. Most countries have similar laws against torture and torture by proxy. Even many with poor human rights records, such as Saudi Arabia, have made it illegal—though the laws are often ignored in such countries.

Torture is likewise addressed by many international agreements on human rights and war. The United Nations Convention Against Torture (UNCAT) forbids "any act by which severe pain or suffering, whether physical or mental, is intentionally inflicted on a person," whether for information, punishment, coercion, intimidation, or discrimination. It permits only suffering that is incidental to legal punishment. The document states that torture can be justified by "no exceptional circumstances whatsoever." Torture is also forbidden by the UN Universal Declaration of Human Rights, which addresses cruel punishment, and outlawed by the Rome Statute of the International Criminal Court, which classifies it as a crime against humanity. Finally, the Geneva Conventions protect all prisoners of war, whether military or civilian, from violence.

In addition to the legal restrictions, there is a strong precedent of intolerance for torture. The United States historically has considered torture a war crime and prosecuted others for abusing prisoners of war. The country's highest politicians routinely call prisoner abuse a human rights violation and condemn countries that use it. In the months leading up to the 2003 U.S. invasion of Iraq, supporters of the war argued that Saddam Hussein's use of torture against his own people justified American intervention. Nevertheless, the United States and certain other Western countries have resorted to torture as a counterterrorism tactic in recent decades. The contemporary debate around torture is largely centered on the United States because of its use of "extraordinary rendition" and the abuse of prisoners in Cuba, Iran, and Afghanistan. It has also attracted much attention because top government officials have defended the practice and advanced arguments justifying its use against terrorists.

Extraordinary Rendition

Extraordinary rendition, or the extrajudicial transfer of a detainee from one country to another, is extremely controversial not only because of the possible use of torture in the receiving country, but also because it involves sending suspected terrorists to other countries for their interrogation, thereby evading the American legal system and media. The United States has captured terrorists outside its borders at least as early as 1987, when the Federal Bureau of Investigation (FBI) and Central Intelligence Agency (CIA) cooperated in arresting the hijacker Fawaz Yunis after luring him into international waters near Cyprus. The capture set a precedent for the extraordinary renditions of the mid-1990s. The Clinton Administration authorized the CIA to capture terrorists hiding outside U.S. jurisdiction, even when doing so meant illegally making arrests inside the borders of other sovereign states. The primary targets were members of al-Qaeda, but the program was limited to arrest and conventional interrogation. The target remained the same during the George W. Bush Administration, but extraordinary rendition was used more frequently and became a program for torturing the arrested subjects.

Although the CIA has captured many of the suspected terrorists and operated the network of transit sites that are used to move them secretly, torture usually has been done by proxy. Detainees are given to foreign governments with the understanding that they will be tortured for information. In one of the most famous cases of post-9/11 torture, Canadian citizen Maher Arar was arrested at John F. Kennedy airport in New York approximately a year after the attacks and, after being interrogated in Tunisia, was sent to Syria to be tortured by that country's intelligence service. Arar reported being held in Syria for ten months and subjected to harsh physical tortures. He was also forced to confess to being a member of al-Qaeda.

Torture by proxy is a way of keeping its use a secret but does not provide any legal protection for the countries that employ it. UNCAT and 18 U.S.C. § 2340 forbid the extradition of detainees to countries where they may be tortured and U.S. authorities are required to assess this risk based on that state's human rights record. Arresting suspected terrorists in foreign countries has strained relations between the United States and members of the European Union. According to the Council of Europe, approximately 100 people in EU territory have been kidnapped by the CIA and extradited to secret prisons elsewhere for torture. This has also implicated some American allies, particularly the United Kingdom. Any country that knowingly allows the CIA to transport prisoners for torture is likewise in violation of UNCAT.

Abu Ghraib

The United States is known to have tortured suspected terrorists and insurgents in military prisons based in Cuba, Iraq, and Afghanistan. The Abu Ghraib prisoner abuse scandal is probably the most famous case; the photographs taken there in the early 2000s were irrefutable evidence of detainee abuse. Although the inquiry into the incident placed the blame on the soldiers directly involved, reports suggested that torture was systemic and authorized at higher levels. Former prisoners, human rights organizations, and even guards have found instances of prisoner abuse at other U.S. facilities. In 2002, several prisoners at the Bagram Theater Internment Facility in Afghanistan were severely beaten and two were killed. The Guantánamo Bay facility in Cuba, which has housed suspected terrorists since the invasion of Afghanistan, is often at the center of the debate over torture, as there have been numerous reports of torture being used there.

The pervasiveness of torture may be due, at least in part, to official government policy and the Bush Administration's rhetoric supporting it. The administration sought to find ways around torture laws by contesting its definition and reinterpreting the laws in place to prevent it. One tactic used by defenders of "enhanced interrogation" was to argue that some practices that leave no physical signs of harm, such as water boarding (simulated drowning), stress positions, sleep deprivation, and various forms of psychological torture, are not really torture. Water boarding emerged at the center of this debate about what constitutes torture when in 2007 it was revealed that the CIA and Department of Justice had approved the technique for use against many suspected members of al-Qaeda.

A different approach was used to exploit loopholes in the laws regarding torture. In 2002, Deputy Assistant Attorney General John Yoo and Assistant Attorney General Jay Bybee issued a memo that authorized harsh interrogation for terrorists. They found a legal basis for this in UN resolutions and U.S. law that defined torture as the intent to inflict severe pain. Thus, according to their memo, as long as the interrogator's intent is to gain information and not to inflict pain, the means used for gathering information are legitimate. A third justification for torture, invoked by Secretary of State Donald Rumsfeld in defense of the detention center at Guantánamo Bay, is that the Geneva Conventions do not apply to terrorists because they are not uniformed soldiers. Therefore, the reasoning goes, they should be classified as illegal combatants rather than prisoners of war.

One prominent form of psychological torture in the war on terror, and perhaps the most difficult to clearly identify as torture, is the expression of gross disrespect for the culture and religious values of detainees. This has included defacing the Koran, exposing prisoners to sexually oriented magazine articles, and forcing them to perform acts that conflict with their religious values. The photographs from Abu Ghraib show prisoners being forced to be naked and simulate homosexual acts—both serious violations of Islamic morality. The photos themselves, taken at this prison and others, were an important part of the torture because they could be used to blackmail prisoners who were released. In the intensely honor-conscious Iraqi culture, the threat of showing these pictures to friends and family members is a powerful way of compelling obedience. Likewise, women soldiers were sometimes used as interrogators, a particular humiliation to men of a culture with strong patriarchal values. Beyond that, the female interrogators violated Islamic rules by touching the men in a sexual manner, showing them menstrual blood, and exposing themselves.

Other Countries

The United States has not been alone in torturing suspected terrorists. Many other countries also routinely violate prohibitions on torture. Russia, Israel, the Netherlands, and the United Kingdom are a few of the countries that forbid torture but have been accused of using it as part of their counterterrorism and counterinsurgency programs. Although the United Kingdom has not used torture to the same extent as the United States, some government officials may have knowingly allowed the United States to use its airports to transport prisoners for extraordinary rendition. In 2005, British soldiers in Iraq were found guilty of torturing prisoners in Basra. One of the prisoners, Baha Mousa, died while in British custody, and others were seriously injured. Earlier charges of torture had surfaced in the context of British counterterrorism operations in Northern Ireland. During the early 1970s, at least fourteen Irish prisoners were subjected to intense noise, food and water deprivation, hooding, wall standing, and sleep deprivation.

Russia reportedly tortured Chechens during its occupation of the region in the 1990s and 2000s. Many of the alleged incidents involved rape and the delivery of electrical shocks to Chechen women in order to intimidate the insurgents. Russia is unique in that torture is commonly used internally, against soldiers in its military. However, this is the result of internal factionalism and does not reflect national policy. The Israeli government has admitted to torturing Palestinian prisoners using psychological techniques between 1988 and 1992, during the First Intifada. Methods included sleep and sensory deprivation, confinement in small spaces, and exposure to extreme temperatures. Human rights organizations have documented more recent incidents as well. Even the Dutch military, known for its humanitarian response to insurgencies, has been accused of torturing Iraqi prisoners. As with the United States and United Kingdom, its methods were primarily psychological, including sleep deprivation, sensory deprivation, and exposure to loud music. Because it is illegal, it is difficult to gather reliable information on the use of torture, especially in countries that have centralized control over the media. However, human rights reports give some idea of the magnitude. Amnesty International found evidence of torture or cruel punishment in more than 150 countries between 1997 and 2000.

The contravention of laws and international agreements suggests that torture is a powerful weapon and that extralegal action may be justified, yet there is no definitive evidence to support this. There have been incidents of criminals and terrorists revealing information under torture, but also many cases of terrorists and insurgents revealing valuable information after being subjected to legal forms of interrogation. It is unlikely that there will ever be any strong empirical support for either side. Experimental research is impossible given the ethical rules that govern academic research. Information provided by those who have used torture may provide some insight into its effectiveness, but this information comes from a biased source. Those who practice torture have a strong incentive to show that it works, while those who favor other methods of interrogation have a strong incentive to show that torture is unnecessary.

Given this uncertainty, the academic debate on torture in the war on terror is largely concerned with the moral issue. The discussion often raises the hypothetical situation of the "ticking bomb," which focuses on the ultimate question of whether torture is permissible in situations where it is certain to prevent a deadly attack. Proponents argue that such situations justify the use of torture, while opponents claim that these situations are extremely rare and that, when torture is used, it is just as likely to provide false information.

The change in U.S. political leadership in January 2009 caused a shift in the government's position on torture, with the Barack Obama Administration taking steps to eliminate torture—including water boarding—at all American military and intelligence facilities. Nevertheless, many of the Bush Administration's programs remained in place. During the election campaign in 2008, Obama had pledged to close the Guantánamo Bay detention facility on his first day in office, as part of his program to reverse the Bush Administration's allegedly illegal or unethical counterterrorism measures. President Obama initially took steps to keep this promise, issuing an order that the camp had 120 days to review detainees' cases and determine how they should be prosecuted. However, the deadline passed while investigators tried to assemble records for each of the detainees, and Obama declined to instate a new deadline. The Guantánamo Bay facility remained in use as of early 2011, with similar facilities operating in Afghanistan.

Marcus Schulzke

See also: *September 11 Attacks*—Political, Legal, and Social Issues; Civil Liberties, Civil Rights, and National Security; Imprisonment and Legal Status of Detainees.

Further Reading

Danner, Mark. *Abu Ghraib: The Politics of Torture.* Berkeley, CA: North Atlantic Books, 2004.

Greenberg, Karen J., ed. *The Torture Debate in America.* New York: Cambridge University Press, 2006.

Grey, Stephen. *Ghost Plane: The True Story of the CIA Rendition and Torture Program.* New York: St. Martin's Griffin, 2007.

Levinson, Sanford, ed. *Torture: A Collection.* New York: Oxford University Press, 2004.

McCoy, Alfred W. *A Question of Torture: CIA Interrogation, from the Cold War to the War on Terror.* New York: Macmillan, 2006.

Rejali, Darius. *Torture and Democracy.* Princeton, NJ: Princeton University Press, 2007.

Sharrock, Justine. *Tortured: When Good Soldiers Do Bad Things.* Hoboken, NJ: John Wiley and Sons, 2010.

Wittes, Benjamin. *Law and the Long War: The Future of Justice in the Age of Terror.* New York: Penguin, 2009.

U.S. Economic Impact

Conceptually, the economic costs to the United States stemming from the 9/11 terrorist attacks can be broken down into several categories, depending largely on their nature (direct and indirect) and on the time period examined (immediate, short term, medium term, and long term). The short-term, direct costs are clearly the easiest to identify and measure. Estimates covering longer periods of time and focused mainly on indirect costs require numerous assumptions concerning counterfactuals and hence are on less firm ground.

Immediate and Short Term: Direct Effects

The September 11 attacks inflicted casualties and material damages on a far greater scale than any other terrorist aggression in recent history. Lower Manhattan lost approximately 30 percent of its office space, and a number of businesses ceased to exist. Close to 200,000 jobs were destroyed or relocated out of New York City, at least temporarily. The destruction of physical assets was estimated in the national accounts to total $14 billion for private businesses, $1.5 billion for state and local government enterprises, and $700 million for the federal government. Rescue, cleanup, and related costs have been estimated to amount to at least $11 billion, for a total direct cost of $27.2 billion.

Immediate and Short Term: Indirect Effects

Immediately following the attacks, leading forecast services sharply revised downward their projections of economic activity. The consensus forecast for U.S. real gross domestic product (GDP) growth was instantly downgraded by 0.5 percentage points for 2001 and 1.2 percentage points for 2002. The implied projected cumulative loss in national income through the end of 2003 amounted to 5 percent of annual GDP, or $500 billion. In the end, however, the impact of the attacks proved far less damaging to GDP, which economists later estimated amounted only to between about 0.5 percent and 1 percent of GDP, or roughly $50 billion to $100 billion.

With production disrupted in some areas (airlines) and consumers increasingly cautious, real GDP shrank in the third quarter of 2001. But in the fourth quarter, demand held up better than initially predicted, and GDP increased. However, private sector fixed investment registered a steep decline, and inventories were slashed. Offsetting these forces were household consumption, (helped by falling energy prices), government spending, and rising house prices. Some sectors or firms actually witnessed an increase in demand, notably those firms in the area of security and information technology. Still, while overall demand proved fairly resilient, a number of sectors were hit hard, with declining output and profits continuing into the midterm.

Overall, the short-term adverse economic impact of the attacks was far less than feared initially, thanks in large part to good economic crisis management. The Federal Reserve, the administration, and Congress acted quickly to restore confidence, inject liquidity, and provide resources to deal with the consequences of the attacks. The Federal Reserve, by lowering the price of credit and temporarily providing vast amounts of liquidity, helped safeguard the integrity of the financial system and saved many firms from bankruptcy.

Medium Term

The fact that the attack was premeditated and therefore could be repeated has had a significant impact on five main areas: (1) insurance; (2) airlines; (3) tourism and other industries associated with travel; (4) shipping; and (5) defense and security expenditures. In turn, developments in these areas have had a broader effect on wide areas of economic activity.

Insurance

The losses from the terrorist attacks for the insurance industry (including reinsurance) are estimated at between $30 billion and $58 billion, with the main uncertainty concerning liability insurance. By comparison, the losses associated with Hurricane Andrew's 1992 damage in Florida came to around $21 billion. Even if the final cost is close to the lower estimate, insured losses in 2001 are likely to have been the highest ever.

Following the attacks, most primary insurers increased their premiums and curtailed or dropped altogether coverage for terrorism-related risk. The increases in insurance premiums have adversely affected several key industries. The strongest impact has been on aviation, but other sectors, including transportation, construction, and tourism and energy generation, have also been affected. Overall, it is estimated that commercial property and liability insurance rates have been raised by 30 percent on average.

Airlines and Tourist Industry

The U.S. airline industry was already in a weak financial position before the attacks, with rising debt ratios and falling returns on investment. Even with cutbacks in service on the order of 20 percent and significant government support of roughly $5 billion in short-term assistance and $10 billion in loan guarantees, airline passenger traffic has apparently remained below normal. A total of 100,000 layoffs occurred, and employment in October and November 2001 fell by 81,000 (almost 8 percent). Equity valuations compared to the overall market illustrate these difficulties. In the year following the attacks, the U.S. airline sector lost about 20 percent of its relative value.

Related industries were also been badly affected, such as hotels, tourism, car hire, travel agents, restaurants, and civilian aircraft manufactures. For example, hotels reported higher vacancy rates, and employment in the sector as a whole fell by 58,000 (about 3 percent) in October and November following the attacks. A year after the attacks, relative equity values for hotels and leisure facilities were off by about 15 percent.

Shipping

Tighter security requirements and a series of surcharges have also affected the cost of transporting goods by sea and air. International sea shipments have encountered stricter notification requirements and more frequent Coast Guard inspections and tug boat escorts. The result has been increased costs and longer waiting times. For airfreight, higher security-related costs at airports led to the introduction of security charges and higher commercial insurance premiums. These cost increases were offset in part by a decline in fuel prices and the sharp deceleration in demand following the attacks. Still, airfreight rates, for example, were about 10 percent higher at the end of the year, suggesting that the increased costs directly attributable to higher security may be in the range of 15 to 20 percent.

Security and Military Spending

The president requested a significant increase in security-related programs in the context of the budget for fiscal year 2003. Additional spending of $448 billion was proposed for national defense (an increase of 14 percent from the previous year). In addition, the president asked Congress for an appropriation of $38 billion for homeland security, compared to $20 billion spent in 2001. This appropriation seeks to improve the preparedness of first responders (firefighters, police officers, and rescue workers), enhance defenses against biological attacks, secure borders, and improve information sharing, and it includes $8 billion for domestic defense spending. Over the next five years, defense spending jumped by about 20 percent, or $60 billion annually in constant dollars, much of it related to antiterrorism security. This figure did not, of course, include the costs of the wars in Afghanistan and Iraq (the first a direct result of September 11 and the latter an indirect result), which, by 2010, had amounted to just over $450 billion and $800 billion, respectively. Meanwhile, it is estimated that overall homeland security costs rose by about $44 billion annually between 2001 and 2005. Of this amount, about one-third went to protecting critical infrastructure and other assets, one-third to border and transportation security, and the rest to a variety of other tasks.

Other cost factors that are more difficult to calculate in dollar terms as a result of the 9/11 terrorist attacks include increased investor wariness, a rise in transaction costs, higher operating expenses to meet enhanced security needs, and the costs of maintaining greater inventories for fear that terrorist attacks could disrupt the just-in-time deliveries that had become so integral to the global economy.

Although the immediate and short-term effects of the terrorist attacks were shown to be considerable, medium- to longer-term effects have been much more difficult to calculate, essentially because the various costs associated with heightened security and increased investor concerns have been affected by other events, including further terrorist attacks, such as those in Madrid, London, and Mumbai in 2004, 2005, and 2008, respectively, and the wars in Afghanistan and Iraq. In addition, the normal ups and downs of the economy, such as the housing-fed boom of the mid-2000s and the financial crisis and recession of the latter years of the decade, further complicated calculations. Still, economists estimate that the direct medium- and long-term costs of 9/11 are probably in the hundreds of billions, a remarkable figure given that the cost of the operation to al-Qaeda has been estimated at about $200,000.

Robert Looney and James Ciment

See also: *September 11 Attacks*—Global Economic Impact; U.S. Aid and Relief; Cleanup and Rebuilding; Victim Relief. *Counterterrorism*—Financial Counterterrorism.

Further Reading

Alexander, Dean C., and Yonah Alexander. *Terrorism and Business: The Impact of September 11, 2001.* Ardsley, NY: Transnational, 2002.
Devol, Ross, and Perry Wong. "Metropolitan Economies." *The Milken Institute Review* (First Quarter 2002).

Morgan, Matthew J., ed. *The Impact of 9/11 on Business and Economics: The Business of Terror.* New York: Palgrave Macmillan, 2009.

U.S. Congress. Joint Economic Committee. "The Economic Costs of Terrorism." Washington, DC: U.S. Government Printing Office, May 2002.

Victim Relief

The deaths and destruction resulting from the September 11 attacks created a serious financial emergency for thousands of survivors. Both private charities and the federal government responded to the situation by offering various forms of aid. The American Red Cross and Safe Horizons, a Manhattan-based group, handed out emergency aid to those who had lost relatives or suffered property damage as a result of the attack. However, given the need for speedy assistance and the difficulty of checking requests for aid, the relief efforts were vulnerable to fraudulent claims. Six months after the tragedy, New York authorities had uncovered dozens of false claims involving more than $1 million in aid. By the end of April, forty-seven individuals had been charged by the Manhattan district attorney with falsely reporting the deaths of family members in order to obtain money from government and private charities. It was alleged that fraudulent claims were made for nonexistent individuals as well as for persons who were still alive or who had died earlier.

In addition to private charitable efforts, a federal fund was established to compensate the families of individuals who had died in the attack. The September 11th Victim Compensation Fund was created only a few days after the attack, as part of legislation enacted in order to bail out the airline industry. Washington, D.C. attorney Kenneth Feinberg was appointed special master of the fund, in charge of administering all aspects of the program. It was decided that the fund would pay the surviving family members $250,000 for each death, plus an additional $50,000 for the deceased's spouse and $50,000 for each dependent of the deceased. This was considered compensation for their pain and suffering. In addition an estimate was made of how much each victim would have earned over the rest of his or her lifetime. Essentially, this part of the compensation process attempted to measure expected (but discounted) future earnings. Therefore, survivors of older workers were awarded less than those of younger workers, and survivors of high-paid workers were awarded more than those of low-paid workers. Also, the value of life insurance policies, pensions, and other death benefits was deducted from the award.

The compensation rules were criticized on several grounds. The victims' families had to waive the right to sue the airline industry in order to receive payment, with the payments being far lower than that awarded to airline crash victims. Since many of those killed or injured at the World Trade Center were highly paid financial professionals, their families argued that had a court considered each case individually, they would have received much higher amounts. However, those who were unhappy with the amount of the award could appeal in an informal hearing. Feinberg, who worked pro bono for three years, personally presided over 900 of the 1,600 hearings. In the end 97 percent of the families participated in the program, receiving a total of $7 billion; the average payout was $1.8 million.

The Victim Compensation Fund was only one source of compensation for those harmed, and the total amount paid out by the government, insurance companies, and charitable groups was unprecedented. According to a RAND study published in November 2004, a total of $38.1 billion was given to individuals and businesses affected by the attacks. New York businesses received the largest share, almost $24 billion, while $10.6 billion went to emergency responders and other individuals killed or injured. The RAND study found that the average compensation received from all sources (insurance, employers, and charities, as well as the Victim Compensation Fund) was $3.1 million for civilians killed or injured, and $4.1 million for emergency responders.

Christopher Hewitt

See also: *September 11 Attacks*—Emergency Response: Police, Firefighters, and Medical Personnel; Victims and Survivors.

Further Reading

Dixon, Lloyd, and Rachel Kaganoff Stern. *Compensation for Losses from the 9/11 Attacks.* Santa Monica, CA: RAND, November 2004.

Morgan, Matthew J., ed. *The Impact of 9/11 on Business and Economics: The Business of Terror.* New York: Palgrave Macmillan, 2009.

Security and Defense

America's security and defense posture changed radically in the wake of the terrorist attacks of September 11, 2001. Those attacks—perpetrated by foreign nationals who had exploited vulnerabilities in the nation's security apparatus and procedures—led to two major responses. The first was an expansion and enhancement of domestic and international security operations; the second was an expansion of the government's capacity to monitor people living in the United States—citizens and especially visitors and resident aliens. As the articles in this subsection of the encyclopedia reveal, these changes were both qualitative—administrative reorganization, new agencies, and new missions for existing security and military organizations—and quantitative, as more personnel and money were earmarked to protect the country against terrorists and terrorist events.

At home, the most far-reaching security changes came almost immediately. Recognizing the weaknesses of a largely privately run security system at the nation's airports, Washington federalized airport security with the establishment of the Transportation Security Administration just two months after 9/11. There was a general recognition, however, that airports did not represent the country's only vulnerability to terrorist attack. Borders, ports, coastland, immigration, internal transportation—they all presented their own problems in an age of terrorism. To better focus and coordinate antiterrorism efforts—as well as to enhance the nation's response to natural disasters—Congress passed the Homeland Security Act of 2002, the most fundamental transformation of the nation's security apparatus since the beginning of the Cold War. The legislation established the cabinet-level Department of Homeland Security, which subsumed most of the agencies charged with security broadly defined. At the same time, the act led to the reorganization of existing agencies, including the separation of immigration policing from naturalization, so as to better focus the former on border security and the monitoring of immigrant traffic.

At the same time, with the USA PATRIOT Act, the government moved to enhance the powers of local, state, and national security organizations to monitor citizens and aliens alike. Such moves were justified by the George W. Bush Administration as necessary in an age in which enemies—bent on wholesale carnage—lived and operated within American society. But civil libertarians countered that, while the threats were real, the powers granted to the government to spy on citizens, hold suspects, and regulate people's daily lives were too expansive, while the checks placed on those powers were too weak.

Abroad, the United States adopted a new doctrine of preventive military engagement, which the Bush Administration argued was necessary in an age when rogue regimes harbored terrorists and pursued weapons of mass destruction. The implications of this new doctrine were twofold. First, regimes that did not support U.S. and international efforts to fight terrorism—such as the Taliban regime in Afghanistan—became, in effect, enemies of the United States. Second, in an age of proliferating weapons of mass destruction, the costs of waiting for rogue states (or terrorist groups) to act before going on the attack were too high, or, as Bush himself put it so ominously in a speech a year after 9/11, "we cannot wait for the final proof [of an enemy regime's intent to attack the United States], the smoking gun that could come in the form of a mushroom cloud." The results of the new Bush doctrine were two wars, in Afghanistan and Iraq, which began with quick successes for the U.S. military before they turned into long-term and rather bloody counterinsurgency wars—wars that some critics have argued have weakened America's security by alienating enemies and draining resources that could be better spent on improved homeland security.

Whether supportive or critical of these changed arrangements, most experts agree that the war on terrorism has wrought a transformation of the nation's domestic security system and its military, including the impact this security has on the ordinary lives of American citizens, which is likely to be as far-reaching and as lasting as those that accompanied America's last decades-long security challenge—the Cold War.

James Ciment

See also: *September 11 Attacks*—Civil Liberties, Civil Rights, and National Security; Airport Security; Armed Forces Missions; Homeland Defense: Organization and Policy; Hunt for al-Qaeda and Terrorist Networks; Immigration Policy and Border Defense; Intelligence Community: Pre-9/11 Failures and Successes; Intelligence Community: Response to 9/11; National Guard Missions; Special Events Security; Terror Threat Warnings. *Counterterrorism*—Asymmetric Warfare; Drone Attacks and Assassinations, Counterterrorist; Law Enforcement, Counterterrorist; Special Operations; Technology, Terrorist and Counterterrorist; U.S. Response to Weapons of Mass Destruction.

Further Reading

Alden, Edward. *The Closing of the American Border: Terrorism, Immigration, and Security Since 9/11.* New York: Harper, 2008.

Ball, Howard. *U.S. Homeland Security: A Reference Handbook.* Santa Barbara, CA: ABC-CLIO, 2005.

Etzioni, Amitai. *How Patriotic Is the Patriot Act? Freedom Versus Security in the Age of Terrorism.* New York: Routledge, 2004.

Herman, Susan N., and Paul Finkelman, eds. *Terrorism, Government, and Law: National Authority and Local Autonomy in the War on Terror.* Westport, CT: Praeger Security International, 2008.

Howard, Russell, James Forest, and Joanne C. Moore. *Homeland Security and Terrrorism: Readings and Interpretations.* New York: McGraw-Hill, 2006.

Morgan, Matthew J. *The American Military After 9/11: Society, State, and Empire.* New York: Palgrave Macmillan, 2008.

Airport Security

On September 11, 2001, the world entered a new era of airborne violence and terrorism when four airplanes were used by terrorists to attack the United States. All four planes were used as high-explosive bombs, two striking and destroying New York City's World Trade Center Twin Towers, one striking the Pentagon in Washington, D.C., and one failing its mission when passengers fought back inside the aircraft, forcing it to crash in a Pennsylvania field. More than ushering in a new age of vulnerability for Americans both at home and abroad, the attacks of 9/11 brought about sweeping and unparalleled changes to air travel. Prior to 9/11, airline travel was unfettered by regulation and was a relaxing way to travel (with the exception of holidays and certain long weekends when passengers jostled for boarding position). After the 9/11 attacks, airline travel would never again be the same.

Legal and Enforcement Agency

On November 19, 2001, President George W. Bush signed into law the Aviation Transportation Security Act, Public Law 107-71 (2001), the most comprehensive federal law covering air transportation security ever enacted in the United States. ATSA 107-71 established a new federal agency, the Transportation Security Administration (TSA), under the Department of Transportation, and headed by Secretary Norman Mineta. The TSA was shortly reassigned to the Department of Homeland Security (DHS). In July 2010, John S. Pistole was named the fifth director of the TSA. The primary responsibilities of the TSA are to secure airports and airlines from terrorist and criminal activity. Provisions of the law apply to all areas of airport and airline operations. Specific provisions are presented throughout this article and are referenced as (ATSA).

Airplane and Flight Security Measures

One of the first preventive measures taken to guard against the use of airplane attacks was to establish no-fly zones over large cities, certain types of facilities (e.g., nuclear power plants), military installations, and other critical areas of the country. Some of these areas are off-limits entirely to any civilian aircraft. Other aircraft must file a flight plan and receive permission from the Federal Aviation Administration (FAA) prior to entering this restricted airspace. Failure to do so is a federal violation, and violators will initially be greeted by military aircraft scrambled to intercept them. Military AWACS (Airborne Warning and Control System) aircraft now patrol the air corridor between Washington D.C., and New York City on a twenty-four-hour, seven-days-a-week basis.

The federal air marshal program was placed under the TSA and significantly expanded. Started in 1968 and expanded in 1985 under Public Law 99-83, after two Shiite Muslims hijacked TWA 847 and killed a U.S. Navy diver, air marshals now ride disguised as passengers on most domestic and international flights. The air marshals serve as in-flight police officers with full police authority, including the authority to use deadly force under the same guidelines as any U.S. law enforcement officers.

Airplane cockpit doors have been reinforced with steel, attack-proofed, and hardened to stop small arms and some rifle fire. All cockpit doors must be closed and locked prior to leaving the gate and may not be opened by the aircrew or passenger-side personnel (airline or civilian) until arriving and gating at their destination. In addition, pilots and flight crews undergo training to protect and defend against armed threats. In several instances, passengers have intervened to attack potential terrorists and criminals. Two of the most notorious involved Richard Reid and Umar Farouk Abdulmutallab. On December 22, 2001, Richard Reid tried to ignite a shoe bomb aboard American Airlines 63 from Paris to Miami. Passengers were able to subdue and hold him until landing. On December 25, 2009, Umar Farouk Abdulmutallab attempted to detonate plastic explosives hidden in his underwear aboard Northwest Airlines 253 from Amsterdam to Detroit. A passenger, Jasper Schuringa, grabbed and detained him until other passengers could assist. Abdulmutallab was secured until the airplane landed in Detroit. Other security measures proposed for aircraft (and in place as of 2010) include cameras watching the passenger compartment, "knock-out" gas in the passenger compartment, fuel-absorbing foam in the fuel tanks, bombproof containers for suitcases and other cargo, in-flight emergency phone systems, and stronger runway alert perimeter defense systems. As noted in *U.S. News and World Report* soon after the attack, the airline industry and the public have come a long way since the publication in 2000 of recommendations for security measures (e.g., matching each bag in the hold with a domestic passenger) in an FAA-funded study that was strongly resisted by the airlines.

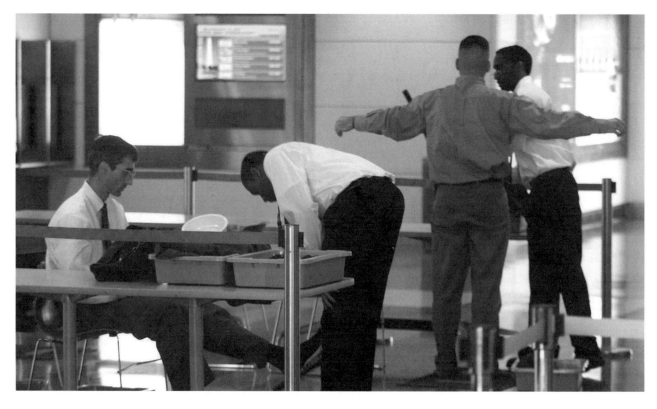

Sweeping federal legislation after 9/11 created the Transportation Security Administration to protect the safety of the American traveling public. Among the many security measures implemented by TSA was tighter screening of air passengers and cargo. *(Mark Wilson/Getty Images)*

In 2003, the TSA implemented one of the most controversial of all airline security programs when then administrator James Loy approved a program to arm airline pilots and other crew members. Pilots, copilots, and navigators can, at their discretion, be trained and carry firearms in flight to defend their aircraft. In 2003, President Bush expanded the program to include cargo plane aircrews and certain other flight crew members. As of 2008, it was estimated that at least 10 percent of airline pilots were armed, with more arming themselves every month.

The 9/11 Commission Act (2007) required DHS to establish a system to screen 100 percent of all cargo flown on passenger aircraft by August 2010. In February 2009, TSA agents were screening about 50 percent of all domestic cargo and had increased the rate to 75 percent by May 2010. Additional screening measures require that all passenger jets be searched at least once per day, both inside and out. All outside doors and hatches and the cargo holds must be visually inspected. Inside, all closets, galleys, trash containers, overhead storage areas, lavatories, seats, seat backs, cushions, life vests, and other areas must be searched. Any materials brought aboard by maintenance, food crews, service personnel, and others must also be searched. One-third of all aircraft will require employee checks involving either a manual pat-down search or metal detector. Any suspected lapse of security around an aircraft will mandate the repetition of all these procedures.

Terminal and Passenger Security

Immediately following September 11, National Guard troops were mobilized to assist in terminal security. In May 2002, the National Guard was replaced by police officers and private security firm screeners at every screening station. By 2005, all had been replaced with TSA federal screeners (ATSA). Passenger screening has been one of the most contentious of all airline security measures, as the screening techniques and procedures are the most individually intrusive. Passenger screening uses hand searches, metal detectors, X-ray machines, and chemical analysis (for potential explosive material residue). After Richard Reid's shoe-bomb attempt, all passengers are required to remove their shoes prior to screening. In 2006, a trio of British-born al-Qaeda-trained terrorists led by Ahmed Abdulla Ali were plotting to blow up seven or more airplanes using a series of liquid bombs disguised in soft-drink containers. At least seven flights between London and the United States and Canada were to be targeted at approximately the same time. As a result of this plot, the TSA instituted the 3-1-1 rule for carry-ons. A passenger may carry one 3.4-ounce bottle, one quart-sized clear zip-top bag, and one bag per passenger in the screening bin. In 2010, most of the world had accepted the 3-1-1 rule for passengers. In addition, many other items are prohibited aboard aircraft (ATSA). Presently, the list of prohibited items numbers in the hundreds and includes box cutters, scissors, nail clippers, all knives, pool cues, hand tools, snow skis and poles, and toy weapons.

The newest technology used to screen passengers is Advanced Imaging Technology (AIT), or full-body scanners. These machines are replacing the time-honored X-ray and hand-scanning procedures used in most airports. In December 2009, only nineteen U.S. airports had full-body scanners and only six of those airports used them as the primary screening method. Following the attempted bombing of Northwest Airlines 253, the TSA increased the budget and planned deployment of AITs to more than 1,800 units serving most U.S. airports. The TSA plan is to eventually have AITs at every airport, to be used as the primary screening method. Most problematic with the introduction of these machines is the cost—each unit costs between $130,000 and $170,000. Cast Scope machines are going into service at many airports to scan casts and artificial limbs for weapons and explosives. Baggage is screened by hand, X-ray, and explosive-detection systems. Technology is improving the ability to detect weapons in baggage as well. More than 900 Advanced Technology X-ray Systems, which allow for bags to be scanned from multiple angles, are currently in use. Explosive Trace Detection systems, which use chemical swabs on bags to test for explosives, are being replaced by more advanced explosive-detection systems, which are similar to MRIs. Under the American Recovery and Reinvestment Act of 2009, airports are on track to reach 100 percent cargo screening in passenger airplanes during the 2010–2014 budget cycle. Topographic Explosive Detection Systems are being developed and purchased by airlines and airports to meet this goal.

Finally, the no-fly lists are being revised, updated, and expanded in the wake of the May 2010 Times Square bombing attempt. Faisal Shahzad attempted to detonate a homemade bomb in Times Square, then tried to board a flight to the Middle East. He had boarded his airplane and was waiting for departure when he was caught. Given his near escape, the government revised and improved the no-fly notification procedures to more rapidly and readily identify no-fly passengers.

Private Airplanes and Airports

The largest and most significant weakness in America's airport and airplane defense system is in the private sector. The United States has more than 20,000 small airports and more than 220,000 private aircraft that are exempt from any federal security regulations or indus-

try scrutiny. From these airports, flights go through no screening and search procedures, planes are not inspected, pilots and passengers are not screened or subjected to any security procedures, no pilot-license-review procedures are in place, the no-fly lists do not apply, and there are no other security measures in place. Even in flight, these planes are not subject to any scrutiny. For example, planes flying at lower altitudes under visual flight rules are not required to file a flight plan. This lax security can have disastrous results. In February 2010, Joseph Stack, distressed over past taxes, flew a small single-engine airplane from one of these airports into an Austin IRS building. In addition to himself, Stack killed a worker inside the building.

Problems and Remaining Issues

Airline passengers are resistant to more rigorous behavioral screening and more personal scrutiny. In a nation of free will, free speech, and other constitutionally guaranteed freedoms, the public finds intense personal scrutiny unacceptable. As security tightens, resistance increases. Likewise, airlines are loath to do anything that may increase passenger apprehension and unrest. Faced with a deep recession and tightened economy, airlines are having to increase prices and fees to meet rising costs. Any security measures that cost money are put on the back burner and most likely will not be implemented. Government mandates, laws, and programs to increase airport and airline security cost money, and it is money that is not available. For example, the fiscal year 2011 federal budget includes $214.7 million for 500 AIT units. Triple that figure is needed, say many experts. The 2011 DHS budget includes more than $1 billion to increase airport security (total over $8.2 billion). This money is divided among technology, explosive-screening K-9 teams ($71 million) and 350 more TSA behavior-detection officers ($20.2 million).

Wayman C. Mullins

See also: *September 11 Attacks*—Immigration Policy and Border Defense.

Further Reading

Clark, Kim, and Dana Hawkins. "A Wing and a Prayer." *U.S. News and World Report,* September 24, 2001.

Croft, John. "Runaway Security Fees Spark Industry Ire." *Aviation Week and Space Technology,* April 15, 2002, 55.

Fiorino, Frances. "Airline Crews to Be Taught New Defensive Measures." *Aviation Week and Space Technology,* January 28, 2002, 48.

Mann, Paul. "Air Defense Key to Homeland Mission." *Aviation Week and Space Technology,* May 6, 2002, 26.

Transportation Security Administration. www.tsa.gov.

Armed Forces Missions

The fundamental mission of the U.S. military is to fight and win the nation's wars when diplomatic and other efforts to resolve a crisis have failed. Yet, as a result of the September 11, 2001, terrorist attacks on the World Trade Center and the Pentagon, the armed forces entered a new era. For most of our history, except for unique events such as the Japanese surprise attack on Pearl Harbor on December 7, 1941, and the World Trade Center bombing in 1993, the United States has been generally immune from direct attack by foreign enemies. Domestic terrorist attacks such as the Oklahoma City bombing have generally been considered law enforcement issues and do not directly involve America's military. Even during the height of the Cold War, the well-known policy of mutually assured destruction brought some measure of reassurance to the public because there was a general understanding that if the Soviet Union attacked, we would execute an immediate, massive retaliation. That comfortable reassurance vanished once the terrorists brought the war to American soil and once it was realized that all of the nation's assets, including the armed forces, must have an active role in the defense of U.S. national interests. Those interests and, therefore, the missions of U.S. armed forces, include the following:

- Protecting the physical security of U.S. territory and that of U.S. allies and friends
- Protecting the safety of U.S. citizens at home and abroad
- Protecting the economic well-being of U.S. society
- Protecting U.S. critical infrastructures—including energy, banking and finance, telecommunications, transportation, water and power systems, government, and emergency services—from disruptions intended to cripple their operation

Strategy for Military Transformation

Since the founding of the republic, the United States has embraced the fundamental and enduring goals of maintaining the sovereignty, political freedom, and independence of the United States, with its values, institutions, and territory intact; protecting the lives and personal safety of Americans, both at home and abroad; and promoting the well-being and prosperity of the nation and its people. The aim of the Department of Defense's (DOD's) "transformation strategy" is to ensure U.S. military preeminence well into the twenty-first century. Much about the future security environment is uncertain, such as the identity of the nation's adversaries and the precise ways in which they will threaten U.S. interests. However, some aspects of the emerging threat environment are already clear. A number of states will have the capability to threaten U.S. vital interests through coercion, cross-border aggression, or other hostile actions.

Other states will face internal humanitarian crises and ethnic conflict, which may require the U.S. military to respond quickly while minimizing the risk of American and noncombatant casualties. Whether in the context of a major theater war or smaller-scale contingencies, future opponents are likely to threaten to use or will actually employ asymmetric methods such as terrorism, cyberattacks on critical computer-based networks, and weapons of mass destruction—or combinations of all three methods—in an attempt to offset the conventional superiority of the U.S. military. "Transformed" military forces are needed because the strategic environment is changing; such changes are possible primarily because technologies that are changing the civilian world are changing the military sphere as well. More tailored forces and increasingly precise weaponry and targeting will allow greater massing of effects with less massing of forces, thus decreasing the vulnerability of U.S. forces. In short, U.S. forces must exploit revolutionary technologies in order to protect citizens at home and project power abroad in the twenty-first century.

Joint Vision 2020 and Full-Spectrum Dominance

Joint Vision 2020 is the DOD program name for the continuing transformation of America's armed forces. It builds upon and extends the conceptual template established by Joint Vision 2010, and it establishes full-spectrum dominance as the overarching objective for a transformed U.S. military. Full-spectrum dominance is the ability to defeat any adversary and control any situation across the full range of military operations, whether operating unilaterally or in combination with multinational and interagency partners. The full range of operations includes maintaining a posture of strategic deterrence. It also includes theater engagement and presence activities, conflict involving employment of strategic forces and weapons of mass destruction, major theater wars, regional conflicts, smaller-scale contingencies, and those ambiguous situations residing between peace and war, such as peacekeeping and peace enforcement operations. In the next twenty years, adversaries will probably not challenge U.S. strengths but will probably seek to attack the United States and its interests through asymmetric means. They could identify vulnerable areas and devise means to attack them. The potential of such asymmetric approaches is perhaps the most serious danger the United States faces in the immediate future.

Critical Overseas Missions: Promoting Regional Stability

The DOD promotes regional stability by reassuring friends and allies of U.S. commitment, facilitating regional cooperation, supporting democratization, and enhancing transparency.

The DOD seeks to prevent conflicts and other threats by limiting the spread of dangerous military technologies, combating transnational threats, and providing security reassurance. Examples of these efforts include the U.S.-North Korean Agreed Framework, the Cooperative Threat Reduction Program with Russia, Ukraine, Kazakhstan, and other new independent states of Eurasia, and the Chemical Weapons Convention. The DOD combats transnational threats through a number of measures: missions to prevent terrorism, efforts to reduce U.S. vulnerability to terrorist acts, and programs to decrease the production and flow of illegal drugs to the United States.

A vital aspect of the military's mission in shaping the international security environment is deterring aggression and coercion in key regions of the world on a daily basis. The ability of the United States to deter potential adversaries in peacetime depends on several factors:

- A declaratory policy and overseas presence that effectively communicate U.S. security interests and commitments throughout the world
- A demonstrated will to uphold U.S. security commitments when and where they are challenged
- Conventional war-fighting capabilities across the full spectrum of military operations, including both forces forward deployed and forces rapidly deployable on a global scale
- A demonstrated ability to form and lead effective military coalitions

Most Dangerous Mission: Responding to Crises

Despite the DOD's best efforts to shape the international security environment, the U.S. armed forces will occasionally be called upon to respond to crises in order to protect national interests, demonstrate U.S. resolve, and reaffirm the nation's role as a global leader. Therefore, U.S. forces must also be able, either unilaterally or as part of a coalition, to execute the full spectrum of military operations, from deterring an adversary's aggression or coercion in crisis to conducting concurrent smaller-scale contingency operations to fighting and winning major theater wars. While deterring aggression and conducting smaller-scale contingency operations are intense missions, fighting and winning major theater wars are the most stressing missions for U.S. forces. In order to protect American interests around the globe, the armed forces must continue to overmatch the military power of regional states with interests hostile to the United States. Some states possess nuclear, biological, or chemical weapons that may be used to intimidate neighbors or deter U.S. or international intervention.

Antiterrorism Mission

The terrorist threat has changed markedly in recent years for a number of reasons, including changing terrorist motivations; the proliferation of technologies of mass destruction; increased access to information and information technologies; and a perception that the United States is not willing to accept casualties. As a result of the dynamic environment influencing terrorism, demonstrated by the attack in 2000 on the USS *Cole* and the 9/11 attacks on the World Trade Center and the Pentagon, the United States must continue to improve its ability to stay ahead of terrorists' increasing capabilities.

The DOD's program for combating terrorism has four components: antiterrorism, counterterrorism, terrorism consequence management, and intelligence support. Antiterrorism consists of defensive measures used to reduce the vulnerability of individuals, forces, and property to terrorist acts. Counterterrorism consists of offensive measures taken to prevent, deter, and respond to terrorism. Terrorism consequence management consists of measures to mitigate the effects of a terrorist incident, including those resulting from the use of a weapon of mass destruction. Finally, intelligence support consists of the collection, analysis, and dissemination of all-source intelligence on terrorist groups and activities to protect, deter, preempt, or counter the terrorist threat to U.S. personnel, forces, critical infrastructures, and interests.

The DOD has completed interagency agreements delineating security responsibility for military personnel in more than 120 countries. The DOD's antiterrorism training program, which reaches all levels of DOD personnel, is constantly being refined. The Combating Terrorism Readiness Initiative Fund provides an important means for the chairman of the Joint Chiefs of Staff to help combatant commanders meet emergency and other unforeseen high-priority requirements. Defense intelligence organizations are engaged in an aggressive day-to-day mission to better alert decision makers to potential terrorist attacks, to strengthen their close working relationships with other elements of the national intelligence community, and to increase intelligence exchanges with U.S. friends and allies.

In the area of counterterrorism, U.S. armed forces possess a tailored range of options to respond to terrorism directed at U.S. citizens, interests, and property, both domestically and overseas. The DOD can employ the full range of military capabilities, including rapid-response Special Operations Forces that are specifically trained, manned, and equipped to preempt or resolve terrorist incidents. In the area of terrorism consequence management, the DOD strives to deter and, when necessary, minimize the effects of a weapon of mass destruction incident.

The DOD has created, and is continually refining,

an effective response capability. In the early 2000s, the DOD established the position of assistant to the secretary of defense for civil support to provide policy guidance and the Joint Task Force Civil Support to assume operational responsibility for the DOD's consequence management support to civil authorities for weapons-of-mass-destruction incidents within the United States and its territories and possessions.

Future Missions

The United States must structure and manage its military forces to meet the fundamental challenge of future missions. It must maintain near-term capabilities to support U.S. strategy while simultaneously undergoing necessary transformations to shape and respond for the future. In the face of evolving threats and challenges, the United States must maintain military superiority as a means of achieving its objective of creating an international environment that is peaceful, prosperous, and compatible with U.S. interests and ideals. Acquiring superior technology and exploiting it to the fullest is key to maintaining superior forces. U.S. forces must be capable of operating across the spectrum of conflict by meeting the challenges posed by smaller-scale contingency operations as well as major theater wars that include significant asymmetric terrorist threats.

Stephen C. Malone

See also: *Modern Terrorism*—Afghanistan: U.S. Invasion and War; Iraq: U.S. Invasion and Post-Saddam Hussein Era. *September 11 Attacks*—Hunt for al-Qaeda and Terrorist Networks; National Guard Missions.

Further Reading

Berkowitz, Bruce. *The New Face of War: How War Will Be Fought in the 21st Century.* New York: Free Press, 2003.

Mahnken, Thomas G. *Technology and the American Way of War.* New York: Columbia University Press, 2008.

Morgan, Matthew J. *The American Military After 9/11: Society, State, and Empire.* New York: Palgrave Macmillan, 2008.

Paquette, Laure. *Counterinsurgency and the Armed Forces.* New York: Nova Science, 2009.

Sapolsky, Harvey M., Benjamin H. Friedman, and Brendan Rittenhouse Green, eds. *US Military Innovation Since the Cold War: Creation Without Destruction.* New York: Routledge, 2009.

Homeland Defense: Organization and Policy

Counterterrorism attained unprecedented salience and criticality in the public policy realm in the aftermath of the September 11, 2001, terrorist attacks. The magnitude of this tragedy demonstrated that America had not adequately prepared for such an eventuality. Consequently, the federal government undertook a massive effort to restructure and expand its counterterrorism and homeland security policies. Toward this end, on October 8, 2001, President George W. Bush issued Executive Order 13228, which established the Office of Homeland Security. In essence, homeland security is a comprehensive effort designed to safeguard the nation's population, property, government, and critical infrastructure. It seeks to accomplish this task by preparing for, protecting against, and managing the consequences of terrorist attacks and related crises. Counterterrorism involves *offensive* measures taken to prevent, deter, and respond to terrorism. It differs from antiterrorism, which includes *defensive* measures used to reduce the vulnerability of individuals and property to terrorism.

Background

The issues of counterterrorism and homeland security had actually received considerable attention prior to September 11, 2001. However, most of this attention was confined to policy think tanks and various blue-ribbon panels. Furthermore, although President Bill Clinton had placed counterterrorism high on his domestic agenda for much of his tenure, his approach was incremental and not sweeping. Much of the impetus for these efforts actually came from the perceived threat of domestic right-wing extremists and self-styled citizen militias. The April 19, 1995, bombing of the Murrah Federal Building in Oklahoma City was seen as a harbinger of further domestic terrorism. Some of President Clinton's more notable policy initiatives in the area of counterterrorism on which current homeland security efforts build were as follows.

First, President Clinton issued Presidential Decision Directive (PDD) 39 in 1995, which was the first directive to make terrorism a national top priority. This policy further articulated and defined the roles of members of the U.S. counterterrorism community. The Federal Bureau of Investigation (FBI) was designated the chief government agency responsible for investigating and preventing domestic terrorism, and the Federal Emergency Management Agency (FEMA) was named the lead agency for consequence management within U.S. territory. Pursuant to PDD 39, a specialized interagency team—the Domestic Emergency Support Team—was created to provide expert advice and guidance to the FBI on-scene commander and coordinate response measures. This directive was later augmented by PDD 62, which created a more systematic and integrated approach to fighting terrorism by establishing the National Coordinator for Security, Infrastructure Protection and Counter-Terrorism, which oversees a broad variety of relevant policies and programs. However, insofar as responsibility for counterterrorism activities and homeland security remained primarily with the individual agencies, the coordinator position was basically ineffectual.

Soon thereafter, new legislation was passed, including the Anti-Terrorism and Effective Death Penalty Act of 1996, which contained the most thoroughgoing measures theretofore aimed at combating terrorism. The various new laws and initiatives nearly doubled the amount of money spent on counterterrorism to $11 billion a year. Much of the money went to the FBI, whose antiterrorism budget jumped from $78 million to $609 million a year. Furthermore, between fiscal years 1993 and 2000, the number of FBI special agents assigned to counterterrorism programs increased from 550 to 1,669—approximately a 224 percent increase.

To better coordinate strategies among federal agencies, the FBI established its Counterterrorism Center in 1995. Eighteen federal agencies maintain a regular presence at the center and participate in its daily operations. The center combats terrorism on three fronts: international terrorism operations both from within the United States and in support of extraterritorial investigations, domestic terrorist operations, and countermeasures relating to both domestic and international terrorism.

In 1998, the FBI received a mandate in PDD 63 to establish the National Infrastructure Protection Center as the means by which to integrate personnel from state and local public safety agencies and representatives of the private sector to prevent, deter, and investigate attacks on the nation's critical infrastructure.

The U.S. Department of Justice made efforts to enhance homeland security as well and in 1998 announced the creation of the National Domestic Preparedness Office—a multiagency center composed of representatives from various federal agencies as well as state and local law enforcement and public safety agencies—whose primary mission is to serve as a clearinghouse for information to state and local officials on how to develop preparedness strategies for their communities, especially with issues concerning weapons of mass destruction (WMD).

Finally, in early 2001 the United States Government Interagency Domestic Terrorism Concept of Operations Plan (CONPLAN) was created to provide overall guidance to federal, state, and local agencies on how the federal government would respond to terrorist threats and attacks involving WMD. The primary agencies involved in CONPLAN include the Department of Justice, FEMA, the Department of Defense, the Department of Energy, the Environmental Protection Agency, and the Department of Health and Human Services.

Advisory Panels

These efforts notwithstanding, various government officials, policy analysts, and blue-ribbon panels argued that they were not enough to protect the country against the "new terrorism," which was thought to be more indiscriminate and potentially more lethal than the terrorism of the past. Many of these entities advanced suggestions to safeguard the American homeland and issued reports that recommended the creation of a federal agency that would coordinate these efforts. For example, the Gilmore Commission recommended the creation of a National Homeland Security Agency, which would have responsibility for "planning, coordinating, and integrating various U.S. government activities involved in homeland security." Furthermore, the commission recommended assisting so-called first responders (e.g., police, firefighters, and EMT personnel) so that they could better counter and respond to terrorist attacks; enhancing health and medical capacities so that the nation's health-care workers could adequately respond to casualties resulting from terrorism; strengthening immigration and border controls; improving security against cyberattacks and enhancing the security to America's critical infrastructure; and finally, clarifying the use and role of the military in regard to homeland security.

The United States Commission on National Security/21st Century, more popularly known as the Hart-Rudman Commission, called for the creation of a National Homeland Security Agency by merging several agencies responsible for homeland security into one consolidated agency. The new agency would be a cabinet-level department. The Gilmore Commission advocated an alternative approach, which would establish a focal point in the Executive Office of the President to coordinate homeland security and counterterrorism activities. This was similar to the approach that President George Bush eventually chose.

Office of Homeland Security

Homeland security and counterterrorism cut across so many different sectors that it is extremely difficult to consolidate all of these functions in one agency. For example, nearly fifty federal agencies play some role in these areas. Furthermore, these efforts are complicated by both the federal system and the separation of powers inherent in the American government. Therefore, the Bush administration created the Office of Homeland Security as an agency within the Executive Office of the President that would coordinate these security efforts. Specifically, as President Bush explained, the purpose of the office was "to coordinate the executive branch's efforts to detect, prepare for, prevent, protect against, respond to, and recover from terrorist attacks within the United States."

First, America's borders must be secured. To strengthen border security, the U.S. Customs Service was granted more personnel, new technology, and a substantially increased budget. Moreover, efforts were made to improve transportation security by assigning federal security personnel for screening duties at the nation's airports, and the number of federal sky marshals for airlines was increased. The Immigration and Naturalization Service was also granted more personnel and was required to implement a new entry-exit system to track the arrival and departure of non-U.S. citizens. Finally, the Coast Guard received substantially increased funding and was ordered to improve coordination with other port entities and to provide increased protection for high-risk vessels and coastal facilities.

Second, support for first responders was increased. To support this effort, President Bush proposed an allocation of $3.5 billion to enhance the homeland security response capabilities of first responders. This amount was a greater than tenfold increase in federal funding over what had previously been budgeted.

Third, in order to defend against bioterrorism, the government introduced initiatives that focus on three areas: (1) strengthening infrastructure by improving state and local health systems; (2) improving response by enhancing the federal government's capabilities to communicate and coordinate with state, local, and private agencies in the event of a bioterrorist attack; and (3) developing new vaccines, medicines, and diagnostic tests through increased research and development. To meet the requirements for these new efforts, President Bush's 2003 budget called for $5.9 million in funding for defending against bioterrorist attacks—a 319 percent increase from the 2002 level.

Finally, the government sought to improve technology systems and protect critical infrastructure systems. Toward this end, the government announced that it would create partnerships among the government and the owners and operators of the nation's critical infrastructure. Critical infrastructure includes those physical and cyber-based systems that are essential for the day-to-day operations of the economy and government and includes, inter alia, transportation, electrical power systems, gas and oil pipelines, water and sewage systems, communications systems, and emergency systems. Because much of the nation's critical infrastructure is privately owned and operated, the cooperation of its proprietors is essential to developing an adequate homeland defense plan.

Indicative of the government's commitment to deal with the crisis, $10.6 billion was dedicated for homeland security in a Fiscal Year 2002 Emergency Supplemental Bill. More than 4,000 agents along with 3,000 support staff were assigned to the investigation of the September 11 attacks—the single largest investigation in the history of the FBI. Roughly fifty-six Joint Terrorism Task Forces and 100 Anti-Terrorism Task Forces were established to better coordinate investigations and improve communications among federal, state, and local law enforcement.

The government also sought to encourage citizen engagement to deal with the crisis by creating several

Created in response to the September 11 attacks and the disconnects among agencies that allowed them, the cabinet-level Department of Homeland Security consolidated all federal bodies charged with safe-guarding America. Tom Ridge was its first secretary. *(Alex Wong/Getty Images)*

grassroots Citizen Corps organizations. These included (1) the Medical Reserve Corps, which was comprised of health-care professionals to augment the efforts of local health officials in areas affected by a crisis; (2) Operation TIPS (Terrorist Information and Prevention System), which allowed transportation workers, postal workers, and public utility employees to identify and report suspicious activities; (3) Community Emergency Response Teams, which enabled individual Americans to participate in training in their local communities to prepare for and respond to crises; (4) Neighborhood Watch programs; (5) the Volunteers in Police Service Program, in which citizen volunteers were permitted to assist their local police in performing nonsworn functions and, in doing so, free up police to perform vital frontline duty in the event of an emergency; and (6) the Patriot Readiness Center, which helped retired federal workers return to active service.

President Bush also created a Homeland Security Council on which he, Governor Tom Ridge, the cabinet secretaries, and other high-ranking officials involved in domestic security served. The new council is analogous to the National Security Council insofar as it seeks to involve key representatives from various agencies for which homeland security is a high-priority mission. The September 11 attacks prompted other parts of the government to redouble their efforts toward counterterrorism homeland security and to reconsider how they deal with these issues.

Federal Emergency Management Agency

The Federal Emergency Management Agency, which former president Jimmy Carter created by executive order in 1979 to respond to regional and national disasters, was increasingly oriented toward dealing with terrorism and its consequences. For example, in 1999 FEMA was given the responsibility of implementing the Federal Response Plan, which established a process and structure for a coordinated and systematic delivery of federal assistance to address the consequences of major disasters or emergencies. Included in the Federal Response Plan were several provisions for terrorism, chief among which was the responsibility to ensure that the government could adequately respond to the consequences of terrorism involving WMD. Toward this end, FEMA was given responsibility for crisis management, which refers to measures that "identify, acquire, and plan the resources needed to anticipate, and/or prevent, and/or resolve a threat or act of terrorism," and consequence management, which refers to measures that "protect public health and safety, restore essential government services, and provide emergency relief to governments, businesses, and individuals affected by the consequences of terrorism."

Shortly after the September 11 attacks, FEMA director Joe M. Allbaugh focused more of FEMA's attention on these issues as the agency began coordinating its activities with the newly created Office of Homeland Security. These two agencies were responsible for helping to ensure that the nation's first responders were adequately trained and equipped to deal with WMD.

Department of Defense

Traditionally, the U.S. military has concerned itself with projecting a forward presence, that is, preparing for military operations outside of the continental United States. Throughout the 1990s, the U.S. Department of Defense favored a strategic approach that prepared for the capability of fighting two simultaneous major wars. However, the September 11 attacks revealed a significant flaw in America's defense military strategy. Consequently, the Department of Defense reconsidered this strategy and undertook measures to deal more thoroughly with counterterrorism and homeland security. The military's new role in homeland security necessitated a redesign of its strategy to one that allowed for fighting one major war while contemporaneously protecting the American homeland.

As part of this new strategic thinking, then secretary of defense Donald Rumsfeld announced the creation of a new Northern Command, which would have primary responsibility over air patrols over the United States, naval vessels guarding the sea coasts, and emergency responses in the event of terrorist attacks. To meet this challenge, the Department of Defense had to address several threats related to homeland security, including countering the threat posed by WMD; protecting the nation against cyberattacks; ensuring national missile defense against ballistic and cruise missiles against the United States; ensuring the continuity of government; maintaining border and coastal defense; and providing for the continuity of military operations and force protection.

Although the Posse Comitatus Act of 1878 proscribes the involvement of the military in law enforcement and intelligence-gathering operations, exceptions are permitted in the event of a national emergency. Shortly after the September 11 attacks, Reserve and National Guard personnel were activated to provide security to American airports. President Bush also approved the use of special military tribunals to streamline the trials of suspected foreign terrorists, for they allow for greater secrecy and faster trials than ordinary criminal courts. The United States has not convened such tribunals since World War II, when the U.S. military secretly tried German saboteurs. In 2004 and 2006, the Supreme Court issued decisions ruling these special military tribunals unconstitutional. Congress responded with the Military Commissions Act of 2006, which created a new system of tribunals in accordance with the military's Uniform Code of Justice.

Congress

To meet the exigencies of the new terrorist threat, Congress passed the USA PATRIOT Act, which was signed into law by President Bush on October 26, 2001. The thrust of the new law was to give authorities more options for surveillance with less judicial supervision. It contains several features that should help authorities combat terrorism. First, it authorizes the use of so-called roving wiretaps to tap any electronic communications device that a suspected terrorist may be using. Second, it permits surveillance of a suspect's Internet activity and gives the FBI greater latitude in conducting secret searches of suspects' homes. Third, it allows for greater sharing of information among grand juries, prosecutors, and intelligence agencies. Fourth, it expands the powers of the Immigration and Naturalization Services—now Immigration and Customs Enforcement—to detain immigrants suspected of terrorist activities. Fifth, it gives the government greater power to penetrate banks suspected of being involved in the financing of terrorist groups and activities. Finally, the new law statutorily creates new crimes, enhances penalties, and increases the length of statutes of limitation for certain crimes. Many of the surveillance provisions had sunset clauses that caused them to be suspended by the end of 2005, unless further legislation was forthcoming. In March 2006, Congress reauthorized the Patriot Act, maintaining most of these provisions, while adding new citizen protections in response to civil liberties concerns.

One complicating factor for Congress in dealing with counterterrorism and homeland security is that at least nine congressional committees and twenty-six subcommittees have jurisdiction in one way or another on this issue. To better coordinate efforts with the executive branch, then House Speaker J. Dennis Hastert established a Terrorism and Homeland Security Working Group under the House Select Committee on Intelligence. After the September 11 attacks, this body was elevated to the status of a subcommittee. The subcommittee receives briefings from senior government officials and experts in the area of terrorism and homeland security. The body plans legislative reforms in the areas of intelligence and law enforcement to deal with terrorism.

What Is to Be Done?

A well-articulated and overarching strategy is needed to create clarity, set priorities, identify threats, and define requirements so that the government can organize homeland security effectively. Some observers have pointed out that in the past the absence of such a strategy hindered the nation's counterterrorism efforts and in doing so left the nation vulnerable to the attacks that were visited upon New York City and Washington on September 11, 2001. A comprehensive threat assessment and analysis is necessary as the basis for developing national strategy. Terrorism expert Ruth David has outlined several key elements critical to the formation of an effective homeland security policy. First, deterrence is necessary to discourage would-be adversaries from attacking the United States. Second, prevention must deny adversaries the means to attack. Third, preemption must deny adversaries the opportunity to attack. Fourth, crisis management and consequence management are necessary to mitigate its effects. Fifth, attribution is essential to identifying those responsible for the attack. Finally, a swift and appropriate response is necessary to demonstrate resoluteness and to discourage subsequent attacks.

Fundamental to these new counterterrorist initiatives is improving upon the current system of intelligence gathering and analysis. The extremely well-coordinated attacks of September 11 underscored the gaping hole in the area of human intelligence. Since 1976, the FBI

has officially conducted surveillance of extremist and potentially violent groups under the attorney general's guidelines, which were established after misconduct and abuses arising from the defunct counterintelligence program in the 1960s, in which government intelligence agencies spied on and harassed legal protest groups. According to these guidelines, in order for investigation of a group to commence, evidence of a criminal predicate (i.e., a probable cause of criminal wrongdoing) was required. An investigation could not be opened solely on activities protected by the First Amendment. These guidelines marked a significant departure from traditional policy in that they moved federal law enforcement away from its preventive functions.

The enormity of the September 11 attacks impelled the government to reexamine and recalibrate this policy. As a result, new guidelines allow the FBI to enter public places and forums, including publicly accessible Internet sites, in order to observe and gather information. Furthermore, under the new guidelines, field office directors are allowed to initiate terrorism investigations without approval from headquarters. These new measures caused consternation in some quarters, most notably from civil libertarians who fear that the FBI will resume domestic spying against politically unpopular dissident groups. Such fears were borne out in 2005, when it became public that the government had examined the Internet-based and mobile phone communications of thousands of citizens without first obtaining a warrant from special national security–oriented tribunals established under the Foreign Intelligence Surveillance Act of 1978, a violation of that act.

This revelation indicated that the Department of Justice had shifted away from an emphasis on due process to preventive investigations. Toward this end, in November 2001 Attorney General John Ashcroft instructed federal prosecutors to arrange interviews with approximately 4,800 men between the ages of eighteen and thirty-three who were of Middle Eastern descent. This was a voluntary effort on the part of those interviewed, and its purpose was to cull information that might alert authorities to potential terrorist attacks. The Justice Department was also believed to have detained more than 1,100 people in the first year or so after 9/11 as part of its investigation of terrorism. Many of those detained were held on immigration charges. Fewer than 100 were held on other criminal charges. In addition, as many as two dozen people were detained as material witnesses because they may have had relevant information related to ongoing grand jury investigations. Finally, the FBI also considered loosening its guidelines pertaining to the investigation of extremist groups.

With regard to funding, the government has demonstrated that it is prepared to underwrite the cost of the war on terrorism. Funding to combat terrorism nearly quadrupled, as the $13 billion that was originally budgeted for this effort in fiscal year 2002 was increased to $50 billion.

The war on terrorism presents a new challenge to the United States. Essential to meeting the demands of this challenge is a well-funded agency that has the statutory authority to effectively coordinate the nation's homeland security efforts. Toward this end, on June 6, 2002, President Bush announced in a national address his desire to consolidate several federal agencies—including the Coast Guard, Immigration and Naturalization Service, Customs Service, FEMA, Border Patrol, and the Secret Service among others—into a cabinet-level department, the Department of Homeland Security, to coordinate the efforts to protect the nation against terrorism. This initiative constituted the most ambitious governmental reorganization since the creation of the Department of Defense in 1947.

The Homeland Security act Bush asked for passed Congress on November 19, 2002. Not only did it fold a number of existing agencies, such as FEMA (formerly an independent agency), into the new department, but it also consolidated and reorganized others. For example, the former U.S. Customs Service and Immigration and Naturalization Service, of the Treasury and Justice departments, respectively, were reconstituted as U.S. Immigration and Customs Enforcement, to focus on security issues. The division of the Immigration and Naturalization Service focusing on providing services to new and prospective Americans became U.S. Citizenship and Immigration Services. The relatively new Transportation Security Administration, set up in November 2001 to federalize airline and airport security, was pulled in from the Department of Transportation.

In 2004 came a further a reorganization of the federal government's security operations, though one far less sweeping than that which created the Department of Homeland Security two years earlier. In an effort to better coordinate intelligence gathering and utilization and address the failure of various agencies to provide one another with critical information about the 9/11 terrorists prior to the attacks, the Intelligence Reform and Terrorism Act of 2004 created a new presidential adviser, the director of national intelligence, to oversee and coordinate the activities of some of the federal government's intelligence agencies. But the fact that the law left the powerful National Security Agency outside the new office's bailiwick—and failed to adequately address what powers would be retained by the director of central intelligence—has meant, say critics, that the post of the director of national intelligence remains a very weak one, as well as merely adding another layer of management to an already overly bureaucratized intelligence system.

George Michael and James Ciment

See also: September 11 Attacks—Airport Security; Immigration Policy and Border Defense; National Guard Missions.

Further Reading

Cilluffo, Frank, et al. *Defending America in the 21st Century: New Challenges, New Organizations, and New Policies.* Washington, DC: Center for Strategic and International Studies, 2000.

Davis, James Kirkpatrick. *Spying on America: The FBI's Domestic Counterintelligence Program.* Westport, CT: Praeger, 1992.

Hoge, James F., and Gideon Rose, eds. *How Did This Happen? Terrorism and the New War.* New York: Public Affairs, 2001.

Howard, Russell, James Forest, and Joanne C. Moore. *Homeland Security and Terrorism: Readings and Interpretations.* New York: McGraw-Hill, 2006.

Kettl, Donald F. *System Under Stress: Homeland Security and American Politics.* Washington, DC: CQ Press, 2007.

Noftsinger, John B., Jr., Kenneth F. Newbold, Jr., and Jack K. Wheeler. *Understanding Homeland Security: Policy, Perspectives, and Paradoxes.* New York: Palgrave Macmillan, 2007.

Radvanovsky, Robert, and Allan McDougall. *Critical Infrastructure: Homeland Security and Emergency Preparedness.* Boca Raton, FL: CRC Press/Taylor and Francis Group, 2010.

Talbot, Strobe, and Nayan Chandal, eds. *The Age of Terror: America and the World After September 11.* New York: Basic Books, 2001.

Hunt for al-Qaeda and Terrorist Networks, 2001–Present

In the aftermath of the September 11, 2001, terrorist strikes against the United States, the international hunt for al-Qaeda and its affiliated terrorist networks began in earnest. U.S. forces invaded Afghanistan and defeated and scattered major Taliban and al-Qaeda formations, although the Taliban reasserted itself in many rural regions of the country over the next ten years and al-Qaeda found sanctuary in the poorly governed tribal areas of northwest Pakistan.

During this time, the United States redoubled its hunt for senior and sub-senior commanders and operatives of al-Qaeda Central and related global terrorist affiliates in more than sixty countries worldwide, with a strategic focus on Afghanistan and Pakistan, Yemen, and Southeast Asia. While many al-Qaeda leaders continued to elude captivity, the United States and its allies had numerous successes, culminating in the May 2, 2011 (May 1 in the United States) raid on Abbottabad, Pakistan, which resulted in the death of al-Qaeda's founder and ideological leader, Osama bin Laden.

Status

In the initial attack against al-Qaeda strongholds in Afghanistan, a number of the organization's leaders were

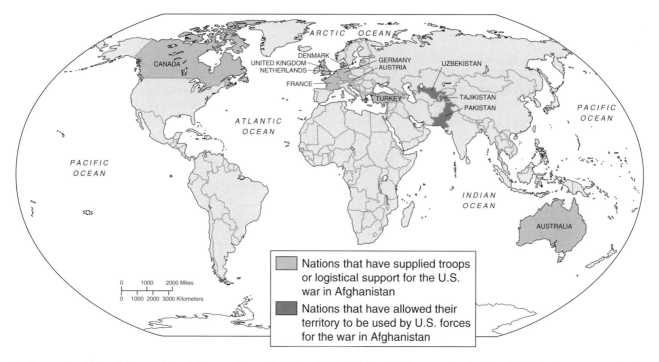

In its war in Afghanistan and hunt for members of al-Qaeda, the United States received extensive help from sympathetic allies. NATO allies in Australia provided logistical support, while strategically located countries in Central and South Asia, including Pakistan, Tajikistan, and Uzbekistan, allowed U.S. forces to operate from their territory.

killed or captured. Among the former were Egyptian Mohammed Atef, the organization's master military planner, while the latter included the Saudi-born Abu Zubaydah, alias for Zayn al-Abidin Muhammad Husayn, al-Qaeda chief terrorism trainer. Over the next several years, more than 500 mid- and low-level al-Qaeda operatives were arrested in the Middle East and Pakistan, 250 in Europe, 150 in Asia, 75 in Eastern Europe and the former Soviet Union, 50 in Latin America, and 50 in sub-Saharan Africa.

U.S. military and intelligence units remained unrelenting in their pursuit of al-Qaeda Central's leadership. In the nine-year period from the spring of 2002 to the spring of 2011, the United States inflicted significant manpower losses on the higher echelons of the organization. Because of U.S. and allied military operations and Predator/Reaper missile strikes, this period yielded the death or capture of 200 or more al-Qaeda Central (and Taliban) senior commanders, senior ideologists, senior trainers, and senior financiers, as well as sub-commanders.

In October 2010, as a direct result of U.S. special forces operations worldwide, Predator and Reaper drone reconnaissance and strike operations in Afghanistan and Pakistan, and related U.S. strategic reconnaissance and attack operations in Iraq, Yemen, and other countries, al-Qaeda, the Taliban, and affiliate militant Islamic organizations suffered serious losses to their senior and

mid-level leadership cohorts, adversely affecting the organizations' ability to launch well-planned and sustained strategic strike operations against the United States and European and other allied nations worldwide.

In going after bin Laden, himself, however, the Barack Obama Administration opted instead for the May 2011 commando raid on his compound in Abbottabad, Pakistan—an action that led to bin Laden's death. This would provide confirmation and hard evidence that, in fact, U.S. forces had killed the organization's founder and ideological leader.

Despite previous losses, al-Qaeda Central retained its ability to recruit and retain high-quality personnel for senior and sub-senior levels of the organization. This, according experts, is a function of its deep appeal among radical and disaffected youth in the Muslim world. Al-Qaeda has also recruited new personnel by capitalizing on the family and tribal ties of current members. For example, it recruited a new global chief of operations, a former Pakistani special forces commander with close ties to Pakistan's intelligence community named Mohammad Ilyas Kashmiri. Among the operations Kashmiri is believed to have helped plan, both prior to and during his tenure with al-Qaeda, are the assassination of former Pakistani prime minister Benazir Bhutto in 2007, the Mumbai attacks of 2008, and the assault on Pakistan's general military headquarters the following year—three of the most spectacular terrorist operations of the latter part of the decade. Moreover, say experts, based on the prior replacement history of high-level personnel by al-Qaeda Central, Kashmiri already has highly capable subordinates ready to replace him should the Central Intelligence Agency or a Reaper missile strike terminate him.

Despite its resiliency, al-Qaeda may find its ability to recruit dampened by the death of Osama bin Laden. Polls among Arab youth find that while al-Qaeda as an organization had lost much of its appeal, bin Laden still remained an iconic figure of resistance to the West and corrupt Arab regimes, especially among those inclined toward Islamist radicalism.

Afghanistan and Pakistan

The international hunt for al-Qaeda Central, the Taliban senior leadership core, and related militant Islamic terrorist franchises, affiliates, and operational personnel has had its territorial focus in Afghanistan and Pakistan, areas with large concentrations of al-Qaeda and Taliban forces who survived the U.S. and allied operations in 2001. During the U.S. special forces–led operations in 2001 and immediately thereafter, al-Qaeda and Taliban terrorist infrastructures were severely disrupted in Afghanistan to the extent that communications between senior leaders and middle-management operatives were impaired, limiting their ability to plan and implement global and regional terrorist operations against the United States and its allies. U.S. special forces then continued the active patrolling of Pakistani and Afghan border areas with the assistance of local Afghan troops. Ironically, of course, the leader of al-Qaeda, bin Laden himself, was killed in an upscale suburb of the Pakistani capital of Islamabad, where it is believed he had been living since the middle of the last decade.

During the early period of the war in Afghanistan, U.S., British, Canadian, and Afghan forces enjoyed some limited military success against entrenched al-Qaeda and Taliban forces at the battle of Shah-i-Kot in mountainous Khost Province, as well as in nearby Paktia Province. However, al-Qaeda and Taliban forces quickly fled across the border into Pakistan's poorly governed Federally Administered Tribal Areas under the cover of night, bypassing the U.S.-supported 600-man force of local Afghans guarding border areas near Khost Province and the 12,000 Pakistan army troops watching a fifty-mile stretch of mountain passes and valleys in the same area.

According to many experts, however, the George W. Bush Administration's decision to invade Iraq to bring about the downfall of the Saddam Hussein regime in March 2003 forced the United States to withdraw military personnel from the hunt and to reduce the material resources required to solve the immense political, economic, and security problems of Afghanistan. The U.S. strategic political, economic, and military withdrawal allowed the Taliban and al-Qaeda to rebuild their political, ideological, and military presence and operations in Afghanistan in preparation for America's return to the country.

In 2009, the new Barack Obama Administration decided that it was in U.S. national security interests that al-Qaeda Central and its erstwhile Taliban and other militant Islamic allies not be allowed to further consolidate and restore their national and regional territorial and ideological control of Afghanistan. As a direct result, the Obama administration decided to renew U.S. commitment to establishing democracy and stability in one of the most war-devastated countries in the international system. After winding down its political and military occupation of Iraq (while maintaining 50,000 troops to assist Iraqi military and security forces in a country-wide training capacity in their security operations until 2011), the United States committed in December 2009 at least 100,000 troops to Afghanistan, to supplement the standing NATO troop formations and other allied forces. The strategic objective of the new administration is to pacify Afghanistan through classical counterinsurgency doctrine and activities, combining civilian economic and infrastructure investment after securing territory through military pacification operations.

However, the U.S. commitment is limited by a specific timetable for troop withdrawals, to begin in July 2011, complicating U.S. pacification planning. Given the standing withdrawal timetable according to U.S. officials, the immediate pacification strategy is to eliminate as many mid-level Taliban commanders throughout Afghanistan as possible, in order to force the Taliban's senior leadership to negotiate a peace treaty before the U.S. troop pullout begins. With the death of bin Laden in May 2011, the pressure for the United States to pull out of Afghanistan grew more intense. Many felt the raid proved that good intelligence and narrowly focused special operations raids were a more effective way to fight al-Qaeda than mass counterinsurgency operations, such as those in Afghanistan.

As recently as late 2010, however, U.S. and NATO leaders were trying a new counter-insurgency strategy, allowing senior commanders of the Taliban and the allied Haqqani network to enter Afghanistan from Pakistan in order to begin negotiations with the Hamid Karzai government. Officials hoped that many of the Pakistan-based commanders could be drawn into the Afghan government, further isolating al-Qaeda's central leadership in Pakistan's tribal regions.

Yemen

In the 1980s, thousands of Yemeni tribal recruits flocked to join al-Qaeda to fight in the holy war against the Russians in Afghanistan. When the holy warriors returned to Yemen as national heroes, many fought in the brutal Yemeni civil war in 1994. At the war's end, some joined the Islamic Army of Aden-Abyan, while others joined the national army and security forces. Osama bin Laden maintained close personal, financial, and religious ties with members of the Islamic Army of Aden-Abyan and with the holy warriors who fought with him in Afghanistan, the ancestral home of Osama bin Laden's family. The well-executed attack on the USS Cole in 2000 demonstrated the major presence of al-Qaeda cells in Yemen, initiating a joint investigation by the Federal Bureau of Investigation (FBI) and the Yemeni domestic security agency. The cooperation of Ali Abdullah Saleh, president of Yemen, in the maritime investigation was mitigated, however, by tribal politics, suspicion of U.S. interests, great poverty, reluctance by the Yemeni security and intelligence services to share al-Qaeda information with the United States, and the deep roots of radical militant Islam in Yemen. The 2002 death of Samir Ahmed Mohammed al-Hada, a Yemeni al-Qaeda operative who blew himself up before he could be captured by Yemeni security forces, was indicative of the dedication of some Yemenis to radical militant Islam and al-Qaeda, as well as their deep hatred of the United States.

Although the government of Yemen has been willing to cooperate over the past eight years with the United States for economic, financial, and military reasons, the tribes of Yemen are not generally inclined to do so and, say experts, probably will not in the future, making it difficult in the long run for the United States to capture al-Qaeda operatives there. The al-Qaeda infrastructure in Yemen has been disrupted, U.S. security officials believe, but it continues to possess the leadership and the resources to severely threaten the Yemeni government.

Despite the growing popular opposition to President Ali Abdullah Saleh in early 2011, the government's crackdown on opponents, and, ultimately Saleh's resignation, the Obama Administration continued to strengthen the U.S. strategic commitment to the country and to the oil-rich region's stability (initiated by the George W. Bush Administration). It also committed to more military-training personnel and economic and security assistance resources toward the rebuilding the political, economic, and military capacity of Yemen. Yemen is especially important to al-Qaeda Central because of its territorial proximity to Saudi Arabia, because of its past and current capacity as a high-quality manpower recruitment pool, and because Yemen's collapse would be a strategic win for al-Qaeda Central.

Singapore and Southeast Asia

The global reach of al-Qaeda in the immediate post-9/11 era was further demonstrated in Singapore when an al-Qaeda sleeper cell of thirteen operatives was found to be planning to blow up the U.S., Australian, British, and Israeli embassies in the city-state in December 2001. The well-trained al-Qaeda unit (of which eight members had received advanced terrorist training in Afghanistan) managed to avoid formal and informal

contacts with members of affiliated Islamic groups and local mosques in Singapore, conceal its existence, and engage in secured military planning there. The United States and allied surveillance of the notorious al-Gamaa al-Islamiyyah, or the Islamic Group, in Singapore began with a post–September 11 tip-off that Muhammad Aslam Yar Ali Khan was an al-Qaeda operative. Khan subsequently fled to Afghanistan, and information was developed on the Singapore bombing plot. It was also determined that a militant Muslim cleric in Indonesia, Abu Bakar Baasyir, provided religious guidance to members of al-Gamaa al-Islamiyyah, which planned the Singapore embassy bombings and had close ties with their brethren in Indonesia, Malaysia, and the Philippines, all cooperating in the recruitment, training, and support of the holy warriors in Afghanistan.

The most prominent Islamic militant groups in Southeast Asia include Jemaah Islamiah (active in Indonesia, Malaysia, the Philippines, and Singapore), Malaysian Mujahideen Group (active in Malaysia and Indonesia), Abu Sayyaf (active in the Philippines), Moro Islamic Liberation Front (the Philippines), and Laskar Jihad (active in Indonesia). These groups use the Internet for propaganda purposes, to recruit, train, and radicalize militants, and to raise funds for their nefarious activities. The October 2002 Bali bombings by Jemaah Islamiah in Indonesia are a primary example of the active nature of the militant Islamic threat in Southeast Asia.

During the period 2002–2011, there was hard evidence that al-Qaeda Central maintained close communications and personal contacts with the leadership of Southeast Asian terror groups, providing logistical support and military policy advice. Al-Qaeda Central also drew financial support from the Southeast Asian region. Moreover, there remains a close strategic relationship between al-Qaeda Central and the senior leadership of Jemaah Islamiah and with other radical militant Islamic organizations that, most experts confirm, will continue productively well into the future.

Europe

The most important regional center for planning, financing, and implementing global al-Qaeda operations is Europe. The majority of global al-Qaeda middle managers, terrorist operatives, and sleeper cells are allegedly hidden within the significant Muslim and Arab populations in Germany, Belgium, Italy, France, Spain, the Netherlands, Britain, and Spain. The planning and financing of al-Qaeda's September 11 strike against the United States occurred in Germany and Spain, with operational assistance from al-Qaeda cells in Britain, Italy, France, and Belgium. The European investigations into al-Qaeda's structure and financial methods have resulted in multiple arrests and judicial hearings for al-Qaeda middle managers and lower-level terrorist operatives in Germany, Spain, Britain, Italy, and France. The co-operation between the United States and the European Community has provided investigators with a broader understanding of the wide-ranging operations of al-Qaeda in Europe, as well as data on the background of the nineteen al-Qaeda personnel who participated in the September 11 strike.

In this context, there has been improved information sharing on the identities of the al-Qaeda middle managers in Europe, who provided the identification papers and financial support for the U.S. strike. The data reveal that the al-Qaeda terrorist infrastructure in Europe has gone underground to regroup, representing a dangerous long-term strategic threat to both the European Community and the United States. Between September 2001 and May 2011, al-Qaeda greatly strengthened its multifaceted presence throughout Europe, and the literature indicates that it has been responsible for the majority of the military terrorist attacks in Europe, including the Madrid train bombings in Spain on March 11, 2004, the Chechen terrorists' killing of 300 people in southern Russia in early September 2004, and the London transit-system bombings that killed 54 British citizens on July 7, 2005. In addition, the assassination of prominent European critics of al-Qaeda and Islam continues. Recent warnings by al-Qaeda Central suggest the imminent use of Mumbai-style strike teams to fire indiscriminately in the central cities of Britain, France, and other European states with the purpose of causing maximum population losses and economic damage, which is consistent with the advanced terror campaigns waged by al-Qaeda and its affiliated terrorist organizations in the past.

Sub-Saharan Africa

Al-Qaeda's strategic interest and operational presence in sub-Saharan Africa has been and remains a historical constant. Sub-Saharan Africa's general geographical proximity to the Middle East and Europe, its strategic importance to the United States, and the large Muslim populations in eastern Africa, western Africa, southern Africa, and the Horn of Africa have also greatly influenced al-Qaeda's strategic calculations. On August 7, 1998, al-Qaeda assault teams struck simultaneously at the U.S. embassies in Nairobi, Kenya, and Dar es Salaam, Tanzania, causing great loss of life and signaling al-Qaeda's military capability of striking at American targets anywhere. Since that time, al-Qaeda has strengthened its operational presence, recruitment, and ideological and training activities in eastern and western as well as northern Africa, sending in senior trainers and senior ideologists and providing significant logistical assistance and financial support to al-Qaeda Central's affiliates and franchises in Somalia, Sudan, Kenya, Nigeria, Niger, and other African states. The increasing activities of al-Qaeda Central's affiliates in Somalia and very recently in Nigeria point to future problems for U.S. interests in sub-Saharan Africa.

United States

In the aftermath of the September 11 attacks, the search for al-Qaeda's senior leaders, middle managers, terrorist operatives, and sleeper cells has been conducted by the U.S. Office of Homeland Security (later Department of Homeland Security) and the U.S. intelligence community, with the FBI as the lead federal domestic investigation agency. The FBI's search for al-Qaeda's middle-management operatives and active terrorist cells has been very difficult. Moreover, the search for al-Qaeda sleeper cells has not been entirely successful, since their members have apparently blended deeply into U.S. society. The arrests of the twentieth al-Qaeda operative linked to the September 11 attacks, Zacarias Moussaoui, and of Richard Reid, the shoe-bomb suspect who sought to blow up a transatlantic flight, do represent domestic successes for U.S. authorities, as, of course, does the killing of Osama bin Laden himself in May 2011. The U.S. Department of Defense has led the way in the location, arrest, and detention of senior and mid-level al-Qaeda and Taliban leaders and operatives caught in Afghanistan and Pakistan, with a majority of these detained at Guantánamo Bay, Cuba. The FBI and the Department of Defense have gathered a treasure trove of information on al-Qaeda, preventing attacks against Americans and American interests.

In the period 2001–2011, the long-standing recruitment activities directed at American citizens by al-Qaeda Central was a major security headache for U.S. domestic intelligence agencies, especially with regard to U.S. citizens with dual citizenship from sub-Saharan African countries and other areas of the world. The United States was fortunate to capture José Padilla, an American al-Qaeda Central operative who sought to use radioactive material to cause great damage in the United States; that thwarted scheme, and the December 2009 apprehension of the Nigerian chemical bomber Umar Farouk Abdulmutallab, who tried to blow up a Northwest Airlines airplane bound from Amsterdam to Detroit, are just two of the most prominent cases of al-Qaeda Central terrorist activities in the United States.

It is clear that U.S. governmental efforts to prevent such attacks in the future hinges on better real-time information about al-Qaeda Central's ever-changing strategic intentions and military capabilities as well as those of its militant Islamic affiliates and franchises. In the area of weapons of mass destruction (or a damaging cyberwarfare attack) and their potential use by al-Qaeda Central against American targets, it is a matter of when and not if, according to some U.S. experts. It is clear that America's timely collection and expert utilization of strategic information capabilities to target and prevent higher-order mass-destruction attacks, as al-Qaeda has promised, will demand the successful operational penetration of al-Qaeda Central.

Michael J. Siler

See also: *Modern Terrorism*—Afghanistan: U.S. Invasion and War; Pakistan: Islamist Struggle; Philippines: Marxist and Islamist Struggles; Yemen: Civil War and Islamist Terrorism. *September 11 Attacks*—Armed Forces Missions; Pursuit and Death of Osama bin Laden; National Guard Missions.

Further Reading

Cigar, Norman. *Al-Qaida's Doctrine for Insurgency: Abd Al-Aziz Al-Muqrin's "A Practical Course for Guerrilla War."* Washington, DC: Potomac Books, 2009.

Gunaratna, Rohan. *Inside al-Qaeda: Global Network of Terror.* New York: Berkley, 2003.

Hoffman, Bruce. *Combating Al Qaeda and the Militant Islamic Threat.* Santa Monica, CA: Rand, 2006.

———. *Islam and the West: Searching for Common Ground, the Terrorist Threat and the Counter-Terrorism Effort.* Santa Monica, CA: Rand, 2006.

Jenkins, Brian Michael. *Building an Army of Believers: Jihadist Radicalization and Recruitment.* Santa Monica, CA: Rand, 2007.

———. *Terrorists Can Think Strategically: Lessons Learned from the Mumbai Attacks.* Santa Monica, CA: Rand, 2009.

Johnston, Alastair. "Thinking About Strategic Culture." *International Security* (Spring 1995): 33–64.

Long, Jerry Mark. *Strategic Culture, Al-Qaida, and Weapons of Mass Destruction.* McLean, VA: SAIC, 2006.

Pursuit and Death of Osama bin Laden, 1998–2011

In the early morning hours of May 2, 2011 (May 1 in the United States), a team of U.S. special forces launched a raid on a residential compound in Abbottabad, Pakistan, and killed Osama bin Laden, founder and leader of the al-Qaeda terrorist network. The operation ended a nearly decade-long effort to bring to justice the mastermind of the September 11, 2001, terrorist attacks on New York and Washington, D.C. While bin Laden's death was celebrated by millions of Americans and was said to bring a sense of closure to the families and friends of 9/11 victims, it also raised new questions about the ongoing U.S. war on terrorism.

Background

U.S. efforts to capture or kill bin Laden actually predated 9/11 by several years. In the wake of al-Qaeda attacks on the U.S. embassies in Kenya and Tanzania in 1998 and the USS Cole in Yemen in 2000, President Bill Clinton ordered cruise missile attacks on terrorist training camps in Taliban-controlled Afghanistan, where bin Laden had been living since being ejected from Sudan in 1996. After the 9/11 attacks, President George W. Bush launched an invasion of Afghanistan, both to overthrow

the Taliban government and to destroy al-Qaeda. The rapid toppling of the regime in Kabul forced bin Laden and other al-Qaeda leaders to flee to the mountainous region near the Pakistan border, pursued by U.S. special forces. But bin Laden eluded them. Many critics argued that the Bush Administration, increasingly distracted by the buildup to war in Iraq, had not put the necessary resources into the hunt, relying on its Afghan allies, the anti-Taliban Northern Alliance forces, to do the job.

For the next several years, U.S. military efforts in the war on terrorism shifted away from the pursuit of bin Laden, who was believed to be hiding in caves in the tribal areas of Pakistan. There, it was said, he enjoyed the protection of the Pashtun peoples, many of whom continued to support the Taliban resistance in Afghanistan and Pakistan. Periodically, bin Laden would release audio and videotapes to the media, calling on his supporters to continue their jihad against the West.

Intelligence Breakthroughs

Still, progress in the pursuit of bin Laden was being made on the intelligence front, thousands of miles from the Afghanistan-Pakistan border in the various terrorist detention centers run by the United States and its allies in the war on terror. According to U.S. officials, an al-Qaeda suspect—a Pakistani national named Hassan Ghul, captured by Kurdish forces in Iraq and held at a secret CIA facility in Poland in 2004—divulged information about Abu Ahmed Kuwaiti, the nom de guerre of a top bin Laden courier. The information would prove crucial. To avoid detection, bin Laden and other top al-Qaeda leaders had ceased using electronic communications, maintaining connections to their supporters and the outside world through human messengers.

Using that information and pieces of evidence gleaned from other detainees, the CIA by 2007 was able to establish the real identity of Kuwaiti, a protégé of 9/11 mastermind Khalid Sheikh Mohammed. Over the next two years, agents came to learn that Kuwaiti and his brother, another trusted al-Qaeda operative, were active in Pakistan. By August 2010, the CIA had tracked the courier to a large residential compound in the city of Abbottabad, about 40 miles north of the capital of Islamabad. For the next eight months, the CIA closely monitored the compound, verifying that it was the hideout of bin Laden and his family, studying the layout, and tracking the routines of its inhabitants. How long bin Laden was living there is open to conjecture, though most experts say he probably moved in in 2006, after the hideout was modified with new security features, including barbwire-topped walls reaching 18 feet.

With bin Laden's location confirmed, the question became how to get him. President Barack Obama dismissed the idea of an aerial attack by Predator drone or a bombing raid, concluding that it was important for the United

After more than a decade of searching, U.S. intelligence finally found al-Qaeda leader Osama bin Laden at a walled compound in Abbottabad, Pakistan. On May 2, 2011, U.S. special operations forces raided the compound and killed bin Laden. *(Aamir Qureshi/AFP/ Getty Images)*

States to prove to al-Qaeda supporters that it had captured or killed bin Laden. Such proof, advisers felt, could only come by obtaining his body and then using DNA tests and facial measurements to corroborate his identity.

Raid in Abbottabad

By late April 2011, President Obama had made the decision to send in a team of approximately two dozen special-forces commandos—most of them members of the Navy Sea, Air, and Land's (SEALs) elite Team 6. Aboard twin Blackhawk helicopters, specially modified for stealth, the team flew from a base in Afghanistan to Abbottabad, located about 110 air miles from the border. Almost immediately upon arrival, one of the helicopters lost control and went down, an event that led some in the White House Situation Room, who were following the raid in real time, to fear for the mission's success. (Team 6 members partially blew up the helicopter to prevent its top-secret technology from falling into Pakistani hands.)

The fears proved unfounded. The team quickly located bin Laden on the third floor of the compound and killed him with a shot to the head, along with several others. One of bin Laden's wives was shot in the leg, though government officials later dismissed initial reports that she had served as a "human shield" for him. After 40 minutes on the ground, the team left on the single Blackhawk helicopter that was still operational, along with bin Laden's body and a treasure trove of paper and

electronic records. Experts believed that these materials would help intelligence officials in their pursuit of other al-Qaeda targets.

Upon the arrival of the helicopter back in Afghanistan, U.S. officials took DNA and facial measurements that, according to the White House, proved that the body was that of bin Laden. Because Islamic custom dictates that a peson must be buried within 24 hours of death, the body was then transported to a U.S. aircraft carrier, prepared according to Islamic ritual, and buried in the north Arabian Sea. The burial at sea was intended to prevent a gravesite becoming a shrine for bin Laden supporters.

News of bin Laden's death—conveyed to the American people by Obama in an unusual late-Sunday-night media address—produced spontaneous celebrations in front of the White House and at Ground Zero, the former site of the World Trade Center in New York City. Supportive messages poured in from leaders around the globe, with the near unanimous verdict that the world was "a better place because of the death of Osama bin Laden."

Questions and Implications

Questions about the raid and the larger U.S. war on terrorism were raised almost immediately. Some wondered why Team 6 had made no serious effort to capture rather than kill bin Laden; the commandos had been ordered to kill him only if he posed a risk to his captors—specifically, they were to make sure that he did not have an explosive device hidden on his person. Others questioned

In the White House Situation Room, President Barack Obama (second from left) and his national security team watch the 40-minute U.S. assault on Osama bin Laden's compound in Pakistan in a real-time video feed. *(MCT/Getty Images)*

Obama's decision not to release the death photos of bin Laden, which would have quelled all doubts tht he had been killed. "We don't trot this stuff out as trophies," the president explained in a television interview broadcast days later. Moreover, he said, releasing such images would have provided propaganda tools to al-Qaeda and its supporters.

Another issue was the manner in which the intelligence that led to bin Laden's capture had been obtained. Some wondered whether controversial interrogation methods, such as water boarding, had helped in extracting key information from detainees. CIA officials denied accusations of torture but did admit that other enhanced-interrogation methods, such as sleep deprivation, nudity, and food restrictions were used. Then there was the matter of Pakistan, America's troubled ally in the war on terrorism, which Washington kept in the dark about the Abbottabad raid until the special operations team was out of Pakistani air space. To many in media and policymaking circles, as well as the public at large, it stretched credulity that Pakistani military and intelligence officials did not know of bin Laden's whereabouts, given that he had been living for years in an upscale bedroom community favored by retired military men and home to the country's leading military academy. This question only added to lingering doubts in Washington about Pakistan's commitment—and the commitment of its intelligence services—to the U.S.-led struggle against al-Qaeda and Islamist terrorism.

The biggest question of all, of course, was the meaning of bin Laden's death for the future. Virtually all experts agreed that it did not mean an end to the al-Qaeda threat;

indeed, it was believed to heighten the risk of terrorist attack in the near term, whether in retaliation or as a reaffirmation of resolve. Within days of the Abbottabad raid, a statement released by al-Qaeda's "General Command" confirmed bin Laden's death and declared that the terrorist group would "continue on the path of jihad."

For the longer term, there was much debate regarding the implications of bin Laden's demise for the ongoing U.S. war on terrorism. Should America shift its priorities from counter-insurgency to counterterrorism? In other words, did the Team 6 raid prove that good intelligence and small, special operations attacks on specific terrorist targets are a more effective—not to mention less expensive—way to fight al-Qaeda and its affiliates than the large and costly Afghanistan counter-insurgency effort? For the time being, the Obama Administration's answer was no. But the argument that the death of bin Laden provided an ideal justification for winding down America's Afghanistan military commitment sooner rather than later was likely to gain cogency among an American public increasingly disenchanted with the war.

James Ciment

See also: *September 11 Attacks*—Al-Qaeda; Bin Laden, Osama; Torture; Hunt for al-Qaeda and Terrorist Networks. *Counterterrorism*—Special Operations.

Further Reading

"After Osama bin Laden: They Got Him: What the Death of the Movement's Figurehead Means for al-Qaeda, Pakistan, Afghanistan—and the West." *The Economist*, May 5, 2011.

Booth, Robert, Saeed Shah, and Jason Burke. "Osama bin Laden Death: How Family Scene in Compound Turned to Carnage." *Guardian* (United Kingdom), May 5, 2011.

Dilanian, Ken. "Trail to Bin Laden Began with CIA Detainee, Officials Say." *Los Angeles Times*, May 5, 2011.

Mazzetti, Mark, Helene Cooper, and Peter Barker. "The Death of Osama bin Laden: Behind the Hunt for Bin Laden." *New York Times*, May 2, 2011.

Immigration Policy and Border Defense

Nondomestic terrorism can afflict the United States in one of two ways: either through actions committed by foreigners living within the territory of the United States—such as the September 11, 2001, terrorist attackers—or through attacks by terrorists attempting to enter, or send weapons or explosives into, the United States, as was the case with the so-called Christmas Day bomber of 2009, a Nigerian national who attempted to blow up a U.S.-bound jet from Amsterdam, or the attempted UPS bombings of 2010, in which explosives were placed aboard U.S.-bound flights originating in Yemen. Because these threats come from abroad or from noncitizens living in the United States, combating them usually means addressing the issues of immigration, customs, and border security policy.

The threat from foreign terrorists is nothing new in U.S. history. In the early decades of the United States, foreign-born anarchists were involved in a number of terrorist activities, including bombings and assassinations. In 1919, at the height of America's first so-called Red Scare, 249 noncitizens were deported, many of them simply for their radical views but some because of alleged involvement in terrorist activities.

With the arrival of radical Islamist terrorism on American shores in the 1990s came concerns about the laxity of immigration law and the inability of the U.S. government to prevent terrorists from getting into the country—legally on tourist or student visas or illegally with falsified documents—and then remaining here illegally long after their visas had expired. For instance, Omar Abdel Rahman, the so-called blind sheikh from Egypt and inspirational leader for the 1993 World Trade Center bombers, came to the United States on a tourist visa, despite being on a State Department terrorism watch list, and then stayed illegally. Kuwaiti-born Pakistani national Ramzi Yousef, the mastermind of the attack, got into the United States with a falsified Iraqi passport and then asked for asylum as a political refugee from Saddam Hussein's regime.

In December 1999, customs inspectors at Port Angeles, Washington, discovered explosives inside the car of an Algerian national living in Canada named Ahmed Ressam, who was planning on setting them off at Los Angeles International Airport in the so-called millennium bomb plot. Then came the terrorist attacks of September 11, 2001, in the aftermath of which it was learned that all nineteen hijackers were all foreign nationals (fifteen of whom came from Saudi Arabia) who had entered the United States legally, mostly with tourist visas. The organizers and "pilots" for the attacks had mostly entered well before the attacks and overstayed their visas, whereas those being utilized as muscle, to prevent crew members or passengers from interfering with the hijackings, came in shortly before the attacks.

Since September 11, there have been other attempted attacks against airliners perpetrated by foreign terrorists entering or trying to enter the United States with tourist visas or because they have come from countries, such as the United Kingdom, from which the United States does not require visas. These include the so-called shoe bomber, Richard Reid, a British-born Muslim convert of Jamaican descent, who tried to blow up a Paris-to-Miami flight in December 2001, and Nigerian national Umar Farouk Abdulmutallab, who tried to blow up an Amsterdam-to-Detroit flight on Christmas Day 2009 while traveling to the United States on a multiple-entry visa. While various U.S. intelligence agencies were aware that Abdulmutallab was a potential threat—having been notified as such by the young man's banker father—he was not on the no-fly list maintained by the U.S. government.

In response to the 1993 World Trade Center bombing and the September 11 terrorist attacks, Congress passed legislation and the various agencies of the federal government enacted policies and undertook measures to prevent potential or suspected terrorists from entering the country and to force them to leave once they are in the United States. Title 4 of the 1996 Anti-Terrorism and Effective Death Penalty Act included mechanisms to bar aliens on government terrorism lists from entering the country and to remove those that are already in the United States. In addition, it narrowed the asylum provisions, which allowed suspected terrorists to remain in the country as prospective political refugees. The USA PATRIOT Act, passed in the immediate wake of September 11, broadened law enforcement agencies' power to detain immigrants suspected of involvement in terrorism activities and gave immigration authorities enhanced powers to deport them. Similar provisions were included in immigration-oriented pieces of legislation, including the Border Protection, Anti-Terrorism and Illegal Immigration Control Act of 2005 and the REAL ID Act of the same year. While both of these acts increased the government's capacity to deport those suspected of terrorist activities, they largely focused—at least in their antiterrorism provisions—on detecting the false or elapsed documentation suspected terrorists use to get into and stay in the country. While few criticized such efforts to ferret out potential terrorists, many critics of these acts questioned the political motivations of their sponsors, who utilized fears of terrorists entering the country to call for tougher sanctions against illegal aliens and the construction of a fence along the border with Mexico. As these critics noted, no suspected terrorist had ever entered the United States from Mexico, whereas the vast majority had come to the United States with perfectly legal visas.

Yet another immigration-related antiterrorism measure taken by the government was the reorganization of the immigration and customs services under the Homeland Security Act of 2002. Under that landmark piece of legislation, the U.S. Customs Service and the enforcement components of the Immigration and Naturalization Service were folded into a single agency, U.S. Immigration and Customs Enforcement, and placed under the Department of Homeland Security. (The naturalization component of the old Immigration and Naturalization Service was put into a separate U.S. Citizenship and Immigration Services agency.) At the same time, the U.S. Customs and Border Protection, with its mandate to defend the nation's land borders, was also placed under the Department of Homeland Security. This reorganization was effected, in part, to heighten and coordinate the antiterrorist component of immigration regulation, customs activities, and border enforcement.

Steven Camarota and James Ciment

See also: *September 11 Attacks*—Political, Legal, and Social Issues; Civil Liberties, Civil Rights, and National Security; Airport Security; Homeland Defense: Organization and Policy.

Further Reading

Alden, Edward. *The Closing of the American Border: Terrorism, Immigration, and Security Since 9/11.* New York: Harper, 2008.

d'Appollonia, Ariane Chebel, and Simon Reich, eds. *Immigration, Integration, and Security: America and Europe in Comparative Perspective.* Pittsburgh, PA: University of Pittsburgh Press, 2008.

Winterdyk, John A., and Kelly W. Sundberg, eds. *Border Security in the Al-Qaeda Era.* Boca Raton, FL: CRC Press, 2010.

Intelligence Community: Pre-9/11 Failures and Successes

Like the Japanese attack on Pearl Harbor in 1941, the September 11, 2001, terrorist attacks against the United States spurred many questions in the media, among the political establishment, and in the public at large. Primary among them was how such an assault could have occurred on the territory of the United States—that is to say, why and in what ways did the country's intelligence establishment fail to recognize the threat. In the months that followed the attacks, there was a growing crescendo of opinion that a definitive investigation was needed.

After some initial reluctance, President George W. Bush established, in late 2002, a commission—consisting of five prominent Republicans and five prominent Democrats and co-chaired by Lee Hamilton, a former Democratic Indiana congressman with extensive experience in foreign policy matters, and Thomas Kean, a highly respected former Republican governor of New Jersey—to conduct such an investigation. The National Commission on Terrorist Attacks upon the United States, better known as the 9/11 Commission, examined all aspects of U.S. counterterrorism policy—from diplomacy to military action—but its best-known findings concerned the U.S. intelligence establishment and its operations, including data collection, information processing, intelligence analysis, intelligence dissemination, and management of the total intelligence effort. Overall, it sought to unearth the failures and successes of America's "early-warning system" regarding terrorist actions.

In July 2004, the commission released its report to the public. The report identified a number of problems, as well as some successes, in America's intelligence efforts at combating Islamist terrorism generally and al-Qaeda in particular.

As the study indicated, the attacks were "a shock, but they should not have come as a surprise." As a string of attacks against American targets at home and abroad—beginning with the first bombing of the World Trade Center in 1993 and running through the suicide attack on the USS *Cole* in Aden harbor, Yemen, in 2000—indicated, Islamist terrorists were intent on inflicting as much damage and as many casualties as they possibly could. Moreover, the report noted that the intelligence community had its successes in thwarting other attacks, most notably a plot by Ramzi Yousef, one of the perpetrators of the 1993 World Trade Center bombing, to blow up a dozen U.S. airliners over the Pacific. Thus, American officials were aware of both the threat and the ambitions of Islamist terrorists prior to 9/11.

This became especially evident after the simultaneous bombings of the U.S. embassies in Kenya and Tanzania in 1998, an operation that demonstrated the capability of Islamist extremists to mount a devastating and sophisticated operation over a great geographic area. Moreover, the bombings revealed the al-Qaeda organization, which carried out the attacks, as the leading terrorist threat facing the United States. In the wake of the East Africa bombings, Osama bin Laden, the head of al-Qaeda, began putting into operation a plan brought to him by operative Khalid Sheikh Mohammed to conduct an attack using up to ten airliners against U.S. targets. The specifics of such an attack were not known to U.S. intelligence prior

The independent commission appointed to investigate the events of 9/11 and America's readiness issued its final report in July 2004. The commission called for structural changes and closer cooperation in the federal intelligence and law enforcement communities. *(Associated Press)*

to 9/11, but the community was aware, at least by the spring and summer of 2001, that al-Qaeda planned to execute a major terrorist assault on U.S. soil. This was conveyed to Bush in a now famous presidential daily brief from August 2001, headlined "Bin Laden Determined to Strike in US."

According to the 9/11 Commission report, many within the intelligence community had uncovered several relevant facts about al-Qaeda and the threat it posed to the United States. But the report's authors also found that there was a general failure to put all of the information together. For example, there had been no National Intelligence Estimate on terrorism since the mid-1990s. Still, the Central Intelligence Agency had scored some significant successes in disrupting al-Qaeda operations prior to 9/11, including the arrests of several operatives. In addition, there were many operations ongoing at the

time of the attack to capture or kill bin Laden and his top lieutenants. The report said, though, that the CIA had lacked the capacity to conduct the kinds of paramilitary operations necessary to destroy al-Qaeda operations in countries that offered the terrorist organization safe haven, such as Afghanistan.

The report cited a number of reasons to explain such failures of intelligence and counterterrorist operations, including a lack of funding, an organizational structure that made it difficult for information to flow up the chain of command, and bureaucratic rivalries that hampered the sharing of information among various branches of the American domestic and international security establishment. Such deficiencies made it particularly hard to deal with the most significant security threat of the late twentieth and early twenty-first centuries—the rise and growth of transnational terrorist organizations like al-Qaeda.

Moreover, the intelligence community in particular and the U.S. security establishment in general experienced major failures in management, most notably, in the government's inability to make sure that information and intelligence were shared among various agencies and that duties were assigned efficiently across agencies—from the CIA to the FBI to the State Department to the Pentagon and to other domestic security agencies, such as the Border Patrol and Customs.

In the final analysis, the commission members said, "the most important failure was one of imagination." Policy makers in general did not fully appreciate the kind of radical new threat al-Qaeda and transnational terrorism represented. Thus, they failed to restructure America's intelligence and security apparatus to deal with it in an effective way.

James Ciment

See also: *September 11 Attacks*—Civil Liberties, Civil Rights, and National Security; Government Spying and Privacy Issues; Intelligence Community: Response to 9/11. *Counterterrorism*—Intelligence, Counterterrorist.

Further Reading

Clarke, Richard. *Against All Enemies: Inside America's War on Terror.* New York: Free Press, 2004.

Kean, Thomas H., and Lee Hamilton, with Benjamin Rhodes. *Without Precedent: The Inside Story of the 9/11 Commission.* New York: Vintage, 2007.

National Commission on Terrorist Attacks Upon the United States, 2004. www.9-11commission.gov.

Intelligence Community: Response to 9/11

In the context of the intelligence failures associated with 9/11 and the assessment of Iraq's current capabilities with weapons of mass destruction, both federal legislation and responsible executive departments initiated major investigations of causes and resolutions. Some of the changes that resulted appear to have been generated mostly as a political response to post-9/11 public pressure and may therefore have less than permanent status. However, other initiatives appear to have some staying power. The creation of the Office of the Director of National Intelligence (ODNI), which was a revision of authority at the top, was transformative, of course, although the practical and political implications are still unfolding. This change altered the structure and administration of the intelligence community, including the CIA, the multifunctional intelligence agencies operating under the aegis of the Department of Defense (DOD), and the other intelligence agencies of the federal government. Although this reorganization was supposed to consolidate the many administrative mechanisms of the intelligence community into one centralizing and efficient unit, it appears—at this early juncture—to have increased bureaucracy as much as or more than efficiency. Indeed, it is not yet clear what the exact role of the ODNI is in given contexts and whether it has more than nominal authority over the budgets of the various, more lavishly funded intelligence agencies of the DOD.

Another institutional change, the creation of the Office of Homeland Security, was initially intended to consolidate virtually all federal, domestic-based counterterrorist activities into one coordinating body. Indeed, most of the federal counterterrorist activities not assigned to the FBI are theoretically coordinated here—with some exceptions. However, the agency functions at this juncture more as an analytical center and a coordinating body—with relatively few operational responsibilities.

The passage of the Patriot Act established new guidelines for the investigation of presumed criminal activity as well as for the collection of intelligence information functions under the legal doctrine of "search and seizure" under the Fourth Amendment to the Constitution. The effect of this legislation, a significant revision of the Foreign Intelligence and Surveillance Act of 1978, was to allow law enforcement and intelligence agents relatively quick and convenient access to private information—without prior court authorization and specific and timely documentation on affected persons or locations. The Fourth Amendment to the Constitution establishes the constitutional parameters for the search and seizure of private property by legal authorities in the commission of their official duties. However, both the Foreign Intelligence and Surveillance Act of 1978 and the more recent Patriot Act are intended to allow court-initiated latitude when authorities can justify a temporary suspension of constitutional guarantees for the sake of collecting timely evidence of suspected criminal acts. The Patriot Act has come under intense scrutiny for stretching this latitude to include roving wiretaps and post hoc court authorizations on the basis of stipulated intelligence requirements against potential terrorist threats.

FBI and CIA

The FBI responded to 9/11 with a heightened interest in the area of counterterrorism, a willingness to move aggressively into the arena of intelligence—as opposed to criminal investigation—and a desperate desire to stave off any inclination by the government for the creation of a new agency focused on counterintelligence. Consequently, the FBI hired an abundance of new—mostly inexperienced—intelligence analysts and created in September 2006 the National Security Division, currently staffed at about 320 employees. In addition to the FBI, the Department of Justice has augmented its staff, both at headquarters and regionally, to include dedicated antiterrorist capabilities.

In spite of a major reorganization of the total effort against terrorism, the CIA remains a key player. However, it also lost several key responsibilities: It is no longer responsible for the president's daily brief, the key foreign news digest for the president. In addition, the CIA lost its nominal role as head of the intelligence community, now a function of the ODNI. On the other hand, the CIA's dominant role as the head of foreign-based human intelligence has been reemphasized under the ODNI—after a relative diminishment of its traditional monopoly in this arena in favor of DOD-based human intelligence efforts under the George W. Bush Administration. The CIA has also benefited, de facto, from the so-far relatively successful struggle of the ODNI against the traditional dominance of the DOD in defining intelligence budgets. Ironically, the CIA's loss of titular status as head of the intelligence community (and the budget) has resulted in real gains against the traditional dominance of the DOD over the whole intelligence community. The CIA has also made some major inroads as the most responsive organization for emerging counterterrorism crises, beginning with very successful and timely agency efforts to lead the attack in the early stages of the War in Afghanistan in 2001 and continuing with the success of the Predator program against remote targets in western Pakistan.

The National Counterterrorism Center (NCTC), a multiagency fusion center operating under the aegis of the ODNI, is intended to ensure that all vital information is duly shared among and disseminated to decision makers in a timely and effective fashion. This organization was initially established by Executive Order 13354 under the CIA as the Terrorist Threat Integration Center. It was subsequently codified and renamed to reflect a strong congressional mandate for a fully integrated, government-wide effort against the terrorist threat as described in the Intelligence Reform and Terrorism Prevention Act of 2004.

The director of the NCTC serves as the counterterrorism mission manager for the intelligence community under the direction of the ODNI and provides guidance in identifying critical intelligence issues, knowledge gaps, and resource problems. The NCTC also creates and develops strategic counterterrorist plans designed to establish priorities and performance objectives.

The NCTC is currently staffed by upward of 500 personnel representing more than sixteen agencies. It is primarily responsible for several key activities:

- The president's daily brief, which provides the president with the latest summaries of topical intelligence developments
- The National Terrorism Bulletin, an issue-focused summary for general dissemination throughout the intelligence community
- The Terrorist Identities Datamart Environment, an authoritative repository of information on the identities of international terrorists
- Situational Awareness, a fully manned and dedicated information center for 24/7 incident reporting and tracking
- Coordination of collaboration among members of the Homeland Threat Task Force, informing key policy makers on terrorism threat issues on a weekly basis
- Multiagency pursuit units, which have been developed to focus on four regional sleeper threats

Recent terrorist events—in particular, an attempted plane bombing by a Detroit-bound Nigerian student in December 2009—have raised the issue of the NCTC's cost-effectiveness. As a result of this event, the NCTC was tasked to create a process for thoroughly and exhaustively prioritizing terrorist threats, identifying follow-up activities by responsible agencies, and enhancing the database of identified threat personalities. The recently upgraded Terrorist Identities Datamart Environment system is more streamlined, relatively automatic, timely, and user-friendly.

Other terrorism-focused "fusion" centers and joint programs have been established throughout the intelligence community at the federal, state, and local levels—all with the same goal of effective collaboration.

Back to Basics

The thrust of the intelligence reform criticism that emerged from 9/11 was eventually transformed into law and administrative actions according to several basic policy orientations and values. On a more fundamental level, some of these changes addressed underlying cultural issues. Following is a review of the major themes.

For a number of reasons, one of the consistent intelligence reform themes is that the United States needs more of the basic elements: more collection (spies), more special forces–oriented operations, more analysts, and more political priority and public awareness. The presumed problem is a lack of dedicated resources and mission focus. Another rationale is that more organizations might encourage the prospect that at least one of them will get it right when it counts by not ignoring a warning indicator or succumbing to the seductions of groupthink or stultifying cultural paradigms, such as the insidious assumption that an attack can't happen in the United States. Thus, the FBI added more analysts to its underresourced terrorist section and the Justice Department built up its own analytical capability by hiring cadres and fostering analytical units around the country. In addition, a whole new, cabinet-level Department of Homeland Security was added with a largely analytical and counterterrorism coordination mission.

Contractor-Based Intelligence

An offshoot of the push for more intelligence resources is the recent and large-scale use of contractors—in place of traditional, government-based professionals. Contractors now serve throughout the intelligence community as analysts, technicians, and even intelligence collectors. According to one recent study, government outsourcing of intelligence activities to private contractors is a $50 billion-per-year business. Reportedly, it now consumes up to 70 percent of the intelligence budget. This development resulted from the relatively sudden abundance of new funding opportunities in the wake of 9/11, the previous retirement of many experienced senior intelligence professionals after the Cold War in the 1990s, and the resurgent status of experienced human intelligence professionals as a result of new kinds of threats, such as international terrorism, insurgencies in remote and unfamiliar social systems, and the advent of dangerous new technologies (i.e., weapons of mass destruction) in third world countries. In addition, terrorism has reawakened an interest in several issues, such as cultural approaches to social science and foreign area studies. Unfortunately, these kinds of intellectual interests and skill sets have not generally been sustained or recruited for by the intelligence community for decades, and the necessary understanding and skills were consequently to be found mainly in the private sector and academia.

Because much of what the intelligence community does involves technological development for application against a wide range of threats, heavy emphasis is placed on contractors with expertise in information technology and high-level clearances. In addition, after 9/11, many of the existing information technology–focused companies, from tiny "Beltway bandits" to giant aerospace corporations, used their personal contacts and corporate networks with the intelligence community to develop new opportunities—in spite of the obvious gap between terrorist threat issues and computer software expertise. One point of commonality was the critical need after 9/11 for analysts with technical (i.e., information technology) familiarity who could apply those practical skills to the burgeoning needs for current intelligence. Many information technology types were hired as intelligence analysts by large aerospace / information technology companies, such as CACI, BAE Systems, SAIC, and Booz Allen Hamilton, to fill the need, and several former CIA-based senior managers were hired by the corporate giants to attract agency contracts and recruit new employees. In an effort to stay on top of the need for technological innovation, the CIA created one enterprise, In-Q-Tel, as a technology-incubation center that invests in promising new areas of research.

Localism: State and Local Intelligence Functions

Many state agencies have established intelligence warning centers that employ professional analysts for threat awareness tracking and data fusion. Although many of these centers appear to provide legitimate warning functions, it is not yet clear how they will perform over the long run or even in more routine crisis situations. A crucial question is whether they will simply provide the counterterrorism effort with more bureaucracies for stovepiping information—hoarding it until organizational interests, such as bureaucratic survival and personal and program agendas, become clear—in live-action settings or political budget debates.

Another theme was that the local police should be more involved as the first line of defense against the insidious nature of the terrorist threat. Local community organizations incorporated new police responsibilities and capabilities for collecting and disseminating intelligence on potential threats. Much of this new involvement probably developed both from the media's dramatic indulgence in the imagery of 9/11 and from genuine patriotism. However, it was also probably partly motivated by a willingness of the federal government to spend vast sums of money on counterterrorism programs, without serious reference to a realistic analysis of needs (i.e., risk of an attack).

Grassroots Intelligence

A positive outcome of 9/11 was to encourage popular involvement on a mass level: the man on the street as well as the local police, fire, and emergency worker. The premise is that more citizen awareness and local cooperation—the eyes and ears of the private citizen—bring more tools to bear on a common problem. The local-ist theme also incorporated the idea that every citizen is a potential security asset—as well as a potential victim. Thus, in this conception, Richard Reid, popularly known as the shoe bomber terrorist, was identified in the act of attempting to set off a bomb on an airplane on December 22, 2001, by a flight attendant, precisely because she was acutely aware of the aerial threat in that early, post-9/11 timeframe. Indeed, private citizens played key roles in averting numerous incidents prior to September 11, 2001, most notably when a part-time U.S. Customs inspector detained Ahmed Ressam, the convicted would-be perpetrator of the Los Angeles International Airport bombings in December 1999. Moreover, several of the nineteen perpetrators of 9/11 were encountered by the police—at least two for traffic issues—and it is at least conceivable that these local contacts could have resulted in timely arrests had the police been aware of all of the possible and relevant intelligence that could have been available from comprehensive intelligence dissemination had it occurred in a timely and efficient manner.

Culturalism

An offshoot of the localism theme is an emphasis on culture, particularly with respect to international terrorism, where the threat is quite obviously related to foreign ideas, values, and beliefs. In the context of intelligence, this implies investing more in university- and defense-based foreign-area and language programs and enhancing internal training programs for new and better-educated recruits. Unfortunately, much of this training is less useful than commonly understood, because language training cannot generally transcend the limitations of ethnic or region-specific dialogue. Also, military-style quick-and-dirty training in foreign-area programs is adequate for cultural understanding but not for mastery of a complex topic. On the other hand, virtually all of the intelligence agencies were forced by 9/11 to acknowledge the need for more language capabilities, not least by finding people who were native born or first-generation immigrant speakers of the highest-priority languages.

Intellectual Training and Academic Intelligence

Most of the immediate response to 9/11 was intended to shore up capabilities against impending threats, traditionally the domain of "current intelligence." However, the intelligence business also requires a more strategic focus. In the 9/11 context, it is about not only where adversaries will strike, but why young men are attracted to terrorist groups—a strategic issue, particularly when viewed from the perspective of development over time. In this context, academia has made some attempts to enhance and deepen understanding of relevant global and regional issues. In addition, some programs have been designed to emphasize certain disciplinary concepts of specific relevance to terrorism, such as the application of anthropology-based concepts with extremist ideologies and terrorism. In addition, some of the traditional academic programs in social science have expanded their offerings, not without controversy, to include these issues in their curricula. Also, in the context of pre-9/11 intelligence failures, many new programs are being offered at major universities on terrorism, intelligence studies, and related subdisciplines, such as homeland security and counterinsurgency.

Information Sharing and Collaboration

The 9/11 Commission recognized that responsible federal agencies did not share relevant counterterrorism information in a timely and integrated fashion. Traditionally, intelligence personnel have tended to report information mainly, if not strictly, to their authority chains: a pattern known as "stovepiping." The effect is to restrict vital information within narrow channels; information is confined largely to insiders, and access for outsiders is discouraged. Although stovepiping has been recognized for some time as problematic (and is officially out of favor), in contrast to fusing information between and within agencies, it is a deep-seated habit.

The move toward centralized fusion organs emphasizes the value of sharing: people of diverse backgrounds and enhanced communication skills can generate good ideas—better conceived, more creative—and do it more quickly. Fusion centers are intended to enhance communication among disparate groups with the use of close working quarters, by eliminating physical barriers and by using a variety of technologies to enhance cognitive awareness (e.g., using large flat screens with zoom capabilities and an array of communications media linked to collectors, analysts, and coordinators). Although the verdict is still out on their total effectiveness, such centers certainly appear to enhance the situational awareness required for current intelligence-based responses to threats.

Unfortunately, the relative status of many intelligence fusion centers is not clear: some are high priority and career enhancing; others are more aptly described as analytic "backwaters"—but this characterization is probably now obsolete. At least since 9/11, analysts are no longer considered out of the mainstream of activity. Examples of fusion centers are the NCTC, the CIA's Counterterrorism Center, the Justice Department-administered Joint Terrorism Task Force, and the now defunct Iraq Survey Group.

An important possible issue is that fusion could create new possibilities for mediocrity—or worse—by encouraging groupthink—the tendency for disparate individuals conjoined in functional working groups to feel pressure toward a common mind-set that actively discourages the consideration of different core values, different beliefs, or unpopular opinions. For intelligence planning and analysis activities, groupthink can be anathema to constructive analysis because it can inhibit the consideration of alternative hypotheses. An example of possible groupthink on the political level was the relative deprioritization of international terrorism in the early months of the Bush Administration (i.e., the perceived threats from Iraq and the emergence of the Chinese military as a regional power were apparently considered far more important by the neoconservatives who influenced the president's thinking at the time), and this belief set could have placed certain constraints on strategic-level discussions about how to address the perceived threat of al-Qaeda.

Imagination

The perceived need for enhanced levels of imagination stems from the idea that we must be consistently smarter than the terrorists, and that outthinking them requires the ready application of more unconventional, innovative tactics. The problem with this concept is that it tends to underestimate our opponents and to deny them the same potential mental agility. It also appears to indulge a classic American tendency to assume that we can always fix any problem and that we can accomplish it without casualties. The implication of this technological approach to problem solving is to try to solve human problems with fixes that don't always work well, such as the use of satellite reconnaissance against terrorist groups in urban areas. On the other hand, an inhibiting bias against technology could have prevented the drone-based Predator technology, which has provided both excellent intelligence and perhaps our best weapon (i.e., the Predator-Hellfire missile combination) against extremely remote al-Qaeda terrorist groups. An alternative to technological fixes is the development of analytical think tanks, in which individuals try to outthink their terrorist counterparts through role-play by developing models of existing behavior in order to enhance understanding of behavior and by challenging old ideas, technologies, and tactics with innovative approaches.

Planning Issues: Scenarios and Realities

From a planning perspective, the issue of terrorist scenarios involves a decision maker's assumptions about the world, the threats that he or she chooses to address, and the strategic-level operational choices or options he or she is faced with in the planning process. For example, if a nation's leader chooses to shut down commercial aviation and impose significant aerial "caps" over major cities on the basis of terrorist threats, this decision will have cost impacts on resources available for other issues. In addition, if a leader raises any threat issue too often, his or her credibility is likely to suffer over time (the cry-wolf syndrome).

For the intelligence professional, planning scenarios are relevant if analytical contributions, such as finished intelligence or ongoing consultation, can increase exposure to and influence with policy makers. More influence is generally desirable because it might facilitate decisions that provide more resources for collection purposes or increase intelligence participation in the development of operational scenarios. The job of actually creating policy is generally reserved for the top leadership or his or her advisers, perhaps informed by intelligence provided by the ODNI or CIA. Thus, President Bush's national security advisers, Condoleezza Rice and Stephen Hadley, working under the aegis of the president's policy guidance, defined the appropriate scenarios. According to Richard Clarke, the special assistant on terrorism under Bush, Rice, accurately reflecting the orientations of top political leadership in the administration, was not inclined to prioritize international terrorism against competing, state-centric issues.

Current Scenarios

As of early 2011, al-Qaeda had failed to follow up on the attacks of September 11, 2001, in the United States. No subsequent attack, attempted attack, or even realistic planning scenarios that we know of has even approached the magnitude of 9/11. On the other hand, numerous terrorist attacks have been accomplished in the United States, and some have been successful. However, they were virtually all relatively small-scale, and their execution was frequently bungled. In addition, the current status of the specific—as opposed to the global terrorist network—threat from al-Qaeda is currently unclear. The wide range of failed terrorist attempts since the 9/11 attacks suggests that intelligence efforts have benefited from both good fortune and significantly enhanced capabilities. The identification of the radiation bomber, José Padilla (aka Abdullah al-Muhajir), on the basis of intelligence obtained from a computer hard drive confiscated in Afghanistan was the result of an aggressive, foreign-based collection effort. On the other hand, the failed attempt by a Nigerian student, Umar Farouk Abdulmutallab, the so-called underwear bomber, to bomb an airliner on Christmas Day 2009—only to be thwarted by faulty technology and the flight crew—indicates that chance often plays a critical role in the outcome of contemporary terrorist events.

The November 2010 intelligence tip from Saudi sources on a bomb-laden aircraft headed to the United States from Yemen indicates that intelligence is the key to successful counterterrorism. In that incident, two packages advanced through four countries—in spite of airport detection systems—before the intelligence tip triggered a frantic search. The reputation and pride of the U.S. intelligence community received a major boost in May 2001 with the killing of Osama bin Laden at a residential compound in Abbottabad, Pakistan, that U.S. intelligence agents had identified and confirmed in a years-long mission that focused on a courier carrying information to and from the site. As the events of the previous decade made clear, however, the greatest danger in counterterrorist intelligence lies in underestimating the ongoing threat.

Raymond Picquet

See also: *September 11 Attacks*—Pursuit and Death of Osama bin Laden; Civil Liberties, Civil Rights, and National Security; Government Spying and Privacy Issues; Intelligence Community: Pre-9/11 Failures and Successes; Intelligence, Counterterrorist.

Further Reading

Betts, Richard K. *Enemies of Intelligence: Knowledge and Power in American National Security.* New York: Columbia University Press, 2007.

Jervis, Robert. *Why Intelligence Fails: Lessons from the Iranian Revolution and the Iraq War.* Ithaca, NY: Cornell University Press, 2010.

National Commission on Terrorism Attacks Upon the U.S. (The 9/11 Commission). *The 9/11 Commission Report. Final Report of the National Commission on Terrorism Attacks Upon the United States.* Washington, DC: U.S. Government Printing Office, 2004.

Odom, William E. *Fixing Intelligence: For a More Secure America.* New Haven, CT: Yale University Press, 2003.

Sageman, Mark. *Understanding Terror Networks.* Philadelphia: University of Pennsylvania Press, 2004.

Legislation

In the wake of the terrorist attacks of September 11, 2001, the U.S. Congress passed and President George W. Bush signed into a law a number of key pieces of legislation relating to the attacks and to the prevention and prosecution of terrorist acts. The main bills include the USA PATRIOT Act of 2001, the Homeland Security Act of 2002, the SAFETY Act of 2002, the Intelligence Reform and Terrorism Act of 2004, the Border Protection, Anti-Terrorism and Illegal Immigration Control Act of 2005, the REAL ID Act of 2005, and the Military Commissions Act of 2006. Along with these terrorism-fighting pieces of legislation came other acts to compensate victims, the most important of which was the Air Transportation and Safety and System Stabilization Act of 2001.

Pre-9/11 Legislation

The United States has long been plagued by terrorism, largely of the domestic kind. In response, the government has enacted a number of important antiterrorist laws, most notably Reconstruction-era laws aimed at curbing the violent excesses of the Ku Klux Klan and other white supremacist organizations. In the modern era, the two most important pre-2001 pieces of legislation were the Foreign Intelligence Surveillance Act of 1978 (FISA), enacted in the wake of revelations of abusive domestic spying practices by U.S. intelligence agencies, and the 1996 Antiterrorism and Effective Death Penalty Act, signed into law by President Bill Clinton in response to the Oklahoma City bombing of the previous year and the first World Trade Center bombing, in 1993. Among other things, FISA established a special court to issue wiretapping and other national security–related warrants. The act returned to the news in 2005, when it was learned that in order to monitor mass Internet and cell phone traffic, the Bush Administration had largely bypassed Foreign Intelligence Surveillance courts. Along with new restrictions on federal habeas corpus laws in death penalty cases (the Antiterrorism and Effective Death Penalty Act) came key provisions regarding terrorism, including expanded rights to sue foreign governments that support terrorism, mechanisms for combating the financing of terrorism, and expanded powers for the federal government to bar or remove aliens suspected of involvement in terrorist groups or activities.

USA PATRIOT Act

Arguably the most controversial—and among the most sweeping—of post-9/11 terrorist-related pieces of legislation was the USA PATRIOT Act, an acronym for Uniting and Strengthening America by Providing Appropriate Tools Required to Intercept and Obstruct Terrorism Act, passed on October 26, 2001, just six weeks after the attacks. Much of the bill was not particularly controversial, allowing for enhanced border security, better anti–money laundering procedures, enhancements to existing compensation procedures for victims of crime, and improved coordination among various government agencies involved in domestic and foreign intelligence gathering. More controversial were the domestic surveillance provisions, which included roving wiretaps, so-called sneak-and-peek search warrants, and more powers to the Federal Bureau of Investigation to gain access to documents aimed at determining suspicious patterns of activities of U.S. citizens, including the books they check out of libraries. The roving wiretap provision aimed to bring existing wiretap legislation into the modern communications age by allowing for warrants that targeted individuals across multiple communications platforms, from landlines to cell phones to Internet connectivity. The sneak-and-peek warrants allowed investigators to search private premises without the knowledge of the owner or occupant, in order to obtain information about

evidence—the warrants did not allow for the seizure of evidence—that could then be used to obtain a traditional warrant to seize such evidence. While supporters of these provisions, including the Bush Administration's Justice Department, argued that these new rules were needed to more effectively fight a new kind of terrorist enemy—which lived clandestinely in America and used its modern communications infrastructure—civil libertarians argued that they gave government overly broad powers to spy on law-abiding citizens. In March 2006, the Patriot Act was reauthorized, partly to deal with certain parts of the first act, which had sunset provisions or had been struck down as unconstitutional by the courts. For example, new civil liberties protections were placed into the provisions of the original act that dealt with roving wiretaps.

Government Reorganization

In 2002, Congress passed and Bush signed the Homeland Security Act, the most sweeping reorganization of the federal government since the National Security Act of 1947, which created the Department of Defense. With the aim of better coordinating the various government mandates and agencies involved in protecting U.S. territory, the act created a cabinet-level Department of Homeland Security, which absorbed, introduced, and reorganized agencies once spread across several departments, including Immigration and Customs Enforcement, the Federal Emergency Management Agency, the U.S. Coast Guard, and the all-new Transportation Security Administration, which federalized airport and airline security. Much like the Homeland Security Act, the Intelligence Reform and Terrorism Act of 2004 included a reorganization of the government, albeit somewhat less sweeping. Aimed at correcting the lack of coordination among intelligence-gathering agencies that some experts said had been a key reason the government failed to prevent 9/11, the act created the new position of director of national intelligence, to oversee the various intelligence-gathering agencies, and the National Counterterrorism Center, to coordinate government activities in that area of security. Both reorganizations have been criticized by many—Homeland Security for focusing too much on terrorism at the expense of ordinary natural disasters, as witnessed by the federal government's failure to deal more effectively with the 2005 Hurricane Katrina disaster; and the Intelligence Reform and Terrorism Act for adding more levels of bureaucracy to intelligence gathering. Far less controversial has been the SAFETY Act, an acronym for the Support Anti-terrorism by Fostering Effective Technologies Act, of 2002, which granted increased legal liability protection to companies developing or providing qualified antiterrorism technologies. The goal of the bill was to foster new technologies in the securities field.

Immigration and Terrorism

As security against illegal immigration and terrorism often overlap, a number of pieces of legislation dealing with the former include provisions concerning the latter. Among these has been the Border Protection, Antiterrorism and Illegal Immigration Control Act of 2005. Largely aimed at stemming the flow of illegal immigrants into the country—including through the construction of an enhanced border fence with Mexico—the law included provisions aimed at stopping potential terrorists from illegally entering the country through enhanced documentation verification. Similarly, the REAL ID Act, also of 2005, included antiterrorist elements within a bill aimed largely at preventing illegal immigrants from obtaining employment or government benefits. Among these were new rules that allowed the government to more easily deport illegal aliens suspected of involvement in terrorist activities and organizations.

The last of the major post-9/11 pieces of antiterrorism legislation was the 2006 Military Commissions Act, a response to the U.S. Supreme Court's *Hamdan v. Rumsfeld* decision of the same year, which held that military commissions set up by the Bush Administration to try "enemy combatant" detainees held at Guantánamo Bay, Cuba, were unconstitutional and in violation of the Geneva Conventions, to which the United States is a signatory. The act placed such trials in conformity with the Uniform Code of Military Justice. While challenged by detainees several times, the law largely has been upheld by the courts.

Compensation

In addition to these various security measures, Congress passed legislation aimed at aiding the victims of the 9/11 disaster, the most important of which was the Air Transportation and Safety and System Stabilization Act, passed just eleven days after the attacks. Not only did it provide U.S. airlines, hard hit by the disaster's aftermath, with billions in loan guarantees, but it also created a victim compensation fund that eventually awarded some $7 billion to the families of those who died in the disaster, in exchange for an agreement not to sue the affected airlines for damages. A bill to provide some $6 billion to cover the health costs of emergency responders and cleanup personnel affected by the toxins produced by the 9/11 disaster was passed by Congress at the end of 2010.

James Ciment

See also: *September 11 Attacks*—National Political Response; U.S. Foreign Policy; Political, Legal, and Social Issues; Civil Liberties, Civil Rights, and National Security. *Counterterrorism*—International Law and the War on Terrorism.

Further Reading

Etzioni, Amitai. *How Patriotic Is the Patriot Act? Freedom Versus Security in the Age of Terrorism.* New York: Routledge, 2004.

Fein, Bruce. *Constitutional Peril: The Life and Death Struggle for Our Constitution and Democracy.* New York: Palgrave Macmillan, 2008.

Moore, John Norton, and Robert F. Turner, eds. *Legal Issues in the Struggle Against Terror.* Durham, NC: Carolina Academic Press, 2010.

Wong, Kam C. *The Impact of USA Patriot Act on American Society: An Evidence Based Assessment.* New York: Nova Science, 2007.

National Guard Missions

In the wake of the September 11, 2001, terrorist attacks, the missions required of the U.S. National Guard came under comprehensive review, as the guard came to be utilized in a number of homeland security operations. Then, as the United States launched wars in Afghanistan and Iraq in 2001 and 2003, respectively, the guard was deployed to foreign battlefields to a degree unprecedented in the nation's history. All of this was a far cry from the traditional duties of the guard, that is, responding to civil disturbances and natural disasters.

The National Guard is the organized militia reserved to the states by the Constitution of the United States under article 1, section 8. In peacetime, the governor of each respective state or territory commands the National Guard. When ordered to active duty for mobilization or called into federal service for emergencies, units of the guard are under the control of the appropriate service secretary.

The militia clause reserves the appointment of officers and the authority of training the militia (according to congressionally prescribed standards) to the states. In 1903, Congress officially designated the organized militia as the National Guard and established procedures for training and equipping the guard to active-duty military standards. The National Guard has two roles—one as part of the nation's entire military force and the other in the respective states for emergency response and community support missions. This dual state-federal role for the National Guard is based on a constitutional mandate. The relationship is unique and sets the National Guard apart from other military reserve forces.

Unlike U.S. reserve forces, the National Guard is comprised of two segments, the Army National Guard and the Air National Guard. These two organizations are regulated under title 32 of the U.S. Code, as opposed to title 10, which regulates the activities of the active-duty forces of the United States and the five U.S. reserve forces (army, navy, air force, Marine Corps, and Coast Guard). The primary role of the National Guard is to provide trained and ready forces to support the governor of the state in which they reside. The Air National Guard and Army National Guard are comprised of approximately 485,000 members, with armories and training facilities in more than 3,300 communities. Upon federalization, the National Guard becomes an active-duty force subject to the requirements of title 10 and no longer belongs to the governor. The National Guard unit's chain of command becomes the same as that of the active-duty forces.

Long-Standing Missions

The National Guard's routine missions during a natural or man-made disaster are familiar to the public. National Guardsmen routinely report for duty in the event of riots, floods, hurricanes, tornadoes, and forest fires. The local National Guard armory is often used for community activities and as an operations center in the event of a crisis. The National Guard operates in a broad spectrum of operations ranging from local routine support to overseas combat duty as required in the Department of Defense's war plans. In the homeland security role, this adaptability is useful because the National Guard is legally and organizationally flexible enough to take on the missions of key asset protection and civil disturbance, maintain air sovereignty, respond to incidents involving weapons of mass destruction (WMD), and operate national missile defense systems.

In a role that is perhaps not as well publicized, the National Guard is regularly used to support the Customs Service in searching the millions of shipping containers that enter the nation's ports annually. Assisting federal and local law enforcement heavily involves the National Guard in the nation's counterdrug program in aerial surveillance and road improvements, providing support personnel to the Department of Defense's Joint Task Force North. The National Guard provides counterdrug support in 580,000 square miles (103,994 square meters) of the southwestern United States as well as Puerto Rico and the U.S. Virgin Islands.

New Responsibilities

Prior to September 11, 2001, the National Guard was at the forefront of the Department of Defense's effort to improve homeland defense. The Defense Against Weapons of Mass Destruction Act of 1996, sponsored by Senators Sam Nunn, Richard Lugar, and Pete Domenici, mandated the enhancement of domestic preparedness and response capability for terrorist attacks involving nuclear, radiological, biological, and chemical weapons. The legislation provided funding to improve the capability of the federal, state, and local emergency response agencies to prevent and, if necessary, respond to domestic terrorist incidents involving WMD. It also required the Department of Defense to develop plans to enhance the nation's defenses against WMD. One of the impor-

tant by-products of these plans was the establishment of the National Guard WMD Civil Support Teams (CSTs). Although these teams have had several names during their evolution, the importance of their mission cannot be overstated. These teams are designed to provide incident commanders with the ability to detect the presence of chemical and biological agents, as well as residual radiation that may be present after an explosion involving nuclear or radioactive materials.

Since the inception of the congressional mandate, the National Guard has aggressively moved ahead to activate and train CSTs. The first ten were established geographically so that each Federal Emergency Management Region would include a team. The second group of seventeen was established to ensure that all major population centers in the United States had at least one CST within 300 miles (482 kilometers). During fiscal year 2001, Congress funded five additional teams, bringing the total to thirty-two teams. Congress's long-term goal is to have at least one CST in each state plus one in each territory (Guam, Puerto Rico, U.S. Virgin Islands) and the District of Columbia, for a total of fifty-four highly trained teams designed to enhance U.S. homeland defense capabilities. These teams are composed of twenty-two highly trained Army and Air National Guard personnel who are on full-time active duty. These guardsmen have been trained in a variety of skills in the disciplines of medicine, communications, and nuclear, chemical, and biological defense.

Unique Capabilities

The Army National Guard's GuardNet XXI, along with the Air National Guard's Warrior Network, have combined to become Network America. This network is the backbone for the delivery of voice, video, and other data, including the Distributive Training Technology Program, to the National Guard. It can be made available to civilian emergency responders, as well as hospital and emergency medical personnel desiring to participate. The National Guard also works through the Department of Justice's Office of Justice Programs and with the Public Health Service to establish the Early Responders Distance Learning Training Center, located on the campus of St. Joseph's University in Philadelphia. The goal is to link the WMD curricula being developed with the National Guard's distance-learning infrastructure to provide standardized and validated training to the emergency response community at the state and local level.

In attempting to coordinate the National Guard's support to the nation and to obtain the resources needed to provide this support, the National Guard Bureau has established a WMD coordination office and has staffed it so that it can coordinate with all federal agencies involved in homeland defense and WMD issues. These agencies include the Federal Bureau of Investigation, Department of Justice, Federal Emergency Management Agency, Office of Justice Programs Office for State and Local Domestic Preparedness Support, Technical Support Working Group, U.S. Army's Training and Doctrine Command, Homeland Defense Center of Excellence, and U.S. Army Soldier and Biological Chemical Command.

Since 2001 the National Guard has also established a WMD coordination office in each state and territory and the District of Columbia. This office coordinates with the National Guard Bureau's Weapons of Mass Destruction Program Office and at the state level with state and local response and support entities. The mission of this office is to ensure full and proper integration of National Guard capabilities into local and state WMD response plans. The State Weapons of Mass Destruction Program Office coordinates National Guard participation in interagency and joint WMD exercises and assists as requested with the development of local and state needs assessments. Liaison is maintained with the appropriate federal agency representatives such as the Federal Bureau of Investigation and the Federal Emergency Management Agency in the states.

Since September 11, 2001, the National Guard has continued its service to the nation with even more intensity. National Guard soldiers and airmen have been deployed to the airports to bolster security. The WMD CST continue to train and deploy to exercises and National Security Special Events such as national political conventions and Super Bowls. In addition, both the George W. Bush and Barack Obama Administrations have deployed small numbers of National Guard troops to provide support for the U.S. Border Patrol along the border with Mexico.

The National Guard has also taken on a major part of the military missions in Afghanistan and Iraq since those wars were launched in 2001 and 2003, respectively. Hoping to ease the strain on the military of fighting two wars simultaneously, George W. Bush and Secretary of Defense Donald Rumsfeld opted for a strategy of utilizing National Guard units to bolster troop numbers in both conflicts. In 2005, roughly 40 percent (50,000) of all U.S. troops in Iraq and 55 percent (16,000) in Afghanistan were members of the National Guard. By the beginning of 2011, however, the numbers had fallen significantly to roughly 10,000 National Guard troops in Iraq and about another 6,000 in Afghanistan. At that time, the Iraq contingent represented approximately 8 percent of U.S. military personnel, whereas the Afghanistan contingent represented roughly 17 percent. (All of these figures do not include the reserve forces of the various military branches.) While the numbers were relatively small given the overall National Guard level of 460,000, some critics of using the National Guard for such missions pointed to the strains on the guards in those states sending relatively large contingents.

Stephen C. Malone and James Ciment

See also: *Modern Terrorism*—Afghanistan: U.S. Invasion and War; Iraq: U.S. Invasion and Post-Saddam Hussein Era. *September 11 Attacks*—Security and Defense; Armed Forces Missions; Hunt for al-Qaeda and Terrorist Networks.

Further Reading
Doubler, Michael D. *The National Guard and the War on Terror: Operation Iraqi Freedom.* Arlington, VA: National Guard Bureau, Office of Public Affairs, Historical Services Division, 2008.

Klerman, Alex. *Rethinking the Reserves.* Santa Monica, CA: RAND, 2008.

Waterhouse, Michael, and JoAnne O'Bryant. CRS Report for Congress: National Guard Personnel and Deployments: Fact Sheet. January 17, 2008.

Special Events Security

Security considerations and counterterrorism efforts have long been of paramount importance at high-profile events in the United States. However, it was not until May 1998 that the U.S. government began to formally designate certain events as receiving critical federal support.

Developments prior to May 1998 actually set the foundation for U.S. policy on special-event security. In April 1995, President Bill Clinton introduced Presidential Decision Directive (PDD) 39, which set forth counterterrorism responsibilities for key federal agencies. PDD 39 reinforced the lead agency role for the Federal Bureau of Investigation (FBI) for domestic terrorist attacks or threats that had existed for many years. However, PDD 39 also further clarified the roles of the FBI and other federal agencies. Under PDD 39, the FBI assumed lead federal agency responsibilities for crisis management, which involves efforts to prevent, preempt, or terminate terrorist threats or acts, and to apprehend and prosecute perpetrators. The Federal Emergency Management Agency was designated the lead federal agency for consequence management, which involves efforts to respond to the consequences or potential consequences of a terrorist incident.

In May 1998, President Clinton also announced PDD 62, which expanded the U.S. government's counterterrorism framework established in PDD 39. It provided further clarifications of the counterterrorism responsibilities for various federal agencies. One important development in PDD 62 was that the U.S. Secret Service was designated the lead federal agency for designing, planning, and implementing federal security efforts at National Security Special Events (NSSEs).

Since then, the Secret Service, the FBI, and the Federal Emergency Management Agency have all worked closely to coordinate federal security and counterterrorism efforts at a number of events. Since May 1998, dozens of events have received the NSSE designation, including international summits held on U.S. soil, various political conventions, Super Bowls, presidential inaugurals, and the 2002 Winter Olympic Games in Salt Lake City.

While security coordination, planning, and implementation for each of these events have been considerable, expensive, and resource intensive, the 2002 Salt Lake City (SLC) Winter Olympics—the first to take place in the wake of September 11—exceeded the earlier NSSEs in scope and scale. The federal government spent $310 million for counterterrorism support to the SLC Olympics (nearly triple the amount spent during the 1996 Atlanta Summer Olympics). The 2002 SLC Winter Olympics received official NSSE designation in August 1999; security preparations in coordination with the FBI actually began shortly after the International Olympic Committee selected SLC as the recipient for the Winter Olympics in June 1995. Almost every conceivable security precaution and measure was implemented at the SLC Winter Olympics, including joint federal, state, and local intelligence sharing, as well as command and control centers. Aerial no-fly zones were extended for forty-five miles (72 kilometers) outside of SLC, while various detection and monitoring systems were in place to provide notice against chemical, biological, and radiological weapons threats. In addition, thousands of federal personnel were deployed for a variety of security and response functions, including almost 10,000 military personnel (active duty, reserve, and National Guard). A similarly large number of responders from Utah, SLC, and other local jurisdictions also participated in response and security efforts.

Given the continued concern over possible terrorist attacks sponsored by operational al-Qaeda elements already in the United States, or from other domestic or international terrorist groups, it can be expected that a number of high-profile events may be considered for an NSSE designation in the future.

Meanwhile, security at special events overseas has also become an increasingly complex and expensive endeavor, as a history of Olympic Games since SLC attests. When Athens put in its bid for the 2004 Summer Olympics, it estimated security costs at $122 million. That was before September 11, however; in the end, it cost the Greek government and other entities $1.8 billion to secure the games. Fearing actions by homegrown terrorists, including Muslim separatists, as well as international terrorists, the Chinese government spared little expense in securing the 2008 summer games, ultimately deploying a 150,000-strong security contingent, plus 290,000

volunteer patrollers to watch over the games, the athletes, and visitors, though some of these were deployed to prevent peaceful protests in the authoritarian state and many of the volunteer patrollers offered routine aid and assistance to visitors. Ultimately, more than $2 billion was spent on security for the games, or about 5 percent of the $40 billion total cost of hosting the games. At the much smaller and more remote Winter Olympics in and around Vancouver in 2010, security costs amounted to $720 million. While visitors and athletes sometimes complain of the stifling atmosphere produced by the heavy security measures, they have in fact worked, as no Olympics since Atlanta in 1996, at which a domestic antiabortion terrorist set off a bomb that killed two persons, have been marred by a significant terrorist act.

Javed Ali and James Ciment

See also: *September 11 Attacks*—Security and Defense; National Guard Missions.

Further Reading

Fisher, Eric. "Super Bowl Security Blitz." *Washington Times,* January 30, 2002.
Lichtblau, Eric. "Tranquil Winter Olympics Serving as Blueprint for Security Operations." *Los Angeles Times,* March 5, 2002.
Shenon, Philip. "U.S. Is Requesting Tighter Security at Utah Olympics." *New York Times,* January 29, 2002.
"Statement of John Magaw, Deputy Director, Federal Emergency Management Agency, the 2002 Winter Olympics in Salt Lake City, Utah: Cooperation Among Federal, State, Local, and Private Agencies to Address Public Safety Concerns Before the Committee on the Judiciary, United States Senate, May 31, 2001."

Terror Threat Warnings

In the aftermath of the September 11 terrorist attacks and the anthrax incidents that began in October 2001, the Bush Administration was faced with a difficult dilemma: how best to inform the U.S. public, the private sector, and state and local governments about potential or actual threats in the United States or to U.S. interests abroad, while at the same time preventing further public anxiety and determining which threats were the most credible and of sufficient importance to merit broadcast to a national audience.

On October 11, the Federal Bureau of Investigation (FBI) issued the first terror alert. This alert, however, failed to include any specifics regarding the "who, what, where, when, and how" details critical to assessing the immediacy or credibility of a particular threat. Despite this warning, the administration faced criticism from state and local government officials and individual

Beginning in January 2003, the U.S. government employed a color-coded scale to warn the public of the risk of terrorist attack at a particular time. In April 2011, a two-level system providing more specific information replaced the original scale. (Scott Olson/Getty Images)

citizens regarding the ambiguity of the threat warning. On October 29, 2001, the FBI issued a second threat warning that additional terrorist attacks in the United States or against U.S. citizens abroad were possible within that following week. Government officials indicated that the warning was based on credible information regarding possible al-Qaeda activity. At this time, it was also revealed that the U.S. intelligence community had developed a highly classified "threat matrix" that listed sixty to eighty terrorist threats received each day and assessed by analysts to be of sufficient credibility to pass along to senior administration officials. In early November 2001, it was revealed that senior FBI officials actually opposed the issuance of the threat alert on October 29 but were overruled by the attorney general and the FBI director.

On December 3, 2001, the administration issued its third terror alert. This alert was based on credible evidence that suggested attacks might be launched in December, given that major religious events (Christmas, Ramadan, and Hanukkah) all fell within this month. Again the alert was criticized for being vague about the particulars of any threat. By January 2002, the administration extended the December 2001 threat alert to March 11, 2002—the six-month anniversary of the September 11 attacks.

By early 2002, the administration began exploring mechanisms that would help provide additional clarity, specificity, and reassurance regarding future terrorist threats. The Office of Homeland Security was tasked with creating and implementing a new threat advisory system. By mid-March 2002, this new system was unveiled. The system had five levels: green (the lowest level), blue, yellow, orange, and red. Each level triggered specific actions by federal agencies and state and local governments; however, the system was still considered a work in progress, and its recommended activities were not binding upon state and local governments. Under this system, the attorney general set the alert levels, after consultation with U.S. law enforcement agencies, the intelligence community, and the director of the Office of Homeland Security.

In the years since 9/11, the terror threat warnings fluctuated between yellow (elevated) and red (severe). (There had never been a period since the system went into effect when the level was set at green.) For the most part, yellow predominated, though there had been eight times when the warning was set at orange (high), usually in response to critical events, such as the start of the Iraq War in March and April of 2003 or as a result of intelligence, such as from August to November 2004, when U.S. security officials feared the possibility of attacks on financial institutions and other targets in the New York City and Washington, D.C., areas. There had been only one period when the level was set at red. This was in response to the disruption of what British law enforcement said was a serious threat to blow up aircraft bound from the United Kingdom to the United States.

Over the years, the security threat warnings were criticized for a variety of reasons. Some critics said they offered little protection, as most people came to disregard them. Others warned of their politicization, noting that the longest period an orange level was ever in effect—from August 1 to November 10, 2004—coincided with a presidential election season in which the incumbent George W. Bush stressed his security credentials in the war on terror.

For these reasons, the Barack Obama Administration decided to update the terror warning system. In January 2011, it implemented the new National Terrorism Advisory System, which worked alongside the old system through April, when it completely replaced it. Under the new system, the color coding was replaced by two categories—"elevated threat" and "imminent threat," the latter a higher level of alert. In addition, the Department of Homeland Security will also provide much more detailed information about the nature of the threat, as well as recommended actions that individuals, businesses, communities, and government agencies can take to deal with the threat.

Javed Ali and James Ciment

See also: *September 11 Attacks*—Security and Defense; Homeland Defense: Organization and Policy.

Further Reading

Ball, Howard. *U.S. Homeland Security: A Reference Handbook.* Santa Barbara, CA: ABC-CLIO, 2005.

Ervin, Clark Kent. *Open Target: Where America Is Vulnerable to Attack.* New York: Palgrave Macmillan, 2006.